D0370355

THE GREEN GUIDE
Provence

Ménerbes Photo: © Franck Guziou/hemis.fr

MICHELIN

THEGREENGUIDE **PROVENCE**

Editoral Director	Cynthia Clayton Ochterbeck
Editoral Manager	Gwen Cannon
Contributing Writer	Terry Marsh
Production Manager	Natasha George
Cartography	Peter Wrenn
Photo Editor	Yoshimi Kanazawa
Proofreader	Sean Cannon
Interior Design	Chris Bell
Layout	Nicole D. Jordan, Natasha George
Cover Design	Chris Bell, Christelle Le Déan
Cover Layout	Michelin Travel Partner, Natasha George

Contact Us

Michelin Travel and Lifestyle North America
One Parkway South
Greenville, SC 29615
USA
travel.lifestyle@us.michelin.com
www.michelintravel.com

Michelin Travel Partner
Hannay House
39 Clarendon Road
Watford, Herts WD17 1JA
UK
✆01923 205240
travelpubsales@uk.michelin.com
www.ViaMichelin.com

Special Sales

For information regarding bulk sales,
customized editions and premium sales,
please contact us at:
travel.lifestyle@us.michelin.com
www.michelintravel.com

Note to the reader Addresses, phone numbers, opening hours and prices
published in this guide are accurate at the time of press. We welcome corrections
and suggestions that may assist us in preparing the next edition. While every
effort is made to ensure that all information printed in this guide is correct and
up-to-date, Michelin Travel Partner accepts no liability for any direct, indirect or
consequential losses howsoever caused so far as such can be excluded by law.

HOW TO USE THIS GUIDE

PLANNING YOUR TRIP

The blue-tabbed PLANNING YOUR TRIP section at the front of the guide gives you **ideas for your trip** and **practical information** to help you organize it. You'll find tours, a host of outdoor activities, a calendar of events, information on shopping, sightseeing, kids' activities, and more.

INTRODUCTION

The orange-tabbed INTRODUCTION section explores Provence's **Nature** and geology. The **History** section spans prehistory through Roman colonisation to today. **Architecture**, the **Arts** and **Literature** are highlighted, while **Provence Today** delves into modern Provence.

DISCOVERING

The green-tabbed DISCOVERING section features Principal Sights by region, highlighting the most interesting local **Sights**, **Walking Tours**, nearby **Excursions**, and detailed **Driving Tours**. Admission prices shown are normally for a single adult.

ADDRESSES

We've selected the best hotels, restaurants, cafes, shops, nightlife and entertainment to fit all budgets. See the Legend on the cover flap for an explanation of the price categories. See the back of the guide for an index of where to find hotel and restaurant listings in this guide.

Sidebars

Throughout the guide you will find blue, peach and green-colored text boxes with lively anecdotes, detailed history and background information.

😊 A Bit of Advice 😊

Green advice boxes found in this guide contain practical tips and handy information relevant to your visit or a sight in the Discovering section.

STAR RATINGS★★★

Michelin has given star ratings for more than 100 years. If you're pressed for time, we recommend you visit the ★★★, or ★★ sights first:

★★★ **Highly recommended**
★★   **Recommended**
★   **Interesting**

MAPS

- 😊 Principal Sights map.
- 😊 Region maps.
- 😊 Maps for major cities and villages.
- 😊 Local tour maps.

All maps in this guide are oriented north, unless otherwise indicated by a directional arrow. The term "Local Map" refers to a map within the chapter or Tourism Region. A complete list of the maps found in the guide appears at the back of this book.

© Bertrand Gardel/hemis.fr

PLANNING YOUR TRIP

INTRODUCTION TO PROVENCE

© José Antonio Moreno/age fotostock

CONTENTS

DISCOVERING PROVENCE

© Bertrand Gardel/hemis.fr

5

Welcome to Provence

Along the Mediterranean Coast in the southeastern corner of France, nestled next to Italy, lies beautiful Provence. It gets its name from the fact that it was the first Roman province outside Italy. But today the name is synonymous with serene landscapes and rich history. Provence's western border is the Rhône River, one of the country's major commercial routes. Inside these boundaries are mountains comparable to the Alps, plains and reserves that attract natural life, sandy beaches, and arable land with bountiful crops.

Flamingos in the Camargue

©Javier Gil/Fotolia.com

MARSEILLE AND AROUND
(pp106–165)

Marseille and its coastline of blue inlets lie sparkling in the sun. The large city of Marseille is a bustling port with quaint buildings in the Vieux Port. While tourism is important, Marseille is a thriving industrial city, where the commercial port still aids in oil pressing, soap-making and flour milling. Yachts bobbing in the Vieux Port, fish restaurants lining the quays, beaches within biking distance, and the vast sweep of the Mediterranean adding a briny tang to the air: these are just some of the components that make Marseille so compelling.

AIX AND SAINTE-VICTOIRE
(pp166–187)

Sophisticated and serene, Aix-en-Provence bubbles with religious and art history, just as the natural thermal springs bubble below the town. This town is home to many Provençal elements, from Roman ruins to 17C creativity to 20C art, and a little 21C shopping. Highlights include the lovely Cours Mirabeau walkway and Ste-Victoire, which was and remains an inspiration to artists.

ARLES AND THE CAMARGUE
(pp188–213)

It is difficult to think of any area as wide-ranging in its appeal as the history-soaked town of Arles, with the vast, watery wilderness of the Camargue at its door. A river port valued by the Romans (Julius Caesar included), Arles has archaeological and architectural treasures by the score, as well as links to Van Gogh. Walking, biking, horse riding and boating open up the world of the Camargue nature and zoological reserve, dense with wildlife, including more than 400 species of birds.

THE ALPILLES AND THE MONTAGNETTE *(pp214–251)*

The great outdoors is the appeal of the Alpilles, Provence's majestic limestone hills. This land is pristine, preserved and protected for the most part, so that the flora and fauna are similar to what they were centuries ago when people first began to flock here. At the highest elevations, the views are full of stately bare rock formations. Further down, olive, almond and pine trees flourish. Montagnette is a smaller mountain range, but no less bucolic. Once a camping ground for Roman soldiers, the Montagnette is now planted with classic Provençal herbs.

AVIGNON AND THE PAYS DE SORGUES *(pp252–285)*

Provence is nothing without its papal history, and Avignon brims with it. The Palais des Papes is renowned as a home to seven popes in the 14C. Those residents helped transform Avignon from a city of little importance to Provence's centre of culture, history and religion. The Avignon Festival is internationally known and attracts the biggest names in theatre and performance. A short distance east of Avignon, the pretty towns built around the river Sorgue are worth exploring.

ORANGE AND AROUND *(pp286–311)*

In the northwest corner of Provence, Orange and its surroundings are sometimes overlooked by visitors making a dash south. A sad mistake. The town, the gateway to the Midi, has two remarkable UNESCO Roman monuments, while nearby Vaison-la-Romaine harbours an immense area of Gallo-Roman remains. Red wines from here are rustic and now in demand around the world. A sea of vines greets you on the way to the medieval Enclave des Papes, stretching right across the Ouvèze valley to the slopes of the Dentelles de Montmirail.

COMTAT VENAISSIN AND MONT VENTOUX *(pp312–333)*

Lying between the Rhône and the Durance rivers and the mightiest mountain in Provence, the Comtat Venaissin and Ventoux are delightful areas. At their heart lies Carpentras, as interesting for its Jewish past as for the bountiful weekly market today. Around it to the north, east and south spreads countryside enriched both by the fields and orchards that have made this area famous for vegetables and fruit, and by a whole series of fascinating villages. Above it all looms magnificent Mont Ventoux.

Carpentras

© Alain Hocquel/L'ADT Vaucluse Tourisme

LUBERON AND AROUND *(pp334–383)*

Postcard-perfect villages with quaint homes and narrow streets populate the towns of the Luberon region, which may be why it was the ideal setting for Peter Mayle's *A Year in Provence* books. The climate is classic, sun-blessed Mediterranean, which produces remarkable views of the landscapes. *Bories* (dry-stone huts), rock quarries and fields filled with lavender make up the backdrop of this region. In the foreground precariously perched clusters of quintessential hamlets, with houses, cafés and shops, greet visitors.

Roman ruins in the Quartier de Puymin, Vaison-la-Romaine

©S. Sauvignier/MICHELIN

Calanque d'En-Vau
© Bertrand Gardel/hemis.fr

Michelin Driving Tours

① PROVENCE AND THE ROMAN EMPIRE ROUTE

233km/145mi leaving from Orange.
This itinerary starts at **Orange** with a visit to the triumphal arch, the magnificent Roman Theatre and the museum just opposite. From there, continue on to the extraordinary archaeological site at Vaison-la-Romaine. Other sites on the itinerary include a triumphal arch at Carpentras, remains of the Roman wall in Avignon, the Roman monuments of the Plateau des Antiques and the ancient city of Glanum, situated just outside St-Rémy. Then it's on to Arles: the amphitheatre, the Roman Theatre, the mysterious Cryptoporticus, Constantine's baths, the melancholy necropolis of Les Alyscamps, and the fascinating Musée de l'Arles et de la Provence Antiques. To extend the trip northwards, head towards Nîmes for the amphitheatre; the Temple of Diana; the Maison Carrée; and the vestiges of the city's fortifications, the most impressive example of which is the Tour Magne. The Castellum, a Roman water distribution tank, is an appropriate introduction to the majestic Pont du Gard, the most spectacular part of the ancient aqueduct that brought water from the Eure fountain near Uzès to Nîmes. This Roman aqueduct crosses 50km/31mi of hinterland.
(♿*For more information about Nîmes and the Pont du Gard, see Michelin Green Guide Languedoc Roussillon Tarn Gorges).*

② NATURAL WONDERS OF THE VAUCLUSE

258km/160mi leaving from Carpentras, after visiting the old town.
Starting at **Carpentras**, admire the views and landscapes of the Dentelles de Montmirail, and stop in the picturesque village of Malaucène. Choose a clear day to climb Mont Ventoux and enjoy the spectacular views. From the Nesque gorges, carry on to the remarkable ochre quarries of Colorado de Rustrel, gateway to the Luberon. Climb the Mourre Nègre summit, and acquaint yourself with Mount Luberon and the *villages perchés* (hilltop villages) of Bonnieux, Roussillon (where ochre reigns) and Gordes, with its stepped alleyways and the surprising *village des bories*. Stop in Fontaine-de-Vaucluse, where you can see the resurgent spring of the Sorgue River. It comes to the surface here after curving its way below the Vaucluse plateau, while you were winding your way above.

Driving through lavender fields, Mont Ventoux in the background

©Arco Digital Images/Tips Images

③ BEAUTIFUL VILLAGES IN THE LUBERON

128km/79.5mi leaving from Cavaillon.

Don't go anywhere without tasting the famous melons of **Cavaillon**. Then set out to visit the town: the synagogue and Jewish museum in the lower town; and the antique shops at L'Île-sur-la-Sorgue. If your memory is in high gear, you may wish to recite the poems of Petrarch in Fontaine-de-Vaucluse, his retirement home in the 14C.

The curious group of drystone huts known as the *village des bories* may inspire you to write some poetry of your own. In the village of Gordes, go up and down the *calades*, the steep staircases that serve as streets, and admire the view of the Calavon valley. The Abbey of Sénanque is nestled in a lavender field nearby, a heavenly place in more ways than one.

Explore Roussillon, with its ochre-coloured buildings and extraordinary quarries from which ochre was extracted, as well as the workshop where the pigment was processed with time-consuming and complex techniques. Visit Saturnin-lès-Apt, with its mill and cherry orchards, before going to Apt, where you can enjoy crystallised fruits and the large Saturday market.

Climbers will appreciate the rock spur of Buoux, but you can, too, by just resting in the charming hamlet at the base. To round off your tour, take a walk in the cedar forest of Bonnieux before visiting Lacoste and the lovely hillside villages of Ménerbes and Oppède-le-Vieux.

④ CAMARGUE

228km/141.6mi leaving from Arles.

Start in **Arles** with a visit to the Museon Arlaten, founded by the legendary local poet Frédéric Mistral. Next board a boat for a relaxing trip down the Rhône. Off starboard, you can catch a glimpse of the unique and beautiful ecosystem of the Camargue. Discover the intricate network of marshes and streams, and the fabulous flora and fauna of the wetlands. Visit the salt marshes of Salin-de-Giraud, and walk the footpaths of the Domaine de la Palissade (the only area of the delta not to have been enclosed by dykes) to Piémanson beach near the mouth of the Rhône. Learn more about the birds and flora on the footpaths around La Capelière or take a seat aboard the small train in Méjanes and visit the shores of the Vaccarès lagoon. The Musée de la Camargue is devoted to the customs of the region's inhabitants; the bird sanctuary at Pont-de-Gau offers a unique opportunity to become better acquainted with the unusual and rare birds that frequent the lagoons.

Take a stroll through the streets of Les Saintes-Maries-de-la-Mer, with its white houses nestled around the imposing fortified church, before going to the walled city of Aigues-Mortes, either via the Sylvereal bridge or by boat. Savour some fish soup and other local specialities in the port of Grau-du-Roi before starting the return journey to Arles.

On the way back, explore the profusion of reeds that conceal the Scamandre lagoon, and then stop to contemplate the sculptures adorning the façade of the Abbey of St-Gilles, a masterpiece of Provençal Romanesque architecture.

⑤ PAINTERS AND AUTHORS OF PROVENCE

250km/155mi leaving from Baux-de-Provence.

What better place to start this tour devoted to artists than the magnificent town of Baux, which has inspired many painters and writers? It is only fitting to make the pilgrimage to Maillane where the great master of the Félibrige movement, Frédéric Mistral, was born and lived, before going to admire the paintings of Auguste Chabaud in Graveson. A visit to the Château of Tarascon will evoke the pageantry of the court of

King René, and be sure to stop off at Tartarin's house before going to explore the landscape and the mill of Fontvieille, which inspired the author Alphonse Daudet.

In Arles follow the footsteps of Vincent van Gogh: visit the foundation that bears his name and the hospice where he was interned, which has been faithfully reconstructed. The Picasso donation in the Musée Réattu is well worth a visit for the remarkable modern sculpture and fine photographic collection.

To learn more about the late 19C Provençal school, go to the Musée Ziem in Martigues, while the Musée des Beaux-Arts in Marseille will deepen your appreciation of the great Baroque master Pierre Puget.

Classical Aix-en-Provence is the place to go to follow in Cézanne's footsteps (as well as finding out more about Vasarely) and to re-read Zola, who described the city (under the name of Plasson) as the birthplace of the Rougon family in his Rougon-Macquart series of novels. And if you're curious, why not visit Salon to find out what the future holds in Nostradamus' prophecies?

⑥ THE MOUNTAINOUS SHORE AND THE COUNTRYSIDE BEYOND MARSEILLE

290km/180mi leaving from Marseille.

This itinerary is the ideal opportunity to use your walking shoes—or your flippers! After you take a pleasant stroll through the Panier and Notre-Dame de la Garde quarters of old Marseille, the Chaîne de l'Estaque provides creeks and *calanques* with some superb seawater for swimmers and divers. Niolon, in particular, is ideal for divers, while the tiny beaches of Ensuès-la-Redonne are good for catching sea urchins and spotting octopuses *(pourpres)*. If you prefer to swim without octopuses, head for Carry-le-Rouet, Sausset-les-Pins or Carro.

Aix-en-Provence is a good place for an evening stroll when the light falls on the façades of the old *hôtels particuliers*. Trace Cézanne's footsteps by exploring Ste-Victoire, where the steep footpaths provide some superb views from the Croix de Provence. A visit to the Royal Monastery at St-Maximin makes an ideal prelude to an excursion on the Ste-Baume massif, which attracts pilgrims, ramblers and climbers who enjoy the challenge of its steep rock faces. The bucolic St-Pons park offers a pleasant rest in the shade before returning to the sea at La Ciotat and travelling up the Corniche des Crètes. Finally, at Cassis, get on a boat for a voyage of discovery to the sumptuous *calanques*.

LOCAL DRIVING TOURS

Listed below are sights within the Discovering Provence section of the guide that you can find included on local driving tours.

When and Where to Go

WHEN TO GO
SEASONS

The region of Provence is blessed with mild weather throughout the year, especially along the coast. The rhythm of the seasons fluctuates somewhat, especially in the spring; even in winter the temperature can rise or fall dramatically in one day.

Spring

High pressure from Siberia abates from February on, allowing the Atlantic rains to fall. These rains are less violent than those in the autumn and bright and clear days are frequent. The mistral (see Winds), especially in March, can provoke a surprising chill for those who are not used to the whims of a Provençal spring.

Summer

This is the season. In these three or four months, the heat and lack of rain attract sun-loving crowds to this popular region. It rains no more than 70mm/2.75in and the daily temperature consistently reaches 28°C/82.4°F. The dry heat is not overpowering; its constancy is explained by the presence of a hot air mass from the Sahara, protected from the west's humid depressions by the Massif Central.

Autumn

The reflux of high pressure of tropical origin opens the way to Atlantic depressions. From mid-September to late November, rain appears; sometimes violent rainstorms provoke flash floods. The rainfall can amount to more than 100mm/3.94in in 1hr (annually 600mm/23.6in).

Winter

The cold season – which is often sunny – is relatively mild and dry. The temperature can drop 10°C/18°F in a few hours because of the mistral. The Mediterranean's liquid mass reduces the cold front and prevents snowfalls except on the peaks.

WINDS

The wind is an essential part of the Provençal climate. The best known is the mistral (mistrau means master in Provençal, thus master-wind). This strong, dry, cold northwesterly wind sweeps down when the pressure is high over the mountains. It can rage like a storm, then disappear as suddenly as it arrives. Two other common winds in this region are the southeast marin, bringing rain and fog, and the southwest labech, bringing rainstorms.

CLIMATE

Writers have acclaimed Provence's temperate climate, low rainfall and exceptional light. Nonetheless, weather conditions are changeable from year to year. Provence's land relief and the sea play an important role. Maritime Provence enjoys a more agreeable climate (less rain and hotter) than the hinterland, where altitude modifies the temperature considerably. But the dominant factor remains the long periods of sunshine (more than 2 500hr per year) in the region.

WHAT TO PACK

As little as possible!
Cleaning and laundry services are available everywhere and most personal items can be replaced at reasonable cost.
Try to pack everything in one suitcase and a carry-on bag. Take an umbrella – and an extra tote bag for packing new purchases, shopping at the open-air markets, carrying a picnic, etc.
Be sure luggage is clearly labelled and old travel tags removed.

WHERE TO GO
ONE WEEK

With good international access, Marseille makes a convenient starting point. Explore the city first, then drive northwest to Arles for its Roman amphitheatre. From here you can take in delightful St-Rémy-de-Provence before heading north to Avignon to see the Pope's Palace. Allow a day there before moving east to relax in the Luberon countryside, having a look at some of its hilltop villages and perhaps one of its two magnificent abbeys. You should have time for a full day in historic Aix-en-Provence before returning to Marseille.

TWO WEEKS

A two-week tour could incorporate everything on the one-week itinerary but allow for more exploration at the northern end of the loop (and more downtime, too). Begin with Marseille, then Arles and the Camargue followed by Les Baux-de-Provence as well as St-Rémy. Avignon comes next, requiring at least a day if you want to see more than the Pope's Palace and the old streets within the ramparts. From there, sample the delights of the wine capital, Châteauneuf-du-Pape, followed by Orange with its famous Roman Theatre. The ravishing Dentelles de Montmirail will provide refreshing walks and soothing views, leading on to more history at Vaison-la-Romaine before you head south again.

During the second week, visit Carpentras and mighty Mont Ventoux, then see the lovely Luberon including villages like Gordes and Roussillon as well as the 12C abbeys of Senanque and Silvacane. You should squeeze in Apt also, with its great market if the timing is right, before moving on to Aix-en-Provence. Try to take in Cézanne country around Montagne Ste-Victoire as well as the architectural gems of the city itself. After all that, you'll deserve a lazy stop on the coast, perhaps in picturesque Cassis, before you go back to Marseille.

HISTORICAL ITINERARIES

In France, several driving itineraries that encompass sights of historical interest have been officially designated "Routes historiques" by the Fédération nationale des Routes historiques de France (*www.routes-historiques.com*).

Unfortunately, none of these routes cross the Provence region, but below are some itineraries with important historical value that can be accessed in this region:

♦ **Route du Patrimoine Juif**
ADT Vaucluse Tourisme.
℘04 90 80 47 00.
www.provenceguide.com.

♦ **Route Historique des Vaudois en Luberon**
3 rue du Four. 843000 Merindol.
℘04 90 72 91 76.
www.chateaux-france.com/route-vaudois.

♦ **Via Domitia** *(for cyclists only)*
Comité Régional du Tourisme Provence-Alpes-Côte d'Azur
℘04 91 56 47 00.
www.decouverte-paca.fr.

Historical itineraries are signposted along country roads. All of them are detailed in handbooks available from local tourist offices.

PAINTERS' PATHS, WRITERS' FOOTSTEPS

The **Route des Peintres de la Lumière en Provence** offers an introduction to the region through the various sites painted by artists who created radiant works suffused with light (*see Introduction, p90*).
For details, enquire at the *Comité Régional du Tourisme Provence-Alpes-Côte d'Azur (℘04 91 56 47 00; www.decouverte-paca.fr/us)*.
The tourist offices in Aix-en-Provence, St-Rémy-de-Provence and Arles (*see Aix-en-Provence, St-Rémy-de-Provence, Arles)* have information on thematic itineraries – **"In the steps of Cézanne" (Aix), "The places painted by Vincent van Gogh" (St Rémy)** and **"Arles et Vincent van Gogh" (Arles).**

Cassis viewed from Cap Canaille

©Didier Zylberyng/Travel Pictures

In Aubagne, you can walk or take a bus tour to explore the life of writer/film-maker **Marcel Pagnol**: enquire at the tourist office in Aubagne (&*see Aubagne*).

For a tour of the sites that inspired **Alphonse Daudet**'s famous *Lettres de Mon Moulin*, enquire at the tourist office in Fontvieille (&*see Les Alpilles*).

NATURE PARKS

Parc Naturel Régional de Camargue
&*See La Camargue.*
Mas du Pont de Rousty, 13200 Arles.
&04 90 97 10 82.

Parc Naturel Régional du Luberon
&*See La Montagne du Luberon.*
60 place Jean-Jaurès, BP 122, 84404 Apt Cedex. www.parcduluberon.fr.

MARINE PARKS

Marine parks (*www.aires-marines.fr*) feature preserved areas where fishing and diving activities, as well as boat anchoring are strictly regulated and where experiments with artificial reefs are being carried out. The aim of these parks is to fulfil a number of well-defined objectives, such as:

♦ protecting the natural environment (controlling all activities concerned with the development and survival of plant and animal species);

♦ exploiting the available resources (immersion of artificial reefs to encourage the growth of flora and fauna);

♦ installing blocks to hinder illicit trawling;

♦ and providing information to increase public awareness of ecological issues.

Parc Marin de la Côte Bleue
Lying west of Marseille harbour, it laps the Massif de la Nerthe, a rocky mountain range separating the Étang de Berre from the sea.
Information: Observatoire du Parc Marin de la Côte Bleue, , plage du Rouet, 31 avenue Jean-Bart, BP 42, 13620 Carry-le-Rouet. &04 42 45 45 07. www.parcmarincotebleue.fr.
Or from local tourist information centres in Carry-le-Rouet, Ensuès-la-Redonne, Martigues, Le Rove and Sausset-les-Pins.

Parc National des Calanques
The major marine park in the region is this brand new national park. Established in 2012, it spreads out over the marine areas of Marseille, Cassis and La Ciotat.
Information: Etablissement public du Parc national des Calanques
Bât A4 - 2 Impasse Paradou, 13009 Marseille &04 20 10 50 00.
www.calanques-parcnational.fr.

Lavender field, Valréas

© Alain Hocquel/LADT Vaucluse Tourisme

An Important Reminder

Never forget that the marine environment is extremely fragile and needs to be respected by all those who venture near it.
Make a point of observing the following rules:

- Dispose of plastic bags on shore in closed containers.
- Throw any fish you have caught back into the sea.
- Do not damage or remove the long, green *posidonia* leaves that cleanse seawater by renewing its oxygen.

OLIVES AND THE OIL INDUSTRY

There are several types of olives in Provence – *see Oil-rich Alpilles panel, p216*. To learn more about the olives and oils of the region, contact the Institut du Monde de l'Olivier, 40 place de la Libération, 26110 NYONS. ℘04 75 26 90 90. www.huilesetolives.fr. For driving itineraries, Provence offers thematic circuits that focus on the olive in various areas. These tours include visits to olive groves, mills, presses and museums in the area. *Information:* Association Française Interprofessionnelle de l'Olive, 13626 Aix-en-Provence Cedex. ℘04 42 23 01 92. www.afidol.org.

LAVENDER FIELDS

Created by the Regional Tourist Committee of the Provence-Alpes-Côte d'Azur area, the **Route de la Lavande** enables you to visit many places associated with the growing and processing of lavender around Mont Ventoux, the Luberon and the Provençal Drôme. This circuit is complemented by various festivities, such as Fête de la Lavande in Sault between mid-August, and the **Corso Nocturne de la Lavande** in Valréas at the beginning of August.
For more information on lavender, visit www.grande-traversee-alpes. com/routes-de-la-lavande.

TRUFFLES

The Vaucluse is the main truffle-producing region. If you are here from mid-November to mid-March, you can enjoy a visit to the winter truffle markets that take place in the morning. *See Black Diamonds panel p314.*

- **Carpentras**
  The most important truffle market of the Vaucluse, runs from mid-Nov–mid-Mar, Fri 9am.
- **Richerenches**
  An important market: mid-Nov–mid-Mar, every Sat from 10am.

WINE VISITS

Many wine cellars *(caves)* are open for visits all over the wine-producing regions of Provence. Some individual producers and co-operatives also offer themed tastings, vineyard walks, cycle rides and so on.

For details, check with the appropriate tourist offices, or check the websites of the wine organisations listed below. Also consult Michelin's *The Wine Regions of France.*

Wine festivals are held in countless wine villages throughout the region. Again, details are easily obtainable from tourist offices or wine s*yndicat* websites. ◖*See Gateway to Wine panel, p254.*

Côtes-du-Rhône Wines
Inter Rhône,
6 rue des Trois Faucons, 84024 Avignon Cedex 1. ℘04 90 27 24 00. www.rhone-wines.com.
Inter Rhône produces an excellent guide, *Tourism & Vineyards in the Rhône Valley,* as well as smaller information booklets and brochures. Suggested itineraries detailed in these include L'Enclave des Papes; Orange to Vaison-la-Romaine; the Dentelles de Montmirail; Châteauneuf-du-Pape; around Avignon; the Ventoux and the Luberon.

Ventoux Wines
AOC Ventoux, Maison des Vins 388 ave Jean-Jaurès, 84206 Carpentras. ℘04 90 63 36 50. www.aoc-ventoux.fr.

Luberon Wines
Les Vins AOC Luberon, boulevard du Rayol, 84160 Lourmarin. ℘04 90 07 34 40. www.vins-luberon.fr.

Côtes-de-Provence, Coteaux d'Aix-en-Provence, and Coteaux du Varois en Provence Wines
Conseil interprofessionnel des vins du Provence, Maison des Vins, RN7, 83460 Les Arcs sur Argens, ℘04 94 99 50 10. www.vinsdeprovence.com.
The umbrella organisation for these *appellations* provides a range of useful information related to wine tourism.

Cassis Wines
Maison des Vins Cassis,
Route de Marseille, 13260 Cassis. ℘04 42 01 15 61. www.maisondesvinscassis.com.

Harvesting, Dentelles de Montmirail

© V. Giller/L'ADT Vaucluse Tourisme

What to See and Do

OUTDOOR FUN
MARINAS

Most of the seaside resorts lying between Le Grau-du-Roi and La Ciotat (&see Where to Stay) have well-equipped marinas. The main ones, running from west to east, are: Aigues-Mortes, Le Grau-du-Roi, Port-Camargue, Les Saintes-Maries/Port Gardian, Port-St-Gervais to Fos-sur-Mer, Martigues, Les Heures Claires at Istres, Carro, Sausset-les-Pins, Carry-le-Rouet, L'Estaque, Le Frioul, Marseille Pointe Rouge and Le Vieux Port, Cassis and La Ciotat.

Le Grau-du-Roi, Marseille, Port-St-Gervais to Fos-sur-Mer, Cassis and Port-Camargue have been awarded the Pavillon Bleu d'Europe (Blue Flag), granted on the basis of the following criteria: clean site and surroundings, special equipment and amenities, reception and information services, educational facilities.

Most seaside resorts have sailing schools where courses are organised. In season, you can hire boats with or without a crew.

For further information, contact the local harbour-master's office or the **Fédération Française de Voile** (01 40 60 37 00. www.ffvoile.fr).

SCUBA DIVING

Marseille and its surroundings have always been a privileged setting for diving activities. It was here that Jacques-Yves Cousteau and Émile Gagnan achieved their record-breaking performances that paved the way for modern diving with the invention of the aqualung.

The most popular spots for deep-sea diving are the *calanques* around Marseille, where the seabed is truly a feast for the eyes. Despite subsequent damage caused by pollutant waste, excessive harpoon fishing and the combing of wrecks for their valuable archaeological significance, the *calanques* still provide exceptional interest for divers with their abundance of multicoloured fish, gorgonia, sponge, purple sea urchins, crayfish and mother-of-pearl.

Six exceptional sites can be explored: Le Chaouen, a Moroccan cargo ship, which ran aground on the Île de Planier (off Marseille); La Drôme, a shipwreck lying at a depth of 51m/168ft; Le Liban, a liner that sank in front of the Île Maïre in 1903; Les Impériaux, a site renowned for its huge gorgonian fish; La Cassidaigne, a seaway teeming with fish at the foot of the lighthouse (4 nautical miles from Cassis), and Île Verte, an islet with luxuriant vegetation and waters teeming with fish.

This sport requires lengthy and challenging training, which can only be provided by fully qualified instructors holding nationally recognised diplomas. For a list of clubs offering scuba-diving courses, contact the local branch of the **Fédération Française d'Études et de Sports Sous-Marins** (04 91 33 99 31. www.ffessm.fr). This organisation publishes the magazine *Subaqua* every two months. The Centre UCPA in Niolon is Europe's biggest training centre for deep-sea diving (04 91 46 90 16). Books about diving can be found at the Librairie Maritime bookshop (*26 quai de Rive-Neuve, 13007 Marseille;* 04 91 54 79 40). The Centre Cassidain de Plongée (06 71 52 60 20. www.cassis-calanques-plongee.com) in Cassis offers one-to-one first dives (*Baptême*) in English for €65. Also check out Plongée Passion Carry (04 42 45 08 00. www.plongee-passion-carry.com) on the Côte Bleue, which offers first dives in English from €68.

SEA FISHING

Although the Mediterranean is not the busiest fishing spot in France, shoals of rock fish abound: red mullet, conger and moray eels as well as numerous octopuses, spider crabs, various squid and even the odd crayfish. In shallow, sandy waters there are skate, sole and dab. Offshore, shoals of sardines, anchovies and tuna fish intermingle with sea bream, bass and grey mullet. No permit is necessary for sea angling, provided that the day's catch is for personal consumption only.

BOAT TRIPS

Leaving from Marseille, you can visit the Château d'If, the Îles du Frioul and the *calanques*; leaving from Cassis, you can visit the *calanques* at Port-Miou, Port-Pin and En-Vau. &See *Les Calanques*.

Leaving from La Ciotat, you can visit the Île Verte (&*see La Ciotat)*. The excursions leaving from La Ciotat are on board a catamaran-type boat offering views of the sea depths cruising among the *calanques* of La Ciotat, between Cassis and Marseille. For details contact **Les Amis des Calanques** (&*06 09 35 25 68. www.visite-calanques.fr).*

Tiki III (&*04 90 97 81 68. www.tiki3.fr),* leaving from Les Saintes-Maries-de-la-Mer, will take you along the River Rhône between March and November. The trip offers an insight into the Camargue of the *gardian*: herds of bulls and horses grazing on the plains; herons, flamingos and egrets on the banks of the tamarisk-dotted river. In Le Grau-du-Roi, you can hire a boat (&*licence required in some cases)* to cruise the canals from **Cap 2000** (*ZA Port de Pêche. &04 66 51 41 54)* or **A2M** at Port-Camargue (&*04 66 53 35 18).* Sea lovers will enjoy the Nautiques de Port-Camargue (&*04 66 51 81 65. www.lesnautiques.com),* a nautical fair devoted to used boats that takes place in March or April.

WALKING

Exploring Provence on foot is an enchanting way of discovering the all-encompassing brightness of Provençal light as it sets off the beauty of the landscape to perfection, both in its natural, unspoiled state, and featuring the evidence of humankind's passage through village and countryside. Leave the car behind and experience

a different, more relaxed pace of life in a landscape that rings with the echoes of days gone by.

Many long-distance footpaths (*sentiers de Grande Randonnée* – GR) cover the area described in this guide. The GR 4 crosses the lower Vivarais country as far as Mont Ventoux; to climb up the mountain, you can start in the Bédoin Forest and follow GR 91 and 91B (information in the Bédoin tourist office: &*04 90 65 63 95. www.bedoin. org).* GR 42 leads along the valley of the Rhône; GR 6 follows the River Gard as far as Beaucaire and then plunges into the Alpilles and Luberon ranges; GR 9 takes the line of the north face of Mont Ventoux, then crosses the Vaucluse plateau, the Luberon range, Montagne Ste-Victoire and the massif of Ste-Baume. Further variations on the above are offered by the GRs 63, 92, 97 and 98. Besides the long-distance footpaths, there are short- to medium-distance paths ranging from walks of a few hours to a couple of days (*Petit Randonnée* – PR).

The **Fédération Française de la Randonnée Pédestre** publishes "topo-guides" available from its information centre (&*01 44 89 93 93;. www.ffrandonnee.fr).* The regional guides describe long-distance trails (GR, for *Grande Randonnée* and GRP for *Grande Randonnée de Pays)* and shorter ones (PR – *Petite Randonnée)* in detail, with distances and approximate times. **Cicerone Press** in the UK (*www.cicerone.co.uk)* publish two up-to-date walking guidebooks: *Walking in Provence – West (ISBN: 978-1-85284-616-9),* covering Drôme Provençal, Vaucluse and Var, and *Walking in Provence – East (ISBN: 978-1-85284-617-6),* covering Alpes Maritimes, Alpes de Haute-Provence and Mercantour.

Another source of maps and guides for excursions on foot is the **Institut national de l'information géographique et forestière (IGN)**. Their website (*www.ign.fr)* is available in English. Among their publications, that you can order online are France

😊 A Bit of Advice 😊

A French bylaw rules that access to forests and other wooded massifs is strictly forbidden between 1 July and the second Saturday in September, and when winds blow at over 40kph/25mph.

903, a map showing all of the GRs and PRs in France; the *Série Bleue* and *Top 25* maps, at a scale of 1:25,000 (1cm = 250m), which show all paths as well as refuges, campsites and beaches for a specific area.

In Provence itself, you can find many of the publications cited above in book shops, at sports centres or outdoor equipment shops, and elsewhere. For information on walking the *calanques*, contact **Les Excursionnistes Marseillais** (*16 r. de la Rotonde, 13001 Marseille.* 📞*04 91 84 75 52. www.excurs.com*).

HORSE RIDING

The **Comité national de Tourisme Équestre** (📞*02 54 94 46 80. www.ffe. com*) is a useful source of information if you would like to plan a riding holiday. The website lists horse-friendly holiday cottages, riding trails and riding centres. It also publishes "l'Estafette" (€6.20 for a year – four issues), a review of local events and information on maps for riders, children's activities etc, and the catalogue *Cheval Nature*, where you will find further information including the addresses of riding centres (*Centres de Tourisme Équestre*) region by region, and practical tips on holidays for kids, insurance and more.

Riding is a favourite pastime in the **Camargue**. Go to Ranch La Brouzetière (*rte d'Arles, 13460 Les Saintes-Maries-de-la-Mer.* 📞*06 16 59 51 24*). if you dream of riding one of the famous white horses on the plain, in the marshes or along the beach, the ranch offers half-day rides for €45 and full-day rides (*lunch not included*) from €80.

Another good place on the way into Les Saintes-Maries-de-la-Mer is Les Écuries de l'Auberge Cavalière du Pont des Bannes (*rte d'Arles, 13460 Les Saintes-Maries de la Mer.* 📞*06 63 65 26 08. www.ecuries-cavaliere. camargue.fr*), which has highly qualified instructors and offers riding lessons; 4hr rides cost €100 (*including lunch, but no beverage*). On the Espiguette road there are several stables: Écurie des Dunes (📞*04 66 53 09 28. www.ecuriedesdunes.com*),

Camargue horses

© M. Raynaud/Comité Régional de Tourisme Provence-Alpes-Côte d'Azur

Mas de l'Espiguette (📞04 66 51 51 89. *www.masdelespiguette.com*), Ranch du Phare (📞04 66 53 10 87), Ranch Lou Seden (📞04 66 51 74 75) and Abrivado Ranch (📞04 66 53 01 00; *www. abrivadoranch.fr*).

CYCLING

For general information concerning cycling in France, contact the **Fédération Française de Cyclotourisme** (📞01 56 20 88 88. *www.ffct.org*). Off-road enthusiasts should contact the **Fédération Française de Cyclisme** (📞01 49 35 69 00. *www.ffc.fr*) and request the *Guide Officiel des Sites VTT-FFC*. The IGN (*www.ign.fr*) offers Map 906 (*Randonnées à vélo*). The websites provide addresses of local clubs and a calendar of events.

A favourite challenge is to tackle Mont Ventoux by bike. Contact the tourist office in Bédoin for details of trails (📞04 90 65 63 95. *www.bedoin.org*). Local tourist offices have a list of cycle hire firms (including some SNCF train stations).

Europbike Provence (*1 r. Philippe-Lebon, Arles*. 📞06 38 14 49 50. *www. europbike-Provence.net*) offers bike rental seven days a week. It has offices in Arles, Avignon and Aix-en-Provence. If riding on roads, make sure you have your wits about you.

SKIING

You can practise both downhill and cross-country skiing at the Mont-Serein resort (the secondary peak of Mont Ventoux, 1 445m high). *For details, contact the reception chalet/ tourist information desk at the ski resort Chalet d'Accueil: 📞04 90 63 42 02. www.stationdumontserein.com.*

ROCK CLIMBING

Rock climbing is possible all year up the Dentelles de Montmirail or the cliffs in the *calanques* near Marseille. 🙂*Access to the calanques is forbidden from 1 July to the second Saturday in September.* The local branch of the **Club Alpin Français**

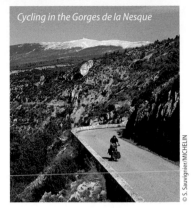
Cycling in the Gorges de la Nesque

© S. Sauvignier/MICHELIN

Marseille-Provence (📞04 91 54 25 84. *http://cafmarseille.free.fr*) organises accompanied climbing trips.

General information can be obtained from the **Fédération Française de la Montagne et de l'Escalade** (📞01 40 18 75 50. *www.ffme.fr*).

For the Dentelles de Montmirail, contact the tourist information centre of Gigondas (📞04 90 65 85 46. *www.gigondas-dm.fr*).

CANOEING/KAYAKING

Canoeing is a good way to explore the less accessible stretches of the Durance and Sorgue rivers in Provence. Sea kayaking in the calanques is a major activity in the region. The **Fédération départementale de canoë-kayak du Vaucluse** (📞04 26 03 17 25 or 06 11 52 16 73. *www.canoe-paca.fr* or *www. canoe-vaucluse.fr*) and the **Fédération départementale de canoë-kayak des Bouches-du-Rhône** (📞04 91 76 51 41) can provide local information. Between Fontaine-de-Vaucluse and Isle-sur-la-Sorgue, a 8km/5mi trip on the Sorgue will enable you to discover the beauty of the local landscape. Contact **Kayak Vert Aqueduc** in Fontaine-de-Vaucluse (📞04 90 20 35 44. *www.canoe-france.com*).

In conjunction with the **Fédération Française de Canoë-Kayak** (📞01 45 11 08 50. *www.ffck.org*), IGN publishes Map 905 called *Canoë-Kayaken France*, which lists all the different excursions, classifying them in terms of difficulty. It is also great to make an excursion to the rivers of Ardèche, Cèze and the Gardon. Bear in mind that the stretch of the Ardèche between Charmes and Sauze has been designated a natural reserve and special rules are enforced: no windsurfing, no boats with more than three people allowed, compulsory life jackets. Camping is possible only in Gaud and Gournier, for no longer than two nights.

For further practical information, contact the **Maison de la Réserve** at Gournier (*04 75 04 36 38. www.gorgesdelardeche.fr*).

The **Association de Protection des Gorges de l'Ardèche** publishes a plastic-coated map showing difficult stretches of river and possible refuelling stops along the river. It can be found at local tourist information centres.

For a trip in the area around Bagnols-sur-Cèze, contact the association **CAPCANOE** (*route de Barjac, 30500 St-Ambroix. *04 66 24 25 16. http://capcanoe.com*). There is a choice of three routes along the River Cèze (4, 8 and 29km/2.5, 5 and 18mi) and a route of 14km/8.7mi through the Cèze gorges.

Upstream from the Pont du Gard, you can safely practise canoeing on

Canoeing on the Sorgue

© Alain Hocquel/L'ADT Vaucluse Tourisme

the Gardon (4 trips of 4, 8, 11 and 22km/2.5, 5, 7 and 14mi). Contact **Kayak Vert** in Collias (*8 chemin Saint-Vincent, 30210 Collias. *04 66 22 80 76. www.canoe-france.com*).

BULLFIGHTING EVENTS

The Camargue area, and especially the famous Camargue bull, have always been at the heart of French bullfighting or bull running. *Courses camarguaises* involve men called *raseteurs* chasing a bull around an arena in a bid to remove a rosette (*cocarde*) from between its horns. The bull is not killed, and the beasts take part in the games year after year, often becoming famous in their own right: some even have a statue erected in their native village! The major event takes place in Arles – the *Cocarde d'Or* – on the first Monday in July. Local newspapers give the dates for events in other locations. You can also find information on the website of the Fédération Française de la Course Camarguaise (*www.ffcc.info*) or at www.camargue.fr.

Originally, bullfighting was a Spanish tradition, but it gradually spread to Provence in the 18C. *Corridas* and *novilladas* are usually held during *férias*, large celebrations that bring huge crowds to the arenas and create a lively atmosphere in the town centre: *abrivados* (bulls are let loose on the streets), *peñas* (brass bands) playing along pavements and in the *bodegas* (bars), dances, etc. Arles stages the famous *Féria de Pâques* at Easter. In Saintes-Maries-de-la-Mer, the *corridas* are performed on horseback (*Féria du Cheval*). To attend a *corrida* or a *novillada*, it is best to book in advance by contacting one of the following offices: **Arles:** *Arènes d'Arles, BP 42, 13633 Arles Cedex* (*08 91 70 03 70 – charge of €0.225/min. www.arenes-arles.com*) *and Domaine de Méjanes* (*04 90 97 10 10. www.mejanes. camargue.fr*). **Saintes-Maries-de-la-Mer:** *Arènes des Saintes-Maries-de-la-Mer* (*04 90 97 85 86*). The best seats are on the side of the arena.

ACTIVITIES FOR KIDS 👨‍👧

In this guide, sights of particular interest to children are indicated with a Kids symbol (👨‍👧). Some attractions offer discount fees for children. Here are a few sights and activities that children especially should enjoy – and they make a change from a day at the beach.

OK Corral (∞€22, child €20. ☎04 42 73 80 05. www.okcorral.fr), situated between Aubagne and La Ciotat, this Wild West theme park features fun rides in a super setting.

Amazonia near Bagnols-sur-Cèze in the Gard (∞€15, child €14; €13/€12 in low season. ☎04 66 82 53 92. www.parcamazonia.fr) is another theme park, with an Aztec-Mayan theme.

The **Bonbon Museum** (☎04 66 22 74 39; www.haribo.com) in Uzès offers children a sweet treat.

Just south of Gordes in the Vaucluse, the **Village des Bories** (∞€6, children, 12–17, €4. ☎04 90 72 03 48. www.gordes-village.com) is now a museum that showcases rural life in its old stone dwellings, some 500 years in age.

At **Parc du Cosmos** (∞€13, children, 6–15, €10. ☎04 90 25 66 82. www.parcducosmos.eu) in Les Angles, near Villeneuve-lès-Avignon, the stars and planets are the featured performers.

Outside Aix-en-Provence, **Greasque mining centre** (∞€3, free under 6 yrs. ☎04 42 69 77 00. www.ville-greasque.fr), a museum inside a formerly active (1922-1960) coal mine, offers insight into the life of a miner.

West of Villeneuve Lez Avignon, a 19C castle houses a fascinating collection of bicycles and motor bikes on display in the **Musée du Vélo et de la Moto** (∞€6, child €5. ☎04 66 57 65 11). Exotic creatures can be found at **La Barben Zoo** (∞€15, children, 3–12, €10. ☎04 90 55 19 12. www.zoolabarben.com) near Salon-de-Provence. If you are in the area at the end of June, be sure to attend the **Fête de la Tarasque** in Tarascon, an enchantment for all ages.

SIGHTSEEING
FROM ABOVE

One way of discovering the beautiful landscapes of Provence from above is gliding. The following companies organise trips throughout Provence:

♦ **Association Vélivole de Carpentras**, BP 08, 84210 Pernes les Fontaines. ☎04 90 60 08 17. http://planeurs.carpentras.pagesperso-orange.fr.

♦ **Aéro-Club St-Rémy-les-Alpilles**, chemin du Romanin, 13210 St-Rémy-de-Provence. ☎04 90 92 08 43. www.aeroclub-alpilles.fr.

♦ **Centre de Vol à Voile de la Crau**, Aérodrome de Salon-Eyguières, 13300 Salon-de-Provence. ☎04 90 42 00 91. www.planeur13.com.

General information can be obtained from the Fédération Française d'ULM (☎01 49 81 74 43. www.ffplum.com).

FROM BELOW GROUND

Provence is packed with many **archaeological sites** that welcome voluntary diggers in summer. Every spring, the magazines *Archeologia*, *L'Archéologue* and *Archéologie* list sites that are looking for new recruits. Contact regional archaeology departments *(Services Régionaux de l'Archéologie)* for details.

♦ **Ardèche and Drôme**: DRAC Rhône-Alpes, 6 quai St-Vincent, 69283 Lyon Cedex 01. ☎04 72 00 44 00. www.culturecommunication.gouv.fr/Regions/Drac-Rhone-Alpes.

♦ **Bouches-du-Rhône, Var and Vaucluse**: DRAC Provence-Alpes-Côte d'Azur, 23 boulevard du Roi-René, 13617 Aix-en-Provence Cedex 1. ☎04 42 16 19 00, www.culturecommunication.gouv.fr/Regions/Drac-Paca.

♦ **Gard**: 5 rue de la Salle-l'Évêque, CS 49 020, 34967 Montpellier Cedex 2. ☎04 67 02 32 00. www.culturecommunication.gouv.fr/Regions/Drac-Languedoc-Roussillon.

Aperitifs and liqueurs from Provence

© S. Sauvignier/ MICHELIN

Shopping

VALUE ADDED TAX

There is a **Value Added Tax** (VAT) in France of 19.2 percent on almost every purchase (books and some foods are subject to a lower rate). However, non-European visitors who spend more than €175 in any one participating store can apply for a refund of the VAT. Usually, you fill out a form at the store, showing your passport.

Upon leaving the country, you submit all forms to customs for approval (they may want to see the goods, so if possible don't pack them in checked luggage).

The refund is usually paid directly into your bank or credit card account, or it can be sent by mail. Big department stores that cater to tourists provide special services to help you; be sure to mention that you plan to seek a refund before you pay for goods (no refund is possible for tax on services).

If you are visiting two or more countries within the European Union, submit the forms on departure from only the last EU country. The refund is worthwhile for those visitors who would like to buy fashion, furniture or other fairly expensive items, but remember, the minimum amount must be spent in a single shop (though not necessarily on the same day).

People travelling **to the USA** cannot import plant products or fresh food, including fruit, cheeses and nuts. It is acceptable, however, to carry tinned products or preserves. Among the souvenirs you might like to bring home are the famous *santons* figurines from Aubagne, Arles or Marseille. Tarascon is known for its Provençal cloth, although it can be bought throughout the entire region. Provence is celebrated for its candied fruit (Apt, Aix) or its olive oil (Alpilles region).

SPECIALITIES FROM PROVENCE

Crafts and Workshops

Numerous craft workshops can be found along the coast and inland, representing a wide variety of cottage industries. Most of them welcome visitors during the summer, but it is always advisable to book in advance.

Alcohol

♦   Distillerie Liqueur Frigolet (Élixir du Révérend Père Gaucher), 26 rue Voltaire, BP 88, 13160 Châteaurenard. ℘04 90 94 11 08. www.frigoletliqueur.com.

Antiques

l'Isle-sur-la-Sorgue boasts no fewer than 160 antiques dealers, with shops in five separate "villages".

- The largest one is the Village des Antiquaires de la Gare, 2 bis avenue de l'Égalité, 84800 L'Isle-sur-la-Sorgue. ℘04 90 38 04 57. www.levillage desantiquairesdelagare.com.
- Galerie des Antiquaires de Lignane, RN 7, Lignane, 13540 Puyricard. ℘04 42 92 38 28. www. curiositel.com/aix_en_ provence/antiquaires_ lignane.htm.

Provençal Cloth

- Annie Sotinel, hameau Les Pourquiers, D156 *(behind the Huppe farm)*, 84220 Gordes. ℘04 90 72 05 71.
- Souleiado, 39 rue Charles-Deméry, 13150 Tarascon. ℘04 90 91 76 05. www.souleiado.com.
- Les Olivades, 5 avenue du docteur Barberin, chemin des Indienneurs 13103 St-Étienne-du-Grès. ℘04 90 49 19 19. www.lesolivades.fr.

Provençal Furniture

- Meubles Melani, route d'Eyguières, Pont de Crau, 13200 Arles. ℘06 15 09 49 50. www.meubles-melani. com (tour of workshops for small groups by appointment).
- Meubles Bonjean, 747 route de l'Isle-sur-la-Sorgue, 84250 Le Thor. ℘04 90 33 82 94 (tours during the week).

Santons and Faïence Pottery

- Santons Marcel Carbonel, 49 rue Neuve-Sainte-Catherine, 13007 Marseille. ℘04 91 13 61 36. www.santonsmarcelcarbonel.com.
- Maison Chave *(santons)*, 37 rue Frédéric-Mistral, 13400 Aubagne. ℘04 42 70 12 86.
- Santons Fouque, 65 cours Gambetta, 13100 Aix-en-Provence. ℘04 42 26 33 38. www.santons-fouque.com.
- Les Deux Provençales *(santons and faïence)*, 2 boulevard Émile-Combes, 13400 Aubagne. ℘04 42 01 39 62. www.lesdeux provencales.com.

- Poterie Ravel (faïence), avenue des Goums, 13400 Aubagne. ℘04 42 82 42 00. www.poterie-ravel.com.
- Vernin Carreaux d'Apt Matières et Idées (clay tiles), Le Pont Julien, 84480 Bonnieux. ℘04 90 74 00 47.

Soaps

- Savonnerie Marius Fabre, 148 avenue Paul-Bourret, 13300 Salon-de-Provence. ℘04 90 53 82 75. www.marius-fabre.fr.

Sweets

- Confiserie Léonard Parli (calissons d'Aix), 35 avenue Victor Hugo, 13100 Aix-en-Provence. ℘04 42 26 05 71. www.leonard-parli.com.
- Confiserie du Mont Ventoux (Berlingot sweets), 1184 avenue D-Eisenhower, 84200 Carpentras. ℘04 90 63 05 25. www.berlingots.net.

PROVENÇAL MARKETS

Provence's picturesque markets enliven city streets and village squares. Find high-quality local produce and crafts (fruit and vegetables, flowers, spices, herbs, olives, honey, cheese, fabric); and stallholders with broad southern French accents!

Aix-en-Provence – Traditional market on place Richelme daily. General market on place des Prêcheurs and place de la Madeleine Tuesdays, Thursdays and Saturdays.
Flower market on place d'Hôtel de Ville Tuesdays, Thursdays and Saturdays.
Flea market on place Verdun Tuesdays, Thursdays and Saturdays.

Apt – Traditional market Saturdays. Farmers' market Tuesdays (May–November).

Arles – Traditional market Wednesdays (boulevard Émile-Combes) and Saturdays (boulevard des Lices and boulevard Clemenceau).

Flea market on boulevard des Lices the first Wednesday of each month.

Aubagne – Traditional market on cours Voltaire, Tuesdays, Thursdays and weekends. Flea market at La Tourtelle the last Sunday of each month.

Avignon – Traditional market daily except Mondays at les Halles (*www.avignon-leshalles.com*). Flower market on place des Carmes, Saturdays. Flea market on place des Carmes, Sundays.

Market in Avignon
© Illustrez-vous/Fotolia.com

Beaucaire – Traditional market, Thursdays and Sundays.

Bédoin – Provençal market, Mondays.

Cadenet – Farmers' market, Mondays and Saturdays.

Carpentras – Traditional market around the station, daily. Truffle market Fridays (November–March).

Cavaillon – Traditional market, Mondays.

La Ciotat – Handicraft market every evening 8pm to midnight at the Vieux Port in July and August.

Fontvieille – Handicraft market, once a week 4pm to 9pm in June, July and August.

Gardanne – Traditional market in the town centre Wednesdays, Fridays and Sundays.

Graveson – Farmers' market on place du Marché, 4pm to 8pm Fridays May–October (*www.lemarchepaysan.com*).

L'Isle-sur-la-Sorgue – Traditional market Thursdays and Sundays. Flea market on avenue des Quatre Otages, Sundays.

Marseille – ♿See Marseille, Addresses.

Orange – Traditional market Thursdays.

Pertuis – Traditional market Fridays. Farmers' market Wednesdays and Saturdays.

St-Rémy-de-Provence – Traditional market Wednesdays on place de la République and place Pélissier.

Les Stes-Maries-de-la-Mer – Traditional market on place des Gitans Mondays and Fridays.

Salon-de-Provence – Traditional market on place Morgan and along the cours, Wednesdays. Flea market on place Morgan the first Sunday of each month.

Tarascon – Traditional market in the town centre Tuesdays.

Vaison-la-Romaine – Traditional market Tuesdays. Provençal market in the upper town Sundays (June–September).

Valréas – Traditional market Wednesdays and Saturdays.

FAIRS AND EXHIBITIONS

Arles – Santons Fair (*Salon International des Santonniers*) November–January.

Aubagne – Santons and Ceramics Fair (*Foire aux Santons et à la Céramique*), July and August and early December to early January.

L'Isle-sur-la-Sorgue – Antiques Fair (*Foire aux Antiquités*) Easter Sunday and the Sunday around 15 August.

Marseille – International Fair in September. Santons Fair (*Foire aux Santons*) at La Canebière from the last Sunday in November to 31 December.

Books and Films

BOOKS
PERSONAL EXPERIENCE

Village in the Vaucluse – *Laurence Wylie (3rd ed. Harvard University Press, reprinted 2005).* Written by Wylie, a sociologist, in the years following World War II, this is a sincere, in-depth look at rural France in the years of post-war recovery.

Two Towns in Provence – *M F K Fisher (Vintage, new ed. 2002).* This is a reissue under one cover of *A Considerable Town* (Marseilles) and *Map of Another Town* (Aix-en-Provence). Well known for her cookbooks and treatises on culinary arts, she has here set down parts of her life story when she was living in southern France in the 1950s.

A Year in Provence, Toujours Provence, Provence Encore, Provence A-Z – *Peter Mayle (Alfred A. Knopf).* These best-selling books have been credited with stirring up interest in Provence and all things Provençal, including house renovation and the game of *boules*.

The Magic of Provence: Pleasures of Southern France – *Yvonne Lenard (Broadway Books, 2002).* Lenard is an American with French origins who, after a teaching stint in Aix, decided to stay on in the Luberon. She tells some entertaining stories about local characters and events, and closes most chapters with a doable recipe.

FOOD AND WINE

The Provence of Alain Ducasse – *Alain Ducasse and François Simon (Assouline Pub. 2000).* This hardback, coffee-table book is by a Michelin-starred chef whose love for the region of Provence is apparent in every page. In addition to recipes, luscious photographs, information about regional products (flowers, olive oils, herbs, etc.), there are tips on finding the best markets, café terraces, wineries and gardens.

Patricia Wells at Home in Provence: Recipes Inspired by her Farmhouse in France – *Patricia Wells, photographs by Robert Freson (Prentice Hall, 1996).* Lovers of French fare, whether prepared at home in the kitchen or savoured in restaurants both grand and humble, are well acquainted with Wells' reviews and recipes.

Markets of Provence: A Culinary Tour of Southern France – *Dixon Long, Ruthanne Long, photographs by David Wakely (HarperCollins, 1995).* This book offers ways to really blend in with the local life by discovering the daily markets (and asking vendors about their specialities), visiting vintners or finding the freshest goat cheese and bread. It even includes directions to favoured picnic spots.

Flavours of Provence: Recipes from the South of France – *Clare Ferguson (Ryland, Peters & Small, 2007).* Great cookbook full of regional information and authentic recipes.

FICTION

Hotel Pastis – *Peter Mayle (Penguin, 1994).* More Mayle, anyone? This one is a tale of fun, love and outlandish schemes in the sunny south: the best of Mayle's novels.

The Sacred Pool – *L Warren Douglas (Baen Books, 2001).* Set in the early Middle Ages and greatly inspired by folklore, full of magic and mysticism, and offers an interesting perspective on history.

Toujours Dead – *Susan Kiernan-Lewis (Abdale Books, 2001).* A whodunnit that does it in the setting of a quaint village in Provence, and involves the handsome heir to an ancient vineyard, who also happens to be a great cook.

Jean de Florette and Manon des Sources – Marcel Pagnol, translated by W Evan Heyningen (Prion Books, 2004).

These two books, which follow one another in sequence, are acclaimed works of French literature, and admirable in their faithfulness to the region's character. Visit Pagnol's home in Aubagne to get a real feel for them.

REGIONAL INTEREST AND ART

The Most Beautiful Villages of Provence– Michael Jacobs, photographs by Hugh Palmer (Thames and Hudson,1994). The villages of Provence are especially photogenic, drenched in colour, bright with flowers, fountains sparkling in the squares.

Colours of Provence – Michel Biehn (Stewart, Tabori & Chang, 1997). This intriguing book is divided into chapters entitled "Red", "Orange", "Yellow", "Green", "Blue" and "White, Black & Gray". The text ventures from Van Gogh and Picasso, to local fabric designs and other crafts, delving into the realm of flower and herb gardens. The photographs of landscapes, villages, interiors and objects illustrate personal reminiscences, historical anecdotes, and descriptions of local culture, poetry, folklore and cuisine.

Crafts of Provence: Projects and Inspiration from the South of France – Amelia Saint George (Conran Octopus, 2000). If you are not quite ready to realise your dream of retiring to southern France, here is a book that will advise you on transforming your home into a bright and sunny place that will make you feel like you're on holiday there. Fabrics, ceramics, tiles and gardens are discussed at length and some DIY projects are outlined.

The Women Troubadours – Meg Bogin (W W Norton paperback, 1980).

This book casts a new light on the famous 12C poetry of Provence: finally we get a peek at courtly love from the feminine perspective.

The Memoirs of Frédéric Mistral – Frédéric Mistral, translated by George Wickes (W W Norton, 1988).

This book was first published in Provençal in 1906 under the title *Moun espelido: Memori e raconte*. The region's best-loved bard, Mistral was awarded the Nobel Prize for literature in 1904 and founded the Félibrige association of poets to protect and revitalise the Provençal language. His memoirs are a charming collection of proverbs and stories, hyperbole and myth. Mistral gives us a look at the ordinary people of his time, singing and telling tales, and delights the reader with examples of medieval and modern Provençal poetry.

The Letters of Vincent van Gogh – Vincent van Gogh, translated by Arnold Pomerans (Penguin Classics, 2003). These letters are a precious companion to art book reproductions (see below) and will certainly move any reader interested in Van Gogh's paintings.

Van Gogh in Provence and Auvers – Bogomila Welsh-Ovcharov (Universe Publishing, 2008). This oversize book has 270 excellent reproductions of the artist's paintings, focused on his 15 months in Arles and the last feverish days of his life in Auvers, where he painted 70 pictures in as many days. The text provides insight and analysis of Van Gogh's achievements.

The Yellow House – Martin Gayford (Penguin, 2008). Gauguin and Van Gogh go mad in Arles (literally, for the latter). An account of their ten-week, masterpiece-producing stay in the city in 1888.

Cézanne in Provence – Evmarie Schmitt (Prestel, 1995). This series is popular for the quality of the text and the reproductions. The artist's work was deeply rooted in his native region, and the 50 paintings reproduced here emphasise the landscapes in particular, but his *Bathers* and still lifes are also included.

LITERATURE IN FRENCH

Jean de Florette, Manon des Sources, Marius, Fanny, César, Topaze, La Gloire de mon Père, Le Château de ma Mère, Le Temps des Secrets, Le Temps de l'Amour by M Pagnol *(Éditions de Fallois, collection Fortunio).* Atmospheric, bittersweet tales set in Marseille or its surrounding countryside.

Lettres de mon Moulin, Tartarin de Tarascon by A Daudet *(Paris, Presses Pocket).* The first is a nostalgic look at 19C village life; the latter is a fictional tale of hunting Tarascon's mythical monster.

GENERAL INTEREST

Caesar's Vast Ghost – Lawrence Durrell (Faber & Faber, 2002). Part history, part colourful memoir, part poetry by British author who lived in the Gard.

French Dirt – Richard Goodman (Workman, 2005). An American's tales of gardening, and living, near Avignon.

New Gardens in Provence: 30 Contemporary Creations – Louisa Jones *(Stewart, Tabori & Chang, 2006).* Stunning book on Provence's beautiful gardens.

The Roman Remains of Southern France – James Bromwich *(Routledge, 1996).* All you need to know about the Roman remains in the area.

Wild France: A Traveller's Guide edited by Douglas Botting and Simon Rigge. *(Sheldrake, 2000).* Ideal companion for outdoor types.

Cock and Bull Stories: Folco de Baroncelli and the Invention of the Camargue – Robert Zaretsky *(University of Nebraska, 2004).* Examines the history of France's Wild West.

Provence: Style of Living – Jerome Coignard (Hachette Illustrated, 2003). A stylish look at some beautiful homes.

FILMS

White Mane (1953) by Albert Lamorisse. A short film about a boy and his Camargue horse (filmed near Stes-Maries-de-la-Mer).

Borsalino (1970) by Jacques Deray. Belmondo and Delon in Marseille-based crime caper.

Caravan to Vaccarès (1974) by Geoffrey Reeve. Charlotte Rampling pouts her way through mediocre action thriller set in the Camargue.

French Connection II (1975) by John Frankenheimer. Action thriller starring Gene Hackman, as Popeye Doyle chases smugglers in Marseille.

Jean de Florette (1986), Manon des Sources (1986) by Claude Berri. Breathtaking interpretations of Pagnol's novels with Depardieu, Béart, Montand and Auteuil.

My Father's Glory (1990), My Mother's Castle (1990) by Yves Robert. More of Pagnol's depiction of early 20C French provincial life.

Marius and Jeannette (1997) by Robert Guédiguian. Gritty love story set in the suburbs of Marseille.

Taxi (1998) by Gérard Pirès. A lighthearted action comedy set in the streets of Marseille, written by Luc Besson.

La ville est tranquille (2000) by Robert Guédiguian. Social and political drama set in Marseille.

A Good Year (2006) by Ridley Scott. Russell Crowe plays a City boy turned wine-maker in the predictable film of Peter Mayle's book.

La fille du puisatier (2011) by Marcel Pagnol. This film, whose title translates as *The Well-Digger's Daughter*, is a remake of Pagnol's classic 1940 version based on his eponymous novel. Directed by Daniel Auteuil, who also stars in it, the film centres on Provence.

Calendar of Events

The list below is a selection of the many events that take place in the region. Contact local tourist offices for further details.

TRADITIONAL CELEBRATIONS

2 FEBRUARY
Marseille – Candlemas Procession (*Fête de la Chandeleur*) in the Basilique St-Victor (*http://marseille.catholique.fr*).

SUNDAY BEFORE LENT
Graveson – Carnival Procession of Floats (*Corso carnavalesque*; *www.graveson-provence.fr*).

EASTER WEEKEND
Arles – *Féria de Pâques*. Bullfights (*www.feriaarles.com*).

1 MAY
Arles – Gardians' Festival (*www.arlestourisme.com*).

24 AND 25 MAY
Saintes-Maries-de-la-Mer – Gypsy Pilgrimage (*Le Pèlerinage*) on 24 May, procession and blessing of the sea on 25 May (*www.saintesmaries.com*).

St-Rémy-de-Provence – Transhumance Festival. Sheep procession to the mountains (*www.saintremy-de-Provence.com*).

23 JUNE
Valréas – Feast of Little St John (*Foire de la St Jean; www.ot-valreas.fr*).

THIRD WEEK IN JUNE
Martigues – **Le Grau-du-Roi** –
Cassis – Fishermen's Festival on St Peter's Day. Water jousting and sardine scoffing.

LAST WEEKEND IN JUNE
Tarascon – Tarasque Festival. Folklore procession led by the mythical Tarasque monster (*www.tarascon.org*).

LAST FRIDAY IN JUNE
Arles – *Pegoulado*. Night-time procession in traditional costume (*www.arlestourisme.com*).

EARLY JULY
Marseille – International Folklore Festival at Château-Gombert (*www.roudelet-felibren.com*).

Gypsy Pilgrimage, Saintes-Maries-de-la-Mer

©Haga Library/JTB/Photoshot

Transhumance Festival, St-Rémy-de-Provence

© Camille Moirenc/hemis.fr

FIRST SATURDAY IN JULY
Martigues – Venetian Festival. Fireworks display and evening flotilla of decorated boats (*www.martigues-tourisme.com*).

FIRST SUNDAY IN JULY
Châteaurenard – Festival of St Eligius (*Défile d'Or St Eloi*). St Eligius' cart, decorated and drawn by 40 horses in Saracen harness (*http://ot.chateaurenard.com*).

FIRST MONDAY IN JULY
Arles – *Cocarde d'Or*. Provençal-style bullfights (*www.arles tourisme.com*).

ABOUT 14 JULY
Les Saintes-Maries-de-la-Mer – *Festival du Cheval*. Competitive events, games in the arena, gypsy flamenco music (*www.festival ducheval.camargue.fr*).

MID-JULY
Carpentras – *Corso nocturne fleuri*. Evening procession of floats (*www.carpentras-ventoux.com*).

MID-JULY–MID-AUGUST
Valréas – *Festival des Nuits de l'Enclave*. Concerts, markets and parades. (*www.ot-valreas.fr*)

LAST WEEK OF JULY
Graveson – Feast of St Eloi. Bull races and *pétanque* competitions (*www.graveson-provence.fr*).

MID-AUGUST
St-Rémy-de-Provence – Feria. Provençal-style bull runs (*abrivados*) and *courses camarguaises* (*www.saintremy-de-Provence.com*).

AROUND 20 AUGUST
Monteux – Festival of St John's firework display. Concerts and activities all week (*www.monteux.fr*).

FIRST SUNDAY IN SEPTEMBER
Aix-en-Provence – Blessing of the Calissons in the Église St-Jean-de-Malte (*www.moinesdiocesains-aix.cef.fr*).

WEEKEND AROUND 22 OCTOBER
Les Saintes-Maries-de-la-Mer – October Gypsy Pilgrimage (*www.saintesmaries.com*).

EARLY DECEMBER
Istres – Shepherds' Festival. Shepherds march through the streets with their herds (*www.istres.fr*).

24 DECEMBER

Allauch – Midnight Mass in Provençal. Shepherds come down from the hill of Notre-Dame du Château.

Les Baux de Provence – Shepherds' Festival. Midnight Mass in Provençal.

Arles – Christmas Eve watch and Midnight Mass in Provençal.

St-Michel-de-Frigolet, **Tarascon**, **St-Rémy-de-Provence** – Midnight Mass in Provençal.

Les Saintes-Maries-de-la-Mer – Midnight Mass with offerings.

Séguret – Enactment of the Li Bergié de Séguret Mystery.

FESTIVALS

JULY

Fontaine-de-Vaucluse, **L'Isle-sur-la-Sorgue**, **Lagnes**, **Le Thor** – *Festival de la Sorgue*. Music, theatre, dance (*www.paysdessorgues.fr/festivites*).

Villeneuve-lès-Avignon – International Events at the Charterhouse Theatre (*www.chartreuse.org*).

Îles du Frioul – *Festival MIMI*. Jazz, variety entertainment, folklore (*www.amicentre.biz*).

Avignon – Festival of Theatre, Dance and Music (*www.festival-avignon.com*).

Aix-en-Provence – International Festival of Opera and Music (*www.festival-aix.com*).

JULY–AUGUST

Valréas – Evenings of the Papal Enclave (*Nuits de l'Enclave des Papes*). Theatre and concerts (*www.ot-valreas.fr*).

EARLY JULY–LATE AUGUST

La Tour d'Aigues – Festival of South Luberon (*www.chateau latourdaigues.com*).

JULY–SEPTEMBER

Luberon region – Luberon International String Quartet Festival (*www.quatuors-luberon.org*).

Arles – International Photography Festival (*Les Rencontres d'Arles; www.rencontres-arles.com*).

St-Rémy-de-Provence – Organ Festival. Organ concerts (*http://organa2000.free.fr*).

MID-JULY–EARLY AUGUST

Orange – *Chorégies*. Opera, symphonic concerts (*www.choregies.asso.fr*).

Vaison-la-Romaine – *L'Été de Vaison*. Theatre, dance, music concerts (*www.musiquesdanslesvignes.com*).

SECOND FORTNIGHT IN JULY

Carpentras – *Les Estivales*. International Festival of Theatre, Opera and Dance (*www.carpentras-ventoux.com*).

Marseille – The Marseillaise Pétanque Competition held in Parc Borély.

Salon-de-Provence – Jazz Festival (*www.salon-de-Provence.org*).

MID-JULY–LATE AUGUST

Martigues – International Folk Festival (*www.martigues-tourisme.com*).

La Roque-d'Anthéron – International Piano Festival (*www.festival-piano.com*).

THIRD WEEK IN SEPTEMBER

St-Maximin-la-Ste-Baume – Autumn Festival. Organ concerts (*www.st-maximin.fr*).

OCTOBER

Marseille – *Fiesta des Suds*. Two weeks of world music with high-profile performers

EARLY NOVEMBER

Vaison-la-Romaine – Gastronomic Festival (*www.vaison-la-romaine.com*).

Know Before You Go

USEFUL WEBSITES

**www.ambafrance-us.org,
www.ambafrance-uk.org**
The French embassies in the US and UK provide basic information (geography, demographics, history), a news digest, business-related information, pages for children and on culture, language study and travel.

www.franceguide.com
The French Tourist Office website is packed with practical information and tips for travelling to France. Choose your country of origin and then click the French region you're interested in. You'll find links to individual sites for the Gard, Vaucluse and Bouches-du-Rhône plus contact details for local tourist boards and offices.

www.france-travel-guide.net
A practical and developing website for the traveller, written by a Francophile travel writer. Includes essential information, as well as a wide range of regional and local content.

www.Provencebeyond.com
Useful site, which as well as providing general information on Provence, has details of local transport.

www.Provenceguide.co.uk
The lively website of the Vaucluse tourist board has information on accommodation, restaurants, markets, and upcoming events.

www.Provencefoodandwine.com
An independent website run by a passionate food and wine lover, with details of her latest discoveries: restaurants, shops, wine makers, etc.

http://int.rendezvousenfrance.com
This corporate website offers general, yet rich, information aimed at an international audience.

TOURIST OFFICES

For information, brochures, maps and assistance in planning a trip to France, travellers should apply to the official French Tourist Office or Maison de France in their own country.

AUSTRALIA – NEW ZEALAND
Sydney
Level 13, 25 Bligh Street (level 13), Sydney, NSW 2000, Australia.
℘61 (0)2 9231 6277
http://au.franceguide.com.

CANADA
Montreal
1800 avenue McGill College, Suite 1010, Montreal, Quebec H3A 3J6.
email: canada@franceguide.com
http://ca-en.franceguide.com.

SOUTH AFRICA
Sandton
C/O Air France, Village Walk Office Tower Bldg (3rd Floor),
Maud and Rivonia Road,
Sandton
℘00 27 11 523 82 52
http://za.franceguide.com

UNITED KINGDOM
London
Lincoln House, 300 High Holborn, London WC1V 7JH.
℘09068 244 123 (60p/min)
http://uk.franceguide.com.

UNITED STATES
Three offices are are available.
http://us.franceguide.com
New York – 825 Third Avenue, 29th Floor (entrance on 50th Street), New York, NY 10022
℘+1 (514) 288 1904.
Chicago – Consulate General of France, 205 North Michigan Avenue, Suite 3770, Chicago, IL 60601 ℘+1 (312) 327 0290.
Los Angeles – 9454 Wilshire Boulevard, Suite 210, Los Angeles, CA 90212 ℘+1 (310) 271 6665.
http://us.franceguide.com.

LOCAL AND REGIONAL TOURIST OFFICES

Visitors may also contact local tourist offices for more precise information, and to receive brochures and maps. The addresses, telephone numbers and websites of local tourist offices are listed after the symbol ▯ in the Orient Panels of the Principal Sights in the *Discovering* section of this guide. Below are addresses for the regional tourist offices and the *départements* tourist offices for Provence.

COMITÉ REGIONAUX DE TOURISME

Provence-Alpes-Côte d'Azur
Maison de la Région,
61 La Canebière - CS 10009,
13231 Marseille Cedex 01.
℘04 91 56 47 00.
www.decouverte-paca.fr.

COMITÉ DÉPARTEMENTAL DU TOURISME

Bouches-du-Rhône
Le Montesquieu, 13 rue Roux-de-Brignoles, 13006 Marseille.
℘04 91 13 84 13.
www.visitprovence.com.

Vaucluse
12 rue Collège-de-la-Croix, BP 50147, 84008 Avignon Cedex 1.
℘04 90 80 47 00.
www.provenceguide.com.

Signs in Avignon
© Alain Hocquel/CADT Vaucluse Tourisme

INTERNATIONAL VISITORS
EMBASSIES AND CONSULATES IN FRANCE

♦ **Australia Embassy**
4 rue Jean-Rey, 75015 Paris.
℘01 40 59 33 00.
www.france.embassy.gov.au.

♦ **Canada Embassy**
35 avenue Montaigne, 75008 Paris.
℘01 44 43 29 00.
www.amb-canada.fr.

♦ **Eire Embassy**
4 rue Rude, 75116 Paris.
℘01 44 17 67 50. Fax: 01 44 17 67 50. www.embassyofireland.fr.

♦ **New Zealand Embassy**
7 ter rue Léonard-de-Vinci,
75116 Paris.
℘01 45 01 43 44.
www.nzembassy.com.

♦ **South Africa Embassy**
59 quai d'Orsay,
75343 Paris Cedex 07.
℘01 53 59 23 23.
www.afriquesud.net.

♦ **UK Embassy**
35 rue du Faubourg St-Honoré,
75383 Paris ℘01 44 51 31 00;
www.ukinfrance.fco.gov.uk/en
UK Consulate: 18bis rue d'Anjou,
75008 Paris ℘01 44 51 31 00

♦ **USA Embassy**
2 avenue Gabriel, 75382 Paris
℘01 43 12 22 22; www.amb-usa.fr
USA Consulate: 2 rue St-Florentin,
75001 Paris ℘01 43 12 22 22.

♦ **USA Marseille Consulate General**
Place Varian Fry, 13286 Marseille Cedex 6. ℘04 91 54 92 00,
Fax 04 91 55 56 95 (from outside France) or 04 91 55 09 47 (from inside France).

DOCUMENTS
Passports
Nationals of countries within the European Union entering France need only a national identity card (a passport for UK nationals). Nationals of other countries must be in possession of a valid national **passport**. In case of loss or theft, report to your embassy or consulate and the local police.

Visas
No **entry visa** is required for Canadian, US or Australian citizens travelling as tourists and staying for up to 90 days, except for students planning to study in France. If you think you may need a visa, apply to your local French consulate. US citizens are advised to consult www.travel.state.gov for entry requirements, security and other information including contact numbers of US embassies and consulates. In an emergency call the **Overseas Citizens Services** ℘1-888-407-4747 (℘1-202-501-4444 from overseas).

CUSTOMS
In the UK, **HM Revenue & Customs** (www.hmrc.gov.uk) publishes *A Guide for Travellers* on customs regulations and duty-free allowances.
US citizens should view *Tips for Traveling Abroad* online *(http://travel.state.gov/travel/tips/tips_1232.html)* for general information about visa requirements, customs regulations, medical care, etc. There are no customs formalities for holidaymakers bringing their caravans into France for a stay of less than six months. No customs document is necessary for pleasure boats and outboard motors for a stay of less than six months but the registration certificate should be kept on board.
The **US Customs Service** offers a publication *Know Before You Go* for US citizens to consult and download at www.customs.ustreas.gov (click on "Travel").
Australians will find customs information at www.customs.gov.au.

DUTY-FREE ALLOWANCES	
Spirits (Whisky, gin, vodka, etc.)	10l/2.6gal
Fortified Wines (Vermouth, port, etc.)	20l/5.28gal
Wine (not more than 60l sparkling)	90l/23.7gal
Beer	110l/29gal
Cigarettes	800
Cigarillos	400
Cigars	200
Smoking tobacco	1kg/2.2lb

For **New Zealanders**, "Advice for Travellers" is at www.customs.govt.nz. Persons living in a member state of the European Union are not restricted with regard to purchasing goods for private use, but the recommended maximum allowances for alcoholic beverages and tobacco are listed in the table above.

HEALTH
First aid, medical advice and chemists' night service are provided by chemists/drugstores *(pharmacie)* identified by the green cross sign. Since the recipient of medical treatment in French hospitals or clinics must pay the bill, it is advisable to take out comprehensive insurance coverage. Nationals of non-EU countries should check with their insurance companies about policy limitations. Reimbursement can then be negotiated with the insurance company according to the policy held. All prescription drugs should be clearly labelled; it is recommended that you carry a copy of the prescription.
British and Irish citizens, if they are not already in possession of an **EHIC** (European Health Insurance Card), should apply for one before travelling. The card entitles UK residents to reduced-cost medical treatment. Apply at UK post offices, call ℘0845 606 2030, or visit *www.nhs.uk*. You pay upfront but

can reclaim most of the money (see website for details). **Americans** concerned about travel and health can contact the International Association for Medical Assistance to Travelers, which can also provide details of English-speaking doctors in different parts of France: *℘716 754-4883. www.iamat.org.*

ACCESSIBILITY

The sights described in this guide that are easily accessible to people of reduced mobility are indicated by the symbol ♿. On French TGV and Corail trains there are wheelchair spaces in 1st-class carriages available to holders of 2nd-class tickets. On Eurostar and Thalys special rates are available for accompanying adults. All airports are equipped to receive physically disabled passengers. Disabled drivers may use the EU blue card for parking entitlements.

Many of France's historic buildings, including museums and hotels, have limited or no wheelchair access. Older hotels tend to lack lifts.

Tourism for All UK (*℘0845 124 9971; www.tourismforall.org.uk*) publishes overseas information guides listing accommodation that they believe to be accessible but haven't inspected in person.

Information about accessibility is available from French disability organisations such as **Association des Paralysés de France** (*17 bd. Auguste-Blanqui, 75013 Paris; ℘01 40 78 69 00; www.apf.asso.fr*). Useful information on transportation, holidaymaking, and sports associations for the disabled is available from the French-language website www.handicap.fr. In the UK; www.radar.org.uk is a good source of info and support, and the US website www.access-able.com provides information on travel for mature travellers or those with special needs. The **Michelin Green Guide France** and **Michelin Camping and Caravanning in France** indicate hotels and campsites with facilities suitable for people with physical disabilities.

Getting There

BY AIR

You can currently fly direct from the UK to:

Nîmes Airport (*℘04 66 70 49 49*) with Ryanair (*℘0871 246 0000; www.ryanair.com*).

Avignon (*℘04 90 81 51 51; www.avignon.aeroport.fr*) with Flybe (*℘0871 700 2000; www.flybe.com*).

Marseille (*℘04 42 14 14 14; www.marseille.aeroport.fr*) with Ryanair, easyJet (*℘0871 244 2377; www.easyjet.com*), British Airways (*www.ba.com; ℘0844 493 0787*) and Air France (*℘0871 66 33 777; www.airfrance.com*). No North American airlines currently fly direct to Provence, so you'd need to go to Paris and get a connecting flight or train. American Airlines (*℘1 800 433*

7300; www.aa.com), Delta (*℘1 800 221 12 12; www.delta.com*) and Continental (*℘1 800 231 0856; www.continental.com*). All fly from the US to Paris.

BY SEA
FROM THE UK OR IRELAND

There are numerous **cross-Channel services** (passenger and car ferries, hovercraft) from the United Kingdom and Ireland, as well as the **Eurotunnel** rail shuttle through the Channel Tunnel (*℘08705 35 35 35; www.euro tunnel.com*). To choose the most suitable route between your port of arrival and your destination use the *Michelin Tourist and Motoring Atlas France, Michelin map 726* (which gives travel times and mileages) or Michelin maps from the Local series (with the yellow cover). To compare prices, see www.ferrysavers.co.uk or contact:

- **Brittany Ferries** ✆0871 244 0744 (UK); 0825 828 828 (France). www.brittanyferries.com. Services from Portsmouth, Poole and Plymouth.
- **Condor Ferries** ✆01202 207216, www.condorferries.co.uk. Services from Weymouth, Poole and Portsmouth.
- **DFDS Seaways** now incorporate Norfolk Line and have taken over some LD Lines routes. They operate routes between Dover and Calais, Dover-Dunkerque Portsmouth-Le Havre and Newhaven-Dieppe. ✆(UK) 0871 574 7235 and 0800 917 1201; www.dfdsseaways.co.uk.
- **LD Lines** Services from Portsmouth and Newhaven are now operated by DFDS Seaways.
- **MyFerryLink** is what became of SeaFrance. ✆0844 2482 100. www.myferrylink.com. Services between Dover and Calais.
- **Norfolk Line** Norfolk Line is now part of DFDS Seaways.
- **P&O Ferries** ✆08716 642 121 (UK), or 0825 120 156 (France), www.poferries.com. Services between Dover and Calais.

BY RAIL

Eurostar (✆08432 186 186; www.eurostar.com) operates a 2hr15min daily service via the Channel Tunnel from **London** (St Pancras) and Ebbsfleet International in Kent to **Paris** (Gare du Nord) or **Lille** (1hr20min). You can then catch a connecting train, the high-speed **TGV**, from **Paris** (Gare de Lyon) to **Marseille** (3hr15min) or **Avignon** (2hr40min). You can also catch a train south from **Lille**, which is convenient as you just have to change platforms and not stations. In May 2015 Eurostar introduced a direct service from London to Marseille. All services throughout France can be arranged through **Voyages-SNCF** in the UK: Personal callers are welcome to drop into Voyages-SNCF Travel Centre, 193 Piccadilly, London W1J 9EU. Telephone: 0844 848 5 848. www.voyages-sncf.com.

Train tickets in France must be validated (composté) by using the orange automatic date-stamping machines at the platform entrance (failure to do so may result in a fine).

BY COACH/BUS

Eurolines has regular overnight services from London and Paris to Marseille, Avignon and Nîmes. For further information go to www.eurolines.com or call ✆0871 781 8178.

Getting Around

BY TRAIN/RAIL

France's rail system (SNCF) is an efficient and inexpensive way of getting between cities and larger towns. The TGV (train à grande vitesse) network is ever-expanding – see www.tgv.co.uk for a route map. Provence is well served by the TGV: it stops at Nîmes, Arles, Avignon, Aix-en-Provence, Miramas, Montélimar and Marseille. To help you get around during your stay, information on local train schedules and ticket prices can be seen at www.voyages-sncf.com. You'll find many offers and discounts: if you're travelling with children look out for the Découverte Enfant ticket, which allows a 25 percent discount on travel for up to four people accompanying one child under 12.

BY COACH/BUS

Getting around by bus is a cheap way of seeing Provence, but services can be infrequent or at odd hours (to coincide with the school run). For bus timetables in the Gard see www.edgard-transport.fr, for the Bouches-du-Rhône see www.lepilote.com and for the Vaucluse see www.vaucluse.fr (all websites in French). You'll find up-to-date information in local bus stations and at some tourist offices.

BY CAR
ROUTE PLANNING

The area covered in this guide is easily reached by main motorways and national routes. **Michelin map 726** indicates the main itineraries as well as alternative routes for avoiding heavy traffic during busy holiday periods, and gives estimated travel times. **Michelin map 723** is a detailed atlas of French motorways, indicating tolls, rest areas and services along the route; it includes a table for calculating distances and times. The latest Michelin route-planning service is available at **www.ViaMichelin.com**. Travellers can calculate a precise route using such options as shortest route, a route avoiding toll roads or the Michelin-recommended route. The site also provides tourist information (hotels, restaurants, attractions). The roads are very busy during the holiday period (particularly weekends in July and August) and, to avoid traffic congestion, it is advisable to follow the recommended secondary routes (signposted as Bison Futé – itinéraires bis). The motorway network includes rest areas (aires) and petrol stations, usually with restaurant and shopping complexes attached, about every 40km/25mi, so that long-distance drivers can stop for a rest regularly.

DOCUMENTS

Driving licence – Travellers from other European Union countries and North America can drive in France with a valid national or home-state driving licence. An **international driving licence** is useful but not obligatory.

Registration Papers
For the vehicle, it is necessary to have the registration papers (logbook) and a nationality plate of an approved size.

Insurance
Certain motoring organisations (AA, RAC) offer accident insurance and breakdown service schemes for members. Check with your current insurance company for coverage while abroad. Because French autoroutes are privately owned, your European Breakdown Cover service does not extend to breakdowns on the autoroute or its service areas – you must use the emergency telephones, or drive off the autoroute before calling your breakdown service.

RULES OF THE ROAD
Regulations
The minimum driving age is 18. Traffic drives on the right. All passengers must wear **seat belts**. Children under the age of 10 must ride in the back seat. Headlights must be switched on in poor visibility and at night; dipped headlights should be used at all times outside built-up areas. Use sidelights only when the vehicle is stationary. In the case of a **breakdown**, a red warning triangle or hazard warning lights are obligatory, as are **reflective safety jackets**, one for each passenger, and carried within the car. it is now compulsory to carry an in-car **breathalyser kit**, too; you can be fined if you do not. UK right-hand drive cars must use headlight adaptors.

In the absence of stop signs at intersections, cars must **give way to the right**. Traffic on main roads outside built-up areas (priority indicated by a yellow diamond sign) and on roundabouts has right of way. Vehicles must stop when the lights turn red at road junctions and may filter to the right only when indicated by an amber arrow.

The regulations on **drinking and driving** (limited to 0.50g/l) and

RENTAL CARS – RESERVATIONS IN FRANCE		
Avis France:	☎ 08 20 05 05 05	www.avis.fr
Europcar:	☎ 08 25 35 83 58	www.europcar.com
Budget:	☎ 08 25 00 35 64	www.budget.com
Hertz:	☎ 08 25 861 861	www.hertz.com
SIXT:	☎ 08 20 00 74 98	www.e-sixt.com
CITER:	☎ 08 25 16 12 20	www.citer.fr

speeding are strictly enforced – usually by an on-the-spot fine and/or confiscation of the vehicle.

Speed Limits
Although liable to modification, these are as follows:
- **Toll motorways** (autoroutes) 130kph/80mph (110kph/68mph when raining);
- **Dual carriageways and motorways without tolls** 110kph/68mph (100kph/62mph when raining);
- **Other roads** 90kph/56mph (80kph/50mph when raining) and in towns 50kph/31mph;
- **Outside lane on motorways** during daylight, on level ground and with good visibility – minimum speed limit of 80kph/50mph.

Parking
In towns there are zones where parking is either restricted or subject to a fee; tickets should be obtained from the ticket machines (horodateurs – small change necessary) and displayed inside the windscreen on the driver's side; failure to display may result in a fine, or towing and impoundment. Other parking areas in town may require you to take a ticket when passing through a barrier. To exit, you must pay the parking fee (usually there is a machine located by the exit – sortie) and insert the paid-up card in another machine which will lift the exit gate.

Tolls
In France, most motorway sections are subject to a toll (péage). You can pay in cash or with a credit card.

VEHICLES
Car Rental
There are car rental agencies at airports, railway stations and in all large towns throughout France. Most European cars have manual transmission; automatic cars are available only if an advance reservation is made. Drivers must be over 21; between ages 21–25, drivers are required to pay an extra daily fee; some companies allow drivers under 23 only if the reservation has been made through a travel agent. Rental agencies have offices all over France; to find the one near where you want to rent, consult the websites in the coloured box above.

Petrol/Gasoline
French service stations dispense:
- sans plomb 98 (super unleaded 98)
- sans plomb 95 (super unleaded 95)
- diesel/gazole (diesel)
- GPL (LPG).

Petrol (gasoline) is considerably more expensive in France than in the USA. Prices are listed on signboards on the motorways; it is usually cheaper to fill up after leaving the motorway; check the large hypermarkets on the outskirts of town. You can pay by card at the pump using credit/debit cards, including Maestro.

Where to Stay and Eat

WHERE TO STAY
FINDING A HOTEL

Turn to the **Addresses** within individual sight listings for descriptions and prices of typical places to stay (**Stay**) and eat (**Eat**) with local flair. The key at the back of the guide explains the symbols and abbreviations used in these sections. To enhance your stay, hotel selections have been chosen for their location, comfort, value for money, and, in many cases, their charm.

Prices indicate the cost of a standard room for two people in peak season. For an even greater selection, use the red-cover **Michelin Guide France**, with its well-known star-rating system and hundreds of establishments throughout France.

The **Michelin Dormez insolite en France** guide describes 170 unusual addresses (tree houses, tipis, yurts, etc.) for all budgets and tastes.

Be sure to book ahead, especially for stays during the high season: Provence is a very popular holiday destination. You can also contact the tourist offices for further information on all kinds of accommodation in their respective areas, such as hotel-châteaux, bed-and-breakfasts, etc.

Another resource, which publishes many catalogues listing holiday villas, apartments or chalets in each *département*, is the **Fédération Nationale des Locations de France Clévacances** (*54 bd de l'Embouchure, BP 52166, 31022 Toulouse Cedex 2; ℘05 61 13 55 66, www.clevacances.com*).

For good-value hotels, **Fédération Internationale des Logis** is one of the best organisations to contact (*℘01 45 84 70 00; www.logishotels.com*).

Relais & Châteaux provides information on booking in luxury hotels with character: *℘0825 825 180. www.relaischateaux.com.*

ECONOMY CHAIN HOTELS

If you need a place to stop en route, chain hotels can be useful, as they are relatively inexpensive and generally located near the main road.

While breakfast is available, there may not be a restaurant; rooms are usually small, with a television and bathroom. Central reservations in France (0,34 €/min):

- **Akena** ℘01 69 84 85 17 www.hotels-akena.com
- **B&B** ℘0 892 782 929 www.hotel-bb.com
- **Campanile** ℘0 892 230 591 www.campanile.com
- **Hotel F1** ℘0892 685 685 www.hotelf1.com
- **Ibis Budget** ℘0 892 688 900 http://ibisbudgethotel.ibis.com
- **Kyriad** ℘0 892 230 591 www.kyriad.fr

RENTING A COTTAGE, BED AND BREAKFAST
Rural Accommodation

The **Maison des Gîtes de France** is an information service on self-catering accommodation in France. *Gîtes* usually take the form of cottages or apartments decorated in the local style where visitors can make themselves at home, or bed and breakfast accommodation *(chambres d'hôtes)* which consists of a room and breakfast at a reasonable price.

🖹℘01 49 70 75 75, www.gites-de-france.com. From the website, you can order catalogues for different regions illustrated with photographs of the properties, as well as specialised catalogues (bed and breakfasts, chalets in skiing areas, farm stays etc). You can also contact the local tourist offices, which may have lists of other properties and local bed and breakfast establishments.

The **Fédération Française des Stations Vertes de Vacances**, 6 rue Ranfer-de-Bretenières, BP 71698, 21016 Dijon Cedex ℘03 80 54 10 50; www.stationsvertes.com, is able to provide details of accommodation, leisure facilities and natural attractions in rural locations selected for their tranquillity.

HOSTELS, CAMPING

To obtain an **International Youth Hostel Federation** card (there is no age requirement, and there is a "senior card" available too), you should contact the IYHF in your own country for information and membership applications. There is an online booking service *(www.hihostels.com)*, which you may use to reserve rooms as far as six months in advance. There are two main youth hostel *(auberges de jeunesse)* associations in France, the **Ligue Française pour les Auberges de Jeunesse** *(67 rue Vergniaud, bâtiment K, 75013 Paris; ℰ01 44 16 78 78; www.auberges-de-jeunesse.com)* and the **Fédération Unie des Auberges de Jeunesse** *(27 rue Pajol, 75018 Paris; ℰ01 44 89 87 27; www.fuaj.org)*. The Federation has an informative website providing online booking.

There are numerous officially graded **camping sites** with varying standards of facilities throughout Provence. The **Michelin Camping and Caravanning in France** guide lists a selection of campsites (two guides are available in French: *Guide Camping & Hôtellerie de plein air France* and *Guide Escapades en camping-car France)*. The area is very popular with campers in the summer months, so it is wise to reserve in advance. Are you going hiking, skiing or kayaking and want a rustic place to stay overnight? Then visit *www.gites-refuges.com*, which provides details of accommodation in France's national parks including the Luberon. You can print out a guide to the Provence region for €5.

THALASSOTHERAPY

Thalassotherapy uses the virtues of **sea water** to prevent or cure certain disorders and to improve general fitness and well-being. The healing and relaxing properties of the marine climate (iodine, radiant light, etc.), sea water, sea mud, algae and sand have given rise to a variety of therapeutic cures: fitness programmes, beauty treatments, therapy for relief from backache, stress and addiction to smoking. The mild Mediterranean climate is a good place to rest and restore your energy. There are various thalassotherapy centres in the region, at **Marseille** and **Les Saintes-Maries-de-la-Mer**. Or contact the national association for information: **France Thalasso** ℰ06 66 85 64 50. www.france-thalasso.com.

WHERE TO EAT

A selection of places to eat in the different locations covered in this guide can be found in the **Addresses** appearing in the section entitled

Camping van in the Alpilles

© Norbert Eisele-Hein/age fotostock

Discovering Provence. The key at the back of the book explains the symbols and abbreviations used in the Addresses. We have highlighted an array of eating places primarily for their atmosphere, location and regional delicacies. Prices indicate the average cost of a starter, main dish and dessert for one person. Use the red-cover **Michelin Guide France,** with its well-known star-rating system and listings of hundreds of establishments throughout France, for an even greater choice. If you would like to experience a meal in a highly rated restaurant from the **Michelin Guide**, be sure to book ahead. In the countryside, restaurants usually serve **lunch** between noon and 2pm and **dinner** between 7.30 and 10pm. It is not always easy to find something in between those mealtimes, as the "non-stop" restaurant is still a rarity in the provinces. However, a hungry traveller can usually get a sandwich (usually a filled baguette) in a café, and ordinary hot dishes may be available in a brasserie. Throughout France, the culture leans more towards sitting and eating than to grabbing a sandwich on the go, so it's worth planning ahead if you're unsure.

In French restaurants and cafés, a service charge is included. Tipping is not necessary, but French people often leave the small change from their bill on their table, or about 5 percent for the waiter in a nice restaurant.

For information on local specialities, see the section on Food and Wine in the next chapter, Introduction to Provence.

Basic Information

BUSINESS HOURS

Most of the larger shops are open Monday to Saturday from 9am to 6.30 or 7.30pm. Smaller, individual shops often close for 1–2hr at lunch daily and open half day on Monday. Food shops – grocers, wine merchants and bakeries – are generally open from 7am to 6.30 or 7.30pm; some open on Sunday mornings. Many food shops close between noon and 2pm and on Monday. Hypermarkets usually stay open non-stop until 8pm or later. Many museums are closed on Monday or Tuesday.

DISCOUNTS

Some towns and cities sell passes, available from local tourist offices, which allow entry to several museums and monuments. In **Marseille**, you can get a one- or two-day *City Pass* for €24 or €31 respectively, which allows entry to 11 museums, a free trip on the little tourist train, a free guided tour of the city, a free boat trip to If Island or Frioul Islands, discounts or freebies in some shops and free access to the bus, tramway and metro system. In **Arles**, you can get a *Passeport Liberté* (valid for one month) for €10, which allows entry to four monuments and one museum. Tourist offices will have details of any special passes or discounts applicable to their town or area.

The **World Youth Student & Educational Travel Confederation** (WYSE) (www.wysetc.org), the global administrator of the International Student Identity Cards (www.isic.org), is an association of student travel organisations around the world. WYSE Travel Confederation members collectively negotiate benefits with airlines, governments, and providers of other goods and services for the student community, both in their own country and around the world. The non-profit association sells international ID cards for students and youth under age 25 (who may get discounts on museum entrances, for example).

ELECTRICITY

The electric current is 220 volts/50hz. Circular two-pin plugs are the rule. Adapters and converters (for hairdryers, for example) should be bought before you leave home; they are on sale in most airports. If you have a rechargable device (video camera, portable computer, battery recharger), read the instructions carefully or contact the manufacturer or shop. Sometimes these items only require a plug adapter, in other cases you must use a voltage converter as well or risk ruining your device.

EMERGENCIES

European Emergency Call: ☎112

OTHER EMERGENCY NUMBERS
Police: ☎17
Fire Brigade (Pompiers): ☎18
Ambulance (SAMU): ☎15

MAIL/POST/INTERNET

Main post offices usually open Monday to Friday 9am–noon and 2pm–7pm, Saturday 9am–noon. **Stamps** (timbres) are also available from newsagents and bureaux de tabac. To save time, buy a timbre prioritaire. Stamp collectors should ask for timbres de collection in any post office.

A helpful website is www.laposte.fr; it can calculate the cost to send a letter from France anywhere in the world, depending on its weight. **Internet** is widely available in France. Most hotels now offer Wi-Fi access and usually free of charge, although this may not apply in more rural areas.

France	Letter	(20g) €0.66
UK	Letter	(20g) €0.83
North America	Letter	(20g) €0.98
Australia	Letter	(20g) €0.98
New Zealand	Letter	(20g) €0.98

MONEY
CURRENCY

There are no restrictions on the amount of currency visitors can take into France. Visitors carrying a lot of cash are advised to complete a currency declaration form on arrival, because there are restrictions on currency export: if you are leaving the country with more than €10 000, you must declare the amount to customs.

BANKS

Banks are generally open 9am–noon and 2pm–4pm and branches are closed on either Monday or Saturday. Banks close early on the day before a bank holiday.

A passport is necessary as **identification** when cashing traveller's cheques in banks. Commission charges vary, and hotels usually charge more than banks for cashing cheques.

One of the most economical ways to obtain money in France is by using an **ATM** to get cash directly from your bank account or to use your credit cards to get cash advances (but be aware that your bank will charge you for this service). Be sure to remember your PIN; you will need it to use cash dispensers and to pay with your card in most shops, restaurants, etc. Code pads are numeric; use a telephone pad to translate a letter code into numbers. PINs have four digits in France; enquire with the issuing company or bank if the code you usually use is longer. Visa is the most widely accepted **credit card**, followed by MasterCard; other cards, credit and debit (Maestro, Plus, Cirrus, etc.) are also accepted in some cash machines.

Not widely accepted in France, American Express might be accepted in premium establishments. Some credit cards don't charge for transactions made abroad (apart from withdrawing money from ATMs).

Most places post signs indicating the cards they accept; if you don't see such a sign, and want to pay with a card, ask in advance. Cards are widely accepted in shops, hypermarkets, hotels and restaurants, at tollbooths and in petrol stations.

If your card is **lost or stolen**, call one of the following 24-hour hotlines in France:

American Express: ☎01 47 77 72 00
MasterCard: ☎0 800 90 13 87
Visa: ☎0 800 90 11 79

You must report any loss or theft of credit cards or traveller's cheques to the local police, who will issue a certificate to you (useful proof to show the issuing company).

PUBLIC HOLIDAYS

See the box below for a list of major public holidays in France. There are other religious and national festivals days, and a number of local saints' days, etc. On all these days, museums and other monuments may be closed or may vary their hours of admission. In addition to the usual school holidays at Christmas and in the spring and summer, there are long mid-term breaks (10 days to a fortnight) in February and early November; most attractions tend to be crowded at such times.

PUBLIC HOLIDAYS	
1 January	New Year's Day (Jour de l'an)
Mon after Easter Sun	Easter Monday (Pâques)
1 May	Labour Day
8 May	VE Day
Thu 40 days after Easter	Ascension Day (Ascension)
7th Sun after Easter	Whit Monday (Pentecôte)
14 July	**Fête Nationale** France's National Day (or Bastille Day)
15 August	Assumption (Assomption)
1 November	All Saints' Day (Toussaint)
11 November	Armistice Day
25 December	Christmas Day (Noël)

SMOKING

Since the beginning of 2008, smoking has been forbidden in all public places in France, especially bars, restaurants, railway stations and airports. Ironically this has created a problem for non-smokers who want to sit outside on a terrace to enjoy the open air, where smoking is not prohibited.

TELEPHONES
PUBLIC TELEPHONES

Most public phones in France use pre-paid phone cards (télécartes), rather than coins. Some telephone booths accept credit cards (Visa, MasterCard/EuroCard). Télécartes (50 or 120 units) can be bought in post offices, branches of France Télécom, bureaux de tabac (cafés that sell cigarettes) and newsagents and can be used to make calls in France and abroad. Calls can be received at phone boxes where the blue bell sign is shown; the phone will not ring, so keep your eye on the little message screen. Some public telephones have internet access.

NATIONAL CALLS

French telephone numbers have ten digits. Paris and Paris region numbers begin with 01; 02 in northwest France; 03 in northeast France; 04 in southeast France and Corsica; 05 in southwest France.

INTERNATIONAL CALLS

To call France from abroad, dial the country code (+33) + 9-digit number (omit the initial 0). When calling abroad from France, dial 00, then dial

INTERNATIONAL DIALLING CODES	
Australia	☎61
New Zealand	☎64
Canada	☎1
United Kingdom	☎44
Eire	☎353
United States	☎1

the country code followed by the area code (☞ *see box below*), minus the first 0, and number of your correspondent. To use your **personal calling card** dial:

AT&T ℘0800 99 00 11
Sprint ℘0800 99 00 87
Verizon ℘0800 99 00 19
Canada Direct ℘0800 99 00 16
BT ℘0800 99 02 44
International information
US/Canada: ℘118 700
International operator ℘00 33
12 + country code
Local directory assistance ℘118

MOBILE/CELL PHONES

Dual- or tri-band mobile phones will work almost anywhere In France, but at international roaming rates. If you are staying for an extended period you might consider renting a mobile phone locally, including Black-berries and iPhones – www.cellhire.fr. A number of service providers now offer the facility to use home-country units rather than paying roaming charges, but make a daily charge for this. If you plan to make regular use of a mobile phone while abroad, this is worth considering.

TIME

WHEN IT IS **NOON IN FRANCE**, IT IS	
3am	in Los Angeles
6am	in New York
11am	in Dublin
11am	in London
7pm	in Perth
9pm	in Sydney
11pm	in Auckland

France is 1hr ahead of Greenwich Mean Time (GMT). France goes on daylight-saving time from the last Sunday in March to the last Sunday in October. In France "am" and "pm" are not used, but the 24-hour clock is widely applied.

Terrace of a café Aix-en-Provence

© M. Raynaud/Comité Régional de Tourisme Provence-Alpes-Côte d'Azur

TIPPING

Since a service charge is automatically included in the price of meals and accommodation in France, any additional tipping is up to the visitor, generally small change, and generally not more than 5 percent. Taxi drivers and hairdressers are usually tipped 10–15 percent.

As a rule, prices for hotels and restaurants as well as for other goods and services are less expensive in the French regions than in Paris.

Restaurants usually charge for meals in two ways: a *menu*, that is a fixed price menu with two or three courses, sometimes a small pitcher of wine, all for a stated price or à la carte, the more expensive way, with each course ordered separately.

Cafés have very different prices, depending on where they are located. The price of a drink or a coffee is cheaper if you stand at the counter (*comptoir*) than if you sit down (*salle*), and sometimes it is even more expensive if you sit outdoors (*terrasse*).

CONVERSION TABLES

Weights and Measures

EU	US	UK	
1 kilogram (kg) 6.35 kilograms 0.45 kilograms	**2.2 pounds (lb)** 14 pounds 16 ounces (oz)	**2.2 pounds** 1 stone (st) 16 ounces	*To convert kilograms to pounds, multiply by 2.2*
1 metric ton (tn)	**1.1 tons**	**1.1 tons**	
1 litre (l) 3.79 litres 4.55 litres	**2.11 pints (pt)** 1 gallon (gal) 1.20 gallon	**1.76 pints** 0.83 gallon 1 gallon	*To convert litres to gallons, multiply by 0.26 (US) or 0.22 (UK)*
1 hectare (ha) **1 sq kilometre (km²)**	**2.47 acres** 0.38 sq. miles (sq mi)	**2.47 acres** 0.38 sq. miles	*To convert hectares to acres, multiply by 2.4*
1 centimetre (cm) **1 metre (m)**	**0.39 inches (in)** 3.28 feet (ft) or 39.37 inches or 1.09 yards (yd)	**0.39 inches**	*To convert metres to feet, multiply by 3.28; for kilometres to miles, multiply by 0.6*
1 kilometre (km)	**0.62 miles (mi)**	**0.62 miles**	

Clothing

Women	EU	US	UK		Men	EU	US	UK
	35	4	2½			40	7½	7
	36	5	3½			41	8½	8
	37	6	4½			42	9½	9
Shoes	38	7	5½		Shoes	43	10½	10
	39	8	6½			44	11½	11
	40	9	7½			45	12½	12
	41	10	8½			46	13½	13
	36	6	8			46	36	36
	38	8	10			48	38	38
Dresses	40	10	12		Suits	50	40	40
& suits	42	12	14			52	42	42
	44	14	16			54	44	44
	46	16	18			56	46	48
	36	6	30			37	14½	14½
	38	8	32			38	15	15
Blouses &	40	10	34		Shirts	39	15½	15½
sweaters	42	12	36			40	15¾	15¾
	44	14	38			41	16	16
	46	16	40			42	16½	16½

Sizes often vary depending on the designer. These equivalents are given for guidance only.

Speed

KPH	10	30	50	70	80	90	100	110	120	130
MPH	6	19	31	43	50	56	62	68	75	81

Temperature

Celsius (°C)	0°	5°	10°	15°	20°	25°	30°	40°	60°	80°	100°
Fahrenheit (°F)	32°	41°	50°	59°	68°	77°	86°	104°	140°	176°	212°

To convert Celsius into Fahrenheit, multiply °C by 9, divide by 5, and add 32.
To convert Fahrenheit into Celsius, subtract 32 from °F, multiply by 5, and divide by 9.
NB: Conversion factors on this page are approximate.

Useful Words and Phrases

Sights

	Translation
Abbaye	Abbey
Beffroi	Belfry
Chapelle	Chapel
Château	Castle
Cimetière	Cemetery
Cloître	Cloisters
Cour	Courtyard
Couvent	Convent
Écluse	Lock (Canal)
Église	Church
Fontaine	Fountain
Halle	Covered market
Jardin	Garden
Mairie	Town Hall
Maison	House
Marché	Market
Monastère	Monastery
Moulin	Windmill
Musée	Museum
Parc	Park
Place	Square
Pont	Bridge
Port	Port/harbour
Porte	Gateway
Quai	Quay
Remparts	Ramparts
Rue	Street
Statue	Statue
Tour	Tower

Natural Sites

	Translation
Abîme	Chasm
Aven	Swallow-hole
Barrage	Dam
Belvédère	Viewpoint
Cascade	Waterfall
Col	Pass
Corniche	Ledge
Côte	Coast
Forêt	Forest
Grotte	Cave
Lac	Lake
Plage	Beach
Rivière	River
Ruisseau	Stream
Signal	Beacon
Source	Spring
Vallée	Valley

On the Road

	Translation
Parking	Car park
Permis de conduire	Driving licence
Est	East
Garage	Garage (for repairs)
Gauche	Left
Autoroute	Motorway/ Highway
Nord	North
Horodateur	Parking meter
Essence	Petrol/Gas
Station d'essence	Petrol/Gas station
Droite	Right
Sud	South
Péage	Toll
Pneu	Tyre
Ouest	West
Sabot	Wheel clamp
Passage clouté	Zebra crossing

Time

	Translation
Aujourd'hui	Today
Demain	Tomorrow
Hier	Yesterday
Hiver	Winter
Printemps	Spring
Été	Summer
Automne	Autumn/Fall
Semaine	Week
Lundi	Monday
Mardi	Tuesday
Mercredi	Wednesday
Jeudi	Thursday
Vendredi	Friday
Samedi	Saturday
Dimanche	Sunday

Numbers

	Translation
0	zéro
1	un
2	deux
3	trois
4	quatre
5	cinq
6	six
7	sept
8	huit
9	neuf
10	dix
11	onze
12	douze
13	treize
14	quatorze
15	quinze
16	seize
17	dix-sept
18	dix-huit
19	dix-neuf
20	vingt
30	trente
40	quarante
50	cinquante
60	soixante
70	soixante-dix
80	quatre-vingt
90	quatre-vingt-dix
100	cent
1000	mille

Shopping

	Translation
Banque	Bank
Boulangerie	Baker's
Grand	Big
Boucherie	Butcher
Pharmacie	Chemist
Fermé	Closed
Sirop pour la toux	Cough mixture
Cachets pour la gorge	Cough sweets
Entrée	Entrance
Sortie	Exit
Poissonnerie	Fishmonger's
Épicerie	Grocer's
Librairie	Newsagent, Bookshop
Ouvert	Open
Poste	Post office
Pousser	Push
Tirer	Pull
Magasin	Shop
Petit	Small
Timbres	Stamps

Food and Drink

	Translation
Bœuf	Beef
Bière	Beer
Pain	Bread
Petit-déjeuner	Breakfast
Beurre	Butter
Fromage	Cheese
Poulet	Chicken
Dessert	Dessert
Dîner	Dinner
Poisson	Fish
Fourchette	Fork
Fruits	Fruit
Verre	Glass
Glace	Ice cream
Glaçons	Ice cubes
Jambon	Ham
Couteau	Knife
Agneau	Lamb
Déjeuner	Lunch
Salade	Lettuce salad
Viande	Meat
Eau minérale	Mineral water
Salade composée	Mixed salad
Jus d'orange	Orange juice
Assiette	Plate
Porc	Pork
Restaurant	Restaurant
Vin rouge	Red wine
Sel	Salt
Cuillère	Spoon
Sucre	Sugar
Légumes	Vegetables
Eau	Water
Vin blanc	White wine
Yaourt	Yoghurt

UNESCO World Heritage Sites

Provence boasts four World Heritage Sites, that is, sites deemed to be of outstanding value to humanity. Arles' Roman (amphitheatre, theatre, Alyscamps) and Romanesque (St-Trophime Church) remains have been protected by the organisation since 1981. Orange's well-preserved Roman theatre, probably the best-remaining example of its kind, and Roman triumphal arch are also included. The Pont du Gard aqueduct near Nîmes has been protected since 1985 and is fêted as a magnificent feat of Roman engineering, standing almost 50m/164ft high. Avignon's Papal Palace and bridge stand to remind us of the city's prominent role in the 14C when it was the home of the then popes. These sites will be protected and preserved as shining examples of Provence's contribution to European development for many generations to come.

For further information, see http://whc.unesco.org.

Personal Documents and Travel

	Translation
Aéroport	Airport
Carte de crédit	Credit card
Douane	Customs
Passeport	Passport
Voie	Platform
Gare	Railway station
Navette	Shuttle
Valise	Suitcase
Billet de train/d'avion	Train/plane ticket
Portefeuille	Wallet

Commonly Used Words

	Translation
Au revoir	Goodbye
Bonjour	Hello/good morning
Comment	How
Excusez-moi	Excuse me
Merci	Thank you
Oui/non	Yes/no
Pardon	I am sorry
Pourquoi	Why
Quand	When
S'il vous plaît	Please

USEFUL PHRASES

Do you speak English?
Parlez-vous anglais?

I don't understand
Je ne comprends pas

Talk slowly
Parlez lentement

Where's ...?
Où est ...?

When does the ... leave?
À quelle heure part ...?

When does the ... arrive?
À quelle heure arrive ...?

When does the museum open?
À quelle heure ouvre le musée?

When is the show?
À quelle heure est la représentation?

When is breakfast served?
À quelle heure sert-on le petit-déjeuner?

What does it cost?
Combien cela coûte-t-il?

Where can I buy a newspaper in English?
Où puis-je acheter un journal en anglais?

Where is the nearest petrol/gas station?
Où se trouve la station d'essence la plus proche?

Where can I change traveller's cheques?
Où puis-je échanger des traveller's chèques?

Where are the toilets?
Où sont les toilettes?

Do you accept credit cards?
Acceptez-vous les cartes de crédit?

Arènes, Arles

INTRODUCTION TO PROVENCE

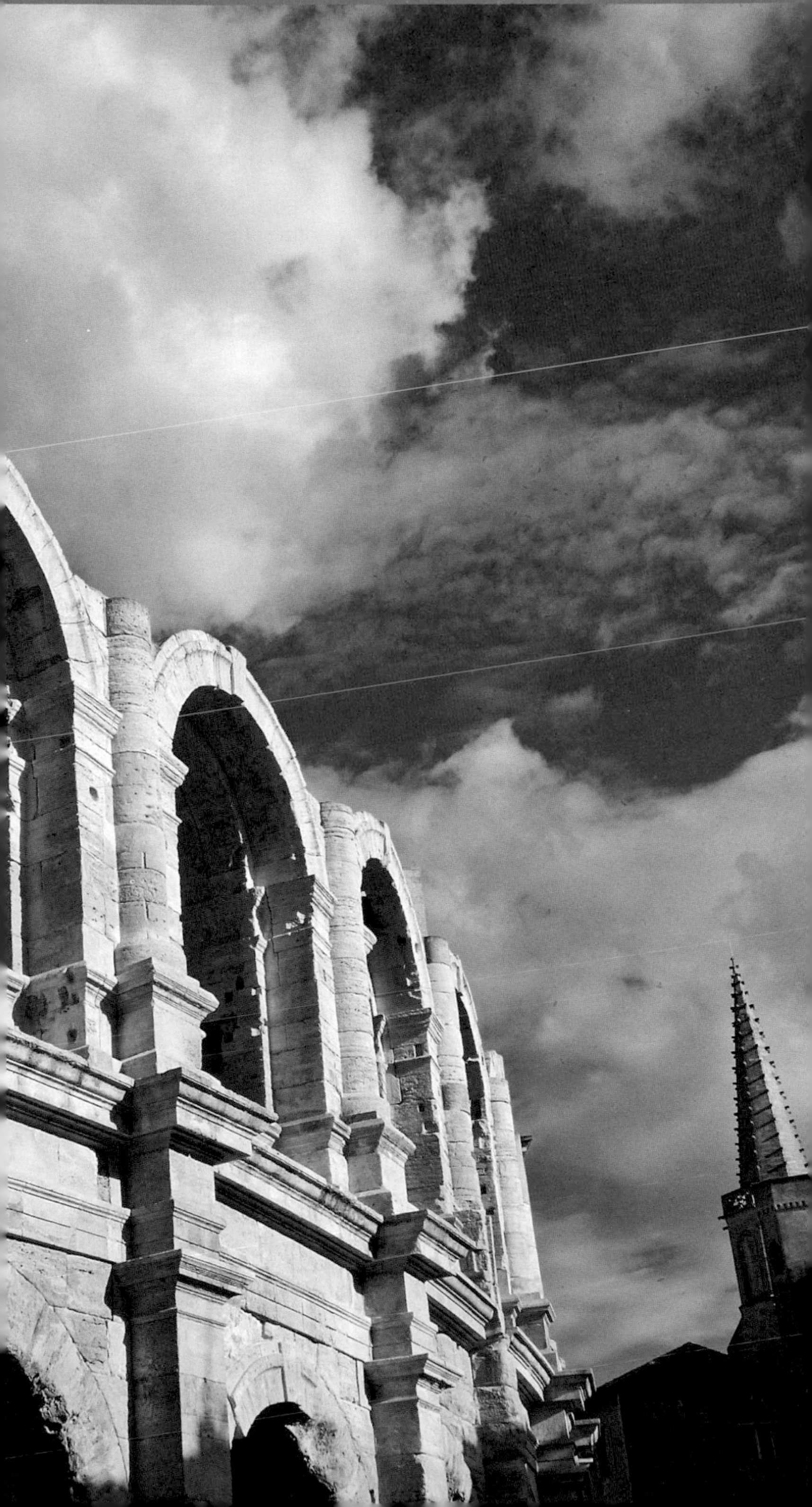

Provence Today

Provence is famous the world over for its colourful landscapes and its relaxed way of life, along with its mouthwatering regional produce and cuisine; it's precisely these desirable attributes that drive a thriving tourist industry. The region still retains a strong cultural identity, most evident in its year-round events calendar, in spite of increased industrialisation and farming.

21ST CENTURY

The beginning of this century has seen Provence posing a familiar question to itself: how to combine modern development and growth, with Marseille being the second-largest city in France, while maintaining its fiercely proud Occitan identity, which has inspired artists and visitors and provided a melting pot for Mediterranean culture throughout its long history?

POPULATION

Provence has a population of around 4.5 million inhabitants, of which 850,000 inhabit the metropolitan area of Marseille, and of which 50 percent are of working age. The region boasts a growing population with around 55,000 births and around 20,000 marriages per year. Provence also enjoys a higher life expectancy at birth than the rest of the country. Interestingly, it has also become popular with second-home owners, with twice the percentage of second homes than the national average.

LIFESTYLE

The Provençal way of life is synonymous with a tranquil and easy-going charm, epitomised by its Mediterranean climate and alluring scenery. It is fused with bustling markets that can be found on any day of the week in most areas, where the wares of local artisans and fresh farm produce create a forum for communal life, and by the festivals or *férias*, which bring communities together in celebration.

RELIGION

Roman Catholicism is the religion of the majority of France, while there are also significant minorities who practise Islam, Protestantism and Judaism. *Laïcité*, the French concept regarding the separation of Church and State, allows citizens the freedom to practise the religion of their choosing. In this context, religion is seen as a private matter and people generally refrain from discussing their beliefs openly.

SPORT

As well as enjoying France's passion for sports such as football and cycling, Provence also enjoys regional sports such as *pétanque*, a form of bowls played with steel *boules*, which developed from the 17C sport called *jeu provençal*. *Courses camarguaises*, a bloodless (at least for the bulls!) form of bullfighting where *raseteurs* snatch rosettes called *cocardes* from the head of a young bull, are regularly contested in villages as well as during festivals, especially in Arles.

MEDIA

As well as Marseille-based newspapers such as *La Provence* and *La Marseillaise*, the region is also served by the *France Bleu Provence* radio station (103.6 FM) along with local television stations.

ECONOMY

Of all the regions of France, Provence is perhaps the place where the local economy has undergone the greatest changes in the past 50 years. These changes have come about due to the transformation of the agricultural sector, increased industrialisation – especially along the coast – adaptation to large-scale tourism, and urbanisation.

FACETS OF AGRICULTURE

Rural life in the past depended mainly on three crops – wheat, vines and olives. These, with other produce such as fruits, vegetables, almonds, honey, and the keeping of goats and some sheep, ensured the existence of small farmers. Although under threat from more intensive agriculture, this traditional polyculture has survived to a striking degree in Provence, as can be seen not just at the main weekly markets but also at the increasing number of farmers' markets where small producers sell directly to the public.

Early Produce
The alluvial soil of the Rhône plain, the high mean temperature, and irrigation schemes favoured the development of early market gardening and fruit growing, producing several crops a year in the Comtat Venaissin and Petite Crau. The whole region is now divided up into parcels of land protected from the *mistral* winds by screens of cypress trees and reeds.

Strawberries, especially from Carpentras; cherries, especially from Venasque; melons, especially from Cavaillon; figs, especially from Caromb; potatoes from Pertuis; garlic from Piolenc and asparagus, tomatoes, peaches and apricots from all over Provence are eagerly sought in markets throughout France and the world.

Early produce, picked in the morning, is either sold to a private packer or sent to a cooperative where it is sorted, graded, packed and conditioned. Cooperatives have been established in places such as St-Rémy, Châteaurenard, Barbentane, Cabannes and St-Andiol, west of Cavaillon, among others.

From the main railway hubs (Châteaurenard, Cavaillon, Carpentras, Barbentane, Avignon), high-speed trains transport the early produce up the Rhône Valley to Paris and other large cities.

Cereals and Vineyards
The area between Arles and Tarascon, once the centre for growing wheat in Provence, now produces maize, rape seed and rice as well. The windmills dear to Alphonse Daudet have been replaced by modern milling machinery.

Vineyards are extremely important, for a very part of the extensive and important Southern Rhône wine region falls within Provence. While Châteauneuf-du-Pape remains its most celebrated *cru*, many other villages within the Côtes du Rhône

have steadily risen in stature in recent years, while lesser-known *appellations* like the Ventoux and Luberon have become much more dynamic.

Lavender and Lavandin
The delicate scent of lavender is characteristic of Provence. This plant is well suited to the climate and calcareous soils of Provence and Haute-Provence (&see The Green Guide French Alps). *Lavandin*, a more productive but less fragrant hybrid, is cultivated on the lower slopes (400–700m) and in the valleys. Today, approximately 8 400ha/20 748 acres of lavender are cultivated as well as 2 350ha/5 805 acres of *lavandin*. The harvest takes place from July to September according to the region. Though mostly mechanised, the inaccessible or closely planted older fields are still picked by hand. After drying for two to three days, the picked lavender is sent to a distillery. One hundred kilos (220lb) of lavender blossom are needed to produce one litre (0.2gal) of essence (the same amount of *lavandin* flowers yields 10l/2.6gal).

Lavender essence is reserved for the perfume and cosmetic industries, whereas the hybrid *lavandin* is for perfumed laundry, soap and cleaning products. Lavender fields can be spotted on the Vaucluse plateau near Sault.

Almonds and Olives
Almond trees, which grow all round the shores of the Mediterranean, were first imported into France from Asia in 1548. The development of later-blossoming

Bouquets of lavender, Bouches-du-Rhône

© Taylor Richard/Sime/Photononstop

varieties has led to increased cultivation. The most famous form of local almond confectionery is the *calisson* from Aix, a lozenge-shaped sweet made from ground almonds and puréed melon, and coated in white sugar icing.

Silvery-green olive groves are a common sight in many parts of Provence, and especially in the Alpilles. Sometimes, in the olive plantations, old trees have been cut low to the ground and four suckers can be seen growing in a crown-like shape; these create handsome new trees. Provence is famous for the quality of its olives, olive oils and olive-based products such as *tapenade*, a spread made from puréed black olives, anchovies and capers.

Truffles

The truffle is an edible, subterranean fungus that develops from the myce-lium, a network of filaments invisible to the naked eye. They live symbiotically with the roots of trees, in particular the *chêne vert* (green oak) that grows wild in many parts of Provence, most notably in the Vaucluse. Some truffles are harvested from around the roots of trees in the wild, while others are dug up under trees which have been impregnated with truffle spores, then planted in small plantations known as *truffières*. The advantage of these impregnated trees (which are sold by nurserymen as saplings) is that they become productive more rapidly and reliably than do trees in the wild. Different kinds of truffles are unearthed, depending on the season, with the help of specially trained dogs.

Lime Trees and Herbs

Although found in most parts of France, the lime tree *(tilleul)* is cultivated mainly in Provence between Buis-les-Baronnies and Carpentras. Today it is mostly planted in orchards and pruned, rather than found lining French roads.

The flowers are picked in June, depending on the blooming, dried in a shaded, airy dry room, then sold in bags or by the ounce for tea. Aromatic herbs used in cooking (*herbes de Provence*) are also widely grown. While rosemary and thyme flourish in their wild state on the scented scrubland known as *garrigue* as well as in market gardens, marjoram, lemon balm and especially basil are widely cultivated. As fresh herbs are now generally preferred to dried ones for flavour, some growers are specialising in many different varieties of a single herb. One grower who sells her produce each week at the Coustellet farmers' market cultivates 40 different kinds of basil.

Stock Raising

Sheep raising is an essential resource of all Mediterranean rural economies. Wool, no longer profitable, was abandoned and the sheep are now reared for meat.

Pastis in Provence

Inextricably linked to the game of *boules*, *pastis* is usually imbibed around apéritif time, on the outdoor terraces of cafés. It made its first appearance in Marseille in 1922 after aniseed beverages were rehabilitated (they had been banned since 1915 because they were likened to absinth). Proper *pastis* is produced by leaving various aromatic plants (anise, star anise, liquorice, etc.) to macerate in alcohol. By the late 1930s, brands had already made a name for themselves: Capon, Pernod, Cap Anis, Stop-Anis, but especially Ricard (locals will ask for "*un Ricard*" rather than "*un pastis*"). During World War II, *pastis* was sold in small packets on the black market: mixing the concentrated powder with half a litre of 90% proof alcohol and the same quantity of water would produce a litre of *pastis*. Demand for bottled *pastis* soared once again in the 1960s. Today there are some chic new brands on the market. You'll find a superb selection at **La Maison du Pastis**, 108 quai du Port, Marseille (℘*04 91 90 86 77. www.lamaisondupastis.com*).

The merino variety from Arles is predominant in the Bouches-du-Rhône *département*; however, the area allocated to it diminishes daily. The sheep graze on the meagre *coussouls* from the Plaine de la Crau from mid-October to mid-June. They are then moved up to Alpine pastures. Once a picturesque procession through villages and rugged countryside (known as transhumance), the transfer of the sheep is now done in trucks. In the *garrigues*, flocks of sheep graze on the sparse vegetation. They spend the summer in Larzac, or in the Lozère mountains.

The Camargue is famous for the black bulls and white horses that live in semi-liberty in herds called *manades*.

FISHING

Fishing is a traditional activity in the area around Marseille. Although water pollution can cause adverse effects, fishermen in these areas annually catch several thousand tonnes of sardines, anchovies, red mullet, mackerel and eel as well as more local varieties such as *grondin* and *rascasse*. The sight of sailor-fishermen unloading their catch still remains one of the most attractive scenes in ports such as Martigues and Cassis as well as Marseille itself.

In Marseille, the port of Saumaty, located at the foot of the Estaque, can shelter as many as 180 trawlers and offers all the necessary equipment for the preservation of fish.

Small fishing boats still supply the fishmongers of Marseille's Vieux Port. The hustle and bustle and the sing-song cries of the stallholders create a lively, timeless atmosphere that seems to have come straight out of Marcel Pagnol's novels.

INDUSTRIALISATION

In the 1930s, Provence witnessed spectacular industrial development. Around Étang de Berre a vast industrial complex was built: oil refineries, and chemical, aeronautic and metal works. Its centre was the Bassins de Fos complex, inaugurated in 1968.

From Marseille to Aix, industrial zones have multiplied and offer a vast range of activities: from soap-making plants to the most modern electronics factories. The hydroelectric installations of the lower valleys of the Rhône and Durance have also contributed to profound economic upheavals. Hydroelectric production combined with nuclear (*Marcoule*) production has allowed France to strengthen its energy potential. Moreover, the domestication of the two undisciplined rivers has resulted in the possibility of irrigating an immense agricultural area, until then hindered by drought. All these transformations have made Provence one of France's great industrial zones juggling between two types of industry: **traditional**: minerals (ochre, bauxite, lignite), shipbuilding, foodstuffs, soap-making (Marseille area), building materials, construction and saltworks; **modern**: petroleum and its derivatives, aeronautics, electronics, nuclear and chemicals.

Light industries have also developed: packaging in Valréas and Tarascon; confectionery in Aix and Apt.

Ochre

Up to the time of the Second World War, the Apt-Roussillon area was one of the main mining and treatment regions in France for ochre (an earthy red or yellow, and often impure, iron ore essentially used as a pigment for paints or as a wash applied for its protective value). The mineral beds can at times be 15m thick. Ochre in its natural state is a mixture of argillaceous sand and iron oxide. To obtain a commercially pure ochre product, the mineral is first washed and the impurities, which tend to be heavier, settle on the bottom. The lighter weight "flower", which is made of iron oxide and clay, is passed through the filter and into settling tanks. There, after drying, it assumes the look of ochre. It is then cut into blocks. After drying, the ochre is crushed, sifted and at times baked in ovens to darken the pigmentation and obtain a reddish-orange colour. This process is called ochre calcining. The ochre then becomes an unctuous, impalpable powder used commercially.

Although the production of ochre in the mines around Roussillon has diminished drastically, the bright yellow and red cliffs on which the village stands, and the glowing colours of its ochre-washed houses, still make a memorable sight.

Olive Oil

Typically, Provençal oil has always been olive oil. Besides playing an essential part in cooking, it is also used for soap and cosmetics. While vast numbers of olive growers continue to supply their fruit to a local co-operative, in recent years more and more have begun to set up as small, independent, artisan producers of top-quality oil – echoing the trend in the wine which has seen many good grape growers begin to bottle under their own label. The quality of the oil depends on the quality of the fruit and the treatment (number of pressings). Once picked, the olives are crushed whole with the pit, either by a millstone, hammer mill or roller.

The paste obtained is then distributed on a trolley's nylon discs. The trolley, now loaded, is placed on the sliding piston of a hydraulic press that exerts pressure on the paste, resulting in a mixture of oil and water that is collected in tanks and then pumped into centrifugal machines where the oil and water will be separated. The oil that comes out of the machine is a virgin oil obtained by a first cold-water pressing. The residual pulp *(grignon)* can be pressed again, yielding more oil, though of a lesser grade and taste.

In the past the olive paste was spread by hand onto coconut mats *(scourtins)* which were stacked under the press. For a long time the presses were worked by hand and a horse turned the millstone. The residual pulp was remashed with lukewarm water: a mixture of refined and virgin oil was obtained, classed as second quality and called second pressing. Today, as in the past, the residual pulp treated with chemical solvents in Italy produces oil used for cutting or soap-making. Before this last pressing the olive pit can be separated from the pulp: the pit is ground down into powder and is used by the baker and pastry cook; the pulp is used for compost.

Salt Marshes

The Camargue has two large salt marshes: one is south of Aigues-Mortes and spreads over 10 000ha/24 700 acres; the other lies south of Salin-de-Giraud and covers more than 11 000ha/27 170 acres.

Already improved by the monks in the 13C, the marshes increased salt production in the mid-19C, progressed and then decreased. The present-day

Olives and olive oil at a market, Cassis

© Ruth Tomlinson/Robert Harding

Playing boules

©Brigitta L. House/MICHELIN

annual production is c.850 000 metric tons. *Fleur de sel de Camargue*, made from hand-harvested crystals that form on the salt pans when conditions are right, is a gourmet speciality of the region, sold in all delicatessens.

GOVERNMENT

France is split on an administrative level into 22 metropolitan and four overseas *régions*, which are administered by elected regional councils. These are furthermore divided into 100 *départements* (equivalent to a district or county), in turn administered by general councils. Provence encompasses an area included in three *régions*, consisting of six *départements*: **Gard** in the Languedoc-Roussillon *région* to the west; **Drôme** and **Ardèche** in the Rhône-Alpes *région* to the north *(covered in Green Guide Languedoc Roussillon Tarn Gorges)*; and **Bouches-du-Rhône**, **Var** and **Vaucluse** in the Provence-Alpes-Côte d'Azur *région* to the east.

POPULAR GAMES
BOULES

This popular game is emblematic of Provence: long lazy evenings and animated debates. Contests are played between teams of three *(triplettes)* or four *(quadrettes)*, amid attentive and enthusiastic spectators. The *pointeurs* have to throw their balls, which

are weighted with iron, as near as possible to a smaller ball *(cochonnet)*, which has been set at the end of the bowling ground; the *tireurs* have then to dislodge the balls of the opposing team by striking them with their own. The most skilful succeed in doing this and in taking the exact place of their adversary *(faire le carreau)*. Over short distances play is *à la pétanque*, standing within a circle, feet together. Over longer distances, above 10m, the game is called *la longue*; the *tireurs* take a running start and throw their balls after having made three hopping steps from the throwing point.

Among all these shirt-sleeved players, the two Provençal types form a real contrast. One, a native of the mountains, somewhat reserved and distant, shows his pleasure or his disappointment by a smile or frown. The other enacts quite a little drama, which has been happily described:

"Here then is the last ball; it rolls out before the player and you can watch its progress in his face; he broods over it, protects it with his gaze; gives it advice, strives to make it obedient to his voice, hurries or slows its course, encourages it with a gesture or urges it on with a heave of his shoulder, slackens it with his hand; perched on tiptoe, his arm flung out, his face animated by a wealth

of varying emotions, he wriggles his body in bizarre undulations; one could almost say that his soul had passed into the ball."

Play is frequently held up by noisy, heated arguments about the distances separating the various balls from the *cochonnet*. Play resumes once measurements have been taken, often with small branches or twigs broken off a nearby tree.

CARD GAMES

The unforgettable scene in the *Bar de la Marine*, where a group of locals take part in a game of *manille*, with the colourful dialogue that typified Marcel Pagnol's work, exemplifies the importance of card games in Provençal society. Provence was the first place in France where playing cards appeared.

Minutes drawn up by a Marseille notary, dated 30 August 1381, prohibiting a merchant of the city from playing *nahipi* or *naïbi*, a sort of Happy Families card game, attest to the fact. This card game is nowadays considered the ancestor of modern-day tarot. Following their likely origins in the imperial Chinese court, playing cards reached the Occident during the course of the 13C, via Venetian bankers and merchants, or via the hordes of Tartars from central Asia. Venetian artists, hitherto devoted to religious and secular canvases, succumbed to this trend of painting on card and parchment. Marseille was soon drawn to the charms of this new pastime, as was the Comtat Venaissin, with its close ties with Italy.

The 15C gave rise to the game *cinq cents*, also known as the *Marseillais*. The first "professional" card makers appeared around 1631. With the development of new xylographic and typographic processes, replacing wooden printing moulds with copper ones, card production continued to increase dramatically, reaching a rate of 180 000 packs a year by the end of the 17C. The 18C was for Marseille the epoch of **tarot**, which originated in Italy. Apart from the set manufactured by Jean Noblet in Paris

during the 17C, the oldest tarot cards, said to have been made in Marseille, actually appeared in Avignon in 1713, a city where card makers were exempt from tax.

This privilege was removed in 1754, at which time Marseille established itself as the leading manufacturer. Marseille tarot, the French version of Venetian tarot, from which it copied 78 signs, provided the game with its definitive form, principally under the aegis of the master tarot maker **Nicolas Conver**, who produced a particularly attractive set of cards in 1760. The *Tarot de Marseille*, which was adopted by clairvoyants and soothsayers alike, was also to act as a support for another regional game in the 18C, the **Portrait de Marseille**.

However, the following century the Camoin company, with its exports worldwide, was to distance itself from its competitors by producing over a million sets a year, based on traditional expertise acquired over more than two centuries. The company finally closed its doors in 1974, though its sparkling creations can still be admired in the large collection housed in the Musée du Vieux-Marseille.

FESTIVALS AND COSTUMES
FESTIVALS

The people of Provence have always had a taste for celebration. In the past it was the men who were in charge of the festivities. The fairs, either secular or religious (remnants of Christian celebrations mixed with pagan tendencies), were numerous. There are the feast days that occur throughout the year, and the larger festivals, more or less traditional, attracting thousands of people in a typically colourful Provençal atmosphere.

In April and September, Nîmes and Arles try to outdo each other with their famous *férias*, via the *corrida* (bullfights) or *courses camarguaises,* where men called *raseteurs* attempt to grab a rosette *(cocarde)* from between a bull's horns. The latter continues to take place throughout the summer in arenas across the Camargue.

Also in the Camargue, the *Féria du Cheval* in July celebrates the region's four-legged friends – the horse and, of course, the bull.

In canal town Martigues, the Venetian Water Festival includes a nocturnal procession of decorated boats as well as water jousting.

Families will love the Tarasque Festival in Tarascon at the end of June, which celebrates the killing of a mythical medieval monster.

And of course there are the theatre, opera and dance festivals. Be it Avignon, Aix-en-Provence, Orange, Vaison-la-Romaine, Carpentras, Salon-de-Provence or Arles, each of these cities is the venue for an annual artistic festival of top quality (✆*see Planning Your Trip – Calendar of Events*).

FARANDOLES

Most of the festivals are a wonderful opportunity to listen to the fife and *tambourin* so delightfully characteristic of the Provence region. The **farandole** is a Mediterranean dance that dates back to the Middle Ages if not to Antiquity, and was danced throughout Arles country. Young men and women, holding either each other's hands or a handkerchief, dance to a six-beat rhythm. The typically Provençal instruments played by the *tambourinaires* are the **galoubet**, a small three-holed flute that produces a piercing sound, and the **tambourin**, a type of drum 75cm high and 35cm wide, beaten by a *massette* held in the right hand while the other hand holds the *galoubet*. On the drum itself, the head of which is made from calfskin, is stretched the *chanterelle*, a thin strand of hemp or a violin string that produces a rasping sound, poetically called the "song of the cicada".

CHRISTMAS IN PROVENCE

Celebrations surrounding the end of the year begin on 4 December, the feast day of St Barbe, and end at Candlemas on 2 February. The locals start by sowing their "Christmas wheat" *(lou blad de Calendo)* on 4 December. When it starts to sprout, they place it above the fireplace. Three weeks later, people use it as decoration beside the crib or as a centrepiece for the long banquet table. Preparations for the crib take place on the Sunday before Christmas, but it is only at midnight on 25 December that the infant Jesus is laid in the crib. That same night, the whole family ritually performs *Cacho-Fio*, a ceremony during which a Christmas log *(bûche de Noël)* is blessed with a fortified wine and taken round the house three times, before being burned. The family may then be seated to begin their Christmas feast. The table, covered with three overlapping tablecloths, is laid with three chandeliers and three saucers containing the Christmas wheat, as well as 13 loaves of bread. The meal ends with the traditional 13 desserts (*mendiants*: walnuts and hazelnuts, figs, almonds and raisins; fresh fruit; black and white nougat; *pompe à huile*, a flat, brittle loaf made with olive oil).

Midnight Mass starts with *lou Pastrage*: the shepherd, the miller and the ancestors enter the church, where the priest lays the infant Jesus in the crib. Then the bells are rung, inviting the procession of shepherds to enter the church: they draw a small cart with a lamb, an offering made to the infant Jesus. Mass continues with a series of Christmas songs and carols, which retraces the steps of Joseph who was seeking refuge for the night.

On 31 December, Provençal people always celebrate the New Year *(an nou)* together as a family. On the first Sunday in January, they pay tribute to the Magi and throughout the month of January, in honour of the Three Wise Men, they eat Twelfth Night cake *(galette des rois)*, a crown-shaped bun decorated with crystallised fruit and containing a lucky charm *(fève)*.

These Christmas festivities end on 2 February with Candlemas *(Chandeleur)*, the feast marking the Purification of the Virgin Mary and the presentation of Christ in the Temple 40 days after his birth. Celebrations involve a procession of green church candles. In Marseille, people also eat *navettes*, small boat-shaped biscuits that evoke the arrival of the Saintes Maries.

PROVENÇAL COSTUMES

It was thanks to the commercial relationship between Marseille and the Mediterranean ports of the Levant that Provence discovered Oriental fabrics. Since the end of the 17C, it has made these its own by adopting printed floral calicos and stitching and quilting techniques. The characteristic patterns of colourful motifs now known as "Provençal prints" are the result of a long evolution of methods and fashions. Traditional costume in Arles is but one example of the different costumes traditionally worn in Provence in the past, and still sometimes donned for festivals. It is a reminder of the diversity of the clothing worn by the various social milieux of days gone by: the fisherman's wife of the Vieux Port of Marseille, with the flaps of her coif blowing about in the wind; the flower girl; the country farmer's wife; the washerwoman; or the peasant woman with her striped underskirts, her huge apron of deep purple canvas and the *capuche* or *capelino*, which envelops her head.

In their traditional festive costume (there is an excellent collection in the Museon Arlaten in Arles), women from Arles wear long colourful skirts and a black under-blouse *(eso)* with tight sleeves; on top, a pleated shirt is covered with a shawl either made of white lace or matching the skirt. There are different varieties of headdress, all worn on top of a high bun: *à la cravate* (white percale knotted like rabbits' ears); *à ruban* (with a lace-trimmed velvet ribbon); or *en ailes de papillon* ("butterfly wings" of lace).

The men's costume is less colourful. They wear a white shirt knotted at the collar by a thin tie or ribbon, sometimes covered by a dark-coloured vest upon which hangs a watch chain; canvas trousers are held at the waist by a wide red or black woollen belt. They wear black felt hats with a wide, tilted brim.

FOOD AND WINE
A SUCCULENT CUISINE

The delicious cooking of Provence is based around fresh, local produce: garlic, olive oil, fish, vegetables, fruit and goat's cheeses. Although they also feature, meat and poultry are generally of secondary importance.

Bouillabaisse

This famous Provençal dish traditionally comprises "the three fishes": the spiny

Arlésiennes festival costumes

© bapaume/Bigstockphoto.com

Three Traditional Recipes

Tapenade - This olive, anchovy and caper-flavoured paste is eaten either as an hors-d'œuvre or as an accompaniment to an apéritif and is spread on slices of bread. In a mortar, place two handfuls of stoned black olives, 2–4 anchovy fillets, 2 soup-spoonfuls of capers, 1 crushed garlic clove, a pinch of thyme, and ground black pepper to taste. Crush until you get a rough paste. Add a dessert-spoon of mustard if desired, juice from a quarter of a lemon, a dash of brandy (optional), and mix. Lastly, add enough olive oil to give the paste a nice spreading consistency.

Artichauts à la Barigoule - The term *barigoule* is Provençal for mushroom; the name of the dish comes from the manner in which the artichokes are cut, giving them the appearance of mushrooms. Select a dozen small fresh artichokes and remove the largest leaves. Cut off the top two-thirds of the remainder and cook in an open casserole dish over a low heat with some sliced onions and carrots; add some olive oil. After 20–25min, add two glasses of dry white wine, two glasses of stock, two cloves of garlic and a few bacon cubes. Add salt and pepper, then cover once more and simmer for 50min. Serve the artichokes in the sauce. **Serves 4**.

Daube Provençale - Allow two days for the preparation of this dish. Marinate half a pound of beef cut up into pieces in red wine together with an onion cut in four, a clove of garlic, a bunch of mixed herbs *(bouquet garni)*, salt and pepper. The next day, fry some bacon *(lard)* in hot olive oil, using a casserole dish. Add a chopped onion and two sliced carrots as well as two crushed tomatoes. After browning these, mix in with the meat and continue to fry. Pour in a glass of red wine and bring to a boil. Add two more glasses of water and the garlic, the *bouquet garni* and the peel of an orange. Season with salt and pepper. After the boiling point is reached, turn the heat down and leave to simmer very slowly for up to five hours.

scorpion fish, gurnard and conger eel *(rascasse, grondin, congre)*. Cooks add as many other fish as are available: sea bass *(loup)*, turbot, sole, red mullet *(rouget)*, monkfish *(lotte)* and crustaceans such as crabs, spider crabs *(araignées de mer)*, mussels *(moules)* and sometimes spiny lobsters *(langoustes)* or crayfish. These sea delights are cooked together very rapidly in a *bouillon*, emulsified with a small quantity of olive oil and seasoned with salt, pepper, onion, tomato, saffron, garlic, thyme, bay leaf, sage, fennel, orange peel, and maybe a glass of white wine or Cognac – the magic of the results depends on the seasoning.
A *rouille* (pronounced *roo-EE*), a thick garlicky mayonnaise with a dash of cayenne pepper, is served at the same time to sharpen the dish and give it colour.
In a restaurant one is usually presented with a soup plate and toast with which

to line it. Some people then spread some of the toast with the *rouille*; others mix it directly into the thickened bouillon soup that arrives in a tureen. To your plateful of toast, *rouille* and soup, you then add bits of the assorted cooked fish and crustaceans.
Bouillabaisse is a main dish. The fish must be fresh and the dish freshly prepared. It is not a stew: the actual cooking time is only 10 minutes.

Aïoli

The other great Provençal speciality is a mayonnaise made with garlic, egg yolks, lemon juice, olive oil and sometimes mustard. It is served with hors-d'œuvres, asparagus and other vegetables, and also as a sauce with *bourride*, the fish soup made from angler fish *(baudroie)*, sea bass *(loup)* and whiting *(merlan)*. It is also the name of a complete dish consisting of steamed vegetables (carrots, potatoes and green beans), fish (cod) and boiled eggs served with the mayonnaise.

Fish and Shellfish

Local fish dishes include red mullet *(rouget)* cooked whole, sea bass *(loup)* grilled with fennel or vine shoots, and *brandade de morue*, a thick and creamy mash of pounded cod, olive oil and milk, seasoned with crushed garlic.

Fish specialities are associated with individual towns. For Marseille, in addition to *bouillabaisse*, there are clams *(clovisses)*, iodine-rich sea-squirts *(violets)*, mussels *(moules)* and sea urchins *(oursins)*, all of which you will find easily in the small restaurants around the Vieux Port. In St-Rémy you will encounter the *catigau*, a dish of grilled or smoked Rhône eel in sauce. In the Camargue, look for *tellines* (tiny clams) served with a pungent sauce.

Fruit and Vegetables

With a sunny climate and suitable soil, Provence produces an astonishing diversity of vegetables and fruits all year round, providing the basis for its varied and strongly seasonal cuisine. Asparagus, cherries and strawberries in spring; tomatoes, courgettes, aubergines, peppers, garlic, apricots, peaches, melons and figs in summer; saffron and grapes in autumn; olives in winter – these are the staple ingredients. They are cooked in a wide variety of ways. Vegetables feature in gratin dishes baked in the oven *(tians)*, soups, salads, stews, fritters or stuffed vegetables. Fruits are enjoyed raw or cooked, perhaps in a gratin or a more international (but fashionable) crumble, sometimes with lavender flowers or verbena leaves scattered on top.

Honey is also extremely important in cooking. Half a dozen different kinds are widely produced in Provence, including lavender, rosemary, acacia and the richest style, chestnut.

Olives

All over Provence, olives of different kinds are grown. Some are harvested early, while they are still green; others are left to darken and ripen fully, when they are black. They must then be "cured" with salt to tame their naturally bitter flavour, before being used in the kitchen.

Olives add a tangy richness to countless recipes: that is one reason you will see them laid out in all their infinite variety at every market. The other reason is

The Herbs of Provence

The famous *herbes de Provence* form, along with garlic and olive oil, the basis of the region's cuisine. Coupled with the magic touch of the chef, these fresh ingredients will add their own personality to the frugal yet fully flavoured and characteristic cooking of Provence.

Among these note: **savory**, often used to flavour goat's or sheep's cheeses; a mix of **thyme** and **bay**, which, combined with tomatoes, aubergines, courgettes, red and green peppers, and onions, is used to make the popular ratatouille (vegetable stew), as well as being an ideal addition to grilled and roast meats; **basil**, which, when crushed with garlic, olive oil, and occasionally bacon and parmesan cheese, is an important ingredient in the preparation of the famous *pistou*; **sage**, its clear, velvety leaves boiled with garlic to make the traditional *aigo-boulido* broth to which nothing more than olive oil and slices of bread are added; **rosemary**, a perfect seasoning for vegetable gratins and baked fish, also used in herbal teas to ease digestion; **wild thyme**, particularly suited to wild rabbit dishes, but which also brings out the best in vegetable soups and tomato-based recipes; **juniper**, an irreplaceable seasoning for pâtés and game; **marjoram**, ideal for stews; **tarragon**, used to spice up white sauces; **fennel**, with its aniseed taste, a superb accompaniment to fish dishes.

White nougat of Provence

© Soleil Noir/Photononstop

that an apéritif in Provence would seem naked without a bowl of olives, or some little toasts on which to spread olive paste *(tapenade)*.

Cheeses

Provençal artisanal cheeses abound in the weekly markets throughout the region, as well as in speciality shops *(fromageries)* and covered markets, such as Les Halles in Avignon. Many artisan cheese producers are happy to sell direct from their farm.

Provence is renowned for its sheep- *(brebis)* and goat's *(chèvre)* milk cheeses, which often come in the form of small discs: fresh *(frais)*, *crémeux* (creamy and a little more mature) and *sec* (hard and decidedly mature). These cheeses impart the flavours of the aromatic plants upon which the sheep and goats grazed, enriching their milk.

A tasty salad is *salade de chèvre chaud*: well-dressed salad greens are topped with toasted slices of baguette covered in melting goat's cheese, herbs and a drizzle of olive oil.

Specialities

Among the numerous Provençal specialities are *pieds-et-paquets* (lamb tripe and feet) from Marseille; *gardianne de taureau*, bull stew from the Camargue; Aix's *calissons* (almond paste sweets with sugar icing); and *berlingots,* candies from Carpentras. Look out for the crystallised fruits for which Apt was once famous.

Nougat is also a Provençal strength, given the quality of local honey and almonds. Bear in mind that the best quality white nougat should not look bright white in colour but creamy in tone.

WINES

It was the Greeks who first cultivated vines in Provence on the hills around Massalia (present-day Marseille) and the lower Rhône Valley. The Romans continued to grow grapes and make wine right across the region, consolidating a tradition which has continued to this day, despite the ravages wrought by phylloxera, the vine pest which decimated vineyards towards the end of the 19C.

Rather confusingly, in wine circles the term "Provence wines" relates mainly to wines produced in the area southeast of the territory covered by this guide (▶*For more information on the wines of Provence, see the Michelin Green Guide The Wine Regions of France)*, although some Provence *appellations* do fall within the scope of this book, at least in part. While red wines are becoming a little more important in most of these areas, the main focus is on rosé, an enormous success internationally as well as in France in recent years.

Provence Appellations

Near Marseille, the wines of **Cassis** have a splendid reputation, particularly the flower-scented, mineral-edged dry whites. The outskirts of Aix-en-Provence are home to the minuscule **Palette** *appellation*, dominated by famous Château Simone. The **Coteaux d'Aix-en-Provence** and **Côtes de Provence** are celebrated, above all, for the rosés with which the very word Provence has become synonymous throughout the world of wine, although warm reds and dry, lively whites are increasing in importance. The **Les Baux-de-Provence** *appellation* produces stylish red, white and rosé wines, many of them from organically cultivated grapes, near the town of the same name.

Southern Rhône Appellations

By far the biggest vineyard area encompassed in the Provence of this guide falls within the Southern Rhône. This is essentially **red wine country**, dominated by the heat-loving Grenache

Bottles of Châteauneuf-du-Pape

© V. Gillet/ADT Vaucluse Tourisme

grape blended with other grapes including Syrah and Mourvedre.

At its heart is the vast sweep of the **Côtes du Rhone**, especially famous for **Châteauneuf-du-Pape** but increasingly recognised for the quality of wines from other villages including **Gigondas**, **Vacqueyras**, **Rasteau**, **Cairanne** and **Beaumes-de-Venise**. According to the region's hierarchy of quality, its best wines have the right to put the name of their village on the label; next best in quality come wines labelled Côtes du Rhône-Villages; and ranked below these are straightforward Côtes du Rhône.

Also under the umbrella of the Southern Rhône are the so-called "satellite" *appellations* of the **Ventoux** and the **Luberon**, both sources of increasingly polished wines from up-and-coming producers. Indeed, quality right across the region has improved strikingly over the last decade or two. Young producers these days are more open-minded than their fathers or grandfathers, and more likely to realise that they stand a better chance of making a decent living by producing small quantities of good wines than large quantities of inferior quality which will sell only at a rock-bottom price, if at all.

Across all of these Southern Rhône *appellations*, red wines account for well over 90 percent of production. Even so, **whites and rosés** can be refined and delicious, especially in summer. As is the local tradition, these too are made from a blend of several grape varieties. The front runners are Grenache Blanc, Clairette, Bourboulenc, Marsanne and Roussanne for whites and the usual red varieties for the rosés.

Dessert wines are represented by **Rasteau**, with its red or amber robe, and by **Muscat de Beaumes-de-Venise**, renowned for its golden robe and flowery, grapey aromas. These styles are made from very ripe, late-picked grapes whose fermentation is halted at a certain point by the addition of grape spirit.

For more information about the wines of the Southern Rhône, see *Orange and Around*.

History

TIME LINE
PREHISTORY TO THE ROMAN CONQUEST

BCE

c.90 000–40 000 Neanderthal Man occupies coastal Provence.

c.30 000 Modern early humans (Cro-Magnon) settle in the region, leaving traces, such as the cave paintings in Grotte Cosquer (👁 see Cassis).

c.6000 Neolithic-impressed pottery: the first potters begin turning to agriculture and settle on the sites of Châteauneuf-les-Martigues and Courthézon.

c.3500 Chassey culture: the appearance of stock-raising farmers living in villages.

1800–800 Bronze Age. Ligurian occupation.

8C–4C Progressive installation of the Celts.

c.600 Founding of Massalia (Marseille) by the Phocaeans (👁 see Marseille).

4C Massalia is at its apex; travels of the Massaliote, Pythéas, into the northern seas.

218 Hannibal passes through Provence and crosses the Alps.

125–122 Conquest of southern Gaul by the Romans. Destruction of Entremont and founding of Aix.

102 Marius defeats the Teutons at Aquae Sextiae (Aix).

58–51 Conquest of *Gallic Comata* ("long-haired Gaul") by Julius Caesar.

27 Augustus establishes the Narbonensis.

AD

2C Nîmes at its apex.

284 Narbonensis is divided into two provinces: Narbonensis on the west bank of the River Rhône, and Viennoise on the east bank.

4C Arles at its apex; establishment of the dioceses.

416 Jean Cassien, from the Far East, founds the Abbaye de St-Victor in Marseille.

THE COUNTY OF PROVENCE

471 Arles taken over by the Visigoths.

536 Provence ceded to the Franks.

8C–10C Saracens, Vikings and Magyars terrorise the land.

843 By the Treaty of Verdun Provence, Burgundy and Lorraine are restored to Lothair (one of Charlemagne's grandsons).

855 Provence is made a kingdom by Lothair for his third son, Charles of Provence.

879 Boso, Charles the Bald's brother-in-law, is King of Burgundy and Provence.

973 Expulsion of the Saracens from Provence.

1032 Provence is annexed by the Holy Roman Empire; the Counts of Provence, however, retain their independence; the towns expand and assert their autonomy.

1125 Provence divided up between the Counts of Barcelona and Toulouse.

c. 1135 First mention of a consulate in Arles.

1148 Sénanques abbey is the first Cistercian monastery established in Provence.

1229 By the Treaty of Paris, Lower Languedoc returns to France; founding of the royal seneschalship in Beaucaire.

1246 Charles of Anjou, brother of St Louis (Louis IX), marries Beatrice of Provence, the Count of Barcelona's

	daughter, and becomes Count of Provence.
1248	St Louis embarks from Aigues-Mortes on the Seventh Crusade.
1274	Cession of the Comtat Venaissin to the papacy.
1316–1403	The popes and schismatic popes at Avignon. Papal Schism (1378–1417).
1337–1453	Hundred Years' War.
1348	Clement VI buys Avignon from Queen Joan I. Great Plague epidemic.
1409	University of Aix founded.
1434–80	Reign of Good King René, Louis XI's uncle (see Aix-en-Provence).
1450	Jacques Cœur sets up his trading posts in Marseille.
1481	Charles of Maine, nephew of René of Anjou, bequeaths Provence to Louis XI.

THE ESTATES OF PROVENCE

1486	The Estates of Provence meet at Aix to ratify the union of Provence to the Crown.
1501	Inauguration of the Parliament of Aix as Supreme Court of Justice with limited political authority.
1524–36	Provence is invaded by the Imperialists (soldiers of the Holy Roman Empire).
1539	Edict of Villers-Cotterêts decrees French as the language for all administrative laws in Provence.
1545	Suppression of Vaudois heretics from Luberon.
1555	Nostradamus publishes his astrological predictions, Centuries.
1558	The engineer Adam de Craponne builds a canal.
1567	Michelade tragedy occurs in Nîmes.
1622	Louis XIII visits Arles, Aix and Marseille.

1660	Solemn entry of Louis XIV into Marseille.
1685	Revocation of the Edict of Nantes. Huguenots flee France.
1713	Under the Treaty of Utrecht the Principality of Orange is transferred from the House of Orange-Nassau to France.
1720	The Great Plague, which originated in Marseille, decimates Provence.
1763	Peace of Paris ends French and Indian War (1754–63), marking the end of France's colonial empire in North America.
1771	Suppression of Aix's Parliament.

FROM THE REVOLUTION TO THE PRESENT

1789	The French Revolution; Storming of the Bastille.
1790	The constitutional Assembly divides southeast France into three départements: Basses-Alpes (capital: Digne), Bouches-du-Rhône (capital: Aix-en-Provence), Var (capital: Toulon).
1791	Avignon and Comtat Venaissin are annexed to France.
1792	500 Marseille volunteers parade in Paris to the song of the Rhine Army, called "La Marseillaise".
1815	Battle of Waterloo; Napoleon's fall.
1854	Founding of the Provençal literary school: Félibrige.
1859	Frédéric Mistral publishes the Provençal poem Mirèio.
1904	Frédéric Mistral wins the Nobel Prize for Literature.
1932	Paul Ricard introduces pastis on a commercial basis in Marseille.
1933	Founding of the Compagnie Nationale du Rhône for the harnessing of the river.
1942	Germany invades Provence.

Avignon TGV station opened in 2001

© J-C.&D. Pratt/Photononstop

1944 15 August: Allied troops land on the Côte d'Azur. 22–28 August: General de Montsabert and his troops aided by the Resistance movement liberate Marseille from German occupation.

1962 First hydroelectric power stations of the Durance begin operating.

1965 Construction of Bassins de Fos complex begins.

1970 A 6–A 7 motorways link Paris and Marseille. Creation of the Parc Naturel Régional de Camargue.

1977 Marseille's Métro system begins service. Creation of the Parc Naturel Régional du Luberon.

1979 Creation of Mercantour National Park.

1981 The TGV, France's high-speed train, links Paris to Marseille.

1991 Cave paintings and engravings dating from the Upper Paleolithic Era are discovered in the Calanque de Sormiou, south of Marseille; now known as the Grotte Cosquer.

1993 Olympique de Marseille become the first French football team to win the European Cup.

1994 A painted cave, known as the Grotte Chauvet, is discovered in the Ardèche gorges.

1997 Creation of the Verdon Regional Natural Park.

1999 Marseille celebrates its 2,600th birthday.

2000 Avignon is one of nine cities designated a European Capital of Culture.

2001 The new TGV Méditerranée line south of Valence opens, making Paris a mere 3hr away from Marseille.

2004 The Millau Viaduct, the world's highest car bridge, opens west of Avignon, facilitating faster travel to southern France.

2006 Aix-en-Provence marks the centenary of the death of artist, and former resident, Paul Cézanne.

2007 Nicolas Sarkozy is elected President of France and Marseille is one of ten French cities to host Rugby World Cup matches.

2009 France assumes full membership of NATO.

2012 Creation of the Parc National des Calanques. François Hollande is elected President of France.

2013 Marseille-Provence becomes European Capital of Culture.

2015 Eurostar operate a direct service from London to Marseille.

HALLMARKS OF DIVERSITY

Provence is the product of one of the most highly used crossroads of the Mediterranean world, where ancient, medieval and modern meet. Provence received migrations and invasions from diverse peoples including the Bronze-Age Ligurians, the Iron-Age Celts, the early Greeks, Romans, Visigoths and Arabs. No lesser diversity greets the visitor today, as Provence has become a desirable tourist destination.

PRE-ROMAN SOUTHERN GAUL
Origins: A Melting Pot

During the Bronze Age (1800–800 BCE) Ligurians, the probable descendants of the native Neolithic population in northern Italy and southeastern France, inhabited the region. Celts began to infiltrate the area in the 7C, though their mass influx did not occur until about the 5C–4C. In the 7C, the first Greeks were also settling in the area. Phocaeans – Greeks from Phocaea in Asia Minor (Ionia, near Izmir in modern Turkey) – founded Massalia (Marseille) around 600 BCE in agreement with a Celtic tribe. This period represents a mixing of populations that established ancient Provence's roots in the Celtic-Ligurian civilisation. These diverse populations settled progressively in *oppida*, fortified hill sites. Nages, near Nîmes, St-Blaise overlooking the Golfe de Fos, and Entremont, near Aix, were important settlements and fortified townships.

Greek Presence

Greek settlement and influence is an essential part of the history of Provence's civilisation. The Rhodian Greeks most likely gave their name to the great Provençal river (Rhodanos). However, the Phocaeans were the first to establish a permanent colony: **Massalia**. Massalia rapidly became a powerful commercial city, which founded in turn a number of trading posts – Glanum, Avignon and Cavaillon – and had commercial exchanges with the people of the north (wine and pottery for pewter from Armorica and agricultural products and livestock from Brittany). The colonists brought with them a number of improvements, such as a wine and olive oil industry, the introduction of coinage, and more intricate architecture. But by the 2C, relations between the natives and the Phocaeans from Massalia were deteriorating. The Salian Confederation, which had grouped together the Provençal population, rose against Massaliote imperialism.

Rome and Massalia

During the Second Punic War (218–201 BCE), Massalia supported Rome whereas the Salian Franks helped Hannibal cross the region in 218. In 154 Massalia, worried about the threat of attack by the Gauls, obtained the protection of Rome. In 130 BC the powerful Arverni empire threatened southern Gaul's security, Gaul being the key trading centre

Roman mosaics, Musée Départemental Arles Antique

©S. Sauvignier/MICHELIN

between Italy and Spain. Rome came to Massalia's aid in 125 and the Roman legions easily conquered the Vocontii and Salian Franks, toppling their capital, Entremont. In 123, date of the founding of Aquae Sextiae (Aix-en-Provence), the Arverni and Allobroges suffered a bloody defeat. The consul Domitius Ahenobarbus relaxed the boundaries of a new province, **Gallia Transalpine**, which became **Narbonensis** (from the name of the first Roman colony of Narbonna) in 118. Massalia remained independent and was recognised as a territory. The Roman domination, which at one time was threatened by the Cimbrian and Teuton invasions in 105 (disaster at Orange) and halted by Marius near Aix in 102, spread irreversibly over the region, not without abuse and pillaging.

ROMAN COLONISATION
Pax Romana
Gaul Transalpine rapidly became integrated in the Roman world and actively supported the Proconsul Caesar during the Gallic Wars (58–51 BCE). Marseille, as a result of having supported Pompey against Caesar, was besieged in 49 BCE, fell, and lost its independence. The important Roman towns were Narbonne, Nîmes, Arles and Fréjus. Romanisation accelerated under Augustus, and the Narbonensis was reorganised in 27 BCE. Antoninus Pius' reign (2C) marked the apogee of Gallo-Roman civilisation. Agriculture remained Provence's principal activity and trade enriched the towns. Arles profited the most from Marseille's disgrace. Urban affluence was reflected in a way of life entirely focused on comfort, luxury and leisure. Excavations have given us a glimpse of that life.

Arles, the Favoured City
After the troubled times of the 3C, the 4C and 5C brought considerable religious and political transformation. Christianity triumphed over the other religions after the conversion of Constantine. Arles became his favourite town in the west.

Marseille remained a commercial centre. Aix became an administrative capital. Nîmes declined, and Glanum was abandoned.

Rural areas suffered from the general impoverishment of the Gallo-Roman world. Large landowners placed heavy demands, and insecurity led to the resettlement of fortified hill sites, such as St-Blaise.

FALL OF THE ROMAN EMPIRE TO PAPAL AVIGNON
Invasion after Invasion
Until AD 471, the date Arles was taken by the Visigoths, Provence had been relatively free from invasions. The Burgundian and Visigoth domination (476 to 508) was followed by the Ostrogoth restoration, a period of some 30 years whereupon the Ostrogoths considered themselves the mandatories of the Far Eastern emperor and revived Roman institutions: Arles thus recovered its praetorian prefects. Religious life continued to progress; several synods were held in Provence towns (Vaison-la-Romaine).

The Bishop of Arles, St Caesarius, had a vast following in Gaul. In 536, Provence was ceded to the Franks and followed the same uncertain destiny as other provinces, tossed from hand to hand according to the Merovingian dynastic divisions. Decline was rapid.

The first half of the 8C was chaotic and rife with tragedy: Arabs and Franks transformed the region into a battleground. In 855 Provence was made a kingdom, its limits corresponding more or less with the Rhône basin. It soon fell into the hands of the kingdom of Burgundy, whose possessions spread from the Jura to the Mediterranean and were under the protection of the Holy Roman Emperors, who inherited it in 1032. This was a major date in the region's history as it made Provence a part of the Holy Roman Empire, with the area west of the Rhône under the aegis of the counts of Toulouse.

Occitanian Provence

The 10C and 11C marked a major shift in the evolution of Provence's civilisation, which until then was deeply defined by its Greco-Roman past. A new society developed out of the feudal anarchy. Rural life, henceforth, was concentrated in the hillside villages – Luberon, Ste-Baume and the Vaucluse mountains – which depended upon the seigneuries. Many towns sought to recover a degree of autonomy. The Oc language spread. Close links were established between Provence and Languedoc.

The failure of Occitania facilitated Capetian intervention. The Albigensian heresy resulted in the delayed union of the Catalan and Toulousain peoples, who until then had been fighting over Provence against the invaders from the north. The defeat at Muret in 1213 dashed all hope of a united Occitania.

Louis VIII's expedition (siege of Avignon in 1226) and the Treaty of Paris in 1229 brought about the founding of the royal seneschalship in Beaucaire: the west bank of the Rhône was part of France. In the east, the Catalan Count, Raimond Bérenger V, maintained his authority and endowed Provence with administrative organisations. The towns became powerful locally: as early as the 12C they elected their own consuls, whose power increased to the detriment of the traditional lords (bishops, counts and viscounts). In the 13C they sought their independence.

House of Anjou's Provence

The marriage of **Charles of Anjou**, St Louis' brother, to Beatrice of Provence, Raimond Bérenger V's heir, in 1246 linked Provence to the House of Anjou. Charles had large political ambitions: he interfered in Italy and conquered the kingdom of Naples in 1266 before turning towards the Far East.

In Provence, Charles of Anjou's government was very much appreciated. It re-established security.

Honest administration managed public affairs, and prosperity returned. Concerning the territories, Comtat Venaissin was ceded to the papacy in 1274 by the King of France and evolved separately. Charles I's successors, Charles II and Robert I, continued their father's and grandfather's political ideas and political order, and peace reigned during the first half of the 14C. Aix was raised to administrative capital with a seneschal and a court where the officers who presided were in charge of the finances of the county.

The key city was henceforth Avignon, where the Bishop Jacques Duèze, elected pope in 1316 under the name John XXII, established himself. French-born Pope Clement V was already resident in Comtat Venaissin and benefited from the protection of the King of France. Thus John XXII's decision was confirmed by his successor Benedict XII, who began the construction of a new papal palace. The popes' stay in Avignon, which lasted almost a century, brought expansion and extraordinary brilliance to the city.

FROM ANNEXATION TO THE FRENCH CROWN
The End of Provence's Independence

After the second half of the 14C, Provence entered a difficult period. Famine and plague (which struck in 1348), pillaging road bandits, and political uncertainty brought about by the slackness of Queen Joan (granddaughter to King Robert; she was assassinated in 1382), badly damaged Provence's stability. The population was decimated, the country in ruins. After a violent dispute over succession, Louis II of Anjou (nephew to the King of France, Charles V), aided by his mother, Marie of Blois, and the pope re-established the situation (1387).

Pacification was temporarily slowed by the activities of a turbulent lord, Viscount Raymond de Turenne, who terrorised the country (1389–99), pillaging and kidnapping. His lairs were the fortresses of Les Baux and Roquemartine. Peace was not achieved until the early 15C.

Louis II of Anjou's (d. 1417) youngest son, **King René**, inherited the county at the death of his brother in 1434. He was primarily concerned with the reconquest of the kingdom of Naples but every attempt of his failed, whereupon he turned all his attention to Provence (1447) and came to love it. His reign left happy memories; it coincided with a political and economic restoration that was felt through all of France. King René was a poet and had a cultivated mind fed by his love of the arts. He attracted a number of artists to Aix, who came to take up where the popes' Avignon had left off. His nephew Charles of Maine briefly succeeded him. In 1481 Provence ceded to Louis XI of France and the region's history was henceforth interlaced with that of the kingdom of France.

Vaudois and Huguenots

The Reformation spread in the south of France as early as 1530, thanks largely to the impetus from merchants and pedlars. Through the Rhône and Durance valleys and Vivarais, Protestantism was stimulated by the brilliance of the Vaudois Church located in the Luberon village communities.

The Vaudois heresy went back to the 12C: a certain Peter Waldo or **Valdès**, a rich merchant from Lyon, had founded a sect in 1170 preaching poverty, Evangelism, refusal of the sacraments, and ecclesiastical hierarchy. Excommunicated in 1184, the Vaudois had since been pursued as heretics. In 1530 they were targeted by the Inquisition, and in 1540 the Aix Parliament decided to strike hard by issuing a warrant for the arrest of 19 Vaudois from Mérindol. François I temporised and prescribed a deferment. Instead of calming things down, the religious controversy came to a head. The heretics pillaged Abbaye de Sénanque in 1544. As a riposte, the *Parliament*'s president obtained royal authorisation to enforce the Mérindol warrant and organised a punitive expedition. From 15 to 20 April 1545 blood ran through the Luberon village streets: 3 000 people were massacred, 600 were sent to the galleys, and many villages were razed.

Nevertheless, Protestantism continued to spread, especially west of the Rhône in Vivarais, Cévennes, Nîmes and Uzès. East of the Rhône it was Orange (a Nassau Family principality since 1559) that became a Reformation stronghold. In 1560, numerous churches and abbeys (St-Gilles, Valbonne charterhouse) were pillaged by the Huguenots; violence gave rise to more violence and with it the capture of Orange (1563) by the Catholic partisans. This in turn was answered by the fall of Mornas.

During these tumultuous times Provence and Languedoc-Cévennes split, taking different paths. Provence opted for Catholicism, and the Catholic League recruited fervent partisans in such cities as Aix and Marseille (both of which would have liked to become an independent republic). On the Rhône's opposite shore the situation was different. The people, influenced by the merchants and textile craftsmen who kept the Reformation alive, generally tended to believe in the Protestant movement and Nîmes was its capital.

The violent Wars of Religion in southern France brought about a conflict between two peoples of opposing mentalities who were to clash again during the Camisard Insurrection (1702–04).

18C TO THE PRESENT DAY

In the 18C, Provence experienced a golden age for agriculture and commerce. The 19C was a less successful period: industrialisation progressed but rural life suffered from the failure of the silkworm farms, and phylloxera, which spread through the vineyards.

In the face of these changes, **Frédéric Mistral** sought to defend the Provençal identity and its traditions. When he died in 1914, Provence was nevertheless wholeheartedly engaged in modernisation.

In the 21C, Provence is now a successful society, relying on heavy industry, agriculture and tourism. The region is renowned for its cultural events, its climate and its products (wine, honey, rice) as well as for its multiculturalism.

Architecture

TRADITIONAL RURAL STYLE

The Provençal country house, whether a *mas*, a *bastide* or an *oustau*, features the following characteristics:

- a shallow sloping roof of Roman style; curved terra-cotta tiles, with a decorative frieze under the eaves, composed of a double or triple row of tiles embedded in the wall and known as a **génoise**;
- stone walls, more or less smoothly rendered (pink or lavender), with no windows on the north side and those on the other three sides just large enough to let in light but keep out the summer heat;
- a north–south orientation, with sometimes a slight turn to the east to avoid the direct blast of the *mistral*; cypresses serve as a windbreak to the north, plane and lotus trees provide shade to the south;
- floors covered with red or brown terra-cotta tiles *(mallons)*;
- vaulting in dried stone or masonry that completely replaced floorboards.

The **Provençal mas** is a large, low farmhouse rectangular in plan with a sprawling low roof covering the living quarters and annexes. The walls are made of stone taken from the fields or from the Plaine de la Crau, with ashlar-stone surrounding the openings. Traditionally, it is divided into two parts by a corridor, for in times past, one side was for the master and the other for the farmer *(bayle)*. This was repeated on the ground floor and on the upper storey. The kitchen is level with the courtyard, and functions as the centre of the house in spite of its small size. Upstairs are bedrooms with tiled floors, and the attic. The outbuildings and other rooms are used for various purposes according to the importance of the *mas* and the agricultural vocation of the region. The ground floor sometimes has a vaulted cellar facing north. This cellar could be used as stables, shed, storeroom, sheep's pen (at times separated from the *mas*), bread oven or cistern. Above it, the attic space once served as the cocoonery for silkworms, and also as a barn (above the sheep's pen) and dovecote.

The **mas of the Bas Vivarais** are slightly different. They have an attractive pattern of stonework and an additional storey. In a traditional farm, the ground floor, covered by solid vaulting, contains the stables for the smaller animals and the storeroom for wine-making tools. In the cold-room, harvested products as well as hams and sausages are kept. A stone staircase opens on to a **couradou**, a terrace that is generally covered, and leads to the stone or terra-cotta-tiled kitchen. The cocoonery was often off the *couradou* and until c.1850 was an essential part of the Vivarais *mas* architectural conception. The sleeping quarters are off the kitchen, and a small wooden staircase leads to the attic. In the wealthier *mas* this may be a spiral staircase in a turret with the bedrooms on the upper floor. Annexes were often added to the living quarters, such as bread oven, barn, and, in the chestnut region, a chestnut dryer, **clède** (or *clédo*). Nowadays, it is hard to find a *mas* occupied by a traditional farming family. Many of these properties have been bought up for use as holiday homes and have been completely transformed to accommodate modern desires: a jacuzzi where sheep once rested; a TV room where the silkworms once spun; or a microwave where the bread oven stood.

An **oustau** is a typical Provençal farmhouse smaller in size than a *mas* but with the same layout. In the upper Comtat it is called a *grange*. In the past these barn-like buildings were progressively enlarged to house the family, which formed a clan, and the workers. It was small in size, but people compensated for the lack of surface area by adding upper storeys.

A **bastide** is built of fine ashlar-stone and displays regular façades with symmetrical openings. Most often its layout is square in plan with a hipped roof.

Architecture A–Z

Acroterion: ornaments placed at the apex and ends of a pediment of a temple.

Ambulatory: aisle around the east end of a church.

Apse: rounded termination of the central nave opening onto the east end.

Archivolt: arch moulding over an arcade or upper section of a doorway.

Blind arcading: sequences of arches applied to a blank wall for decoration.

Brattice: temporary wooden gallery or parapet for use during a siege.

Caryatid: carved female figure used for support.

Chevet: French term for the east end of a church.

Cippus: small pillar used to mark a burial place.

Claustra: stone railings with vertical bars.

Coffered ceiling: vault or ceiling decorated with sunken panels.

Crocket: carved ornament in the form of a curled leaf or cusp used in Gothic architecture.

Diaphragm arch: transversal arch used to relieve side walls.

Entablature: projecting crown of a façade.

Exedra: niche with a bench around the wall.

Flamboyant: 15C phase of French Gothic architecture; named after the tapering (flame-like) lines of the window tracery.

Fluting: vertical, shallow grooving decorating a column or pilaster.

Foliated scrolls: sculptural or painted ornamentation depicting foliage.

Fresco: mural paintings executed on wet plaster.

Gable: triangular part of an end wall carrying a sloping roof; or steeply pitched ornamental pediments in Gothic architecture.

Génoise: decorative frieze under the eaves, composed of a double or triple row of tiles embedded in the wall.

Historiated: decorated with figures of people or animals.

Hypocaust: an underground furnace for heating.

Jambs: supporting pillars flanking a doorway.

Keystone: middle and topmost stone in an arch or vault.

Lintel: horizontal beam or stone slab surmounting a door or window frame.

Mascaron: medallion carved in the shape of a human head.

Modillion: small console supporting a cornice.

Mullion: vertical post dividing a window.

Narthex: interior vestibule of a church.

Peristyle: columns surrounding or fronting a building.

Pietà: Italian term for the Virgin Mary with the dead Christ on her knees.

Pinnacle: slender upright structure crowning a buttress, gable or tower.

Piscina: washbasin for sacred vessels.

Predella: base of an altarpiece, divided into small panels.

Pulpitum: front section of the stage in an antique theatre.

Retable: ornamental structure set up above and behind an altar.

Rood screen: open screen separating areas reserved for clergy (chancel) and laity (nave).

Rosette: circular window with ornamental tracery radiating from the centre to form a rose-like pattern.

Stucco: decoration of powdered marble, plaster and strong glue.

Transom light: upper section of a door or window.

Triptych: three decorated panels hinged together.

Voussoir: wedge-shaped stone forming part of an arch or vault.

Unlike the *mas*, the *bastide* was not necessarily a farmhouse. Thus, its conception was more luxurious, using decorative elements such as wrought-iron balconies, exterior staircase and sculpture.

The **gardian's cabin**, the typical Camargue dwelling of bygone days, is a small building (10m x 5m) with a rounded apse at one end. The cob walls are low. Only the front façade, with its entrance door, is built in rubble to hold a long ridge beam supported by another piece of wood sloped at a 45° angle, and crossed by a piece of wood to form a cross. Thatched with marsh reeds *(sagnos)*, these cabins usually had just two rooms divided by a wall of reeds: the dining room and bedroom.

CELTIC-LIGURIAN

Ligurians and Celts settled in fortified hill sites known as *oppida*, such as Nages, Entremont and Roquepertuse, and created towns organised on a regular plan. Within the fortified walls stood a group of uniform dwellings, a type of hut in unfired stone and brick.

Celtic-Ligurian sculpture honoured, above anything else, the cult of the dead warrior, the town's hero, whom they represented in the form of warriors' statues seated cross-legged with people either free-standing or in relief. An important ritual consisted of setting the severed heads of the conquered peoples, or at least the carved version, in the stone lintels. The sculpture exhibited at Roquepertuse perfectly demonstrates this Celtic form of expression.

Analysis of pottery shards confirms that Roquepertuse was densely occupied from the final Neolithic Era (3000 BCE) to around 200 BCE, the date of the last destruction of the site. The most prosperous period was between the end of the 4C BCE to the end of the 3C BCE, characterised by the widespread use of delicate Mediterranean dishes (cups and pitchers of either painted or unpainted clay, and black glaze from the 3C BCE). From being confined to a single sanctuary, as was long believed, Roquepertuse, which is still the subject of detailed research, is in fact a vast complex stretching from the *oppidum* in the north to the sloping village in the south.

Hellenistic influence was also crucial for the region; it directly influenced the native peoples, accelerating the development of their economy and society. Greek construction techniques are evident in the building of St-Blaise and Glanum. Numerous pottery fragments and Greek black figure vases were excavated at Arles, and the stelae found in rue Négrel in Marseille are the oldest examples (second half of the 6C BCE) of Greek sculpture in France.

ROMAN CULTURE

Throughout Provence, towns were built on the Roman urban plan. They all boasted remarkable public and private buildings, some of which are still well preserved, giving them a charm all their own. Without dropping Hellenistic influence entirely, the great Provençal towns took Rome as their model.

TOWNS

Most of the towns were built on either native Hellenistic or Gallic sites. And yet, very often, the desire to settle in a particular spot was that of a colony of veteran legionnaires, as was the case in Nîmes and Orange, who were soon after joined by the civilian population. The urban foundation was laid according to precise rules: having determined the future town centre, two major streets were traced – the *cardo maximus* (north–south orientation) and the *decumanus maximus* (east–west orientation). This created a regular grid pattern in which the grids were squared with sides some hundred square yards wide. This geometric exactitude could appear only on sites where the local topography was suitable, such as in Orange or Arles as opposed to Nîmes and Vaison-la-Romaine.

Where previous edifices had existed, they were razed, as at Glanum, to make room for the new buildings. These towns were not surrounded with walls except at Nîmes, Arles and Orange, which were granted the honour of surrounding themselves with ramparts (permission obtained from Rome). Defensive walls did not appear until the end of the 3C BCE Such walls were built with towers and gates corresponding to the main streets.

STREETS

The main streets were lined with pavements, at times 50cm high and bordered by porticoes that protected the people from sun and rain. The roadway, paved with large flagstones laid diagonally, was crossed at intervals by stepping stones laid at the same level as the pavements but between which horses and chariot wheels could pass and pedestrians could cross over above the dust and mud. Gutters also ran alongside the road and were slightly rounded.

FORUM

The forum, a large paved open space surrounded by an arcade, was the centre of public and commercial life in a Roman town. Government offices were located round the forum. These included a temple devoted to the imperial cult, a civil basilica (a type of town hall where judicial and commercial affairs were conducted), the *curia* or headquarters of local government, and, at times, a prison.

At Arles the forum had the particularity of being lined with a vast underground gallery, *cryptoporticus*, the origin of which remains a mystery.

THE ART OF BUILDING

The art of building was very advanced with the Romans. The rapidity with which their buildings went up was due not so much to the number of people working on a site as to the special training of the workers, their organised working methods, and the use of lifting devices, such as levers, hoisting winches and tackles, that moved heavy materials into place.

BUILDING MATERIALS

For building materials the Romans used the local limestone, which was not hard to dress; stones were easily extracted and shaped into blocks. Romans originally adopted the method of using large blocks of stone without mortar:

Architectural terms

ORANGE – Roman Theatre (early 1C BC)

Side entrance for secondary roles

Royal Doorway for lead roles

Backstage wall (scaenae frons) used for decorative props, the only one still standing in Western Europe

Superimposed colonnades

Foyer: reception area for spectators

Stage (scaena) with wooden flooring

Orchestra (orchestra) fitted with movable seats for senators and other dignitaries

Gradins (cavea) divided into sections (maeniae) separated by aisles

©R. Corbel/MICHELIN

Religious architecture

VAISON-LA-ROMAINE – Plan of the Ancienne Cathédrale Notre-Dame-de-Nazareth (11C)

This cathedral is a typical example of Provençal church architecture, consisting of a nave without a transept ending in a semicircular apse.

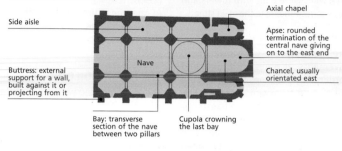

Side aisle

Axial chapel

Apse: rounded termination of the central nave giving on to the east end

Chancel, usually orientated east

Buttress: external support for a wall, built against it or projecting from it

Nave

Bay: transverse section of the nave between two pillars

Cupola crowning the last bay

Vertical section of a Romanesque Provençal church

The two following drawings reflect the type of Romanesque church most frequently encountered in Provence.

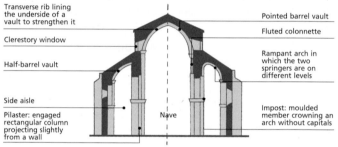

Transverse rib lining the underside of a vault to strengthen it

Pointed barrel vault

Fluted colonnette

Clerestory window

Rampant arch in which the two springers are on different levels

Half-barrel vault

Side aisle

Impost: moulded member crowning an arch without capitals

Pilaster: engaged rectangular column projecting slightly from a wall

Nave

Abbaye de SILVACANE – Vaulting in the Chapter-house (13C)

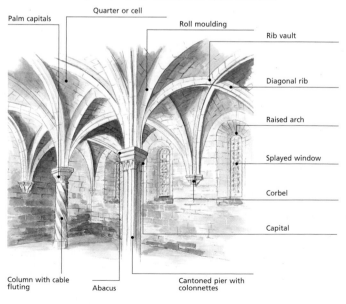

Palm capitals

Quarter or cell

Roll moulding

Rib vault

Diagonal rib

Raised arch

Splayed window

Corbel

Capital

Column with cable fluting

Abacus

Cantoned pier with colonnettes

©R. Corbel/MICHELIN

Abbaye de MONTMAJOUR – Chapelle Ste-Croix (12C)

The quadrilobed plan of the Chapelle Ste-Croix, based on a Greek cross and representative of 12C Provençal architecture, can be seen in several other buildings of the area.

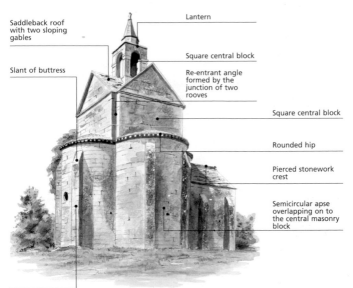

Saddleback roof with two sloping gables

Lantern

Square central block

Slant of buttress

Re-entrant angle formed by the junction of two rooves

Square central block

Rounded hip

Pierced stonework crest

Semicircular apse overlapping on to the central masonry block

Buttress

CARPENTRAS – South Door of the Ancienne Cathédrale St-Siffrein (late 15C)

The South Door, known as the Jewish Door, is Flamboyant or late Gothic: this is evidenced by the window tracery and its sinuous, tapering lines evoking tongues of flame.

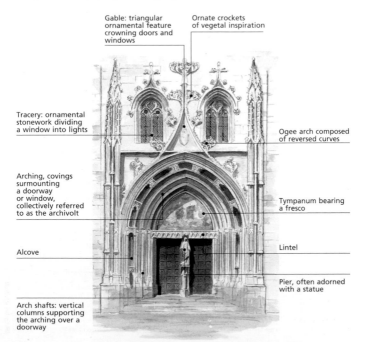

Gable: triangular ornamental feature crowning doors and windows

Ornate crockets of vegetal inspiration

Tracery: ornamental stonework dividing a window into lights

Ogee arch composed of reversed curves

Arching, covings surmounting a doorway or window, collectively referred to as the archivolt

Tympanum bearing a fresco

Alcove

Lintel

Pier, often adorned with a statue

Arch shafts: vertical columns supporting the arching over a doorway

©R. Corbel/MICHELIN

**Abbaye de ST-MICHEL-DE-FRIGOLET – Retable in the Chapelle
Notre-Dame-du-Bon-Remède (17C)**

This 11C chapel is richly decorated with Baroque panelling dating from the 17C. At the far end stands an imposing altarpiece.

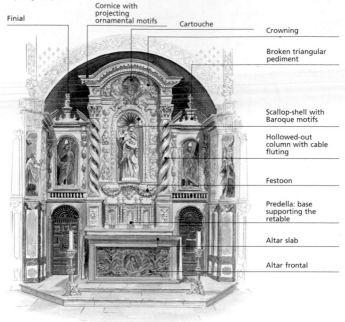

Finial

Cornice with projecting ornamental motifs

Cartouche

Crowning

Broken triangular pediment

Scallop-shell with Baroque motifs

Hollowed-out column with cable fluting

Festoon

Predella: base supporting the retable

Altar slab

Altar frontal

UZÈS – Organ in the Cathédrale St-Théodorit (18C)

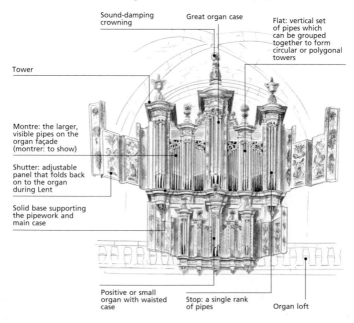

Sound-damping crowning

Great organ case

Flat: vertical set of pipes which can be grouped together to form circular or polygonal towers

Tower

Montre: the larger, visible pipes on the organ façade (montrer: to show)

Shutter: adjustable panel that folds back on to the organ during Lent

Solid base supporting the pipework and main case

Positive or small organ with waisted case

Stop: a single rank of pipes

Organ loft

©R. Corbel/MICHELIN

TARASCON – Fortified castle (14-15C)

Machicolations: projecting parapet with openings through which missiles were thrown at the enemy

Merlo

Crenel: open space between two merlons

Loophole

Outer bailey: courtyard lying outside the castle perimeter but protected by its ramparts; it housed the quartermasters' lodgings and could serve as a refuge for the population in the event of a siege

Arrow slit

Fixed bridge

Moat: defensive ditch encircling the towers and curtain wall

Curtain wall: enclosing rampart connecting two bastions or towers

Battered wall which recedes as it rises, forming a slant

PORT-DE-BOUC – Fort (17C)

This fort was built by Vauban in 1664. Its defensive system allows for a great many salients and bastions in order to avoid both dead angles and areas lacking artillery.

Rampart walk

Steep, narrow flight of steps backing on to the fort

Barracks

Look-out turret

Re-entrant angle in an outer rampart formed by the junction of two wings

Raised terreplein reserved for heavy artillery pieces

Salient

Battered wall

©R. Corbel/MICHELIN

Civil architecture

AIX-EN-PROVENCE – Pavillon de Vendôme (17-18C)

The main façade features the "great order" advocated by Palladio as early back as the Renaissance, characterised by the display of three superimposed orders: Doric, Ionic and Corinthian.

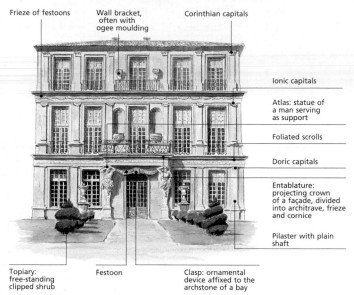

Frieze of festoons

Wall bracket, often with ogee moulding

Corinthian capitals

Ionic capitals

Atlas: statue of a man serving as support

Foliated scrolls

Doric capitals

Entablature: projecting crown of a façade, divided into architrave, frieze and cornice

Pilaster with plain shaft

Topiary: free-standing clipped shrub

Festoon

Clasp: ornamental device affixed to the archstone of a bay

MARSEILLE – Water tower of the Palais Longchamp (19C)

Seeking inspiration from Bernini's work in Rome, the architect Espérandieu built a monumental fountain whose decoration draws heavily upon the aquatic theme.

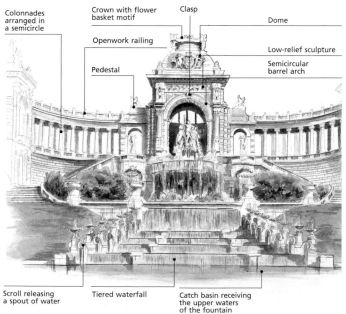

Colonnades arranged in a semicircle

Crown with flower basket motif

Clasp

Dome

Openwork railing

Low-relief sculpture

Semicircular barrel arch

Pedestal

Scroll releasing a spout of water

Tiered waterfall

Catch basin receiving the upper waters of the fountain

©R. Corbel/MICHELIN

the stones were held together by their weight, and with dowels or cramps. But builders then revolutionised wall construction by introducing the use of concrete, a manufactured material not unique to any one country. Concrete could be used in the construction of buildings throughout the empire, giving a uniformity and similarity to their edifices.

They also used concrete to fill in cracks or joints, or give to a public building a uniform surface, such as at the Maison Carrée and Amphitheatre in Nîmes, or to wedge the stones together allowing the expansion of a vault.

ORDERS

The Roman architectural Orders derived from the Greek Orders but with some variation. Roman Doric, still called the Tuscan Order, the simplest and most solid, was found on the monuments' lower storeys. Too severe, it was rarely used by the Romans. The Ionic Order was very elegant but not ornate enough for the Roman architects. It was the Corinthian Order that Romans used frequently because of the richness of its ornamentation. The Composite Order was a combination of the Ionic and Corinthian Orders.

ROOFS

Public buildings sometimes had rectangular-shaped roofs held by colonnades inside the rooms. But more often the Romans used rounded vaulting in corridors and galleries where the walls were parallel, groined vaulting in square rooms, and the dome in circular rooms.

PUBLIC BUILDINGS

The inhabitants of Roman towns enjoyed bloody combats as much as more peaceful theatrical representations.

Due to the influence of Christianity, gladiator fights were forbidden in 404. The games were abandoned at the same time.

AMPHITHEATRES

The amphitheatre (the **arena** was the name of the sand floor) had two tiers of arcades on the outside surmounted by a low storey called the attic. Posts were fixed on the attic to carry a huge adjustable awning, the *velarium*, to shelter the spectators from the sun and rain. The arcades were divided by rectangular pillars decorated with engaged half-columns on the first storey. Inside, enclosing the arena, a wall protected the spectators in the front rows from the wild animals released in the ring. The *cavea* – terraces for the spectators – was divided into *maenia* – tiers of seats generally in groups of four, individually separated by a passage. The seats were strictly allocated, those nearest the arena being for the men with a superior social station. The first *maenia* were reserved for consuls, senators, magistrates and members of local guilds (such as the boatmen of Arles). In another section sat priests, knights and Roman citizens, whereas freemen and slaves sat in the attic. The arcades and three circular gallery-promenades, and the hundreds of staircases and passages, allowed spectators to reach or leave their stepped seats directly. At Nîmes it took less than five minutes for the audience of 20 000 to leave via exits known as *vomitoria*.

THEATRES

The Roman theatre, in the form of a half-circle lengthened by a deep stage, was divided into three sections: the *cavea* (auditorium) built in the hollow of a hillside, as in Orange, and crowned by a colonnade; the orchestra, the

Doric Order, Ionic Order, Corinthian Order

©R. Corbel/MICHELIN

semicircular section in front of the stage with movable seats reserved for dignitaries; the stage flanked by side rooms, rectangular in shape, which were higher in level than the orchestra. At the back of the stage was a wall (which was as high as the *cavea*) with three doors through which the actors entered.

The stage wall was the finest part of the building. Its decoration included several tiers of columns, niches containing statues (the central niche contained the emperor's statue), marble facing and mosaics. Behind this were the actors' dressing rooms and store rooms. Beyond these again was a portico open to the garden through which the actors entered the theatre. In it, spectators would stroll during the intermissions or take shelter from rain. As in the arenas, a huge adjustable awning, known as the *velum*, could be opened to shelter the spectators from the sun and rain.

Theatrical scenery and machinery were ingenious. Some scenes were fixed; some were superimposed and uncovered by sliding others sideways. The curtain was only 3m/9.8ft high. It dropped into a slit at the beginning of the play and rose at the end. The basement contained the machinery and communicated with the stage through trapdoors on which the actors could rise from or sink into the ground. Other machines, mounted in the flies, lowered gods or heroes from the heavens, or raised them into the clouds.

The effects men knew how to create were smoke, lightning, thunder, ghosts, and the accompaniment of apotheoses. All sorts of means were used to obtain perfect acoustics. The mouths of the actors' masks were little megaphones. The large sloping roof over the stage threw the sound downwards, and the upward curve of the seats received it smoothly.

The colonnades broke up the echo, and carefully graduated sounding-boards under the seats acted as loudspeakers. One detail shows how far these refinements were carried: the doors on the stage were hollow and made like violins inside. When an actor wished to amplify his voice he would stand against one of these sound-boxes.

CIRCUSES

These were the largest public sites in the Roman world, about four times longer than an amphitheatre, one end of which was oval shaped; they were used for chariot and horse races. The one in Arles was big enough to race about 12 chariots at a time and all that remains of it now is the obelisk that stands in front of St-Trophime church, which was once the finishing line.

TEMPLES

The temple stood on a podium surrounded by columns and consisted of two rooms: the *pronaos* (a vestibule) and the *cella* (a place for the statue of the divinity). The prime example of a

Triumphal arch of Glanum, mausoleum on the left

© Magdalena Jankowska/iStockphoto.com

temple is the Maison Carrée at Nîmes. In the countryside there were small local temples, *fana* (singular *fanum*).

TRIUMPHAL ARCHES

The arches in Orange, Glanum, Carpentras and Cavaillon resemble the triumphal arches of Rome, raised in honour of victorious generals, but these were built to commemorate the founding of the cities in which they stand and the exploits of the veterans who settled there. They had either one or three openings. The columns decorating the four sides and flanking the central arch were all engaged; later on they became detached. The upper storey was decorated with statues, horse-drawn chariots, and their feats of arms, usually in gilt bronze.

BATHS

The Roman baths, which were public and free, were also centres of physical culture, casinos, clubs, recreation centres, libraries, lecture halls and meeting places, which explains the amount of time people spent in them. Decoration in these great buildings was lavish: columns and capitals picked out in bright colours, mosaic ornaments, coloured marble facings, richly coffered ceilings, mural paintings and statues.

CENTRAL HEATING

The bath's functioning demonstrated the Romans' understanding of the canalisation of water and its subsequent heating. Water was brought from the mountains via aqueducts and placed into cisterns and then distributed by a lead-pipe and cement system of canals; evacuation was conducted through a network of drainpipes.

To heat air and water a number of underground furnaces (hypocausts) like bakers' ovens, in which roaring fires were kept going, were used. The hot gases circulated among the brick pillars supporting the stone floors of rooms and baths, and rose through flues in the walls to escape from chimneys. In this way the rooms were heated from below and from the sides as in

modern buildings. The warmest room, facing south or west, had large glazed windows and was used as a solarium. Water at three different temperatures – cold, lukewarm and hot – circulated automatically by thermo-siphon.

BATHER'S ROUTE

The bather followed a medically designed route. From the *apodyterium* (changing room), where he would have left his clothes and anointed his body with oil, he entered the *palaestra* (a gymnasium of sorts), where he would warm up performing physical exercises. Then came the *tepidarium* (a lukewarm room), where he thoroughly cleaned himself by scraping his skin with small curved metal spatulas *(strigiles)* that prepared him for the *caldarium* (hot room), where he took a steam bath. He then proceeded into the hot swimming-pool. Having been massaged, he once again returned to the *tepidarium* before continuing on to the *frigidarium* (cold bath) to tone up the skin.

Thoroughly revived, the bather dressed and proceeded to take advantage of the baths' other activities, such as lectures, sports, gossip, and the like.

THE ROMAN TOWNHOUSE

Numbers below correspond to the illustration p84.

Excavations at Vaison-la-Romaine, Glanum or the Fountain quarter in Nîmes have uncovered Roman houses of various types: small bourgeois houses, dwellings (several storeys high) for rent, shops open to the street, and, finally, large, luxurious patrician mansions.

Mansions had modest external appearances owing to their bare walls and few windows. But the interiors, adorned with mosaics, statues, paintings and marbles, and sometimes hot baths and a fish pond, reflected the wealth of their owners.

A vestibule and a corridor in the mansion led to the atrium. The **atrium (1)**, which opened onto the street through a vestibule containing the porter's lodge, was a large rectangular court, open in the middle to the sky *(compluvium)*. A basin called the *impluvium*, under the open section, caught rainwater. Rooms opened off the *atrium*: a reception room **(2)**, a private oratory, a *tablinum* or study, and a library of the head of the family.

The **peristyle (3)** was a court surrounded by a portico (a gallery with a roof supported by columns) in the centre of the part of the house reserved for the family. They reached it from the *atrium* along a corridor called the *fauces*. Here the peristyle was generally made into a garden with basins lined with mosaics, fountains and statues. The living quarters opened all around it: bedrooms, *triclinium* (dining room **4**) and *oecus* (main drawing room).

The annexes included the kitchen with a sink and drain, baths, and a flush lavatory. Other buildings housed slaves' quarters, attics, cellars, stables, etc.

Roman townhouse

RURAL HOUSING

Experts are just beginning to examine this kind of dwelling. The towns must have been numerous and the settlement of these sites by Romans was done on pre-existing sites. The cadastral plan of Orange seems to show that the Romans tried to organise their territory into square-shaped lots called *centuries*.

The most common type of house was the villa, 40 of which have been discovered in Provence.

AQUEDUCTS

Grandiose like the Pont du Gard or more modest like Barbegal, aqueducts played an important role in daily life as they carried the water from their source to the town.

ROMAN ROADS

As soon as they settled in Provence, the Romans decided to design and build a reliable network of terrestrial means of communication that would ensure supremacy over the lands they had conquered, while at the same time encouraging the exchange of both goods and ideas. The layout of these roads usually coincided with that undertaken by the Gauls or with the paths *(drailles)* traditionally used by herds of cattle. They were cobbled only at the entrance to cities (country ways were surfaced with small, flat stones arranged tightly together) and dotted with stone or wooden bridges (Pont Julien at Bonnieux, Pont Flavien at St-Chamas), military milestones (1 Roman mile = 1,481m/0.92mi) and relay posts. Three great Roman roads cut across Provence: the Aurelian Way *(Via Aurelia)*, the Domitian Way *(Via Domitia)* and the *Via Agrippa*.

The first connected Rome to the River Rhône, running along the coast through the towns of Antibes *(Antipolis)*, Fréjus *(Forum Jilii)*, Aix-en-Provence *(Aquae Sextiae)* and Salon-de-Provence *(Salo)*, before joining up with the Domitian Way in Tarascon *(Tarusco)*. The *Via Domitia*, which headed towards Spain, helped link northern Italy to southern Gaul. It served the cities of Briançon *(Brigantium)*, Gap *(Vapicum)*, Sisteron *(Segustero)*, Apt *(Aptia Julia)*, Cavaillon *(Cabello)*, Tarascon *(Tarusco)*, Nîmes *(Nemausus)*, Béziers *(Julia Baeterrae)*, Narbonne *(Noarb)* and Perpignan *(Ruscino)*. Finally, the Via Agrippa was a network built by Marcus Vipsanius Agrippa which started at Arles *(Arelate)* and extended towards Lyon, following the left bank of the Rhône and crossing Avignon *(Avenio)* and Orange *(Arausio)*.

ROMAN INFLUENCE

The brilliant Gallo-Roman civilisation took a long time to disappear after the fall of the Western Empire. The ancient public buildings remained standing and the architects of the Middle Ages took inspiration from them to build churches and monasteries.

A dark age followed (5C–10C) when few buildings were erected, of which only isolated specimens now remain, such as the small baptistries at Aix and Venasque. Early Romanesque art, which developed from Catalonia to northern Italy in the 10C and 11C, did not leave significant examples, either.

The 12C was for Provence one of its most outstanding historic periods during which it underwent a brilliant architectural renaissance. Churches, remarkable for the bonding of their evenly cut stones with fine mortar work, appeared everywhere. Their style was closely linked to a school which had evolved in the area between the River Rhône, the Drôme, the Alps and the Mediterranean. This school knew how to capture different influences: from Roman Antiquity came the use of vaults and especially decoration; from Languedoc came the carved portals; from Lombardy came the Lombard arcade or the lions adorning the base of doors; and from Auvergne came the dome on squinches over the nave and in front of the apse.

Below are the essential characteristics of the Romanesque style, the best examples of which were the great sanctuaries in the Rhône Valley: Cathédrale de la Major in Marseille, St-Trophime in Arles, St-Gilles, Cathédrale Notre-Dame-des-Doms in Avignon, Cathédrale Notre-Dame in Orange, and the church in Le Thor.

CHURCHES AND CHAPELS PLAN

Provençal Romanesque churches have descended directly from the Roman basilica and Carolingian church. Their general appearance was of a solid mass. Transepts were rare and shallow. Often there was a single nave with side chapels hollowed out of the thickness of the walls. The east end took the form of an apse with two flanking apsidal chapels, where there were side aisles. Only the great pilgrimage churches of St-Gilles (in St-Gilles) and St-Trophime (in Arles) have ambulatories.

Minor buildings (Chapelle Ste-Croix in Montmajour; St-Sépulcre in Peyrolles) present a quadrilobed plan.

BELL TOWERS

The bell tower is an imposing, most often square, sometimes octagonal structure, that dominated the dome above the transept crossing. It was sometimes placed above the bay preceding the apse or on the façade. It was decorated with blind arcading known as Lombard arcades or fluted pilasters in the Antique style, or sometimes both.

Detail of the west front, St-Trophime, Arles

© Zoonar/Lothar Hinz/age fotostock

SIDE WALLS

The walls were usually bare except for the cornice and the plain side doors. Massive buttresses, between which were set the windows of the nave, relieved the austere monotony of the exterior.

WEST FRONTS AND DOORS

The west front was generally plain, opened by a door surmounted by an *oculus* as the main door was often located on the south side sheltered from the *mistral*. The doors were probably the architectural element most influenced by ancient Greek and Roman art; sometimes they were decorated with a *fronton* directly influenced by the ancient temples, such as the porch at Notre-Dame-des-Doms and the Chapelle St-Gabriel near Tarascon.

During the 12C, façades became more ornate, preceded at times by a porch: a large carved tympanum over a horizontal lintel began to be featured. The doorways of St-Gilles and St-Trophime, superbly carved examples, rivalled in quality, size and beauty the Gothic cathedral masterpieces of northern France.

INTERIOR

Upon entering the Provençal Romanesque church the visitor is struck by the simplicity and austerity of the inside structure, enhanced only by some carved mouldings and cornices, barely visible in the dimly lit interior.

CHANCELS

This is the part of the church reserved for the clergy. It was usually oven vaulted and linked to the transept crossing with rounded barrel vaulting.

NAVES AND VAULTS

The lofty structure of the building's interior, moderate though it was, was remarkable for the purity of its lines.

The nave was roofed with pointed barrel vaulting in which the downward thrust was more direct than that of the rounded arches, which tended to splay the wall outwards.

The barrel vaulting had already been used in the Roman era, having replaced the easily flammable wooden roofing, used from the 5C to the 11C, which had caused the destruction of many buildings. It was buttressed by pointed arches, also called transverse arches, which came down on thick engaged pilasters in the side walls or down onto slender pillars lining the nave.

The nave was sometimes lined with aisles with quarter-circle or pointed barrel vaulting, which acted as buttresses.

Owing to the height of the side aisles there were no tribunes but a decorative band of blind arcading, made of rounded arches, with three arches to each bay, the central arch pierced by a lancet window, which let in very little light. Where the churches had but a single nave the side walls were quite thick in order to compensate for the missing side walls and balance the whole structure.

TRANSEPTS AND DOMES

The construction of the transept was a difficult problem for the architects in the Romanesque period. The groined vaulting made by the crossing of the nave and aisle vaulting had to be of great height in order to support the heavy weight of the central bell tower; the problem was solved by placing a dome on squinches over the crossing in the style of the Auvergne School.

Decoration

Interior decoration was as austere as exterior decoration: decorated capitals usually ornamented with stylised leaves, friezes with interlacing and foliated scrolls, fluting and rope moulding.

The capital with leaves of the Romanesque style was an adaptation of the ancient Corinthian capital: it was formed by a group of leaves arranged according to the style of the Romanesque period (interlacing and stylised decoration). The most picturesque of these capitals were historiated, inspired by religious stories taken from the Old and New Testaments. The cloisters offer the best examples:

St-Trophime with its magnificent corner pillars adorned with statues of saints is remarkable. Fine capitals can also be found in the cloisters of Montmajour and St-Paul-de-Mausole (fantastic animals) and the apse of the church at Les Stes-Maries-de-la-Mer. There are also fragments of carved decoration worth seeing: in Avignon's cathedral there is the bishop's throne; in Apt's cathedral there is the altar.

ABBEYS

Provence boasts several fine abbeys. The Benedictine Abbaye de Montmajour near Arles, founded in the 10C, forms a superb architectural ensemble illustrating the evolution of Romanesque forms from the 11C to 13C. It includes two churches (an upper church and crypt or lower church), two chapels and cloisters. Its annexes showcase the characteristic Provençal style: simplicity in the monumental size, the volumes of which were inspired by the Antique style, carved decoration similar to St-Trophime, and perfection in the stone bonding. Cistercian art was represented by three sister abbeys: Sénanque, Silvacane and Le Thoronet (⏾ see the Michelin Green Guide French Riviera, for Le Thoronet).

Sober elegance, austerity and lack of ornamentation were the required rules of the Cistercians, a reformed monastic order founded by St Bernard of Clairvaux. St Bernard had denounced the fanciful nature of Romanesque sculpture, which could distract the monks at prayer. The Cistercians imposed an identical plan everywhere, and they themselves directed the construction.

GOTHIC STYLE
EVOLUTION

Romanesque art survived longer in Provence than it did in the rest of France. In spite of the relatively early appearance of Gothic, limited to two buildings (crypt of St-Gilles, porch of St-Victor in Marseille) and quadripartite vaulting as early as pre-1150, Gothic art was late in taking hold in Provence.

In the early 13C the new vaulting was used to cover buildings only in the Romanesque style. The only buildings entirely in the 13C Gothic style are to be found in Aix: the central nave of Cathédrale St-Sauveur and Église St-Jean-de-Malte, the former priory of the Knights of Malta.

In the mid-14C, there began a new step in Gothic evolution: a school of architecture called the Papal Gothic style began developing in Avignon. The popes attracted to their court artists from different regions of France, Germany, Flanders and Italy.

During the 15C the cardinals embellished Villeneuve-lès-Avignon with palaces (livrées), churches and cloisters; aisles and chapels were added to certain churches. St-Trophime was altered; the Romanesque apse was replaced by an ambulatory and radiating chapels.

The main Gothic churches include: Palais des Papes (Clementine, Grand or Clement VI Chapel), St-Didier, St-Pierre, St-Agricol, Couvent des Célestines, all in Avignon; St-Laurent in Salon-de-Provence; Cathédrale St-Siffrein in Carpentras; the basilica of St-Maximin-la-Ste-Baume; the church in Roquemaure; and especially the charterhouse and church in Villeneuve-lès-Avignon.

ARCHITECTURE

The Gothic style is marked by the systematic use of quadripartite vaulting and pointed arches. This innovative style, which originated in northern France, revolutionised construction by concentrating the weight of the structure on four pillars directed by stringers and transverse arches. Due to the absence of flying buttresses (characteristic of northern Gothic), the thrust of the vaults was assured by the massive buttresses between which chapels were built.

Inside, the nave was relatively dark, almost as wide as it was high, and ended in a narrower polygonal apse. Its width better accommodated the primary function of the church: Dominican preaching. The wall surfaces required painted decoration.

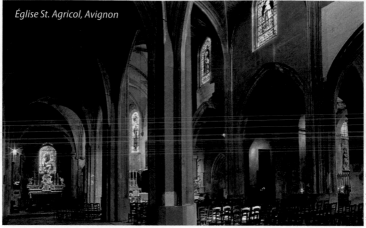

Église St. Agricol, Avignon

© Yann Guichaoua/Tips Images

Église St-Didier in Avignon is considered the best example of southern Gothic in the region, whereas in a building like the basilica in St-Maximin-la-Ste-Baume, southern and northern influences appear. The church of the Couvent des Célestines in Avignon is entirely northern Gothic in style.

Religious edifices were not the only examples of Gothic art in Provence. Civic and military buildings also held an important place. The Palais des Papes in Avignon was one of buildings in the 14C that accommodated the demands of luxury and comfort with those of defence and security.

DECORATION

The austere elegance of Provençal Gothic churches is underlined by their lack of decoration.

Fine Arts

PAINTING

The Avignon region was for over two centuries (14C–15C) the great centre of Provençal painting. Already in the 13C the frescoes of the Ferrande tower recalled the miniatures painted during St Louis' reign. In the 14C the popes decorating the palace sought out the great Italian masters: **Simone Martini** from Siena and **Matteo Giovanetti** from Viterbo (&see the Michelin Green Guide Italy).

The charterhouse in Villeneuve-lès-Avignon also contains fine works by Giovanetti. Once the popes had left Avignon, Italian influence diminished, but artistic life underwent a renaissance in the mid-15C. Good King René was a patron of the arts and attracted master-craftsmen – artists and architects – to his court. Fresco painting lost ground to the Avignon School of panel painting. Artists from the north, Flanders and Burgundy, painted splendid masterpieces such as the Triptych of *The Annunciation* (1443–45) in Aix's Ste-Marie-Madeleine Church and *The Coronation of the Virgin* (1453–54) by Enguerrand Quarton, which is exhibited in the Musée Pierre de Luxembourg in Villeneuve-lès-Avignon.

Nicolas Froment, King René's court painter from Languedoc, painted the famous *Triptych of the Burning Bush* (in Aix's Cathédrale St-Sauveur). Avignon's Petit Palais contains a remarkable collection of lovely 14C and 15C paintings (Avignon and Italian Schools).

SCULPTURE

In the 14C, sculpture consisted of recumbent figures (John XXII in Avignon's Notre-Dame-des-Doms, Innocent VI in Villeneuve-lès-Avignon's charterhouse, and Cardinal Lagrange in the Petit Palais in Avignon), corbels, keystones and slender capitals. Archaic in style, they tended to draw on the Romanesque tradition.

RENAISSANCE

Although the Rhône Valley was the principal route by which personalities of the Italian Renaissance entered France, Provence remained virtually untouched by the movement.

CLASSICAL PERIOD

The 17C and 18C, by contrast, produced a large number of buildings. They were dignified and austere in design without distinctive regional characteristics. The so-called Jesuit style developed in the Comtat Venaissin churches, bringing with it Italian monumental features such as ornate retables or altarpieces, panelling and baldachins, often obscuring the church's architectural lines. Avignon became the major centre once more, with local artists such as the Mignards and Parrocels producing religious pictures, and **Jacques Bernus** of Mazan carving for churches throughout the region.

In the Gard, there was a great drive to rebuild churches damaged during the Wars of Religion (Église St-Gilles). An entirely novel element was the building of townhouses by the old and new moneyed nobility, the magistracy and others: a few remain in Avignon and Nîmes but the finest line the streets of Aix. These well-proportioned, dignified stone houses are distinguished by doorways coroneted with ironwork balconies often supported by robust caryatids or muscular atlantes. The artists of these works were sculptor-decorators **Jean-Claude Rambot** (1621–94) and **Jean Bernard Toro** (1672–1731), both contemporaries of **Pierre Puget** (*see box below*), the 17C Baroque artist and architect from Marseille. The 18C saw the continuation of the towns' and cities' embellishment programme, which had begun the previous century: in Nîmes the engineer J-P Mareschal designed the splendid Jardin de la Fontaine.

Among the painters of that period, two stand out: **Carle Van Loo**, who was

Pierre Puget (1620–94)

This highly skilled, multifaceted artist began his career as a young sculptor in Italy, where he trained under Pietro da Cortona. In 1645 Fouquet commissioned him to execute the doorway for the town hall in Toulon – it was to be one of his first great masterpieces. Between 1660 and 1668, the most brilliant period in Puget's career, he was living in Genoa. He was called back to Paris by Colbert, who entrusted him with the decoration of ships' prows belonging to the fleet in Toulon. Wary of the plots and intrigues of Versailles, he chose to live away from the French Court and devoted himself to the ornamentation of several Provençal cities, such as Aix and Marseille. His work is said to be forceful rather than elegant, and his statues, often of monumental proportions, artfully convey power, movement and pathos. His style is strongly reminiscent of Italian Baroque (Bernini, Cortone), and he succeeded in gracing Provence with a personal and highly original touch at a time when the country was largely dominated by Classicism.

His paintings (*Achilles' Education*) and sculptures (*The Faun*, *The Plague in Milan*), are displayed at the Musée des Beaux-Arts in Marseille, as well as at the Louvre Museum in Paris (the famous *Milon de Crotone* sculpture). His architectural feats include the ovoid dome of the Vieille Charité chapel in Marseille.

susceptible to Provençal charm, and **Claude Joseph Vernet**, the painter of seascapes and ports.

19C

The art of architects and civil engineers was mostly practised in the Marseille region where **Henri-Jacques Espérandieu** erected the new Cathédrale La Major and Basilique de Notre-Dame-de-la-Garde, in the fashionable late-19C Romano-Byzantine style, and Palais Longchamp. Roquefavour Aqueduct is a superb civil engineering project that brings to mind the ancient Roman Pont du Gard. The Rove Underground Canal also represents an incredible feat.

Around this time painting benefited from an explosion of talented artists all fascinated by the luminous beauty of the Provençal countryside. The first to study the landscapes of Provence were **J A Constantin** (1756–1844) and **François-Marius Granet** (1775–1849). The Landscape School inspired by **Émile Loubon** (1809–63) also explored the notion of light with painters such as **Paul Guigou** (1834–71), a forerunner of Impressionism, and the Marseille artist **Adolphe Monticelli** (1824–86). This School ceased to exist around 1870 and was replaced by the painters known as "Naturalists": **Achille Emperaire** (1829–98) and **Joseph Ravaisou** (1865–1925)

in Aix; **Clément Brun** (1868–1920) and **Paul Sain** (1853–1908) in Avignon; **Joseph Garibaldi** (1863–1941), **Jean Baptiste Olive** (1848–1936) and **Alphonse Moutte** (1840–1913; strong realistic scenes of local fishermen) in Marseille. Finally **Félix Ziem**, a resident of Martigues, one of the first to paint in the hills beyond the fishing village of L'Estaque, chose to use colour in its own right and not to create light effects.

VAN GOGH

Vincent van Gogh (1853–90), son of a Dutch Calvinist pastor, admirer of Millet and Rubens and influenced by the art of Japanese Ukiyo-e prints, was attracted to Impressionism, and brought his strong personality to his work.

In February 1888, he decided to settle in Arles, seeking a "different light". The two years he spent discovering Provence (Arles, Les Stes-Maries-de-la-Mer, Les Baux, St-Rémy) correspond to an intense period of creativity: he sought to express with colours and dramatic forms the "terrible human passions" that tormented him and caused him to suffer. He painted intensely the light and forms of Provence: landscapes (*View of Arles with Irises*, *The Alyscamps*, *Starry Night over the Rhône*, *Crau Plain*, *Boats along the Beach*) and portraits (*Portrait of an Old Provençal Peasant*, *L'Arlésienne*, *Madame Ginoux*).

Gulf of Marseille seen from L'Estaque *(c.1885) by Paul Cézanne*

©Imagestate/Tips Images

His quarrel with **Paul Gauguin**, who had joined him in October 1888, plunged him into despair and madness; he was cared for at St-Paul-de-Mausole near St-Rémy-de-Provence and continued to paint (*Wheatfields*, *Cypresses*, *Starry Night*, *Olive Trees*, *Self-Portrait*). He returned to Paris in May 1890 and committed suicide two months later. He left an enormous legacy of work, of which his Provençal period is perhaps the most intense and fascinating.

CÉZANNE

Paul Cézanne (1839–1906), unlike Van Gogh, was from Provence. Son of an Aix-en-Provence banker, he left his studies to take up painting. Introduced to the Parisian Impressionists by his friend, the writer Émile Zola, he began as a Romantic studying Delacroix, whose theory of colours he adopted. Having assimilated the Impressionist techniques, he rapidly went beyond them as early as 1879 and began his constructive period; he experimented with large dabs of luminous colour and simple geometric forms. "Everything in nature is modelled after the sphere, the cone and the cylinder", he wrote. He painted still lifes and portraits in which colour and form determined the painting's organisation.

After 1890, he hardly ever left his native Provence. He devoted all his energy to capturing the Montagne Ste-Victoire on canvas, painting it some 60 times without ever being entirely satisfied with his work. His research continued until his death and opened the way to Cubism.

20C

Clearly, for Cézanne, it was impossible for a painting to convey the full brilliance and subtleties of light; only colour could presume to fulfil that role. These views gave rise to a movement that influenced many late 19C and early 20C painters. Provence was now attracting numerous artists who settled in L'Estaque, following in the footsteps of Cézanne. The first was **Paul Signac** (1863–1935), who applied his Pointillist technique to Provençal colour (instead of the fine brushwork used in the north of France); here he opted for square, oblong touches, more suitable for catching the vivid sunlight).

The Fauves found inspiration in this radiant Provençal setting. Their works played with colours and lines ignoring perspective and chiaroscuro. Matisse, Dufy and Derain all spent time in Provence, together with native artists from the region like **Charles Camoin** (1879–1965), **Auguste Chabaud** (1882–1955), **Alfred Lombard** (1884–1973) and **Louis-Mathieu Verdilhan** (1875–1928). Around 1906 **L'Estaque** became the privileged meeting place of those artists who were later dubbed the Cubists. **Georges Braque** and **Pablo Picasso** worked together closely in Sorgues; the product of this joint venture was revolutionary, pictorial compositions touching on abstraction.

After World War I, a new generation was experimenting with novel theories, such as Expressionism and Surrealism. **André Masson**, father of spontaneous drawing (a technique that enabled him to break from figurative conventions), settled in the Aix region until his death in 1987 and drew a series entitled *Provençal Landscapes*. **Victor Vasarely** (1906–97) opened a foundation at Gordes to continue his research into optics and kinetics.

CONTEMPORARY TIMES

Today, many of the region's young artists have studied at the École d'Art de Lumigny in Marseille. There are contemporary art museums in the region that showcase recent works: the best being the Musée d'Art Contemporain in Marseille. Musée Réattu in Arles, Maison René-Char in L'Isle-sur-la-Sorgue and Collection Lambert in Avignon all have permanent and temporary exhibitions focusing on modern art.

Marseille's status as European Capital of Culture 2013 shows how contemporary art and culture have become an important part of life in the region.

Decorative Arts

PROVENÇAL FURNITURE

It was during the 15C that Provençal furniture, until that time considered to be of unsophisticated design, began to follow the lead set by Italy, with the introduction of delicate sculptures, finished off with a Spanish-influenced style of heavily chiselled wrought iron and copper keyholes. The 18C and beginning of the 19C heralded the *grande époque* of Provençal furniture, with the main production centres scattered between the lower valley of the Rhône and the mid-section of the Durance. The period from the Second Empire onwards was characterised among other things by excessive sculptured decoration.

In lower Provence, the Louis XV style reigned absolute from the middle of the 18C onward. Artisans preferred working with walnut, resorting if necessary to the use of box, olive, cherry or pear wood. The pieces of furniture, with their irregular curves, pronounced bends, and curled legs and bases, are generally of quite slender proportion, with an abundance of storage units. They include: the **paneiro** or openwork bread bin; **manjadou** or meat safe decorated with ornamental spindles; **estagnié** or pewter cupboard; **verriau**, for glasses; and **saliero** or salt container. The following original items also stand out: the elegant **buffet à glissants**, or sliding sideboard; **radassier**, a large straw-seated sofa adorned with esparto leaves or sprigs of rye, such as those of the *à la capucine* armchairs, distinguishable by their trapezoid seat, setback arm rests, and concave-strutted back. Ornamentation is based on abundant and deep mouldings and sculpted motifs with overriding importance given to vegetation in different forms: acanthus leaves, flower baskets, branches of olive or oak; and the addition of small, curved candle-rings to the angles and to the crest tops. The best-known decorative style is from Arles, a production centre of particular character, where the *paneiro* or bread container, the first mobile cabinets, and *à la capucine* chairs originated.

In upper Provence, sombre lines and décor triumph over furniture of a more rustic style, remaining steadfast throughout the period of influence of the Renaissance and Louis XIII styles. Craftsmen in this part of the region preferred working with mulberry, pine or limewood. Furniture not seen in lower Provence, such as the *vaisselier* or dresser, and the *banc à dossier* or backed bench, are a testimony to the influence of the neighbouring Dauphiné. Simple wall cavities also tend to replace the use of small storage units in evidence in lower Provence.

THE SUPREMACY OF CLAY

The abundance of excellent-quality clay in Provence has given rise to a number of large ceramic centres in the region: the mottle decoration of **Apt** and **Avignon** faïence; Allemagne-en-Provence and Moustiers (*see Michelin Green Guide French Alps)*; La Tour d'Aigues; and above all, **Marseille**, where clay has been worked into vessels, both useful and decorative, since ancient times. Under Louis XIV, the wars that emptied the kingdom's coffers resulted in the banning of the use of gold and silver dishes, thus providing an opportunity for the faïence industry.

In 1679, the Fabre pottery works at **St-Jean-du-Désert** between Aubagne and Marseille transformed its production to that of faïence under the influences of **Joseph Clérissy**, who was from an Aubagne family that had moved to Moustiers. Its blue "Chinese-style" cameos drew inspiration from the first pieces of porcelain imported into France from China. Although St-Jean-du-Désert saw its importance decline after the Great Plague, other earthenware works started to spring up, many of which employed the sharp fire technique. **Fauchier** created *fleurs jetées*, designs of flowers painted in a seemingly haphazard fashion, and used a distinctive yellow enamel background decoration. The works of **Leroy** are recognisable for their fantastic creatures and human figures set on a background of star-like flowers.

The second half of the 18C represented the zenith of Marseille earthenware, mainly as a result of the activities and talent of **Pierrette Candellot**, a colourful personality originally from Lyon, and the wife of the Marseille pottery manufacturer **Claude Perrin**. Following his death in 1748, his widow, known as **La Veuve Perrin**, guided the family business towards the mild firing technique, consequently obtaining pieces of exceptional quality. She perfected the ornamental Marseille style, introduced fish motifs and sea landscapes, and developed an unusual sea-green background. She also drew inspiration from contemporary trends in jewellery design.

After Veuve Perrin, the last great Marseille earthenware producers were **Joseph-Gaspard Robert** and **Antoine Bonnefoy**, both of whom were able to give to faïence an ornamental refinement that until that time had been the prerogative of porcelain. Bonnefoy is famous for his trademark *bouillabaisse* motifs and pastoral scenes reminiscent of the Rococo paintings of François Boucher. Robert created floral motifs set off by black butterflies and a gold border; his dishes bordered in red, white and blue were the last great series to come out of Marseilles. Ultimately, a combination of the competition from porcelain makers, the Revolution, and the blockade by the English naval fleet sounded the death knell for Marseille's faïence industry.

THE CHRISTMAS CRÈCHE

Christmas cribs (*crèche* means crib) have a long tradition in Provence, although it was not until the late 18C that they became common and developed a typically local character. A few 18C groups, often highly original and beautifully modelled, may still be seen at a collector's or in a church, but most are now in museums (Musée du Vieil Aix, Musée du Vieux Marseille, Museon Arlaten in Arles, and the Musée National des Arts et Traditions Populaires in Paris).

CHURCH CRIBS

Christmas was not an important festival in the early church. Nativity scenes did not form part of the medieval celebrations except for rare low reliefs of the Adoration of the Shepherds or the Kings as in the St-Maximin crypt.

In 1545 the Council of Trent sought to advance the Counter-Reformation through the encouragement of popular piety. The practice of setting up a crib in church arrived in Provence from Italy in the 17C. There is a particularly beautiful crèche from this period in the church of St-Maximin; the carved figures, about 50cm/20in high, are of gilded wood. In the 18C, bejewelled wax figures were introduced with glass eyes and wigs.

Only the head, arms and legs were carved and attached to a richly dressed articulated frame. In the 19C, new materials were introduced, including printed or painted cardboard cut-outs with gaily coloured clothing, figures made from spun glass, cork, clay and even bread dough. By then, all the Provençal churches had adopted the Christmas crib of dressed figures. This kind of crib can still be seen today.

PERFORMANCE CRIBS

At Midnight Mass in many churches – Séguret, Allauch, Isle-sur-la-Sorgue and Marseille – a Nativity play is performed. In Gémenos, children in costume place an infant Jesus in a straw-filled manger. In Les Baux, a little cart, decorated with greenery and bearing a newborn lamb, is drawn into church by a ram and accompanied by shepherds. The procession is headed by angels and fife and tabor players, while the congregation sings old Provençal carols.

TALKING CRIBS

The 18C passion for marionettes was adapted to produce talking cribs in which mechanical figures enacted the Nativity to a commentary and carols. People came from far and wide to see and hear the talking cribs of Marseille and Aix. Characters were added to the already numerous cast and, as imagination ran wild, historical accuracy and relevance vanished: reindeer, giraffes and hippopotamuses joined the other animals in the stable, and the pope was made to arrive in a carriage to bless the Holy Family. It must have been a sight to see a Napoleon puppet, accompanied by his soldiers and a man-of-war firing salvoes, arriving at the manger! Another new idea came to those presenting a crib close to Marseille station: the Three Kings travelled to the scene in a steam train!

Santon figure, St-Rémy-de-Provence
©S. Sauvignier/MICHELIN

SANTON CRIBS

The *santon* cribs are the most typical of Provence. They first appeared in 1789 at the time of the Revolution when the churches were closed. **Jean-Louis Lagnel** (1764–1822), a church statue-maker from Marseille, had the idea of making small figures that families could buy at little cost. Labelled *santouns* (little saints) in Provençal, and *santoni* in Italian, abbreviated from *santibelli* (beautiful saints), these figurines had an immediate and wide appeal. They were modelled in clay, fired and naïvely painted in bright colours.

Limited at first to biblical personages, they were soon joined by men and women from all walks of life, dressed in local costume: the Holy Family, the Shepherds and their sheep, the Three Kings, the knife grinder, the fife and tabor player, the smith, the blind man and his guide, the fishwife, the wetnurse, the milkmaid, the huntsman, fisherman and even the mayor!

So great was the figurines' success, as virtually every family began to build up a collection, that a Santons Fair *(Foire des Santonniers)* was inaugurated in Marseille, which is still held on the Canebière from the last Sunday in November to Epiphany. Aubagne was also famous for its *santons*. *Santon* makers established workshops in towns throughout Provence, whereas in the country, men and women made figures in the long winter evenings. The craft reached its peak in the 1820s and 1830s, which is why so many of the characters appear in the dress of that period.

The *santons* of Provence are now known the world over, and many families like to add to their collection of characters each year and set up displays during the Christmas holidays.

Literature

Provence is an ancient civilised land, Greco-Latin then Occitanian, a fact that has never stopped influencing poets and writers who expressed themselves in Provençal.

LANGUAGE OF THE TROUBADOURS

The Romance languages evolved out of Vulgar Latin spoken at the end of the Roman Empire. These were Italian, Romanian, Catalan, Spanish, Portuguese, and, in France, the Oïl language *(langue d'oïl)* in the north and the Oc language *(langue d'oc)* in the south. "*Oïl*" and "*Oc*" were the words used for "yes" in the north and south, respectively. This distinction, which was formed as early as the Merovingian period, was advanced enough in the 10C and 11C for the two languages to enter into literature separately. Occitan, which appeared in Latin texts for the first time in the 11C, owed its place and influence to the success of 12C courtly literature. The art of the **troubadours**, which developed in the feudal courts of Périgord, Limousin and Gascony, was not confined purely to Provence but encompassed all of Occitania, from Bordeaux to Nice.

These troubadours (*trobar* means to find) were inventors of musical airs, both melodies and words in the Oc language, and they created a linguistic community independent of political divisions: Jaufré Rudel from Blaye, Bernard de Ventadour from Limousin, Peire Vidal from Toulouse, and from Provence, Raimbaut of Orange, the Countess of Die, Raimbaut of Vaqueiras and Folquet of Marseille.

Under the Provençal or Limousin name, Occitanian was appreciated by noble foreigners and most of the European courts. The essential inspirational force of the troubadours was love, not passionate love but courtly love, where the patience and discretion of the poet-lover finally won over the lady who accepted the homage of her vassal. Using sound, word pattern, and stanza-structure, these poems told of the troubadours' anxieties and hopes.

PROSE AND POETRY

The courtly poem declined in the 13C, its themes having been exhausted. It was replaced by satirical poems known as *sirventès* and prose that told of the lives of the troubadours (the famous *vidas*). This period is marked by the European influence of French, by the setting up of the Inquisition, and by the expansion of the Capetian monarchy.

Occitan, nevertheless, retained its importance. It is said that **Dante** (c.1265–1321) almost used it to write his *Divina Commedia* and that it was the language spoken at the pontifical court of Avignon. With Latin, Occitan was, in the Middle Ages, the only written administrative language. And yet, beginning in the 14C, regional differences began appearing in written texts, and French was gradually adopted in its place. Occitanian literature became popular in Italy where it was revived thanks to Dante and returned in force into the Rhône Valley in the form of a sonnet with **Petrarch** (1304–74). Exiled in

Avignon, Petrarch fell passionately in love with the lovely Laura de Noves in 1327. His *Il Canzonière* (1348) were a group of sonnets where he expressed his unrequited love for her. The poet, who had retired to Fontaine-de-Vaucluse, also wrote descriptions of Provençal life in his letters; he spoke of shepherds, the Sorgue fishermen, and his climb to Mont Ventoux.

The fatal blow fell upon the Occitan language in 1539, with the adoption of the Edict of Villers-Cotterêts, which decreed that for all administrative purposes the French language, the dialect spoken in the Île de France, and thus Paris, should be used. In spite of that, Occitan survived until the 19C in the theatre, poetry, short stories and legends, chronicles, and didactic and erudite works (dictionaries and anthologies).

One of the regional popular writers of the 16C was **Bellaud de la Bellaudière**. Born in Grasse around 1543, he lived a very active life as a soldier; he was also opposed to the Huguenots. When he was in prison, he wrote 160 sonnets, his *Œuvres et Rimes*. His poetry – inspired by Marot, Rabelais and Petrarch – was essentially personal, owing to its familiar realism. His work renewed the Occitan language, and he inspired and was joined by Claude Bruey, Raynier from Briançon and François de Bègue.

In the 17C, when the moralist Vauvenargues was born in Aix, and Madame de Sévigné resided at Grignan, **Nicolas Saboly** was composing Provençal **Noëls**: charming, simple works of popular poetry. These happy yet pious canticles, touching and devout, depicted the entire world running in the night towards the newly born baby Jesus. In Saboly's lifetime, church services were still held in Occitan in rural villages as well as in the cities. When French dramatist **Jean Racine** resided in Uzès in 1661, he had a great deal of difficulty making himself understood. Until the Revolution, Occitan was the language spoken daily; only a small elite spoke French, and even then they were bilingual.

And yet, the use of Occitan declined steadily, breaking up into different local dialects.

THE FÉLIBRIGE

In the late 18C, Occitan, weakened by the centralised state, was reborn through literature. In 1795, Abbot Favre made history with his *Siège de Caderousse* (*Caderousse's Seat*), a satirical poem written in dialect, amusing because of its Rabelais-like truculence. In the 1840s Occitan experienced an explosion: **Joseph Roumanille** (1818–91), a teacher in Avignon and the author of a work *Li Margarideto* (1847), awakened in the young **Frédéric Mistral** (1830–1914) a passion for Provence, its culture, history and Oc language.

As early as 1851, Mistral began writing *Mirèio*. In 1852 the first congress of future *Félibres* was held in Arles. On 21 May 1854, at the castle of Fort-Ségugne, seven young poets writing in Provençal (Roumanille, Mistral, Aubanel, Mathieu, Tavan, Giéra and Brunet) founded the Félibrige. *Félibre* was a word taken from an old song meaning doctor. Félibrige was an association whose goals were to restore the Provençal language and to codify its spelling. It published a periodical *Armana Provençau,* which spread its ideas.

In 1859 Mistral published *Mirèio*, an epic poem of 12 cantos that brought him immense success. Lamartine praised his work and Charles Gounod made it into an opera in 1864. Mistral's literary works included *Calendau* (1867), *Lis Isclo d'or* (1875), *Nerto* (1884), *La Reino Jano* (1890), *The Song of the Rhône* (1896) and *Lis óulivado* (1912). In 1904 he was awarded the Nobel Prize for literature.

Mistral was also a fine philologist who patiently collected the scattered elements of the Oc language and recorded their spelling in a monumental dictionary, *Lou Trésor du Félibrige*, published in 1878–86. It still serves as a reference book. The Félibrige brought together Occitanian poets and novelists as different as Alphonse Daudet, Paul Arène, Félix Gras, Baptiste Bonnet, Joseph d'Arbaud, Charles Rieu, Dom Xavier de Fourvière, Jean-Henri Fabre, Folco de Baroncelli-Javon and Charles Maurras (political theorist). During the same period, renowned writers of French included Jean Alcard (a member of the Academy, who wrote *Maurin of the Moors*); Émile Zola, who went to secondary school in Aix and who in his Rougon-Macquart series described the evolution of a family from the south; and Edmond Rostand, born in Marseille, who wrote the unforgettable *Aiglon*.

THE PRESENT

Although Provence is always present in their works, many of the contemporary writers have gone beyond the regional level and joined the ranks of the top French writers: Jean Giono from Manosque; Marcel Pagnol (*Jean de Florette*, *Manon des Sources*) from Aubagne; René Barjavel from Nyons; acclaimed poet René Char from Isle-sur-la-Sorgue; and Marie Mauron.

Provençal as a spoken language regressed, while as a language of culture – successor to the troubadours and Félibres – it progressed. Admittedly the local dialects remain but they are most often ignored by the young and are more prevalent in rural than in urban areas. At the same time, the centralising and unifying role of the state has enhanced the language: the Oc language is recognised in official teaching programmes.

Continuing with the work of the Félibrige society, the goal of the Institut des Études Occitanes (Institute of Occitanian Studies), while still promoting the use of authentic everyday speech, is to seek the unity of a common language, and to restore to Occitania the status it enjoyed in Middle Ages when it extended beyond political limits from the Atlantic to the Mediterranean.

LEGENDS AND TALES

The legends and tales of Provence are a colourful account of its history and geography. These stories depict regional people, customs, institutions, lifestyles, beliefs, monuments and sites. The Greco-Roman heritage

Sorcery

Rare were the villages that did not have at least one *masc* or *masco*. These people had the power to bewitch humans and animals. If a baby stopped suckling, if horses stopped for no apparent reason, if hunting dogs lost their scent, they had been *emmasqués*. Méthamis, in Vaucluse, is still – even today – a sanctuary of Provençal sorcery. To fight against evil spells a *démascaire* was called in. This person was often a shepherd, because the shepherd was a holder of supernatural powers, but was said to be a sworn enemy of sorcerers, someone who held the secrets of nature. The *démascaire* was good and broke the evil spell. He was also a bone-setter and cured sickness with plants.

Other ways of warding off evil spells were possible, such as wearing a piece of clothing inside out or back to front, throwing salt into the hearth, or reciting different invocations while crossing oneself at the same time. To protect houses from the evil eye, the custom was to cement a vitrified pebble into the wall. On the sheep-pen door people nailed a magic thistle. Some places are totally magical and mysterious, such as Garagaï at Vauvenargues, a bottomless chasm where strange things happen. Between Arles and Montmajour is the fairies' hole, peopled with supernatural beings.

shows in Provençal legends, in which the wondrous accompanies daily life in its humblest activities, where the gods are omnipresent and miracles occur at their behest.

ANCIENT MYTHS

For the ancient Greeks, the western Mediterranean was awe-inspiring, yet at the same time, frightening. Each evening the sun set with Apollo's chariot. **Heracles**, Zeus' son, had been to this land and had married Galathea from Gaul. Endowed with incredible strength, he had opened the passages through the Alps. To protect his son's passage through Provence, Zeus showered his enemies with stones and boulders, which became a desert, the Crau. The attraction of this western Mediterranean land inspired the Phocaeans later to found a colony here. The legend of **Protis** and **Gyptis** illustrates this episode. The Marseille navigator **Pytheas** is said to have sailed in 4 BCE, between the columns of Heracles (Straits of Gibraltar), across the waters to Cornwall and on to Iceland.

LEGENDS OF THE SAINTS

Christianity, too, brought its collection of stories. A thousand-year-old tradition ascribes the conversion of Provence in the 1C to the miraculous landing of a boat from Judaea bearing **Lazarus**, **Mary Magdalene**, **Martha** and disciples of Christ. With **St Victor** and **Cassien** they formed a sort of mystic Provençal state and are credited with many wondrous acts. Among the most dramatic is Martha's defeat of the Tarasque monster (&see Tarascon).

Local saints were not in short supply either. Legend has it that **St Mitre**, the beheaded martyr, picked up his head, kissed it, and bore it to the cathedral (&see Aix-en-Provence). Then there is **St Caesarius**, who captured a puff of sea air in his glove and carried it back to Nyons country. From that moment, a light wind began to blow over the region; the local people took heart and started to cultivate the land. The prosperity of Nyons country dates from this period, and the advantages of the local climate have made it a perfect place for growing olives.

TROUBADOUR TRADITION

The legends of Provence were inspired by epic poetry (*chansons de geste*) and courtly prose.

Pierre of Provence, a valiant knight and talented troubadour, lived at his father's court in the Château de Cavaillon. Seeing her portrait, the knight fell in love with Princess Maguelone, daughter of the King of Naples, and set out to find her. Received at the Neapolitan court, he was victorious in a series of tournaments where he wore Maguelone's colours. But one day Pierre was kidnapped by Barbary pirates and taken to Tunis where he was imprisoned for seven years. Having served his term, he was finally able to set sail for Provence, but not far from Aigues-Mortes, his boat sank. Mortally wounded, he was brought to the local hospital, headed by Princess Maguelone herself, who had sought through charitable works a way to forget her unhappy love. The lovers met and recognised each other. Pierre was cured. Not all endings were so happy. One day **Guillem de Cabestaing**, a son of a noble and well-known troubadour, came to sing at the court of the lord of Castel-Roussillon, an ugly, vulgar old man who had a lovely young wife named Sérémonde. Love kindled quickly between these two young people. The lord, having discovered this, killed the handsome Guillem in an ambush, ripped out his heart, and served it to his wife for dinner. Sérémonde responded with: "My lord, you have served me such delicious fare that nothing could ever equal it and so I swear before Christ, in order to keep the taste fresh for all time, I will never eat again." She then threw herself from the top of a cliff in Roussillon. As her blood spread it coloured the soil, bringing about the origin of ochre.

CHILD HEROES

A great number of Provençal legends recount the memorable exploits of children and adolescents gifted with a force and extraordinary ingenuity. They generally appeal to Almighty God, the intervention of the saints or magic. This is the case of the shepherd boy **Bénézet**, who built the bridge at Avignon after experiencing a vision in 1177. **Jean de l'Ours**, so-called because he had been brought up with a bear, was another. At the age of 12 he conceived the idea of journeying round France. He forged himself a stout iron staff and, thus armed, killed the horrible dragons that kept a young princess in an enchanted castle. **Guihen l'Orphelin** (the orphan), thanks to his mysterious white hen, which he would stroke while murmuring a special incantation, could become invisible. He was able to free a king and the king's daughter, both of whom had been imprisoned by a wicked baron. To thank him the king promised his daughter to Guihen, and they lived, of course, happily ever after.

Nature

Renowned for its laid-back Mediterranean lifestyle, Provence is blessed with natural treasures that range from rocky coastal creeks to the back-country's chalk outcrops, irrigated by the Rhône and her tributaries. This sun-kissed land, where the scent of rosemary and thyme fills the air, provides the ideal refuge for cicadas, which hum among its *garrigues*, olive groves and pine forests.

REGIONS AND LANDSCAPES
TOPOGRAPHY
Formation of the Land

Approximately 600–220 million years ago, during a period called the Primary Era, what is now Provence was covered by a sea that surrounded the continent of Tyrrhenia, contemporary with the Massif Central. Tyrrhenia was formed by crystalline rocks. Vestiges of this land mass included the Maures, Corsica, Sardinia and the Balearic Islands. During the Secondary Era (220–60 million years ago), erosion gradually levelled Tyrrhenia; the Cretaceous Sea covered practically the whole region.

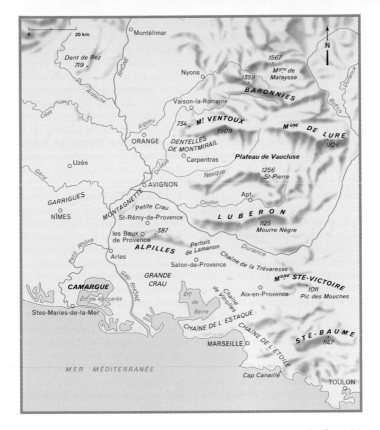

Variations in sea level were caused by materials from the Primary strata carried down by rivers and deposited at the bottom of the sea, forming sedimentary deposits composed either of limestone (e.g. from Orgon) or marl and transformed into regular, parallel layers of rock (strata) in a strip of land lying east to west; this was the Durancen Isthmus. The Tertiary Era (60–2 million years ago) was marked by important tectonic upheavals that uplifted the sedimentary cover and created the young folded mountains of the Alps and Pyrenees. The strata were uplifted and folded in an east–west direction, giving rise to the Provençal secondary mountains north of Marseille, Toulon and Draguignan (Ste-Baume, Ste-Victoire, Mont Ventoux, Baronnies, Alpilles, Luberon). The sea level rose to the present-day Rhône Valley, and while the Alpilles chain was thrust upwards, the Crau plain sank.

During the Quaternary Era (beginning about 2 million years ago) land mass development continued: Tyrrhenia was submerged beneath the present-day Mediterranean Sea, leaving the Maures, Esterel and Canaille mountains. The relief adopted the form it has now, the Rhône corridor emerged, widened and became an important travel route. The subsiding Crau plain modified the course of the River Durance so that it deviated to join the Rhône. Erosion during glaciation and interglacial periods put the final touches to the landscapes (calanques).

Plains

The plains, such as the Rhône delta, were formed by the constant deposits of alluvial sediments that reclaimed territory from the sea. These plains first spread over the Rhône's east bank, **Comtat Venaissin**, then spread over both banks. On the west side of the river the plains extended to the Lower Languedoc dominated by the *garrigues* near Nîmes. To the east they became the fertile **Petite Crau** and **Grande Crau**. Romans, medieval monks and small property holders throughout the centuries have improved the land with drainage and irrigation systems.

Two regions, especially, have profited from such systems: Comtat Venaissin and Petite Crau. Market gardens now cover the land creating a fine pattern of tiny plots separated by windbreaks of tall cypress and lower screens of reeds. The **Grande Crau**, separated from Camargue by the Grand Rhône, is an immense desert of pebbles and boulders between which grow tufts of grass known locally as *coussous*. It was used traditionally for the winter pasturing of large flocks of sheep. The expansion of the industrial zone of Fos and the clearing of the land of stones as well as the irrigation systems have transformed the area; it has lost its pastoral image and with it much of its charm. Olive groves, almond trees, vineyards and undulating grassland make up the new wealth of these areas.

The **Camargue** is a man-made delta of recent alluvium or silt formed by the Rhône, which holds the sea back by means of dykes. The wetland thus created is one of France's most picturesque regions. The *sansouires*, vast salt marshes, give the area the appearance of an untamed expanse.

Plateaux and Mountains

The Provençal plains are flanked or penetrated by folded mountain chains lying east to west that rise quite abruptly, blocking the horizon. The relief often appears confused, presenting an undisciplined alternation of limestone heights and partitioned-off fertile basins: Apt country, Aigues country (south of Luberon), Aix country (irrigated by the Provence canal) where very varied crops (grain, vineyards, fruit, market gardening) are cultivated. East of the Rhône, from north to south, different landscapes follow one after the other.

The western fringe of the **Baronnies** forms a complicated structure of hills and slopes of pure beauty wherein reign olive groves and the hybrid *lavandin*. Unique to Provence, the rocky summits of the **Dentelles de Montmirail** display a finely carved-out relief (*dentelle* means lace) of oak and pine forest with vineyards carpeting the slopes. Backed up against the Baronnies is **Mont Ventoux**, an imposing limestone massif that dominates the Comtadin plain at a height of 1,912m.

The **Vaucluse plateau**, also known as the Vaucluse hills, is a vast arid land of karstic relief devoted to raising sheep and to the cultivation of lavender. This limestone countryside is potted with chasms and carved out by gorges. An underground hydrographic network, still largely uncharted, penetrates the limestone and opens out at the Fontaine de Vaucluse.

The **Montagne du Luberon** stretches over some 60km/37mi. Cut in half north to south by the Lourmarin combe, it culminates in the Grand Luberon at Mourre Nègre (alt 1,125m). This region has some rugged but beautiful mountain sides to which villages cling precariously. There is a striking contrast between its wild, forest-clad north face and its more cultivated south face. In the middle of the Rhône plain stand two picturesque ranges: La **Montagnette** and Les **Alpilles**.

East of Aix, **Montagne Ste-Victoire**, a limestone mass pockmarked with caves and chasms, dominates the Aix basin, whereas to the southeast the Trévaresse and Vitrolles ranges bar it from the Étang de Berre. This lagoon is closed to the south by **Chaîne de l'Estaque** and is separated from the St-Mitre hills by the Caronte depression.

The **Chaîne de l'Étoile**, Chaîne St-Cyr and Massif Marseilleveyre surround Marseille, whereas on the horizon looms the long rocky barrier of the **Massif de la Ste-Baume**, which reaches an altitude of 1,147m at the Ste-Baume signal station.

West of the River Rhône, the Cévennes foothills lie north to south receding in the river's direction and the vine-carpeted plain via the *garrigues* of Nîmes. A series of desolate limestone plateaux cut by canyons and gouged out by sometimes huge chasms succeed in tiers; it is an arid, rocky terrain only fit for grazing sheep. *For more information about this region, see Michelin Green Guide Languedoc Roussillon Tarn Gorges.*

Waterways

On its Provençal passage, the Rhône receives water to the west from the Ardèche and Gard rivers, which come down from the Cévennes, and to the east from the Aigues, Ouvèze and Durance rivers, which come down from the Alps. They all have the same appearance: a trickle of water in an oversized stony bed during periods of drought, a torrent of foaming water during rain storms. The Cévennes receive rainfalls of unusual severity – a single downpour can exceed the annual rainfall of Paris.

For the tributaries of the east that come down from the Alps, it is the melting snows that multiply the volume of water. The Durance, for example, expands up to 180 times its usual volume. Fortunately these spates occur in the spring, when the Ardèche and Gard rivers are low. On the other hand, the Durance is almost dry in winter and autumn while the rains from the Cévennes expand the tributaries of the west bank.

Coastline

From the Languedoc coast to the Marseille *calanques*, the form of the coastline changes often. As far as the Golfe de Fos, the shoreline is marked by vast lagoons separated from the sea by narrow sand bars: the mass of alluvial deposits dropped by the Rhône and shaped by the coastal currents has formed offshore bars closing off the lagoons. The encroachment of sand has pushed old ports like Aigues-Mortes inland.

At the Chaîne de l'Estaque, limestone relief reappears and cuts the coastline. From Marseille to La Ciotat the littoral is cut into a great number of coves, of which the deepest and most uneven are called **calanques** – they are in fact the submerged extremities of the valleys when the sea level rose after the Quaternary Era's glacial period. Steep cliffs, brown and reddish rocks plunge vertically into the sea from which emerge a number of nearby islands. With small well-sheltered ports and lovely wild creeks, the *calanques* are nirvana for deep-sea divers and climbers.

The Sea

The Mediterranean is the bluest of European seas. This deep cobalt, in painters' parlance, arises from the great limpidity of the water.

The surface water temperature varies between 20°–25°C/68°–77°F in summer, falling to only 12°–13°C/53°–55°F in winter. At a depth of 200–4,000m the temperature is a constant 13°C/55°F, an important factor in the climate: this great liquid mass cools the area in summer and warms it in winter. As a result of very rapid evaporation, the water is noticeably saltier than that of the Atlantic. The sea's tide is very slight, averaging 0.25m, and yet strong winds can cause variations in height of as much as 1m. This relative stability has singled out the Mediterranean as base level for all the French coast's altitudes.

A calm sea, with short, choppy waves, the Mediterranean can suddenly become violent. When the *mistral* wind rises, often with little or no warning, dangerous storms can surprise unsuspecting yachts people.

FLORA

In addition to its beautiful country-side, backdropped by a luminous sky, Provence possesses a unique natural habitat.

Climate and Zones

All vegetation is closely dependent on climatic conditions. In Provence, flowering occurs during the spring, although there is a second blossoming in the autumn that goes on well into winter. The dormant period is during the summer, when the climate's heat only permits plants that are especially adapted to resist drought to grow, such as those with long taproots, glazed leaves that reduce transpiration, bulbs that act as reservoirs of moisture and a protective perfumed vapour. The olive tree and holm oak mark out the distinctly Mediterranean zones, known as *garrigues*. In Haute-Provence the *garrigues* disappear to be replaced by forest cover (downy oak, Scots pine, beech) and moors (broom, lavender, boxwood).

Olive Trees

The Greeks brought olive trees to Provence 2,500 years ago because they grow equally well in limestone or sandy soils. The olive has been called the immortal tree since, grafted or wild, it will continually renew itself. Those grown from cuttings die relatively young, at 300 years of age. Along the coast the trees reach gigantic dimensions, attaining 20m in height, their domes of silver foliage 20m in circumference and trunks 4m round the base. The olive tree – there are more than 60 varieties – will grow at altitudes of up to 600m, mainly on valley floors and hillsides, often mingling with almond and fig trees. Its presence marks the limit of the Mediterranean climate. It begins to bear fruit between 6 and 12 years of age and is in full yield at 20–25 years; it is harvested every two years. Locals cultivate early vegetables in the shade of the light-coloured, evergreen foliage of the olive tree.

Oak Trees

There are several varieties of oaks.
The **holm oak** (*Quercus ilex*) has a short, thick-set trunk with a wide-spreading thick dome. It grows on arid, calcareous soil at less than 1 000m. It is an evergreen oak, the leaves of which remain a fine dark green. In stunted form it is a characteristic element of the *garrigues* in association with all sorts of shrubs and aromatic plants.

The **kermes**, or scrub oak, is a bushy evergreen shrub rarely exceeding 1m in height. It has a trunk of grey bark with a thick dome of shiny, tough, ragged and prickly leaves. Its name, kermes, comes from the scale-insect that lives on its branches and from which a bright red dye is obtained. The tree can grow on stone-free dry soil but prefers fertile, cool soil.

The **downy oak** or **pubescent oak** (*Quercus pubescens*) is a deciduous tree; the undersides of the leaves are covered with dense short white hairs. It requires more water than the evergreens noted above. The downy oak can be found in the valleys and on the more humid mountain slopes. It is at times found with the maple, service tree and rowan. In its undergrowth grows a variety of shrubs and flowers, most notably the orchid. Truffles develop around the roots of this tree.

Pine Trees

The three types of pine found in the Mediterranean can be easily distinguished by their shape.
The **maritime pine** (*Pinus pinaster*) grows on limestone soil; its foliage is dark blue-green, the bark an orange-red.
The **umbrella** or **stone pine** (*Pinus pinea*) is one of the Mediterranean's most characteristic sights; it owes its name to its easily recognisable shape. It is often found growing alone.

Olive tree

©R. Corbel/MICHELIN

Almond tree

©R. Corbel/MICHELIN

The **Aleppo pine** *(Pinus halepensis)* is a Mediterranean species that grows well in the chalky soil along the coast. Its foliage is light and graceful; its grey bark-covered trunk twists as it grows.

Other Provençal Trees

Streets and squares are shaded by the smooth-barked **plane trees** or the dark green canopy of the branching **lotus tree** *(micocoulier),* which yields a fruit mentioned by Homer in the *Odyssey* as inducing a state of dreamy forgetfulness and loss of desire to return home – hence lotus-eaters.

The outline of the dark **cypress**, a coniferous evergreen, marks the Mediterranean landscape with its tapered form pointed towards the sky. It is often planted in serried ranks to form a windbreak.

The rosaceous species, the most common **almond tree** in Provence, bears lovely early spring blossoms.

The noble elm tree has practically disappeared from the landscape.

Forest Cover

There are not many forests in Provence and those that exist grow especially in the mountain ranges below 1,600m.

Fine forests of holm or downy oak grow in Grand Luberon, on Montagne Ste-Victoire, and on the Vaucluse plateau. Petit Luberon is covered with a cedar forest. Beech tree forests grow on the north face of the Massif de la Ste-Baume. A moor of broom spreads along the limestone peaks.

The designation of the word "forest" beyond these areas indicates copses carpeting vast areas north of the Durance.

Garrigues

The word comes from the Provençal language – *garriga* – and defines an area of second-growth vegetation that appears on calcareous soils in the Mediterranean region following the destruction of the forest. Areas of *garrigue,* small or sometimes more extensive, can be found in most parts of Provence. The sparse vegetation is mostly composed of holm oaks, stunted downy oaks, thistles, gorse and cistus, as well as lavender, thyme and rosemary. Short dry grass also provides pasture for sheep in some places.

Environmental Threats

The natural habitat of Provence is under constant attack due to the influx of tourists, and to industrial and urban development.

Forest Fires

The Provençal forest is particularly vulnerable to fires (those of 1979, 1985 and 1986 were catastrophic), the majority of which are due to negligence or arson (most recently in 2005). Over time, these fires gradually disrupt the ecological balance. The oak forests are receding and the soil remains barren for a long period of time. Fire prevention and public awareness (especially that of tourists) will best help combat this devastating problem.

Dial 18 to reach the Fire Department (pompiers).

Pollution

The fast-developing urbanisation and industrialisation programmes in Provence have dealt a heavy blow to the beauty of many natural sites.

The Fos-sur-Mer industrial complex spreads out over the Plaine de la Crau; the area around Étang de Berre, especially its eastern side, has become the bustling suburb (airport, refineries, etc.) of Marseille. In 1957, owing to the high level of polluted water, fishing was strictly forbidden in the lagoon. Discharge of used water from the surrounding towns, St-Martin-de-Crau's rubbish tip and Marseille's main sewer flow into the Calanque Cortiou were all harmful.

Sadly, increased traffic in the region has necessarily resulted in the construction of more and more road networks that are cutting up the countryside and diminishing natural land.

Plage du Prado from the Ferris wheel at the Escale Borely, Marseille
© Bertrand Gardel/hemis.fr

No matter what time of year it is, Marseille and its coastline of blue inlets lie sparkling in the sun. Even though it is France's second-biggest city with a population of close to one million people and a sprawling industrial hinterland, it feels like a holiday town. Yachts bob in the Vieux Port, fish restaurants line along the quays, beaches are within biking distance and the vast sweep of the Mediterranean adds a briny tang to the air… All helping to make Marseille so compelling.

Founded in 600 BCE by Greeks who made Massalia a prosperous trading centre, then developed by the Romans, Marseille is the most important port in France – a busy, pulsating city, multi-layered and multicultural. Yet paradoxically (and engagingly), it feels more like a village, or a collection of villages, for its *quartiers* all have their own identity, their own local characters. Even the Vieux Port, the nerve centre of it all, has a small-town feel, with stallholders and customers at the morning fish market exchanging salty wisecracks.

Highlights

Marseille's history has endowed it with fascinating buildings enshrining its long past: museums, churches, lavish villas, grandiose warehouses. But visitors should focus on its new riches too because it has more to offer now than ever before. Designated European Capital of Culture 2013, it acquired a whole new cityscape, a new sense of style, helping it finally to shrug off its old reputation for crime and grime.

Mediterranean Flavours

Although the vibrant flavours of the Mediterranean permeate all of Provence, Marseille and its surrounds are gastronomically a step ahead. Nowhere else has such a bounty of fish: no wonder this is the home of *bouillabaisse*. But, with a quarter of Marseille's population originating from other countries, the city's food is also brilliantly diverse, intriguingly exotic. Right in the centre, souk-like streets smell of Moroccan spices, Egyptian flatbread, Turkish coffee, Tunisian dates. *Pastis*, Provence's favourite apéritif, is another Marseille speciality, and the delicious wines of Cassis come from vineyards half an hour away.

Captivating Calanques

To the southeast, the small port of Cassis is dubbed the St Tropez of the Marseille coast because, although quieter and less fashionable, it has a pretty harbour and a well-heeled clientele. It is one of the departure points for boat trips to the calanques; but you don't have to come here, or to nearby La Ciotat, to enjoy these narrow inlets of water, so picturesque with their juxtaposition of dazzling white rock against turquoise sea. They are all the way along the coast.

Small Towns, Vast Mountain

Less well known is La Côte Bleue to the northwest, an area of oil refineries and heavy industry which has still managed to cling on to attractive little towns like Martigues with its silvery canals and sardine feasts. For a change from the sea and summer crowds, there is fresh air of a different kind, a cool forest and wide vistas up on the Massif de la Sainte-Baume.

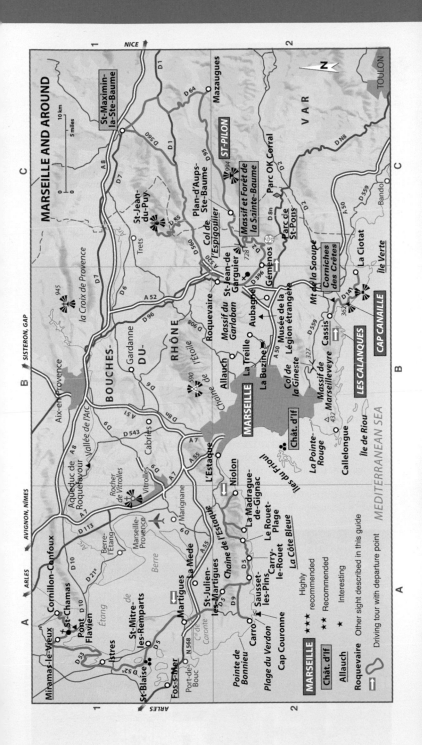

MARSEILLE AND AROUND

NICE

TOULON

SISTERON, GAP

AVIGNON, NÎMES

ARLES

MEDITERRANEAN SEA

MARSEILLE

Chât. d'If

ST-PILON

Massif et Forêt de la Sainte-Baume

CAP CANAILLE

LES CALANQUES

Corniches des Crêtes

V A R

BOUCHES-DU-RHÔNE

MARSEILLE ★★★ Highly recommended

Chât. d'If ★★ Recommended

Allauch ★ Interesting

Roquevaire Other sight described in this guide

Driving tour with departure point

N

10 km

5 miles

St-Maximin-la-Ste-Baume

Mazaugues

Plan-d'Aups-Ste-Baume

Parc OK Corral

994

St-Jean-du-Puy

Col de l'Espigoulier

Parc de St-Pons

La Ciotat

Île Verte

Mt de la Saoupe

362

Cassis

327

Massif de Marseilleveyre

432

Île de Riou

Callelongue

La Pointe-Rouge

Îles du Frioul

Chât. d'If

Col de la Gineste

Musée de la Légion étrangère

La Buzine

La Treille

Aubagne

Gémenos

St-Jean-de-Garguier

728

306

Massif du Garlaban

Roquevaire

806

590

Chaîne de l'Étoile

Allauch

Gardanne

Cabriès

Vitrolles

Rocher de Vitrolles

Aqueduc de Roquefavour

Aix-en-Provence

la Croix de Provence

945

Trets

L'Estaque

Chaîne de l'Estaque

Niolon

La Madrague-de-Gignac

Le Rouet-Plage

Carry-le-Rouet

Sausset-les-Pins

Carro

Cap Couronne

Pointe de Bonnieu

Plage du Verdon

La Côte Bleue

Port-de-Bouc

Fos-sur-Mer

St-Blaise

Miramas-le-Vieux

Istres

St-Mitre-les-Remparts

St-Chamas

Cornillon-Confoux

Pont Flavien

La Mède

Martigues

St-Julien-les-Martigues

Étang de Berre

Berre-l'Étang

Marseille-Provence

Marignane

Vallée de l'Arc

D1

D64

D560

A8

D7

D95

D560

D2

A50

N8

D559

D141

D559

D559

A50

A50

D2

D8n

D2

D96

D6

D7

A52

D96

D543

D9

A7

A55

A7

D8n

A51

A8

D113

D10

D5

D5

D9

D5

D21e

D10

D52a

D53

N568

107

Le Silo

©Boris Horvat/AFP/Getty Images

European Capital of Culture 2013

Marseille-Provence celebrated its shiny status as European Capital of Culture in 2013 with a year-long programme of 400 cultural events. Drawing on countries all around Europe and the Mediterranean to showcase creative endeavour, this cultural feast rippled out from Marseille to Arles and Aix-en-Provence, encompassing not just art and architecture, theatre and music, cinema and dance but literature, photography, popular culture, circus arts and gastronomy.

As exciting as this diverse calendar of events was the way in which Marseille has metamorphosed physically into a worthy culture capital. A €660 million programme involving some of the world's most talented architects has delivered an enormous boost to the city's cultural infrastructure. Long after 2013, visitors continue to enjoy striking new buildings like MuCEM, the Museum of European and Mediterranean civilisations designed around Fort St Jean on the Vieux Port by Rudy Ricciotti; Stefano Boeri's spectacular waterfront exhibition space and auditorium La Villa Méditerranée; the modern art space FRAC (Fonds Régional d'Art Contemporain) created by Kengo Kuma and Toury Vallet; Le Silo, a concert venue in a converted dockside grain silo; and the Panorama building, a new contemporary art space in the Friche de la Belle de Mai, the old tobacco factory that is now a hip artists' hang-out.

The renovation of handsome old buildings for the 2013 celebrations also brought lasting benefit, along with the partial pedestrianisation of the Vieux Port. Even GR2013, a 200km/125mi circuit (accessible from Aix-en-Provence TGV station) designed by a group of artist-walkers to encourage walkers to explore the transition from city to countryside in a new way, continues to hold its appeal. But just as important as these physical enhancements is the city's new mood of confidence. As a capital of buzzing creativity, Marseille sparkles even more than before. *www.mp2013.fr.*

MuCEM

© C. Chillio/Comité Régional de Tourisme Provence-Alpes-Côte d'Azur

Marseille ★★★

Bouches-du-Rhône

Twenty-six centuries of history have made Marseille the oldest of the great French cities. It has always been fiercely independent, resulting in its isolation from the national community until the 19C. Even today, although proud of being France's second city, it has retained its own distinct character: a combination of authenticity and hardworn clichés. The distinctive local dialect, the cries of the fishmongers on the Vieux Port, the exotic African markets... all combine to create the soul of Marseille. Yet the city where Le Corbusier conceived daring urban architectural schemes in the 1940s and 50s continues to look to the future with dazzling redevelopment projects like "Euroméditerranée" and a raft of inspiring new buildings (see panel opposite). This forward-thinking approach has helped Marseille to graft a dynamic future onto its multi-layered past.

OLD MARSEILLE

☛ WALKING TOURS

1 VIEUX PORT ★★

▶ Begin at the Vieux Port, to which all streets lead.

The Phocaeans landed in this creek in 600 BCE. It was here that, until the 19C, all Marseille's maritime life was concentrated. The quays were constructed under Louis XII and Louis XIII. In the 19C, the depth of two fathoms was found to be insufficient for steamships of large tonnage and new docks were built. Where the rue de la République meets the Vieux Port, you will see the Renaissance façade of the **église Saint-Ferréol** (the Augustine church), reconstructed in 1804.

▶ **Population:** 850 726.

⚬ **Michelin Map:** 340: H-6.

ⓘ **Info:** 11 La Canebière, Marseille. ℰ08 26 50 05 00. www.marseille-tourisme.com.

▶ **Location:** For an overview, take a **tour** or board the **Petit Train Touristique** at the Vieux Port which is right in the centre of the city (& see Addresses). A **City Pass** (from the tourist office, 1 day €24, 2 days €31) covers guided tours, access to many museums and also public transport. **Gare St-Charles** is the main station. Although the Canabière is the city's central artery, **rue Saint-Ferréol** is the main shopping street.

🅿 **Parking:** As in any big city, parking spaces are usually difficult to find. There are several underground car parks, but consider taking the convenient metro system (& see Addresses). Or pick up a bike at one of the many stands (www.levelo-mpm.fr).

☺ **Don't Miss:** The Vieux Port, the old Panier district, the Corniche with its glamorous bourgeois villas, and a boat trip over to Château d'If for a fantastic view of Marseille from the sea.

🕐 **Timing:** Start at the Vieux Port. From here you can get the metro, a bus (no 83 for the Corniche) or a ferry to your chosen destination.

👥 **Kids:** Petit Train Touristique; Natural History Museum; an Olympique de Marseille soccer match; Château d'If; supervised beaches such as Plage du Prophète, Borély or Pointe-Rouge.

Marseille's Colourful History

The Founding of Massalia – Around 600 BCE galleys manned by Phocaeans (Greeks from Asia Minor) landed on the coast in Lacydon creek, which is now the Vieux Port. The Greeks, who were expert traders, quickly made the city prosperous. After their defeat by the Persians in 540 BCE, the city became home to several different colonies of people. They set up busy trading posts at Arles, Nice, Antibes, Agde, Le Brusc, the Hyères islands, and inland at Glanum, Cavaillon and Avignon. With the Celtic–Ligurians, intense trade concentrated on arms, bronze objects, oil, wine, salt, and most likely slaves and ceramics. Masters of the sea between the straits of Messina and the Iberian coast, and dominant in the Rhône valley, the Massalians controlled trade in amber and raw metals in particular: silver and pewter from Spain or Brittany, copper from Etruria. After a period of eclipse, the city regained its splendour in the 4C. The coastal region was developed and planted with fruit and olive trees and vines. Greek sailors pushed further south as far as Senegal and to the north explored the Baltic coast as far as Iceland. Massalia was administered as a republic and widely recognised as a cultural centre.

The excavations around the Vieux Port and the Bourse commercial district have enabled historians to establish the layout of the town: it covered 50ha/124 acres and was built facing the sea on the hills of St-Laurent, Moulins and Carmes. It was surrounded by ramparts and featured two temples (one celebrating Artemis and the other Apollo), as well as several other monuments.

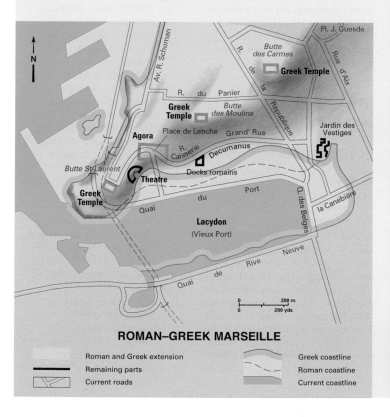

ROMAN–GREEK MARSEILLE

- Roman and Greek extension
- Remaining parts
- Current roads
- Greek coastline
- Roman coastline
- Current coastline

Rome Comes to Massalia's Aid – The Romans, taking advantage of the occasion to acquire more influence, entered Provence in 125 BCE, rescuing Massalia for the Salian Franks and beginning their conquest. For three years battles raged as the Salian Frankish tribe harassed the land, but Roman tenacity triumphed. Transalpine Gaul was founded with Aix and Narbonne as colonies. Massalia remained an independent republic allied to Rome; it kept a strip of territory along the coast.

Roman Marseille – At the moment when the rivalry between Caesar and Pompey was at its height, Marseille was forced to decide for one or the other of the two Roman generals. It backed Pompey, making the wrong choice. Besieged for six months, the town at last fell in 49 BCE; Caesar stripped it of its fleet, its treasures and its trade. Arles, Narbonne and Fréjus were enriched with its spoils. Nevertheless, Marseille remained a free city and maintained a brilliant university, the last refuge of Greek teaching in the West.
After the invasions, Marseille remained an active port which continued to trade with the Far East; it was the object of violent rivalry between the barbarian leaders. In 543 the plague arrived in Gaul for the first time and the town's decline began in the 7C. Pillaging by the Saracens, the Greeks and Charles Martel pushed the town back behind the fortifications of the bishopric on St-Laurent hill.

Maritime Development – As early as the 11C the old Phocaean city mobilised all its shipping resources and put its shipyards to work. In 1214 Marseille became an independent republic, but only for a short time, as in 1252 it submitted to the rule of Charles of Anjou. During this prosperous period (12C–14C), during the Crusades, Marseille competed with Genoa for the rich supply trade in war material and food to the Crusaders. Not only did the city reap great profit from this, but it was granted ownership of a section of Jerusalem with its own church.
Marseille, now rich again, sought new outlets. Its sailors began to trade along the Catalan coast and often sailed as far as the Levant, Egypt and North Africa. In the early 15C prosperity was undermined by crises which came to a head in 1423 when the fleet from Aragon pillaged the city. Under the influence of two clever merchants, the Forbin brothers, trade started up again. Jacques Cœur installed the main office of his bank here.

The Great Plague – In the early 18C Marseille's population was about 90,000. It had profited from an edict of franchise since 1669 and from a monopoly of trade with the Levant. It subsequently became a huge warehouse of imported products (textiles, food products, drugs), and was preparing to launch into trade with the West Indies and the New World, when in May 1720 it fell victim to a dreadful curse. A ship coming from Syria, the *Grand St-Antoine*, was stricken with several cases of the plague. When it arrived in Marseille, it was put under quarantine at the Île de Jarre. Despite the precautions taken, the epidemic struck the town in circumstances which are still unclear. The *Parliament* at Aix forbade all communication between Marseille and the rest of Provence under penalty of death. Despite this and the construction of a "Plague wall" 28km/17.4mi long, ordered by the papal vice-legate, the plague spread to Aix, Apt, Arles and Toulon. In two years 100,000 people died, 50,000 of whom were from Marseille.

Commercial Activity – In only a couple of years the city had re-established its demographic and economic energy. By 1765 the city had returned to the

1720 demographic level with approx. 90,000 inhabitants. Trade flourished with Latin America and the West Indies; Marseille began importing sugar, coffee and cacao. Industrialisation began and fortunes were made with soap- and glass-making, sugar refining, glazed earthenware (faïence) and textiles.

The city welcomed the Revolution with enthusiasm. In 1792, volunteers from the city popularised the *"Marseillaise"*, composed by a young army officer, Claude-Joseph Rouget de Lisle (&see sidebar p119). Marseille was the first city to demand the abolition of the monarchy. The tyranny of the Convention, however, became unbearable for Marseille and it rebelled. Under the Empire, Marseille became Royalist, the city's trade having been hard hit by the continental blockade. Under the Second Empire, Marseille became Republican; urban projects were undertaken (the opening of the present rue de la République, construction of Palais Longchamp, Notre-Dame de la Garde basilica, the Cathedral, Pharo Palace and park). The conquest of Algeria put an end to the Barbary pirates, and the opening of the Suez Canal in 1869 contributed to the stimulation of economic activity.

Marseille Today – The German-Italian bombing of 1940 and that of the Allies in 1943–44 to prepare for their landing in Provence caused widespread damage and fatalities. In January 1943, under the pretext of public health, the Nazis evacuated 40,000 inhabitants from the old district in order to raze the streets between rue Caisserie and the Vieux Port. After the Liberation Marseille threw all its energy into reconstruction programmes. The most striking project of this period was the **Cité Radieuse**, built between 1947 and 1952 on boulevard Michelet. Nicknamed the *Maison de Fada* or crazy house, this complex by **Le Corbusier** has a bold and innovative design. It is now much studied by architects worldwide and is open to the public.

Today, after a period of economic decline, Marseille has embarked on a dynamic new era of development. Exciting building and regeneration projects on a vast scale are transforming a city which had become down-at-heel into an edgy, gleamingly modern metropolis. But along with its colourful old port, Marseille has managed to retain its salty soul.

©Sami Sarkis/age fotostock

Unité d'Habitation, Cité Radieuse by Le Corbusier

Quai de La Fraternité, Vieux Port

© Camille Moirenc/hemis.fr

Cross over to the **quai du Port**, skirting the "Corps-de-Ville", the heart of the old city of Marseille, bombed by the Nazis in 1943 on hygiene grounds after the evacuation of 40,000 people. Only a few exceptional buildings were spared, including the Hôtel de Ville. Around them stand blocks of flats with arcades built after the war by Fernand Pouillon.

Hôtel de Ville
pl. Villeneuve de Bargemon.
A town hall has existed on this site since the 13C. The present building and its façade, an example of Provençal Baroque architecture, date from the middle of the 17C.
The king's coat of arms above the main entrance is a copy of a work by **Pierre Puget** exhibited in the Musée des Beaux-Arts (&*See Longchamp District, p125*).

Musée des Docks Romains★
10 pl. Vivaux. ◗*Open daily Jun–Sept except Mon 10am–6pm; rest of year 10am–5pm.* ◗*Closed public holidays.* ◉*No charge.* ✆*04 91 91 24 62.*
During reconstruction work in 1947 the remains of some commercial Roman warehouses used for storing *dolia* (large earthenware jars) were uncovered, dating from the 1C to the 3C. The museum contains objects found on the site, which date from the Greek period to the Middle Ages. A model reconstruction

illustrates the site and its surroundings. The warehouse complex consisted of a ground-floor level opening out onto the quay, and a first-floor level, which was probably connected by a gateway to the main street of the city, which is now rue Caisserie. The ground floor housed the *dolia* for grain, wine and oil. The history of trade in Marseille is retraced in the museum with the help of ceramic- and metalware and amphorae, retrieved from shipwrecks, and coins and measures. A potter's kiln demonstrates how amphorae were made.

Notice the 16C **Maison Diamantée** (*r. de la Prison*). Currently closed for renovations, it houses the Musée du Vieux Marseille.

▷ Take a few steps into Grand Rue; no 27 bis is the Hôtel de Cabre.

Hôtel de Cabre
27 bis Grand Rue.
Built in 1535 and spared when much of the district was destroyed in 1943, this is one of the oldest houses in the city. Its Gothic, composite style is typical of civil Marseille architecture.
Returning to Place Daviel, notice the former Law Courts building, the **Pavillon Daviel** (mid-18C). It has a beautiful wrought-iron balcony decorated in the style typical of

Marseille known as *à la marguerite* or daisy style, and a harmonious façade of pilasters.

The imposing **Hôtel-Dieu** which dominates the port is typical of hospital architecture of the second half of the 18C; note the arrangement of space and the superimposing of its arcaded galleries.

▷ From here go towards the Quartier du Panier.

Le Panier★

Built on the Moulins hill on the site of ancient Massalia, the Panier district is all that remains of old Marseille since the Liberation. In the past its inhabitants, the majority of whom were of modest means and lived mainly from the sea, made the most of their tiny plots of land by constructing tall buildings. Just at the time when it was gradually becoming something of a ghetto, Le Panier reaped the benefits of a large renovation and development programme to turn the restored Vieille Charité into a **museum** (&*see below right*). The area, with its narrow streets dissected here and there by flights of steps and where the tall façades are gradually regaining their former colours, is best explored on foot, preferably between shopping and lunchtime, at the end of the morning: the **Montée des Accoules**,

symbol of the area, but also **rue du Panier**, rue Fontaine-de-Caylus, rue Porte-Baussenque, rue du Petit-Puits, rue Ste-Françoise, rue du Poirier, and rue des Moulins which leads to place des Moulins. This charming and highly picturesque quarter of Marseille can be seen as a melting pot where Naples, Catalonia and the Mediterranean coast mingle with the French West Indies, Vietnam and the Comoro Islands to produce scenes which delight the senses: washing hangs from windows, the air is full of the scents of basil and *ratatouille*, and bursts of Marseille French, with its inimitable turns of phrase, can be heard everywhere. In recent years, trendy restaurants, art galleries and boutiques have begun to open in Le Panier, giving it a dynamic new edge.

Centre de la Vieille Charité★★

2 r. de la Charité. ◐*Open daily except Mon 10am–6pm.* ◐*Closed 1 Jan, 1 May, 1 Nov, 25 and 26 Dec.* ℘*04 91 14 58 80. http://vieille-charite-marseille.com.* This well-restored former hospice is a fine architectural unit built from 1671 to 1749 based on the plans of Pierre and Jean Puget. The buildings, created originally to shelter the deprived, stand around the central **chapel★**, a fine Baroque building with an ovoid dome by Pierre Puget. The façades looking on

Centre de la Vieille Charité

© C. Chillio/Comité Régional de Tourisme Provence-Alpes-Côte d'Azur

to the courtyard present three storeys of arcaded galleries in elegant pink and yellow-tinted Couronne stone.

The rich and varied collection, bringing together some 900 artefacts from the Near East, Greece, Etruria and Rome, makes this one of the few provincial museums able to offer an almost complete picture of ancient Mediterranean civilisations.

Nowadays the building houses the **Musée d'Archéologie Méditerranée-nne**, the museum of African, Oceanic and native American art (MAAOA), a poetry centre and a variety of exhibitions. At the time of printing, it houses the Musée des Beaux-Arts collection (see Longchamp District, p126).

Musée d'Archéologie Méditerranéenne★

First floor, north wing.

Egypt: Spanning the beginning of the Old Kingdom (2700 BCE) to the Coptic period (3C and 4C AD), this collection of approximately 1,600 pieces provides a complete overview of art, funerary rites, religion and daily life in Pharaonic Egypt.

Near East: Assyrian pieces from the palace of Sargon II at Dur-Sharukin (present-day Khorsabad) and the Assurbanipal Palace at Nineveh.

Cyprus: With as many as 185 artefacts, the collection of Cypriot antiquities is the largest to be found in any French provincial museum. It includes pieces of pottery with a shiny red surface bearing incised or light relief decoration dating from the Early Cypriot Bronze Age, Mycenaean-type funerary objects crafted in the Late Cypriot Bronze Age, and turned ceramic pieces decorated with concentric circles from the Cypriot Geometric period.

Greece, Magna Grecia: Statues of marble Cycladic idols precede an exhibit dating from the Minoan civilisation; ceramics decorated with geometrical motif friezes are characteristic of the 9C and 8C BC. Corinthian works influenced by Eastern art (aryballos and alabaster: perfume vases ornamented with animal or floral motifs), black-figure ceramics, red-figure ceramics and sculptures of a naked young man *(kouros)* or a clothed young woman *(koré)*.

Etruria, Rome: Ceramics in *bucchero nero*, where the carefully smoothed black paste rivals the shine of the silver pieces; funerary painting from Chiusi and Tarquinia, sculpture in Vulci stone, *korés* from Cerveteri and Veii.

Roquepertuse and the Celtic-Ligurians: Roquepertuse is situated in the commune of Velaux (north of Vitrolles) where various excavation projects have unearthed a remarkable archaeological collection. This includes painted, sculpted and engraved fragments, statues of warriors sitting cross-legged, huge birds and the bicephalous **Hermes★**, a magnificent sculpture of two heads attached by a mortice and tenon joint. The "broken heads" portico consists of three monolithic pillars, the upper part of which is hollowed out with cephaliform cavities which were intended to hold skulls.

Musée des Arts Africains, Océaniens et Amérindiens (MAAOA)★★

Second floor, north and east wings.

After the Musée de l'Homme in Paris, this museum has the richest collection of artefacts from Africa, Oceania and the Americas of any museum in France. The works are exhibited on one side against a black background, illuminated by indirect lighting, while the opposite exhibit provides the corresponding explanatory text.

Go round the left side of the Vieille Charité, turn left and left again into rue de l'Évêché, then turn right to reach the Major.

Cathédrale de la Major

pl. de la Major. Open Jan–mid-Jun Tue 10am–6.30pm, Wed–Sat noon–6.30pm, Sun 9.30am–6.30pm; mid-Jun–mid-Sept daily except Mon 10am–6.30pm; ret of year daily except Mon 10am–6pm. 04 91 90 01 82.

A huge and sumptuous construction started in 1852 in Roman-Byzantine

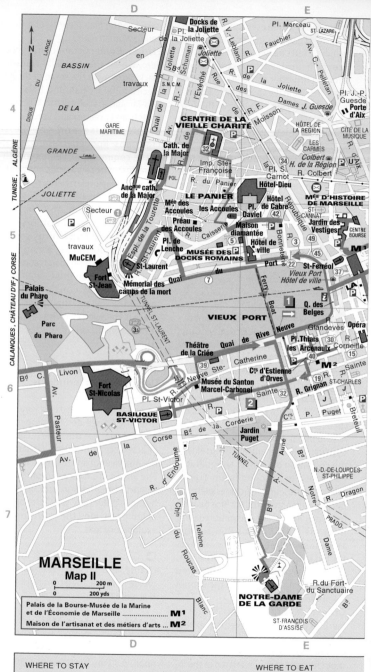

MARSEILLE
Map II

0	200 m
0	200 yds

Palais de la Bourse-Musée de la Marine
et de l'Économie de Marseille .... **M¹**
Maison de l'artisanat et des métiers d'arts ... **M²**

WHERE TO STAY			WHERE TO EAT	
Hôtel Azur............................	⑯	Hôtel Relax.....................	㉚	Axis.............................. ①
Hôtel Edmond Rostand........	⑲	Hôtel Vertigo..................	㉜	Bateau-Restaurant
Hôtel Hermès......................	㉒	New Hôtel Vieux Port......	㊲	Le Marseillois.............. ③
Hôtel Le Ryad....................	㉗	Radisson Blu Hotel...........	㊴	Café des Épices.............. ⑤

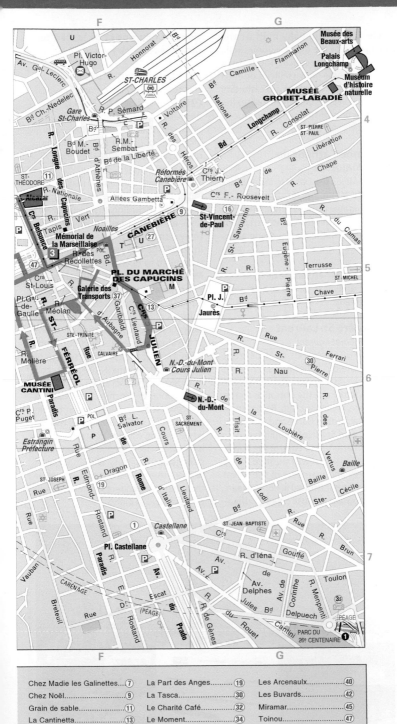

Chez Madie les Galinettes....⑦	La Part des Anges............⑲	Les Arcenaulx...............⑩
Chez Noël.........................⑨	La Tasca.........................㉚	Les Buvards.................㊷
Grain de sable.................⑪	Le Charité Café.............㉜	Miramar......................㊺
La Cantinetta..................⑬	Le Moment....................㉞	Toinou........................㊼
La Casertane..................⑮	Le Resto Provençal........㊲	Une Table, au Sud........㊾

style. It was originally built at the instigation of the future Napoleon III, who wished to reconcile the Church and the people of Marseille in one fell swoop. Sadly, part of the old cathedral (&see below) was destroyed during the construction of this rather pompous building.

Ancienne Cathédrale de la Major★

pl. de la Major. ⊶*Closed to the public.* The "Old Major", in stout contrast, is a fine example of mid-11C Romanesque architecture. Only the chancel, transept and one bay of the nave and side aisles remain.

◐ Go past the esplanade de la Tourelle and make for the small church of St-Laurent.

Belvédère St-Laurent

Parvis de Saint-Laurent. Located on the parvis of St-Laurent church, the old fishermen's parish of the St-Jean district, it offers a fine **view★** of the Vieux Port, the entrance to the Canebière, the Étoile chain, Basilique de Notre-Dame de la Garde and the **Forts St-Jean and St-Nicolas**. Built by Louis XIV in an attempt to control the town. The Fort St-Nicolas was stormed on 30 April 1790 and members of the Royal Family were imprisoned in Fort St-Jean, which now hosts **Musée des Civilisa-** tions de l'Europe et de la Méditerranée (&see below).

Fort Saint-Jean-MuCEM

Fort Saint-Jean, Quai du Port. ◷*Open daily except Tue May–Jun and Sept–Oct 11am–7pm; Nov–Apr 11am–6pm; Jul–Aug 9am–8pm (Fri in May–Oct until 10pm).* ◷*Closed 1 May and 25 Dec.* ⊛€8. ℘04 91 59 06 88. *www.mucem.org.* This important museum is a major ongoing project. It encompasses some older buildings including the Tour du Roy René and Fort St-Jean. A new wooden tower, the Tour d'Assaut, was built in 2007. The whole complex, which is scheduled to open mid-2013, is called **MuCEM (musée des Civilisations de l'Europe et de la Méditerranée)**. This national museum is dedicated to the cultures of Europe and the Mediterranean, bringing together the collections of the Musée des Arts et Traditions Populaires and of the European section of the Musée de l'Homme. The architect is Rudy Ricciotti (winner of the 2006 Grand Prix National de l'Architecture). Under a latticework of reinforced concrete, the space will act as a screen to filter the sun while playing with the concept of "seeing without being seen", and contrasting strength with fragility. With its views of the fort, the sea and the port, one after the other, the architect says MuCEM will be a "vertical casbah".

Villa Méditerranée and the Cathédrale de la Major, the Ancienne Cathédrale de la Major on far right

© C. Chillio/Comité Régional de Tourisme Provence-Alpes-Côte d'Azur

The "Marseillaise"

On 20 April 1792, Revolutionary France declared war against Austria. In Strasbourg, General Kellerman asked Claude-Joseph Rouget de Lisle, a talented captain and composer-songwriter in his spare time, to write "a new piece to celebrate the departure of the volunteers"; the *Chant de Guerre pour l'Armée du Rhin* (War Song for the Rhine Army) was written on the night of 25 April. Soon adopted by a batallion from Rhône-et-Loire and carried south by commercial travellers, the Chant was heard in Montpellier on 17 June.

On 20 June, a young patriot from Montpellier on assignment in Marseille, François Mireur, sang it during a banquet offered by the Marseille Jacobin club, located at rue Thubaneau. Enthusiasm was such that the text of the song was distributed to 500 national guards from Marseille, who had been called to arms for the defence of Paris. Re-named *Chant de Guerre aux Armées des Frontières* (War Song for the Border Armies), the anthem was sung at each of the 28 stages of the journey towards the capital, with increasing success and virtuosity.

On 30 July, the impassioned verses sung by these warm southern voices, ringing out across the St-Antoine district, were referred to by the electrified crowd as the Chant des Marseillais (Song of the Marseillais). A few days later, the new anthem, on the storming of the Tuileries, was given its definitive name. The *Marseillaise* became the national anthem on 14 July 1795 and once again, after a long period of eclipse, on 14 February 1879.

Fort St-Jean also includes an old *blockhaus*: it is in this remnant of the German occupation that a **Memorial to the death camps (Mémorial de camps de la mort)** has been installed. Dedicated to all the victims of Nazi barbarity, it recalls the round-up of 22 January 1943 when 804 Marseille Jews were deported to the Sobibor extermination camp in Poland, from which none returned. Some days later the head of the Gestapo in France, Karl Oberg, announced that the city's old quarters would be destroyed "with mines and fires". Twenty-five thousand inhabitants of the Vieux Port were evacuated by the French police and deported to internment camps in Fréjus. When they returned, they found a vast expanse of ruins: 1,494 apartment blocks occupying 14ha/35 acres had been dynamited by the occupying forces. The video on the ground floor and the exhibition on the first floor of **photographs from Nazi archives** taken at the time of the destruction of the Vieux Port re-create this period.

On the second floor, you may spend some time in silent contemplation in front of the urns containing the ashes and earth of 18 concentration and death camps. &*Quai de la Tourette (right beside Fort St-Jean).* ⊙*Open Jun–Sept 11am–6pm; rest of year 10am–5pm.* ⊙*Closed Sun, Mon and public holidays.* ⊛*No charge.* ✆*04 91 90 73 15.*

Place de Lenche

This lively square whose façades are embellished with wrought-iron balconies is located on the presumed site of the agora of the Greek town; there is an interesting view of Notre-Dame de la Garde and the Théâtre de la Criée.

▶ Go to the landing stage of the legendary Ferry-Boat, which takes you to quai de Rive Neuve.

2 RIVE NEUVE

Quai de Rive-Neuve

It was only relatively recently that the shallows that inconvenienced this part of the port were dredged and the quayside improved. Surrounded by beautiful buildings in Neoclassical style, the quai de Rive-Neuve is nowadays livelier than its opposite bank.

▶ Enter the shipyard district via place aux Huiles.

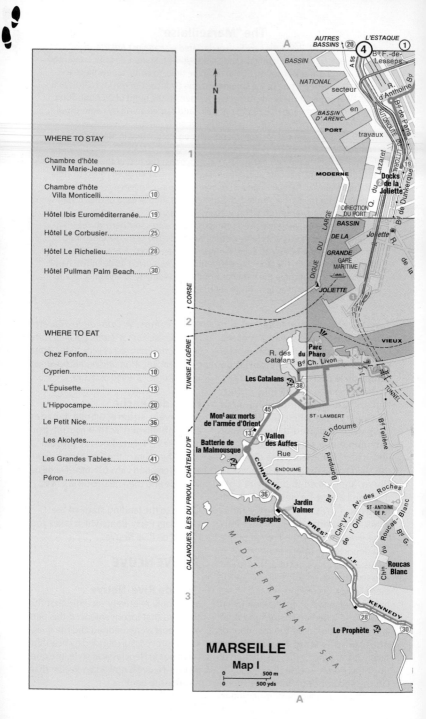

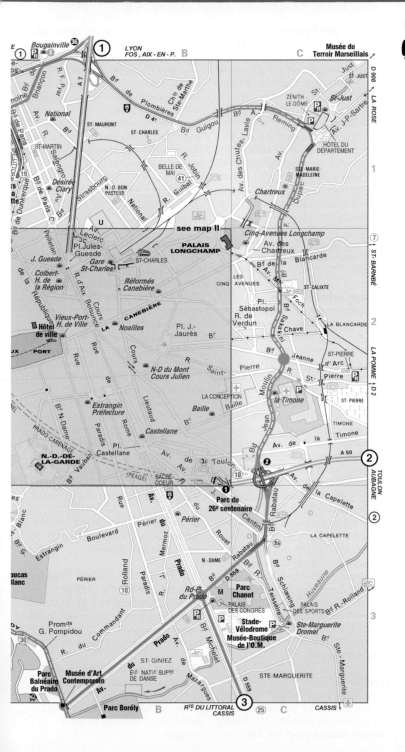

Quartier des Arcenaulx

In the Italian-style **cours Honoré-d'Estienne-d'Orves** are several cafés and restaurants, as well as the remains of the Arsenal's buildings, at no **23** and no **25**.

Carré Thiars

This network of streets around the pleasant 18C square of the same name developed on the site of the old naval yard. Now it is a lively area full of restaurants serving the cuisine of many different countries. Bars and nightclubs keep it busy until the small hours.

▷ To reach the basilica take rue Marcel-Paul (steps) and rue Sainte on the right.

Abbaye Saint-Victor★

3 r. de l'Abbaye. ○*Open daily 9am–7pm.* ◎*No charge, visit to the crypt €2.* ℘*04 96 11 22 60. www.saintvictor.net.*
It is in this church that Marseille's famous religious festival, the Fête de la Chandeleur, has been celebrated on 2 February every year since the Middle Ages. Candles, green in colour to symbolise the virginity of the Virgin Mary, are blessed and taken home by the thousands of pilgrims who attend. The basilica is the last relic of the famous abbey known as the "key to Marseille harbour", founded in the early 5C by St John Cassian, a monk from the Far East, in honour of St Victor, patron saint of sailors and millers, who suffered martyrdom in the 3C by being slowly ground between two millstones. The sanctuary, destroyed in a Saracen raid, was rebuilt in c.1040 and subsequently remodelled and strongly fortified.
From the outside it is truly a fortress. The porch, which opens into the Tour d'Isarn, is roofed with heavy pointed vaulting (1140) which is among the oldest in Provence.

Crypt★★

The most interesting part is the 5C basilica, erected by St Cassian, which was submerged when the 11C church was built. Near it are the cave of St Victor

and the entrance to the catacombs where, since the Middle Ages, St Lazarus and St Mary Magdalene have been venerated. In the neighbouring crypts a remarkable series of ancient pagan and Christian sarcophagi can be seen. In the central chapel, near the so-called St-Cassian sarcophagus, is a shrine (3C) discovered in 1965, which contained the remains of town martyrs on the tomb of which the abbey was built.

▷ Go down rue Neuve Ste-Catherine and the steps which lead to quai de Rive-Neuve.

♣♣ Musée du Santon Marcel-Carbonel

47–49 r. Neuve-Ste-Catherine. ○*Open 10am–12.30pm, 2–6.30pm: Jan–Nov Tue–Sat, Dec Mon–Sat.* ○*Closed public holidays.* ◎*€2.* ℘*04 91 54 26 58. www.santonsmarcelcarbonel.com.*
At the back of the shop, this small private museum holds the private collection of one of Marseille's great *santon* makers (◖*see Introduction, p94*), **Marcel Carbonel**. Particular highlights: pieces made by well-known *santonniers* (Lagnel, Neveu, Devouassoux, Paul Fouque, Puccinelli, etc.) and the clothed figures created by the priest, Abbé Sumien (1912). More exotic models are displayed on a little mezzanine (crèches from Japan, Alaska and Mexico). Next door (no 47), the workshop may also be visited.

▷ Immediately on your left, take the narrow walkway and steps leading to the quai de Rive-Neuve.

You will soon pass the **Théâtre National de Marseille-La Criée**, whose reputation has been made by the Marcel Maréchal company. It is located in the former fish auction house *(criée)*, which was moved near to L'Estaque in 1975.

▷ Take the car or the no 60 bus from cours Jean Ballard to go up to the basilica. To reach it on foot take boulevard Aune (at the end of cours Pierre Puget) and walk through the park.

GETTING AROUND TOWN

METRO: The metro is the most convenient mode of transport; the two lines operate Mon–Fri 5am–11pm (last departure from the terminus 10.30pm); 5am–1am Sat–Sun (last departure 12.30am). Tickets cover travel on tram, bus and metro, and are valid for multiple journeys within one hour (**Ticket Solo €1.50**). These options for several trips provide better value: 1 day (**Pass Journée €5.20**, good until midnight on the day first validated), 3 consecutive days (**Pass 3 Jours €10.80**). **Transtick €3** for 2 journeys, €13.40 for 10 journeys. Free maps from the ticket office. *℘04 91 91 92 10. www.rtm.fr.*

FERRY BOAT: Trips daily from one side of the Vieux Port to the other (saving you about 800 paces!): place aux Huiles to the town hall. *No charge.*

Basilique de Notre-Dame de la Garde★★

Leave the car on "Plateau de la Croix" (free parking). ⏲*Open Apr–Sept daily 7am–7.15pm; Oct–Mar daily 7am–6.15pm. ℘04 91 13 40 80. www.notredamedelagarde.com.*

Now restored, this famous basilica gleams resplendent in the bright Marseille sun. It was built by Espérandieu in the mid-19C in the then fashionable Romano-Byzantine style. It stands on a limestone outcrop (*alt 162m*) on the site of a 13C chapel also dedicated to Our Lady. Surmounting the belfry (60m high) is a huge gilded statue of the Virgin. The interior is faced with multicoloured marble, mosaics and mural paintings by the Düsseldorf School. Numerous ex-votos cover the walls, while in the crypt there is the lovely Mater Dolorosa in marble carved by Carpeaux.

A magnificent **panorama★★★** can be enjoyed from the parvis of the basilica.

③ THE CANEBIÈRE

Built as Marseille expanded in the 17C, this wide avenue – the city's central artery – derives its name from a hemp rope factory (hemp: *canèbe* in Provençal) which once existed here.

For more information about this famous boulevard, see the sidebar on p128.

▷ Leaving the Vieux Port, keep to the footpath on the left-hand side.

Palais de la Bourse-Musée de la Marine et de l'Économie de Marseille

Palais de la Bourse, 9 la Canebière. ⏲*Open daily 10am–6pm. €2. ℘04 91 39 33 21. www.ccimp.com.*

This maritime and commercial museum displays models of sailboats and steamships; paintings, watercolours, engravings and plans illustrate marine history and the history of the port of Marseille, from the 17C to the present.

▷ Continue up la Canebière, keeping to the footpath on the left-hand side. To the right of rue St-Ferréol a covered passageway and escalator lead to the Centre Bourse shopping centre, which houses the Musée d'Histoire de Marseille.

Belfry, Basilique de Notre-Dame-de-la-Garde

© Frank Rossbach/age fotostock

Musée d'Histoire de Marseille★

Square Belsunce, Centre Bourse. ◐*Open Tue–Sun 10am–6pm.* ◐*Closed 1 Jan, 1 May, 1 Nov, 25–26 Dec.* ✆€5. ☎04 91 55 36 00. www.marseille.fr/siteculture/les-lieux-culturels/musees/le-musee-dhistoire-de-marseille.

This museum traces the history of Marseille in its Provençal context from prehistoric to Gallo-Roman times through archaeological finds, documents and models. The model of Greek Marseille in the 3C and 2C BCE shows the horn shape of the ancient port, complete with slipways. A Roman merchant vessel dating from the 3C, preserved through freeze-drying, shows the wide range of wood used in naval construction of the time: the keel is made of cypress, the stem of umbrella pine, the keys and plugs of olive or ilex, and the planking and interior covering of larch and Aleppo pine.

Going back along the Canebière, several buildings are remarkable for the **quality of their architecture**, recalling the past glory of the street, especially on the right-hand side: the mid-18C rocaille façades of buildings between rue St-Ferréol and cours St-Louis; the Baroque-style building (1671–72) on the corner of cours St-Louis (no **13**), which was to have formed one side of the Place Royale designed by Pierre Puget, but never finished; and two typical Second Empire buildings, no **53** (now a department store) and no **62** (Hôtel Noailles). At no **58** cours Belsunce is the glass canopy of the famous **Alcazar** theatre which, after lying abandoned for decades, has now become the city's main library, the **Bibliothèque Municipale à Vocation Régionale** (**BMVR**).

▷ Go down to the shopping area which extends south of the Canebière. Turn right into boulevard Garibaldi and then immediately left.

Cours Julien

Until 1972 this was the Marseille wholesale market for fruit and vegetables. It has now been renovated and here you will find specialist restaurants, antique shops, fashion boutiques, galleries and so on. The streets leading off to the east of the cours, such as rue de Bussy-l'Indien, rue Pastoret, rue Crudère and rue Vian, are slightly on the "fringe", their façades covered with artists' graffiti (note the front of La Maison Hantée, rue Vian). The clubs and cafés come to life as night falls.

▷ Take the footbridge spanning cours Lieutard to reach rue d'Aubagne.

Rue d'Aubagne, which also has its share of unusual establishments (e.g. the grocery shop at no **34**), leads to the "belly of Marseille", still lively, even if of less economic importance. Rue du Musée and rue Rodolph-Pollack specialise in exotic and African hairdressers; **place du marché des Capucins**, opposite Noailles metro station, is a hub for local stall holders or *partisanes*. The air rings with their loud cries, urging passers-by to purchase their lemons and beans. In the narrow **rue Longue-des-Capucins** the atmosphere is part souk, part flea market. With a fascinating mix of traders, from African countries especially, selling their foodstuffs here, the air is full of different scents: spices mingled with freshly baked flatbreads, coffee, dates, pitted or marinated olives, anchovies, herbs and dried fruit.

Rue des Halles-Charles-Delacroix (a former fish market, now demolished), lined with grocery stores and shops selling exotic wares, leads to rue Vacon, where Provençal fabrics are displayed, as well as to "Saint-Fé", the rue St-Ferréol, which is the main pedestrian-only shopping street of the city (♿ *see Addresses*).

Musée Cantini★

19 r. Grignan. ◐*Open Tue–Sun 10am–6pm (Thu 10pm).* ◐*Closed 1 Jan, 1 May, 1 Nov 25–26 Dec.* ☜*Guided tours available (1hr).* ✆€5. ☎04 91 54 77 75.

Housed in the 17C Hôtel de la Compagnie du Cap Nègre, which was donated to the city, this museum specialises in 20C art after World War II until 1960, with particular attention to Fauvist, early Cubist, Expressionist and Abstract art, including works by Matisse, André Derain (*Pine Forest, Cassis*), Raoul Dufy (*Factory in the Estaque*), Alberto Magnelli (*Stones no 2*, 1932), Dubuffet (*Striking Woman*), Kandinsky, Chagall, Jean Hélion and Picasso. The presence of a number of Surrealist artists in Marseille during the last war is represented with paintings by André Masson (*Antille*, 1943), Max Ernst (*Monument to the Birds*, 1927), Wilfredo Lam, Victor Brauner, Jacques Hérold, Joan Miró and rare drawings by the Marseille artist Antonin Artaud.

The port of Marseille, a local subject of inspiration along with l'Estaque, is represented on canvases by Marquet, Signac and the Marseille specialist in this subject, Louis Mathieu Verdilhan (1875–1928). Finally, the collection features a few works by 20C artists who defy classification: Baltus (*The Bather*), Giacometti (*Portrait of Diego*) and Francis Bacon (*Self-Portrait*).

▶ Return to the Canebière and take rue Paradis, a busy shopping street, on the right.

LONGCHAMP DISTRICT
Musée Grobet-Labadié★
140 bd Longchamp. Closed for renovation. ℘04 91 62 21 82.

The bourgeois interior of this town house has been preserved, with its fine Flemish and French (16C–18C) tapestries, furniture, 18C Marseille and Moustiers faïence ware, religious gold and silver plate, wrought-iron work and old musical instruments. Fine paintings hang on the walls: Flemish, German and Italian Primitives, French School covering the 17C–19C. The museum is enriched by a collection of drawings by European schools from the 15C to the 19C.

Palais Longchamp
Metro Longchamp-Cinq-Aves.

This remarkable building with its monumental fountains was constructed by the Nîmes architect **Henri Espérandieu** from 1862 to 1869, to celebrate the completion of the Durance to **Marseille canal**. A true hymn to the glory of water, it mixes many different architectural styles and has an attractive garden at the upper level. It is linked by colonnades to the Musée des Beaux-Arts and the Musée d'Histoire Naturelle.

Musée des Beaux-Arts
Left wing of the Palais Longchamp.
Open Tue–Sun 10am–6pm. Closed 1 Jan, 1 May, 1 Nov, 25–26 Dec. ℘04 91 14 59 30.

Palais Longchamp

©Dan Talson/Fotolia.com

The Alcazar Music Hall

Even though it closed down long ago, the renowned Alcazar music hall is still cherished by the people of Marseille and has become something of a legend.

The Alcazar first opened its doors in 1857 on the present cours Belsunce and for over a century was the home of variety shows. Here, against a backdrop of Moorish-inspired décor, mime artists, pastoral players, "Marseille review" entertainers, music-hall celebrities, fortune tellers, bawdy comedians, local eccentrics and, in later years, rock stars, all took the stage. The operettas of Vincent Scotto and Sarvil, performed by well-known French singers, developed their own style here, while at the same time the spirit of the Alcazar carried more than a hint of Marcel Pagnol.

The music hall reached its zenith between 1920 and 1950, with such artists as Mayol, Mistinguett, Rina Ketty and Maurice Chevalier, a regular performer here since his very first appearance at the age of 16. Raimu, Fernandel, Tino Rossi and Yves Montand all made their debuts at the Alcazar, the last in a Western-style repertoire which dubbed him the "young swing star of 1941".

Performing at this mythical venue was indeed a test: the audience here, as in the nearby Opéra, was merciless and would not tolerate a single note out of key or any vocal weakness, seizing the first opportunity to heckle, shout jibes or burst into raucous laughter. The performers nonetheless appreciated the foresight and generosity of the theatre: stars tried out their shows at the Alcazar before heading up to Paris. The Alcazar closed down in 1964: one of the last celebrities to triumph there was the French pop singer Johnny Hallyday.

On the first floor, a gallery is devoted to **16C and 17C painting** from the French School (exquisite *Virgin with rose* by Vouet), the Italian School (Pérugin, Carrache et le Guerchin), and the Flemish School (Snijders, Jordaens and several Rubens works including *The Wild Boar Hunt*).

Provençal artists such as Michel Serre, Jean Daret, Louis Pinson and Meiffren Comte are also represented. Pride of places goes to **Pierre Puget** for a wide range of work: paintings such as *Sleep of the Infant Jesus* and *Achilles and the Centaur;* sculptures *(The Faun)* and bas-reliefs like *The Plague in Milan* or *Louis XIV on Horseback*. In the stairway are murals by Puvis de Chavannes.

On the second floor, several rooms focus exclusively on **French painting of the 18C and 19C**. The 18C is represented by fine canvases by Nattier, Verdussen, Watteau de Lille, Carle Van Loo, Françoise Duparc, Greuze, Joseph Vernet *(A Storm)* and Mme Vigée-Lebrun *(The Duchess of Orléans)*. Among the 19C works, the most compelling include paintings by Courbet *(Stag at the Water)*, Millet, Corot, Girodet, Gros, Gérard, Ingres, David and the Provençal artists Guigou and Casile. Honoré Daumier, born in Marseille in 1808 and well known as a caricaturist, was also a sculptor, as this museum reveals – a little-known facet of a prodigious talent.

🧍🧍 Musée d'Histoire Naturelle★

Right wing, Palais Longchamp. 🕐*Open Tue–Sun 10am–6pm.* 🕐*Closed public holidays.* 🎟€8. ☎04 91 14 59 50. www.museum-marseille.org.

Rich zoological, geological and prehistorical collections are exhibited. Four hundred million years of history of the Provence-French Riviera region are retraced, and a safari museum illustrates the diversity of the animal kingdom throughout the world. A gallery is devoted to Provençal flora and fauna. The various **aquariums** present a standing exhibition on water habitats under the title "Eaux vives, du Verdon aux Calanques".

LA CORNICHE★★

*⌖ You can drive up the Corniche
but it is almost impossible to find a
parking place. The 83 bus goes from
the Vieux Port as far as the Prado beach,
and from there the 19 bus goes on to
the Pointe-Rouge beach.*

Jardin du Pharo

bd Charles Livon.
This park is situated on a promontory
above the entrance to the Vieux Port.
Enjoy the **view** from the terrace near
the Pharo palace, built for Napoleon III.
There is an underground auditorium in
the park.

Corniche Président-J.-F.-Kennedy★★

This Corniche runs for nearly 5km/3mi –
almost entirely along the seafront. Be
sure to have a look at the elegant villas
built by wealthy families at the end of
the 19C. Level with the **Monument
aux morts de l'armée d'Orient** *(60
Corniche Kennedy)*, attractive views open
out towards the coast and the islands. A
viaduct crosses the picturesque Vallon
des Auffes.

Vallon des Auffes

*Access through boulevard des
Dardanelles, just before the viaduct.*
This tiny fishing port, crowded with
traditional boats and ringed with small
fishermen's cottages, seems worlds
away from hectic city life rather than
just a matter of minutes. Come here
for dinner at a little restaurant on the
front, watch the sun go down in a blaze
of crimson over the water and you will
have discovered one of Marseille's most
seductive (yet little known) attractions.

Jardin Valmer

This looks so much like a private estate
that many people walk straight past the
gate. But Jardin Valmer is indeed a public garden – the most elegant in the city.
Crowned by the **Villa Valmer**, a sumptuous néo-Renaissance-style *bastide*
built in 1865 by a wealthy industrialist *(a
guided tour can be arranged through the
tourist office)*, the park offers dramatic

Vallon des Auffes

© M. Raynaud/Comité Régional de Tourisme Provence-Alpes-Côte d'Azur

views of the Mediterranean from the
hills of Marseilleveyre in the south to
the pointe de Carry in the north. In the
heat of the summer you will especially
appreciate the dense shade created by
the luxuriant vegetation – the diversity
is reminiscent of the most beautiful gardens of the Côte d'Azur. Arbutus trees,
olive trees and green oaks mingle with
exotic species (palms, pistachio trees
etc) brought back from the east by the
first owner.

▲▲ Promenade de la Plage

This is the extension of the Corniche
to the south, running alongside the
plages Gaston-Defferre, a leisure area
bordered by gardens with children's
playgrounds which contains pleasure
pools and artificial beaches. On the
other side of the road there are several
restaurants.
The Pointe Rouge, on the opposite side
of the Prado roundabout, with its replica
of Michelangelo's *David*, is an important
sailing centre.

Château Borély – Musée des Arts décoratifs, de la Faïence et de la Mode

*134 av. Clot-Bey. ⏱Open Tue–Sun
10am–6pm. ✆04 91 55 33 60.*
Built between 1767 and 1778 by the
Borély, a family of wealthy merchants, the château
houses the town's Museum
of Decorative Arts.

The **park**, with its network of paths, extends to the east with beautiful **botanical gardens** (av. du Prado; ⬤ open Mar–Oct daily 10am–noon, 1pm–6pm; Nov–Feb daily 10am–noon, 1.30pm–6.30pm. ✆€3. 📞04 91 55 25 06). A popular place for a Sunday stroll, except when it is the venue every year for the extremely popular world championship of boules.

▶ Continue on avenue Pierre-Mendès-France and avenue de la Pointe-Rouge. From avenue de Montredon, enter the Parc de Montredon.

Musée de la Faïence★

157 av. de Montredon (not on map). ⬤Open Tue–Sun Jun–Sept 11am–6pm; Oct–May 10am–5pm. ⬤Closed public holidays. ✆€3. 📞04 91 72 43 47.

Set up in the Château Pastré, a fine 19C mansion built at the foot of the Marseilleveyre massif, this museum is devoted to the art of ceramics, from the early Neolithic era up to the present day.

A great many of the collections feature exhibits from Provence, and particularly Marseille, where the manufacturing of faïence pottery was considerable in the late 17C and 18C. Marseille aside, you will be able to compare the styles of work from other leading pottery centres: Moustiers, La Tour d'Aigde, Aubagne, Apt and Le Castellet.

ADDITIONAL SIGHTS
The Port

It is worth having a look at Le Port (as distinct from the Vieux Port), as this is one of the parts of Marseille that has undergone the most dramatic transformation in recent years. To reach it from the Vieux Port, walk up the **rue de la République**, a long street whose fine apartment blocks from the Napoleon III era have been magnificently restored as part of the "Euroméditerranée" project. As long ago as the 1840s the Vieux Port had become inadequate, with ships crowded four or five rows deep, so in 1844 the construction of a new dock at La Joliette was authorised. Later the docks of Lazaret and Arenc were built and the port area was enlarged through the addition of further docks to the north.

The city retained some traditional Marseille activities, based on maritime trade industries: oil pressing, soap-making, flour milling, semolina production and metalworking. However, the two World Wars, the fact that larger ships could no longer use the Suez canal, and decolonisation dealt Marseille a heavy blow. Reconversion and modernisation, mainly in the oil and chemical sectors, brought about a shift in the main industrial activities to the area around the Étang de Berre and the Golfe de Fos.

La Joliette Docks

Access: Metro Joliette. Entrance at place de la Joliette, through the administrative buildings.

Situated between the new port of La Joliette and the railway line, these warehouses were built from 1858 to 1863, based on an English design.

La Canebière

The fame of this street spread all over the world, thanks to sailors of every nationality who visited the great Mediterranean port of Marseille and walked along its grandest thoroughfare. The operettas of Vincent Scotto and popular songs from the inter-war years also contributed to making this avenue an iconic symbol of the bustling city. During its period of glory, which lasted from the 1870s until the 1940s, the Canebière was lined with fashionable hotels, restaurants and department stores. In the wake of the German Occupation, however, it lost a considerable amount of its prestige. It has been slow to regain its former splendour, but in recent years progress has been made. Cutting a swathe up the city centre, it is seen by every visitor, anyway.

Almost 400m long, they are the embodiment of Marseille's economic heyday as the Gateway to the Orient. The use of stone, brick and cast iron in the construction, which nowadays is a specific feature of this type of architecture, was intended to prevent the risk of fire.

Renovated some years ago by the architect Eric Castaldi, the Joliette docks now encompass performance and exhibition spaces. The most recent enhancement to the area is the **Cité de la Méditerranée**, an exciting urban development encompassing dynamic new buildings (the most striking is the glass tower of the CMA-CGM headquarters designed by Zaha Hadid) and renovations like **Le Silo**, a 1930s grain silo that has been converted into a performance space.

👥 Museum and shop of OM and Vélodrome Stadium visit

3 bd Michelet, under the Stade Vélodrome, Metro Rond-Point-du-Prado. 👣*Guided tours of the stadium on request; bookings at Tourist Office.* 📞*04 91 23 32 51. www.om.net.*

Situated in the Vélodrome Stadium beside the souvenir shop is a mini-museum dedicated to the famous club OM (Olympique de Marseille).

Thousands of football fans come to gaze at the three windows devoted to the club, which feature the replica of the 1993 European Cup and scores of other trophies (the oldest from 1924). At the entrance, a wall of imprints reveals the hands of Barthez and the feet of Papin and Djorkaeff, among others.

Musée d'Art Contemporain

69 av. d'Haifa (not on map) Metro: Rond-Point-du-Prado, then bus no. 23 or 45: alight at Haïfa-Marie-Louise. 🕐*Open Tue–Sun Jun–Sept 11am–6pm; Oct–May 10am–5pm.* 🕐*Closed Mon, public holidays.* 💶€3. 👣*Guided tours €3.50.* 📞*04 91 25 01 07.*

A huge thumb by César marks the entrance to the museum of modern art housed in a building created from identical modules that have been jux-taposed. The permanent collection, which concentrates on French artists and gives pride of place to artists born or living in Marseille, brings together the different trends in contemporary art from the 1960s to the present day: structured movements, such as New Realism, the Support-Surface or Arte Povera group, but also eclectic work from the 1980s and maverick art which resists all attempts at classification.

This rewarding collection includes work by **César**, Richard Baquié, Jean-Luc Parent, **Daniel Buren**, the complex creative approach of Martial Raysse, Jean-Pierre Raynaud, **Tinguely**, Yves Klein, contributions by Robert Combas and **Jean-Michel Basquiat** as well as exhibits of the sometimes underrated art of our culture: cartoons and graffiti.

👥 Musée du Terroir marseillais

5 pl. des Héros (not on map). 🕐*Open Tue–Fri 10am–1pm, 2–5pm, Sat–Sun 2–5pm.* 🕐*Closed holidays.* 💶€4 (children, 7–14yrs €2).* 📞*04 91 68 14 38. www.musee-provencal.fr.*

Situated in **Château-Gombert** (in the 13th *arrondissement*), on a large square shaded by plane trees, this museum re-creates Provençal daily life in the 18C and 19C. In the kitchen, with its original chimney flue and *pile* (sink), you will see Marseille faïence, pewterware, *terralhas*, *tians* in terra-cotta, mortars for crushing garlic and so on. In the living room and bedroom, furniture typical of the region includes a long sofa known as a *radassier*. Note the fine collection of *santons* and crèches. You can sample various Provençal dishes at **La Table Marseillaise** (*imp. Ramelle;* 📞*04 91 05 30 95)*, the restaurant in one wing of the museum.

L'Estaque

🔶*Consult the regional map (p107). To reach this outlying area of Marseille (10km/6.25mi north of the Vieux Port), take the car or bus 35 from the Vieux Port.*

😊 **Good to know** – The **chemin des peintres**, leading from the jetty in the port, has eight panels at intervals tell-

L'Estaque port

© Laurent Giraudou/hemis.fr

ing the story of this popular quarter and the pictures painted in it. A number of avant-garde painters made the village of L'Estaque famous between 1870 and the First World War. It was partly here that the foundations of modern art were laid – especially Cubism from 1908 to 1910 – by Cézanne, Renoir, Braque and Dufy. Marseille people are now attracted here by the fish shops and restaurants, as well as the odd stall that continues to make *chichi frégi* – delicious doughnuts. You can enjoy a **panoramic view** from the place de l'Église in the old town. From here take in the ports and islands, and the picturesque rooftops of the old village, to see what attracted the artists.

EXCURSIONS
Îles du Frioul
Sea crossing: leaves from Quai des Belges, Vieux Port. For times, contact Frioul If Express 𝄞*04 91 46 54 65. www.frioul.if-express.fr.*

Château d'If★★
Accessible by boat from Frioul If Express (www.frioul-if-express.com). ⏲*Open late May–mid-Sept daily 9.30am–6.10pm; late Sept–Mar Tue–Sun 9.30am–4.45pm; Apr–mid-May daily 9.30am–4.45pm.* ⏲*Closed 1 Jan, 25 Dec.* ☞€*5.50 (18-25yrs €4).*

𝄞*04 91 59 02 30. www.if.monuments-nationaux.fr.*
Alexandre Dumas (1802–70), the popular 19C French author of *The Three Musketeers*, gave this castle literary fame by imprisoning three of his heroes here: the Man in the Iron Mask, the Count of Monte Cristo and Abbé Faria. Built rapidly from 1524 to 1528, Château d'If was an outpost destined to protect the port of Marseille. In the late 16C the castle was encircled by a bastioned curtain wall. After falling into disuse, it became a state prison where Huguenots and various political prisoners were held; their cells can be visited.
The **panorama★★★** from the old chapel terrace is remarkable, taking in the harbour, the city and the Ratonneau and **Pomègues** islands, linked by the new port of Frioul.

Massif des Calanques★★
☞*See Les Calanques.*

Chaîne de l'Estaque★
☞*See La Côte Bleue.*

Château de la Buzine
West on the D 2. 56 traverse de la Buzine, La Valentine. ⏲*Open Jun–Sept 11am–6pm; rest of year daily except Mon 10am–6pm.* ☞€*8.* 𝄞*04 91 45 27 60. www.chateaudelabuzine.com.*
The fine restored façade of this Second Empire *bastide* attracts fans of Pagnol: the writer/cinematographer bought it in 1941, having recognised it as "my mother's château" from his childhood. He planned to create a "Cinema City" here. The City of Marseille, the current owner, has now brought this project to fruition, honouring the work of Pagnol and of local cinema. Marseille architect André Stern was in charge of the redevelopment.

ADDRESSES

🛏 STAY
🛌 **Hotel Vertigo** – *2 r. des Petites-Maries.* 🚉*Gare-St-Charles.* 𝄞*04 91 91 07 11. www. hotelvertigo.fr. 18 rooms.* Situated in the historic Belsunce neighbourhood, this

simple place offers various types of accommodation from hostel-style sharing to twin or double rooms. Nicely renovated.

Hôtel Relax – *4 r. Corneille.* ⋒*Vieux Port.* ℘*04 91 33 15 87. www.hotelrelax.fr. 21 rooms.* Situated near Marseille's shopping area and a 2-minute walk from Vieux Port, the location is ideal. Rooms are small but well kept and air-conditioned.

Hotel Le Richelieu – *52 Corniche Kennedy.* ℘*04 91 31 01 92. www.lerichelieu-marseille.com.* ▣. *19 rooms and 2 suites.* Charming hotel on the Corniche near the Catalans beach. Seven types of rooms and prices with or without views (and bathrooms!).

Hôtel Azur – *24 cour Franklin Roosevelt.* ⋒*Réformés.* ℘*04 91 42 74 38. www.azur-hotel.fr. 18 rooms. Restaurant*⊜⊜. Very near the Canabière, this hotel is in typical Provençal style. Rooms are spread across four floors; some open on to the garden, where you can have breakfast. Friendly staff.

Hôtel Hermès – *25 r. Bonneterie.* ⋒*Vieux Port.* ℘*04 96 11 63 63. www.hotel marseille.com. 28 rooms.* Unpretentious, centrally located hotel with small, well-kept rooms; those on the fifth floor have a terrace overlooking the quayside. Panoramic rooftop sundeck.

Hôtel Edmond Rostand – *31 r. du Dragon.* ⋒*Castellane.* ℘*04 91 37 74 95. www.hoteledmondrostand.com. 15 rooms.* Clean, simple contemporary rooms at a reasonable price in a quiet neighbourhood.

Hôtel Ibis Euroméditerranée – *25 bd de Dunkerque.* ℘*04 91 99 25 20. 192 rooms.* Straightforward rooms, but air-conditioned and comfortable. A good base to explore the recently transformed area between Joliette docks and rue de la République.

Chambre d'hôte Villa Marie-Jeanne – *4 r. Chicot.* ⋒*Cinq Avenue Long Champs.* ℘*04 91 85 51 31. 3 rooms.* A 19C building in a residential quarter of the city. Traditional, elegant Provençal touches, old-fashioned furniture with modern amenities.

Hôtel Le Ryad – *16 r. Sénac de Meilhan.* ⋒*Vieux Port.* ℘*04 91 47 74 54. www.leryad.fr.* ▣. *9 rooms. Restaurant*⊜⊜⊜. Step off the Canebière and into Morocco! Cosy and elegant, with a tea room and Moroccan restaurant.

Chambre d'hôte Villa Monticelli – *96 r. du Cdt-Rolland.* ⋒*Rond-Point-du-Prado.* ℘*04 91 22 15 20. www.villa monticelli.com. 5 rooms.* This Art Deco villa in the Prado area has small but tastefully decorated rooms. Only a stroll from the beach.

Hôtel Le Corbusier – *280 bd Michelet.* ℘*04 91 16 78 00. www.hotelle corbusier.com. 21 rooms.* ▣. *Closed 1 week in Jan. Restaurant*⊜⊜. Architects and designers love this unique hotel in Le Corbusier's innovative 1940s apartment block, La Cité Radieuse (a short bus ride from the centre). Rooms all have original features and accessories and there's a 360-degree view from the roof. The excellent restaurant, Le Ventre de l'Architecte, has similar period décor.

New Hôtel Vieux Port – *3 bis r. Reine-Elisabeth.* ⋒*Vieux Port.* ℘*04 91 90 76 24. www.new-hotel.com. 42 rooms.* Well located just a few steps from the Vieux Port, this hotel, recently refurbished, has rooms decorated with exotic themes: Pondicherry, Rising Sun, Arabian Nights, Vera Cruz or Tropical Africa.

Hôtel Pullman Palm Beach – *200 corniche J.-F.-Kennedy.* ℘*04 91 16 19 00. 160 rooms. Restaurant*⊜⊜⊜. Facing the Île du Château d'If, this stylish contemporary hotel has a nautical feel. Extremely comfortable, well-equipped rooms all with sea view. The very modern restaurant gives the sunny flavours of the south a new twist.

RadissonBlu Hotel – *38 quai de Rive Neuve.* ⋒*Vieux Port.* ℘*04 88 92 19 50. www.radissonblu.com. 189 rooms. Restaurant*⊜⊜⊜. Right by Vieux Port, this smart, designerish hotel, between Fort St-Nicolas and Théâtre de la Criée, is furnished beautifully and provides the latest high-tech gadgets. Immaculate, bright rooms, some with harbour views.

🍴 EAT

Les Buvards – *34 Grand'Rue.* ⋒*Vieux Port.* ℘*04 91 90 69 98. Closed Sun lunch.* Unpretentious bistro with simple food and an interesting selection of wines to drink in or take away.

Le Charité Café – *2 r. de la Charité.* ⋒*Colbert.* ℘*04 91 91 08 41. Open 9am–5pm, closed Mon.* A pleasant brasserie right beside the Vieille Charité. Salads, *plats du jour*, afternoon tea etc.

Les Grandes Tables de la Friche – *41 r. Jobin (Friche de la Belle de Mai).* ℘*04 95 04 95 85. Open lunch Mon–Fri; dinner Thu–Sat, closed Sun. Bar open Fri–Sat from 5pm.* Out from the centre, this is a key address for Marseille's trendy, artistic types. It is part of the Friche de la Belle de Mai, an artists' colony housed in an old tobacco factory, hence the post-industrial-chic feel of the restaurant's vast dining room with its raw concrete and stainless steel. This café-"neo-brasserie" serves retro-style comfort food.

⊜ **La Part des Anges** – *33 r. Sainte.* ⬟*Vieux Port.* ✆*04 91 33 55 70. www.lapart desanges.com.* This cosy, old-fashioned wine bar has an excellent selection of wines by the glass or bottle to enjoy on the spot or take away. It also serves simple food. Lively in the evening.

⊜ **Le Resto Provençal** – *64 cours Julien.* ⬟*Cours-Julien.* ✆*04 91 48 85 12. Closed Sun, Mon, Thu eve.* A cosy place with Provençal specialities including sea bream soup and fig tart.

⊜ **Toinou** – *3 cours St-Louis.* ⬟*Noailles.* ✆*0 811 45 45 45. www.toinou.com. Closed Sun afternoons.* This famous Marseille fishmonger has been here nearly 50 years. Right at the stall in cours St-Louis, the restaurant allows you to sit down and enjoy some shellfish or a fine seafood platter, washed down with a little glass of chilled white wine. Home deliveries.

⊜⊜ **Les Akolytes** – *41 r. Papety. Bus 83, 54.* ✆*04 91 59 17 10. Closed Sat lunch and Sun.* Opened by three young people, this trendy spot focuses on "gastronomic tapas". The fashionable modern interior matches the clientele, especially in the evening. Fantastic sea views are a bonus, and after dinner you can enjoy a walk on the plage des Catalans, just opposite.

⊜⊜ **Axis** – *8 r. Sainte-Victoire.* ⬟*Castellane.* ✆*04 91 57 14 70. www. restaurant-axis.com. Closed Sat lunch, Sun, Mon eve.* The seasonal, contemporary-style cuisine makes this establishment worth a detour. Modern décor, with views of the chefs in action. Charming welcome.

⊜⊜ **Le Café des Épices** – *4 r. Lacydon.* ⬟*Vieux Port.* ✆*04 91 91 22 69. Closed Sat eve, Sun and Mon. Reservations advised.* This tiny, trendy restaurant seats just 20, but the esplanade terrace and its olive grove in the background are delightful, as is the creative cuisine.

⊜⊜ **La Cantinetta** – *24 cours Julien.* ⬟*N.-D.-du-Mont.* ✆*04 91 48 10 48. Closed Sun, Mon.* This young Italian restaurant is making a reputation for itself for its surprisingly spot-on food that uses all fresh ingredients, and for its bistro décor and pleasant garden. Excellent value for money. Booking strongly advised.

⊜⊜ **La Casertane** – *71 r. Francis-Davso.* ⬟*Vieux-Port.* ✆*04 91 54 98 51. Closed Mon–Sat dinner and Sun.* A stone's throw from the Vieux- Port, this restaurant and delicatessen delights its regulars with antipasti and copious pasta dishes at very reasonable prices. Do keep a bit of room for the excellent traditional tiramisu. You can shop for goodies before you leave.

⊜⊜ **Chez Madie Les Galinettes** – *138 quai du Port.* ⬟*Vieux Port.* ✆*04 91 90 40 87. Closed Sat lunch in Jul, Sun.* Near the museums of Old Marseille, this Povençal restaurant with terrace sits on the Vieux Port. Traditional dishes.

⊜⊜ **Chez Noël** – *174 la Canebière.* ⬟*Réformés-Canebière.* ✆*04 91 42 17 22. Closed Mon, Aug.* Some say that these are the best pizzas in Marseille. The décor is just a touch dowdy, but the atmosphere is great. A small family business that is going strong.

⊜⊜ **Cyprien** – *56 av. de Toulon.* ⬟*La Castellane.* ✆*04 91 25 50 00. Closed 23 Jul–4 Sept, 24 Dec–5 Jan, Mon eve, Sat lunch, Sun, public holidays.* This restaurant near the place Castellane offers classic, tasty cuisine and a décor to match. Interior adorned with floral touches and paintings.

⊜⊜ **L'Hippocampe** – *151 plage de l'Estaque (L'Estaque).* ✆*04 91 03 83 78 . Closed Sun dinner, Mon.* From outside this restaurant doesn't look that great, but the dining room overlooking the Vieux Port and the terrace right beside the water make it worthwhile. Salads, beef kebabs and Provençal specialities. A singer, too, on Friday and Saturday evenings and on Sunday at midday.

⊜⊜ **La Tasca** – *102 r. Ferrari.* ⬟*N.-D.-du-Mont.* ✆*04 91 42 26 02. www.latasca.fr. Closed Sun, Mon.* Opposite the Poste à Galène theatre, La Tasca is *the* place to go for a tapas evening. Tucked away, a large garden is open year-round. Good Spanish tapas, with traditional plates of jamon Serrano y manchego (Serrano dry-cured ham and cheese), *tortillas y patatas bravas* (Spanish omelette with potatoes) and some 65 other varieties of tapas.

⊜⊜⊜ **Les Arcenaulx** – *25 cours d'Estienne-d'Orves.* ⬟*Vieux Port.* ✆*04 91 59 80 30. www.les-arcenaulx.com. Closed 11–17 Aug, Sun.* Dine surrounded by the books, which cover the walls of this restaurant: it's combined with a bookshop and publishers, located in the original warehouses of the 17C Arsenal des Galères. Large terrace and sun-kissed cooking.

⊜⊜🍴 **Bateau-Restaurant Le Marseillois** – *quai du Port-Marine, just by the Town Hall.* 🚇*Vieux Port.* 🕿*04 91 90 72 52. Closed Feb.* Impossible to eat any closer to the water than in this 19C schooner moored opposite the *mairie.* Provençal cuisine, with seafood a speciality.

⊜⊜🍴 **Chez Fonfon** – *140 r. du Vallon-des-Auffes.* 🕿*04 91 52 14 38. www.chez-fonfon.com. Closed 2–23 Jan, Mon lunch, Sun.* The dining room of this renowned restaurant is a landmark in the tiny harbour of the Vallon des Auffes. Freshly caught fish is its speciality, needless to say.

⊜⊜🍴 **Le Moment** – *5 pl. Sadi Carnot.* 🚇*Vieux-Port.* 🕿*04 91 52 47 49. www.le moment-marseille.com. Closed Sun and Mon eve.* Run by talented chef Christian Ernst, this ultra-modern restaurant near the Vieux Port also offers top-notch takeaway food and cookery classes. Exciting cooking in refined surroundings.

⊜⊜🍴🍴 **l'Épuisette** – *156 r. du Vallon des Auffes.* 🕿*04 91 52 17 82. Closed 5 Aug–5 Sept, Sun–Mon.* Perched on rocks beside the sea in the picturesque Vallon des Auffes, this restaurant has long been a Marseille favourite, especially for fish. Wonderful seascapes and attentive staff.

⊜⊜🍴🍴 **Miramar** – *12 quai du Port.* 🚇*Vieux Port.* 🕿*04 91 91 10 40. www. bouillabaisse.com. Closed Sun and Mon.* This 1960s-style restaurant on the Vieux Port is famous for its bouillabaisse and other fish specialities. High prices do not deter faithful customers!

⊜⊜🍴🍴 **Péron** – *56 corniche J.-F.-Kennedy* 🕿*04 91 52 15 22. www.restaurant-peron.com. Closed 1 week Mar, 1 week Nov.* In a great location on the Corniche, this well-known restaurant, decorated in the style of a transatlantic steamer, has giddy views out to the îles du Frioul. Mediterranean cooking in a modern vein.

⊜⊜🍴🍴 **Une Table, au Sud** – *2 quai du Port (1st floor).* 🚇*Vieux-Port.* 🕿*04 91 90 63 53. www.unetableausud.com. Closed Aug, 3–11 Jan, Sun–Mon.* This colourful restaurant delights both the eye and the taste buds, thanks to inventive cuisine with delicious southern accents. No terrace, so book a window table for a view over the Vieux Port.

⊜⊜🍴🍴 **Le Petit Nice** – *Anse de Maldormé (small laneway at side of 160 corniche J.-F.-Kennedy).* 🕿*04 91 59 25 92. www.passedat.fr. Closed 1–20 Jan, Feb school holidays, Whitsun holidays.* Chef Gérald Passédat's refined and inventive cooking (of fish and seafood especially), combined with magical sea views, a soigné atmosphere and well-trained staff, has made this restaurant a top address.

NIGHTLIFE

Bar de la Marine – *15 quai Rive-Neuve.* 🚇*Vieux Port.* 🕿*04 91 54 95 42. Open noon–midnight.* The setting for Marcel Pagnol's *Marius et Fanny* trilogy, you're more likely to find the beautiful people having a drink here these days. A great spot for pre- or post-dinner drinks – if you can get a seat.

Café de la Banque – *24 bd Paul-Peytral,* 🚇*Estrangin-Préfecture.* 🕿*04 91 33 35 07. Noon–9.30pm, closed Sun and public holidays.* Perfect place to meet for a drink on the terrace; there's a brasserie-type ambience with uniformed waiters and a chic, pseudo-intellectual clientele.

La Caravelle – *34 quai du Port.* 🚇*Vieux-Port.* 🕿*04 91 90 36 64. 7am–2am.* There's a wonderful view of the Vieux Port from the mini-balcony of this bar on the first floor of an old apartment block. Inside, the 1930s décor has a certain charm; light food at lunchtime and apéritifs with tapas from 6pm. Jazz concerts and exhibitions too.

L'Escale Marine – *22 quai du Port.* 🚇*Vieux-Port.* 🕿*04 91 91 67 42. 10am–8pm.* An unusual café-shop with a selection of Marseille gourmet products (*terrines, tapenades, anchoïades*), which you can buy to take away or sample on the little terrace with a drink.

ENTERTAINMENT

The magazine **Marseille L'Hebdo** provides full listings. New edition from kiosks every Wednesday. Listings also in the booklet *In Situ* available from the tourist office and Espace Culture.

Le Cabaret Aléatoire – *41 r. Jobin (Friche de la Belle de Mai). Bus 49.* 🕿*04 95 04 95 09. www.cabaret-aleatoire.com.* Concerts, performances, clubbing… Given over to electronic music, rock and funk, this performance space is a key address for Marseille nightlife. Appropriately, it's right in the heart of the Friche de la Belle de Mai.

Le Poste à Galène – *103 r. Ferrari, Mo Cours-Julien.* 🕿*04 91 47 57 99. www. leposteagalene.com.* One of the city's most celebrated concert halls, where the singer Anaïs and many others made their debut. Rock or vaguely trash ambience, as you'd expect of the La Plaine quarter, popular with Marseille night owls.

Le Son des Guitares – *18 r. Corneille, Mo Vieux Port.* ℘*04 91 23 31 14.* A tiny music café where Corsicans nostalgically gather to enjoy their native guitarists. Dancing on certain evenings.

Football – Follow the OM cult on match evenings at the Vélodrome Stadium, or at the OM café on the quai des Belges where matches are screened live, or in one of the many cafés which broadcast matches to feverish fans. On other dates hunt for pennants, scarves and other souvenirs in one of the OM shops (opposite the stadium or on the Canebière).

TAKING A BREAK

Café Debout – *46 r. Davso.* ◖*Vieux-Port.* ℘*04 91 33 00 12. 8.30am–7.30pm, closed Sun.* Tiny outlet of an old Marseille coffee company, highly prized for its classy selection of coffees, teas and chocolates. You might want to try Harrar coffee, the favourite of French poet Arthur Rimbaud.

Torréfaction Noailles – *56 La Canebière.* ◖*Vieux-Port.* ℘*04 91 55 60 66. www. noailles.com. 9am–5pm.* This old Marseille coffee-roasting company has opened cafés in various parts of the city. With its lively atmosphere, freshly roasted coffees and Canebière location, this one is especially worthwhile.

TOURS

Guided Tours – *By reservation at the tourist office.* €*8.* Multi-language guided tours (2hr) take place on most days.

Le Grand Tour (bus) – *Leaves from quai du Port daily, on the hour from 10am.* ℘*04 91 91 05 82.* Hop-on-hop-off bus tour (1hr 30min circuit) with audio commentary in several languages that takes you around all the major sights.

⛟ Little tourist train – *Leaves from quai du Port.* €*8 (children, 3–11, €4).* ℘*04 91 25 24 69. www.petit-train-marseille.com.* There are two itineraries: to Notre-Dame de la Garde going past the Basilica of St-Victor (year-round); and to Le Panier, the old town (Apr–Oct).

EVENTS

Programmes are listed in local newspapers (*La Provence*: *www.la Provence.com*; *La Marseillaise*: *www. lamarseillaise.fr*), and the tourist office also distributes a small monthly magazine, *In Situ*.

Festival de Marseille – *Jun–Jul.* ℘*04 91 99 02 50. www.festivaldemarseille.com.* Theatre, music and dance festival takes place in atmospheric venues in the city.

Fiesta des Suds – *www.dock-des-suds.org.* In late October, this world music festival brings 50 000 spectators to Marseille and vibrates with the music and traditions of the Mediterranean.

Folklore – International Folklore Festival at Château-Gombert takes place in early July (*www.roudelet-felibren.com*).

Pétanque World Championships – Preliminary games in Parc Borély, finals at the Vieux Port. A very popular event frequented by celebrities who, after a few throws, let the champions take over. First week in July (*www.fipjp.com/en/world-championships*).

Santons Fair – Extensive selection of the finest *santons* in Provence, on the Canebière, end Nov–end Dec.

SHOPPING
MARKETS
Fish – every morning on quai des Belges. Food – Mon–Sat morning cours Pierre Puget, place Jean-Jaurès (la Plaine), place du Marché-des-Capucins and ave du Prado. **Flower** – Tue and Sat morning bd La Canebière; Fri morning ave du Prado. **Book** – Second Sat/month cours Julien outside the Palais des Arts. **Flea** – Sunday morning ave du Cap-Pinède.

Marchés de Noël – Nov–Dec various city-centre locations.

BOOKS
Librairie-galerie-restaurant des Arcenaulx – *25 cours d'Estienne d'Orves.* ◖*Vieux-Port.* ℘*04 91 59 80 40. www.les-arcenaulx.com.* Home of publisher Jeanne Laffitte. Specialises in books on Marseille, Provence and food; old and rare books. Quality gifts and restaurant.

Librairie Maritime Outremer – *26 quai de Rive-Neuve.* ◖*Vieux-Port.* ℘*04 91 54 79 26. www.librairie-maritime.com. Tue–Fri 9am–12.30pm, 2pm–6.30pm, Sat 10am–12.30pm, 2.30pm–6pm.* People who are passionate about the sea can satisfy their longing to discover more about marine life in this bookshop. Great stock of books, nautical maps, models, lithographs and other sea-related objects.

Savon de Marseille

©S. Sauvignier/MICHELIN

CLOTHES

The main shopping street is rue
St-Ferréol, which has many individual and
chain boutiques plus Galeries Lafayette.
Adventurous dressers might like to visit
Marseille's well-known designer, **Madame
Zaza** *(73 cours Julien (M)Cours-Julien. ℘04
91 48 05 57)*, for colourful, daring outfits.

HERBS

Au Père Blaize – *4-6 r. Méolan, Mo Noailles.
℘04 91 54 04 01. www.pere-blaize.fr.
Tue–Sat 9.30am–12.30pm, 2.30pm–6.45pm.
Closed Aug.* This old pharmacy cum
herbalist, established in 1815, is brimming
with aromatic and medicinal plants. Star
anis, marjoram, thyme, basil, rosemary,
ash, marshmallow, canne de Provence.
Lovely all-wooden décor.

SANTONS

Santons Marcel Carbonel – *47–49 r.
Neuve-Ste-Catherine. (M)Vieux Port. ℘04 91
13 61 36. www.santonsmarcelcarbonel.com.
Closed Sun. Guided tours on request.* Visit the
workshop where the *santons* are made.

SOAP

La Compagnie de Provence – *18 r.
Caisserie. (M)Vieux Port. ℘04 91 56 20 94.
www.lcdpmarseille.com. Open 10am–7pm,
closed Sun.* A vast range of products based
on Marseille soap with attractive modern
packaging; other bathroom accessories
too. The smell here is wonderful.

Savonnerie de la Licorne – *34 cours Julien.
(M)Cours-Julien. ℘04 96 12 00 91. www.
soap-marseille.com. Mon–Fri 9am–7pm, Sat
10am–7pm.* The only artisan soap producer
in the centre of town. A dozen perfumes
including rose, violet and pastis.

SWEET TREATS

Four des Navettes – *136 r. Sainte.
(M)Estrangin Préfecture. ℘04 91 33 32 12.
www.fourdesnavettes.com.* Flavoured
with orange-flower water, the hard little
biscuits known as *navette*s have long
been a local tradition – a protection,
apparently, against plague and other
catastrophes. The city's oldest bakery has
been guarding the recipe for 200 years.

PASTIS

La Maison du Pastis – *108 quai du Port.
(M)Vieux-Port. ℘04 91 90 86 77. www.
lamaisondupastis.com. Open daily in
summer 10am–7pm; winter 11am–6.30pm.*
This small, bright yellow shop on the
Vieux Port is a great place to get to grips
with Marseille's best-loved aperitif. You
can taste different styles, some created by
small, artisan producers.

ACTIVITIES

Swimming – Marseille's public
beaches: plage des Catalans (volleyball
tournaments); plage de Malmousque and
plage du Prado (kite-flying); also plage de
la Pointe-Rouge or plage de Montredon.

Les Calanques★★★

Bouches-du-Rhône

The Massif des Calanques, with Mont Puget (565m) its highest peak, stretches almost 20km/12.4mi between Marseille and Cassis. With its weather-worn pinnacles, it has long attracted nature lovers for its wild beauty. However, its unique character and exceptional charm stem above all from its famous *calanques*, a series of deep, narrow indentations chiselled out along the coastline, creating a majestic union of aquamarine sea, blue sky and white rocks. Les Calanques were classified as a National Park (Parc Naturel National) in 2012. *Some paths dangerous for children.*

- **Michelin Map:** 340: H-6 to I-6.
- **Info:** *see Marseille* and *Cassis*.
- **Location:** East of Marseille, stretching 20km/12.4mi between Goudes and Cassis.
- **Don't Miss:** Lunch in the sun in the fishing village of Goudes.
- **Kids:** A Calanques boat trip.

EXCURSIONS

Goudes

▶ Leave Marseille by the promenade de la Plage.

This old fishing village in Marseille's eastern suburbs marks the starting point of the *Calanques* coast. Rocky scenery, a tiny beach and a number of small restaurants popular with locals line the shore.

▶ Continue as far as Callelongue where the tarmac road ends.

Callelongue

This inlet with several *cabanons*, a restaurant, diving centre and shelter for a small flotilla of boats is the *calanque* nearest to Marseille which features in most boat-trip programmes. *(45min). From there you can get to the calanque of Marseilleveyre and its little pebble beach.*

Sormiou★

(45min) Leave Marseille on either ave de Hambourg or chemin de Sormiou. Park in the car park (€3) at the entrance to the tarmac road blocked off to vehicles. Walk down to the calanque. Considered by the Marseille people to be among the best *calanques*, Sormiou has numerous *cabanons*, a small port, a sandy beach and two restaurants.

Calanque de Sormiou

© Chris Hellier/age fotostock

Background

What is a Calanque?

The word *calanque* (from the Provençal *cala* meaning steep slope) describes a narrow and steep-sided coastal valley bored into solid rock by a river and later submerged during cycles of flooding. Fluctuations in sea level have resulted from the alternation of glaciation and deglaciation on the earth's surface over the course of the past two million years. The most recent rise in the water level, an average of 100m, occurred 10,000 years ago, flooding caves inhabited by prehistoric man. The *calanques*, none of which is longer than 1.5km/0.9mi, extend towards the open sea via large underwater valleys. Although they can be compared to the *abers* of Brittany, they should not be confused with fjords, which are shaped by glaciers.

A Fragile, Remarkable Site

The absence of any form of surface water and the area's dryness can be explained by the permeability of the limestone, the proliferation of faults, and low levels of rainfall. The sun's glare on the high, bare rocks and the area's sheltered position away from the *mistral* combine to create an exceptionally hot microclimate on the southern slopes of the Massif des Calanques, conditions that occasionally result in winter temperatures 10°C higher than those on its northern side. Some typically tropical and extremely rare species of vegetation have been able to survive the periods of climatic cooling that occurred during the Quaternary period, creating today a botanical reserve of enormous scientific interest. This may seem paradoxical in an area whose vegetation continues to suffer, mainly from drought, the felling of trees for local lime kilns, excessive grazing and repeated forest fires.

From the time of the first fire ordered by Julius Caesar in 49 BCE to the catastrophic blaze on 21 August 1990 and further fires in July 2009, the forests of the massif have suffered indescribable damage. More protective measures have been introduced in recent years, including, since 1990, the restriction of pubic access during the summer months.

Flora and Fauna

In this semi-arid environment, the best-adapted flora includes copses or thickets of green oaks, viburnum, wild olive trees, myrtle and mastic. In addition to woods of Aleppo pine and stony scrub oak, rosemary and heather-carpeted *garrigue* predominate.

Samphire and sea lavender grow along the coast, replaced higher up the slopes by a thin cushion of plants including the rare Marseille Astragalus or "mother-in-law's cushion" with its fearsome thorns.

Ground where vegetation damage has been widespread may also be home to brachiopods. Europe's largest lizard and longest snake can also be found in the *calanques*: the ocellar lizard can grow to 60cm and the Montpellier grass snake can reach 2m in length.

Birds nest mainly on the coastal cliffs and outlying islands. The most common, the herring gull or *gabian*, which feasts on the rubbish left behind by careless visitors, is rapidly increasing in number. The most rare, Bonelli's eagle (only about 15 pairs remain), is a beautiful diurnal bird of prey with white, grey and dark brown plumage.

It is separated from Morgiou by the **Cap Morgiou**, a viewpoint affording magnificent views of both *calanques* and the eastern side of the massif. Underwater is the opening to the Cosquer cave. 🕭*See panel, p140.*

Morgiou★★

🚶 *(1hr45min) From Marseille take the same route initially as for Sormiou; turn left and follow the "calanque Morgiou" signs (you will pass the famous prison, Les Baumettes). Park near the "sens interdit" (no entry) sign; continue on foot along the paved road.*

A wild setting with tiny creeks for swimming, crystal-clear water, *cabanons* clustered at the far end of the valley, restaurant, small port.

Sugiton★★

🚶 *(45min) From Marseille take bd Michelet as far as Luminy; park in the car park near the École d'Art et d'Architecture and continue on foot along the forest track.*

A small *calanque* with turquoise water, it is well sheltered by its surrounding high cliffs. It is popular with naturists.

En-Vau★★

🚶 *(1hr15min) Access via Col de la Gardiole (Route Gaston-Rebuffat beginning opposite the Carpiagne military camp); leave your car in the Gardiole car park. Other entry available from Port-Miou and Port-Pin calanques, but warning as the drop is extremely vertical and abrupt and the descent can be dangerous.*

The best known and perhaps most picturesque of all the *calanques* with its white cliffs, emerald water and stony beach. It is encircled by a forest of rock pinnacles overlooked by the "Doigt de Dieu" (Finger of God). The beach is both stony and sandy.

Port-Pin★

🚶 *Access via Col de la Gardiole (same directions as En-Vau – 3hr) or Cassis (skirting Port-Miou calanque – 1hr30min).*

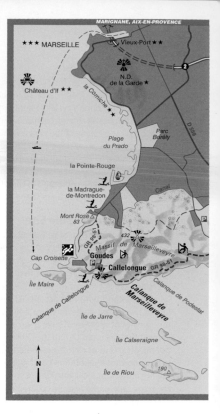

A spacious *calanque* with less steep slopes than those of En-Vau and a sandy beach surrounded by pine trees. This makes a good spot for a family swim.

Port-Miou

🚶*15min: Access from Cassis via the Bestouan car park or the Presqu'île car park, then follow the trail marked in green.*

The longest of the Provençal *calanques* is spoilt somewhat by an old stone quarry. Extracted over a long period, the white, hard stone of Cassis was used in the construction of the Rove tunnel, docks on the Suez Canal, gateways in Genoa's Campo Santo cemetery and the statue of Calendal that stands in the port. Its shelter is appreciated as much today by sailing enthusiasts as it once was by the Romans who baptised it Portus Melius.

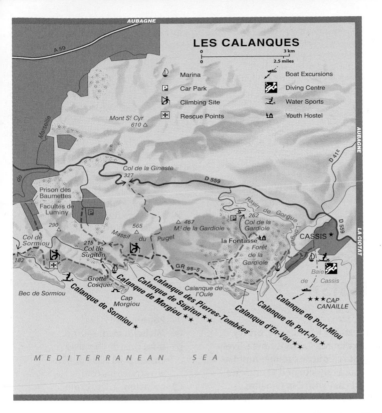

ADDRESSES

⛏/ EAT

⊜⊜ **Nautic Bar** – *13009 Calanque de Morgiou.* ℘*04 91 40 06 37. Closed Jan. (🚫access by car restricted in summer)* 🥢. Offering delightful views, this restaurant provides indoor and outdoor seating overlooking the water. A variety of fish and seafood dominate the menu.

⊜⊜⊜ **Château de Sormiou** – *13009 Calanque de Sormiou.* ℘*04 91 25 08 69. Closed Oct–Mar. (🚫access by car restricted)* 🥢. In a superb location facing the turquoise waters, this place is popular with Marseille people. An old family *cabanon* has been transformed into a restaurant offering straightforward fish cuisine: fish soup, *bouillabaisse,* etc made to order.

BOAT TRIPS

An excursion by boat is a practical way of discovering the *calanques* in summer when access to them by land is strictly controlled. But be aware that the sea can be rough.

From Marseille – Croisières Marseille-Calanques – *quai de la Fraternité, Marseille. www.croisieres-marseille-calanques.com. ℘04 91 33 36 79 (Apr–Nov).*

From Cassis – Les Bateliers de Cassis. *℘04 42 01 90 83. www.calanques-cassis. com.* Departure from the port of Cassis with visits to between three and eight *calanques.* ⊜€*16–27.* Evening trips available in summer.

From La Ciotat – Les Amis des Calanques, *quai Ganteaume. ℘06 09 35 25 68. www.visite-calanques.fr.* Trips in catamarans with glass bottoms. ⊜€*23–29.*

THE CALANQUES

Access – 🚫No access either on foot or by car to the *calanques* between 1 July and the second Sunday in September, or on days when the *mistral* is blowing fiercely. Even when access to the *calanques* is permitted, restrictions may apply in bad weather conditions, particularly on weekends. Spring is the best time to visit.

Diving – Just 30 years ago, the seabed of the *calanques* was considered among the most extraordinary in the western Mediterranean. Although it has since been polluted by effluent and adversely affected by those hunting both for rare fish and the spoils of shipwrecks of archaeological interest, it still holds many attractions for divers like multicoloured fish, sponges, sea urchins, mother-of-pearl. The Marseille tourist office can supply a list of diving clubs.

Walking – There are no direct approach roads by car to the *calanques* with the exception of the less attractive coves of Goudes, Callelongue and Port-Miou. The only way to reach the others is on foot. Footpaths are often steep and rocky: it is advisable to get yourself the IGN map *Les Calanques de Marseille à Cassis (www. ign.fr)*. It is strictly forbidden to pick any

vegetation, stray from marked paths, smoke or light a fire at any time of year. Make sure you are equipped with walking boots and detailed maps; carry water with you and use sunscreen.

Experienced hikers will be tempted to walk the GR 98-51 footpath from Callelongue to Cassis (see local map, p138–139), an incomparable 28km/17.4mi walk (allow 11–12hr) along towering cliffs, with spectacular views of the most secret *calanques*.

Rock climbing – The steep rock faces of the *calanques* rising straight up from the sea are magnificent for climbers of different levels. Contact the Club Alpin Français Marseille-Provence (12 r. Fort-Notre-Dame, 13007 Marseille. ℰ04 91 54 36 94).

Cassis★

Bouches-du-Rhône

Once mainly a fishing port, pretty, pastel-coloured **Cassis** is now a lively and quite chic little summer holiday town. Superbly situated at one end of a wide bay with Cap Canaille towering up behind the harbour, it has good beaches and an attractive waterfront for people-watching. A boat trip to the *calanques* is a worthwhile excursion (see Les Calanques, Addresses).

▸ **Population:** 7 722.
⚙ **Michelin Map:** 340: I-6.
▤ **Info:** Quai des Moulins, Cassis. ℰ08 92 39 01 03. www.ot-cassis.com.
▶ **Location:** 25km/15.5mi E of Marseille.
▯ **Parking:** Your best bet is to visit by bus from Marseille (40min).
☺ **Don't Miss:** The *calanques*, Cap Canaille.

SIGHTS
Beaches
Supervised weekends from early May; daily Jun–mid-Sept.

Two small **beaches** with rocks at either end: one, Grande Mer, with sand and gravel; the other, Bestouan, with pebbles. Both attract swimmers who end up back on the quayside in the evening, tasting the fish and shellfish for which Cassis is famous.

The Grotte Cosquer

This underwater cave, located near the Cap Morgiou headland, was discovered in 1985 by the Cassis diver Henri Cosquer. Scientists quickly proved the authenticity of the cave art, which includes seals, penguins, fish and even human handprints. A neutronic activation dating method, able to analyse minuscule quantities of organic matter, has dated the handprints to 27000 BCE and the animal drawings to approximately 17000 BCE, one or two millennia prior to those found at Lascaux, which are similar in both style and technique. The cave is closed to the public.

Port of Cassis

© M. Raynaud/Comité Régional de Tourisme Provence-Alpes-Côte d'Azur

Village

Although a stay in Cassis is unimaginable without a boat trip to the *calanques*, you should not leave without having strolled in the little streets above which looms the **château**, a medieval fortification which became a military fort from 17C to 19C. Sold by the state in 1881, it was bought by a Var tobacconist, apparently for a very modest sum. After several changes of ownership, the château has recently been turned into a luxury guesthouse. Between the port and the l'église Saint-Michel, renovated old houses tell the story of a fishing village which gradually turned towards tourism in the 20C, eventually embracing it as its main activity.

Today Cassis has only a handful of traditional fishermen selling the fruit of their labours on the quay in the late morning. With 12 estates and a renowned *appellation*, wine production is the other main economic pursuit in Cassis.

Musée municipal méditerranéen d'Arts et Traditions populaires

Place Baragnon. ☜☜ⒸOpen Jun–Sept *10am–12.30pm, 2–6pm; Oct–May 10am–12.30pm, 2.30–5.30pm.* ⒸClosed Sun and public holidays. ☜No charge; guided visits €3. ☏04 42 01 88 66. www.cassis.fr.

Set up in a presbytery dating from the beginning of the 18C, this little museum displays various items of archaeological interest found in the region or in the sea. The collection includes Greek and Roman coins, pottery and amphorae, manuscripts relating to the town and paintings and sculpture by local artists.

🚶 WALKS
👨‍👧 Path of Le Petit Prince

🚶*2hr. Follow the path on the right, with trail marked in blue. Park in the Presqu'île car park (€6), west of the town centre (signposted).*

☺**Good to know** – In summer and some weekends before it, access to the Presqu'île is restricted; a shuttle bus operates from the Gorguettes car park.

Situated on the Presqu'île just before Port-Miou, this pretty path presents no difficulties. With 11 panels at intervals to explain the environment of the *calanques* – flora, fauna, geography etc – it is particularly suitable for families, but do take care as the rocks can be slippery.

🚗 DRIVING TOUR

CORNICHE DES CRÊTES★★
From Cassis to La Ciotat 19km/12mi. Allow 45min.

The stretch of coast road between Cassis and La Ciotat skirts the crests of the Canaille, a limestone range that rises from the sea in white cliffs, some of the tallest in France – 362m at Cap Canaille, and 399m at the Grande Tête.

▶ Leave Cassis in an easterly direction, on the D 559 to Toulon, and during the ascent take a signposted road to the right. At Pas de la Colle, turn left.

Mont de la Saoupe
The **panorama**★★ from the television mast at the top includes Cassis, the Île de Riou and Chaîne St-Cyr to the west, the Chaîne de l'Étoile and Massif de la Ste-Baume to the north, La Ciotat and Cap de Sicié to the southeast.

▶ Return to Pas de la Colle and continue uphill.

Note the views of Cassis and La Ciotat.

Cap Canaille★★★
From the guard rail on the cape there is an outstanding **view**★★★ of the cliff face, Massif de Puget and the *calanques* and Massif de Marseilleveyre.

▶ Beyond Grande Tête, turn right towards the coastguard station.

From the **Coastguard station** (semaphore) the **view**★★★ embraces La Ciotat, Cap Sicié and Cap Canaille (telescope).

▶ Return to the crest road; bear right for La Ciotat.

The descent into town passes quarries, pinewoods, and the "pont naturel", a natural limestone arch.

ADDRESSES

🛏 STAY

🍴🍴 **Hôtel Le Clos des Aromes** – 10 r. Abbé Paul Mouton. ℘04 42 01 71 84. *www.le-clos-des-aromes.fr. Closed 4 Jan–Feb, Wed and Thu lunch. 14 rooms. Restaurant*🍴🍴. Located in the centre of the village, this old building has all the charm of a mansion. Enjoy the Provençal cooking, served on a flower-decked terrace in the summertime. Its rather small bedrooms are colourful and cosy. Mediterranean atmosphere.

🍴🍴🍴 **Hôtel Les Jardins de Cassis**– R. Auguste-Favier. ℘04 42 01 84 85. *www.hotel-lesjardinsde-cassis.com. Closed 7 Nov–20 Mar. 36 rooms.* This pretty Provençal farmhouse sits around a patio and pool. Surrounded by vegetation, pine trees and palms, it offers cosy rooms away from the bustle of the town centre.

🍴 EAT

🍴🍴 **Poissonnerie Laurent**– *5 quai J-J Barthélemy. ℘04 42 01 71 56. Open May–Oct. Closed Mon, and Jan–Feb.* 🍴. An old fishermen's haunt that has been turned into a fish shop and restaurant. Fish specialities, obviously. Tables on the terrace have a nice view of the port.

🍴🍴🍴 **La Vieille Auberge** – *14 quai J-J Barthélemy. ℘04 42 01 73 54. Closed Wed and Feb. Reservations recommended.* Passed from father to son, this lovely inn serves traditional Provençal fare. There is a terrace by the water's edge in summer.

TOURS

Little train tour aboard Le Petit Train de Cassis – *May–Sept daily 11.15am, hourly 2.15pm–6.15pm; Apr, Oct–mid-Nov 11.15am, hourly 2.15pm–5.15pm.* €7 (6-12, €3). ℘06 11 54 27 73. www.cpts.fr. Hop aboard for a 40min commentated tour from the tourist office along the port to the *calanque* of Port-Miou and back.

BARS

xf – *5 quai des Baux. ℘04 42 01 76 09. Open 7am–2am. Closed Tue (off season), 4 Jan–mid-Feb.* Occupying a prime location on the front, this bar attracts some of the celebrities who visit Cassis in the summer, or at least you might see them strolling by.

SHOPPING

Maison des vins – Maison des coquillages – *Rte de Marseille. ✆04 42 01 15 61. www.maisondesvinscassis. com. Open Mon–Sat 9.15am–12.30pm, 2.30pm–7.30pm, Sun 10am–12.30pm (summer 3pm–6pm). Closed public holidays in winter.* Constituting an appellation d'origine controlée (AOC) since 1936, the vineyards of Cassis cover about 170 ha/420 acres, shared among 12 estates. Refined white wines account for 80 percent of production, with rosé and a little red making up the balance. The Maison des vins sells wines from 10 producers, as well as a selection from all over France.

EVENTS

The Cassis Wine Festival and the Feast of St-Éloi *(held the first Sun in September)* offers a good opportunity to sample some excellent local wines.

La Ciotat
Bouches-du-Rhône

La Ciotat, where the houses rise in tiers above the bay of the same name, has been a port since ancient times. Roman occupation, Barbarian invasion and devastation were followed by a revival in the Middle Ages, and from the 16C the provision of a merchant fleet in the eastern Mediterranean. The city continues to fulfil its maritime vocation, particularly by running large shipbuilding yards specialising in oil and methane tankers. However, the worldwide crisis in the shipbuilding industry has scored a direct hit here, and the city is having to adapt to different technologies and to seek new areas of commercial activity, such as tourism. Its beach and fishing port, its cliffs, *calanques* and sea bed attract numerous visitors all year round.

- ▶ **Population:** 33 829.
- ⏱ **Michelin Map:** 340: I-6.
- ℹ **Info:** Boulevard Anatole-France, La Ciotat. ✆04 42 08 61 32. www.laciotat.info.
- ▶ **Location:** Leave the Marseille–Toulon motorway at exit 9 and then follow the D 559 and av. Émile-Bodin, which brings you into town.
- 🕐 **Timing:** This is a pleasant resort for a family holiday outside July and August, when the beaches become packed.
- 👪 **Kids:** Playtime at OK Corral.

SIGHTS
Port Vieux

This old harbour has all the charm of a small fishing port, with its quaysides overlooked by houses painted in bright colours, and lively restaurants.

Église Notre-Dame-du-Port

The church's Baroque façade in shades of pink evokes Italy. From the steps you can see what's going on in the Vieux Port. The modern interior was decorated by local artists: a 22m fresco by Gilbert Ganteaume illustrates scenes from the Gospels, and there are paintings by Tony Roux at the back of the nave. Don't miss the fine *Descent from the Cross* by the Lyon artist André Gaudion (1616).

Musée Ciotaden

1 quai Ganteaume. 🕐*Open daily except Tue: Jul–Aug 4–7pm; Sept–Jun 3–6pm.* 🕐*Closed Mar (enquire about public holiday closures).* ⊛€3.50. *✆04 42 71 40 99. www.museeciotaden.org.*
Inside the former town hall are mementoes and documents about this seafaring town and its past, including a room dedicated to the Lumière brothers.

Parc et Calanque du Mugel

🕐*Open daily Apr–Sept 8am–8pm; Oct–Mar 9am–6pm.* ⊛*No charge. ✆04 42 08 61 32. www.calanques13.com.*

La Ciotat

© C.Chillio/Comité Régional de Tourisme Provence-Alpes-Côte d'Azur

Located at the tip of Cap de l'Aigle, this natural protected area favours abundant and varied vegetation (cork trees, mimosa and arbutus). At the top (steep path), some 155m, there is a lovely view of La Ciotat and its surroundings.

Chapelle Notre-Dame-de-la-Garde

Follow chemin de la Garde for 2.5km/1.5mi by car until you reach a brilliant white housing estate, then 15min on foot.

At the chapel, bear right onto a path which leads to a terrace (85 steps cut out of the rock). The **view**★★ embraces the full extent of La Ciotat bay.

Île Verte★

30min return by boat from Vieux Port.
Departures on the hour May–Jun and Sept Mon–Fri 10am, 11am, noon, 2pm, 3pm, 4pm, 5pm; Jul–Aug 9am–6.45pm; Oct please enquire. Return fare €12. 06 63 59 16 35. www.laciotat-ileverte.com.

The rock at Cap de l'Aigle, so like a bird of prey (*aigle* means eagle) when seen from the small fort on Île Verte, is what gave the point its name.

The Ciotat Calanques

1.5km/0.9mi. Leave La Ciotat along quai de Roumanie, avenue des Calanques and turn left into avenue du Mugel.

These rocky inlets known as *calanques* can also be visited on board a catamaran-type boat with a glass bottom, affording underwater views.

Calanque du Mugel

The inlet is dominated by the rock of Cap de l'Aigle. There is a good view of Île Verte from here.

Calanque de Figuerolles★

15min return on foot.

A short green valley leads to the small clear-water inlet. This curious site is characterised by strangely eroded rocks, including the "Capucin", an isolated crag projecting forwards on the right, and cliffs featuring cavities with sharp edges and a smooth, polished interior.

Clos des Plages

The district has been developed as a resort just north of the Nouveau Port harbour; hotels, outdoor cafés and seaside villas line the beach, making it ideal for family outings. Marking one of the squares open to the sea is a monument to the Lumière brothers, who brought fame to the town with the first showing of a motion picture in 1895. Follow the road towards les Lecques: quite steep paths will lead you to the **plage de Liouquet** (pebbles and reddish cliffs crowned with a pine forest).

EXCURSION
OK Corral

19km/12mi NW on the D 3 then take the N 8 to the left. Open late Mar–early-Nov (check website for specific times and days). €22 (children €20). 04 42 73 80 05. www.okcorral.fr.

Downhill from the N 8, in the centre of a huge pine forest clearing, lies this Wild West-themed amusement park. A chair lift and a small train provide a comfortable tour of the park.

Calanque de Figuerolles

© Yann Guichaoua/age fotostock

Attractions such as Splash Mountain, Serpent Hopi and a rollercoaster at the Gold Rush area offer exciting thrills, but quiet games and rides for all ages are also on offer in the play space. Snack bars, crêperies, drinks stands and picnic areas ensure that visitors are well catered for from the point of view of refreshments.

ADDRESSES

🏨 STAY

Auberge le Revestel– *Le Liouquet (6km/4mi in the direction of Bandol, on the D 559).* ℘*04 42 83 11 06. Closed 16 Jan–9 Feb, Sun eve, Wed. Restaurant*. This bright little inn enjoys a quiet location on the corniche. Bedrooms are simple but comfortable. The dining room offers contemporary regional cuisine and great sea views.

🍽 EAT

Kitch&Cook– *4 pl. Esquiros.* ℘*04 42 03 91 36. www.kitchandcook.com. Closed Sat lunch, Sun.* On a delightful little pedestrianised square, this small restaurant with modern décor offers surprisingly inventive cooking. Ideal for an alfresco lunch.

Les Gourman'dînent– *18 r. des Combattants.* ℘*04 42 08 00 60. Out of season closed Wed, Sat lunch, Sun dinner.* With its large terrace looking straight down on the Vieux Port, this is an attractive spot for food lovers. Refined cuisine with the colours of the south.

SHOPPING

Markets – The **traditional** market is held every Tuesday 8am–noon in place Évariste-Gras and on Sundays at the Vieux Port. In July and August there is a **craft** market every evening from 8pm–1am at the Vieux Port.

Le Palais d'Emma – *4 av. Géry (in front of the old covered market).* ℘*04 42 04 94 45. 9am–1pm, 3–8pm, Dec 8am–8pm. Closed Wed, Sun afternoon.* Trendy retro-style deli offering a good-quality charcuterie, pasta, tapenades etc.

ACTIVITIES

Boat Trip to the Calanques
♿*See Les Calanques, Addresses.*

Parc Régional Marin de la Baie de la Ciotat – Information at the town hall. Famous for the rich diversity of its seabed life, La Ciotat bay is now a protected regional park, thanks to strict measures enforced for its preservation, whereby fishing, deep-sea diving and mooring are strictly regulated.

La Côte Bleue★

Bouches-du-Rhône

The Chaîne de l'Estaque, which divides the Étang de Berre from the Mediterranean, is an unusual limestone formation, arid in appearance and almost uninhabited except for a few small fishing villages sheltered by deep inlets in the steep coastline. The area is much appreciated by the locals from Marseille and is known as the "Côte Bleue", due to the intense cobalt or sapphire blue of its sparkling waters. The Parc Marin de la Côte Bleue, a natural marine reserve, extends along the coast between the ports of Niolon and Carro, at the foot of the Massif de la Nerthe. Note that fishing, scuba diving and mooring are prohibited.

- **Michelin Map:** 340: F-5 to G-5.
- **Info:** East side of marina, along quai Vayssiere, towards the Harbour Office, Carry-le-Rouet. ℘04 42 13 20 36. www.otcarrylerouet.fr.
- **Don't Miss:** A fun way to explore the coastline and its beaches is by train. *See Addresses.*
- **Timing:** Spend a week here at one of the hotels or campsites, or a day visiting the villages by car, bus or train.

🚗 DRIVING TOUR

MARSEILLE TO PORT-DE-BOUC
74km/46mi. About 4hr.

Niolon★
The lovely little village retains a traditional atmosphere where it clings to the hillside above a *calanque* of the same name. It is a good spot for deep-sea diving (*see Addresses: Centre UPCA de Niolon*).

▷ Return to the D 5, which will be on your left. An arid landscape leads to Ensuès. On entering the village turn left and take the D 48D.

La Madrague-de-Gignac
A pretty spot at the end of a *calanque*, with a cluster of small villas underneath pines. From the minuscule port there is a good view across to Marseille.

▷ Returning to Ensuès make a left turn onto the D 5, which goes down the vallon de l'Aigle, bordered by pines and holm oaks in the direction of Carry.

Le Rouet-Plage
Paying car park at weekends, school and public holidays.
This pretty creek with elegant homes dotted through the pine forest to either side leads to a pleasant cove of large stones.

▷ Continue on the D5 in the direction of "Carry Centre".

Carry-le-Rouet
This one-time fishing village is now a seaside resort. Summer residences can be seen in the woods that line the bay. There are plenty of seafood restaurants on the port where you can eat sea urchins, among other specialities.

👥 Sausset-les-Pins
This fishing village and seaside resort has a fine promenade from which you can look across the sea to Marseille. Dominated by the **château** of the Charles-Roux family (1855), this seaside resort depended for many years on fishing, particularly the **seinche au thon ("tuna round-up")**. Every year this extraordinary fishing expedition brought together all the men of the village. They surrounded the banks of tuna with their boats, driving them into a round net. The impressive annual catch has been immortalised by numerous

GETTING THERE

BY CAR: A transverse road cuts across the mountain chain, running along the hinterland (except between Carry and Sausset-les-Pins). Most of the harbours can be reached only down a dead-end road. In the summer, especially during weekends, access to the *calanques* of Niolon and Redonne is sometimes prohibited to reduce the risk of fire in an area with a particularly fragile ecosystem.

BY TRAIN: Between Marseille and Martigues there is a train which makes several stops at the beaches of the Côte Bleue. The train is fun to ride, as it chugs along through tunnels and past gorgeous views of the sea, blowing its whistle to warn daydreamers who enjoy rambling along the tracks!

painters. Today Sausset is better known for its **creeks** and **beaches**, some of them along the attractive promenade de la Corniche and avenue Général-Leclerc.

◐ D 49 leaves the coast and winds its way up the massif. Drive toward La Couronne by way of the D 49B. Turn right before the church and head for Cap Couronne.

Cap Couronne

From the lighthouse on the point there is a view right round to Marseille,

with the Chaîne de l'Estaque in the foreground, the Chaîne de l'Étoile and the Marseilleveyre. The huge beach of La Couronne is popular and is a favourite spot among Marseille's young set.

Carro

The attractive small fishing village and resort lies well protected at the back of a rock-strewn bay. There is a fish market held every morning at the port.

◐ Leave Carro via the D 49 and continue to Les Ventrons.

Calanque de Niolon

© G. Labriet/Photononstopa

Oursinades

The glorious days that usually characterise the winter months are the setting for the "Oursinades", a sea urchin festival which takes place in January in Sausset and February in Carry. The streets around the port are invaded with long tables where people sit down to tuck into sea urchins and other seafood accompanied by white wine. A lively time is guaranteed!

The road climbs through an arid landscape of dark pines against white limestone and, at 120m, looks back *(observation tower)* over the industrial harbour complex of Lavéra, Port-de-Bouc and Fos.

Saint-Julien-les-Martigues

Leaving the town, a path to the left leads to a **chapel**. Attached to the wall on the left-hand side is a Gallo-Roman bas-relief (1C) depicting a funeral scene.

▶ At Les Ventrons turn right onto the D 5 for Martigues.

Martigues
See opposite.

ADDRESSES

STAY

Auberge du Mérou – *Calanque de Niolon, 13740 Niolon, 5km/3mi from Rove, on the road to Niolon.* ℘04 91 46 98 69. www.aubergedumerou.fr. *5 rooms. Restaurant . Closed Sun and Mon eves during low season.* Decorated like cabins in a boat, the rooms look out over the port of Niolon. The restaurant is known for its seafood.

Villa-Arena – *Pl. Camille-Pelletan, 13620 Carry-le-Rouet.* ℘04 42 45 00 12. . *19 rooms.* The elegant façade of this hotel makes an immediate impression and its air-conditioned rooms are spotless and comfortable. Prices may be a little on the high side, but are typical of the area.

EAT

La Pergola – *Calanque de Niolon, 13740 Le Rove. 5km/3mi from village of Le Rove, on road to Niolon.* ℘04 91 46 90 28. *Off season closed Wed, Fri, Sat evenings.* Generous fish dishes at reasonable prices and an unbeatable view of the port of Niolon and Marseille, a pleasure that shouldn't be missed!

Les Girelles – *r. Frédéric Mistral, Sausset-les-Pins.* ℘04 42 45 26 16. www.restaurant-les-girelles.com. *Closed Oct, mid-Jan–mid-Feb, Sun evening low season, Jun–Aug Tue and Wed lunch, Mon.* The terrace bordering the beach is very popular with locals. Inside, there is a pretty model ship and plenty of picture windows that make the most of the view. Appetising and well-presented cooking.

ACTIVITIES

Markets – Sausset-les-Pins has a **traditional** market on Thursday morning at the quai du Port, and Sun morning along av. Armand-Audibert. **Fish** market daily from 9am at quai du Port.

Brousse du Rove – Gaec Gouiran – *17 r. Adrien-Isnardon, 13740 Le Rove.* ℘04 91 09 92 33. *Feb–Oct 8am–noon, 5pm–7.30pm.* . To taste really fresh cheese, make an appointment with M. and Mme Gouiran. They raise the famous Rove goats and produce various different cheeses, from super-fresh to extra-dry, including delicate, perfumed examples of real, pure-goat *brousse du Rove*. A speciality of the area, this unique cheese has its own certified trademark.

Centre UCPA de Niolon – *18 chemin de la Batterie, Le Rove, Niolon.* ℘04 91 46 90 16. www.ucpa-vacances.com. *Closed mid-Nov–mid-Mar.* This is one of Europe's largest diving centres, catering for all levels from beginners to instructors.

Martigues
Bouches-du-Rhône

- ▶ **Population:** 47 544.
- ⟁ **Michelin Map:** 340: F-5.
- ▤ **Info:** Rond-point de l'Hôtel de Ville, 13500 Martigues. ℰ04 42 42 31 10. www.martigues-tourisme.com.
- ⊜ **Don't Miss:** Provençal water jousting on the canals (June–August); and the St Peter's Day Festival (end June).

Martigues was nicknamed "the Venice of Provence" by its past admirers – a description that seems rather exaggerated today, especially in view of its heavily industrial hinterland. Even so, this old fishing village, criss-crossed by canals which link the Étang de Berre with the sea, has managed to cling on to a gentle pace of life in its narrow, brightly coloured streets.

This makes it easy to understand why painters (Corot, Ziem) and writers (Charles Maurras) were captivated by its luminosity and charm. The most attractive area is the quartier de l'Île, separated from the rest of the town by two canals.

WALKING TOUR

Miroir aux Oiseaux★
Pont St-Sébastien on Île Brescon affords a view of the brightly coloured pleasure craft along Canal St-Sébastien. Popular with painters, this spot is known as the Birds' Looking Glass.

Église Sainte-Madeleine-de-l'Île
Built along the Saint-Sébastien canal, this church with its Corinthian-style façade (17C) has a richly decorated interior and an impressive Baroque organ case.

Musée Ziem
bd du 14 Juillet. ⊙Open Jul–Aug 10am–noon, 2.3–6.30pm. Sept–Jun daily except Tue 2.30–6.30pm. ⊙Closed 1 Jan, 1 May, 14 Jul, 15 Aug, 1 Nov and 25 Dec. Guided tours (1hr) on request. €8. ℰ04 42 41 39 60. www.musees-mediterranee.org.
Grouped around the works of Félix Ziem (1821–1911), Impressionist painter of landscapes and oriental scenes, are works by Provençal artists from the 19C and 20C. Fauvist works by Raoul Dufy, André Derain, Francis Picabia and Henri Manguin are displayed. Also exhibited in the museum are collections of local ethnology and archaeology and an exhibition of contemporary art.

Galerie de l'Histoire de Martigues
Hôtel-de-Ville. ⊙Open Jul–Sept 10am–12.30pm, 3–7pm; Oct–Jun Mon–Fri 9am–noon, 1.30–6.30pm, Sat–Sun 2.30–6.30pm. Commentated tours weekends 3pm and 5pm. Closed 1 Jan, 1 May, 25 Dec. No charge. ℰ04 42 44 31 51. www.ville-martigues.fr.
Unbeatable for an understanding of Martigues and its huge transformation over the past 50 years, this modern display uses the latest museum technology to re-create the history of the town and its inhabitants through documents, photographs, models, interactive screens and videos.

Martigues

Chapelle de l'Annonciade

r. du Dr-Sérieux. Guided tours must be booked ahead. 04 42 42 31 10.
This old chapel of the White Pénitents, classified as a historic monument, stands behind the Saint-Geniès church. It will delight fans of Provençal Baroque style, with its gilded panelling, frescoes representing the life of the Virgin, and a painted ceiling whose rich decoration contrasts with the building's sober exterior.

👫 Grand Parc de Figuerolles

Rte. d'Istres (D5), northern approaches to Martigues. 04 42 49 11 42.
Near the étang de Berre, this 130ha/320-acre park has a picnic area, a model farm, fitness trails in the trees *(fee charged)*, and paths through the pine forest for walking, mountain biking, or horseback riding *(fee charged)*. Nearby are a bowling alley and cinema complex.

EXCURSIONS
Beaches

If you don't take a dip in the Étang de Berre, there are six beaches to choose from on the coastal side of Martigues. Most popular is the sandy plage du Verdon (*see La Côte Bleue*), which attracts 11 000 people on summer weekends. Quieter beaches are Carro, Bonnieu *(naturist creek)*, Saulce, Laurons and Sainte-Croix.
The Verdon, Saulce, Sainte-Croix and Laurons beaches are supervised in high season. A cycle route links Martigues with Carro beach.

Fos-sur-Mer

11km/9mi to the west on the N 568. Allow 2hr. Tourist Office: 50 av.Jean-Jaurès. 04 42 47 71 96. www.fos-sur-mer.fr.
Perched on a rocky outcrop, Fos evokes the typical idea of a Provençal village. It is named after the Fosses Mariennes, a canal dug at the mouth of the Rhône by Marius' legions in 102 BCE (*fosse*: canal). The development of the new complex, the largest in southern Europe and which complements the port of Marseille, was begun in 1965 on the

Golfe de Fos. The advantages of the site, some 10,000ha/24,700 acres, are a deep-water channel, a low tidal range, and the stony surface of the Plaine de la Crau that makes an ideal foundation for an industrial estate.

The Village★

The village retains the ruins of its 14C castle, which once belonged to the Viscounts of Marseille, as well as the église St-Saveur (*quartier de l'Hauture*), with its Romanesque nave.
The chief attraction, however, lies in the views from the terrace and rampart garden.

The Port

The combined Marseille-Fos complex is the largest port in France and third-largest in Europe.

🚗 DRIVING TOUR

THE WEST COAST AND L'ÉTANG DE BERRE
113km/70mi round-trip. Allow 1 day.

▶ Leave Martigues by the D 5.

St-Mitre-les-Remparts

The old town, encircled by 15C ramparts, stands just off the road. A network of small streets and alleys leads to the church where there is a view of the Étang d'Engrenier.

▶ Leave St-Mitre-les-Remparts by the D 51.

There is a good view on the right of the Étang de Berre; the road skirts the Étang de Citis before passing the foot of the hill on which stands Chapelle St-Blaise, the east end of which is just visible among the pine trees.

St-Blaise archaeological site
Bouches-du-Rhône. Open Apr–Oct daily except Mon 8.30am–noon, 2–6pm; Nov–Mar 8.30am–noon, 1.30pm–5pm. No charge. 04 42 30 30 83.

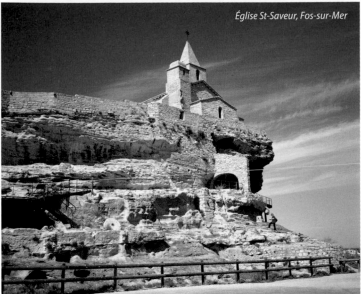

Église St-Saveur, Fos-sur-Mer

©Baier Klaus/age fotostock

The oppidum of St-Blaise (in the commune of St-Mitre-les-Remparts) is a historic site, the wealth of which depended, during the Hellenic occupation, on the working and trading of salt. After abandonment for 400 years, it was reoccupied between the 4C and the 14C.

The settlement of St-Blaise (its ancient name could be Heraclea or Mastramellè) takes the form of a fortified spur, the natural defences of which, tall vertical cliffs, are reinforced by ramparts from the Hellenistic period; these were built on the most accessible side, which overlooks Lavalduc valley.

Etruscan St-Blaise – The oldest traces of human existence date back to early 5000 BCE. The group of small lagoons, which link the east arm of the River Rhône to Berre lagoon, most probably contributed to the discovery of the site by Etruscan sailors in the 7C BCE. They established a trading post and began a successful trade, exchanging salt collected here for wine from Etruria. The settling of the Phocaeans at Marseille in c.600 BCE brought about serious competition between St-Blaise and Marseille; nevertheless, the discovery of Etruscan, Corinthian and Ionian pottery has proved that the settlement progressed.

In the second half of the 7C, the settlement formed a proto-urban town surrounded by a wall. As in Entremont, a lower and an upper town were established. The dwellings were built of stone on a square plan; one in the lower town still has its walls at a height of 0.9m.

A long period of transition (475–200 BCE) then took place, after a fire, marked by the departure of the Etruscans from the trading post, and Marseille took over. It has been suggested that there was a possible period of withdrawal, judging from the absence of human dwellings.

Hellenistic Ramparts★ – From the late 3C to the mid-1C BCE the settlement reached its apex: commerce picked up under the influence of Marseille, which held St-Blaise without, however, making it a colony.

Large projects for levelling of the terrain preceded the establishment of an urban plan and a strong fortified wall. The very high **ramparts★** were raised under the direction of Greek craftsmen between 175 and 140 BCE; they are more than

©S. Sauvignier/MICHELIN

The Étang de Berre

The Étang de Berre (Berre Lagoon), 15 530ha/60sq mi in extent and nowhere more than 9m deep, has been France's principal petroleum port for about the last 80 years. The Canal de Caronte, dredged out where there was once a lagoon of the same name, provides a passage to the Mediterranean, as does the underground Rove section of the Marseille-Rhône canal. The lagoon is fed fresh water by the Arc and Touloubre rivers and the EDF canal (Électricité de France), and is ringed by limestone hills: the Lançon chain to the north, the Vitrolles to the east, the Estaque to the south, and the St-Mitre to the west.

A Bit of History

The region was largely uninhabited when, in 1920, under the San Remo Agreement, France obtained the right to purchase the major part of Iraq's annual crude oil production. The lagoon was transformed into the ideal port for shallow-draught oil tankers, at the same time harbours also began to be developed on the Golfe de Fos: the French BP company set up at Lavéra in 1922–24, Shell-Berre at the Pointe de Berre in 1928 and the Compagnie Française de Raffinage at La Mède in 1934. Esso has had installations in Fos since 1965.

At the turn of the 20C, the peaceful lagoons and deserted Crau plain were an ideal testing ground for pioneer aviators. The very first military aerodrome was established in Istres before World War I and still operates today. Since then it has expanded considerably and now occupies 2,031ha/5,017 acres.

Until 1940, Berre was the most important hydroplane base of the National Marines. When a civil airport was required for Marseille, the Marseille-Provence airport was sited at the east end of the Étang de Berre at Marignane.

The growth in demand for oil, apparent even in 1938, brought about the transformation of Lavéra soon after the war, to enable 90,000-ton tankers to dock and pump their cargoes directly into onshore installations. In the 1960s a new port was constructed at Martigues. The lagoon complex is also the terminal of the South European Oil Pipeline. This line, inaugurated in 1962, supplies a dozen European refineries.

However, the petrol crisis of 1973 led to a slight reduction in the capacity of the refineries, which were obliged to adapt to the fall in demand. The petrochemicals industry has continued to develop in more recent years, contributing to a transformation of the landscape.

The Étang de Berre is also important today because Marseille-Provence international airport, the second most important airport in France in terms of passenger traffic, is sited on its southeastern shore.

1km/0.6mi long and cut by towers and bastions, equipped with three posterns and a gateway and crowned at the top with merlons. The wall was equipped with a system of water evacuation via channels. It had hardly been finished when the settlement underwent a violent siege (dozens of cannonballs have been discovered), which historians are still trying to date.

According to a recent theory, having escaped the control of Marseille a short time after the ramparts were completed, St-Blaise may have been taken over by the Romans during their conquest from 125 to 123 BCE. After this event, St-Blaise went through a period of total decline; after its brief reoccupation in the mid-1C BCE the site was totally abandoned for four centuries.

Palaeochristian and Medieval St-Blaise – With the rise of insecurity at the end of the Roman empire, the Hellenistic fortifications were reused: in the 5C the wall was surmounted by an ornamentation of irregular blocks of stone. Two churches were built: St-Vincent (the apse of which is near the ancient main gate) and St-Pierre (destroyed in the 9C). A necropolis (tombs carved into the rock) extended to the south. The living quarters of this settlement were unfortunately difficult to identify among the other ruins.

In 874, Ugium (the name of the settlement at that time) was destroyed by the Saracens. It recovered slowly, St-Pierre was rebuilt in the 10C, then burned down, then reconstructed again in the 11C (substructures have been found near the chapel of St-Blaise). In 1231, at the plateau's northernmost point a new wall was built to protect the town of Castelveyre (its new name) with its new church Notre-Dame-et-St-Blaise around which the dwellings nestled.

In 1390 Raymond de Turenne's band of brigands pillaged the town. The site was never to be resettled; the last inhabitants settled at St-Mitre. At the end of the spur, a fine view of the Étang de Lavalduc and the Bassins de Fos opens out.

Istres

Despite the town's rapid development, the old village of Istres still retains its Provençal appearance. The **Musée Archéologique d'Istres** (4 pl. José Coto. ⊘ closed for renovation. ℘04 42 11 27 72) presents local history: palaeontology, zoology, prehistory, underwater archaeology, and the economic life of Istres, Fos and Miramas.

▷ Circle the Étang de l'Olivier by way of the D 53 and then turn left onto the D 16, which returns to the Étang de Berre.

Miramas-le-Vieux★

The small town on a flat ledge of rock has preserved its medieval ramparts and the ruins of its 13C castle.

▷ Return to the D 10 and take the D 16 across the way and then the D 70D. At Le Pont-de-Rhaud bear right onto the D 70A.

Cornillon-Confoux

At the centre of the hill village stands a small Romanesque church with a bell gable and modern stained-glass windows by Frédérique Duran. There are good local **views★** from the walk which starts at the church and circles the village.

▷ Take the D 70 and a tourist road on the right to St-Chamas.

Saint-Chamas

This charming village, now with only a few fishing families left, is dominated by a small, triple-arched aqueduct. The church is 17C with a Baroque west front.

Pont Flavien

This bridge, to the south of St-Chamas, crosses the Touloubre in a single span.

ADDRESSES

🏠 STAY

Hôtel Le Castellan– *15 bd Léon Blum, 13800 Istres.* ℘*04 42 55 13 09. www.hotel-lecastellan.com.* 🅿. *17 rooms.*This modern hotel is very close to the étang de l'Olivier. Spacious rooms and attentive staff make up for the rather bland setting.

Clair Hôtel – *57 bd Marcel-Cachin.* ℘*04 42 13 52 52.* 🅿. *32 rooms.* This hotel has been rejuvenated. Leather chairs and old furniture picked up from antique shops still have their place in the plush interior, but they are now combined with ultra-modern conveniences (jacuzzi, air-conditioning, internet).

Hôtel St-Roch – *Av. Georges-Braque, A 55, Martigues-Ferrières exit.* ℘*04 42 42 36 36. www.hotelsaintroch.com.* 🅿. *61 rooms. Restaurant.* Up above the town and shaded by pine trees, this modern hotel has huge rooms which have been completed renovated and which are very well equipped. Pool and solarium.

Hôtel Ariane – *12 av. de Flore, 13800 Istres.* ℘*04 42 11 13 13. www.ariane hotel.com.* ⟓. *49 rooms.* The rooms in this sizeable, reliable hotel are modern and comfortable. Pool, garden and attentive staff.

Chambre d'hôte Embarben – *577 Rte de Grans, 13250 St-Chamas.* ℘*06 84 95 57 16. www.embarben.fr.* ⟓. *6 rooms.* In bucolic parkland with pond and sheep meadow stands this fine *maison de maître.* The delightfully retro rooms have plenty of character. Kitchen garden, orchard and pool.

Chambre d'hôte La Magnanerie – *Imp. de la Glacière, 13450 Grans, 6km/4mi north of Miramas-le-Vieux.* ℘*04 90 55 98 96. www.lamagnanerie-grans.com. Closed Nov–Mar.* ⟓. *4 rooms. Table d'hote.* Right in the centre of the village, this imposing 18C *bastide* has a vast salon and individually decorated rooms. A harmonious mix of polished wood, junk-shop finds, objects from world travels and design pieces creates a unique atmosphere.

🍽 EAT

Pincée de Sel– *29 cours Jean Jaurès, 13800 Istres.* ℘*04 42 55 03 16. Closed Sat lunch, Sun.* A pleasant place to enjoy contemporary cooking at modest prices in a designer setting.

La Bergerie– *Le Guéby Sud, rte de Marseille, 13250 St-Chamas.* ℘*04 90 50 82 29 or 06 60 50 82 29. www.restaurant-la-bergerie.fr.* This restaurant housed in a beautiful stone building serves appetising Provençal cuisine. Attractive, rustic dining room and sweet little terrace.

Les Ombrelles – *Plage de Ste-Croix, La Couronne.* ℘*04 42 80 77 61. Open late Mar–mid-Nov 9am–10.15pm.* With its terrace right above the beach of Sainte-Croix, this is the place where swimmers like to come for an ice cream – but there is also a full menu. Fantastic views.

Le Planet– *Pl. Jean Jaurès, 13450 Grans.* ℘*04 90 55 83 66. Closed Sun and Mon eve.* Tucked away in an old olive oil mill, this small restaurant serves local dishes in a pleasant interior with a vaulted ceiling and stone walls. Nice terrace shaded by plane trees.

Le Bouchon à la Mer – *19 quai Lucien-Toulmond.* ℘*04 42 49 41 41. Closed Sun eve, Mon and Tue lunch.* Just a few steps from the "miroir aux oiseaux" (⏳*see p149*), this restaurant serves classic cuisine in a pretty dining room or on a canal-side terrace.

Le Garage – *20 av. Frédéric-Mistral.* ℘*04 42 44 09 51. www.restaurantmartigues. com. Closed 1–15 Jan, 10–25 Aug, Sat lunch, Sun eve, Mon.* Centrally located with fashionable décor and a modern menu, Le Garage has a young chef at the helm.

Le Rabelais – *8 r. A.-Fabre, 13250 St-Chamas.* ℘*04 90 50 84 40. www.restaurant-le-rabelais.com. Closed Sun eve, Wed eve, Mon.* Expect inventive cooking in this restaurant which occupies a pretty, vaulted room in a restored 17C corn mill. It has a pretty, flower-filled terrace.

La Table de Sébastien– *7 av. Hélène-Boucher, 13800 Istres.* ℘*04 42 55 16 01. www.latabledesebastien.fr. Closed 1 wk Apr, 2 wks late Aug–early Sept, Sun eve, Mon and Tue lunch.* Seductive and extremely creative cooking from a young chef, plus an excellent selection of local wines, either in the renovated dining room or on the terrace.

EVENTS

Festival de Martigues, Danses Musiques et Voix du monde – *www.festivaldemartigues.com.* Theatre, dance, music and song from all over the world, on a floating stage on the canal. First week of July.

Aubagne

Bouches-du-Rhône

Famous for its pottery, Aubagne lies in the verdant basin of the Huveaune valley, dominated to the northwest by the Chaîne de l'Étoile. Although its location has been favourable to industrial expansion and local food production, the once-fortified town has preserved some of its old ramparts and a 12C church remodelled in the 17C. The popular French author, playwright and film-maker Marcel Pagnol (1895–1974) was born here and lived at 16 cours Barthélémy.

A BIT OF HISTORY

Aubagne's pottery tradition, which developed as a result of its clay quarries, dates back to Antiquity. This tradition became established during the Gallo-Roman period with the manufacture of amphorae and ceramics and turned to tile production in the Middle Ages.

In the 19C, the production of *santons* was started and is carried on today in a score of cottage industries dotted throughout the old town. The ceramic coating of ships such as the *Normandie*, the *France* or the *De Grasse* originates from Aubagne's workshops.

WALKING TOUR

The historic centre lies within the ancient fortified ramparts of which a few vestiges remain, including the 14C Gachiou doorway, one of the seven original gates to the medieval city.

The small, narrow streets reveal a number of architectural curiosities – the quaint triangular belfry of the late 17C Chapelle de l'Observance *(place de l'Observance)*, the Tour de l'Horloge and its superb wrought-iron bell tower, the fine, white Baroque front of the Chapelle des Pénitents Blancs and the more Classical façade (1551) of the Chapelle des Pénitents Noirs (chemin de St-Michel).

▶ **Population:** 46 423.
Michelin Map: 340: I-6 or 114 folds 29 and 30.
Info: 8 cours Barthélémy, Aubagne. ℘04 42 03 49 98. www.tourisme-paysdaubagne.fr.
Location: The town is 15min by TER train from Marseille.
Timing: Allow half a day to visit Pagnol sites and *santons* makers.

Birthplace of Marcel Pagnol

16 cours Barthélémy, information from tourist office. &Open Apr–Oct Tue, Thu 2–6pm, Wed, Fri–Sun 10am–1pm, 2–6pm; Nov–Mar Tue–Sun 2–5.30pm. Closed 1 Jan, 1 May, 25 Dec. €3 (under 12s €1.50). ℘04 42 03 49 98.

In this beautiful three-storey bourgeois house with wrought-iron balconies, the apartment which belonged to Marcel Pagnol's father, a teacher, has been re-created. A museum space focuses on Pagnol's childhood with letters, photographs and other relevant material.

Le Petit Monde de Marcel Pagnol

Esplanade Charles de Gaulle. Open Jul–Aug 10am–12.30pm, 2.30–7pm; May–Jun and Sept daily except Sun

Aubagne and the Massif de la Sainte-Baume

© Nicolas Thibaut/Photononstop

10am–12.30pm, 2.30–6pm; Dec–Jan 10am–12.30pm, 2.30–6pm; Mar 10am–12.30pm. ⏱*Closed Feb, Apr, Oct–Nov.* ⬭*No charge.* ☎*04 42 18 19 19. www.marcel-pagnol.com.*
This display consists of a crib with *santons* illustrating the popular characters that feature in Pagnol's films and literary works.

Ateliers Thérèse-Neveu
4 Cour de Clastre. ♿⏱*Open daily except Mon 10am–noon, 2–6pm.* ☎*04 42 03 43 10.*
This huge exhibition hall occupies the former workshop of Thérèse Neveu, a famous *santon* maker from Aubagne. It is devoted to the art of clay and other related industries. It features a standing retrospective on the history of ceramics in the town and hosts temporary exhibitions on a variety of themes associated with *santons* and pottery.

EXCURSIONS
Musée de la Légion Étrangère★
Access via D 2 towards Marseille, turn right on D 44A. ⏱*Open 10am–noon, 2–6pm.* ⏱*Closed mid-Dec–Jan.* ⬭*No charge.* ☎*04 42 18 12 41. www.legion-etrangere.com.*
A must for anybody who is interested in military history. On the ground floor, the great hall opens onto the Salle d'Honneur, with memorabilia belonging to the Legion's great leaders. On the first floor are numerous historical documents, photographs, arms and uniforms, including the wooden hand of Captain Jean Danjou, who led the Legion in their heroic last stand during the Battle of Camarón (1863). Camerone Day is still celebrated by Legionnaires on 30 April.

Chapelle Saint-Jean-de-Garguier
5.5km/3.4mi northeast on D 2, direction Gémenos, then left on to D 396, then D 43D on right.
Dedicated to St John the Baptist, this 17C chapel to which there is a pilgrimage on 24 June has moving ex-votos painted on

wood, canvas and zinc. There are over 300, mainly dating from the 18C and 19C, naive and touching expressions of popular piety.

Le Massif du Garlaban
Sparkling in the sun, this vast, rocky desert is an oasis for ramblers who come to recharge their batteries in the footsteps of Marcel Pagnol. Having spent his childhood summers in the family *bastide*, under the Taoumé and Garlaban summits, the writer and film-maker used these as the setting for many novels and films including the famous *Manon des Sources*. He is still such an important part of the landscape that you will often hear mention of the "hills of Marcel Pagnol". Situated 15km/9.3mi to the east of Marseille, the massif extends over 8,000ha/20,000 acres, spread across **four communes**: Allauch, Aubagne, Marseille and Roquevaire. Allow about 3hrs to explore the massif's hamlets and small towns – or much longer if you are planning to follow Pagnol's example and hike!
⬭ **Warning:** as in all the nature reserves of the Bouches-du-Rhône, access to the massif is strictly controlled from 1 July to mid-September. Open to the public 6am–11am, the area closes when there is a risk of fire. Check before setting out (☎*08 11 20 13 13).* The rest of the year, the same precautions apply on windy days.

La Treille
8km/5mi to the northwest. Leave Aubagne on the D 4, direction Camoins. Cross the village, then keep right to la Treille. ⬭*Warning: parking in the narrow little streets can be stressful! Leave the car at the village entrance and continue on foot to the chemin des Bellons (signposted).*
In the little streets of this charming hamlet it is difficult to believe that you are in the 11th *arrondissement* of Marseille. As a child, Marcel Pagnol spent magical summers at la Bastide-Neuve. The house is still standing, at the end of the chemin des Bellons (⬬*private, plaque on the front wall).* The path climbs on up

into the hills; marked trails take hikers towards the peaks of le Taoumé and le Garlaban and the grotto of le Grosibou, all dear to Pagnol. Later you can visit the writer's grave in the **cemetery**, at the entrance to the hamlet.

Allauch★

16km/10mi to the northwest. Leave Aubagne by the D 2, direction Marseille, then at Valentine turn right on to the D 4A. Surrounded by the Étoile chain of hills and the **massif du Garlaban**, Allauch (pronounced "Allau") is in the outer suburbs of Marseille. Even so, old Allauch exudes the charm of an authentic Provençal village, with its pastel houses and windmills buttressed against the chalk hills. From the **place des Moulins** (with 5 windmills), there are fine **views★** of Marseille.

▲· Musée d'Allauch – *Pl. du Dr-Chevillon.* ᴋ.◐*Open Jun–Sept 9am–12.30pm, 2–6pm; rest of year 9am–noon, 1.30–6pm.* ◐*Closed public holidays.* ◉€3 (under 18 no charge). ℘*04 91 10 49 00. www.musee.allauch.com.* Within the old town hall, this museum focuses on sacred art. A dynamic team and an up-to-the-minute approach which appeals to young people make it particularly worthwhile. You will not be bored exploring the roots of western Christian culture here. The museum's star exhibit: a 14C Romanesque Virgin carved in wood. One room is devoted to the history of Allauch.

ADDRESSES

🏠 STAY

⊜🍴**Hôtel L'Eau des Collines** – *45 rte de La Treille, Camoins-les-Bains, 13011 Marseille.* ℘*04 91 43 06 00. www.hotel-eau-des-collines.fr. 14 rooms. Restaurant*⊜🍴. This family establishment on the road to La Treille benefits from the calm of the surrounding countryside. Rooms are simple but welcoming.

⊜🍴 **Hôtel Les Cigales** – *Rte Enco-de-Botte, 13190 Allauch.* ℘*04 91 68 17 07. www.hotel-lescigales.fr.* ⏚🅿. *6 rooms,*

1 suite. Restaurant ⊜🍴. A relatively new hotel with a family atmosphere between Marseille and Allauch. Quiet rooms and a garden with pool.

⊜🍴🍴**Chambre d'hôte Le Mas des Pins** – *Chemin des Arnauds.* ℘*04 42 84 94 43. Closed Jan.* ⏚🍴. *3 rooms, 2 suites.* In the Aubagne countryside at the foot of the Massif du Garlaban, this is a typical Provençal house surrounded by a large garden with a pool.

⊜🍴🍴**Hostellerie de la Source** – *St-Pierre-les-Aubagne.5km/3mi north of Aubagne by the D 96 or D 43.* ℘*04 42 04 09 19. www.hostelleriedelasource.com.* ᴋ.⏚. *26 rooms.* Standing in wooded parkland with a spring which supplies the hotel, this is a fine buidling from the 17C with a modern annexe. Well maintained, air-conditioned rooms and a lovely pool.

▯/ EAT

⊜**Café des Arts** – *10 r. du Jeune Anacharsis. 6am–midnight.* ℘*04 42 03 12 36.* Nice eating place near cours Foch. Young and animated clientele. Dishes of the day, much appreciated by locals, are served on the terrace or in the dining room.

⊜🍴 **Les Arômes** – *8 r. Moussard.* ℘*04 42 03 72 93. Closed Tue eve, Wed eve, Sat lunch, Sun, Mon.* You will be welcomed like a personal friend in this family restaurant carefully decorated by the lady of the house. The short seasonal menu presents traditional recipes with a modern twist.

⊜🍴🍴**La Ferme** – *La Font de Mai, chemin Ruissatel. 4km/2.5mi north of Aubagne by the D 44.* ℘*04 42 03 29 67. www.aubergelaferme. com. Closed Aug and Feb half term, Sat lunch, Mon and all eves ex Fri and Sat.* Enjoy hearty, generous food based on fresh market produce in this country house opposite Mont Garlaban. The dining-room walls are decorated with plates. A fine terrace is shaded by an oak.

SHOPPING

Markets – Traditional market Tue, Thu, Sat and Sun along *cours Voltaire.* **Antique market** on the last Sun of the month at the Tourtelle wholesale market.

Poterie Ravel – *av. des Goumes.* ℘*04 42 82 42 00. www.poterie-ravel.com. Closed Sun, except in May.* Terra-cotta objects and pottery pieces for the garden and home are found in this place, which has been operating since 1837.

Massif de la Sainte-Baume★★

The longest and highest mountain range in Provence, the Massif de la Sainte-Baume is a huge, craggy wall of chalk and verdant forest rising up behind La Ciotat and Toulon. Regarded by the people of Marseille in ancient times as a sacred mountain associated with fertility rites, it has attracted Christian pilgrims for aeons because Mary Magdalene is believed to have spent the last 33 years of her life here. For many others, it is a place to enjoy spectacular views, wide-open spaces and a protected forest like no other in Provence.

- ⚲ **Michelin Map:** 340: J6.
- ▯ **Info:** www.visitvar.fr/ Provence-cote-azur/massif- de-la-sainte-baume.aspx.
- ▷ **Location:** 20km/12mi inland, east of Aubagne and north of Toulon.
- ☺ **Don't miss:** Sweep- ing views from the summit of Saint-Pilon; Mary Magdalene's grotto and crypt.
- ◷ **Timing**: Go in spring when the Judas trees are in flower. Allow at least half a day.

🚗 DRIVING TOUR

107km/67mi, starting from Gémenos– driving time about 1hr40min with no stops.

Gémenos

On the threshold of the green valley of Saint-Pons, in the valley of l'Huveaune, this beautiful village is worth stopping in for a stroll. It is criss-crossed with little streets and has a **château** dating from the end of the 17C.

▷ Take the D 2, direction Plan- d'Aups-Ste-Baume.

Parc de Saint-Pons★

Leave the car in the car park (⊜no charge) and follow the path along the stream.

An old abandoned mill near a waterfall created by water from the Vaucluse spring of Saint-Pons, a Cistercian abbey founded in 13C and the chapel of Saint-Martin with a Romanesque doorway are tucked into this oasis of freshness which is shaded by abundant vegetation (beech, ash, maple and other species rare in Provence). If possible, come in spring when, lit up by the flowers of the Judas trees, the park shines brightly.

▷ Continue east on the D 2.

Climb up a series of hairpin bends on the south side of the massif, where a deep amphitheatre has been hollowed out. At the **col de l'Espigoulier★** (alt. 728m), there are views of the massif de la Sainte-Baume, the plain of Aubagne, the Saint-Cyr hills and Marseille.

The road descends on the north side, giving views of the Chaîne de l'Étoile and the montagne Sainte-Victoire, separated by the Fuveau lake.

▷ At La Coutronne, turn right on to the D 80.

Plan-d'Aups-Ste-Baume

This pretty little village on the north slope of the massif has an 11C Roman-esque church and the visitor centre for the **Sainte-Baume eco-museum** (at *Nazareth, on the left, after the intersection with the D 480 leading down towards Saint-Zacharie, the building is opposite the Sainte-Baume grotto)*. It aims to preserve the ecosystem of the massif and to explore its geology, besides perpetuating the memory of the human activities carried out here since prehistoric times. *◷Opening hours vary: please check website. ℘04 42 62 56 46. www.ecomusee-sainte-baume.asso.fr.*

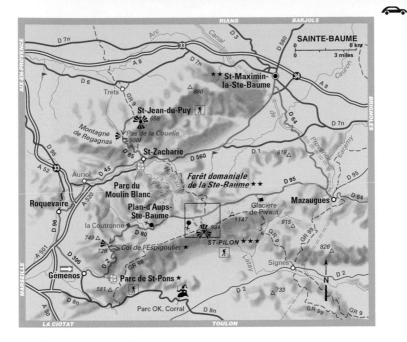

Hôtellerie de la Sainte-Baume

In the entrance, note the doorway to the grotto by Jean Guiramand (16C). In 1972 a chapel was created in a beautiful vaulted room which formerly housed pilgrims. On the left of the *hôtellerie* is the simple cemetery of the Dominicans who died during their time in the monastery. (🕭*To stay in the hôtellerie: see Addresses*).

Access to the grotto

From the 5C, the monks of **Saint-Cassien** lived in this grotto which was already venerated far and wide. It was famous enough to attract throngs of pilgrims, including kings of France (Saint Louis among them), several popes, thousands of lords and millions of the faithful. One of the first public acts of King **René** in Provence was to come to the grotto with his nephew, the future Louis XI. From 1295 onwards, the Dominicans were in charge of the grotto. Their nearby inn was burnt in the Revolution (traces of this can still be seen on the rock face). In 1859 **Father Lacordaire** brought the Dominicans back here as well as to Saint-Maximin. The inn was

rebuilt following his instructions, down on the plateau.
🚶*1hr30min round trip. Two options, indicated on the local map on p160: from the hôtellerie, take the chemin du Canapé to the left of the buildings, passing le Canapé, a huge pile of moss-covered blocks; or for an easier route from the Trois-Chênes crossroads (D 80 and D 95), follow the chemin des Rois.*
These two paths meet at the **l'Oratoire crossroads** (carrefour de l'Oratoire) after a pleasant meander through the magnificent Sainte-Baume forest. From the crossroads, on the right, a wide path leads to stairs carved into the rock and blocked, halfway down, by a door decorated with the fleur de lys escutcheon of France.
On the left, a niche in the rock protects a bronze cross. The staircase *(150 steps)* leads to a **terrace** on the parapet crowned with a stone cross (bronze Pietà, 13th station of the cross). Fine **view★** of the montagne Sainte-Victoire stretching out, on the right, to the mont Aurélien, and below to the Plan-d'Aups, the *hôtellerie* and the dense forest.

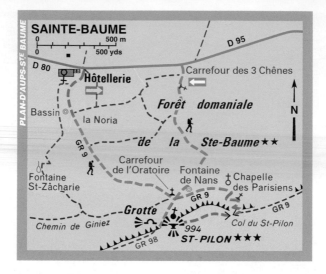

The **grotto** (grotte), in the form of a semicircle, is on the north side of the terrace at an altitude of 946 m. A reliquary to the right of the main altar contains relics of Saint Mary Magdalene found in Saint-Maximin. Behind the main altar in a crevice 3m off the ground – the only dry place in th grotto – is a statue of Mary Magdalene reclining; it was here that penitents came to have their sins forgiven.

Previously, before Christianity put an end to the tradition, people came here to worship fertility goddesses. They marked their visit by putting stones on the path to the grotto, each one representing a longed-for child.

Saint-Pilon★★★

At the Oratoire crossroads, pass in front of the oratory, then take the path on the right (with the red and white markings of the GR 9). This path skirts the abandoned "chapel of the Parisians", zigzags up and turns right at the col du Saint-Pilon. 2hr round trip.
At the summit there was once a pillar (hence the name of Saint-Pilon), later replaced by a small chapel. Here, according to legend, seven times a day the angels brought Saint Mary Magdalene so that she could listen with delight to the "concerts of paradise".

The sister of Martha and Lazarus, **Mary Magdalene** had led an unedifying life until she met Jesus. Captivated, the reprentant sinner followed the Lord. She was at the foot of the Cross on Golgotha and on Easter morning was the first person to whom Jesus revealed himself.

According to Provençal tradition, she was chased from Palestine at the time of the first persecutions of Christians, along with Martha, Lazarus, Maximin and other saints. After they landed at Les Saintes-Maries, Mary Magdalene felt destined to come to la Sainte-Baume. She spent 33 years there in prayer and contemplation.

Feeling her last hour approaching, she went down to the plain where Saint Maximin gave her the last rites and buried her. From Saint-Pilon (alt. 994m), there is a magnificent **panorama**★★★ (orientation table): to the north, you look across the hôtellerie de la Sainte-Baume to the distant outline of Mont Ventoux, the Luberon, the Montagne de Lure, the Briançonnais, Mont Olympe and, closer by, Mont Aurélien; to the southeast, the massif des Maures; to the southwest, the Sainte-Baume range and the bay of La Ciotat; to the northwest, the Alpilles and Montagne Sainte-Victoire.

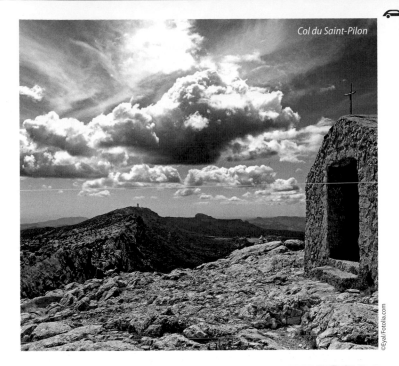
Col du Saint-Pilon

©Eyal/Fotolia.com

▷ Follow the D 95, direction Mazaugues.

At the place known as Les Glacières, the **glacière (ice house) of Pivaut** has been restored *(access via a forest path on the right of the D 95 – can only be seen during group visits).*

Mazaugues

This little Var locality is famous for its **ice houses** which were highly prized in the 19C. When the first frosts arrived, the waters of the nearby springs were diverted into channels which led to terraces of "ice ponds". When winter came, the ice was packed into carts, then "cellared" in ice houses whose inside walls were lined with straw. Once the ice house was full, all you had to do was

A Protected Forest

Covering about 140 ha/346 acres, the **forest**★★ (altitude varying from 680 to 1,000m) has rather unusually been listed as a 'Réserve biologique domaniale' – a state-owned nature reserve. Its main features are giant beeches and huge linden trees mixed with maples whose light leaf canopies meet over the thick, dark branches of yews, spindle trees, holly trees and ivy. Why is it that here, in the middle of Provence, there are trees which would not be out of place in the forests of the Île-de-France? Simply because of the shadow created by the high cliff which dominates the wooded region to the south: it maintains a northern-style freshness and humidity, much appreciated in summer by local people, needless to say. As soon as this rock wall ends, Mediterranean oaks proliferate again. Since time immemorial, no trees have been cut in this treasure of a forest: the main activity has been to ensure the regeneration of a unique heritage and to prevent trees from falling in a dangerous way.

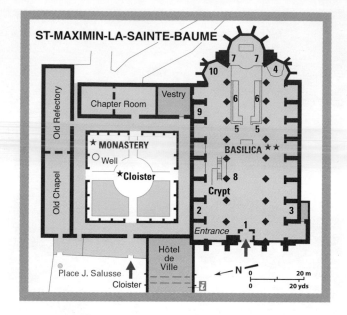

ST-MAXIMIN-LA-SAINTE-BAUME

Old Refectory

Chapter Room

Vestry

★ **MONASTERY**

○ Well

★**Cloister**

Old Chapel

BASILICA ★★

9

10

7   7

4

6   6

5   5

8

Crypt

2

3

1

Entrance

Hôtel
de
Ville

Place J. Salusse

Cloister

N   0   20 m

0   20 yds

close the entrance and wait for the summer. The ice was then taken out with a chisel, as required – much to the delight of town dwellers sweltering in the heat and without any means of preserving foodstuffs. There were at least 17 ice houses in this commune, keeping Toulon and later Marseille supplied with ice throughout the 19C.

Today Mazaugues is the home of the **musée de la Glace**, a reminder of the activity for which this place was blessed by local people during summer heatwaves. It is partly given over to local, artisan methods of ice production, with models, tools etc. So you can follow the route of this rare and ephemeral commodity from its creation to those who used it. ♿🕐*Open Jun–Sept daily ex Mon, 9am–noon, 2–6pm; rest of year Sun 9am–noon, 2–5pm.* �¬*Guided tours (1hr).* ⊛€*2.50, combined admission with Pivaut ice-house €4 .* ℘*04 94 86 39 24.* http://museedelaglace.free.fr.

Ice house near Mazaugues

© DANO/CDT du Var

▷ Take the D 64, direction Saint-Maximin-la-Sainte-Baume.

St-Maximin-La-Sainte-Baume★★

St-Maximin lies at the centre of a small basin, once the bottom of a lake, not far from the source of the Argens in a region of flat depressions; the village is flanked to the north by wooded hills and vineyards and to the south by the mountainous foundations of the Massif de la Ste-Baume. It takes its name from St Maximinus who, according to legend, converted its inhabitants to Christianity and is buried here, on the spot of what subsequently became a Dominican monastery and basilica.

Basilique Sainte-Marie-Madeleine

© Phtothèque WALLIS /CDT VAR

Basilica★★

Pl. de l'Hôtel de Ville . ⏱*Open daily 8.30am–7pm (except during services).* 🎫*No charge.* ☎*04 94 78 00 19. www.lesamisdelabasilique.fr. Allow 45min.*

The Ste-Marie-Madeleine Basilica is constructed on the foundations of a 6C Merovingian church, where in 1279 the alleged tombs of Mary Magdalene and St Maximinus were discovered. The sarcophagus supposedly contained the relics of the saints which were hidden in 716 from the Saracens. The spot was apparently indicated by the saint herself in a dream. In 1295 Pope Bonifacio VIII acknowledged the relics and on the site of the crypt Charles of Anjou had a basilica and monastery built.

He installed the Dominican friars who were in charge of guarding the relics and supervised what soon became a major pilgrimage site.

Exterior

Devoid of transepts and ambulatory, the basilica has a squat appearance reinforced by the absence of a belfry, its incomplete west front, and the massive buttresses reaching the nave walls. It is the most important example of the Gothic style in Provence, combining the influences of the north, such as Bourges, with local architectural traditions.

Interior

The building comprises a nave, chancel and two aisles of remarkable height. The two-storey, 29m-high nave has pointed vaulting; its keystones bear the arms of the Counts of Provence and Kings of France; the very large chancel is closed off by a pentagonal apse.

The aisles, which were only 18m high to allow for a clerestory, end with quadrangular apsidal chapels. The side chapels were raised less than the aisles so as to allow the light to filter through.

1) The organ, which has a double case and still has the pipes saved by Lucien Bonaparte, was made by the lay Dominican Isnard of Tarascon and ranks with the one in Poitiers' cathedral as one of the finest 18C instruments in France.

2) Fine gilded wood statue of John the Baptist.

3) 15C altarpiece of the Four Saints: Lawrence, Anthony, Sebastian and Thomas Aquinas.

4) Rosary altar with 18C gilded wood statue of the Virgin; 16C altar front carved with four low reliefs of Mary Magdalene.

5) 17C wooden choir screen with wrought-iron inlets emblazoned with the arms of France.

6) Choir stall panelling enclosing 94 stalls, decorated with

22 17C medallions of saints of the Dominican Order, carved by Vincent Funel.

7) 17C stucco decoration by J Lombard before which stand, to the right, a terra-cotta of Mary Magdalene's communion, to the left, a marble of the saint's ecstasy and, at the centre, the altar surmounted by a Glory.

8) Pulpit carved in 1756 by the Dominican Louis Gaudet, with representations on the sounding board, of immense size, of the ecstasy of Mary Magdalene, and on the staircase, panels of her life. The rail is cut from a single piece of wood and is a masterpiece in itself.

9) 15C Provençal School predella (lower part of the altarpiece) illustrating the beheading of John the Baptist, St Martha taming the Tarasque and Christ appearing to Mary Magdalene.

10) 16C painted wood **altarpiece★** by Ronzen of the Crucifixion, surrounded by 18 medallions.

Crypt

The crypt was the funeral vault of a late 4C–early 5C Roman villa. It contains four 4C sarcophagi: St Mary Magdalene, St Marcella and St Susan, St Maximinus and St Cedonius. At the back there is a 19C reliquary containing a cranium venerated as that of Mary Magdalene. Four stone tablets depict figures of the Virgin, Abraham and Daniel (c.500).

Royal Monastery★

pl. Jean Salusse. *Guided visits possible; ask at tourist office.*
04 94 86 55 66.
Now the Hôtel Le Couvant Royal (*see Addresses*), the royal monastery was begun in the 13C at the same time as the basilica, and was completed in the 15C. The elegant **cloisters★** (now used for events) include 32 bays. Its garden contains an abundance of foliage: boxwood, yew, lime and cedars. It hosts St-Maximinus Musical Evenings in summer.

The convent buildings include a chapel with vaulting in the form of a depressed arch, the refectory of five bays and the **chapterhouse** (housing the hotel's restaurant) with its pointed vault above slender columns ending in foliated capitals and held by low corbels. The building also houses the town hall.

Saint-Zacharie

This attractive village, which you can admire if you leave the main road leading through it, used to be famous for its ceramics and is proud of its many fountains.

Oratoire de Saint-Jean-du-Puy

On the D 85, just after the pas de la Couelle, a very narrow path goes off to the right, leading after a steep incline to a military radar post. Leave the car there.

15min round trip.

Following a marked trail, you can walk to the oratory: there is a beautiful **view★** of montagne Sainte-Victoire and the plain of Saint-Maximin to the north, the Maures and Sainte-Baume massifs to the southeast and, in the foreground, the montagne de Regagnas, the Chaîne de l'Étoile and the pays d'Aix to the west.

▷ Return to Saint-Zacharie and take the D 45, direction Auriol. Stay on the D 96 until you reach Roquevaire.

Roquevaire

Dominated by its clock tower, this village is famous above all for its **organ** (in église Saint-Vincent) rebuilt with the pipes and wooden panels of the original but incorporating the organ of Pierre Cochereau, former organist at Notre-Dame de Paris. *Guided tour: contact the Association des amis du grand orgue de Roquevaire, 6 av. Pierre-Cochereau, 13630 Roquevaire.* *04 42 04 05 33. www.orgue-roquevaire.fr.*

ADDRESSES

🏠 STAY

Hôtellerie de la Sainte-Baume – *83460 Plan-d'Aups. ℘04 42 04 54 84. 66 rooms.* Surrounded by nature on all sides, this inn at the edge of the state-owned Sainte-Baume forest welcomes pilgrims, hikers and anybody else who feels like retreating from everyday life for a while.

Hôtel Le Parc – *Vallée de St-Pons, 13420 Gémenos. 1km/0.6mi east of Gémenos via the D 2. ℘04 42 32 20 38. www.hotel-parc-gemenos.com.* ▣*. 13 rooms. Restaurant* ⊝⊝*.* In a quiet spot set back from the main road, this hotel has soothing green vistas on all sides. Shady terrace and dining room opening on to the garden. Small, charming rooms.

Hôtel de France – *3–5 av. Albert-ler, St-Maximin-la-Ste-Baume. ℘04 94 78 00 14. 23 rooms.* In what was in former days a coaching inn, this hotel has rooms of various sizes decorated in typical Provençal style. Seasonal cooking in the restaurant.

Hôtellerie du Couvent Royal – *Pl. Jean-Salusse, St-Maximin-la-Ste-Baume. ℘04 94 86 55 66.* ▣*. 67 rooms. Restaurant* ⊝⊝⊝*.* Some of the rooms, monastic in their simplicity, are in the former monks' cells of the old monastery building adjoining the basilica; others are in a modern wing. Meals are served in the capitular room or, if weather permits, in the cloisters.

🍽 EAT

L'Imprévu – *Av. Gabriel-Péri, St-Maximin-la-Ste-Baume. ℘04 94 59 82 36. Booking advised.* Occupying a cheerful, rustic barn, this pizzeria (known as "chez Marie" to the faithful) has a large terrace shaded by plane trees. Marie may suggest some of her pasta specialities, about which she has written a book.

La Restanque – *R. de La Treille, 13360 Roquevaire. ℘04 42 04 21 78. www.restaurant-la-restanque.com.* Above the main square, this place has a fine terrace which is sunny in winter and shady in summer. Pizzas from a wood-fired oven, pasta dishes and Mediterranean specialities.

Château de Nans – *Quartier du Logis (3km/1.8mi from Nans-les-Pins via the D 560). 83860 Nans-les-Pins. ℘04 94 78 92 06. www.chateaudenans.com. Hotel closed Oct–Mar. Restaurant* ⊝⊝⊝*, closed 24 Nov–23 Dec, mid-Feb–mid-Mar, Tue (ex Jul–Aug), Mon.* ⌇*. 5 rooms.* A small 19C castle opposite the Sainte-Baume golf course and fronting on to the road. Classical cooking, served either indoors or out. Attractive, individually decorated rooms; the ones in the tower are the most unusual. Parkland and pool.

SHOPPING

Marché de St-Maximin-la-Ste-Baume – Big market on the Grand-Place Wednesday morning.

Santon and crafts fair – Mid-Nov at Le Couvent Royal, at the Hôtel de Ville and pl. Jean-Salusse (fee charged).

OLIVE OIL

Moulin à huile de la Cauvine – *Quartier de la Cauvine. Between St-Jean-de-Garguier and St-Estève, 13360 Roquevaire. ℘04 42 04 09 30. Open 9am–7pm; closed Sun and public holidays.* A true picture-postcard landscape surrounds this farm. You can fill your basket with seasonal fruits and vegetables on Tuesdays and Fridays. Note: the olive oil produced here and sold at a reasonable price has won a number of awards.

EVENTS

Ice fair – *Last Sun in Feb at Mazaugues.* Exhibitions, discussions, performances and a tasting of artisan ice creams.

International organ festival – *www.orgue-roquevaire.fr.* In Sept–Oct, a prestigious festival which enables people to hear the famous organ of Roquevaire.

Feast of Saint Mary Magdalene – Sunday following 22 July, at the basilica of Saint-Maximin-la-Sainte-Baume. Mass is celebrated and the relics of the saint are carried in a procession in the afternoon.

It may sound far-fetched to suggest that Aix-en-Provence is one of the world's great art capitals, yet this easy-going French provincial town of fewer than 150,000 people has been a glittering centre for art and culture since the early Middle Ages. Ever since the Counts of Provence made Aix their base in the 12C, it has been a refined, civilised place, so rich intellectually and artistically that many a metropolis ten times its size might view it with envy.

Highlights

Long before the Counts arrived, the Romans were here, enjoying life in a settlement built around thermal springs whose therapeutic properties visitors can still sample today. Perhaps, even then, the foundations had been laid for an enlightened town that would flourish in a series of golden ages – the first under Good King René, a fervent patron of the arts in the 15C; the second in the 17C–18C when Aix, teeming with wealthy lawyers, acquired wide avenues of fountains and magnificent mansions; and the third a little over a century ago when artists inspired by Paul Cézanne began to gravitate to the crucible of modern art.

A Walking Town

With so many centuries of prosperity promoting so many exceptional buildings within a manageable scale, Aix-en-Provence is a town to explore on foot. The quaint, narrow streets of the Old Town contrast intriguingly with grand boulevards like the Cours Mirabeau, where wrought-iron balconies on exquisitely elegant houses are supported by columns and caryatids. The nearby Quartier Mazarin is well worth seeing, too, for its wonderfully gracious buildings.

A Musical Feast

In the same way that Avignon has become renowned internationally for its July theatre festival founded in the 1940s (*see Avignon, Addresses*), Aix-en-Provence has built up a global reputation for the music and opera festival launched by visionary Gabriel Dussurget in 1948. The courtyard of the archbishop's palace, setting for the earliest performances, is still a focal point for the festival, which these days attracts more than 60,000 supporters every summer. Young people are especially encouraged to attend.

Cézanne's Mountain

To the east of Aix, the Montagne Sainte-Victoire (affectionately termed "la Sainte") is far more than an imposing limestone mass. For art lovers everywhere it is a powerful symbol, even a rallying point, because it was this mountain that Paul Cézanne painted more than anything else, portraying its craggy landscape in such a radically new way that his influence on 20C art was immense. Picasso, attracted here also, is buried in the park of the Château de Vauvenargues, his home from 1959 to 1962. "Cézanne painted these mountains and now I own them," he said – never, in fact, painting La Sainte-Victoire himself.

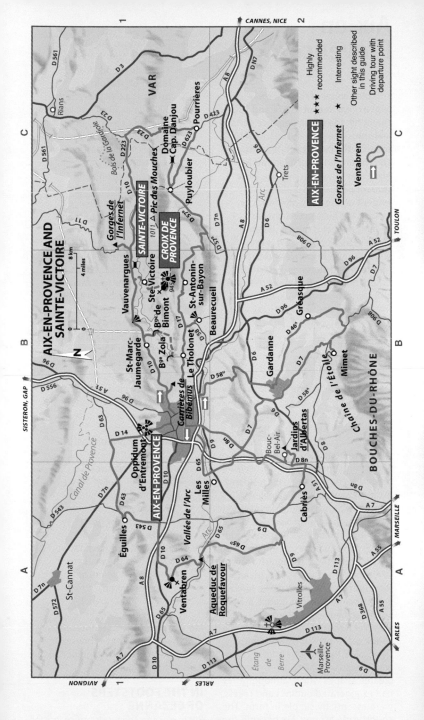

Aix-en-Provence★★★

Bouches-du-Rhône

This old capital of Provence has kept a great deal of its 17C and 18C character: the sober elegance of its mansions, the graceful charm of its squares, the majesty of its avenues, and the loveliness of its fountains. Aix is also a lively city whose large student population is abundantly evident on the busy café terraces. Around old Aix a new town has developed that is both a spa and an industrial complex – it is the largest centre in France and Europe for processed almonds. Part of the production is used to make the cakes and confectionery of Aix, including the local speciality, sugar-iced *calissons*.

CÉZANNE
A BIT OF HISTORY

Born in Aix in 1839, **Paul Cézanne** studied at the Collège Bourbon (now Collège Mignet), where he became friends with Émile Zola. He first chose humanities, then enrolled at the Faculty of Law in accordance with his father's wishes, while at the same time painting and writing poetry in the countryside around Jas de Bouffan. This residence in the midst of parkland, acquired by his father in 1859, was a propitious setting for the development of his artistic work. Although Cézanne became friendly with Impressionist painters in Paris, he was not successful there. It was on his return to Aix that fame came to him, thanks to the good name he had made for himself among painters such as Monet, Manet, Sisley and above all, Pissarro.

However, it was not long before Cézanne shook off Impressionist techniques. Using large, luminous patches of colour and juxtaposing them in new ways, he created shapes which, although they had exaggerated outlines and reliefs, were essentially simple in form. The countryside around Aix became the dominant subject of his painting. Flee-ing Paris in 1870, Cézanne settled at L'Estaque in his mother's house. Finally, in 1904 he achieved recognition in the Paris Autumn Salon.

IN THE FOOTSTEPS OF CÉZANNE

Put in place by the tourist office *(ask for the leaflet)*, this map provides pointers

▶ **Population:** 141 438.

⚬ **Michelin Map:** 340: H-4 or 114 folds 15 and 16 or 528 fold 31 or 524 fold J.

▯ **Info:** Les allées provençales 300 avenue Giuseppe Verdi, 13100 Aix-en-Provence. ☏04 42 16 11 61. www. aixenProvencetourism.com.

▶ **Location:** Take a guided tour of the town (2hr); for information, contact the tourist office (*see above*). Or explore Aix and its surroundings in the footsteps of Cézanne *(see opposite page)*.

▯ **Parking:** Parking is scarce. Avoid the old town and look for spaces on bd. du Roi-René or on bd. Aristide Briand. Try the covered car parks, but these fill up quickly.

⊘ **Don't Miss:** The cours Mirabeau and the old town; place Albertas and the Four-Dolphins fountain; the newly renovated Musée Granet; and, of course, Cézanne's sites.

▲▲ **Kids:** Visit the dinosaur eggs in the Musée d'Histoire Naturelle, a *calisson* or *santon* maker, and the *santons* fair in December.

⊙ **Timing:** Allow half a day for Cézanne's sites and half a day for the old town. Don't miss the markets: you'll come across one every morning.

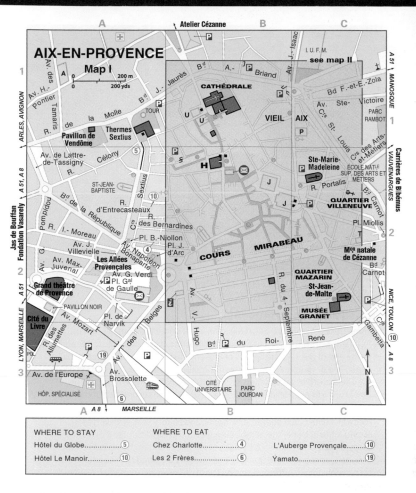

to the places in Aix frequented by the painter (like his **birthplace**, at no 28 rue de l'Opéra), and the places in the surrounding countryside that inspired him, particularly Montagne **Sainte-Victoire** (see Sainte-Victoire).

Good to know – For the three tourist sites mentioned below, the Aix tourist office suggests the Cézanne Pass, a combined one-day ticket (€13; guided tour obligatory for the Bibémus quarries and the jas de Bouffan).

Atelier Paul Cézanne (Cézanne's Studio)★

9 av. Paul-Cézanne, in the north of Aix along av. Pasteur. Open daily Jul–Aug 10am–6pm; Apr–Jun and Sept 10am– *noon, 2–6pm; Oct–Mar 10am–noon, 2–5pm. Closed Sun from Dec–Feb, 1–3 Jan, 1 May, 25 Dec. €5.50. Guided tours (30min) in English daily Apr–Sept 5pm, Oct–Mar 4pm. 04 42 21 06 53. www.atelier-cezanne.com.*

When his mother died in 1897, Cézanne had a traditional Provençal-style house built about 500m from the cathedral, outside the ramparts. It was surrounded by a garden with colourful leafy plants growing right up to the windows of the artist's studio.

The studio, called the Lauves, where he painted *The Bathers*, among other works, has been left as it was at the time of his death in 1906. A few items of memorabilia are on view.

Detail of a portrait of King René (1475) by Nicolas Froment

Musée Granet, Aix-en-Provence. © 2011. White Images/Scala, Florence

Aix-en-Provence

Good King René (1409–80)

Some traces of a prosperous civilisation in Aix under the Roman Emperor Augustus can still be seen in the sophisticated statuary in the Musée Granet. At the end of the 12C, the counts of Provence held a refined and literate court at Aix. The development of the town continued during the 13C, and yet in the 14C its surface area diminished. In 1409 Louis II of Anjou founded the university, but Aix's golden age occurred later, in the second half of the 15C under the reign of Good King René.

A city of 4,000–5,000 people, a bishopric and county seat, Aix exerted a strong influence over the neighbouring countryside, occupied by wealthy townspeople and enhanced by Italian craftsmen. Within the walls lived the burghers, aristocrats and farmers; this category included the shepherds responsible for ensuring a return on livestock investments made by a handful of powerful merchants.

Second son to Louis II and Yolanda of Aragon, René became Duke of Anjou, Count of Provence, and titular King of Sicily and Naples at the death of his older brother, Louis III, in 1434. René spoke Latin, Greek, Italian, Hebrew and Catalan. He played and composed music, painted illuminations with meticulous detail, wrote verses, understood mathematics, astrology and geology. In short, René possessed one of the most universal minds of his time. He was an enlightened patron of the arts, in particular Flemish painters. Dating from his rule are the famous triptychs of the *Annunciation* (said to be by the Master of King René) and the *Burning Bush* painted by Nicolas Froment (of Languedoc origin, he studied in Flanders and Burgundy). By the end of the 15C some 40 artists of quality lived and worked in Aix under contract to René and his nobles. They produced prestigious works of art and contributed to the decoration of mystery plays and popular festivals (such as Corpus Christi, which underwent a brilliant revival).

A man of arts and letters, René did not neglect his obligations as a ruler; he legislated, stimulated commerce and encouraged agriculture. He introduced the Muscat grape into Provence and on occasion cultivated his own vineyards. He was concerned with the health standards of his people and instituted a public service of doctors and surgeons, promulgated a sanitation law and ordained the cleaning up of the different quarters of the city. He was, however, criticised for his heavy taxation as well as his weak currency; the coins he minted, called *parpaillottes*, were of rather base alloy.

At the age of 12, René married Isabelle of Lorraine, who brought him as dowry the Duchy of Lorraine. Their younger daughter, Margaret of Anjou (1430–82), married the English King Henry VI (1421–71), in 1445. Two years after the death of Isabelle (at 44), to whom he had remained tenderly attached for 33 years, René married Jeanne of Laval, aged 21. This second marriage was as happy as the first. Queen Jeanne, who should not be confused with the 14C Queen Joan I of Sicily, was as popular as her elderly husband among the people of Provence.

Having lost both his son and two grandsons, King René sadly observed his nephew Louis XI annex Anjou to the kingdom of France. Thereafter, instead of dividing his time between Angers and Provence, René never set foot outside the land of sunshine and died in Aix in 1480, aged 71. His nephew Charles of Maine, who had been chosen as his heir, died one year later.

The New Faces of Aix

After the union of Provence to France in 1486, a governor appointed by the king lived in Aix. In 1501 the city became the seat of a newly created parliament, and as a result, in the 17C it experienced another period of growth as one of its social classes became prominent – the men of law. These well-to-do judges and lawyers led stimulating lives and consequently proceeded to build magnificent townhouses *(hôtels)* worthy of their name and rank.

At the same time, the urban landscape was transformed: new areas of the city sprang up and developed rapidly (notably the Quartier Mazarin, south of the city); the old ramparts were razed and replaced by an avenue for carriages, which later became cours Mirabeau. In the 18C, the city continued its transformation, with its wide avenues, squares, fountains and new buildings. The county palace was demolished and a law court was built in its place.

Into the Modern Age

After the Revolution, Aix suffered a decline as a result of ever-prospering Marseille, although it retained its court and its university.

It was not until the 1970s that it experienced a two-fold revival: economic, with the installation of high-tech industries; and cultural, with the growing influence of the university and the creation of the music festival. This growth in economic activity and population was accompanied by a major town-planning project, the extension of cours Sextius and cours Mirabeau, of which the Cité du Livre is the first stage, and which will help to redefine Aix in the 21C.

Le jas de Bouffan★

17 rte. de Galice. Leave Aix, in the direction of Lyon, just before the auto-route. Guided visits: Apr–May and Oct Tue, Thu and Sat 10.30am, noon, 2pm (in English) and 3.30pm; Jun–Sept 10.30am, noon, 2pm (in English) and 3.30pm; Nov–Mar Wed and Sat 10am. €5.50. 04 42 16 11 61. *www.cezanne-en-Provence.com.* Acquired by Cézanne's father in 1859, this fine 18C *bastide* on the edge of Aix later provided the painter with memories of his youth and his family. Aged 20, he was allowed to use the downstairs salon as a studio and he painted the four seasons on the walls. Later the plaster was removed in eight sections and preserved. After three years in Paris, he returned – this time to paint outside. The Jas (sheep barn in Provençal) was sold in 1899, two years after the death of Cézanne's mother. Since 'Cézanne 2006', the major com-

Cézanne, who loved Aix

In a letter to his son in 1906, Cézanne described his admiration for Aix:

"I go to the country every day, the motifs are beautiful and so my day is spent more pleasantly here than anywhere else."

memoration marking the hundredth anniversary of the painter's death, the large oval salon has been used for the screening of a film *(17min long)*, made by Gianfranco Iannuzzi and Massimiliano Sicardi, on three walls. In a majestic modern way it covers 40 years of Cézanne's painting at the Jas de Bouffan. The visit ends in the park where the themes of various paintings are pointed out.

Carrières de Bibémus (Bibémus quarries)★

Wear comfortable shoes. The site closes if there is any fire risk. Guided visits: Jan–Mar and Nov–Dec Wed and Sat only, 3pm; Apr–May and Oct Mon, Wed, Fri and Sun 10.30am and 3.30pm; Jun–Sept daily at 9.45am. €5.50.

The quarries were first opened to visitors for 'Cézanne 2006'. The materials used in the visitor scheme (designed by landscape gardeners Philippe Deliau and Hélène Bensoam) blend perfectly into the environment.

Stone was quarried here back in ancient times; you can still see marks of the wheels of ox-drawn carts which were used to transport blocks of stone. Much later, the ochre molasse which was quarried here (a soft stone created from limestone and sand) was used for the construction of Aix mansions, especially in the Mazarin quarter in the 17C and 18C. At the end of the 19C when the stone had been used up and the quarries were abandoned, Cézanne came here to paint the rocks. He produced eleven oil paintings and sixteen watercolours, most of which are in the United States. You can see exactly where he painted the *Red rock (in the Orangerie in Paris)*, two pictures of *Bibémus Quarries* and Mon-

tagne Sainte-Victoire *seen from Bibémus*. Several paths lead from the plateau of Bibémus across the pine forest, providing a wonderful view of the Montagne Sainte-Victoire.

Café-brasserie Les Deux Garçons

53 cours Mirabeau. ℘04 42 26 00 51.

It was in this famous brasserie that Cézanne and his friend Émile Zola came to round off the day after classes at the collège Bourbon (now the collège Mignet at no 41 rue Cardinale). The décor of this café, established in 1792, all gilding, friezes and fancy woodwork, is worth a quick look. Next door, at no 55, you can still see the sign of the hat shop opened in 1825 by Cézanne's father.

WALKING TOUR

OLD AIX★★

Allow half a day, including 1hr30min for Quartier Mazarin.

▷ Start from place du Général-de-Gaulle, known as the "Rotonde", where there is a spectacular fountain.

The ring of boulevards and squares that encircles the old town marks the line of the ancient ramparts. North of cours Mirabeau, the town's focal point, lies Old Aix, tucked between the cathedral and place d'Albertas. The many pedestrian streets criss-crossing this area make it the perfect setting for an exploratory stroll.

Fontaine de la Rotonde

Rising a full 12m, this is a fountain on a monumental scale. Erected in 1860, it marked the entrance to the town. Its pool, 32m in diameter, is surrounded by twelve bronze lions and crowned by the Three Graces in marble: Justice looks towards the cours Mirabeau, Agriculture faces towards Marseille and Fine Arts points towards Avignon.

Photographed by everybody, this fountain is the town's most important symbol and a popular meeting place.

Cours Mirabeau and Fontaine du Roi René

© van der Meer Rene/age fotostock

Cours Mirabeau★★

This wide avenue, shaded by fine plane trees, is the hub of Aix, where a verdant tunnel of foliage protects against the hot Provençal sun.

Built in the 17C on the site of the medieval ramparts, the avenue originally had no shops or boutiques, yet the life of Aix now revolves around this very area. Lining the north side of the street are cafés and shops. A number of bookshops reveal Aix's intellectual and scholarly vocation. On the other side stand the aristocratic façades of the old hotels with their finely carved doorways and wrought-iron balconies supported by caryatids or atlantes from the Puget School.

Hôtel d'Isoard de Vauvenargues – *10 cours Mirabeau.* This mansion was built around 1710 with a wrought-iron balcony and fluted lintel. The Marchioness of Entrecasteaux, Angélique de Castellane, was murdered here by her husband, the president of parliament.

Hôtel de Forbin– *20 cours Mirabeau.* Built in 1656, it has a balcony with beautiful ornamental ironwork.

Fontaine des Neuf Canons– *In the centre of the cours.* It dates from 1691. The term "canon" meant "pipe" in the 13C.

Fontaine moussue – The water is thermal, emerging at a temperature of 18 °C all year, thus encouraging the growth of moss ("moussue" means "mossy"). Dat-

ing from 1734, this fountain is near the junction with rue Clemenceau.

Hôtel Maurel de Pontevès – *No 38.* Now an annexe of the court of appeal, it was here that the Grande Mademoiselle, Anne-Marie de Montpensier, was received in 1660.

Fontaine du Roi René – The work of David d'Angers (19C), this fountain stands at the extreme end of the avenue. The king is portrayed wearing the crown of the Counts of Provence and holding in his hand a Muscat grape – a variety which he introduced to the region.

Hôtel du Poët – *1 pl. Haut du Cours Mirabeau.* This dates from 1730 and closes off the view down cours Mirabeau to the east. The three-tiered façade is decorated with *mascarons* and some pretty ironwork adorns the first-floor balcony.

▷ Take the street to the right of the Hôtel du Poët.

Rue de l'Opéra

There are a number of houses of interest on this street. No **18** Hôtel de Lestang-Parade was built around 1650 by Pavillon and Rambot and remodelled in 1830. No **24** Hôtel de Bonnecorse (or Arlatan-Lauris) dates from the 18C. No **26** Hôtel de Grimaldi was constructed in 1680 after drawings by Puget. And no **28** was Cézanne's birthplace.

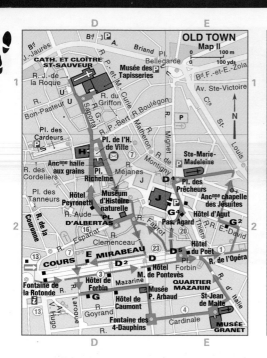

▶ Return towards the Théâtre du Jeu de Paume, turning right and then left into rue Éméric David.

Hôtel de Panisse-Passis
16 r. Éméric David.
Built in 1739, the façade is enhanced by fine wrought-iron and corbelled balconies with fantastically carved heads.

Église Ste-Marie-Madeleine
pl. des Prêcheurs.
The church's west front is modern although the church itself dates from the 17C. At the end of the south aisle, in the fourth chapel, an 18C marble **Virgin★** by Chastel can be seen. The central panel of the 15C **Triptych of the Annunciation★** hangs in the north aisle; it was commissioned around 1443 and is attributed to Barthélemy d'Eyck, an artist who used *chiaroscuro* effects subtly and inventively.

Fontaine des Prêcheurs
pl. des Prêcheurs.
In this square you will find Chastel's 18C fountain. Note the atlantes that decorate the doorway of the **Hôtel d'Agut** at no **2**

(the former residence of Achille Emperaire, a contemporary of Cézanne), before taking rue Thiers, where at no **2** you will find the 17C **Hôtel de Roquesante**.
Rue Thiers leads to the top of cours Mirabeau; take the right-hand pavement. At no **55** note the sign of the hat shop founded by Cézanne's father in 1825.

▶ Turn right into rue Fabrot.

The pedestrian-only rue Fabrot leads to place St-Honoré.

▶ Take rue Espariat.

▲▲ Muséum d'histoire naturelle
6 r. Espariat. ⊙*Open daily except Sun 10am–noon, 1–5pm.* ⊙*Closed public holidays.* ✎€3.50 (under 25 free).
✆04 88 71 81 81. www.museum-aix-en-Provence.org.
This Natural History Museum is housed in the townhouse **Hôtel Boyer d'Éguilles** which was built in 1675, most probably by Pierre Puget. Entrance is through a large *porte cochère* that opens into the main courtyard. The museum houses

interesting collections of mineralogy and palaeontology. The palaeontology section includes general as well as local exhibits, notably a collection of dinosaur eggs from the slopes of Mont Ste-Victoire.

Place d'Albertas★

This square was opened in 1745 and was embellished with a fountain in 1912. It is arranged very much in the style of Parisian squares and has lovely mansions all around it. Concerts are held here every summer.

Hôtel d'Albertas

10 pl. d'Albertas.
Built in 1707, this *hôtel* includes carvings by the sculptor Toro.

▷ Bear right into rue de l'Aude.

Hôtel Peyronetti

13 r. de l'Aude.
Italian Renaissance in style, it dates from 1620.

▷ Follow rue du Maréchal-Foch.

Hôtel d'Arbaud

7 r. Maréchal Foch.
Fine atlantes frame the doorway.

> ### ☙ Aix Pass Cards ☙
>
> The Aix and Pays d'Aix Pass (☞€2 from tourist offices and participating sites) provides valuable discounts to a whole range of museums and other places of interest in and around Aix. It is valid for a full year. A Cézanne Passeport (☞€12), valid for five days, includes admission to Cézanne's studio, the Jas de Bouffan and the Musée Granet, a guided tour of Aix and also a city tour by mini-tram.

Place Richelme

The south façade of the old grain market runs alongside this square, which is broken into sections by two corner statues. ☙*Every morning there is a fresh fruit and vegetable market here.*

Place de l'Hôtel de Ville★

The northwest corner of this attractive square is overlooked by the **clock tower**, which in the 16C used to be the town's belfry. A bell in a wrought-iron cage also dates from the 16C. Each season is represented by a different character. This is also the site of the weekly flower market.

Place d'Albertas

The Marriage of Mirabeau

Aix played an important role in the life of Honoré Gabriel Riqueti, Count of Mirabeau. He married here in 1772 and was divorced here in 1783. It was here, too, that he was elected to the Estates General in 1789.

The fiery Mirabeau was only 23 when he married Mademoiselle de Marignane. The bride was a rich heiress, and among her suitors featured the best of Provence nobility. Mirabeau, although a count, was ill-favoured. With a big head and a face disfigured by smallpox, he was penniless and moreover had a scandalous reputation. But he was aware of the mysterious attraction he held for women. Cynically, he made a show of his good fortune and left his coach at the door of the Hôtel de Marignane *(see Quartier Mazarin)* before spending the night there. After this scandal, a marriage had to take place. But Mirabeau's father-in-law showed resentment by cutting off the young couple's allowance. Mirabeau displayed no embarrassment at this blow and promptly ran up 200,000 *livres* of debts with Aix merchants. Their complaints were such that a warrant was issued sending him under house arrest to Château d'If and subsequently Fort Joux, where he published his *Essay on Despotism*.

Mirabeau returned to Aix in 1783 to answer a summons for separation instituted by his wife. The eminent orator presented his own defence. His prodigious eloquence secured him victory at a first hearing, but he lost on appeal, although it is said that his pleading aroused such enthusiasm and the violence of his language was such that the opposing counsel fainted!

The year 1789 saw the elections to the Estates General. The Count of Mirabeau, who had met with only contempt and rebuff among his peers, decided to represent not nobility but the Third Estate. His election was a triumph and his historic role as an orator began; however, it also marked the beginning of Aix's downfall.

Hôtel de Ville

Built between 1655 and 1670, the town hall was designed by the Parisian architect Pierre Pavillon. Around the splendid paved **courtyard★**, the buildings are divided by pilasters of the Classical order *(see Introduction – Art)*. There is a niche with scrolls on the inside façade.

Ancienne Halle aux Grains

This former grain market was built to the south of the square in the mid-18C. The central part of the building projects forward and is embellished with a pediment carved by Chastel, depicting the Rhône and the Durance. This sculptor spent his life in Aix, a fact evidenced by the many works of art left behind by him. The grain market now houses a post office and administrative centre.

▶ Go along rue Gaston-de-Saporta.

Musée des Tapisseries★

28 pl. des Martyrs de la Résistance. ⏱*Open daily except Tue: mid-Apr–mid-Oct 10am–12.30pm, 1–6pm; mid-Oct–mid-Apr 1.30pm–5pm.* ⏱*Guided tours (1hr) available.* ⏱*Closed Jan, 1 May and 25 Dec.* ⬤€3.50. ✆*04 42 23 09 91.*

Housed in the 17C former archbishop's palace, the Tapestry Museum presents in particular the 19 magnificent tapestries made in Beauvais in the 17C and 18C, including nine famous panels illustrating the life of Don Quixote, after cartoons by Natoire. The courtyard is used for the music festival every July.

Cloître St-Sauveur★

34 pl. des Martyrs de la Résistance (enter through the cathedral). ♿⏱*Open except during religious services: May–Oct 9.30am–noon, 2–6pm; Nov–Apr*

The Legend of Saint Mitre

Mitre was born in 433 in Thessalonica, Greece, from where he emigrated to Aix to lead a humble life. He preached against the adultery of Arvendus, a local Roman magistrate. According to legend, Arvendus framed Mitre sabotaging grapes from his vineyard. Through Mitre's prayers, the grapes miraculously sprouted back on the trees. Accused of witchcraft and beheaded, Mitre picked up his head and carried it to the Église Notre-Dame de la Seds *(located at 22 avenue Jean Dalmas)*, where he passed away. In 1383, his relics were transferred to the Cathédrale St-Sauveur. It is said that a liquid seeped out from the right-hand column supporting his white marble tomb, which was used to cure eye sores.

10am–noon, 2–5pm. ➤Guided tours (20min). ☎04 42 27 07 63. www.cathedrale-aix.net.
These Romanesque cloisters are a delight. The arcades are not buttressed, giving the cloisters a delicate quality. The paired columns and the capitals are adorned with leaves and add elegance to the construction. On a fine corner pillar you will discover a remarkably carved St Peter.

▷ A door northwest of the cloisters gives access to the adjoining cathedral.

Cathédrale St-Sauveur★

Rue Gaston-de-Saporta. ◷*Open except during religious services: May–Oct 9.30am–noon, 2–6pm; Nov–Apr 10am–noon, 2–5pm.* ➤*Guided tours (20min).* ☎*04 42 27 07 63. www.cathedrale-aix.net.*

Triptych of the Burning Bush, Cathédrale St-Sauveur
© Tommaso Di Girolamo/age fotostock

St-Sauveur is a curious building decorated in all styles from the 5C to the 17C. In the Gothic central nave hang two 15C triptychs. Of the first triptych, depicting the Passion, only the central panel is from the 15C. The second series, the **Triptych of the Burning Bush★★**, was made by Nicolas Froment, court painter to King René. The king and his queen are shown kneeling on either side of the Virgin. The Virgin holding the infant Jesus is in the Burning Bush, similar to that in which God appeared to Moses.
Behind the altar, in the Chapel of St-Mitre, hangs the *Martyrdom of St Mitre*, attributed to the School of Nicolas Froment. The doorway is closed by **panels★** *(masked by false doors)* in walnut; this sculpture in wood by Jean Guiramand of Toulon represents the four prophets of Israel and 12 pagan sibyls.
The cathedral's west front includes to the right a door in the Romanesque Provençal style, in the middle a Gothic part (early 16C) and to the left a Gothic bell tower (14C–15C).

▷ Return to cours Mirabeau via place de l'Hôtel de Ville and rue Vauvenargues, rue Méjanes, rue des Bagniers and rue Clemenceau.

Hôtel d'Arbaud-Jouques

19 cours Mirabeau.
Built in 1700, this building displays a finely decorated stone façade with a carved frieze underlining the first floor.

▷ Turn left into rue Laroque and then left again into rue Mazarine which leads to the Quartier Mazarin, a district of orderly design built between 1646 and 1651 by the Archbishop Michel Mazarin, brother of the famous cardinal of the same name.

Quartier Mazarin★
Hôtel de Marignane
12 r. Mazarine.
Late 17C. This *hôtel* was the scene of Mirabeau's scandalous behaviour towards Mademoiselle de Marignane (*see previous page*).

Hôtel de Caumont
3 r. Joseph-Cabassol.
The Darius-Milhaud conservatory of music and dance occupies a fine building with balconies and pediments, dating from 1720.

Musée Paul-Arbaud
2a r. du Quatre-Septembre.
Temporarily closed for renovation.
℘04 42 38 38 95.
www.academiedaix.org.
Housed in a mansion dating from the late 18C, this museum has a collection of local earthenware as well as a library of books relating to Provence.

Fontaine des Quatre-Dauphins★
pl. des Quatre-Dauphins.
At the centre of a small square stands the charming fountain by J.C. Ribaut from 1667.

Église St-Jean-de-Malte
24–26 r. d'Italie. Open daily 10am–noon, 3–7pm. *℘04 42 38 25 70.*
www.moinesdiocesains-aix.cef.fr.
The church, dating from the late 13C, was the chapel of the Knights of Malta, and was Aix's first Gothic building. Although the façade is austere, the **nave★** presents the elegant decorative detail of the High Gothic.

Musée Granet★★
pl. St Jean-de-Malte. Open May–mid-Jun 11am–7pm; mid-Jun–mid-Oct 9am–7pm (Thu noon–11pm); mid-Oct–May daily except Mon 11am–7pm.
Closed 1 Jan, 1 May, 25 Dec.

Guided tours (1hr30min). €5.
℘04 42 52 88 32. www.museegranet -aixenProvence.fr.
The museum's fine collection of paintings includes the legacies of the Aix painter **François Marius Granet** (1775–1849) and works from the great 16C-19C European Schools. One gallery is devoted to Cézanne as well as to Klee, Giacometti, Picasso, Mondrian and other giants.
The collections are arranged chronologically. The **ground floor** covers the period from early primitive painters to the Renaissance, including 18C and 19C sculpture. Works of 17C and 18C Flemish painters include Rembrandt (*Self-Portrait*) and Rubens (*The Feast of Achelous*). The next space is dedicated to artists of the 19C French school, including Philippe de Champaigne (one of its founders), the Le Nain brothers (*The Card Players*), portraits by Rigaud, the Aix painter Claude Arnulphy and the Provençal artists Mignard and Puget.
The Granet room showcases canvases of classical landscapes and the Provençal countryside of the artist's youth. The portrait of Granet by Ingres reigns supreme in the middle of the room. 20C art is represented by the collection *From Cézanne to Giacometti* (71 works). One room is devoted to Cézanne (*The Bathers*), another to Giacometti. The work of Cézanne's contemporaries (*2nd floor*) can be seen. Rare archaeological finds from Entremont (*see p180*) are on show in the basement.

ADDITIONAL SIGHTS
Fondation Vasarely★★
1 av. Marcel Pagnol, Jas de Bouffan.
Open daily except Mon 10am–1pm, 2–6pm. €9. *℘04 42 20 01 09.*
www.fondationvasarely.org.
On the Jas de Bouffan hill west of Aix stands the foundation created by Hungarian artist Victor Vasarely (1906–97), an early practitioner of op art. The vast building, consisting of 16 hexagonal structures, has sober façades decorated with circles on alternating black and white squares. Vasarely first used lines to create optical illusions as far back as 1930; experiments with light

and movement followed in 1955. The work of the op artist's son Jean-Pierre Vasarely is displayed. Better known as Yvaral, he created the Renault logo, worked with holograms and created digitised images, including one of the Mona Lisa exhibited here.

Thermes Sextius
55 av. Des Thermes.
Even if you haven't booked a day of treatments at the **thermes Sextius** *(see Addresses),* see the great hall: the remains of a thermal bath date from the Roman era and, under a slab of glass, a spring from which water emerges naturally at 36°C. Today's baths, spa and thalassotherapy centre occupy the same site as ancient Roman baths that were destroyed in the 19C. An ultra-modern pool (part of the new facilities) blends with architecture from the 18C.

Pavillon de Vendôme
Open daily except Tue: mid-Apr–mid-Oct 10am–12.30pm and 1.30–6pm; rest of year 1.30–5pm. Closed Jan, 1 May, 25 Dec. €3.50 (under 25 free). 04 42 91 88 75.
This country house was built in 1665 for the Duke of Vendôme by Pierre Pavillon and Antoine Matisse. Its façade features beautiful atlantes.
Inside the Classical building is a collection of 17C and 18C Provençal paintings and furniture *(temporarily removed during two annual photography exhibitions).* Outside, the French-style garden is pleasant for a stroll.

DRIVING TOURS

AROUND CÉZANNE COUNTRY★★★
Round trip of 74km/46mi, see Sainte-Victoire.

Vallée de l'Arc
Round trip of 56km/35mi. About 3hr.

▷ Leave Aix-en-Provence on N 65 towards Marseille as far as Les Milles.

Les Milles Memorial
40 chemin de la Badesse. Open 10am–7pm. Closed 1 Jan, 1 May, 25 Dec. €9.50. 04 42 39 17 11. www.campdesmilles.org.
This huge red-brick building, an old tile factory, was the only French camp used for internment, transit and deportation during the Second World War. The German artists and intellectuals who had taken refuge at Sanary-sur-Mer (*see Green Guide to the Côte d'Azur),* and who did not escape at the time of the armistice, came here. The space is being further developed as a memorial and an educational centre – one of the projects undertaken for Marseille-Provence 2013.

▷ Rejoin the D 65, direction Gardanne, then follow the D 8n to Bouc-Bel-Air.

Jardins d'Albertas★
At La Croix-d'Or. Open Jun–Aug daily 3–7pm; May and Sept–Oct Sat–Sun and holidays 2–6pm. €7.50. 04 91 59 84 94. www.jardinsalbertas.com.
These gardens were laid out in 1751 by the Marquis Jean-Baptiste d'Albertas. They blend together different styles including Italian (terraces, antique statues, artificial cave with the Triton fountain), French (flower beds and canals) and Provençal (rows of plane trees).

▷ At San Baquis, turn right onto D60A.

Cabriès
Cabriès is a picturesque hill village with a castle accessed through a clock gateway and a network of narrow streets inside what used to be its fortified town wall.

▷ Take D 8 back to rejoin D 543 and at Calas turn left onto 9B, then D 9. Drive alongside the Réaltor Reservoir, a fine 58ha/143-acre stretch of water set amid lush vegetation, and take D 65D to the right, crossing over the Marseille canal. After Mérindolle, turn left.

Aqueduc de Roquefavour★

Constructed to transport the Canal de Marseille across the Arc valley 12km/7.4mi west of Aix, the 375m long and 83m high aqueduct was completed in 1847 under the direction of Montricher. It comprises three stages – three tiers of arches – supporting the water channel. Its lower level has 12 arches, the middle level 15 arches, and the top level with its 53 smaller arches carries the canal that transports the waters of the Durance to Marseille.

▶ Follow D 65 towards Salon-de-Provence and 300m further on bear right on D 64 uphill.

Top level of Roquefavour Aqueduct (Sommet)

After 2km/1mi bear right on a path towards Petit Rigouès and right again to the keeper's house located on the aqueduct's topmost level.
From the plateau's edge there is a lovely view of the Aix basin, Montagne Ste-Victoire and the Étoile chain. From the car park walk to the top level of the aqueduct where the canal runs.

▶ Return to D 64 and turn right.

Ventabren

This tiny village is dominated by Queen Jeanne's castle, now in ruins. Take rue du Cimetière to the foot of the castle ruins to enjoy the splendid **view** of the Berre lagoon, Martigues, the Caronte gap and the Vitrolles chain.

▶ From D 64A rejoin D 10 on the right, then turn left onto D 543 for Éguilles.

Éguilles

The village, which has a wonderful view of the Arc valley, is situated on the old Aurelian Way, the present D 17. The town hall, an old castle bought by the Boyer d'Éguilles family in the 17C, has a beautiful façade interspersed with mullioned windows on four levels. From the esplanade, there is a magnificent **view** of the Étoile chain, **Les Milles** and the Aix plain through which the TGV Med line passes. Stroll through the village to explore the old wash-houses.

▶ Leave Éguilles to the NE on D 63, and turn right onto D 14. Then take the path to the left up to the plateau d'Entremont.

Oppidum d'Entremont

🕐*Open Jun–Sept daily except Tue 9am–noon, 2–6pm; Oct–May daily except Tue and weekends 9am–noon, 2–5pm.* 🕐*Closed 1 Jan, 1 May, 1 and 11 Nov, 25 Dec.* ✆*04 42 21 97 33. www.entremont.culture.gouv.fr.*
This capital of the Celtic-Ligurian Saluvii *(les Salyens)* resembled a fortified town by 2C BCE, with a surface area of 3.5ha/8.6 acres. It was protected by steep slopes on one side and to the north by

Aqueduc de Roquefavour

© LianeM/Fotolia.com

ramparts with a sturdy curtain wall reinforced with round towers set at regular intervals. Between two of the towers on the ramparts is a gateway where archaeologists think the Saluvii may have displayed the skulls of their enemies.

Excavations have uncovered many artefacts and works of art, proving that the *oppidum* possessed a high level of civilisation. Entremont artefacts may be seen at the **Musée Granet** in Aix.

CHAÎNE DE L'ÉTOILE★
Consult the map on p167.
Allow about 2hrs.
This chain of mountains, which belongs to the small Alps of Provence and is a result of the Pyrenean fold, separates the Arc basin to the north from that of the Huveaune to the east. It extends the Chaîne de l'Estaque beyond the shelf of St-Antoine. In spite of the low altitude of its mountain tops, the chain rises spectacularly above the Marseille plain. Its central crest, which spreads out like a fan, ends at 781m at the Tête du Grand Puech.
Good to know – If you make the stops we suggest, half a day will scarcely be enough to explore this little-known corner of Provence, conveniently situated between Marseille and Aix.

▷ Leave Aix by the southwest (D 58H), then follow the D 58, direction Gardanne.

Gardanne
This important industrial town, with its coal mining, bauxite and cement works, was painted by Cézanne. It is a lively place on market days (Wed, Fri and Sun).

▷ NW of Gardanne on D 7 towards Aix and Valabre.

▲▲ Eco-museum of the Mediterranean Forest
&Open daily except Sat: 9am–12.30pm, 1–5.45pm (Jul–mid-Aug daily 9am–1pm, 1.30–6pm). Closed last 2 weeks of Aug and public holidays. €6.50 (child 5–15, €4.20). 04 42 65 42 10. www.ecomusee-foret.org.
Dedicated to the ecology of this region, this museum has interactive displays,

footpaths and instructive panels, as well as a botanical trail that helps you explore and learn about the flora and fauna in its natural setting. If you're here around midday, there's a nice and inexpensive restaurant in the courtyard for lunch.

Walk along the Gueidan wall
3hrs. Level: easy. Yellow markings. (Details from the tourist office.) Leave from car park at the eco-museum, 2.5km/1.5mi from Gardanne on the D 7.
An ideal little trip to discover the town suburbs, taking in nature and aristocratic life. Still on the D 7, after the eco-museum, you can see **King René's hunting lodge**: a square bastide flanked by four round towers. As it was built in the 16C, the good king was never in it!

▷ Return to the centre of Gardanne and head towards Gréasque on the D 46A.

▲▲ Gréasque mining centre
Car park at entrance. Open Apr–Sept 9am–noon, 2–6pm (Sun and public holidays 6pm); Oct–Mar 9am–noon, 2–5pm. Guided tours (1h30min) possible. Closed Mon–Tue, Thu and certain Sun. €5 (under 12, €3). 04 42 69 77 00.
Set up in an old coal mine, this unusual museum reveals a little-known side of Provence: its mining complex, which had 51 pit heads when at its height. This one has been restored and is crowned by an impressive pit-head frame – a reminder that up to 300 miners worked here between 1922 and 1960. The daily life of the Provençal miner is re-created, and the evolution of his job through different eras is described.

▷ Continue south on the D 46A; 4km further, turn right towards La Valentine to rejoin the D 8. Turn right, direction Gardanne, then left after 3km/2mi.

Mimet
This small hilltop village is undergoing considerable expansion. From its terrace there is a fine **view★** of the Luynes valley, Gardanne and its furnaces.

◉ Return on the D 8 and follow the D 7 (direction Gardanne) to rejoin the D 8N which leads back to Aix.

ADDRESSES

🏠 STAY

🛏🍽 **Hôtel Cardinal** – *24 r. Cardinale. ℘04 42 38 32 30. www.hotel-cardinal-aix.com. 29 rooms.* In an 18C building, in the quiet Mazarin quarter, this hotel has old-fashioned elegance and today's comfort. Its location is perfect for exploring the town on foot.

🛏🍽 **Hôtel des Augustins** – *3 r. de la Masse. ℘04 42 27 28 59. www.hotel-augustins.com. 29 rooms.* Stone vaulting and stained glass are reminders of the origins of this hotel, a stone's throw from cours Mirabeau, which was originally a 15C convent. The rooms, of which two have terraces with rooftop views, are decorated in a modern style.

🛏🍽 **Hôtel du Globe** – *74 cours Sextius. ℘04 42 26 03 58. www.hotelduglobe.com. Closed 20 Dec–20 Jan. 46 rooms.* Rooms are bright, well kept and soundproofed but not luxurious. Good value. Sunny roof-terrace.

🛏🍽 **L'Épicerie** – *12 r. du Cancel. ℘06 08 85 38 68. www.unechambreenville.eu. 5 rooms.* Tucked away in a narrow street near the place des Cardeurs, this adorable guest house is set in a former grocery store. Rooms and suites are tastefully decorated in a contemporary style.

🛏🍽 **Hôtel St-Christophe** – *2 av. Victor-Hugo. ℘04 42 26 01 24. www. hotel-saintchristophe.com. &. 67 rooms. Restaurant 🍽🍽.* This hotel is right in the centre of the city, near cours Mirabeau, and rooms are decorated in either 1930s or Provençal style. The lively Brasserie Léopold, decorated in the Art Deco style, offers regional cuisine and typical brasserie dishes. Pavement terrace in fine weather.

🛏🍽🍽 **Domaine de la Brilane** – *195 rte de Couteron. Leave Aix on N 296 (direction Sisteron), exit 12 (Aix-Les Plataners), then on towards Couteron (signposted). ℘04 42 54 21 44. www.labrillane.com. 5 rooms.* A British banker turned wine producer has made one floor of his fine domaine at the foot of Sainte-Victoire into a comfortable B&B with vineyard views.

🛏🍽🍽 **Le Mas d'Entremont** – *315 rte Nationale 7, 13090 Aix-en-Provence. ℘04 42 17 42 42. www.masdentremont.com. Open mid-Mar–mid-Oct. 20 rooms.* In the hills above Aix, this fine *bastide* nestles in a park with pool, fountains and antique columns.

🍴 EAT

🍽 **Basilic et Citronelle** – *3 r. de l'Opéra. ℘04 42 27 58 77. Open noon–2pm. Closed Sun.* A small, brightly coloured restaurant offering fresh, home-cooked food. The menu changes every day, as do the vegetarian plates, tarts and pastries. Eat in or take away. Booking recommended.

🍽 **Pizza Capri** – *1 r. Fabrot. ℘04 42 38 55 43. Open 6am–1.30pm (Fri–Sat 3.30pm). www.pizza-capri.fr.* Very good pizzeria, also serving panini. Good value for money.

🍽 **La Grignote** – *22 r. Mignet, 13120 Gardanne. ℘04 42 58 30 25. Closed Mon–Thu eve, Sat lunch, Sun.* Close to the cours Forbin, this restaurant focuses on traditional cooking. Air-conditioned dining room and shady terrace.

🍽🍽 **L'Auberge Provençale** – *13590 Meyreuil (near Le Canet-de-Meyreuil). ℘04 42 58 68 54. www.auberge-provencale.fr. Closed Tue–Wed (Jul–Aug). 🅿.* This pretty roadside inn has agreeable dining rooms with a southern feel. Traditional cooking, generous and carefully executed, plus a good list of local wines.

🍽🍽 **Chez Charlotte** – *32 r. des Bernardines. ℘04 42 26 77 56. Closed Aug, Sun–Mon.* Nostalgia sets the tone here; the main dining room's décor is dedicated to the cinema. Focusing on traditional and seasonal cuisine, the owner gives special attention to every dish.

🍽🍽 **Le Formal** – *32 r. Espariat. ℘04 42 27 08 31. Closed Sat lunch, Sun–Mon.* A restaurant occupying 15C vaulted cellars adorned with a collection of contemporary paintings. Inventive, well-presented cuisine.

🍽🍽 **Le Grand Puech** – *8 r. St-Sébastien, 13105 Mimet. ℘04 42 58 91 06. Closed Sun eve and Mon.* In the heart of the old village of Mimet this restaurant serves Florentine specialities. Good selection of pastas. One of the dining rooms has a breathtaking view of the Pilon du Roi.

🍽🍽 **La Table de Muriel** – *42 r. Jean-Jaurès, 13120 Gardanne. ℘04 42 58 14 60. www.latabledemuriel.fr. Closed Mon–Wed eve, Sun, Aug.* Behind a fairly anonymous façade lies a restaurant which pays homage to Provence and the Mediterranean both in its décor and in its food. Local specialities are tinged with Armenian flavours, much to the delight of regular customers.

◕◕ **Les 2 Frères** – *4 av. de la Reine-Astrid. ℘04 42 27 90 32. www.les2freres.com.* As the name suggests, this restaurant is run by two brothers: the older one prepares the fashionable, modern food (his labours are projected onto a screen in the dining room), while his sibling works front of house. Trendy bistro atmosphere.

◕◕◨ **Côté Cour** – *19 cours Mirabeau. ℘04 42 93 12 51. Closed 25–26 Dec, Mon lunch, Sun.* This is a retreat with a luminous, verdant patio-veranda. All the flavours of Provence and Italy are at your fingertips. Try the *aubergines à la parmesane* and the *calamars farcis.*

◕◕◨ **La Cigale** – *48 r. Espariat. ℘04 42 26 20 62. Closed Sun.* In addition to pizzas, classic dishes are on offer. Graceful décor and a terrace in good weather.

◕◕◨ **Chez Féraud** – *8 r. du Puits-Juif. ℘04 42 63 07 27. Closed Aug, Sun–Mon.* Tucked away in a lane in the Old Quarter, an appealing place with typical local cuisine (pistou, daube) and grills.

◕◕◨◨ **Yamato** – *21 av. des Belges. ℘04 42 38 00 20. Closed Mon, Tue lunch.* Guests are made to feel very welcome by Mme Yuriko in this small Japanese restaurant, decorated in traditional Japanese style. Veranda, terrace and garden.

◕◕◨◨ **Pierre Reboul** – *11 Petite-Rue-St-Jean. ℘04 42 20 58 26. www.restaurant-pierre-reboul.com. Closed Sun–Mon.* In the heart of the old town, this elegant contemporary restaurant specialises in delicious and innovative cuisine, with a strong focus on top-quality ingredients.

TAKING A BREAK

L'Instant Thé – *57 r. Espariat. ℘04 42 66 32 97. Open Mon–Sat 8.30am–7.30pm.* A salon de thé opened by a famous Aix pâtisserie. To satisfy all gourmet tastes, there are also some delicious savouries on offer.

NIGHTLIFE

Café des Deux Garçons – *53 bis cours Mirabeau. ℘04 42 26 00 51.* Bordered by plane trees, cours Mirabeau's 13 cafés are very popular. The Deux Garçons, known more familiarly as "le 2 G", is the oldest (1792) and most famous of these cafés.

Cézanne and Zola used to meet here in the afternoons.

La Bastide du Cours – *41–47 cours Mirabeau. ℘04 42 26 10 06. Open 7.30am–2am.* The huge terrace here never seems to empty. A trendy spot where the *jeunesse dorée* of Aix comes to see and be seen.

Château de la Pioline – *260 r. Guillaume-du-Vair, Les Milles. ℘04 42 52 27 27. Open 24hrs.* The bar of this hotel-restaurant (16C) is superbly decorated in the style of the Medicis and Louis XVI. Don't miss the large terrace overlooking the 4ha/10-acre French garden.

SHOPPING

Markets – ♟♟ **Traditional market** every morning in place Richelme and every Tuesday, Thursday and Saturday on place des Prêcheurs and place de la Madeleine. **Flower market** every Tuesday, Thursday and Saturday in place de l'Hôtel de Ville, and in place des Prêcheurs on other days.

Antiques – **Antiques market** every Tuesday, Thursday and Saturday in place Verdun. **Antiques fairs** take place in the centre of town every 1st Sun of the month 9am–6pm. Check with the tourist office.

Crafts – Makers of vases, ceramics, fabrics, baskets and jewellery display their wares on cours Mirabeau at various times throughout the year; check at www.seagoing.com/antiquaires-aix.

♟♟ **Calissons** – Legend has it that these treats were invented to sweeten up Jeanne for her marriage to King René. It seems she felt much happier about her fate after savouring a *calisson* made of almonds, sugar and candied melon. Two exemplary and long-established places to try these delights include:

Calissons Léonard Parli – *35 av. Victor Hugo. ℘04 42 26 05 71. www.leonard-parli.com. Open 8am–7pm (Sat 9am–*

Calissons

© Marc Lerouge/Fotolia.com

12.30am, 3–7pm). Closed 1 and 8 May, Sun;
Calissons du Roy René – *13 r. Gaston-de-Saporta.* 📞*04 42 26 67 86. www.calisson. com. Shop: Open Mon–Sat 9.30am–1pm, 2pm–6.30pm, Sun 4pm–7pm.*

Apéritifs – The definitive shop for Provençal liquors and aperitifs is **Liquoristerie de Venelles**, *36 av. de la Grand-Bégude, 13770 Venelles.* 📞*04 42 54 94 65. www.versinthe.net.* Old-style pastis a speciality. Free tours and tastings.

Santons Fouque – *65 cours Gambetta.* 📞*04 42 26 33 38. www.santons-fouque.com.* Visit the atelier where these figurines are made. 🐚*See Santons Fair, below.*

ENTERTAINMENT

🎭 The monthly arts diary which you can pick up at the tourist office lists shows, exhibitions, talks, guided tours etc..

Grand théâtre de Provence – *380 av. Max-Juvenal.* 📞*0 820 132 013. www. legrandtheatre.net. Box office Tue–Sat 11am–6.30pm and on eve of performances open until end of show.* With the main focus on music and dance, the emphasis here is as much on quality as on variety: operas, recitals, classical concerts, jazz, musical comedies, dance, world music…

Le Pavillon Noir – *530 av. Mozart.* 📞*0 811 020 111. www.preljocaj.org. Box office Wed– Fri noon–6pm, Sat 3pm–6pm.* Since 2006 this concrete-and-glass building has been the home of the Preljocaj ballet company. Dedicated to dance, it houses rehearsal studios and the theatre where performances are held. One rehearsal each month is open to the public free of charge.

Théâtre du Jeu de Paume – *17–21 r. de l'Opéra.* 📞*0 800 000 422. www.lestheatres. net. Box office Tue–Sat noon–6pm.* Twinned with the Gymnase Theatre of Marseille, this beautiful Italianate theatre runs a varied programme.

Cité du Livre – *8–10 r. des Allumettes.* 📞*04 42 91 98 88. www.citedulivre-aix.com. Open Tue–Sat noon–7pm. Closed Sun, Mon.* The City of Books is a bibliophile's dream. Housed in a restored 19C match factory, it is home to the prestigious Méjanes library, holding the substantial 1786 legacy of the Marquis de Méjanes: 80 000 volumes. This space has also opened up new opportunities for artistic creation in Aix. Numerous events and exhibits are organised here.

ACTIVITIES

Thermes Sextius – *55 av. des Thermes.* 📞*04 42 23 81 82. www.thermes-sextius.com. Open 8.30am–7.30pm, Sat 8.30am–6.30pm, public holidays 10.30am–4.30pm. Closed Sun, 25 Dec–1 Jan.* The baths, spa and thalassotherapy centre use Aix's naturally warm water (36 °C) for various treatments: hydromassage, mud wraps, jet showers etc. One-hour, half-day or full-day packages are offered.

Marked trails – You will come across plenty of hikers in the villages of Mimet, Simiane-Collongue *(7km/4.5mi to the west)* and Cadolive *(5km/3mi to the east)* which are the main points of departure for hikes in the Chaîne de l'Étoile.

EVENTS

International Opera and Music Festival – 📞*0 820 922 923. www.festival-aix.com.* Founded in 1948 by Gabriel Dussurget, this prestigious festival takes place every July in the courtyard of the archbishop's palace, which is converted into a theatre for the event. Concerts and recitals are held in the cathedral, the cloisters of St-Saveur and the Hôtel Maynier d'Oppède.
The festival focuses on important operas (in particular those by Mozart) as well as Baroque opera and contemporary music. Among the many illustrious artists who have contributed to the high standards of the festival are conductors Hans Rosbaud and Carlo Maria Giulini and the acclaimed singer Teresa Berganza.

Santons Fair – Figurines by the best local craftsmen can be purchased; *www.santons-fouque.com; end Nov–early Jan along cours Mirabeau.*

Wine Festival – Festival des Vins et Coteaux d'Aix – *cours Mirabeau – last Sun in Jul.* An opportunity to sample the best bottlings from the Aix area.

Journées des plantes rares et méditerranéennes – In the Albertas gardens at Bouc-Bel-Air, last weekend in May.

Les rencontres du 9e art – *www.bd-aix. com. Mar–Apr.* Cartoon festival (exhibitions, animations, films etc).

Festival Tous Courts – *Cité du Livre.* 📞*04 42 27 08 64. www.aix-film-festival.com. Dec.* International competiton for short films with screenings and discussions.

Sainte-Victoire★★★

Bouches-du-Rhône

East of Aix-en-Provence lies Montagne Sainte-Victoire, a limestone range which reaches an altitude of 1 011m at its peak, the Pic des Mouches. Oriented west to east, this range forms on its south side a sheer drop down to the Arc basin, whereas on its north side it slopes gently in a series of limestone plateaux towards the Durance plain. A striking contrast exists between the bright red clay of the foot of the mountains and the white limestone of the high mountain ridges, especially between Le Tholonet and Puyloubier. The mountain, immortalised by Paul Cézanne in his paintings, was depicted about 60 times by the artist.

◔ **Michelin Map:** 340: I-4.

🗊 **Info:** Grand Site Sainte-Victoire, 66, Route de Meyreuil, La Ferme 13 100 BEAURECUEIL. ℘04 42 64 60 90. www.grandsitesainte victoire.com.

◉ **Don't Miss:** The walk up to Croix de Provence.

🕘 **Timing:** Access is restricted Jun–Sept to prevent fires. In summer, bring a hat and water; in winter, a warm jacket.

👪 **Kids:** The Maison de la Ste-Victoire, to find out about the dinosaur eggs found here, now displayed in the Natural History Museum in Aix-en-Provence.

🚗 DRIVING TOUR

AROUND CÉZANNE COUNTRY
Round trip of 74km/46mi. Allow 1 day (not including tour of Aix).

▸ Leave Aix-en-Provence on the D 10 going east; turn right towards the Barrage de Bimont.

Barrage de Bimont
This vaulted dam across the River Infernet is the principal architectural undertaking on the Canal de Verdon extension. It stands in a beautiful, wooded site at the foot of Montagne Ste-Victoire.

🚶 Downstream, superb gorges descend *(1hr there and back on foot)* to the **Barrage Zola** (a dam built by the engineer François Zola, father of the famous author Émile Zola), the second undertaking in the scheme which supplies water to local towns and villages and irrigation to some 60 local *communes*.

▸ Return to the D 10 and turn right. Park the car in the small car park to the right of the road at Les Cabassols farm.

Croix de Provence★★★
🚶 *3hr30min round trip on foot.*
Walk along the Venturiers path, a mule track which rises rapidly through a pine-wood before easing off into a winding path (☞easier walking).
The first staging post is at 900m, the **Notre-Dame de Ste-Victoire priory**, built in 1656 and occupied until 1879. It comprises a chapel and parts of cloisters; a terrace laid in a breach in the wall gives a **view** of the Arc basin and Étoile chain. Bear left of the cloisters to reach the 945m-high summit, Croix de Provence, marked by a 17m cross upon an 11m base. The **panorama★★★** of Provençal mountains includes: Massif de la Ste-Baume and Chaîne de l'Étoile to the south, then towards the right Vitrolles, the Crau plain, Durance valley, Luberon, Provençal Alps and further to the east the Pic des Mouches. To the east on the crest is **Gouffre du Garagaï**, a chasm 150m/492ft deep, a source of legends.

Vauvenargues

Nestling in the Infernet valley, this village has retained its 17C château, which stands on a rock spur. It belonged to **Picasso**, who lived here and is buried in the park in front of the château.

Beyond Vauvenargues, the road follows the steep, wooded **gorges de l'Infernet★** overlooked on the left by the 723m-high Citadelle, and reaches the Col des Portes pass. During the descent, the foothills of the Alps can be seen on the horizon.

At Puits de Rians, take the D 23 to the right, which skirts Montagne Ste-Victoire on its eastern side and crosses the Bois de Pourrières (woods); to your left is the **Pain de Munition** (alt 612m).

▷ In Pourrières turn right towards Puyloubier. Take the D 57B; then turn right onto the D 56C.

Good views of Montagne Ste-Victoire can be enjoyed before the road climbs the slopes of Montagne du Cengle. The D 17, on the left, winds between the imposing mass of Montagne Ste-Victoire and the Cengle plateau.

Domaine Capitaine Danjou

Open daily 10am–noon, 2–5pm.
Closed Jan 1 and Dec 25.
No charge. ℘04 42 91 45 49.
In the château of this wine estate is the Institution for Veterans of the Foreign Legion. In a *bastide* on the estate, you can visit the **Musée de l'Uniforme** (*see also the Musée de la Légion Étrangère, Aubagne*).

▷ Return to Puyloubier and take the D 57B, then go right on the D 56C.

Croix de Provence

© astharoth/Bigstockphoto.com

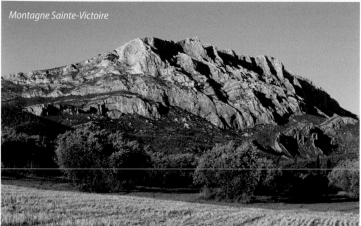

Montagne Sainte-Victoire

© Franck Guiziou/hemis.fr

This picturesque route provides fine views of Montagne Ste-Victoire, the bassin de Trets and the massif de la Sainte-Baume, then crosses the montagne du Cengle before re-joining the D 17, which winds its way towards Aix between Ste-Victoire and the montagne du Cengle.

Saint-Antonin-sur-Bayon

The ♣♣ **Maison Sainte Victoire** (&⊙*open 10am–6pm*. ✍*no charge*. ☎*04 42 66 84 40)* has an exhibition detailing its ecosystem and history (dinosaur eggs). Guided walks are also organised. Before returning to Aix, it is worth making a detour to **Beaurecueil**, which affords the best views of Ste-Victoire, particularly at sunset when the mountain and surrounding countryside are tinted by the sun's rays.

▶ Return to Aix via the "route Paul Cézanne", which goes through Le Tholonet.

ADDRESSES

🛏 STAY

⊜⊜⊜ **Gites Domaine Genty**– *Rte de St-Antonin-sur-Bayon, 13114 Puyloubier. ☎04 42 66 32 44. www.domainegenty.com. ⊟. 4 rooms*. At the foot of the Montagne Ste-Victoire, this is an attractive B&B with four rooms, one gite and a swimming pool.

¶/ EAT

⊜⊜ **Hôtel-restaurant Le Relais de Saint-Ser**– *Chemin départemental 17, 13100 Puyloubier. ☎04 42 66 37 26. www. relaisdesaintser.com. &◻. 9 rooms.* In a dramatic location right up against Montagne Ste-Victoire, at the departure point for the ascent to the Saint-Ser hermitage, this is a pleasant spot surrounded by vines. Excellent local cuisine and bedrooms too. Prices reasonable for this region.

⊜⊜⊜ **Chez Thomé**– *La Plantation, 74 av. Louis-Destrem, 13100 Le Tholonet. ☎04 42 66 90 43. www.chezthome.fr. Closed Sun evening, Mon, Jan. &◻.* One of the best restaurants in the countryside around Aix. Whether you are on the terrace in the shade of a huge *bastide*, or in the lovely dining room, you will enjoy traditional Provençal cooking. Book at weekends.

ACTIVITIES

Walking tour – The **GR 9**, from Les Cabassols to Puyloubier, goes past the Croix de Provence, then follows the ridge up to the pic des Mouches.

Canto-Grihet Equestrian Centre – *Av. Julien-Gautier, 13100 Beaurecueil. ☎04 42 66 97 94. www.canto-grihet.com. Tue–Sun 9.30am–12.30pm, 2pm–5pm. Lesson €40.* In a magnificent setting at the foot of Sainte-Victoire, riding lesssons, courses and treks for all levels from beginners to championship class.

ARLES *and the Camargue*

It is difficult to think of any area as wide-ranging in its appeal as the history-soaked town of Arles and the vast, watery wilderness of the Camargue at its door. A river port valued by the Romans (Julius Caesar included), Arles has archaeological and architectural treasures by the score as well as links with Van Gogh. To the south, the protected Camargue, with its pink flamingoes, white horses, black bulls and unfamiliar birds, is a nature lover's dream.

Highlights

1 Roman **amphitheatre** (perhaps with bulls running): Arles (p194)

2 Magnificent carved doorway of **Église St-Trophime**: Arles (p196)

3 Sarcophagi in the **Musée Départemental Arles Antique**: Arles (p198)

4 **Wildlife and walks** on empty beaches: La Camargue (p203)

5 Pretty **gypsy pilgrimage town**: Les Saintes-Maries-de-la-Mer (p210)

No time is a bad time to visit this part of Provence. In the summer Arles tourist office offers organised walking tours – an excellent way of making sure you don't miss any of its many highlights. Where else can artists and bullfighters be combined in the same day (particularly around Easter)? But other seasons are just as attractive, offering all sorts of festivals.

Archaeology and Architecture

It's impossible to spend time in Arles without picking up on some of its rich heritage. Celtic-Ligurian in origin, then colonised by the Greeks from Marseille and much later, by the Romans, it was a prosperous town through much of its early history because it occupied such an important trading position on the Rhône River. As a result, the city has an abundance of remarkable Gallo-Roman antiquities as well as glorious examples of Romanesque art from the early Middle Ages. Arles has been a UNESCO World Heritage Site since 1981, in recognition of its cultural significance. But it also has an eye to the future, with impressive modern buildings, including the Luma Foundation's extensive restoration of the **Parc de Ateliers**, conceived by prominent US-based architect Frank Gehry; opened in stages through 2014, the site was transformed into a centre for art exhibitions, educational projects and cultural research.

In the Footsteps of Van Gogh

But for all those accolades and accomplishments, Arles may be most synonymous with 19C Impressionist Vincent van Gogh. The home he rented here and Arles street scenes featured in many of his best-known paintings, as did the surrounding landscapes (&see Saint-Rémy-de-Provence for Van Gogh vistas). Any trip to Arles should include a stop at the Espace Van Gogh, once the hospital where he was treated. Art lovers have a treat in store at the Fondation Vincent van Gogh's new location in the **Hôtel Léautaud de Donines**.

Wide Open Spaces

Near Arles, but also worlds away, lies the Camargue, a nature preserve kept in its pristine state through its designation, both in 1927 and in 1970, as a botanical and zoological nature reserve. This watery landscape is home to about 200 bird species and other wildlife, as well as the horses and bulls that are so symbolic of this region.

Abandon your car to explore it on foot, on two wheels, in a boat, or on a small but sure-footed Camarguais horse. After that exertion, you can relax on a sandy beach with hardly a soul in sight near the little town of Les Saintes-Maries-de-la-Mer. Just don't choose 24 May when gypsies come from all over France to honour their patron saint, Sara, who is said to be buried in the local church.

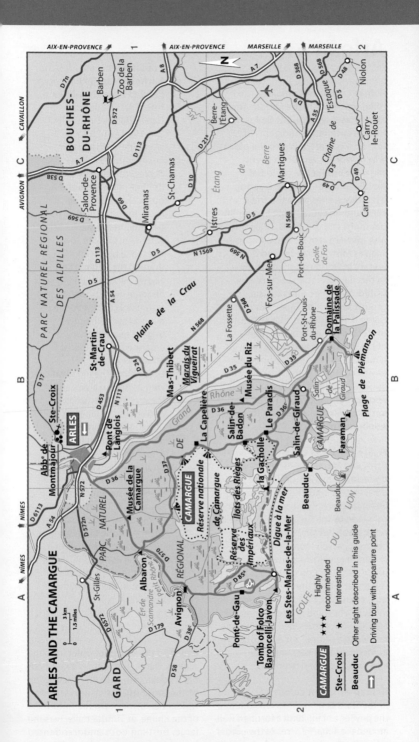

ARLES AND THE CAMARGUE

CAMARGUE
Ste-Croix
Beauduc

★★★ Highly recommended
★ Interesting
▲ Other sight described in this guide
⮕ Driving tour with departure point

0   3 km
0   1.5 miles

Arles★★★

Bouches-du-Rhône

Roman capital and a major religious centre in the Middle Ages, Arles preserves glorious Gallo-Roman antiquities and gems of Romanesque art. It is also the place where Vincent van Gogh spent the most productive period of his life, in 1888–1889, re-creating everyday scenes from the town and surrounding countryside in over 300 paintings and drawings. Arles has also inspired writers and composers such as Mistral, Daudet and Bizet. Its impact in world culture continues to this day: Christian Lacroix, the fashion designer, and musical groups such as the Gipsy Kings are noteworthy Arlésiens. Close to the protected natural environment of the Camargue and good farm land, Arles has also developed as an agricultural centre. Peaches and apricots, the beef of the Camargue's famous bulls, the region's red rice and Arles Merino sheep are its most celebrated products.

A BIT OF HISTORY

Arles and Marseille – The excavations undertaken in 1975 under the Jardin d'Hiver revealed the existence of a Celtic-Ligurian town (known as Theline) colonised by the Greeks from Marseille as early as 6 BCE.

The town, which soon took the name of Arelate, met with new prosperity when in 104 BCE the Consul Marius built a canal that joined the Rhône to the Fos gulf, greatly facilitating navigation. In 49 BCE, when Julius Caesar defeated Marseille, Arles developed economically, becoming a prosperous Roman colony: a crossroads for seven important roads and a major sea and river port.

Roman Arles – A colony of veterans of the Sixth Legion, Arles was granted the privilege of building a fortified wall around the 40ha/99 acres of the official city. A forum, several temples, a basilica, baths and a theatre were built. An

▶ **Population:** 52 661.
◔ **Michelin Map:** 340: C-3 or 528 fold 28 or 524 fold 26.
▤ **Info:** Espl. Charles-de-Gaulle, Bd des Lices, Arles. ℘04 90 18 41 20. www.arlestourisme.com.
◑ **Location:** Stroll along Boulevard des Lices, with its huge plane trees and busy café terraces; the lively atmosphere at its best during the market on Saturdays. The Old Town is reached by passing through the Jardin d'Été and following rue Porte de Laure, with its many restaurants. Take a 90min guided tour of the town to get a quick overview, organised by the tourist office.
☺ **Don't Miss:** The old town with its Roman arena and theatre; the Alyscamps necropolis; the cloisters of St-Trophime and the Musée Départemental Arles Antique.
◔ **Timing:** Arles' public buildings and museums deserve a minimum of two days. Allow at least 30min for Alyscamps alone. The tour of the Crau Plain requires about 3hr.
▲▲ **Kids:** The Roman Amphitheatre; birds of all kinds in the Marais du Vigueirat.

aqueduct brought pure water from the Alpilles. During the 1C, the town developed significantly with the construction of the amphitheatre, shipyards and residential districts. On the right bank of the Rhône, at Trinquetaille, was the large, bustling dockland frequented by sailors, boatmen and merchants. A bridge of boats joined the two banks

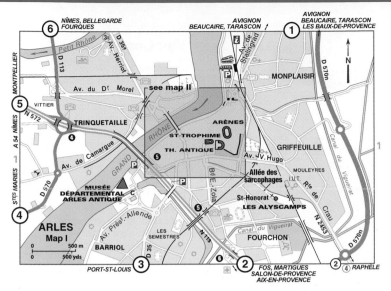

of the river northeast of the town, level with the Bourg-Neuf district.

A Golden Age – In the 5C, Arles was an active industrial centre. Textiles and gold and silver ware were manufactured, ships were built, sarcophagi and arms were made, and imperial money was minted. Wheat, pork meat, olive oil, and dark, concentrated wine from the Rhône valley were all exported. Moreover, stonecarvers, masons and architects from Arles were famous for the quality of their work.

The town had five guilds of boatmen. Some sailed the Rhône, the Durance and the many lakes in the region, using rafts carried on inflated goatskins called *utriculaires*. Other Arlésien watermen sailed the Mediterranean.

Prosperity brought political importance: Emperor Constantine established himself and the expansion of Arles reached its height. The emperor remodelled the northwest district where an imperial palace and the la Trouille baths were built. In AD 395 Arles became the political and administrative capital of the Gauls (made up of Spain, Gaul itself and Brittany). It was also a great religious centre where 19 synods were held, and its bishops were constantly acquiring importance under the protection of imperial rule.

The Decline – In the 8C, the Franks and Saracens fought over the country, causing a great deal of destruction. In the 9C, Arles was but a shadow of its former self when it became the capital of the Kingdom of Arles, which included Burgundy and part of Provence. It was not until the 12C that the town experienced a political and economic revival and acquired the status of a district governed by elected consuls. Its prestige was considerable as the Germanic Emperor Frederick Barbarossa came to the town in 1178 to be crowned King of Arles in the newly completed Romanesque Cathedral of St-Trophime. In 1239 the burghers of Arles submitted to the Count of Provence.

From that time onwards, the town followed the fortunes of the province: political status was transferred to Aix, and Marseille took its revenge and surpassed Arles in economic prosperity.

As long as the Rhône remained the main commercial route, Arles continued to be relatively prosperous. This was even more the case when the land was upgraded by the Crau irrigation project and the drainage of the marshland. However, the arrival of the railway made river traffic obsolete and dealt a severe blow to trade. Until recently Arles was the agricultural market centre for the Camargue, Crau and the Alpilles.

Self-Portrait with Bandaged Ear *(1889)*

©Imagestate/Tips Images

Van Gogh in Arles

Vincent van Gogh (1853–90) came to Arles from Paris on 21 February 1888. He first lived at the Hôtel-Restaurant Carrel at 30 rue Cavalerie before renting a small house, the 'Yellow House' as it came to be known, at 2 place Lamartine. This was where he painted *The Sunflowers* among other works to adorn the walls in preparation for the arrival of his contemporary, Paul Gauguin.

The Café de la Gare around the corner at 30 place Lamartine became the subject for *The Night Café* (all three sites were destroyed during the Second World War). Vincent adapted quickly to Arles. He dreamed of creating a utopian artists' colony. His health improved and he made friends. After much cajoling, Gauguin arrived to stay with him in the Yellow House in October 1888.

Van Gogh's style changed as he moved away from Impressionism. He sought to find "another Japan", as Japanese wood prints fascinated him. The Provençal countryside and its luminosity provided the answer. He painted non-stop: nature, working in the fields, portraits, views of Arles and its surroundings. Among his 200 paintings and 100 drawings were *The Yellow House*, *The Alyscamps*, *L'Arlésienne*, *Crau Plain* and *Langlois Bridge*.

On Christmas Eve 1888, while being plagued by fits of madness and rowing with Gauguin in the street, Vincent's left ear was cut off (whether by him or Gauguin is still in question). He wrapped it in a newspaper and asked a local courtesan called Rachel to "keep this object carefully". Vincent was hospitalised. His fortunes went from bad to worse: Gauguin abandoned him and returned to Paris, his friend Roulin, the postman, was sent to Marseille, and in February 1889 a petition was circulated in Arles demanding that the *fou roux* ('the redheaded maniac') be confined. He finally decided to leave Arles for the asylum at St-Rémy-de-Provence, arriving on 3 May 1889.

Van Gogh's Bedroom in Arles *(1889)*

©Peter Barritt/World Illustrated/Photoshot

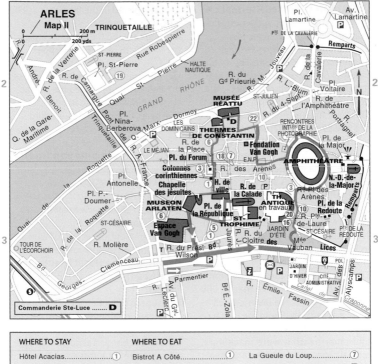

ARLES
Map II

TRINQUETAILLE

Commanderie Ste-Luce .... D

WHERE TO STAY	WHERE TO EAT	
Hôtel Acacias.....................①	Bistrot A Côté....................①	La Gueule du Loup................⑦
Hôtel Calendal...................③	Chez Caro ....③	Le Criquet............................⑩
Hôtel d'Arlatan...................⑥	Ferme-Auberge	Le Cilantro...........................⑯
Hôtel L'Amphithéâtre..........⑩	de Barbegal................④	Querida ....⑱
Hôtel Mireille.................⑲	L'Atelier de	Lou Calèu ....⑳
Hôtel Muette...................㉒	Jean-Luc Rabanel ....⑤	
	L'Autruche.........................⑥	

WALKING TOUR

PUBLIC BUILDINGS
Roman Theatre (Théâtre Antique)★★

r. de la Calade. &⊙*Open daily Mar–Apr and Oct 9am–6pm, May–Sept 9am–7pm; Nov–Feb 10am–5pm.* ⊙*Closed 1 Jan, 1 May, 1 Nov, 25 Dec.* ⊛€6.50 (combined with Arènes). ℘04 90 99 57 01.

Built during Augustus' reign c. 27–25 BCE, this theatre was gradually dismantled. As early as the 5C, it was used as a quarry for the construction of churches. In the 9C it was transformed into a redoubt before disappearing completely under houses and gardens. From 1827 to 1855 it was excavated. The theatre measured 102m in diameter and had a seating capacity of 12 000. It was backed up by a 27-arched portico made up of three levels of arcades, of which only one bay remains.Although little of the original stage survived intact, restoration work carried out in 2010 means that shows can now be staged here using modern equipment.

Turn right by the amphitheatre to the parvis of the **Collégiale Notre-Dame-de-la-Major** *(pl. de la Major.* ⊙*open on certain religious holidays.* ℘04 90 49 38 20)*, an important place for the Confrérie des Gardiens. A terrace allows a fine view of the rooftops of Arles, the Rhône, the Alpilles, and the Abbaye de Montmajour.

▶ Bear right to reach the steps that lead to the amphitheatre.

⚇ Amphitheatre (Arènes)★★

Rond point des Arénes. ♿🕐*Open Mar–Apr and Oct daily 9am–6pm, May–Sept daily 9am–7pm; Nov–Jan daily 10am–5pm.* 🕐*Closed 1 Jan, Feb, 1 May, 1 Nov, 25 Dec.* ⊜€6.50 (under 18 free) *(combined with Théâtre Antique).* ✆04 90 49 36 86. www.arenes-arles.com.

This amphitheatre probably dates from the end of the 1C. Transformed into a fortress during the early Middle Ages, it constituted a system of defence. Later on, the arena was transformed into a town of 200 houses and two chapels, built with materials taken from the building itself, which was mutilated but saved from complete destruction. The excavation and restoration began in 1825. Three out of the four medieval watchtowers remain.

The amphitheatre measured 136m x 107m and could seat more than 20,000 spectators. The arena (69m x 40m), as such, was separated from the tiers by a protective wall. The arena was floored and underneath it were machinery, animal cages and the backstage area. Wander through the upper level of arches in order to understand the building's construction. The spectators would have enjoyed all kinds of games and gladiatorial fighting, which was finally stopped in 404 under the influence of Christianity. Today the amphitheatre hosts bullfighting and cultural events.

It was depicted in the film *Ronin* (1998) with Robert De Niro.
Continue around the amphitheatre past the former 18C **Palais de Luppé**.

▷ Take rue des Arènes to the right of the Palais de Luppé, then the second street on the right, rue Robert-Doisneau, before turning left onto rue des Suisses.

Fondation Vincent van Gogh

Hôtel Léautaud de Donines, 5 pl. Honoré Clair. 🕐*Open during exhibitions Tue–Sun 11am–6pm.* ⊜€9. ✆04 90 93 08 08. www.fondation-vincentvangogh-arles.org.

The permanent collection of works of art assembled in homage to Van Gogh is housed in the **Hôtel Léautaud de Donines** (formerly the Banque de France).

This superb collection includes some of the greatest names in modern culture, such as the painters Francis Bacon, David Hockney, Fernando Botero, Olivier Debré; sculptors Karel Appel and César; photographers Lucien Clergue and Robert Doisneau; writers Viviane Forrester and Michel Tournier; musicians such as Henri Dutilleux; and of course fashion designer and Arles native, Christian Lacroix.

Every year, while the permanent collection is on tour, there is an exhibition

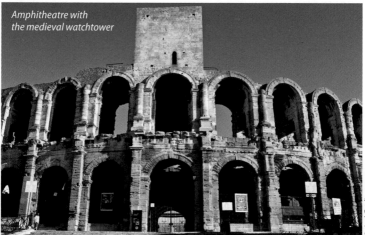

Amphitheatre with the medieval watchtower

©wjarek/Fotolia.com

on the subject of one of these artists, all of whom have made a donation to the foundation.

◆ Continue west on rue des Suisses and turn right onto rue Dominique Maïsto to reach the Réattu museum.

You will pass the former Grand Priory of the Order of the Hospital of St John of Jerusalem (15C), which today houses the Musée Réattu. Take a look opposite at the courtyard of the Commanderie de Sainte-Luce (Social Action Centre).

Musée Réattu★

10 r. du Grand Prieuré. ◷*Open Tue–Sun: Mar–Oct 10am–6pm; Nov–Feb 10am–5pm.* ◷*Closed 1 Jan, 1 May, 1 Nov, 25 Dec..* ◌€8 *(no charge first Sun of month and for under 18 years of age).* ✆*04 90 49 37 58. www.museereattu.arles.fr.*

The museum takes its name from the painter Jacques Réattu (1760–1833), who lived here and whose work is exhibited in the museum's galleries. There are also works from the 16C–18C Italian, French, Dutch and Provençal Schools, as well as a collection of modern and contemporary art. Paintings include those by Dufy, Prassinos, Vlaminck, Sarthou and Alechinsky; and sculpture by César, Richier, Bourdelle and Zadkine. The **Picasso Donation★** is exhibited in three galleries and displays the variety of techniques mastered by Picasso through 57 of his drawings created in 1971. Other exhibitions include an imposing **collection of photographs★**. Many of the 4,000 images were donated by Arles photographer Lucien Clergue, others coming from star guests of the Rencontres Internationales de la Photographie held in Arles every July.

Thermes de Constantin★

r. du Grand Prieuré. ◷*Open daily Mar–Apr and Oct 9am–noon, 2–6pm; May–Sept 9am–noon, 2–7pm; Nov–Feb 9am–noon, 2–5pm.* ◷*Closed 1 Jan, 1 May, 1 Nov, 25 Dec.* ◌€3. ✆*04 90 49 38 20.*

The baths of Arles are the largest (98 x 45m) remaining in Provence. They date from Constantine's era (4C). Enter by the *tepidarium,* through to the *caldarium* with its underfloor furnace which heated the baths and rooms.

◆ Go to rue Maïsto, turn left and left again to reach place and rue de la Sauvage.

Note the old buildings, including the former palace of the Counts of Arlatan de Beaumont (15C), today the Hotel d'Arlatan *(no 26;* ◖*see Addresses).*

Place du Forum

The actual place du Forum is not on the site of the ancient forum, which lay more to the south. Left of the Hôtel Nord-Pinus, two Corinthian columns surmounted by a fragment of pediment are all that remain of a 2C temple.
A street to the left leads to the Plan de la Cour, a small square lined with historical buildings, including the **Hôtel de Podestats** (12C–15C) and the **Hôtel de Ville** (town hall).

Hôtel de Ville

When he rebuilt it in 1675 following the plans of Hardouin-Mansart, the Arles architect Peytret retained the clock tower (16C) inspired by the mausoleum on the Plateau des Antiques (◖*see Saint-Rémy-de-Provence).* Notice in the vestibule *(open to public in daytime)* the almost flat **vault★** – a masterpiece which still mystifies architects. The hall of the Hôtel de Ville gives access to place de la République, in the middle of which stands an obelisk from Arles' Roman circus, moved here in the 17C. The setting is completed with the intricately carved doorway of St-Trophime.

Cryptoportiques★

Access from Hôtel de Ville. ◷*Open May–Sept daily 9am–12.30pm, 2–7pm; Mar–Apr and Oct daily 9am–noon, 2–5pm; Nov–Feb daily 10am–noon, 2–5pm.* ◷*Closed 1 Jan, Feb, 1 Nov, 25 Dec.* ◌€3.50 *(under 18 no charge).*

This double gallery underground, in the form of a horseshoe, dates from the end of the 1C BCE. Two vaulted corridors are separated by a series of huge pillars, and daylight is diffused through skylights. It is not clear whether these substructures of the ancient forum had a purpose apart from ensuring its stability – such as acting as a corn store.

Returning to the Plan de la Cour, then crossing the vestibule of the Hôtel de Ville, you emerge on the place de la République where a fine **obelisk** from the Roman circus in Arles completes the splendid look created by the Classical façade of the Hôtel de Ville and the sumptuous Romanesque doorway of Saint-Trophime.

Église St-Trophime★

12 rue du Cloître. ○*Open Jul–Sept daily 8am–noon, 3–7pm, Sun 9am–1pm, 3–7pm; rest of year 8am–noon, 2–6pm, Sun 9am–1pm, 3–7pm.* ⊜*No charge.* ✆*04 90 18 41 20.*

This church, dedicated to St Trophimus, possibly the first bishop of Arles in the early 3C, was built on a site first occupied by an ancient temple, then, in the Carolingian era, by a church. Its construction began around 1100. In around 1190 the building was enhanced by a magnificent **carved doorway★★**, an example of late Provençal Romanesque style. It displays an ancient Classical arrangement, suggesting the form of a triumphal arch.

Cloître St-Trophime★★

pl. de la République. ○*Open daily May–Sept 9am–7pm; Mar–Apr and Oct 9am–6pm; Nov–Feb daily 10am–5pm.* ○*Closed 1 Jan, 1 May, 1 Nov, 25 Dec.* ⊜*€3.50 (€5.50 combination ticket with les Alyscamps).* ✆*04 90 49 39 53.*

These cloisters, the most famous in Provence for the elegance of their carved decoration, may have been carved with the help of the craftsmen of **St-Gilles**. The best work is to be found in the north gallery *(on the left upon entering)*, particularly on the magnificent corner pillars decorated with large statues and bas-relief. The capitals are adorned

with scenes from the Resurrection and the origins of Christian Arles, as well as foliage. Note especially, on the northeast pillar, the statue of St Paul, his clothing with deeply incised folds, unusually long under the elbows – the work of a craftsman who was familiar with St Gilles' central doorway.

From a later period, the east gallery's capitals and pillars recount the major episodes of Christ's life. The south gallery tells of the life of St Trophimus and the west gallery concentrates on typically Provençal subjects such as St Martha and the Tarasque *(⚲ see Tarascon).* From the south gallery you can see the cloisters, and above, the former chapterhouse and nave.

Dominating the whole stands the stout plain bell tower. Along the east gallery the refectory and dormitory are the location for the famous annual *santons* fair *(Nov–Jan).*

▷ Turn right into rue de la République.

👥 Museon Arlaten★

29–31 r. de la République. ○*Closed for major renovation; reopening 2016.* ✆*04 90 93 58 11. www.museonarlaten.fr.*

This fascinating Provençal Museum was created by the writer **Frédéric Mistral** in 1896 and installed, from 1906 to 1909, in the 16C Hôtel de Castellane-Laval, bought by Mistral with the money he was given when awarded the Nobel Prize for Literature in 1904. Worried by the loss of Provençal identity in the face of national centralisation policies, Mistral wanted to preserve the details of Provençal daily life for future generations. At the entrance to the courtyard you will find a tiled forum with exedra that led to a small 2C basilica.

The Museon, with its attendants in traditional Arles costume, consists of some 30 rooms devoted to the Arles area and organised by theme (including reconstructions of a baby delivery room and Christmas Eve celebrations). This museum is the most comprehensive of its kind in Provence, with furnishings, costumes, ceramics evoking local customs, crafts and music, items of popular devotion, and documents on the Félibrige as well as the history of Arles and its surroundings.

Espace Van Gogh

pl. du Docteur Félix-Rey. ♿ 🕐*Open daily except Mon: Jul–Aug 1–6.30pm (Wed 10am–6.30pm); Sept–Jun Tue–Fri 1–6.30pm, Sat 10am–5pm.* 🕐*Closed public holidays and 25 Dec–1 Jan.* 🚫*No charge.* 📞*04 90 49 39 39.*

This centre was originally a hospital where Van Gogh was treated in 1889; the courtyard is lined with arcades. The site now houses the **Médiathèque d'Arles**, with the city archives, several bookstores, and the school of literary translators, who meet in Arles yearly.

LES ALYSCAMPS★★★

av. des Alyscamps. 🕐*Open May–Sept 9am–7pm; Mar–Apr and Oct 9am–noon, 2–6pm.* 🕐*Closed 1 Jan, 1 May, 1 Nov, 25 Dec.* 🚫€*3.50 (€5.50 combination ticket with Cloître St-Trophime).* 📞*04 90 49 38 20.*

From Roman times to the late Middle Ages, the Alyscamps was one of the most famous necropolises (cemeteries) of the Western world.

In ancient times, when a traveller arrived via the Aurelian Way at the gates of Arles, he made his way to the city's entrance passing along a line of inscribed tombs and mausoleums. And yet the Alyscamps' great expansion occurred during the Christianisation of the necropolis around the tomb of St Genesius, a Roman civil servant, beheaded in 250 for having refused to write down an imperial edict persecuting the Christians. Miracles began to happen on this site, and the faithful asked to be buried here. Added to all this was the legend of St Trophimus, who was buried here.

The transfer of St Trophimus' relics to the cathedral in 1152 reduced the prestige of this cemetery. During the Renaissance, the necropolis was desecrated. City councillors took to offering their guests carved sarcophagi as presents, and monks in charge took funerary stones to build churches and convents and to enclose monastery grounds.

Some sarcophagi are exhibited in the **Musée Départemental Arles Antique** (♿ *see Additional Sights*), permitting a glimpse of the splendour of the Alyscamps in its heyday.

▶ Continue along rue Émile-Fassin to the alley of sarcophagi.

Allée des Sarcophages

A 12C porch, all that remains of the Abbaye St-Césaire, opens onto the avenue bordered with two rows of sarcophagi and also lined with chapels. A number of the sarcophagi are Greek in style with a double-pitched roof with four raised corners. The Roman-style ones are identified by their flat top. Some sarcophagi are carved with three symbols, a plumb line, a mason's level (both signifying the equality of men before death) and a trowel, a type of axe, to protect the sarcophagi from robbers.

Allée des Sarcophages, Les Alyscamps

©De Agostini/World Illustrated/Photoshot

Église Saint-Honorat

Rebuilt in the 12C by the monks of Saint-Victor de Marseille, caretakers of the necropolis, this church is dominated by an impressive bell tower or lantern tower with eight openings on two storeys. Apart from the tower, only the choir, a few side-chapels and a carved doorway remain.

ADDITIONAL SIGHTS
Musée Départemental Arles Antique★★

Follow bd Georges-Clemenceau to the edge of the Rhône, before passing left under the flyover. &⊙*Open Wed–Mon 10am–6pm.* ⊙*Closed 1 Jan, 1 May, 1 Nov, 25 Dec.* ⊛€8 *temporary exhibits (no charge first Sun of month).* ☞*Guided tours available (1hr 30 min).* ℘*04 13 31 51 03. www.arles-antique. cg13.fr.*

Built on the edge of the Rhône, this daring blue triangular building, designed by Henri Ciriani, houses behind its vivid enamel walls a superb collection of ancient art. Its most important exhibit is the earliest known bust of **Julius Caesar★★**, recovered from the bottom of the river Rhône during an archaeological search in 2008. Also worth noting are the colossal **statue of Augustus** (marble torso, limestone drape), which once decorated the theatre stage wall; statues of dancers, altars dedicated to the god Apollo, and a cast of the **Venus of Arles**: the copy of a masterpiece of Hellenistic statuary, the original of which is now displayed in the Louvre. The large **votive shield of Augustus** (26 BCE), a marble copy of the golden Roman shield, shows the extent and speed of Romanisation in Arles. Models illustrate Roman civilisation in imperial times. The museum presents town plans, marked with the important monuments of the Augustan (forum, theatre), Flavian (amphitheatre), Antonine (circus) and Constantine (baths) eras.

Also exhibited is the daily life of the people of Arles, either through objects showing their traditional activities (growing crops, raising animals, craft work) or through sarcophagus reliefs. The economic role of Arles is evoked through the depiction of its road network and both its land and sea trade (sets of amphorae and marine anchors, lead, tin and copper ingots). One area is given over to religions of the time; here you will find a small faun in bronze (1C BCE), and the torso of Sarapis (2C) wrapped in a serpent's coil.

The splendour of the imperial age is exemplified by the **mosaics**, taken from the villas of Trinquetaille (late 2C).

A **footbridge** allows visitors to explore these mosaics, which are either geometrical or illustrate a theme such as the Abduction of Europa or the Four Seasons. Most impressive of all, perhaps, is the remarkable display of **sarcophagi★★**, both pagan and Christian: one of the most important collections after that of Rome. Some of these magnificent marble works, carved predominantly in the 3C and 4C by Arles craftsmen, originate from the Alyscamps necropolis. As well as the sarcophagus known as Phaedra and Hippolytus, note that of the Trinity. This museum also mounts excellent temporary exhibitions.

EXCURSION
Abbaye de Montmajour★

2km/1.25mi N of Arles on the D 17 in the direction of Fontvieille. ⊙*Open Apr–Jun daily 9.30am–6pm; Jul–Sept daily 10am–6.30pm; Oct–Mar Tue–Sun 10am–5pm (last visit 45min before closing).* ⊙*Closed public holidays.* ⊛€7.50. ℘*04 90 54 64 17. www.montmajour.monuments-nationaux.fr.*

On a hill overlooking the Arles plain lie the ruins of Abbaye de Montmajour, full of history and legends, whose buildings represent two different periods: the medieval and the 18C.

The Struggle against the Marshes – The hill was, for a long time, surrounded by marshes. A Christian cemetery was established here and a group of hermits, who looked after the burial ground, were at the origin of the abbey, founded in the 10C under Benedictine rule. The main occupation of these people was

Low-reliefs of a funerary stelae, Musée Départemental Arles Antique

the drainage of the marshland between the Alpilles and the Rhône.

Decadence – In the 17C the abbey consisted of about 20 monks and "religious" laymen, to whom the king granted a position in the community and more significantly part of the revenues. Their tendency towards frivolity provoked a reaction: the congregation of reformed monks of St-Maur, in charge of restoring discipline, sent new monks to the abbey in 1639; the monks who had been expelled then pillaged it. In the 18C the buildings partly collapsed and were replaced by magnificent new constructions. The last abbot, the Cardinal of Rohan, was implicated in the affair of the queen's necklace, with the result that in 1786 Louis XVI proclaimed the suppression of the abbey as retribution.

Fall and Rise of a National Property – In 1791, Montmajour was sold as a national property. It was bought by a second-hand dealer for 62,000 *livres*, payable over 12 years. To help repay the debt the buildings were dismantled: furniture, panelling, lead, timberwork and marble were loaded on carts and sold. In spite of that, the owner was late in her payments and in 1793 the sale was annulled. The abbey was sold for 23,000 *livres* to an estate agent, who broke up the fine stonework and sold the old buildings to people who converted them into lodgings.

During the last century, the people of Arles and the town itself recovered the buildings little by little. In 1872 the restoration of the medieval buildings was started; the 18C buildings remained in ruins. The abbey provided the setting for the film *The Lion in Winter* (1968), starring Peter O'Toole and Katharine Hepburn. The ruins are now a national monument.

Église Notre-Dame★

The 12C building in the main part includes an upper church and a crypt or lower church. The upper church was never completed and consists of a chancel, a transept and a nave with two bays. The **crypt**★ was in part built into the sloping rock and in part raised, because of the slope of the land.

Cloisters★

The cloisters were built at the end of the 12C but only the eastern gallery has preserved its Romanesque characteristics. The capitals bear remarkable historiated decoration which has been associated with that of St-Trophime in Arles.

Monastic Buildings

The remaining buildings include the chapterhouse with rounded barrel vaulting, the refectory with its interesting pointed barrel vaulting *(access from the exterior)* and the dormitory, on the first floor above the refectory.

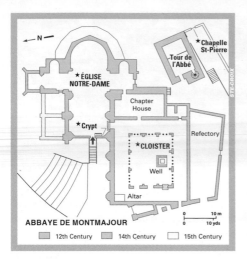

★ Chapelle
St-Pierre

Tour de
l'Abbé

★ ÉGLISE
NOTRE-DAME

Chapter
House

★ Crypt

Refectory

★ CLOISTER

Well

Altar

ABBAYE DE MONTMAJOUR

0   10 m
0   10 yds

| 12th Century | 14th Century | 15th Century |

La Grande Crau

Green countryside gives way to a progressively more barren landscape, devoid of villages, farms and agriculture, apart from the very occasional sheepfold and cabin.

In addition to the encroachment of agriculture from the north, and the installation of several aerodromes, the continued expansion of the Bassins de Fos in the south has radically changed the appearance of the landscape so dear to the writer Mistral.

Chapelle Sainte-Croix★

200m from the abbey on the right, going towards Fontvieille. ⏰*Open Jul–Sept 10am–6.30pm; Apr–Jun 9.30am–6pm; Oct–Mar daily except Mon 10am–5pm.* €7.50. ✆04 90 54 64 17.
This charming little 12C building sits outside the abbey. It is in the shape of a Greek cross – a square with four arms of equal length.

🚗 DRIVING TOUR

TOUR OF THE CRAU PLAIN
93km/58mi. Allow 3hr, excluding the Vigueirat.

▷ Leave Arles on D 453.

St-Martin-de-Crau
The village houses a museum, **l'Éco-musée de la Crau** (*bd de Provence.* ⏰ *open daily except Sun 9am–5pm.* ⏰*closed public holidays.* ⬤*no charge;.* ✆*04 90 47 02 01. www.ceep.asso.fr),* containing an exhibition on this region, which can be explored through guided tours around the nature reserve at Peau de Meau.

▷ Take D 24 south as far as the main road (D 568), where you will head in the direction of Martigues.

▷ At La Fossette turn right and take D 268 to Port-St-Louis-du-Rhône, then turn right onto D 35, and take D 24 to Mas-Thibert.

La Coustière de Crau
Next you reach Coustière de Crau, the damp marshland area of the Crau close to the Grand Rhône where fighting bulls are raised. A Spanish breed, they will end up taking part in the region's *novilladas.*

👥 Marais du Vigueirat★
13104 Mas-Thibert. ♿⏰*Open Apr–Sept daily 9.30am–5.30pm; Feb–Mar and Oct–Nov daily 10am–5pm.* 🗣*Guided tours (1hr) available on foot or by horse-drawn carriage by reservation (2h–4h)* ⬤€11 *(child, under 17, €10).* ✆*04 90 98 70 91. www.marais-vigueirat. reserves-naturelles.fr. Make sure you take mosquito repellent.*
You can visit the marsh alone, on a guided tour along raised footpaths, or in a horse-drawn carriage taking in local birds and animals such as flamingoes, bulls and horses. This protected nature reserve, situated between the Arles canal at Bouc (dug in 1827) and the Vigueirat canal (1642), is the work of a Dutch engineer. Thanks to complex drainage and irrigation systems, the level of the water and its salinity are kept under control, maintaining the

Camargue's ecosystems. Birdlife is especially prolific, including herons of various kinds, mallards, Northern lapwings and Egyptian vultures as well as the region's much-photographed flamingoes.

▶ Return towards Arles via D 35; take the small signposted street to the right.

Pont de Langlois (Van Gogh)

The original bridge, the subject of a famous painting by Van Gogh, was destroyed in 1926. The current bridge, identical to the one in the painting, was rebuilt on the canal that links Arles to Fos.

ADDRESSES

🏨 STAY

🛏🛏 **Hôtel de l' Amphithéâtre** – *5 r. Diderot. ℰ04 90 96 10 30. www.hotel amphitheatre.fr. 33 rooms.* Inside this fine 17C building are cosy, renovated rooms; those in the adjoining mansion are larger and more elegant. Pretty breakfast room.

🛏🛏 **Hôtel de la Muette** – *15 r. des Suisses. ℰ04 90 96 15 39. www.hotel-muette.com. Closed Feb. 18 rooms.* The lovely 12C façade of this small hotel overlooks a little square. Exposed stonework, old beams and the colours of the south in the bedrooms. The breakfast room has interesting bullfighting photos on its walls.

🛏🛏 **Hôtel des Acacias** – *2 r. de la Cavalerie. ℰ04 90 96 37 88. www.hotel-acacias.com. Closed late Oct–end Mar. 33 rooms.* This refurbished hotel near the porte de la Cavalerie has a Camarguaise ambiance downstairs and Provençal décor in its bright rooms.

Plaine de la Crau★★

The Crau plain, which extends over 50,000ha/193sq mi between the Rhône, the Alpilles, St-Mitre hills and the sea, is a grey-white desert of shingle (round rocks) and gravel that in places reaches a depth of 15m.

Cultivation

Since the development of a network of irrigation channels, two areas in the north of the Crau are now cultivated. One stretches from Arles to St-Martin-de-Crau, the other lies to the west of Salon. These two areas are gradually merging, so that a drive along the N 113 from Arles to Salon gives little idea of the stony desert that defines the Grande Crau. Windbreaks of poplar and cypress shelter pastures and fields of fruit and vegetables. There are four crops a year of the famous Crau hay (annual crop approximately 100,000 metric tons) – the last of which is grazed in the fields by sheep wintering on the plain.

Sheep farming

The Grande Crau, resembling a huge steppe, is devoted to sheep farming. The traditional breed is the fine-wooled merino, a cross between the Crau country breed and the Spanish merino introduced into France around the early 19C. About 100,000 head graze on *coussouls* (tufts of fine grass growing between the stones) between mid-October and early June.

The departure for summer pastures (transhumance) takes place when the grazing disappears and water becomes scarce. In the past, the procession of sheep, goats, dogs and donkeys, led by the shepherds, would follow established routes to the Alps. It took 12 days on foot to reach the destination, after passing through many villages, whose inhabitants celebrated the passing of the flocks each year. The return journey, which took place as the first snows began, enjoyed the same festive atmosphere. Nowadays the flock is moved by truck and the area of sheep-grazing land is diminishing.

🛏🍽 **Hôtel d'Arlatan** – *26 r. du Sauvage.* 📞*04 90 93 56 66. www.hotel-arlatan.fr. Closed late Nov–early Apr. 41 rooms.* The past lives on in this gracious 15C mansion thanks to an exhibition of archaeological remains. Rooms are individually decorated using some beautiful old furniture.

🛏🍽 **Hôtel Calendal** – *5 r. Porte-de-Laure.* 📞*04 90 96 11 89. www.lecalendal.com. 38 rooms.* Delightful bedrooms have views of the Théâtre Antique, the Arènes or a lovely garden. In the salon de thé, Provençal salads are just right for a summer lunch.

🛏🍽 **Hôtel Mireille** – *2 pl. St-Pierre.* 📞*04 90 93 70 74. www.hotel-mireille.com. Closed early Jan–end Feb. 34 rooms. Restaurant* 🍽. Out from the centre on the right bank of the Rhône, this hotel has charming Provençal-style rooms. Good service, high-quality breakfasts and a shop selling fine local produce add to its appeal, as do an attractive terrace and pool. Traditional cuisine.

🍴 EAT

🍽 **Querida** – *37 r. des Arènes.* 📞*04 90 98 37 81. www.querida.fr. Open Thu–Mon noon–3pm, 7–11pm.* Just a few steps away from the Arènes, this wine bar has a Spanish feel, thanks in part to the Spanish wines and tapas that it serves. There is a nice patio with a fountain.

🍽 **L'Autruche** – *5 r. Dulau.* 📞*04 90 49 73 63. Closed Sun, Mon.* A friendly couple run this attractive little restaurant. Elegant décor, southern cuisine and a cheerful atmosphere.

🍽 **Chez Caro** – *21 pl. du Forum.* 📞*04 90 97 94 38. www.chezcaro.fr. Closed Tue, Wed.* At this small, unpretentious bistro, the menu changes every other day. It features beautifully presented dishes made from fresh ingredients and cooked by creative, expert hands.

🍽 **Le Criquet** – *21 r. Porte-de-Laure.* 📞*04 90 96 80 51. Closed Mon, early Jan–mid-Feb.* With its beams and stone walls, the dining room of this small restaurant near the Arènes is more appealing than the terrace. The young chef's specialities include *bourride*.

🍽 **La Gueule du Loup** – *39 r. des Arènes.* 📞*04 90 96 96 69. Closed Sun and Mon lunch, Oct–Mar weekends, Apr–Sept.* In the historic centre, it's easy to spot this restaurant by the greenery on the outside. On the first floor, the air-conditioned dining room is pleasantly cool. Provençal cuisine with a focus on fish and Camargue beef. Attentive service.

🍽 **Lou Calèu** – *27 r. Porte-de-Laure.* 📞*04 90 49 71 77. Closed early Jan–mid-Feb, Sun, Mon.* This traditional, popular Arles restaurant is famous for little purple artichokes *à la barigoule*, shrimp tail *mille-feuilles* and all sorts of other delights. Excellent wine list.

🍽 **Bistrot à Côté** – *19 r. des Carmes.* 📞 *04 90 47 61 13. www.bistro-acote.com.* Next door to the Atelier of prominent Arles chef Jean-Luc Rabanel (see below), this more affordable eatery has a relaxed, rather Spanish atmosphere and qualilty produce.

🍽 **Le Cilantro** – *31 Porte de Laure.* 📞*04 90 18 25 05. www.restaurantcilantro. com. Closed Mon (except Mon eve Jul–Aug), Sat lunch, Sun, early Nov and late Feb–early Mar.* Behind the Théâtre Antique, this is a place to enjoy confident, modern cuisine from a talented young chef, either in a smart, contemporary interior or on the terrace.

🍽 **Ferme-Auberge de Barbegal** – *D 33, 13280 Raphèle-les-Arles. Map I.* 📞*04 90 54 63 69. www.barbegal.fr. Open by reservation only Sat, Sun lunch.* ♿🅿🚭. *5 rooms.* The owners of this magnificently restored 300-year-old farm raise sheep and poultry and grow vegetables and olives. Top-quality ingredients for their tasty cooking!

🍽 **L'Atelier de Jean-Luc Rabanel** – *7 r. des Carmes.* 📞 *04 90 91 07 69. www.rabanel.com. Closed Mon, Tue.* Regarded as a true artist in the kitchen, well-known chef Jean-Luc Rabanel serves up innovative, elegant food based on organic local produce in a smart, minimalist setting.

SHOPPING

Markets – Traditional market Wednesday morning bd Émile-Combes, Saturday morning bd des Lices, bd Émile-Combes and bd Clemenceau.

La Camargue★★★

Bouches-du-Rhône

The Camargue, one of the most untouched and romantic regions in Provence, has been largely preserved in its natural state through its designation in 1927 and 1970 as a botanical and zoological nature reserve. Late spring and early autumn are the best times for a visit: wildlife abounds, the sun shines (but not strongly), and there are the famous pilgrimages to Saintes-Maries-de-la-Mer. Just make sure you take plenty of mosquito repellent!

- **Michelin Map:** 339 and 340: B-4 to D-5.
- **Info:** 5 avenue Van Gogh, Saintes-Maries-de-la-Mer. ℘04 90 97 82 55. www.saintesmaries.com. You should also look at www.camargue.fr.
- **Location:** From Arles, the D 570 will take you 27km/16.8mi S to Saintes-Maries-de-la-Mer whereas the D 36 will take you to Le Sambuc and Salin-de-Giraud. In the middle is the Étang de Vaccarès, which you can explore on foot or by bike.
- **Don't Miss:** The Musée de la Camargue to understand local culture; the Camargue Ornithology Park at Pont-de-Gau and the pretty village of Les Saintes.
- **Timing:** A few days would be ideal to sample Camarguais restaurants, visit a working farm and explore the area on horseback, on foot or by bike.
- **Kids:** Horse riding, an afternoon on a vast, sandy beach, Pont-de-Gau Ornithology Park, Domaine Paul Ricard Méjanes.

PARC NATUREL RÉGIONAL DE CAMARGUE

This nature park occupies an area of 85,000ha/328sq mi in the Rhône delta, including the municipalities of Arles and Saintes-Maries-de-la-Mer. The main objective of the park, besides its basic aim of protecting nature, is to allow its occupants to live in their natural habitat, while preserving agricultural activity and strictly monitoring both the hydraulic balance of the region and the growing influx of tourists.

The waters teem with **fish**: pike, perch, carp, bream, and especially eel found in the *roubines*, which are fished with long nets *(trabacs)* composed of three pockets sectioned by passages that get narrower. In the past people lived off their catch. The cistudo, a small aquatic tortoise, and the common snake are also happy in this watery zone.

The **bulls**, black, lithe and agile, with horns aloft, are the stars of the show. They were formerly wild but are now kept in **manades**, the local word for herds of livestock. The *manades*, which contribute to the ecological balance of the Camargue, are tending to decline in favour of agriculture and salt production.

The *mas*, the large farm of several hundred hectares, is managed by a steward *(bayle-gardian)* and numbers an average of 200 horned cattle plus horses. In the spring the round-up *(ferrade)* is a colourful event: the young calves (one year old) are separated from the herd for branding by the *gardians*. They are roped, thrown on to their side, and branded on their left thigh with the mark of their owner.

Camargue **horses** are descended from prehistoric animals, the skeletons of which were discovered in a vast horse cemetery at Solutré (north-northwest of Lyon). Small (not more than 14 hands), they are renowned for their stamina,

Camargue horses
©pigio1958/Fotolia.com

The countryside of Camargue

The Camargue is an immense alluvial plain, the product of the interaction of the Rhône, the Mediterranean and the winds. During the end of the Tertiary Era and the beginning of the Quaternary Period while the sea was receding, waterways transported huge quantities of shingle that piled up along the shore creating a shingle bar dozens of metres wide. On top of this rocky base, marine sediment was deposited after the last glacial period; then, the sea extended to the north shore of the Étang de Vaccarès. However, the landscape changed constantly owing to the conflicting forces of the freshwater Rhône and the sea. The powerful Rhône has shifted its course over the centuries, transporting enormous amounts of alluvial deposits: barriers were formed which isolated the marshes; sandbanks created by the coastal currents closed off lagoons. Every year the Grand Rhône hollows out vast quantities of gravel, sand and mud from its banks and sweeps them to the sea.

The construction of the **sea wall** and the Rhône dikes in the 19C has partially helped to keep this tendency in check. Yet in some places the shoreline keeps advancing, while in others the sea moves it back: the **Vieux Rhône and Petit Rhône** promontories have been swept away by southeasterly storms; Phare de Faraman, a lighthouse 700m inland in 1840, was swallowed up by the sea in 1917 so that a new one had to be built; and Stes-Maries-de-la-Mer, once an inland town, is now protected by breakwaters.

Different Faces of the Camargue

Although the Camargue is one vast plain, it is divided into three distinct regions: cultivated, salt marshes and natural.

The Cultivated Region – North of the delta and along the two arms of its river bed, the Rhône has created banks of fine alluvium *(lônes)* that make up the best soil. This area, the upper Camargue, well drained and tillable, has been improved since the Middle Ages. People have battled against water and high salt levels, accentuated by the evaporation caused by intense summer heat.

Since World War II, great drainage and irrigation projects have been undertaken and have brought satisfactory results. The extent of arable land has considerably increased and large farms predominate. Wheat, vines, fruits, vegetables, maize, rapeseed and fodder are grown in rotation on this productive soil. But the area is known above all for its **rice** production, even if cultivation has dropped drastically in recent times.

Small clumps of white oak, ash, elm, poplar and willow also grow here and there.

The Salt Marshes – These lie near Salin-de-Giraud (11,000ha/27,181 acres) and Aigues-Mortes (10,000ha/24,710 acres), and appear as a chequerboard of evaporation pans and huge glistening mounds of salt. The production of salt goes back to Antiquity and during the Middle Ages created the wealth of salt abbeys like Ulmet and Psalmody. Industrial salt production started in the 19C.

Between March and September a shallow flow of sea water (not more than 30cm deep) is pumped across large "tables" for about 50km/31mi until a saturated solution of sodium chloride has been formed. This is then passed into 9ha/22.2-acre crystallising pans, 12cm deep, divided by dikes (cairels). Between late August and early October, when evaporation is complete, the salt crystals are raked to the edge, washed and piled into huge white glistening mounds (camelles). After further washing, drying and crushing, the salt crystals are ready for use in industry and for animal and human consumption. La Compagnie des Salins du Midi is currently the most important company involved in salt harvesting.

The Natural Region – The wild southern delta comprises a sterile plain dotted with lagoons and smaller pools linked to the sea by a number of channels (graus). A desert of sand and marsh with small dunes lining the coast forms a fascinating nature reserve. Roads cross the Camargue, but for a better idea of this nature reserve, walk along the paths laid out by the regional nature park or nature reserve. These flat expanses, cracked by drought and whitened by the efflorescence of salt, are covered with sparse vegetation known as **sansouire**.

Halophilous (salt-loving) plants, sea lavender and glasswort, green in the spring, grey in the summer, and red in the winter, proliferate and are used to feed the herds of wild bulls. The only shrubs are tamarisks. The reeds serve to make sagno, a screen that protects cultivated land and provides roofing material for the cabins of gardians. The **Îlots des Rièges**, islands that lie at the south end of the Étang de Vaccarès, have lush vegetation, creating a kaleidoscope of colour in the spring: blue thistles, tamarisks, wild daisies and zinerarias, junipers, yellow irises and narcissi.

Fauna

The fauna is exceptional. Besides racoons, otters and beavers (difficult to find), birds reign supreme in this vast marshy land. There are some 400 different species, 160 of which are migratory.

The bird population changes according to the season with migratory birds like teal coming from northern Europe for the winter, or stopping over in spring or autumn, as does the purple heron. Other birds include the egret, grey heron, black-headed gull, herring gull, cormorant, lark, tit, harrier and, finally, the incontestable star of the show, the pink flamingo, instantly recognisable by its pink plumage and long neck. Flamingos live in flocks numbering several thousand and feed on shellfish.

Flamingos

© S. Vinet/MICHELIN

sureness of foot, and lively intelligence. The foals are born brown and turn white only in their fourth or fifth year.

Gardians

The *gardian* is the soul of the *manades*, the cowboy of Camargue, in a large felt hat, carrying a long, three-pronged stick, and watching over his herd. Although the hat and stick are kept more and more for traditional fairs, the horse remains the faithful companion of the *gardian* who is an excellent horseman. His saddle, made locally, must offer maximum comfort and security: padding, fenders which fall along the horse's flanks, cage-like stirrups, pommel in front, and cantle behind.

🚗 DRIVING TOUR

Round trip starting from Arles – 160km/ 99.4mi. Allow one day.

▶ Leave Arles by the southwest (D 570), in the direction of Saintes-Maries-de-la-Mer.

Musée de la Camargue★

D 570, Mas du Pont de Rousty, 13200 Arles. ◷*Open Mar–Oct 10am–12.30pm, 1–6pm; rest of year daily except Tue*

10am–12.30pm, 1–5pm. ⊗€5. ℘04 90 97 10 82. www.parc-camargue.fr.

This museum has been set up in the old sheep-pen of the *mas* at Pont de Rousty and retraces the history of the Camargue region since the formation of the Rhône delta. The periods studied – including Antiquity, the Middle Ages and the 19C – will familiarise you with the traditional activities linked to the Camargue's natural environment.

🚶A footpath of 3.5km/2.2mi through the estate reveals the crops, pasture and marshlands in between the irrigation canals, all of which form a natural part of the grounds of a Camargue *mas*.

Albaron

Albaron, once a stronghold, as can be seen from its fine 13C–16C tower, is now a pumping and desalination station.

Château d'Avignon

◷*Open Apr–Oct Wed–Sun 9.45am–12.30pm, 1.30–5.30pm.* ◷*Closed 1 Jan, 1 May, 1 and 11 Nov, 25 Dec.* ⊗€4. ℘04 13 31 94 54. www.chateaudavignon.fr.

This vast residence with its Classical appearance was modified at the end of the 19C by an industrialist from Marseille, Louis Prat, and is a fine illustration of bourgeois tastes from that period. A tour of the interior reveals beautifully panelled and furnished rooms on the ground floor which are decorated with 18C Aubusson or Gobelins tapestries. A footpath (around 500m) leads visitors past a variety of trees in the garden.

Parc naturel régional de Camargue

Mas du Pont de Rousty - 13200 Arles. ℘04 90 97 10 82. www.parc-camargue.fr.
The Information Centre of the Camargue Regional Park is located on the edge of the Étang de Ginès. Its aim is to make visitors more aware of the fragility of the environment under the park's protection. A permanent exhibition describes the flora and fauna of the Camargue and the working methods and traditions of those who make a living from its natural resources. Large windows overlook the lagoon and marshlands, also giving visitors a good view of many examples of Camargue birdlife as they fly past. Upstairs, there are audiovisual presentations and video films on the subjects of the salt marshes and related activities, pink flamingos and the various projects within the park.

♠♣ Parc Ornithologique du Pont-de-Gau

&♿◷*Hours vary; call or check website for information.* ✆€7.50 *(child 4–12, €5).* ℘*04 90 97 82 62. www.parcornithologique.com.*
This bird sanctuary is next to the information centre. By following a trail marked with explanatory panels and observation posts, you can see first-hand most of the bird species that live in or pass through the Camargue in their natural habitat: nocturnal and diurnal birds of prey, such as the marsh harrier; waders, such as the avocet or the oyster-catcher; grey herons; ducks of all sorts; pink flamingoes, and many more.

Saintes-Maries-de-la-Mer★

♿*See Saintes-Maries-de-la-Mer.*
Take the D 38 W and after 1km/0.6mi, turn left onto a surfaced road. On the left is the **tomb of Folco de Baroncelli-Javon**, the influential writer and

Provençal *gardian*, built in 1955 on the site of his property, the Mas du Simbeu, which was destroyed in 1944.

▷ Return to Les Saintes-Maries-de-la-Mer and head north along the D 85A. At Pioch-Badet, turn right onto the D 570, towards Arles; at the entrance to Albaron, turn right again, onto the D 37, which winds through rice fields. You can make a 4.5km/3mi detour (bear right) to Méjanes.

The road crosses Couvin marsh, a salt-water landscape of stunted plants and swamp. Mas de Cacharel, where the film *White Mane* (1953) was made, stands to the right. The road crosses an expanse relieved by the occasional clump of trees, reeds and isolated *mas*. On the right there is a small viewpoint that looks out over Vaccarès lagoon towards the Rièges islands.

▷ In Villeneuve turn right towards Vaccarès lagoon.

After a small wood the road runs along the lagoon, giving a lovely **view★** over the Camargue, in all its wild splendour.

La Capelière

Chemin de Fiélouse. &♿◷*Open daily except Tue 9am–1pm, 2–6pm (5pm, Oct–Mar).* ◷*Closed 1 Jan and 25 Dec.* ✆€3. ℘*04 90 97 00 97. www.reserve-camargue.org.*
This is the information centre of the **Réserve nationale de Camargue**. The reserve covers more than 13 000ha/ 32 123 acres at the heart of the Rhône delta in the area of the Étang de Vaccarès. The centre offers a permanent exhibition, footpaths (*1.5km/09mi*), and two observatories to help you get better acquainted with the Camargue landscape. To the left, on St-Seren marsh, there is a typical *gardian*'s cabin. The road skirts the Étang du Fournelet.

Salin-de-Badon

◷*Open Apr–Sept 8am–8pm; Oct–Mar 8am–6pm.* ✆€3. ℘*04 90 97 00 97. www.reserve-camargue.org.*

All year round birds flock to this old salt marsh in the thousands. The réserve has laid out footpaths, put up info panels and built three observatories.

▶ After Le Paradis, take the D 36C. After La Bélugue, on the right follow the chemin de Beauduc. (Just about suitable for vehicles, this small road follows the line of a dyke with water on either side.)

👥 Beauduc

One of the most famous beaches in the Bouches-du-Rhône is no more. Or at least, it no longer exists in the guise by which it was known for decades, with a village-like cluster of makeshift cabins at the edge of a vast beach. Previously tolerated although illegal on this part of the protected shoreline, the cabins were removed in 2005. Just a few ramshackle structures escaped the mechanical diggers. The demolition operation has sparked a debate about the disappearance of a certain kind of Mediterranean civilisation, perhaps lacking in sophistication – but not in conviviality! Sadly, the little local restaurant which attracted fans from far and wide has also suffered from the removal of the huts. No more grilled fish: a picnic is vital if you plan to have a day on the beach at Beauduc.

▶ Retrace your steps to Faraman and carry on to Salin-de-Giraud.

Salin-de-Giraud

This small town was developed by two companies involved in salt production. It has pink brick houses with neat gardens and, unusually for these parts, a Greek orthodox church as many of the salt workers were recruited in Greece.

▶ Follow the road skirting the Grand Rhône towards 'Plages d'Arles'.

Viewpoint of the Salt Marsh

The viewpoint beside a salt mound looks out over the Giraud pans and workings. To visit the **Ecomusée du Sel**, take the tourist train that tours the village of Salin-de-Giraud (⏱departs Apr–Sept, 11.30am, 2.30pm, 4pm and 5.30pm. €8. ✆06 70 47 888 12).

Domaine de la Palissade★

⏱Open mid-Jun–mid-Sept daily 9am–6pm; rest of the year 9am–5pm. ⏱Closed Mon, Tue from late Nov–Feb, 1 Jan, 1 May, 11 Nov, 25 Dec. €3. ✆04 42 86 81 28.

This estate, the property of the Conservatoire du Littoral (Society for the Preservation of Coastlines and River Banks), covers 702ha/1,735 acres. It is the only area of the delta not to have been enclosed by dykes. The result is that the scenery reflects the original character of the lower Camargue: alluvial deposits from the old course of the Rhône; riparial shrubs on the present banks; dunes or hummocks; a type of marsh samphire (sansouires in Provençal); fields of sea lavender used for grazing; and beds of reeds and rushes.

Three footpaths thread the estate: one of 1.5km/0.9mi, with info panels, and two others, 3km/2mi and 7.5km/4.7mi, offering fewer explanations but allowing walkers to penetrate the Camargue.

▶ Continue towards Plage de Piémanson.

The road goes along a dyke, through a region of lagoons glistening white with salt. Take the chance to have a dip in the Mediterranean at the vast sandy beach of **Piémanson** (25km/15.5mi).

▶ Head towards Arles through Salin-de-Giraud.

Musée du Riz

Rizerie du Petit Manusclat. ⏱Open daily 9am–12.30pm, 2–6pm. €6. ✆04 90 97 29 44.

If you want to find out everything about rice cultivation in the Camargue, this little museum set up by the Bon family (rice growers for three generaions) is worth visiting. Displays of different rice varieties, tools, models and local flora and fauna are brought to life by the charming and enthusiastic owners.

▶ Take the D 36 and then the D 570, on the right, and head back to Arles.

✖ WALK
Along the Seawall
From the edge of Saintes-Maries-de-la-Mer, the 20km/12mi sea wall is only for those on foot or bike.

The path leads to the **Gacholle lighthouse** (🕐 *open Sat–Sun and school holidays 11am–5pm;* 🚫 *no charge;* 📞 *04 90 97 00 97*) where there is an information point and observatory. Illustrating the Camargue's rich birdlife and landscapes, the walk continues south on a causeway between the two lagoons, the **Étang du Fangassier** and the **Étang de Galabert**. Galabert island is the only nesting site in France for pink flamingos.

ADDRESSES

🛏 STAY

🍽 **Hôtel Le Flamant Rose**– *Rte de St-Gilles, 13123 L'Albaron.* 📞*04 90 97 10 18. www.leflamantrose.camargue.fr. Closed Wed except Jul–Aug. 15 rooms.* Budget accommodation in the heart of the Camargue. The restaurant serves local specialities in a dining room top-heavy with Camarguais décor or in the garden.

🍽🍽🍽🍽 **Le Mas de Peint** – *13200 Le Sambuc. 2.5km/1.5mi out on the road to Salins.* 📞*04 90 97 20 62. www.masdepeint. com. Open late Mar–mid-Nov and Christmas/New Year.* 🅿 ♿ *11 rooms. Restaurant* 🍽🍽🍽🍽. On a vast estate, this superb 17C *mas* fosters Camarguaise traditions with passion. Very comfortable rooms, garden with pool, equestrian centre with private bullring. Retro-chic cuisine: the chef cooks appetising, elegant dishes with a local twist in an open kitchen.

🍴 EAT

😋 **Good to know** – *Gardiane de taureau* is on menus everywhere. It is a beef stew, made by marinading pieces of *taureau de Camargue* (a meat that has had its own *appellation d'origine contrôlée* since 1996) in red wine flavoured with herbs and spices (thyme, bay leaves, parsley, cayenne pepper, cloves), orange zest and garlic.

🍽🍽🍽🍽 **La Chassagnette** – *Domaine de l'Armellière, rte du Sambuc, en Camargue.* 📞*04 90 97 26 96. www.chassagnette.fr. Closed Tue, Wed and Feb–Mar.* This charming restaurant 12km/8mi from Arles serves refined food with an organic and vegetarian focus. Afterward, walk around the organic garden or browse the books in the library while enjoying a tea made with herbs you've picked from the herb garden.

LEISURE ACTIVITIES

Birdwatching – Leave early in the morning, before 10am, or at dusk, Mar–Oct. The best places are the footpaths around La Capelière and the Domaine de la Palissade, the seawall, and the Pont-de-Gau bird park. Just remember to take mosquito repellent if the weather is muggy, and stay quiet!

Courses Camarguaises – These games, where men called *razeteurs* snatch a rosette from between a bull's horns, take place Easter–September. Details from the tourist offices in Arles, Saintes-Maries-de-la-Mer and Aigues-Mortes.

Cycling – The flat Camargue is ideal cycling territory. Pick up details at Arles or Saintes-Maries-de-la-Mer tourist office about five suggested bike routes, varying in levels of difficulty and distance (16–42km/10–26mi).

Horse Riding – Tourist offices have details of many locations offering a wide range of options, from a few hours in the saddle to weekends or full weeks that include meals and accommodation.

Swimming – There are big bathing beaches (some naturist) at Saintes and Piémanson, south of Salin-de-Giraud. You won't have to worry about putting your towel down too close to your neighbour. The nearest person will probably be at least 100mi away!

Walking – The best paths are the **GR 653 footpath**; the sea wall; and the footpaths around Domaine de la Palissade, La Capelière and Salin-de-Badon.

🏇 **Domaine Paul Ricard Méjanes** – 📞*04 90 97 10 10. www.mejanes.camargue.fr. Open May–Sept daily 9am–5pm (6pm summer); Oct–Easter by reservation.* The Camargue in microcosm, the estate includes a bullring with regular *courses*, pony trekking, bike hire, horse-drawn carriages and an electric railway along Vaccarès lagoon.

Saintes-Maries-de-la-Mer★

Bouches-du-Rhône

Between the Mediterranean and the Launes and Impérial lagoons, at the heart of the Camargue, Saintes-Maries-de-la-Mer can be distinguished by its fortified church. A marina extends to the west.

👣 WALKING TOUR

If you stay in Saintes, you will enjoy strolling in narrow streets of dazzlingly white, low houses nestled up against the church, and fall for the charm of a little town which has miraculously escaped the crazy development so often found close to the sea. Unfortunately the charm of certain streets (F.-Mistral and V.-Hugo in particular) has been spoiled by an influx of street traders. To escape the commercial atmosphere, keep to the quiet, white streets away from the centre, on the northern and western fringes of the town. You can be certain of the same tranquillity if you walk along the breakwater which protects

▶ **Population:** 2 296.
🚗 **Michelin Map:** 340: B-5 7.
🗊 **Info:** 5 avenue Van-Gogh, Saintes-Maries-de-La-Mer. ℘04 90 97 82 55. www.saintesmaries.com.
☺ **Don't Miss:** A walk in narrow streets of white-washed houses; the church with its Saint Sara statue.
👫 **Kids:** Discovering the Camargue by bike or paddle steamer.
🕐 **Timing:** It's particularly busy around 24 May when gypsies come to celebrate their patron saint, Sara, who is said to lie buried in the local church.

the town from the ravages of the sea, or by following the **digue à la mer** on foot or by bike. Go as far as the lighthouse, the **phare de la Gacholle**, to enjoy the freedom of the Camargue's vast **beaches**, Beauduc and Piémanson especially (🚗*see La Camargue).*
Take part in an *abrivado,* mingling with the *atrapaires* who fling themselves in front of the *gardians'* horses, then go

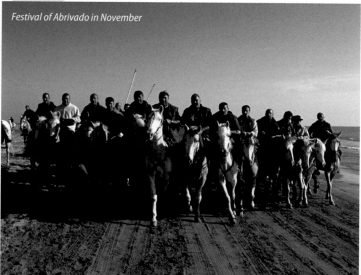
Festival of Abrivado in November

© Camille Moirenc/hemis.fr

Nineteen Centuries of Pilgrimage

According to Provençal legend, the boat abandoned to the waves in c.AD 40 by the Jews of Jerusalem, which, without the aid of sail or oar, landed safely on the shore of Saintes-Maries, carried Mary, the mother of James, Mary Magdalene, Martha and her brother Lazarus, St Maximinus, Mary Salome, the mother of James Major and John, and Cedonius, the man born blind.

Sara, the two Marys' black servant left behind on the shore, wept aloud until Mary Salome threw her mantle on the water so that Sara could walk over it to join the others. The legend continues that after erecting a simple oratory to the Virgin on the shore, the disciples separated; Martha went to Tarascon, Mary Magdalene to Ste-Baume. The two Marys and Sara remained in the Camargue and were buried in the oratory.

The saints' tomb rapidly became the object of a cult attracting pilgrims from afar, while gypsies and other nomads developed a particular veneration for Sara. By the mid-9C the oratory (believed to date from the 6C) had been replaced by a fortified church which, in 869, was being incorporated into the town ramparts under the personal supervision of the Archbishop of Arles, when suddenly the Saracens made a lightning raid and carried off the archbishop. In the short time it took to collect the ransom of 150 *livres* of silver, 150 mantles, 150 swords and 150 slaves, the prelate died; unperturbed, the Saracens returned with the corpse, set it apart on a throne with a great show of respect as if nothing were wrong, and departed with the ransom before the Arlesians discovered their loss.

In the 11C the monks of Montmajour established a priory and in the 12C rebuilt the church, which was at the same time incorporated into the fortifications. At the end of the 14C the church's fortress-like appearance was reinforced by the addition of machicolations. During the Barbarian invasions the saints' remains were buried under the chancel. In 1448, King René ordered the exhumation of the saints, whose relics were then enshrined with great ceremony and have remained the object of a deep and widespread veneration ever since.

on to the bullring and share the thrills of the crowd as the *cocardiers* are hurled against the barriers. For a serene end to the day, you can watch the setting sun light up the watery expanses of the Camargue in flaming colours.

Église Notre-Dame-de-la-Mer★

From the exterior, the massive crenellated walls of this fortified church are decorated with Lombard arcades at the east end. The keep-like structure of the upper chapel, surrounded at the base by a watchpath and crowned by a crenellated terrace, is dominated by a bell gable (restored in the early 20C). On the south side note the images of two fine lions devouring their prey, which are believed to have supported a porch.

Interior

Enter through the small door on place de l'Église. The Romanesque nave is very dark. South of the nave, protected by a wrought-iron railing, is a well of fresh water for use in times of siege. In the third bay on the north side, above the altar, is the boat of the two Saint Marys which is carried in procession by the gypsies in May and the parishioners in October. South of this altar note the Saints' Pillow, a worn block of marble incorporated in a column and discovered during the excavations of 1448 when the saints' relics were found.

Crypt

The altar was built with part of a sarcophagus; it holds the reliquary containing the presumed relics of St Sara. Right of

Aerial view of the Camargue at Saintes-Maries-de-la-Mer

© euroluftbild.de/age fotostock

the altar stands the statue of Sara and ex-votos offered by the gypsies.

Upper Chapel

The chapel is richly panelled in bright green and gold in the Louis XV style. It houses the reliquary shrine of the two Marys. Frédéric Mistral set the final scene of his romance *Mirèio* in the chapel where his heroine, Mireille, came to pray for help.

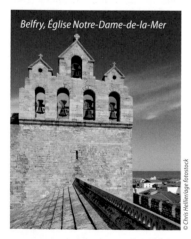

Belfry, Église Notre-Dame-de-la-Mer

© Chris Hellier/age fotostock

Watchpath (Chemin de Ronde)

Access to the roof (53 steps): Apr–Jun 10am–noon, 2–5pm, Sun 2–5pm; rest of the year according to weather conditions. €2.50. 04 90 97 88 77.
Climb to the paved watchpath which encircles the church roof, commanding an unforgettable **view**★ of the sea, the town and the vast Camargue plain.

BEACHES

Yes, you can take a dip at the end of the little white streets: all along the pedestrian promenade skirting the sea, you'll find a succession of small, sandy beaches. The lifeguard post is behind the bullring.

The vast eastern beaches stretch out along the **digue à la mer** *(access: 4km/2.5mi by car, then on foot or by bike)*.

West of the town, there is a sandy beach of more modest proportions, covering 2km/1.2mi. Watersports of all sorts are on offer including windsurfing, dingy sailing, kite-surfing, kayaking; and boats and pedal-boats for hire. There are also sea-fishing trips *(full list of activities available at the tourist office)*.

ADDRESSES

🛏 STAY

Hôtel Méditerranée – *4 av. Frédéric-Mistral.* ☎*04 90 97 82 09. www. hotel-mediterranee.camargue.fr. 14 rooms.* A simple family hotel with plenty of good points: a flower-decked façade, a shady terrace where breakfast is served on fine days, recently decorated rooms, reasonable prices and a good choice of restaurants nearby.

Chambre d'hôte Mazet du Maréchal-Ferrand – *Rte du Bac.* ☎*04 90 97 84 60. www.chambrescamargue.com.* 🅿 🛏. *3 rooms.* A very straightforward place where the owner will immediately put you at your ease. The bedrooms, all on the ground floor, are simple and brightly coloured. Breakfasts are served under the mulberry tree or in a cheerful little room decorated in Provençal colours.

🍴 EAT

Good to know – In Les Saintes-Maries, the restaurants are in a continuous row all the way along the avenue Frédéric-Mistral. Identical menus with *tellines* (tiny clams), *gardiane de taureau*, grilled sea bass, salt-baked fish etc.

Le Bodega Kahlua pub restaurant – *8 r. de la République.* ☎*04 90 97 98 41. Closed mid-Nov–Feb.* ♿. Depending on the time of day, you may decide to drop into this 1930s-style villa for a cocktail, a pizza, charcoal-grilled meat, tapas or Antilles-influenced specialities such as chicken leg "Boucanet".

Bar-Brasserie de la Plage (chez Boisset) – *1 r. de la République.* ☎*04 90 97 84 77. Closed Dec–Jan.* Seafood and shellfish to eat on a terrace shaded by reed screens, or to take away.

SHOPPING

Les Bijoux de Sarah – *12 pl. de l'Église.* ☎*04 90 97 73 73.* Hand-made jewellery. Their speciality is a "gypsy" pendant that is supposed to bring good luck and protect against the evil eye!

Market – Traditional market Monday and Friday in place des Gitans.

EVENTS

Gypsy Pilgrimage – Each May, gypsies from around the world come to celebrate their saint, Sara. After a service in the church on 24 May, her effigy is carried to the sea.

Camargue traditions – 26 May is Baroncelli-Javon Memorial Day; it is one of much celebration and local colour. Camargue *gardians*, with the women of Arles in traditional costume, enjoy local dances, *abrivados*, *courses camarguaises*, etc.

Festival de la Camargue et du Delta du Rhône – One for bird lovers: six days of accompanied walks and exhibitions at the beginning of May. Activities for children, too.

Feria du Cheval – A celebration of all that is equine, held in mid-July *(www. festivalducheval.camargue.fr).*

ACTIVITIES

👓 *See also La Camargue Addresses.*

👥 **Bike riding** – You can discover the Camargue by cycling along the marked 24km/15mi trail which starts in Les Saintes-Maries.

Water sports – With its port and large beaches, Saintes-Maries is a good place to try water sports such as windsurfing, sea kayaking and sailing. The **Ecole de Voile des Saintes-Marie** (on the seafront, behind the bullring) offers lessons and equipment rental *(www.ecoledevoile. camargue.fr).*

👥 **Paddle steamer cruise – Tiki III Mini-Cruise of the Camargue** – *D 38. Departures Apr–Sept at 10am, 2.30pm and 4.15pm; Mar and Oct 2.30pm. Trip (1hr30mn) €12 (under 12, €6).* ☎*04 90 97 81 68. www.tiki3. fr.* Discover the secrets of the Camargue on board *Tiki III*, a paddle-steamer with a rather old-fashioned charm. You can observe the local flora and fauna on this little cruise which includes a stop half-way, with plenty of opportunity to see horses and bulls.

Thalassothery – Thalacap Camargue – *Av. Jacques-Yves Cousteau.* ☎*08 25 12 51 45. www.thalacap.com.* Thalassotherapy centre offering a wide range of treatments.

East of Arles and south of Avignon, the long limestone range of the Alpilles stretches out, creating a white silhouette against a deep blue sky. The hills are the backdrop to a strikingly varied landscape with as many shades of green as you might find on an artist's palette: dark for pines and cypresses, lighter for *Kermes* oaks, vivid for vineyards, silvery for olives. This pretty countryside, which has at its heart some of the most entrancing and historically fascinating towns and villages in Provence, is a nature lover's paradise, claiming to have 960 plant species, 90 bird species and even 19 varieties of bat.

Highlights

1 Roman remains at **Le Plateau des Antiques**: St-Remy-de-Provence (p223)

2 The dramatic **Panorama de la Caume**: Les Alpilles (p232)

3 A walk through medieval streets in the off season: **Les Baux** (p235)

4 Magnificent castle of **King René**: Tarascon (p242)

5 Walking tour of old **Beaucaire** (p249)

Outdoor enthusiasts of all ability levels and interests can find an activity here, from walking to biking to birdwatching. Among the favourites of birdwatchers is the majestic Bonelli eagle, small and brown with a white belly.

Trail options generally include fairly intense walks as well as quick walks as the topography features so many hills and valleys; but there are also some flat stretches for easy biking.

Whatever you decide to do, an outing in the fresh, *garrigue*-scented air of the Alpilles will contrast perfectly with visits to nearby towns.

The Nostradamus Factor

You can follow in the steps of the acclaimed 16C soothsayer by exploring St-Rémy-de-Provence (where he was born) and Salon-de-Provence (where he lived for the last 19 years of his life and published his famous *Prophecies*). There are many other things to see and do in both towns. Salon, less thronged with visitors than some of its neighbours, has a fine old centre where grand houses point to the wealth it enjoyed in medieval times, thanks to its abundance of olive oil. More frequented by tourists, St-Rémy nevertheless remains a quintessential Provençal town with a dreamy atmosphere and houses painted in the pale pastel colours that are typical of this area. It has important Roman remains at the ancient settlement of Glanum.

Medieval War Lords

Spring and autumn are the best times to visit Les-Baux-de-Provence, simply because this citadel, perched dramatically high up on an outcrop of rock, is crammed to bursting point in summer, being one of the most visited tourist sites in Provence. The Lords of Les Baux, who claimed to be descended from the magi king Balthazar, were among the most powerful in the land in the early Middle Ages, controlling 79 towns and villages from their lofty citadel. Les Baux gave its name to the mineral bauxite, which was found here in the 19C.

Off the Main Tourist Trail

To the west are the **Montagnette,** a smaller chain of hills, and two historic towns that should not be missed. On the east bank of the Rhône, Tarascon is the site of Good King René's spectacular castle in the 15C. Its towering bulk, visible for many kilometres, is at odds with an elegant interior testifying to the king's passion for the arts. Just across the river, Beaucaire is an attractive canal-side town with an intriguing past. For centuries it hosted a massive month-long fair, attracting traders of every imaginable kind as well as street performers. That's a memory, but the magnificent 17C and 18C houses of rich merchants are still there to admire.

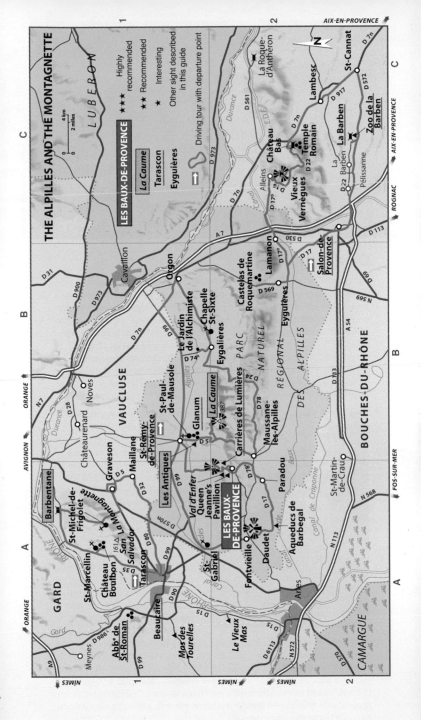

THE ALPILLES AND THE MONTAGNETTE

★★★ Highly recommended
★★ Recommended
★ Interesting

◻ Other sight described in this guide

⬆ Driving tour with departure point

LES BAUX-DE-PROVENCE
La Caume
Tarascon
Eyguières

0   4 km
0   2 miles

215

Alpilles olive grove

© David Martyn/Bigstockphoto.com

Oil-rich Alpilles

Although olive trees flourish all over Provence, few olive-dominated landscapes look quite as ravishing as the Alpilles, or yield such a significant amount of high-quality oil. Granted an *appellation d'origine contrôlée* (AOC) in 1997, the Vallée des Baux produces 25 percent of France's *appellation* olive oil from the fruit of almost a thousand growers. Regulations here stipulate that all AOP (*appellation d'origine protegée*) oils must be blends of several olive varieties. There are five contenders: the soft, buttery Grossane; the light, grassy Salonenque; the leafy Verdale; the punchy Aglandau; and the peppery Picholine, each of them adding subtle nuances to the end result in the same way that different grapes combine to bring layers of complexity to wine.

© C. Chillio/Comité Régional de Tourisme Provence-Alpes-Côte d'Azur

In the Vallée des Baux, the AOP, which has replaced the AOC classification, applies to two distinctly different styles of oil. *Fruité vert* (fruity green), made from olives that are picked and processed on the same day, has the fresh, tangy flavours of green apples or raw artichokes, making it a perfect match for salads of all kinds. *Fruité noir* (fruity black), a less common style that is coming back into fashion, is made from olives that are kept for a few days before being processed. Much richer and more unctuous with mushroomy overtones, it stands up well to *aïoli* and other robustly flavoured Provençal specialities, as well as mushroom and truffle dishes. The outstanding quality of Vallée des Baux oils makes a tasting and shopping detour to some of the best mills (*see Addresses*) essential. You will also find excellent olive oils in many other parts of Provence, and it can be fascinating to compare and contrast their different characteristics. One useful tip: never taste oil with bread (even though it is often offered); it makes even mediocre oils taste better than they should!

Salon-de-Provence★

Bouches-du-Rhône

This attractive fortified town occupied a key defensive position in the Middle Ages. Known as Salon de Crau until 1918 when its name was changed to Salon-de-Provence, it became important agriculturally besides being a centre of traditional soap manufacture. Salon is the seat of the officers' training school for the French Air Force, which was established in 1936. It was also the home of doctor and soothsayer Nostradamus from 1547 to 1566.

▶ **Population:** 43 152.

Michelin Map: 340: F-4.

Info: 56 cours Gimon, 13664 Salon-de-Provence. ℘04 90 56 27 60. www.visitsalondeProvence.com.

○ **Location:** Salon-de-Provence is located half-way between Arles and Aix, in countryside dominated by olive trees.

Don't Miss: Château de l'Empéri, the house of Nostradamus, a trip to La Barben zoo and castle.

○ **Timing:** Allow 2hr or more if you come on market day – Wednesday – on place Morgan.

Kids: La Barben zoo.

WALKING TOUR

TOWN CENTRE
2hr.

Château de l'Empéri
Montée du Puech.
Built on top of Puech rock, this massive castle dominates the old town. Once the residence of the archbishops of Arles, Lords of Salon, the castle was begun in the 10C, rebuilt in the 12C and 13C and remodelled in the 16C; it was transformed into barracks in the 19C but damaged during the 1909 earthquake. A vaulted passage leads to the courtyard decorated with a Renaissance gallery. The 12C Chapelle Ste-Catherine, the main reception room with its finely carved chimney and some 30 rooms, houses the **Empéri Museum**.

Musée de l'Empéri★★
Château de l'Empéri, Montée du Puech.
○*Open daily except Mon: mid-Apr–Sept 9.30am–noon, 2–6pm; Oct –mid-Apr 1.30–6pm.* ○*Closed public holidays.* ⊛€5. ℘04 90 44 72 80.
This museum covers the history of the French army from the time of Louis XIV to 1918. The fine rooms enhance the impressive display of 10,000 items (uniforms, flags, decorations, cutting and thrusting weapons and firearms,

Château de l'Empéri

© Philippe Halle/Dreamstime.com

Nostradamus

Michel de Nostradame (Nostradamus) chose Salon as his home in later life. Born in St-Rémy-de-Provence in 1503, he studied medicine in Montpellier and travelled for 12 years in Europe and the Far East to try to improve the remedies which he kept secret; he also studied esotericism.

The success he achieved with his remedy for the plague epidemics of Aix and Lyon aroused the jealousy of his colleagues. When the epidemics ceased, he retired to Salon in 1547 and took up astrology. His book of predictions entitled *Centuries*, written in the form of verse quatrains, was fantastically successful, attracting the attention of Catherine de' Medici. She came to him and had him read Charles IX's horoscope, showering him profusely with gifts. Nostramadus died in Salon in 1566.

region fertile through the construction of the irrigation canal bearing his name which carries water from the Durance along the original river course through the Lamanon gap.

👤👤 Maison de Nostradamus

11 r. Nostradamus. ⏰*Open Mon–Fri 9am–noon, 2–6pm, Sat–Sun 2–6pm.* ⏰*Closed public holidays.* ⬠€5, *combined admission with Musée de l'Empéri or the Musée Grévin.* ⬠€7.50. ☏*04 90 56 27 60.*

This is the house in which Nostradamus spent the last 19 years of his life. Ten animated tableaux with audiovisual back-up illustrate his life and work.

Église Saint-Michel

The beautiful arched bell tower and the carved tympanum over the doorway will delight enthusiasts of Romanesque sculpture.

Pass through the **porte de l'Horloge** *(rue de l'Horloge)* to reach place Crousillat with its charming 18C fountain, the **Fontaine moussue**.

◗ Continue along rue des Frères-Kennedy, then turn right into rue de Pontis.

Collégiale St-Laurent

r. Maréchal Joffre.

This 14C and 15C church is a good example of southern French Gothic. Inside, admire a monolithic 15C polychrome Descent from the Cross, carved from a single block of stone; the third north chapel contains the tomb of Nostradamus.

🚗 DRIVING TOUR

BETWEEN CRAU AND ALPILLES

Round-trip of 57km/35.4mi. Allow half a day.

◗ Leave Salon-de-Provence on the D 572 heading E. After Pélissanne a small road on the left leads to La

cannons, paintings, drawings, figures on foot or on horseback which illustrate the military past with special reference to the Napoleonic years.

Musée Grévin de Provence

pl. des Centuries. ♿⏰*Open Mon–Fri 9am–noon, 2–6pm, Sat–Sun 2–6pm.* ⏰*Closed public holidays.* ⬠€5. ☏*04 90 56 36 30.*

Some 2,600 years of the history of Provence are retraced here, in the form of 15 waxwork scenes, from the legendary marriage of Gyptis and Protis to the modern day.

Hôtel de Ville

174 pl. de l'Hôtel de Ville.

This elegant 17C mansion with two corner turrets and a carved balcony now houses the town hall. On place de l'Hôtel de Ville stands the statue of Adam de Craponne (1526–76), a native son of Salon and civil engineer, who made the

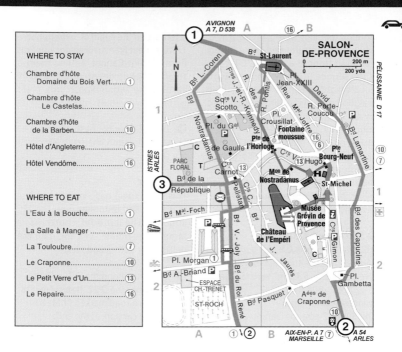

Barben, which occupies a precipitous site in the small Touloubre valley.

Château de La Barben★

rte du château, La Barben. Guided tours only (1hr) Apr–Sept 11am–6pm; 1st 2 weeks in Oct 2–5pm; rest of year hours vary, check website. €9 (child under 13, €6). 04 90 55 25 41. www.chateaudelabarben.fr.

The access ramp to the castle offers a plunging view on to the formal French gardens. The present castle was originally a medieval fortress, built before AD 1000, belonging to the Abbaye St-Victor from Marseille and then to King René, who sold it to the powerful Forbin family. This family owned it for some 500 years and remodelled and enlarged it several

Château de La Barben

© Michel Gotin/hemis.fr

times, especially in the 14C and 17C, when it was transformed into a stately home. In front of a noble 17C façade is the terrace (Henri IV staircase with double flight of stairs), from where there is a good view of the gardens designed by Le Nôtre, and of the Provençal countryside.

Inside, on the second floor, the Empire-style bedroom of Pauline Borghese, Napoleon's sister, and her boudoir ornamented with wallpaper painted by Granet and representing the Four Seasons, are worth noting.

♣♣ Zoo de La Barben★

13330 La Barben. ♿🕐*Open daily 10am–6pm (Jul–Aug 9.30am–7pm; Dec–Jan 10am–5.30pm).* ☞€15, ages 3–12, €10. ✆04 90 55 19 12. www.zoolabarben.com.

This 30ha/12-acre zoo features a number of enclosures in which more than 600 animals roam in relative freedom: big cats, monkeys, elephants, giraffes, bison, zebras and birds of prey. There's a little train to get you around.

▷ Continue east along the D 572.

The road follows the fertile Touloubre valley; after the viaduct carrying the TGV southeast, there is a lovely view of the Trévaresse range.

Saint-Cannat

Before strolling in the village, stop at the **Musée Suffren** (*Espace Suffren, av. Pasteur.* 🕐 *open May–Sept daily except Sat–Sun 3–6pm; rest of year 1st Sun of the month only 3–6pm.* 🕐*closed public holidays.* ✆04 42 57 36 03). It has a collection of archives relating to the history of the commune, with particular

reference to the bailiff of Suffren (1729–1788), a great French navigator who was born in Saint-Cannat. Among them, a small space is devoted to the 1909 earthquake with old postcards, press cuttings, eye-witness reports etc.

▷ Leave St-Cannat by the D 7, in the Avignon direction, then turn left onto the D 917.

Lambesc

This small town has a number of fine mansions and fountains from the 17C and 18C. The large 18C church has a remarkable dome. On a 16C gate is a belfry with a clock and Jack.

▷ Continue along the D 7, in Cazan turn left onto the D 22. 1km/0.6mi SW of Cazan is a road marked Château-Bas, with a car park at the end.

Château-Bas

The fascinating ruins of a Roman temple and chapel stand in a charming site at the far end of the castle (16C–18C) estate. The **Temple Romain** (✆04 90 59 13 16; www.chateaubas.com) probably dates from the late 1C BC, a period characterised by many impressive buildings such as the Commemorative Arch at St-Rémy-de-Provence and the Maison Carrée in Nîmes.

The remains include part of the foundations, the left side wall, a wall ending in a square pilaster, surmounted by a beautiful Corinthian capital, and a 7m fluted column still standing intact. Among the surrounding ruins are a second temple and a semicircular precinct (Roman), probably the ruins of a sanctuary.

Harpagon de Lamanon

Lord of the village which bears his name, the troubadour **Bertrand de Lamanon** was a formidable pamphleteer whose satirical verses *(sirventés)* made his enemies tremble: the bishop of Arles, for one, accused of sins of every kind, knew what that kind of revolt meant! Dear old Bertrand turned especially vicious when Charles d'Anjou deprived him of the monopoly on salt, which he had previously sold for five times more than he had paid for it.

▶ Continue along the D 22 and turn right on to the D 22C.

Vieux-Vernègues

After passing through Vernègues, the uphill road circles the old village, which was destroyed by an earthquake in 1909 (⊶ *the ruins are not open to the public*), and goes on to the small tower from where there is a **panorama★** *(viewing table)* of a large area of Provence.

Follow the winding road to **Alleins**, which has preserved some remains of the city ramparts.

▶ Turn left onto the D 71D and, just after crossing the EDF canal, turn left again on to the D 17D for Lamanon.

Lamanon

Inhabitants of Lamanon are extremely proud of their plane tree, opposite the stadium, because it is 300 years old and has a trunk 8m in circumference. In Provence, the foliage of this tree shades bowls players from the heat of the sun.

You can end your walk with a visit of the little **museum de Calès** opposite the church. There are two rooms of exhibits with information about the troglodyte site (✆04 90 59 54 62 – *Point Tourisme info* – *www.cales-lamanon.fr*).

▶ Continue on the D 17E.

After you have seen the fountains in the pretty village of **Eyguières**, go north on the D569.

Castelas de Roquemartine

Perched high up on a rock, these ruins from various different periods make a very picturesque ensemble. An eyrie like this was just the thing to attract bandits. That was what happened at the end of the 14C when the fortress became the hideout of gangs linked to the sinister Raymond de Turenne.

▶ Return to Eyguières, then follow the D 17 which leads back to Salon.

ADDRESSES

🛏 STAY

⊜⊜ **Hôtel d'Angleterre** – *98 cours Carnot.* ✆04 90 56 01 10. *www.hotel-dangleterre.biz. Closed 20 Dec–6 Jan. 26 rooms.* This hotel near the museums was once a convent. Simply renovated rooms; some are air-conditioned. Breakfast buffet under a glass cupola.

⊜⊜ **Hôtel Vendôme** – *34 r. du Mar.-Joffre.* ✆04 90 56 01 96. *www.hotelvendome.com.* 🅿. *20 rooms.* A peaceful hotel reputed for its comfort. Some rooms open on to the patio.

⊜⊜ **Chambre d'hôte Domaine du Bois Vert** – *474 chemain de la Transhumance, 13450 Grans. 7km/4.3mi S of Salon via D 16 and D 19 for Lançon.* ✆04 90 55 82 98. *www.domaineduboisvert.com.* 🅿⊟. *4 rooms. Closed mid-Nov–mid-Mar.* A park of oak and pine trees surrounds this traditional old house. Rooms have old-fashioned, rustic furnishings. Breakfast is served in the large living room or on the terrace facing the garden. Swimming pool.

⊜⊜⊜ **Chambre d'hôte Le Castelas** – *Vallon des Euores, 13121 Aurons.* ✆04 90 55 60 12. *www.le-castelas.fr.* ⊟. *3 rooms.* Each room is individually decorated. The drawing room on the first floor also has plenty of original furniture, while being comfortable at the same time. The large veranda offers a superb view.

⊜⊜⊜⊜ **Chambre d'hôte Château de la Barben** – *Rte du Château, 13 330 La Barben, 8km/5mi SE.* ✆04 90 55 25 41. *www.chateaudelabarben.fr. 5 rooms. Evening meal for overnight guests.* The castle is open as a Bed & Breakfast inn, showing off beautiful furnishings in its large rooms. Tours of the château are available, children's treasure hunts, walks, hunting, fishing and other activities.

🍴 EAT

⊜ **Le Repaire** – *old village, 13116 Vernègues, 15km/9.3mi NE.* ✆04 90 59 31 64. *http://creperie.le.repaire.monsite.orange.fr. Closed Jan, Mon, Tue (Oct–Mar), Tue (Apr–Sept).* Sitting just steps away from the ruins of the old village that were destroyed in an earthquake in 1909, this eatery has a pleasant setting and pretty terrace in summer. Light fare is served, with a good choice of teas and coffees.

🍷🍷 **Le Petit Verre d'Un** – *17 rue du Verdun.* ✆ *04 90 53 83 62. Closed Wed, Sun.* Expressing its double heritage – Provençal and Lyonnais – with flair, this discreet restaurant is a real find. Everything is fresh, tasty and fairly priced.

🍷🍷 **La Salle à Manger** – *6 r. du Mar. Joffre.* ✆ *04 90 56 28 01. Closed Sun–Mon.* Good-quality food served here. Pleasant ambience and classic décor.

🍷🍷 **La Touloubre** – *29 chemin Salatier, 13330 La Barben.* ✆ *04 90 55 16 85. www. latouloubre.com.* Plane trees shade the vast terrace of this village inn located along a quiet road. Large country-style dining room. Twelve modern rooms available.

🍷🍷 **Le Craponne** – *146 allée de Craponne.* ✆ *04 90 53 23 92. Closed 24 Aug–15 Sept, 24 Dec–4 Jan, Wed and Sun eve, Mon.* The name of this restaurant refers to a benefactor of the region. Dark-wood panelling, yellow walls and rustic furniture. In fine weather, meals served in a small flower-decked courtyard.

🍷🍷 **L'Eau à la Bouche** – *pl. Morgan.* ✆ *04 90 56 41 93.* ♿. *Closed 23 Dec–1 Jan, Sun eve and Mon.* Joined to a fishmongers, this restaurant brings over fish and seafood from the shop before cooking it, so freshness and quality are guaranteed! You will eat either in the simple dining room or on the veranda, which is very pleasant in the summer.

TAKING A BREAK

En Aparthé(s) – *13 pl. E.-Pelletan.* ✆ *04 42 86 35 01. Open Mon–Sat 9am–6.30pm (Mon Tue 3.30pm). Closed Sun.* A warm and welcoming *salon de thé* in Salon which also serves light dishes at lunchtime (savoury tarts, salads etc). Café-bookshop and art gallery here too.

La Case à Palabres – *44 r. Pontis* ✆ *04 90 56 43 21. www.lacaseapalabres.fr. Open Tue–Wed 11am–7pm, Thu–Fri 11am–11pm, Sat 3pm–midnight. Closed Sun, Mon.* This handy and pleasant café is a convivial place where locals like to meet for a drink, perhaps over a game of chess or a book. Light lunchtime food on weekdays. Ice creams and cakes are home-made.

SHOPPING

Market – Large, traditional market on Wednesday morning, pl. Morgan.

Rampal-Patou soaps – *71 r. Félix-Pyat.* ✆ *04 90 56 07 28. www.rampal-latour.com. Mon–Fri 8am–noon, 2pm–6pm. Guided tours Apr–Oct and school holidays, Tue and Fri 10.30pm. Closed 25 Dec–1 Jan.* Since 1828 this artisan company has made Marseille soap the traditional way. It now offers a full range of soap products, both for the body and for the home.

Savonnerie Marius Fabre – *148 av. Paul-Bourret.* ✆ *04 90 53 24 77. www. marius-fabre.fr. Daily 8.30am–12.30pm, 1.30pm–5.30pm (Jul–Aug 6pm). Guided tours Mon, Thu (Jul–Aug Mon–Fri) 10.30am. Closed Sat–Sun, public holidays, 1 Jan, 25 Dec.* This famous brand of soap is still made in the original factory, founded in 1900. Visit the museum and shop.

Domaine du Vallon des Glauges – *Voie d'Aureille, 13430 Eyguières.* ✆ *04 90 59 81 45. www.vallondesglauges.com. Open Jun–Sept 9.30am–12.30pm, 2.30pm–7pm; Oct–May Mon–Sat 9.30am–12.30pm, 2.30pm–6pm. Closed Sun, public holidays.* In a hidden valley tucked beneath the highest point of the Alpilles (Les Opiès: 493m), this estate produces red, rosé and white Coteaux d'Aix-en-Provence wines that have won several awards.

Moulin à huile des Costes – *445 chemin de St-Pierre, 13330 Pélissanne.* ✆ *04 90 55 30 00. www.moulindescostes.com. Shop open Tue–Sat 9am–noon, 3pm–7pm.* Pélissanne is one of the richest communes as far as its wealth of olive groves is concerned. At the Moulin des Costes (18C farmhouse), different oils are produced.

Les Santons de Vernègues – *R. de la Transhumance. 13116 Vernègues.* ✆ *04 90 57 38 40. Open Dec 9am–7pm, Jan–Nov Tue–Sat 9am–noon, 3pm–7pm, Sun 3pm–7pm. Closed 1st week Jul.* In the purest Provençal tradition, Hélène Troussier crafts her *santons* with passion. She sells them in the studio and also works to commission.

ACTIVITIES

Walking or cycling – At the centre of the Tallagard massif, four marked circuits *(3.7km/2.3mi to 7.3km/4.5mi, free map from the tourist office)*, to explore on foot or by mountain bike, will show you traces of the old pastoral way of life, in between pine forests and olive groves.

La Crau gliding centre – *Aérodrome Salon-Eyguières.* ✆ *04 90 42 00 91. www. planeur13.com.* Take a flight in a glider to explore the Alpilles from high above.

Saint-Rémy-de-Provence★

Bouches-du-Rhône

Gateway to the Alpilles, St-Rémy epitomises the essence of Provence: boulevards shaded by plane trees, fountains gracing the squares, charming alleyways, and a festive atmosphere, especially on market day and during traditional fairs. Sitting within a region that is a great fruit and market gardening centre, it is a town of gardeners, and has long specialised in the production and trade of flower and vegetable seeds. St-Rémy's main source of income, however, is tourism, encouraged by the pretty pastel-painted houses on its streets and the presence of impressive Roman ruins.

A BIT OF HISTORY

The village, founded after the destruction of Glanum, developed under the protection of the Abbaye de St-Rémi of Reims, from which its name is derived. Birthplace of the famous astrologist Michel Nostradamus, St-Rémy has been dazzled by the genius of Van Gogh and the inspiration of the Provençal poets from Roumanille to Marie Mauron (1896–1986).

VISIT
Plateau des Antiques★★
1km/0.6mi S of St-Rémy. Allow 2hr.

▶ Leave St-Rémy by the D 5.
🅿*Leave your car in the parking area (high season charge ⊜€4) on the right, in front of the triumphal arch.*

The Roman monuments lie on a plateau below the Alpilles' last foothills. In this pleasant spot, from where the view extends over the Comtat plain, Durance valley and Mont Ventoux, stood the prosperous city of Glanum. It was abandoned after Barbarian invasions at the end of the 3C; two magnificent monuments – the mausoleum and commemorative arch – remain.

▶ **Population:** 10 617.
⌖ **Michelin Map:** 340: D-3 – Regional map, ⌖*see p187.*
ℹ **Info:** Place Jean-Jaurès, 13210 St-Rémy-de-Provence. 📞04 90 92 05 22. www.saintremy-de-Provence.com.
◗ **Location:** Saint-Rémy is 20km/12mi south of Avignon, just north of the Alpilles mountain range.
🅿 **Parking:** Place de la République (except Wed market) or place Jean-Jaurès.
⊛ **Don't Miss:** Plateau des Antiques.
🕐 **Timing:** Count on spending a day here, especially on market day (Wednesday). It's a good base to explore the surrounding area (Avignon, Arles…).

Mausoleum★★

This monument is 18m high and is one of the most outstanding in the Roman world and the best preserved; it lacks but the pine cone finial crowning its dome. For a long time it was believed to have been built as a sepulchre for a noble from Glanum and his spouse. However, the excavations conducted by Henri Rolland have established that it was not a tomb but a cenotaph; that is to say, a monument built in memory of the deceased, around 30 BCE.

Bas-reliefs representing battle and hunting scenes adorn the four walls of the square podium. The first storey, with four arched openings, bears on the frieze (depicting naval scenes) of the northern architrave an inscription which says "Sextius, Lucius, Marcus, sons of Caius of the Julii family, to their parents". This suggests a posthumous dedication from the three brothers in honour of their father and grandfather. The second storey is made up of a rotunda with a Corinthian colonnade which encloses the statues of the two figures.

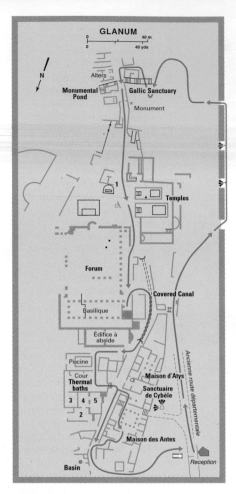

GLANUM

Alters
Monumental Pond
Gallic Sanctuary
Monument
Temples
Forum
Covered Canal
Basilique
Édifice à abside
Piscine
Cour
Thermal baths
3 4 5
2
Maison d'Atys
Sanctuaire de Cybèle
Ancienne route départementale
Maison des Antes
Basin
Reception

Arc Municipal★

Perhaps contemporary with the mausoleum, that is to say the first years of Augustus' reign, this arch is the oldest Roman arch of the Narbonensis region. It indicated, on the main route to the Alps, the entrance to Glanum.

Its proportions (12.5m long, 5.5m wide and 8.6m high) and the exceptional quality of its carved decoration show Greek influence, quite evident at Glanum.

The sole arcade is carved with a lovely festoon of fruit and leaves; inside, it is adorned with a finely carved hexagonal coffered ceiling. On either side of the opening are allegorical symbols of victory and on the sides groups of two

prisoners, men and women, down by the victors' booty. The despondency of these figures is well rendered.

Art historians feel that the unique form of this arch, mutilated very soon after construction, has inspired some of the 12C Romanesque doorways such as St-Trophime at Arles.

Glanum★

rte des Baux-de-Provence.
&☉*Open Apr–Aug daily 9.30am–6.30pm; Sept Tue–Sun 9.30am–6.30pm; Oct–Mar Tue–Sun 10am–5pm.* ☛*Guided tours (1hr30min).* ☉*Closed 1 Jan, 1 May, 1 and 11 Nov, 25 Dec.* ⊛€7.50. ℘*04 90 92 23 79. http://glanum. monuments-nationaux.fr/en.*

The excavations, unearthed since 1921, are located at the main gap of the Alpilles, which dominate them. The site consists of a group of complex structures reflecting several different periods of occupation, grouped by archaeologists into three phases.

Reception

In the visitor centre (ticket office), two models of the site, reconstructed frescoes and various fragments of architecture and domestic objects all help to shed further light on the different phases of the site's history.

Gallic Sanctuary

Set up in terraces facing the rising sun, this sanctuary dates from the 6C BCE. In this area kneeling warriors were uncovered, as well as stelae with carved skulls identical to those found in the great Salian towns.

Nymphaeum

The source around which Glanum possibly developed is marked by a pool with masonry walls of large, Greek-style stones. In 20 BCE Agrippa built a temple next to it, dedicated to

The Three Glanum

The origin of the site is a sanctuary venerated by Celtic-Ligurian people known as the Glanics. This native settlement rapidly came into contact with the merchants of Massalia owing to its location close to two important roads.

Glanon **(or Glanum I)** developed under Hellenistic influence as can be seen in the construction, particularly in the technique of bonding (large carved blocks of stone perfectly set without mortar) in the 3C and 2C BCE. This Hellenistic community included public buildings (temple, agora, assembly hall, a rampart, which was probably ceremonial and controlled the procession to the sanctuary), houses with peristyles, and a fortified district to the south (sanctuary).

The second phase **(Glanum II)** began with the Roman conquest during the late 2C and with the occupation of the country by Marius' army, which stopped the Teutonic army. The town most probably suffered when the Teutons passed through; the new buildings were then made by the bonding of irregular stones and the majority of the public buildings disappeared.

The last phase **(Glanum III)** follows the conquest of Marseille by Caesar in 49 BCE. Romanisation intensified, and under Emperor Augustus the town was rebuilt. In the centre, the old buildings were razed, their debris levelled and filled to make room for a vast horizontal esplanade on which were erected the great public buildings: forum, basilica, temples and baths.

Valetudo, goddess of health (ruins of three fluted columns). A staircase leads to the bottom, still fed with water from the spring.

Fortified Gate

This remarkable Hellenistic vestige used, as at St-Blaise, the Massaliote technique of large, well-matched rectangular blocks of stone with merlons and gargoyles. The ramparts, which succeeded at least two protohistoric ramparts, defended the sanctuary and included a postern with a zigzag passageway and a carriage gate.

Temples

Southwest of the forum *(on the left as you go north)* stood twin temples surrounded by a *peribolos* (a court

Glanum

©D. Chapuis/MICHELIN

enclosed by a wall), the southern section of which partially covered an assembly hall with its tiered seats. These Roman public buildings, the oldest of their kind in Gaul, date back to 30 BCE. Important vestiges of their lavish decoration (blocks of cornice, roof decorations, etc.) as well as exquisite sculpture have been excavated. These vestiges have made it possible, partially, to reconstruct the smaller of the two temples. A monumental fountain **(1)** stood opposite the temples in front of the forum and here a trapezoidal square belonging to a Hellenistic building was laid out, surrounded by magnificent head capital colonnades.

Forum
The forum was built on the ruins of pre-Roman buildings which archaeologists are seeking to identify. It was closed to the north by the basilica (a multipurpose building mostly for commercial and administrative activities), of which 24 foundation pillars remain and under which Sulla's house was discovered. In the house were uncovered mosaics **(2)**, most likely the oldest ones found in Gaul.

South of the basilica lay the forum square, lined on each side by a covered gallery and closed to the south by a great decorated apsidal-ended wall. Discovered under the square were a house and a large Hellenistic building.

Covered Canal
This remarkable work, probably a channel which drained the water from the valley and the town, was so constructed that the stone covering also served as Glanum's main street pavement.

Baths
These baths date back to the time of Julius Caesar. Their clear plan followed the classical route: a *gymnasium* **(3)**, *frigidarium* **(4)**, *tepidarium* **(5)**, *caldarium*, *palestra*, set up for physical exercise and athletic games, once lined with porticoes, and finally a cold swimming pool, possibly supplied with running water.

Maison d'Atys
This house was originally divided into two parts (peristyled court to the north and pool to the south) joined by a large door. Later a sanctuary to Cybele was set up in the area where the peristyle stood; note the votive altar dedicated to the goddess' ears.

Maison des Antes
Beside Maison d'Atys, this lovely Greek-style house, built according to the 2C BC taste, was laid out around a peristyled central courtyard and cistern. The entrance bay of one of the rooms has preserved its two pilasters *(antes)*.

 WALKING TOUR

THE TOWN
Place de la République
Beside the ring road, this square on the site of the medieval ramparts is the heart of the town, animated by its café terraces and its market days.

Collégiale St-Martin
Bd Marceau. Open for organ concerts Apr–Sept and Organa Festival. *06 26 53 70 17. http://organa2000.free.fr.*
This collegiate church with its striking façade was rebuilt around 1820 after it had partially caved in. The only remaining 14C feature is the bell tower crowned with a crocketed spire.
The vestiges of the old 14C fortifications line rue Hoche; here can also be seen the **Maison natale de Nostradamus** (Nostradamus' birthplace) and the 17C **Ancien Hôpital St-Jacques**.

Take boulevard Victor-Hugo and turn left into rue du 8 Mai 1945. In place Jules Pélissier stands the town hall, which was formerly a 17C monastery. Turn right into rue Lafayette, then left into rue Estrine.

Musée Estrine
8 r. Estrine. Open Jul–Sept 10am–6pm; Apr–Jun and Oct 10am–noon, 2–6pm; Mar and 1st 2 weeks of Nov 2–6pm. Closed mid-Nov–mid-

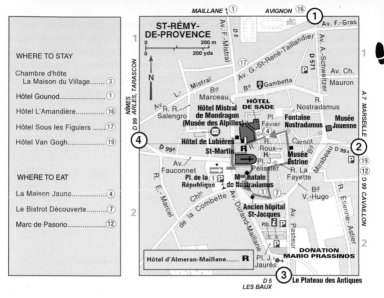

WHERE TO STAY

Chambre d'hôte
La Maison du Village .... ③

Hôtel Gounod .... ①

Hôtel L'Amandière .... ⑯

Hôtel Sous les Figuiers ...... ⑰

Hôtel Van Gogh .... ⑲

WHERE TO EAT

La Maison Jaune .... ④

Le Bistrot Découverte .... ⑦

Marc de Pasorio .... ⑫

Mar. ☎*04 90 92 34 72. www.musees-mediterranee.org.*
This museum is housed in the Hôtel Estrine, a handsome private mansion built in the 18C for Marquis Joseph de Pistoye and subsequently purchased by Louis Estrine. This museum is currently closed for a major refurbishment that is scheduled for completion in mid-2013. It will reopen essentially as a modern art museum with works by St Rémy's most famous painter, Albert Gleizes, and many other prominent artists.

▶ Continue up rue Estrine until you reach the corner of rue Carnot and rue Nostradamus. Note the 19C **Fontaine Nostradamus**, decorated with a portrait of the famous astrologer. A little further on, place Favier is lined with fine 15C and 16C mansions including the **Hôtel Mistral de Mondragon,** home of the Musée des Alpilles.

Musée des Alpilles
pl. Favier. �& ◔*OpenJun–Sept Tue–Sun noon–6pm; Oct–May Tue–Sat 1pm–5.30pm.* ◑*Closed 1 Jan, 1 May and 25 Dec.* ☞*€3.10* ☎*04 90 92 68 24. www.musees-mediterranee.org.*
This little museum is located in the vast 16C Mistral de Mondragon mansion built

around a fine courtyard with a round turreted staircase and overlooked by loggias. The exhibits relate to popular arts and traditions including costumes and old farming techniques. Don't miss the room of traditional Arles costumes (still worn up to the beginning of the 20C). Have a look in the courtyard at the bust of Van Gogh sculpted by Ossip Zadkine.

▶ Return to rue Carnot where you will pass the **Hôtel d'Almeran-Maillane** where Gounod mounted the first performance of Mireille; then, on boulevard Marceau, you will see on the right no 11, the old **Hôtel de Lubières**, also known as the 'maison de amandier' as a sculptor working with almond wood had his studio there.

ADDITIONAL SIGHTS
Donation Mario Prassinos★
Av. Durand-Maillane. ◔*Open Jul–Aug Wed–Sun 11am–1pm, 3–7pm; Sept–Jun Wed–Sun 2–6pm.* ☛*Guided tours (45min) upon request.* ◑*Closed public holidays.* ☞*No charge.* ☎*04 90 92 35 13 www.marioprassinos.com.*
The Greek-born artist Mario Prassinos (1916–1985), who had a studio in Eygalières (☝*see Les Alpilles*), origi-

nally created this series of murals on the theme of supplication for the little chapel of Notre-Dame-de-Pitié, where pilgrims went in times of plague. The artist died of cancer a few days after completing the paintings.

EXCURSIONS
Monastère de St-Paul-de-Mausole
Chemin de Saint-Paul (off the D 5 just before Glanum). 👤🕐*Open Apr–Sept daily 9.30am–7pm, Oct–Dec 10.15am–5.45pm.* 🕐*Closed Jan–Mar, 1 Nov, 25 Dec.* 👥*€4.50.* 📞*04 90 92 77 00. www.saintpauldemausole.fr.*

Located near the Plateau des Antiques, this former monastery is the second most popular tourist site in St-Rémy because of its close association with Vincent van Gogh. Turned into a convalescent home in the mid-18C, it was here that the artist was confined, at his own request, from 3 May 1889 to 16 May 1890. He had a workroom on the ground floor and a bedroom on the first floor. This has been reconstructed and it is a moving experience for visitors to see the window through which Van Gogh contemplated a field of wheat which he went on to paint 15 times.

In the **Champ Van Gogh**, you can admire more than 20 large-format reproductions of pictures which he painted here, including *The Starry Night, The Irises, Olive Grove* and *Self-Portrait.* Saint-Paul is still a care home, so its calm should not be disturbed.

The small church dates from the end of the 12C (18C façade) and has a fine square bell tower with Lombard arcades. Beside it the **cloisters★** have fine Romanesque decoration: the capitals of the small columns are carved with varied motifs (foliage, animals, masks).

Mas de la Pyramide
Chemin des Carrières (200m from the Monastery of St-Paul-de-Mausole). 🔊*Guided tours (1hr) possible.* 📞*04 90 92 00 81.*

This rock-hewn *mas* has an unusual layout. It was built in the old Roman quarries from materials that were also used

for the neighbouring town of Glanum. A **museum** displays tools and agricultural equipment once used by local peasants. At the centre, the vertical "pyramid" rock is a reminder of the ground level of the site before mining began.

ADDRESSES

🛏 STAY

🛏 **Hôtel Van Gogh** – *1 av. Jean Moulin.* 📞*04 90 92 14 02. Closed late Oct–mid-Mar. 21 rooms.* This simple town-centre hotel features rooms decorated with a Provençal note. Those on the first floor have dormer windows. Attractive poolside terrace. Good value.

🛏 **Hôtel l'Amandière** – *av. Théodore Aubanel rte de Noves. 1km/0.6mi NE.* 📞*04 90 92 41 00. www.hotel-amandiere.com.* 🅿 🏊 *26 rooms.* A quiet regional building with a pleasant tree-lined flower garden. Peaceful, practical rooms with a balcony or terrace. Breakfast is served in the winter garden.

🛏🛏 **Hôtel Gounod** – *18 pl. de la République.* 📞*04 90 92 06 14. www.hotel-gounod.com.* Renovated with exuberant Baroque touches, this old hotel where the composer Gounod wrote his opera *Mireille* (1863) is original, central and comfortable, with a pretty garden. It also has a very nice salon de thé (👤*see opposite*).

🛏🛏 **Hôtel Sous Les Figuiers** – *3 av. Taillandier.* 📞*04 32 60 15 40.* 🅿 🏊 *www.hotel-charme-Provence.com. 14 rooms.* Small hotel full of charm and warmth. The stylish rooms (quilts and antique furniture) boast private terraces shaded by a century-old fig tree. Painting workshop.

🛏🛏 **La Maison du Village** – *10 r. du 8 mai 1945.* 📞*04 32 60 68 20. www.lamaisonduvillage.com. 5 rooms.* This 18C house in the heart of the historic centre is delightfully decorated. Superb rooms and enchanting courtyard-terrace.

🍽 EAT

🍽🍽 **Le Bistrot Découverte** – *19 bd Victor Hugo.* 👤📞*04 90 92 34 49. www.bistrodecouverte.com. Closed mid-Feb–mid Mar, Sun eve and Mon (except Jul–Aug.* This characterful bistro with veranda-terrace serves traditional Provençal dishes. Splendid stone-vaulted cellar with a fine wine list; bottles can be sampled on the spot or taken home.

🍽🍽🍽 **La Maison Jaune** – *15 r. Carnot. ☎04 90 92 56 14. www.lamaisonjaune.info. Closed mid-Nov–late Jan, Tue lunch and Mon (summer), Sun eve and Mon (winter).* This well-known restaurant with its yellow façade overlooks the old town. A beautiful place with a large shaded upstairs terrace. Teak furniture and a roof of local tiles. Delicious Provençal cuisine.

🍽🍽🍽🍽 **Restaurant & Bistro Marc de Passorio** – *Hôtel Le Vallon de Valrugues chemin Canto-Cigalo, 1km/0.6mi via 2. ☎04 90 92 04 40. www. restaurant-marcdepassorio.com. Closed Jan; in low season: Sun eve, Tue lunch, Mon. Reservations recommended.* Next door to the elegant restaurant is a bistro where you can sample an interesting blend of classic and modern cuisine prepared by the talented young chef, but at more affordable prices. (There is nothing to stop you from eating in the main restaurant another time!)

TAKING A BREAK

En attendant Gounod – *18 pl. de la République. ☎04 90 92 06 14. Open 7am–7pm.* This café-salon de thé in Hotel Gounod (*☞see opposite*) may be wackily decorated (the owner collects religious statues), but the home-made cakes and ice creams are plain delicious.

SHOPPING

Confiseur Lilamand – *5 r. Albert-Schweitzer. ☎04 90 92 12 77. www. confiserie-lilamand.com. Open Tue–Sat 10am–12.30pm, 2.30pm–7pm (Feb 6pm). Closed Sun, Mon, public holidays except Dec.* Since 1886 this family business has been a top address for traditional candied fruits and jams of the highest quality.

Le Petit Duc – *7 bd Victor-Hugo. ☎04 90 92 08 31. www.petit-duc.com. Open Tue–Sat 10am–1pm, 3pm–7pm; Sun 4pm–6pm.* Using recipes drawn from books of magic spells, the delicacies of Le Petit Duc will surprise you not only for their flavours but also for their names: *oreilles de la bonne déesse* (ears of the good goddess), *pastilles d'amour* (love lozenges) and in particular the town speciality, *pignolat de Nostradamus*.

Joël Durand Chocolatier – *3 bd V.-Hugo. ☎04 90 92 38 25. www.chocolat-durand. com. Open Mon–Sat 9.30am–12.30pm,*

2.30pm–7.30pm (Mon 7pm), Sun 10am–1pm, 2.30pm–7pm. Probably the best-known chocolatier in Provence, Durand is famous for distinctively flavoured chocolates, each named to represent a letter of the alphabet.

Santonnier Laurent-Bourges – *on the D5 to Maillane. ☎04 90 92 20 45. Open daily 9am–7pm. Closed 25 Dec.* From his home in the heart of the countryside, Laurent Bourges dedicated himself to *santon* craftsmanship for almost 50 years until his death in 2008. Now his daughter Marylène Bourgues continues in his footsteps. Visit the studio and learn some of the secrets of this ancient tradition.

ACTIVITIES
WALKING ROUTES

🔍 **Good to know** – Access to the massif is restricted from 1 June to 30 Sept. *Check one day ahead: ☎0811 20 13 13.* In addition to the many maps showing itineraries in the Alpilles *(on sale in bookshops and from newsagents)*, the tourist office has **six maps** detailing walks from Saint-Rémy (1hr30min to 6hr). €2.

Vineyard trail– *Domaine des Terres Blanches, rte de Cavaillon (D 99) about 5km/3mi from town centre. ☎04 90 95 91 66. www.terresblanches.com. 8am–8pm. No charge.* In a beautiful setting surrounded by hills, this organic wine estate suggests **two easy walks** (30min and 1hr30min) among the vines (free illustrated guide in shop). You can also visit the cellars to taste and buy wine.

EVENTS

Feria Provençale – Typical *courses camarguaises* on the weekend of 14–16 August, including *abrivados* and on 15 August the so-called *carreto ramado*, the ritual procession of a cart drawn by 50 horses.

Organa Festival – Performed on the magnificent organ in the Collégiale Saint-Martin *(bd Marceau)*, this annual concert of classical organ music is presented under the auspices of the Association of the Friends of the Organ of Saint-Rémy. For a schedule of concerts, call or check the website. *☎06 26 53 70 17. http://organa2000.free.fr.*

Les Alpilles★★

Bouches-du-Rhône

The limestone chain of the Alpilles, a geological extension of the Luberon range, rises in the heart of Provence between Avignon and Arles. From afar, these jagged crests rising 300–400m appear to be lofty mountains. The arid, white peaks standing out against the blue sky are reminiscent of some Greek landscapes. At the mouths of the dry valleys that cross the mountain chain, olive and almond trees spread their foliage over the lower slopes. Occasionally a dark line of cypress trees breaks the landscape. In the mountains, the gently sloping lower areas are planted with *Kermes* oaks and pines, but often the rock is bare and peppered with a few scraggy bushes covered by *maquis* or poor pasture suitable only for sheep.

Due to the risk of fire, access to the forested areas of the Alpilles is restricted from early June to late September.

- **Michelin Map:** 340: D3-E3 or 528 fold 29.
- **Info:** Nature lovers can plan a guided tour of the Caume by contacting the tourist office in St-Rémy-de-Provence, ℘04 90 92 38 52.
- **Location:** The area is divided between the Alpilles des Baux in the W and the Alpilles d'Eygalières in the E; in the middle is St-Rémy-de-Provence.
- **Don't Miss:** The mill in Fontvieille, made famous by Alphonse Daudet; a tour of the AOC Baux olive oil mills; Christmas markets in Maussane, Mouriès and Eyguières.
- **Timing:** You would ideally spend two or three days exploring the region, particularly at Christmas. If you only have a day, take in two or three villages.

🚗 DRIVING TOURS

LES BAUX ALPILLES★★
Round-trip starting from St-Rémy-de-Provence. 40km/25mi. Allow 4hr.

St-Rémy-de-Provence★
See St-Rémy-de-Provence.

▶ Leave St-Rémy-de-Provence going SW on chemin de la Combette; turn right into Vieux Chemin d'Arles. After 3.8km/2.3mi, turn left at a T-junction on to D 27 (signposted: Les Baux).

Val d'Enfer
Access from the D 27 and D 78G.
A path *(15min)* crosses the Val d'Enfer (Hell Valley), a jagged gorge with views up to twisted rocks which form some of the most dramatic scenery around Les Baux. The caves are still the source of fairytale legends.

▶ After about 5km/3mi, you will reach the top of the Val d'Enfer. Take the road that climbs up on the left (you will see a sign "altitude 110m"). Drive on to the car park. Continue on foot to the viewing table at 500m.

Panorama★★★
Continue along D 27 for about 1km/ 0.6mi and bear right on a steep road (look for parking signs).
This rocky promontory offers the best view of Les Baux and a panorama of Arles and the Camargue, the Rhône valley, the Cévennes mountains, Aix-en-Provence, the Luberon and Mont Ventoux.

▶ Turn around and follow the D 27, direction Les Baux-de-Provence.

❧❧ Carrières de Lumières

By the D 27, 300m N of the village on Route de Maillane. ⏱*Open daily: Mar and Oct–Dec 10am–6pm; Apr–Sept 9.30am–7pm.* ✆€10.50. ✆*04 90 54 47 37. www.carrieres-lumieres.com.*
Albert Plécy (1914–77) chose disused quarries to create the **Cathédrale d'Images**, a place where he could carry out his research on the 'total image'. This has recently been refashioned into the **Carrières de Lumières**, an exciting space whose high rock walls act as giant screens for audiovisual presentations around an annually changing theme.
✎*See also p240.*

▷ Continue on the D 27 to Les Baux-de-Provence; cars must be left in the car park (flat rate €5).

Les Baux-de-Provence★★★
✎*See Les Baux-de-Provence.*

▷ Take the D 78F, then bear left on to the D 78D, which leads back to Paradou.

❧❧ La Petite Provence du Paradou

75 av. de la Vallée des Baux, on right, leaving Le Paradou towards Fontvieille (D 17). ♿⏱*Open daily: May–Sept 10am–6.30pm; Oct–Apr 10am–12.30pm, 2–6pm.* ✆€6 (child under 12, €4.40). ✆*04 90 54 35 75. www.lapetiteProvenceduparadou.com.*
In an interior typical of rural Provence, *santons* are produced here by *santon-makers* from Aubagne. They are dressed in local costumes and some are even mobile. They are arranged into evocative scenes of Provence past, illustrating trades (fisherman, miller, shepherd), festivals, daily life (drinking holes, games of cards), and the like.

▷ Return to the village, taking D 78 to the right through an olive grove.

Aqueducs de Barbegal
🚶*15min round trip on foot: follow the signposts for aqueduc romain.*
Note the impressive ruins, on the left in particular, of a pair of Gallo-Roman aqueducts. The aqueduct branching off to the west supplied Arles with water from Eygalières some 50km/31mi away. The other one cut through the rock and served a 4C hydraulic flour mill on the slope's south side, the ruins of which provide a rare example of Gallo-Roman mechanical engineering.

▷ Go right on D 33.

Olive grove at the foot of the Alpilles

© Franck Guizou/hemis.fr

Le Parc Régional des Alpilles

Since January 2007, 16 communes have joined forces to draw up a charter which will protect the area's flora and fauna and maintain traditional, diversified farming in order to ensure economic development and preserve a unique identity. The park covers a total of 50,000ha/190sq mi between the Durance and Rhône rivers. Today it is the fifth-biggest regional park in the PACA region and the second most important in the Bouches-du-Rhône and the Pays d'Arles. Between the nature reserve of the Luberon to the east and that of the Camargue to the southwest, the living landscape of the Alpilles provides a natural link.

Fontvieille

For centuries, the main industry in this small town, where Alphonse Daudet is remembered for his *Lettres de mon Moulin* (1869), has been the quarrying of Arles limestone.

Moulin de Daudet (Daudet's Mill) – *Allée des Pins (D33)* ◯*Not open to the public.* Between Arles and Les Baux-de-Provence, the admirers of Alphonse Daudet's works can make a literary pilgrimage to his mill, the inspiration for his famous *Lettres de mon Moulin (Letters from my Mill)*, a charming and whimsical series of letters and tales from Provence. A lovely avenue of pines leads from Fontvieille to the mill.

Alphonse Daudet, the son of a silk manufacturer, was born in Nîmes on 13 May 1840 (d. 1897). An outstanding author of tales of Provençal life and member of the Académie Goncourt, he was also a contemporary of such important 19C literary figures as Zola and Mistral. The **view**★ from the mill is an inspiration, embracing the Alpilles, Beaucaire and Tarascon castles, the vast Rhône valley, and the Abbaye de Montmajour.

◗ Among olive and pine trees and fields of fruit and vegetables, the D 33 climbs north again.

Chapelle Saint-Gabriel★

Park on the esplanade. ◌*Don't leave anything visible in the car. Information from the Tarascon tourist office – key available on request.* ☏*04 90 91 19 99.* A busy road nearby does not spoil the delicate charm of this little 12C chapel with its remarkable sculpted façade. The interior is a fine example of Romanesque architecture at its most restrained.

◗ Take the D 32 to Saint-Rémy.

LES ALPILLES D'EYGALIÈRES★★
Round-trip from St-Rémy-de-Provence. 42km/26mi. Allow about 3hr.

The road passes the old monastery of St-Paul-de-Mausole and the Roman monuments of Glanum, before continuing deep into the mountains where the landscape is dominated by pine trees.

◗ After 4km/2.5mi leave the car by the side of D 5 and take the left footpath leading up to the Caume.

Panorama de la Caume★★
⚠*Access is restricted early Jun–Sept. Alt 387m.*
At the top is a television relay mast. 🚶Walk to the southern edge of the plateau to enjoy a vast panorama of the surrounding countryside, including the Alpilles in the foreground and the Crau and Camargue plains. From the northern edge, the view encompasses the Rhône valley, the Guidon du Bouquet with its beak-like outline, Mont Ventoux and the Durance valley.

◗ Return to D 5 and turn left.

The road traverses a pine wood and several small gorges and goes past the **Rochers d'Entreconque**, former bauxite quarries.

#300 04-13-2017 11:09AM
Item(s) checked out to p11048050.

TITLE: Provence.
CALL #: 914.4930484 Prov
BARCODE: 33508013929257
DUE DATE: 05-04-17

Washington-Centerville Public Library
937-433-8091

Chapelle Saint-Sixte, Eygalières

©S. Sauvignier/MICHELIN

▶ Continue on the D 5, heading towards Maussane-les-Alpilles.

Maussane-les-Alpilles

Maussane is a peaceful, unspoiled village in the Baux valley on the southern slopes of the Alpilles. The heart of this charming Provençal village is its huge square, a pleasant place to meet up of an evening in the shade of plane trees.

▶ Leaving the village, turn left on the D 17 and then immediately left again onto the D 78.

The road runs through olive groves at the foot of the Alpilles before rising gently to a low pass from where there is a view of Les Opiès, a hillock crowned by a tower.

▶ At Le Destet, turn left on to D 24, which, as it rises, reveals the crest of La Caume. After 7.5km/4.5mi bear right on to D 24B, which leads to Eygalières.

Eygalières

This small town of narrow winding streets rises in tiers up the hill to an ancient castle keep. Once a Neolithic settlement, it was later occupied by Romans sent to divert the local spring waters to Arles. From the top of the village a view opens out on to the La Caume mountains, the Alpilles and the Durance valley.

Le Jardin de l'Alchimiste

Mas de la Brune (D 99), Eygalieres.
&. ☞☜Guided visits 10am–6pm: May daily; Jun–Sept Sat–Sun and public holidays. ⊜€10. ℘04 90 90 67 67.
www.jardin-alchimiste.com.
The inspiration for the garden around the 16C Mas de la Brune comes from the alchemist and his quest for the philosopher's stone. The garden contains many Mediterranean plants with medicinal properties.

▶ Return to Eygalières and continue on the D 24B, direction Orgon.

Chapelle Saint-Sixte

On a rocky mound which marks the site of a pagan temple dedicated to the waters, this chapel has a fine apse separated from the nave by an arch resting on consoles decorated with the heads of wild boars. Before visiting it, be sure to leave nothing visible in your car.

Orgon

This market town in the Durance plain dominates the ridge which separates the Alpilles to the west and the Montagne du Luberon to the east. It is home to an interesting **church** (Église) from the 14C. The choir and nave are slightly out of alignment.
Crowning the hill overlooking the town to the south *(road subject to restrictions)*, the **Chapelle Notre-Dame-de-Beauregard**'s terrace presents a fine view of the Durance valley and the Luberon mountains.

► Leave Orgon and take the D 7N, returnng to St-Rémy-de-Provence via the D 99.

ADDRESSES

🏨 STAY

◻◻ **Chambre d'hôte Domaine de Saint-Véran** – *13660 Orgon, rte de Cavaillon, 1.5km/1mi north on D 26. ℘04 90 73 32 86. Closed Jan–Feb.* ▱ 🅿 ⬒. *5 rooms.* This fine house stands in a vast park planted with parasol pines and cypresses. All the bedrooms are different and there is a cosy salon as well as a pool.

◻◻ **Hostellerie de la Tour** – *rte d'Arles, 13990 Fontvieille. 9km/5.6mi towards les Baux then take D 78F, then D 17. ℘04 90 54 72 21. www.hotel-delatour.com. Closed Nov–mid-Mar.* 🅿. *10 rooms. Restaurant* ◻◻. A warm welcome and attentive service have made this modest inn popular. The rooms are small, relatively simple, and quite comfortable. The cuisine is good local fare. There is also a decent swimming pool.

◻◻◻◻ **Chambre d'hôte Mas de la Rose** – *rte d'Eygalières, 13660 Orgon, 4km/2.5mi southwest on D 24B. ℘04 90 73 08 91. www.mas-rose.com. Closed Jan–Feb.* ⬒. *8 rooms.* In a bucolic setting, farm buildings dating from the 17C have been prettily converted into a charming guest house. There are landscaped gardens and a pool. Table d'hôte ◻◻◻◻ *(dinner May–Sept, reservation essential).*

🍴 EAT

◻ **L'Ami Provençal** – *35 pl. de l'Église, 13990 Fontvieille. ℘04 90 54 68 32. Closed Feb, Wed in low season, and evenings mid-Sept–Jan and Mar.* Salads are in high demand in this simple restaurant right beside the church and the house occupied by Léo Lelée, the "painter of the Arlésiennes". Fresh market ingredients are used to produce flavours of long ago.

◻◻ **Table du Meunier** – *42 c. Hyacinthe Bellon, 13990 Fontvieille. ℘04 90 54 61 05. Closed 22–27 Dec, mid-Jan–early Mar, autumn half-term, Tue (Sept–Jun) and Wed. Booking recommended.* The regional cooking in the rustic setting of this old mill attracts customers from far and wide. The terrace harbours a real treasure: a chicken house dating from 1765.

◻◻ **La Place** – *65 av. de la Vallée-des-Baux, 13520 Maussane. ℘04 90 54 23 31. Closed Tue, Wed (Oct–Apr).* In an intimate and trendy interior, customers enjoy the cuisine of the south with a modern twist, in two cosy dining rooms or on a shaded terrace.

◻◻ **La Regalido** – *R. Frédéric-Mistral, 13990 Fontvieille. ℘04 90 54 60 22. www.laregalido.com. Closed Mon, mid-Nov–mid-Mar. 15 rooms* ◻◻◻. This fine hôtel-restaurant now offers a lunch menu which is extremely good value, served in a striking setting: an old mill in a luxuriant garden with a terrace. Those with slightly deeper pockets will come back to have dinner and stay the night in one of the lovely bedrooms.

◻◻◻◻ **Bistrot d'Eygalières "chez Bru"** – *Route d'Orgon, 13810 Eygalières. ℘04 90 90 60 34. Booking essential. 9 rooms.* Having made their restaurant in the village an institution, Wout and Suzy Bru have moved 4km/2.5mi out to a stylish modern location with a terrace facing the Alpilles. Chef Wout, who learned his craft in several Michelin-starred restaurants, is known for his innovative cooking. Bedrooms, minimalist in style, are spacious and well appointed.

TAKING A BREAK

Boulangerie Henri Joye – *74 c. Hyacinthe Bellon, 13990 Fontvieille. ℘04 90 54 72 52.* The best baker in the area draws customers from afar with his *navettes*, *fougasses* and speciality breads.

La Maison Sucrée – *R. de la République, 13810 Eygalières. ℘04 90 95 94 15. Open Jul–Aug Tue–Sun midday, Sept-Jun 11am–2pm, 7pm–9.30pm. Closed Mon.* An excellent ice-cream parlour (delicious lavender or passion fruit sorbets), crêperie and salon de thé in the heart of Eygalières.

SHOPPING

Coopérative Oléicole de la Vallée des Baux – *R. Charloun-Rieu, 13520 Maussane-les-Alpilles. ℘04 90 54 32 37. www.moulin-cornille.com. Summer Mon–Sat 9am–6.30pm, winter Tue–Sat 9.30am–6pm.* Based in a 17C mill, this oil co-operative presses olives using traditional equipment. With an artisan approach, it produces a range of virgin oils using the five varieties of olives grown in and around the Vallée des Baux. You can taste before you buy.

Moulin du Mas des Barres – *Petite rte de Mouriès, Quartier de Gréoux, 13520 Maussane-les-Alpilles.* ✆*04 90 54 44 32. Open 9am–noon, 2pm–6pm.* A farm in an idyllic location, amidst olive trees at the foot of the Alpilles. Every year the mill handles the crop of 500 growers to produce its AOP oil. The shop sells tapenade, pistou and olive paste, as well as the oil, of course, in bottles or large flasks.

Moulin Saint-Michel – *Cours Paul-Révoil, at the centre of the village, 13890 Mouriès.* ✆*04 90 47 50 40. www.moulinsaintmichel. com. Open 9am–noon, 2pm–6pm. Closed*

Sun, public holidays and third week of Aug. This mill, now magnificently restored, has been in operation since 1744, crushing the main olive varieties of the Vallée des Baux in order to produce AOP oils. Visits are instructive and the shop sells good local gourmet products.

ACTIVITIES

🚶 **Walking** – Take the 15km/9mi footpath along the Alpilles ridge, from Glanum to Eygalières, via Val St-Clerg, following the GR 6 footpath. Other walks of 1–3hr are available.

Les Baux-de-Provence★★★
Bouches-du-Rhône

Detached from the Alpilles, this bare rock spur – 900m long and 200m wide – has vertical ravines on either side. With a ruined castle and ancient houses right on the top, the spectacular site★★★ of Les Baux is one of the most picturesque French villages and a popular tourist destination. The village gave its name to the mineral bauxite, discovered here in 1822.

A BIT OF HISTORY

A warrior line – The Lords of Les Baux were renowned in the Middle Ages, described by Mistral as "warriors all – vassals never". They were proud to trace their genealogy back to the Magi King, Balthazar, and, so that no one should ignore the fact, boldly placed the star of Bethlehem on their coat of arms. From the 11C the lords were among the strongest in the south of France, having in their control 79 towns and villages. From 1145 to 1162 they warred against the House of Barcelona, whose rights to Provence they contested. Supported for a while by the German emperor, they finally submitted after having succumbed to a siege at Les Baux itself.

They won titles: members of different branches became variously Princes

▶ **Population:** 436.
Ⓒ **Michelin Map:** 340: D-3.
🗉 **Info:** Maison du Roy, 13520 Les Baux-de-Provence. ✆04 90 54 34 39. www.lesbaux deProvence.com.
◖ **Location:** Arriving by the D 78 from Fontvieille, you'll notice the perched houses at the village entrance.
🅿 **Parking:** Leave your car in one of the car parks – the one nearest the village costs €5 for unlimited parking. In summer, unless you get there early, you'll need to park at the side of the road.
⊛ **Don't Miss:** The castle and a walk around the old town.
🕓 **Timing:** Allow about 2hr for a visit. Some shops and restaurants are closed in January.
👪 **Kids:** Firing of the castle's giant catapult (Apr–Sept daily, Oct–Mar weekends).

of Orange, Viscounts of Marseille, Counts of Avellino, and Dukes of Andria (having followed the Capetian Princes of Anjou who were campaigning in southern Italy). One of them married Marie of Anjou, sister of Joan I, Queen

Medieval War Machines

Trebuchet (12C–16C) – With its system of counterweights, this siege engine could make holes in walls more than 200m away. Nicknamed the "war wolf", it could fling stones of up to 140kg in weight – making it among the most feared of weapons.

Couillard (14C–16C) – A type of trebuchet with split counterweights which had a reach of more than 100m and could fire up to 12 rounds per hour. Its name (related to the French word for testicles) reflects its shape!

Bricole (12C) – Lighter than the other weapons, this was operated by women. It was positioned on top of ramparts to bombard enemies below. This stone-throwing device is also the origin of the expression "s'attirer des bricoles", meaning "to get into trouble".

Battering ram – It was roofed over with timber so that assailants were protected from objects hurled down upon them while they propelled it forcefully against walls or doors. Battering rams were already in use in antiquity.

Ballista – This giant crossbow fired out cannonballs or bolts which were loaded into it through a slider mechanism. Like the battering ram, it was widely used by the Greeks and Romans.

of Naples and Countess of Provence. She was destined to tragedy: three times a widow, she died in 1382, smothered by an ambitious cousin.

Turenne, the Brigand – The House of Turenne, from the Limousin, was a great family: two of its members were popes at Avignon, one of whom was Clement VI. Another of its members was the Viscount Raymond de Turenne, nephew of Gregory XI, who became the guardian of his niece, Alix of Baux, in 1372. His ambitions caused civil war in the region. His pillaging and cruelty terrorised the countryside and he was appropriately named the "Scourge of Provence". His chief delight was to force his unransomed prisoners to jump off the castle walls.

The pope and the Lord of Provence hired mercenaries to get rid of the brigands, but the mercenaries themselves ravaged the enemy territories as well as the territories to be protected; as a result their contract was broken and they were paid to leave the area. Pillaging and fighting broke out again quite soon. The King of

France joined Turenne's enemies and in 1399 the "scourge" was surrounded at Les Baux; however, he escaped and fled into France.

The End – Alix was Les Baux's last princess, and on her death in 1426 the domain, incorporated into Provence, became simply a barony. King René granted it to his second wife Jeanne of Laval. Joined with Provence to the French Crown, the Barony revolted in 1483 against Louis XI, who subsequently had the fortress dismantled. From 1528 the Constable Anne de Montmorency, who was titular Lord of Les Baux, undertook a large restoration project on the town, which once again enjoyed a prosperous period. Les Baux then became a centre of Protestantism under the Manville family who administered it for the Crown. In 1632, however, Richelieu, tired of this troublesome fief, had the castle and ramparts demolished and the inhabitants were fined 100,000 *livres* plus the cost of the demolition!

Les Baux-de-Provence

© Pierre Jacques/hemis.fr

🐾 WALKING TOUR

THE VILLAGE★★★
1hr.

A walk through the streets of Les Baux is a magical experience, as long as they are not too crowded or full of souvenir sellers.

▶ Enter through the Porte Mage and turn left towards place Louis-Jou.

Ancien Hôtel de Ville
pl. Louis Jou. ⏰*Open daily 9am–6pm.* 🎫*No charge.* 📞*04 90 54 34 39.*
This deconsecrated 16C chapel, formerly the town hall, still has three rooms with pointed vaulting, which house a **Santon Museum**.

👥 Musée des Santons
⏰*Open 9.30am–5.30pm(high season); off season, contact the tourist office.* 🎫*No charge.*
In this charming little museum was renovated in 2008. Modern museum techniques shed light on the *santon*-making tradition which began in Roman churches in the 13C. In showcases with

😊 Provence PASS 😊

A useful ticket allowing entry to the château and Carrières de Lumières *(Apr–Sept €17.50/€14; Oct–Mar €15.50/€12).* Available from the tourist office.

mirrors which make it possible to see all the little details, you can admire many 'santouns' (small saints in Provençal) – painted or clothed clay models, Neopolitan (17C), and Provençal (19C–20C), as well as a Christmas crèche.

An alley to the right leads to **La porte Eyguières**, which used to be the town's only entrance gate.

▶ Double back the way you came. At the end of rue de la Calade, bear right into rue de l'Église.

Place St-Vincent★
This is a charming, shaded little square. There is a lovely view of the Fontaine valley and the Val d'Enfer from the terrace. In the corner of the square, the Hôtel de Porcelet (Renaissance) houses the Musée Yves-Brayer.

Musée Yves-Brayer★

pl. François-de-Hénain. ⏱*Open Apr–Sept daily 10am–12.30pm, 2–6.30pm; rest of year 11am–12.30pm, 2–5pm.* ⏱*Closed early Jan–mid-Feb.* ⊛€5 *(child, under 18, free).* ☎*04 90 54 36 99. www.yvesbrayer.com.*

The museum displays works by Yves Brayer (1907–90), a figurative painter deeply attached to Les Baux (he is buried in the village cemetery). It is the glowing landscapes of Provence which inspired some of his best paintings, such as *Les Baux* and *Field of Almond Trees.*

In 1974, the painter decorated the walls of the **chapelle des Pénitents blancs** (17C) with pastoral scenes (landscapes of the Alpilles and the Val d'Enfer), and a stained-glass window was based on a design of his.

Flanked on its north side by a graceful campanile, the so-called lantern of the dead, the 12C and 16C **Église Saint-Vincent★ (E** *on map*) is worth a visit. Partly carved out of the bedrock, the simple interior is surprisingly light, with stained-glass windows by Max Ingrand. Coming back up by the rue de l'Église, then rue des Fours, bear left into rue du Château so that you pass the **ancien temple protestant (D)**, incorporating the remains of a dwelling of 1571. On the lintel of one of the church windows,

you can read the Calvinist motto: *Post tenebras lux* ("After darkness, light").

Across the street, the 16C mansion with a beautiful façade decorated with mullioned windows is the Renaissance **Hôtel de Manville (H)**. Donated by the prince of Manville, it now houses the town hall.

Coming back down the Grande Rue, note the Renaissance Maison Jean de Brion: it belonged to Louis Jou (1881–1968), an engraver, editor and printer who devoted his life to the arts associated with books. The **Fondation Louis-Jou (F)** includes early printed books, ancient bindings, engravings by Dürer and Goya, splendid series of wood engravings and works edited by Louis Jou. ☞*Guided tours must be booked 4 days in advance.* ⏱*Closed Jan.* ⊛€3 *(reduced rate €1).* ☎*04 90 54 34 17.*

Returning up the Grande Rue, you will pass the **anciens tours banaux** (communal ovens) **(B)** where the town's inhabitants came to bake their bread, then continue into rue du Trencat, hollowed into the rock, which leads to the château.

Château des Baux-de-Provence★

45min. Access to the citadel via the Musée d'Histoire des Baux, at the end of rue du Trencat. ⏱*Open Jan–Feb*

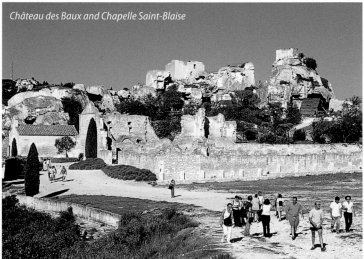

Château des Baux and Chapelle Saint-Blaise

©S. Sauvignier/MICHELIN

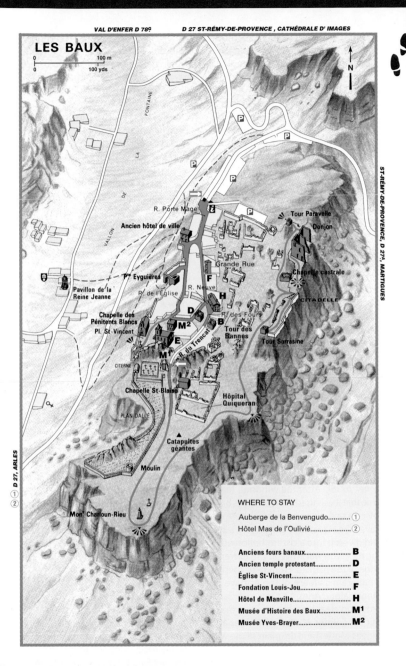

VAL D'ENFER D 78⁹   D 27 ST-RÉMY-DE-PROVENCE , CATHÉDRALE D' IMAGES

LES BAUX

0   100 m
0   100 yds

N

ST-RÉMY-DE-PROVENCE, D 27⁴, MARTIGUES

D 27, ARLES
① ②

R. Porte Mage

Tour Paravelle

Donjon

Ancien hôtel de ville

Grande Rue

Chapelle castrale

Pon Eyguières

Pavillon de la Reine Jeanne

R/ de l'Église

R. Neuve

F

H

CITADELLE

Chapelle des Pénitents Blancs

Pl. St-Vincent

D

M²

B

E

R/ des Fours

R. du Trencat

Tour des Bannes

M¹

CITERNE

Tour Sarrasine

Chapelle St-Blaise

PLAN DALLÉ

Hôpital Quiqueran

Catapultes géantes

Moulin

Mon¹ Charloun-Rieu

WHERE TO STAY

Auberge de la Benvengudo	①
Hôtel Mas de l'Oulivié	②

Anciens fours banaux	**B**
Ancien temple protestant	**D**
Église St-Vincent	**E**
Fondation Louis-Jou	**F**
Hôtel de Manville	**H**
Musée d'Histoire des Baux	**M¹**
Musée Yves-Brayer	**M²**

and Nov–Dec 10am–5pm; Mar and Oct 9.30am–6.30pm; Apr–June and Sept 9am–7.15; Jul–Aug 9am–8.15pm. €10 (child, €8) see combined Provence Pass ticket, p237. 04 90 54 55 56. www.chateau-baux-Provence.com.

Since 1991, the citadel has been the subject of an important restoration project. The excavation work carried out in 1992 allowed three main periods of occupation of the rocky spur prior to the modern era to be determined: the

2C and 1C BCE (second Iron Age), the 5C and 6C (construction of a rampart and scattered dwellings), and the medieval period (construction of a keep).

La Chasse aux Énigmes – A fun questionnaire has been devised so that children aged from 7 to 12 can explore the Château des Baux. A free booklet is handed out at the entrance, and a mystery trail takes children through the castle, looking for hidden clues that reveal its history.

On the way in, pause in front of the two models of the fortress in the 13C and the 16C. They will help you to understand its evolution. Beyond the entrance, in the open air, explanatory notices indicate the historical timelines. For a more detailed understanding of the site, rent an audio-guide.

The **Chapelle Saint-Blaise** was the seat of the woollen carders and weavers' brotherhood from the 12C. Nowadays it houses a small museum devoted to the olive tree. Visitors can watch a video entitled "Van Gogh, Gauguin and Cézanne in the Country of the Olive".

Hôpital Quiqueran was built in the 16C by Jehanne de Quiqueran, wife of the governor of Les Baux, and was in operation until 1787. It is now in ruins.

Now you will climb right up to the huge platform where reconstructions of medieval war machines stand *(see panel, p236)*. After the windmill (each time that it was used the lord of Les Baux levied a tax), alongside which there is a paved area created to collect rainwater and divert it into a cistern hollowed in the rock, you will arrive at the extreme edge of the plateau. From here there is a panoramic **view★** of the Abbaye de Montmajour, Arles, La Crau, the Camargue (in clear weather you can make out Les Saintes-Maries-de-la-Mer and Aigues-Mortes) and the plain all the way to the Étang de Berre.

Look at the monument erected in honour of the poet Charloun Riéu (1846–1924), before heading for the **Citadelle** ruins, towering over the eastern side of the rocky spur. The **Tour Sarrasine** (Saracen Tower) – from the top, a good view of the village and castle – and the **Tour des Bannes** remain to the south, dominating a group of 16C houses. A bay of rib vaulting can still be seen in the **Chapelle castrale** (12C–16C), dedicated to St Catherine.

The **castle** and the **donjon** (keep) (*fairly difficult steps, not recommended for those who suffer from vertigo*) are the remains of a 13C building constructed on the site of the 10C fortress.

There is a magnificent **panorama★★** embracing the Aix countryside, the Luberon, Mont Ventoux and the Cévennes; the tormented shapes of the Val d'Enfer to the north contrast with the gentle countryside of the Vallon de la Fontaine to the west.

Leaning against the northern rampart, the **Tour Paravelle** affords a pretty **view★** of the village of Les Baux and the Val d'Enfer.

ADDITIONAL SIGHTS
Walk around the rock of Les Baux

Allow 45min. Free brochure from the tourist office. Start at the car park, then follow chemin des Trémaïe. There is no shade on the walk so take a hat and water in summer.

This pretty pedestrian loop goes around the rock of Les Baux underneath the château. On it you will see some Gallo-Roman remains (including a bas-relief carved into a block of stone), old quarries open to the sky and a traditional stone hut. Good views of the plain from lower down. The path ends at the Porte d'Eyguières from which steps will take you to rue de la Calade.

Carrières de Lumières

By the D 27, 300m north of the village on Route de Maillane. Open daily Mar–Sept 9.30am–7pm, Oct–Jan 10am–6pm. Closed Feb. €9.50. see combined Provence Pass ticket, p237. 04 90 54 47 37. www.carrieres-lumieres.com.

Replacing the Cathédrale d'Images from March 2012, this benefits from the same quarry setting with its immense spaces. In the half-light, the high limestone walls act as giant three-dimensional screens for audiovisual presentations, making spectators feel like Lilliputians. The theme changes annually, starting with "Gauguin–Van Gogh, Painters of Colour". Cool all year round, so bring a sweater.

Les Baux vineyards

Some wine estates offer guided tours or cellar visits: check with individual domaines.

Enjoying a special microclimate and with particular soils, the vineyards of Les Baux, already known in ancient times but later improved, produce wines of excellent quality. Reds and rosés predominate. Produced in smaller quantities, the white wines are also included in the *appellation* since 2011.

EXCURSION
Queen Jeanne's Pavilion

Vallon de la Fontaine (on the D 78G). A path leads down to the pavilion from Porte Eyguières.

This pretty little Renaissance building was a garden folly built by Jeanne des Baux c.1581. Mistral had a copy made for his tomb at Maillane.

ADDRESSES

🏨 STAY

⊜⊜⊜⊜ **Auberge de la Benvengudo** – *quartier de l'Arcoule (2km/1.2mi southwest of Baux via D 27). ℘04 90 54 32 54. www. benvengudo.fr. Closed Nov–mid-Mar.* 🅿️🔲. *21 rooms. Restaurant*⊜⊜⊜⊜. Nestled in a cluster of olive groves at the foot of the citadel is this charming Virginia creeper-covered inn. Rooms are plush and open on to a flower-filled garden. The dining room and veranda are decorated in Provençal style. Poolside terrace. Dishes are composed around fresh market produce.

⊜⊜⊜⊜ **Hôtel Mas de l'Oulivié** – *Les Arcoules, D 78F, 2.5km/1.5mi southwest of Les Baux. ℘04 90 54 35 78. www.masde loulivie.com. Closed mid-Nov–mid-Mar* ♿🅿️🔲. *25 rooms.* This restored *mas*, whose sustainable practices and support

of local products have earned it the nature reserve designation "Hôtel au Naturel", sits serenely in the middle of an olive grove, right up against the Alpilles. Amazing pool, magnificent gardens, tennis, boules and spa treatments.

🍽 EAT

⊜⊜ **Le Café des Baux** – *r. du Trencat (50m from château entrance). ℘04 90 54 52 69. www.cafedesbaux.com. Open daily Apr–Oct noon–3pm, also evenings Jul–Aug.* A patio shaded by the château, a troglodyte-style dining room and good food make this a worthwhile spot. *Salades gourmandes* and desserts are especially tasty.

⊜⊜⊜⊜ **La Cabro d'Or** – *A short distance from village on Route d'Arles. Open daily Apr–Sept; Oct–Mar. Closed Sun dinner, Mon, Tue lunch only from mid-Oct–Mar. ℘04 90 54 33 21. www.lacabrodor.com. 26 rooms* A member of the prestigious Oustau de la Baumanière hotel and restaurant group, this gorgeous place is slightly less expensive and formal than you'd expect, since it offers exquisite food in a glorious country-house setting. Cookery courses available.

SHOPPING

Castelas – *Mas d'Olivier, quartier Frechier, on the D 27. ℘04 90 54 50 86. www.castelas.com. Open 8.30am–6.30pm. Closed public holidays off season.* Garlanded with awards, the oils produced by Jean-Benoit and Catherine Hugues are ranked among the best in Provence. Excellent English is spoken in the attractive shop beside the mill; good tapenades and other tempting gourmet products are also on sale.

Mas de la Dame – *On the RD 5. ℘04 90 54 32 24. www.masdeladame.com. Open 8.30am–7pm. Closed 1 Jan and 25 Dec.* This 16C property (the oldest wine estate in Les Baux) was mentioned by Nostradamus and painted by Van Gogh. Today it is known mainly for the quality of the organic wines and olive oils produced with attention to detail by sisters Caroline Missoffe and Anne Poniatowski.

EVENTS

Christmas at Les Baux – Midnight Mass is held on Christmas Eve in the church of St-Vincent with a Nativity scene.

Tarascon★

Bouches-du-Rhône

A tradition dating back some 2,000 years has made Tarascon the town of the Tarasque. In the 19C Alphonse Daudet brought fame to the town through his character Tartarin. And yet the city has its own claim to fame in the shape of its magnificent castle, with walls which drop straight down to the swift-flowing Rhône River. The city is on the boundary of a rich market gardening region and has become an important fruit and vegetable dispatching centre. Market day is Tuesday, in the town centre.

CHÂTEAU DU ROI RENÉ★★

Bd du Roi René. ⏰Open daily Jun–Sept 9.30am–6.30pm; Feb–May and Oct 9.30am–5.30pm. ☞Guided tours (1hr) available. ⏰Closed 1 Jan, 1 May, 1 and 11 Nov, 25 Dec. ⊜€7. ☎04 90 91 01 93. www.tarascon.fr.

Its location on the banks of the Rhône, its massive appearance which contrasts with its elegant inner architecture, and its exceptional state of preservation, make this building one of the finest medieval castles in France. In the 13C, the castle, opposite the royal city of Beaucaire, defended Provence's western boundary. Captured by Raymond de Turenne in 1399, it was restored soon after to its owners, the Anjou family;

- ▶ **Population:** 13 297.
- ♿ **Michelin Map:** 340: C-3.
- **Info:** Le Panoramique, av. de la République. ☎04 90 91 03 52. www.tarascon.fr.
- ▶ **Location:** Arrive over the bridge from Beaucaire for the best view of the castle. The town is 17km/10.6mi N of Arles and 23km/14.3mi W of Avignon.
- **P Parking:** Free on the ring road and at the foot of the castle.
- **Don't Miss:** King René's castle, the old town, the Souleiado textile museum and shop.
- ⏱ **Timing:** Allow 2hr to visit the castle followed by a walk around the old town.
- **Kids:** Maison de Tartarin and the Tarasque Festival.

Louis II, father of René, decided to have it entirely rebuilt. From 1447 to 1449, **King René** completed the building, which was his favourite residence, contributing all his taste and refinement to the interior decoration.

It is made up of two independent parts: the seigneurial living quarters on the south side flanked by round towers on the town's side and square towers on the Rhône side, offering a compact mass

Château du Roi René by the Rhône and the spire of Collégiale royale Sainte-Marthe

© Jose Antonio Moreno Castellano/age fotostock

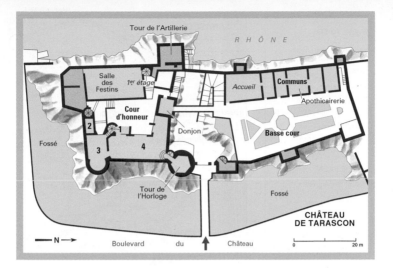

CHÂTEAU
DE TARASCON

of walls rising up 48m; and the inner courtyard on the north side, defended by shorter rectangular towers.

Outer Courtyard (Basse cour)

A wide moat spanned by a bridge (once a drawbridge) isolates the group of buildings from the rest of the city. This section includes the recently restored service buildings, including the Hospital of St-Nicolas' **dispensary**: in a finely panelled 18C room there are 200 apothecary jars.

Main Courtyard (Cour d'honneur)

Enter the seigneurial living quarters through the keep's zigzag passageway to the main courtyard, around which are the apartments with their lovely, finely carved façades adorned with mullioned windows. A graceful polygonal staircase turret **(1)** serves the different floors; near it a niche holds the busts of King René and Jeanne of Laval, his second wife. Note the Flamboyant Gothic screen of the chantry **(2)**; opening on to the corner tower is the lower chapel **(3)**, and above it the upper chapel.

On the town side are the main living quarters, set above a lovely gallery **(4)** with pointed barrel vaulting, and with access to the clock tower.

Seigneurial Living Quarters

in the west wing, which rises above the river, you enter King René's quarters. On the ground floor is the banqueting hall with two large fireplaces; on the first floor are two vast reception rooms with painted wooden ceilings. Continue to the king's bedroom in the southwest tower, with a fireplace and even a hot plate to keep dishes warm (useful, no doubt, when he felt like a snack). On the second floor are the audience chamber and council room, which were vaulted to support the terraces. In these rooms there are several fine 17C Flemish tapestries. Return to the south wing to see the chaplain's room and the royal chapel where, from their oratories, the king and queen could hear the chantry voices.

Terrace

Access via the artillery tower
(Tour de l'Artillerie).
The terrace offers a wide **panorama★★** of Beaucaire, Tarascon, the Rhône, the Vallabrègues dam, the Montagnette hills, the Alpilles, Fontvieille, the Abbaye de Montmajour, Arles and the plain of St-Gilles.

Go back down by the clock tower; the ground floor houses the galley room, so-called because of the graffiti and boat drawings made by past prisoners.

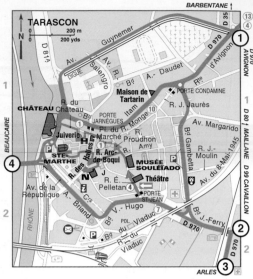

🐾 WALKING TOUR

THE TOWN
Even if it is best known for its castle, the town is also worth a visit for its warm-toned old stone buildings and narrow streets lined with fine mansions, many of whose façades have been carefully restored.

◗ Enter the town by Porte St-Jean and follow rue Pelletan.

On the right note the theatre's Baroque façade, with its chubby-cheeked cherubs.

◗ Continue along rue Proudhon.

A fine mansion (no 39) houses the well-known family business, **Souleiado**, whose shop sells traditional Provençal fabrics printed in bright colours.

Musée Charles-Deméry (Souleiado)★
39 r. Charles Deméry. ◯Open Mon–Sat 10am–6.30pm. ◯Closed Sun off-season and 1 Jan, 8 May, 25 Dec. ⊛€7. ℘04 90 91 40 62. www.souleiado.com.
Since 1806 this old mansion has been the headquarters of a famous

fabric printing business specialising in **indiennes**, the colourful designs which originally reached Provence from the east, hence their name. The museum has almost **40,000 printing blocks**, the oldest dating back to the 18C. Made from wood with brass relief work, they were applied by hand, then hammered with a mallet by workers who printed up to 30m of cotton a day.

In the 19C Provençal interior, scenes from daily life have been re-created, as well as several workshops of the period like the **colours kitchen** where the dyes for the fabrics were prepared. Also on show are **rare pieces of printed fabric**, 18C and 19C Provençal costumes and a worthwhile collection of pottery, faïence and pictures.

◗ Go on down this street.

On the left, just after the **Chapelle de la Persévérance** (17C), partially covered rue **Arc-de-Boqui** begins.

◗ At the end of this street, turn right towards place du Marché.

Hôtel de Ville
pl. du Marché.

This 17C building features an elegantly carved façade enhanced by a stone balcony. The first-floor Salle des Consuls, with its panelling and portraits, may be visited. Rue du Château leads to the interesting **Juiverie**, the town's former Jewish ghetto.

▷ Return to place de la Mairie by rue Robert.

Collégiale royale Sainte-Marthe ★

Erected in the 12C, this collegiate church was largely reconstructed in the 14C, then modified and finally restored after having been damanged in 1944. On the south side it has retained a superb Romanesque doorway whose carved decoration has partly disappeared. Inside, there are paintings by Nicolas Mignard and Pierre Parrocel. In the **crypt** you can see the sarcophagus of Saint Martha (3C–4C.), decorated with carvings. On the stairs on the way down, note the tomb of the old Marshal of Provence, Jean de Cossa – a fine example of the Renaissance style.

▷ When you have gone around the church and had a look at graceful place Fraga, follow rue de l'Ancien-Collège and rue Clerc-de-Molières.

Turn right into rue des Halles, the main street of old Tarascon, where the market was once held. It is lined with pic-turesque arcaded houses (15C). In rue Ledru-Rollin, on the left, are the 17C galleries of the old cloister, the **Cloître des Cordeliers** (◐ *open Mon–Sat 10am–noon, 2pm–6.30pm; ℘04 90 91 38 71*), where exhibitions are held.

ADDITIONAL SIGHTS
♟ Espace Tartarin-Cloître des Cordeliers

Pl. Frédéric Mistral. ◐*Open Mon–Fri 10am–12.30pm, 2–6pm, Sat 1.30–6pm.* ◐*Closed Sun and public holidays.* ⊜*No charge.* ℘04 90 91 98 71.

The famous character created by Alphonse Daudet has finally found a place where he can recover from his adventures. In this interior, refurbished to give the flavour of the 1870s, you will find costumed figures, furniture and documents which re-create the ambience of Daudet's novel.

⬤ DRIVING TOUR

LA MONTAGNETTE
Round-trip of 45km/28mi. Allow 4hr.

▷ Leave Tarascon by the D 80 to the east (in direction of Maillane) and continue along the N 570 via the D 80A, then on the left take the D 32.

Maillane
In the fertile countryside known as the Petite Crau de St-Rémy, Maillane offers the charm typical of a Provençal town with small squares shaded with plane trees and

---

The Tarasque Monster

Tarascon was established on an island in the Rhône as Massalia's trading post. The Romans took it over after the defeat of the Massaliotes. The present castle stands on the site of the Roman camp built by the legionaries. According to a Provençal legend, an amphibious creature periodically climbed out of the Rhône into the town, where it devoured children and cattle and killed anyone attempting to cross the river. To save the town, St Martha came from Les Stes-Maries-de-la-Mer and subdued the beast with the sign of the Cross; the now docile beast was thereupon captured by the townspeople. In celebration of the miracle, Good King René, who often resided in the castle, organised stupendous festivities in 1474. The legend is still recalled in an annual fête.

white houses with tiled roofs. Its renown is largely due to the fame of **Frédéric Mistral**, the Provençal poet and one of the founders of the Félibrige movement.

Musée Frédéric-Mistral

11 av. Lamartine. Guided visits only (45min): Apr–Sept 9.30–11.30am, 2.30–6.30pm; Oct–Mar 10–11.30am, 2–4.30pm. Closed public holidays. €4 (museum only); gardens no charge. 04 90 95 84 19. www.maillane.fr.

This museum is located in the house which Mistral had built and then lived in from 1876 to 1914. Mistral's memory is evoked throughout the various rooms – office, living room, dining room, bedroom – which have been kept as they were at his death.

▶ Continue to Graveson via the D 5, then left onto the D 28.

Graveson

The main street of this charming fortified town runs alongside a canal. There's a good market here every Friday *(May–Oct 4pm–8pm)*.

At the end of cours National, the **Musée Auguste-Chabaud★** (open 10am–noon, 1.30–6.30pm: Jun–Sept daily; Oct–May Sat–Sun and public holidays. closed 1 Jan and 25 Dec. €4. 04 90 90 53 02. www.museechabaud.com) houses a collection of paintings by this artist, sculptor and poet, who was born in Nîmes and died in Graveson in 1955. He found inspiration in the countryside from rural scenes to the festivals of Provence.

To pay further homage to the painter, you can follow the Chabaud walking trail through the streets of the town. About 10 panels with reproductions of his work have been put up on the various places that he painted. *Booklet on sale in the museum.*

Four Seasons garden

Av. de Verdun. Open daily Apr–Sept 8am–8pm, Oct–Mar 8am–6pm. No charge. 04 90 95 88 44. www.graveson-provence.fr.

This public garden on the edge of the village is divided into four sections, each dedicated to a particular season. From the top of the mound in the centre there is a view of the chalk hills of the Montagnette.

Aquatic garden "Aux fleurs de l'eau"

579 rte de Saint-Rémy. Open daily May–mid-Sept (May–mid-Jun, weekends and public holidays only) 10am–noon, 2.30–7pm (1st 2 weeks of Sept 2.30–7pm). Closed late Sept–Apr. €6.50 (under 8 no charge). 04 90 95 85 02. www.auxfleurs deleau.fr.

A dozen pools, three waterfalls, 1km/0.6mi of paths, 2 000 kinds of plants from five continents, many of them aquatic… there's plenty here to delight amateur botanists, or anybody in search of somewhere cool to walk. Children will see frogs, dragonflies and Japanese carp in this well-irrigated and well-organised jungle.

Musée des Arômes et du Parfum

La Chevêche, Petite Rte du Grès (to the south on D 80). Open daily Jul–Aug 10am–7pm; Sept–Jun 10am–noon, 2–6pm. €5.50. 04 90 95 81 72. www.museedesaromes.com.

A few kilometres to the south on D 80, this perfume museum occupies an old *mas* that once belonged to the monks of St-Michel-de-Frigolet. Traditional techniques related to the making of perfume essences are presented and explained in a fascinating exhibition: copper stills, a collection of old flasks, semicircular racks displaying all types of essences *(orgues de parfumier)* and receptacles for catching the essential oils and floral water after distillation *(essenciers)*.

▶ Continue to the D 570 and turn right towards Graveson, then left towards Tarascon. Turn left immediately on to the D 81.

After crossing over the D 970, the road climbs and winds among pines, olive trees and cypresses, in a pleasant setting for a picnic.

Abbaye de Saint-Michel-de-Frigolet

Abbey church and church of Saint-Michel open daily. Cloister and chapter room open only for guided tours (1hr) Sun 4pm. €3.50 (children no charge). 04 90 95 70 07. www.frigolet.com.

The Stations of the Cross are on the way to the abbey entrance. This is flagged by a neo-medieval enclosure which, with its towers, curtain walls, crenellations and machicolations, looks like something out of a Walt Disney cartoon. You can visit the neo-Gothic abbey church built around the **chapelle de Notre-Dame-du-Bon-Remède**, whose Romanesque structure is camouflaged by a profusion of gilded **panels★** donated by Anne of Austria, and pictures attributed to the school of Nicolas Mignard. In the north gallery of the **cloister** (early 12C, restored 17C), there are some Roman remains to admire: friezes, capitals, masks, as well as beautiful modern *santons* carved from the wood of a thousand-year-old olive tree by Charles Toni from Noves. In the **chapter room** (17C) are paintings by Jean Guitton. In the entrance hall, note the striking painting by Wenzel, *The Siege of Frigolet* (1880).

As for the **église Saint-Michel** (12C), it will charm you with its simplicity. It has retained a fine roof of stone tiles, crowned by an elegant, open-work ridge.

Access to the massif is restricted from June to September, and all year when it is windy. A route marked in yellow enables the most energetic visitors to explore the **Montagnette** from Saint-Michel-de-Frigolet, going via Boulbon and the **San Salvador**, which rises to 161m/536ft.

Continue along the D 80 then D 35E.

Barbentane

Built against the north slope of the Montagnette, Barbentane overlooks the plain near the confluence of the Rhône and the Durance and is devoted to market gardening.

The village has retained part of its 14C fortifications and is worth visiting for its castle.

Château★★

Guided tours (45min) Easter–end Oct 10am–noon, 2–6pm. Closed Wed except Jul–Sept. €8. 04 90 95 51 07. www.barbentane.fr.

A Classical 17C façade and terraces with their flower-filled urns overlook formal Italian-style gardens. The interior, enhanced by mementoes belonging to the Marquis of Barbentane, features

Château de Barbentane

© Achim Bednorz/age fotostock

rich 18C decoration of Italian influence. The vaulting, plasterwork, painted medallions, coloured marble, Louis XV and XVI furnishings, Chinese porcelain and Moustiers faïence all add to the charm of this delightful château.

Old Village

All that remains from the fortifications are the two entrance gates, Porte Calendale, which opens on to the Cours, and Porte Séquier above the village.

The 12C Maison des Chevaliers (House of the Knights) has a lovely Renaissance façade composed of a turret and two basket arches topped by a columned gallery. Overlooking the village, the Tour Anglica is the keep of the former castle, built in the 14C by the brother of Pope Urban V, Cardinal Anglic de Grimoard. From the terrace there is a good view of Avignon, Châteaurenard and in the distance Mont Ventoux. A short walk through the pines leads to the well-preserved 18C **Moulin de Bretoul** (Bretoul mill), from where there is a lovely view of the Rhône plain. This is the only remaining example of the many windmills that were formerly in this region.

▶ Leave Barbentane to the south, on the D 35.

Boulbon

An impressive fort dominates the town, which is laid out against the Montagnette hillside. In the cemetery, the **chapelle Saint-Marcellin** (11–12C) contains some fine sculptures. ℘04 90 43 95 47. ☞Guided tours can be booked at the town hall.

▶ Return to Tarascon on the D 35.

ADDRESSES

🏠 STAY

☞ **Hôtel du Viaduc** – 9 r. du Viaduc. ℘04 90 91 16 67. www.hotelduviaduc.com. 🅿. 16 rooms. Situated within easy walking distance of the town centre, this simple hotel is well fitted out. In good weather, breakfast is served on the shaded terrace.

☞☞ **Hôtel Les Échevins** – 26 bd Itam. ℘04 90 91 01 70. www.hotel-echevins.com. Closed Nov–Mar. ♿. 40 rooms. Restaurant☞☞. Guests will enjoy this 17C dwelling with its family atmosphere. Modest but well-maintained rooms. Beautiful staircase with wrought-iron railing. Colourful veranda-restaurant and traditional cuisine.

☞☞ **Hôtel Le Mas des Amandiers** – rte d'Avignon, 13690 Graveson, 1.5km/0.9mi. ℘04 90 95 81 76. www.hotel-des-amandiers.com. 🅿. 28 rooms. Rooms at this hotel, amid almond groves, have rustic furniture; the dining room is Provençal in style. Swimming pool and "botanic" garden.

☞☞ **Hôtel Cadran Solaire** – 5 r. du Cabaret Neuf, 13690 Graveson. ℘04 90 95 71 79. www.hotel-en-Provence.com. Closed Nov–Mar (except for reservations). 🅿. 12 rooms. A sundial adorns the pretty façade of this former coaching inn. Natural tones, rush matting on the floor and country furniture.

☞☞☞☞ **Chambre d'hôte Rue du Château** – 24 r. du Château. ℘04 90 91 09 99. www.chambres-hotes.com. ⛱. Closed Nov–Mar. 4 rooms. Staying in this carefully restored 18C house, situated in a quiet road leading to the château, is like going back in time. Breakfast is served on the flower-decked patio. A dream of a place.

🍽 EAT

☞☞ **Bistrot des Anges** – pl. du Marché. ℘04 90 91 05 11. ♿. Closed evenings and Sun. Likeable restaurant in Provençal style with a summer terrace and light fare from a changing menu which relies heavily on fresh, local produce.

☞☞ **Le Théâtre** – 4 r. E.-Pelletan. ℘04 90 91 41 44. www.restaurantdutheatre.com. Closed Mon, Tue lunch and mid-Nov–mid-Dec. Opposite the theatre, this small restaurant uses ultra-fresh ingredients for its family-style dishes, offered at keen prices.

EVENTS

Fêtes de la Tarasque – This very ancient festival runs from the last Friday in June for four days. In a big procession the monster (☞see panel on p245) appears, dragged along by knights (tarascaïres) and accompanied by Tartarin. Various musical and traditional events end with a spectacular firework display beside the Rhône.

Beaucaire★

Gard

Formerly a stronghold of the Counts of Toulouse, Beaucaire kept watch over Tarascon across the river. It became famous for its fair, which attracted huge crowds for centuries. Now prized for its fine old buildings and canal-side setting, it has been designated a"Ville d'Art et d'Histoire".

▸ **Population:** 15 946.
⊙ **Michelin Map:** 339: M-6.
▣ **Info:** 24 Cours Gambetta, 30301 Beaucaire. &04 66 59 26 57. www.ot-beaucaire.fr.
◖ **Location:** 14km/8.7mi N of Arles; 24km/15mi S of Avignon.
▣ **Parking:** On the banks of the canal.
⚏ **Kids:** Les Aigles de Beaucaire, Le Vieux Mas.

 WALKING TOUR

OLD BEAUCAIRE★
www.ot-beaucaire.fr

◖ Take rue Hôtel de Ville (to the right of cours Gambetta), which leads to place Georges Clemenceau.

Hôtel de Ville
r. de l'Hôtel de Ville.
The town hall is a late-17C mansion by Mansart with a central block flanked by wings outlined with a high, balustraded wall; carved flower garlands surround the windows, and the grand staircase in the courtyard rises behind a double portico of Ionic columns.

Église Notre-Dame-des-Pommiers
Note the curved façade, typical of the Jesuit style in vogue in the 18C and inside a majestic dome on pendentives. From rue Charlier, you can see a frieze recessed into the upper part of the wall – all that remains of the Romanesque church which this one replaced. It depicts the Last Supper, Judas's kiss, the Way of the Cross and the Resurrection.

◖ A small arched passageway leads to rue de la République.

Beaucaire Fair

The fair, launched in 1217 by **Raymond VI of Toulouse**, originally lasted one week. It became a great medieval fair and, at its peak in the 18C, it lasted a month every July when as many as 300,000 people gathered to do business, roister and celebrate. So prestigious was the fair that the prices negotiated there served as a reference throughout the kingdom. Streets specialised in single commodities after which many were named: Beaujolais was a wine street; Bijoutiers was a jewellers' row; rue des Marseillais was where oil and soap were sold. On the quayside, traders proffered an array of produce including cocoa, coffee and dates.

The fairground, on the large flat expanse between the castle cliff and the river, was set with stalls offering everything from perfume to pottery. It was also a horse fair. Circus acts with everything from acrobats to elephants amazed onlookers. This huge success was almost certainly due to the town's position at a crossroads of land and river routes, aided by Louis XI's decree which made it a free port. Today, the Beaucaire Fair is re-created during the "Estivales" Festival, which still attracts a crowd.

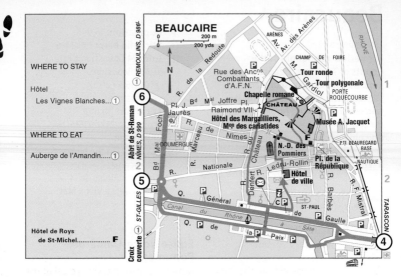

Hôtel des Clausonnettes

21 r. de la République.
Note the Classical façade of this 18C building which backs onto the castle *(try to enter the courtyard).*

Hôtel des Margailliers

23 r. de la République.
This magnificent 17C dwelling with its carved façade is known as the "house of caryatids" because of the caryatids flanking its porch.

▷ A little further on.

Hôtel de Roys de Lédignan

r. de la République.
A fine 18C mansion. The street emerges onto **place de la République**, a square with arcades. In the centre is a statue of the *drac*, the local mythological monster which is Beaucaire's answer to Tarascon's Tarasque.

▷ Go back along rue de la République, then take the street on the right side that leads up to the castle.

Château★

Montée du Château. ⓘ*See Musée Auguste-Jacquet hours.* ℘*04 66 59 71 34.*
Built in the 11C on the site of a Roman camp and remodelled in the 13C, the castle was dismantled in the 17C on the orders of Cardinal Richelieu. It stood on top of the hill protected by ramparts. It is still possible to walk around, discovering en route the very unusual **polygonal tower**, the sheer drop from the **curtain walls** and the beautiful round tower in one corner. The small Romanesque chapel has a charming sculpted tympanum.

Musée Auguste-Jacquet

In the castle. ⓘ*Open daily except Tue: Apr–Oct 10am–12.30pm, 2–6pm; Nov–Mar 10am–noon, 2–5pm (Sat–Sun 9am–noon, 2–5pm).* ⓘ*Closed public holidays.* ⊛€5.50 (child under 12, €2). ℘04 66 59 90 07. www.beaucaire.fr/ spip.php?article65.
In the fortifications of the château, this museum has an archaeological section with items from prehistoric times up to the Gallo-Roman period. It also evokes old Beaucaire in an interesting way with a re-created bourgeois interior, costumes, headwear, utensils, ceramics from Saint-Quentin-la-Poterie (near Uzès) and documents about the fair.

▷ Return to cours Gambetta via place Raimond-VII, then via rue du Château and the street extending from it, rue Denfert-Rochereau.

EXCURSIONS
Mas Gallo-Romain des Tourelles

4km/2.5mi to the west. Leave Beaucaire by the rocade (ring road), then take the D 38 towards Bellegarde. After 4km/2.5mi, turn right for the Mas des Tourelles. &. Open Apr–Jun and Sept daily 10am–noon, 2–6pm (except Sat am and Sun am); Jul–Aug Mon–Sat 10am–noon, 2–7pm (Sun 2–7pm); Oct daily 2–6pm; Nov–Dec and Feb–Mar, Mon–Sat 2–5.30pm; Jan, Sat 2–5.30pm. Closed 1 and 11 Nov, 24 Dec–3 Jan. €6 (under 18, free) 04 66 59 19 72. www.tourelles.com.

Arranged around a flower-filled courtyard are the buidings of this 17C farm which stands on the site of a Gallo-Roman villa, farm and pottery workshop. There are fascinating displays of archaeological material discovered here, as well as information about wine production in the Gallo-Roman period. The Cella Vinaria is a reconstructed Roman wine-cellar complete with giant press, stone vat and large earthenware jars. Mas des Tourelles produces some wines made according to Roman techniques (they taste unusual!), as well as modern Costières de Nîmes wines.

Abbaye de St-Roman★

5km/3mi northwest on the road to Nîmes. Open Jul–Aug daily 10am–1pm, 2–7pm; Apr–Jun and Sept–Oct Wed–Sun 10am–1pm, 2–6.30pm (Tue 2–6.30pm); late Oct–Mar Sat–Sun and school holidays 2–5.30pm. Closed 1 Jan, 24–25 Dec. €5.50. 04 66 59 19 72. www.abbaye-saint-roman.com.

An attractive path up through *garrigue* leads to the entrance of this extraordinary troglodyte monastery which stood on a limestone peak dominating the Rhône valley.

Abandoned in the 16C, it evolved into a fortress which was demolished in 1850. A marked trail leads to the chapel containing the tomb of Saint Roman.

The **view★** from the terrace takes in the Rhône, Avignon, Mont Ventoux, the Luberon, the Alpilles and, in the fore-

ground, Tarascon and its castle. On the way back down you will see a vast hall, and the monks' cells, carved out of the rock, complete the picture of a place which is spellbinding in its simplicity.

Le Vieux Mas

6.5km/4mi south on D 15 (to Fourques), then a small road to the right towards Mas Taraud, which you follow for 2km/1mi to Mas Végère. &. Open Apr–Sept daily 10am–6pm (Jul–Aug daily 10am–7pm); Oct–Mar Wed, Sat–Sun and public and school holidays 1.30–6pm. Closed Dec–Jan except Christmas holidays. €9 (child 3–15, €6.50) 04 66 59 60 13. www.vieux-mas.com.

Turkeys, geese, ducks and cattle are raised in this traditional *mas* where life seems to have stopped around 1900. Staff dressed in period costume demonstrate old tools and techniques.

ADDRESSES

☞ STAY

Hôtel Les Vignes Blanches – 67 av. de Farciennes. 04 66 59 13 12. www.lesvignesblanches.com. &. Closed 2 Jan–8 Feb. 57 rooms. Restaurant. A well-run hotel in a modern complex near a busy road. Welcoming bistro and dining room with traditional menu.

☞ EAT

Auberge de l'Amandin – 1076 chemin de la Croix de Marbre. 04 66 59 55 07. www.auberge-amandin.com. Open Tue–Sun lunch, Thu–Sat dinner. In an attractive old *mas* with a pretty garden and pool-side terrace, deft cooking uses the best local ingredients, in season.

EVENTS

Market – Thursday and Sunday.

Les Fêtes de la Madeleine – This July festival re-creates the glorious past of the Beaucaire Fair. Entertainment includes *abrivados*, *novilladas* and *corridas*.

Les Rencontres Equestres Meditérranéennes – Equestrian competitions and musical evenings, in July.

In many ways, Avignon is the heartbeat of Provence, standing at its centre not just geographically but also from the point of view of religion, art and cultural history. Few cities make such a powerful impression. Rising majestically above the Rhône, it looks immediately imposing: stout medieval ramparts, fine old houses, exquisite churches and, towering above them all, the massive bulk of the Popes' Palace and the slender golden Virgin glinting on top of the cathedral.

Highlights

Although the popes made Avignon the headquarters of the Catholic Church for less than a century, from 1309 to 1377, their influence is still palpable today, not only in the fortified palace that occupies the same space as four standard French cathedrals, but in the whole fabric of a city that developed and prospered with their patronage. Avignon's old centre is filled with treasures because art and architecture have been fostered here for more than 700 years. On a brief visit it may seem too busy to enjoy, with traffic choking the narrow streets and the Place de l'Horloge bustling with people; but take the time for a long, slow walk, and you will find plenty of quiet corners where it is easy to imagine what Avignon must have been like at the height of its splendour.

On the World Stage

Today the city is as famous for its theatre festival as for its papal past. A major event on the world calendar of culture, the Avignon Festival, founded in 1946 by theatre director Jean Vilar, attracts huge crowds every July. With an ambitious main programme of events and a fringe festival too, the festival stages performances all over the place, making the city feel like one immense theatre.

The Cardinals' Choice

Across the river stands Villeneuve Lez Avignon, a twin town of a sort. While the popes lived in Avignon, the cardinals crossed the Rhône to Villeneuve which, as its name suggests, was a brand-new development in the early 14C. Built in a dominating position above Pont St Bénezet, it was soon to acquire wonderfully grand mansions worthy of church dignitaries, as well other significant buildings added during a period of affluence that lasted five centuries.

Riverside Charm

A short distance east of Avignon, two pretty towns built around water are worth exploring. L'Isle-sur-la-Sorgue is famous today for its remarkable concentration of antique dealers, but it may have been its rich history as a centre for the manufacture of silk, paper and leather that drew them here in the first

Antique market, L'Isle-sur-la-Sorgue

© Hervé Lenain/hemis.fr

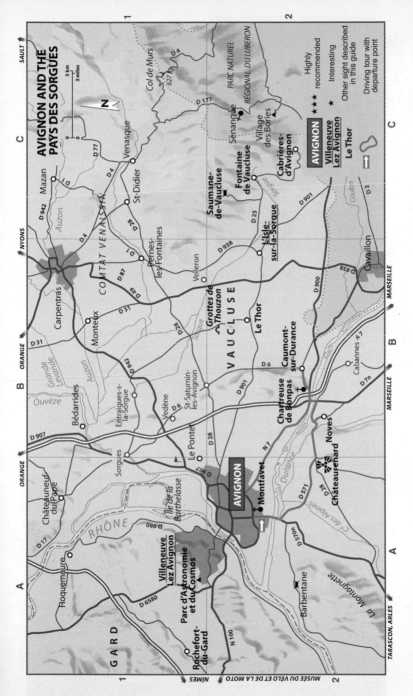

AVIGNON AND THE PAYS DES SORGUES

N

5 km
3 miles

SAULT

1

2

Legend

★★★ Highly recommended

★ Interesting

● Other sight described in this guide

➡ Driving tour with departure point

AVIGNON

AVIGNON
Villeneuve
Lez Avignon
Le Thor

C

PARC NATUREL RÉGIONAL DU LUBERON

Col de Murs
627

Venasque

Mazan

St-Didier

Pernes-les-Fontaines

Sénanque

Fontaine de Vaucluse

Saumane-de-Vaucluse

Village des Bories

Cabrières-d'Avignon

L'Isle-sur-la-Sorgue

Cavaillon

MARSEILLE

COMTAT VENAISSIN

Carpentras

Monteux

Velleron

Grottes de Thouzon

Le Thor

Caumont-sur-Durance

VAUCLUSE

Entraigues-s-la-Sorgue

St-Saturnin-les-Avignon

Vedène

Chartreuse de Bonpas

Cabannes

Noves

Bédarrides

Sorgues

Le Pontet

Châteaurenard

Montfavet

AVIGNON

Barbentane

La Montagnette

Roquemaure

Châteauneuf-du-Pape

Île de la Barthelasse

RHÔNE

Villeneuve Lez Avignon

Parc d'Astronomie et du Cosmos

Rochefort-du-Gard

NÎMES

MUSÉE DU VÉLO ET DE LA MOTO

TARASCON, ARLES

GARD

place. Fontaine-de-Vaucluse is proud to have been a refuge for the love-stricken poet Petrarch; but in the summer heat, the coolness of the celebrated fountain where the River Sorgue gushes out of the ground may be an even greater lure.

253

Châteauneuf-du-Pape vineyard

© V. Gillet/L'ADT Vaucluse Tourisme

Gateway to Wine Country

Ever since the Avignon popes made Châteauneuf-du-Pape their summer retreat in the 14C, planting well-sited vineyards to ensure a supply of the excellent wine that their lifestyle required, Avignon has been the gateway city to one of the most important wine regions in France.

The Southern Rhône stretches in all directions from within a few kilometres of the city walls. Châteauneuf-du-Pape remains its most internationally renowned *appellation*, famous both for voluptuously rich, heady red wines and for vineyards carpeted with *galets*: smooth round stones like outsize potatoes. But these days many other wine villages across the vast sweep of the Côtes du Rhône are producing impressive wines, often at very reasonable prices.

Reds predominate, based mainly on the heat-loving grape Grenache with help from Syrah, Mourvèdre and other varieties traditionally used in the Châteauneuf-du-Pape mix. Gigondas, Vacqueyras, Rasteau, Cairanne, Séguret, Sablet, Beaumes-de-Venise: here are some of the names that visitors should seek out, not just on wine labels but on signposts, because these are picturesque old villages clinging to limestone ledges in the jaggedly dramatic Dentelles (&see Dentelles des Montmirail). The Ventoux and Luberon *appellations* to the southeast are thrilling wine territory these days too, thanks to a new generation of quality-focused producers.

What a huge vat of excitement there is to sample on Avignon's doorstep! The Southern Rhône has more than 7,000 wine growers – far too many for a representative selection to be squeezed into this guide – so plan to do a spot of research and visit at least a few. For more information, access *www.vins-rhone.com*.

Séguret vineyards

© David Martyn/Bigstockphoto.com

Avignon★★★
Vaucluse

Designated city of art and culture, on the borders of three *départements* (Bouches-du-Rhône, Gard and Vaucluse), Avignon stretches in all its beauty along the banks of the River Rhône. Bell towers emerge from a mass of pink roofs and the city is surrounded by ramparts, dominated by the Rocher des Doms, the majestic cathedral and the Palais des Papes. The city is known for its **Festival d'Avignon**, founded in 1947 by actor/director **Jean Vilar** (1912–71). Theatrical events, perhaps not so different from the pageants of the Middle Ages, illustrate various art forms (dance, music and cinema) and use the city's enchanting historical monuments as backdrops.

VISIT
PALAIS DES PAPES★★★
Allow 2hr.
r. Pente Rapide Charles Ansidei.
○*Open daily Mar 9am–6.30pm; Apr–Jun and Sept–Oct 9am–7pm; Jul 9am–8pm; Aug 9am–8.30pm; Nov–Feb 9.30am–5.45pm.* €*11 (Combined ticket with Pont St-Bénézet €13.50).* ℘*04 90 27 50 50. www.palais-des-papes.com.*

The palace is a maze of galleries, chambers, chapels and passages, now empty and deserted. Yet, try to imagine what it was like at the time of the popes. Picture its luxurious furnishings; sumptuous decoration; discreet comings and goings of prelates and servants; changing of the guards in dress uniform; cardinals, princes and ambassadors arriving and departing; the pilgrims gathered in the courtyard waiting to receive the pope's blessing; or to see him leave on his white mule; the litigants and magistrates creating commotion around the pontifical court.

▶ **Population:** 89 683.
ふ **Michelin Map:** 332: B-10.
🛈 **Info:** 41 cours Jean-Jaurès, 84000 Avignon. ℘04 32 7432 74. www.avignon-tourisme.com.
◖ **Location:** Take the sightseeing train (*see Addresses*) or a guided tour of the city for an overview *(contact the tourist office).*
🅿 **Parking:** There are paying and free car parks outside the ramparts – don't try to park in the centre.
✿ **Don't Miss:** Palais des Papes; St-Bénézet bridge; wandering around the narrow streets of the Old Town.
🕓 **Timing:** Allow a couple of days for a visit including half a day for the old town and an hour for the Palais des Papes. Expect crowds during the festival in July.
👥 **Kids:** Boat trips on the Rhône; little sightseeing train.

Construction
This princely residence counts among the largest of its time, with an area of 15 000sq m/3.7 acres. It is both a fortress and a palace and is made up of two buildings joined together: the **Palais Vieux** to the north and the **Palais Neuf** to the south; begun in 1334, its construction lasted 30 years. The Cistercian Benedict XII, brought up in contempt of luxury, had the old episcopal palace razed and entrusted to his compatriot Pierre Poisson the task of building a vast residence that would lend itself to prayer and be well defended. The Palais Vieux thus acquired the appearance of an austere fortress.
Planned around cloisters, its four wings are flanked by towers, the strongest of which, the north tower, Tour de Trouillas, was used as a keep and prison. Clement VI, a great prince of the church, artist and

prodigy, ordered the architect Jean de Louvres to carry out the expansion of the palace. The Tour de la Garde-Robe and two new buildings closed off the main courtyard that preceded Benedict XII's palace.

The exterior was not modified. However, inside, artists sumptuously decorated the rooms, notably the pope's private apartments. The works continued under Clement VI's successors: Innocent VI had Tour St-Laurent built to the south and Tour de la Gache to the west and the decoration completed (fresco on the vault in the Grande Audience); Urban V had the main courtyard laid out with its well and had buildings constructed linking the palace to the gardens, behind the Tour des Anges.

In 1398, and again from 1410–11, the palace was under siege, resulting in the dilapidation of the buildings. Allocated to the legates in 1433, it was restored in 1516 but continued to deteriorate. In a bad state when the Revolution broke out, it was pillaged, with furniture dispersed and statues and sculptures broken. After a particularly bloody episode in 1791, the palace was transformed into a prison and barracks (1810). Occupied by military engineers, it was again mistreated: at least the statutory wash on the walls protected some of the mural paintings.

Unfortunately, in many places, this safeguard came too late: the soldiers had had time to cut the protective coating off the frescoes and sell the pieces to collectors or antique dealers from Avignon.

Exterior

The palace from the outside has the appearance of a citadel built straight out of the rock. Its walls, flanked by ten large square towers, some more than 50m high, are buttressed by huge depressed arches holding up the machicolations: this is one of the first known examples of such military architecture.

Ground Floor

See the map below for a guide to the Ground Floor.

▶ Go through the Porte des Champeaux and enter the former guard room (reception and ticket office).

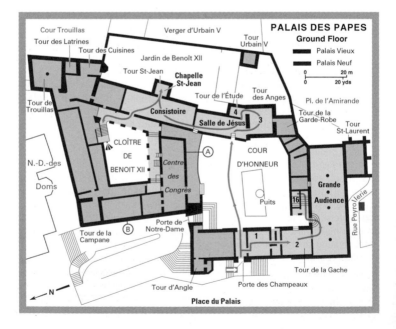

Palais des Papes

© Romain Cintract/hemis.fr

The walls here are decorated with 17C paintings **(1)**.

Petite Audience (2)

In the 17C, when this room was in use as an arsenal, the vaulting was decorated with *grisaille* paintings representing military trophies.

▶ Turn round and go back through the Porte des Champeaux.

Main Courtyard (Cour d'Honneur)

Running along the main courtyard to the north is the Conclave Wing **(A)**, which houses the Conference Centre. The Gothic south wing has a number of irregular openings in its façade and the Indulgence window **(15)** on the first floor. It is used during the summer as a backdrop for the theatrical performances of the Avignon Festival.

Treasury

The **Lower Treasure House** (Trésor Bas) is a vaulted room hollowed out beneath the Tour des Anges. Underneath the flagging were the hiding places where bags of silver and gold, silverware and valuable ornaments were kept. The cupboards on the walls contained the accounts ledgers and archives.

The wealth of the popes was considerable. John XXII bequeathed 24 million ducats to his heirs after 19 years as pope. The size of the papal revenue explains why the most important court dignitary was the Chamberlain, that is, the Minister of Finance.

Grande Trésorerie

This small room has an enormous fireplace decorating the north wall. Take the staircase to the **Salle de Jésus**, which used to serve as antechamber to the Consistoire.

Chamberlain's Bedchamber (3)

Situated on the third floor of the Tour des Anges, just below the Papal Bedchamber, this room is magnificently embellished with a 14C painted beam ceiling and with foliated scrollwork covering parts of the walls. Here, too, there are hiding places concealed in the flags on the floor.

Papal Vestiary (4)

This small room in the Tour de l'Étude was converted into a chapel in the 17C by the vice-legates. The original timberwork was reinforced by a stone vault. The walls feature 18C wood panelling.

Consistoire

To debate the great theories of Christianity, the pope and his cardinals met in council in this vast rectangular hall. It was here that the pope announced

History of the Palais des Papes

Before the Popes – Only a few ruins remain of the monuments which embellished the flourishing Gallo-Roman settlement of Avenio. Following the barbaric invasions of the 5C, Avignon fell into oblivion through the early Middle Ages. Its rebirth occurred in the 11C and 12C, when Avignon took advantage of the feudal rivalries between the Houses of Toulouse and Barcelona to protect and reinforce its independence: like its Italian counterparts, Avignon formed a small city-state. But its commitment in favour of the Albigensians brought about royal reprisals: in 1226, Louis VIII seized the town, ordering its defences to be razed. Nevertheless, Avignon rose again quite quickly, and, in spite of losing its independence, regained its former prosperity under the rule of the House of Anjou.

The Popes at Avignon – Avignon's destiny changed in the early 14C with the exile of the pontifical court to France, bringing with it a century of brilliance.

The court in Rome had become more or less impossible for the popes, who were incessantly the object of political differences. The Frenchman Raymond Bertrand de Got, elected pope under the name of **Clement V** (1305), decided to establish the court in France, where since 1274 the Holy See possessed the Comtat Venaissin. Clement V solemnly entered Avignon on 9 March 1309, though he did not reside here permanently as he preferred the calm of Groseau Priory, near Malaucène, or Monteux castle, not far from Carpentras. He died in 1314. In 1316, the former Bishop of Avignon, Jacques Duèze, was elected. As **Pope John XXII** he established the papacy here; between 1309 and 1377, seven French popes succeeded each other at Avignon, among them **Benedict XII**, who built the papal palace, and **Clement VI**, who purchased Avignon from Queen Joan I of Sicily, Countess of Provence, in 1348.

The Constructive Popes – The city was transformed, and took on the appearance of a vast building site: convents, churches and chapels, not to mention the splendid cardinals' palaces (⚓ *see Villeneuve lez Avignon*), while the pontifical palace was constantly being enlarged and embellished. The university, founded in 1303, numbered thousands of students. The pope wanted to be considered the most powerful ruler in the world. His wealth and munificence shone brilliantly, attracting the notice of the envious, which was why he lived in a fortress and established a line of fortifications to protect the town from mercenary soldiers who pillaged the countryside.

the name of the newly appointed cardinals and received the sovereigns and their ambassadors in great pomp. It was here also that cases proposed for canonisation were examined.

Exhibited in this hall are **frescoes** executed by the great Italian artist **Simone Martini**, which were brought from the porch of Notre-Dame-des-Doms cathedral.

Chapelle St-Jean or Chapelle du Consistoire

This oratory is adorned with lovely frescoes painted from 1346 to 1348 by **Matteo Giovanetti**, Clement VI's official court painter. On leaving the Consistoire, follow the lower gallery of Benedict XII's cloisters and take the staircase to the banqueting hall. There is a fine view of the **Staff Wing (B)**, where people holding various offices lodged with the main servants. From here you will also have a fine view of the Tour de la Campane and of Benedict XII's chapel.

Life in Avignon was pleasant: liberty and prosperity existed and the population jumped from 5,000 to 40,000. A place of asylum for political refugees like Petrarch, the pontifical city also housed a Jewish community. But this tolerance extended, unfortunately, to adventurers, escaped criminals, smugglers, counterfeiters and all kinds of rogues. In these circumstances, the popes thought of returning to Rome; **Urban V** left for the Eternal City in 1367, but hostility in Italy forced him to return to Avignon after three years. **Gregory XI** finally left Avignon in 1376 and died in 1378.

Popes and Schismatic Popes – Hostile to the reforms of the Italian pope **Urban VI**, successor to Gregory XI, the mainly French cardinals of the Sacred College elected another pope, **Clement VII** (1378–94), who returned to Avignon. The Great Schism divided the Christian world; the Avignon pope was recognised mainly in France, Naples and Spain. Popes and schismatic popes mutually excommunicated each other and attempted by any means possible to bring the other down, vying with each other for the papacy's great wealth. **Benedict XIII** (1394–1423) succeeded Clement VII; however, he no longer had the support of the king of France. He fled Avignon in 1403, yet his followers resisted in the palace until 1411. The Great Schism finally ended in 1417 with the election of **Martin V**.

Meanwhile life continued in Avignon as is suggested by the presentation of the *Mystères* (mystery plays enacting an episode of the Scriptures) during Whitsun in 1400, with huge living tableaux and processions that went on for three days and dramatised the Passion of Christ.

Until the Revolution, Avignon was governed by a papal legate and a vice-legate. Intolerance towards the Jews increased: confined to a ghetto, which was locked every night, the Jews had to wear a yellow cap, pay dues, and listen to sermons preached to convert them. Moreover, they were not allowed to mix with Christians, they could only occupy certain positions, and they were under constant surveillance.

Avignon was a society of contrast, with a gulf between the wealthy and poor, as evidenced by the confrontation between them from 1652 to 1659. During the Revolution, Avignon was split between the partisans wanting to belong to France and those who wanted the pontifical state maintained. The former won, and on 14 September 1791 the constitutional assembly voted the union of the Comtat Venaissin to France.

First Floor
See the map on p261 for a guide to the First Floor.

GRAND TINEL OR BANQUETING HALL

Exhibited in this hall, one of the largest in the palace (48m long and 10.25m wide), is a superb series of 18C Gobelins **tapestries**. The immense panelled keel-vaulted roof that takes the form of a ship's hull has been restored. Continue into the **upper kitchen (5)** with its huge chimney in the form of an octagonal pyramid, located on the top floor of the Tour des Cuisines.

This tower was also used as the pantry and provisions storeroom. Next to it, the Tour des Latrines (or Tour de la Glacière – not open to the public) offered common latrines on each floor for the soldiers and staff.

Chapelle du Tinel or Chapelle St-Martial

This oratory is named after the **frescoes** painted in 1344–45 by Matteo Giovanetti of St Martial (an apostle from the

Limousin, Clement VI's native region). They recount the life of the saint using a harmony of blues, greys and browns.

Chambre de Parement

Next to the pope's bedroom, this antechamber, also known as the Robing Room, was used as a small waiting room by those who had been accorded a private interview with the pope. Two 18C Gobelins tapestries hang on the walls.

Next to the Robing Room on the first floor of the Tour de l'Étude you will find Benedict XII's study **(Studium) (6)** with its magnificent tiles. Situated along the west wall of the Robing Room was the pope's private dining room **(7)** called the Petit Tinel. Alongside it was the kitchen (or secret kitchen) **(8)**. The rooms in this section of the palace were entirely destroyed in 1810.

Papal Bedchamber (9)

The walls of this room were richly painted against a blue background: birds entwined in vines and squirrels climbing oak trees. Exotic birdcages were painted in the window embrasures.

Chambre du Cerf (10)

This room, known as the Stag Room, was Clement VI's study and is decorated with elegant **frescoes** painted by various Italian artists. The subjects, illustrated against a verdant background, are hunting, fishing, fruit and flower picking, and bathing scenes. The ceiling in larch wood is very ornate. This intimate and cheerful room had two windows. One offered a fine view of Avignon, and the other overlooked the gardens.

To get to the Chapelle Clémentine, cross the **north sacristy (11)** comprising

Detail of frescoes, Chambre du Cerf

© Alain Hocquel/L'ADT Vaucluse Tourisme

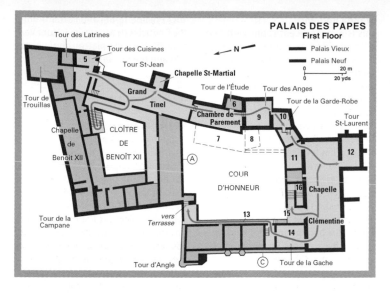

two vaulted bays on diagonal ribs and containing plaster casts of characters who figured significantly in the history of the Avignon papacy. The bridge was built by Innocent VI to link the pope's private dining room with the chapel and led into the east bay.

Grande Chapelle or Chapelle Clémentine

To the right of the pontifical altar, an opening leads into the **Cardinals' vestry (12)** in Tour St-Laurent, where the pope changed vestments when officiating at High Mass. It contains casts of recumbent figures of the popes: Clement V, Clement VI, Innocent VI and Urban V.

In this chapel, the Conclave of cardinals came to hear the Mass of the Holy Spirit before returning to the Conclave Wing **(A)** via a narrow passageway called the **Conclave gallery (13)**, which has elegant vaulting.

The **Conclave** was made up of the college of cardinals, who met ten days after the death of the pope to elect a successor. The first floor of the Palais Vieux was used to receive the cardinals. In order to isolate them from the rest of the world, they blocked up all the doors and windows and did not open them again until they had elected a pope with a two-

thirds majority vote. The word *conclave* is derived from Latin, meaning "under lock and key".

Chamberlain's New Bedchamber (14)

This occupies the far south end of the **High Dignitaries' Wing (C)**, which also houses the bedchamber of the Treasury notaries and the Treasurer's apartment.

Terrasse des Grands Dignitaires

Located on the second floor of the High Dignitaries' Wing, this terrace offers an extensive **view★★** over the upper storeys of the Palais des Papes, the Tour de l'Horloge, the dome of the cathedral, the Petit Palais and, further in the distance, Pont St-Bénézet and the monuments at Villeneuve Lès Avignon.

Turn back in the other direction to come across the loggia opposite the doorway of the Chapelle Clémentine. From the window of this loggia the pope would bless the gathered faithful in the courtyard below **(15)**.

Ground Floor (Palais Neuf)

Go down the **Grand Escalier (16)**. The right-hand flight of stairs is covered with pointed vaulting, a strong example of the bold architectural design typical of that time.

Grande Audience

This is a magnificent room with two aisles divided by a line of columns supporting the pointed arches of the vaulting. It is also called the Palais des Grandes Causes (Palace of the Great Causes), as it was here that the 13 ecclesiastical judges formed the Tribunal de la Rota – *rota* (wheel) comes from the circular bench on which they were seated and which is located in the room's last east bay. Around the judges sat the lawyers and the papal court's public servants. The rest of the room was for the public; seating ran along the whole of the room's wall. On the vaulting against a dark blue background sprinkled with stars is a **fresco of the Prophets**, attributed to Matteo Giovanetti in 1352.

▷ Leave the palace by the Porte des Champeaux.

⚫⚫WALKING TOUR

1 PLACE DU PALAIS AND THE QUARTIER DE LA BALANCE

Allow 4hr for the round-trip circuit of the place du Palais.

"Promenade des Papes"

This walk gives a striking impression of the height of the building. Follow pretty rue Peyrollerie that leads off from the southwest corner and goes under the enormous buttress supporting the Chapelle Clémentine to emerge on to a square in which there is an attractive 17C townhouse. Go along rue Vice-Légat leading to Urban V's orchard, then go through a covered passageway which opens on to cour Trouillas. The Escaliers Ste-Anne leads up to the Rocher des Doms, giving a different view of the palace.

Rocher des Doms★★

There is a well laid-out garden planted with different species on this bluff. From the terraces you will have superb **views★★** of the Rhône and Pont St-Bénézet, Villeneuve Lez Avignon with Tour Phillipe-le-Bel and Fort St-André, the Dentelles de Montmirail, Mont Ventoux, the Vaucluse plateau, the Luberon hills and the Alpilles.

▷ Go back down to the garden, in the direction of the Petit Palais.

Petit Palais★★

pl. du Palais des Papes.

This was formerly Cardinal Arnaud de Via's residence *(livrée)* before being bought by the pope in 1335 to house the bishopric. The building deteriorated during the different sieges imposed upon the Palais des Papes, and had to be repaired and transformed in the late 15C, especially by Cardinal della Rovere, who subsequently became Pope Julius II. Famous guests resided here: Cesare Borgia in 1498, François I in 1533, and Anne of Austria and the Duke of Orléans in 1660.

Musée du Petit Palais

Petit Palais, pl. du Palais des Papes.
🕐*Open daily except Tue 10am–1pm, 2–6pm.* 🕐*Closed 1 Jan, 1 May, 25 Dec.*
✆*€6.* 🖉*04 90 85 44 58.*
www.petit-palais.org.

The first two rooms of this museum contain **Romanesque and Gothic sculpture**. Note the carved figure (at the back of the room), which comes from the late-14C monumental **tomb of Cardinal de Lagrange**.

The realism of the emaciated corpse, which formed the tomb's base, anticipates the macabre representations of the 15C and 16C.

The **Campana collection**, the major treasure of this museum, brings together a group of Italian paintings from the 13C–16C.

The presentation of works by different schools over consecutive periods makes it possible to appreciate the evolution of the Italian style. Note the strong Byzantine influence that still prevailed in the works of the 13C, the Siennese School, represented by Simone Martini and Taddeo di Bartolo, the international Gothic style (Lorenzo Monaco and Gherardo Starnina), the Florentine School, which concentrated on the form of the drawing in balanced compositions where perspective plays an important role, especially with Bartolomeo della Gatta (*Annunciation*), and the rediscovery of Antiquity, c.1500.

The remaining galleries are devoted to the **painting and sculpture of the Avignon School**. Stylistically the Avignon School can be placed midway between the realism of the Flemish School and the stylisation of the Italian Schools. **Enguerrand Quarton** is represented here by the significant *Requin Altarpiece* (1450–55). On either side of a remarkable *Virgin of Pity* (1457) stand the works of Jean de la Huerta *(St Lazarus and St Martha)* and Antoine le Moiturier *(Angels)*.

Cathédrale Notre-Dame des Doms

pl. du Palais des Papes. ⏱*Open daily Easter–Nov 7am–7pm; rest of the year 9am–5.30pm.* ✆*No charge.* ✆*04 90 82 12 21.*

Built in the mid-12C, the cathedral was damaged many times and each time rebuilt and altered. The porch was added in the late 12C and shelters two tympana (a semicircular one surmounted by a triangular one). The magnificent frescoes by Simone Martini which previously decorated it are now located in the Palais des Papes. In the 15C the large bell tower was rebuilt and in 1859 it was crowned with an imposing statue of the Virgin.

Inside, the single nave with five bays is roofed with pointed-barrel vaulting. The Romanesque **dome★** that covers the transept crossing is remarkable: to reduce the area, the master craftsman created a series of projections that supported the dome and its elegant columned lantern.

Hôtel des Monnaies (Mint)

pl. du Palais des Papes.

This 17C townhouse is crowned with a balustrade and has an ornately carved **façade★** of dragons, eagles, the Borghese coat of arms, cherubs and garlands of fruit.

▷ Take the street to the right of the Hôtel des Monnaies to get to the Quartier de la Balance.

Gypsies lived in the **Quartier de la Balance** in the 19C. In the 1970s it was renovated. This *quartier* descends as far as the ramparts and the famous bridge of the French children's song, *Sur le pont d'Avignon*.

Rue de la Balance

This is the Balance district's main street. On one side are old restored townhouses with elegant façades, decorated with mullioned windows. By contrast, on the other side you will witness modern, Mediterranean-style buildings with small flower-bedecked patios and ground-level shopping arcades.

♿♿ Pont Saint-Bénézet★★

6 r. de la Pente-Rapide Charles Ansidei. ♿⏱*Open daily Mar 9am–6.30pm; Apr–Jun and Sept–Oct 9am–7pm; Jul 9am–8pm; Aug 9am–8.30pm; Nov–Feb 9.30am–5.45pm.* ✆€*5 (Combined ticket with Palais des Papes €15.50.* ✆*04 32 74 32 74. www.palais-des-papes.com.*

In reality Pont St-Bénézet was originally a narrow bridge for people on foot or on horseback. It was never the sort of place where people could dance in a ring as in the song lyric, *"Sur le pont d'Avignon l'on y danse tous en rond"*! Indeed, the people of Avignon did their dancing on the island beneath the arches of the bridge, in other words *sous le pont*.

Spanning two arms of the Rhône to Villeneuve Lez Avignon at the base of the Tour Philippe-le-Bel, the bridge was 900m long and was composed of 22 arches.

Legend has it that in 1177, a young shepherd boy, Bénézet, was commanded by voices from heaven to build a bridge across the river at a spot indicated by an angel. Everyone thought he was crazy until he proved his divine guidance by miraculously lifting a huge block of stone. Volunteers appeared and formed themselves as the **Bridge Brotherhood**

Pont Saint-Bénézet and the Palais des Papes

© Alain Hocquel/L'ADT Vaucluse Tourisme

(Frères Pontifes), and funds flowed in. Within eight years they completed the bridge's construction.

Rebuilt from 1234 to 1237, the bridge was restored in the 15C and then broken by the flooded Rhône in the mid-17C. Built on one of the pilings, the **Saint Nicholas Chapel** consists of two separate sanctuaries (one atop the other). One is dedicated to Saint Nicholas, patron saint of ferrymen, and the other *(accessed by the stairs)* to Saint Bénézet. The visit concludes with a small exhibit highlighting the history and iconography of this famous bridge.

Remparts★

The fortifications (4.3km/2.7mi long) were built in the 14C by the popes. From a military standpoint they do not represent first-class work: the towers were open to the town, and parts of the walls had no machicolations. In fact, the popes had simply wanted to build a preliminary obstacle against attack on their palace. The most interesting section is from rue du Rempart du Rhône to the attractive **place Crillon**.

◗ Return to place de l'Horloge via rue St-Étienne bordered by old townhouses, rue Racine to the right, and rue Molière to the left.

② OLD AVIGNON

Start in place de l'Horloge –
allow half a day.

This route explores the churches, museums and the particularly notable townhouses in the part of Old Avignon to the south and east of the Palais des Papes. It also offers you the opportunity to see how much the present contrasts with the past in this lively city.

Place de l'Horloge

The theatre and town hall overlook this vast square right in the heart of Avignon. Shaded by plane trees, it is occupied by a string of open-air cafés and a traditional merry-go-round, much appreciated by visiting and local children. In the little streets around place de l'Horloge there are windows painted with effigies of famous actors – a reminder that for one month every summer Avignon becomes a world capital of theatre. Built in the 19C, the **Hôtel de Ville** town hall has a 14C–15C **clock tower**.

◗ To the left of the Hôtel de Ville, take rue Félicien-David and go around the back of the Église Saint-Agricol. On the way you will see the remains of a Gallo-Roman rampart.

Église Saint-Agricol

Open Mon and Wed–Sat 4–7.30pm.
A wide staircase leads up to the entrance; note the beautifully sculpted 15C façade. Inside are many works of art including a white marble font dating from the mid-15C, paintings by Nicolas Mignard and Pierre Parrocel, and, on the right aisle near the sacristy door, a fine altarpiece by the Avignon sculptor Boachon (1525) depicting the Annunciation.

▷ Take a left on rue Agricol, then a right on rue Bouquerie.

Rue Jean-Viala

The street runs between two 18C mansions housing the *Préfecture* offices and the general council of the *département* (Conseil Général).

Hôtel de Sade

5 r. Dorée.
Elegant mullioned windows overlook the street. In the courtyard there is a fine pentagonal turreted staircase.

▷ Head to rue Bouquerie, take a left, then a right on rue Horace-Vernet, which will take you to rue Joseph Vernet.

Rue Joseph-Vernet

You will see two fine mansions on the right, one of which, the **Hôtel Ville-neuve-Martignan**, houses the Musée Calvet (*see opposite*).

▷ Go to the left on rue Joseph-Vernet.

Musée Calvet★

65 r. Joseph Vernet. *Open Wed–Mon 10am–1pm, 2–6pm.* *Closed 1 Jan, 25 Dec.* *€6 (€7 with Musée Lapidaire).* *04 90 86 33 84. www.musee-calvet-avignon.com.*
This celebrated museum is named after its creator, the physician Esprit Calvet. Highlights include a range of sculptures, a collection of silverware and faience, and French, Italian and Flemish painting from the 16C to the 19C. Note in particular the *Death of Joseph Bara* by David, *The Four Seasons* by Nicolas Mignard, works by Elizabeth Vigée-Le Brun, and the maritime canvases by the Avignon painter **Claude Joseph Vernet** (1714–89). In 2012 three new rooms focusing on Egypt were added.

Muséum Requien

67 r. Joseph-Requien. *Open Tue–Sat 10am–1pm, 2–6pm* *Closed 1 Jan, 1 May, 25 Dec.* *No charge.* *04 90 82 43 51. www.museum-requien.org.*
Nobody with an interest in nature should miss a visit to this museum of natural history. A real Eden, its herbarium contains 200,000 specimens from all over the world.

▷ Take rue Joseph-Vernet to the left.

Musée Calvet

© Peter Richardson/age fotostock

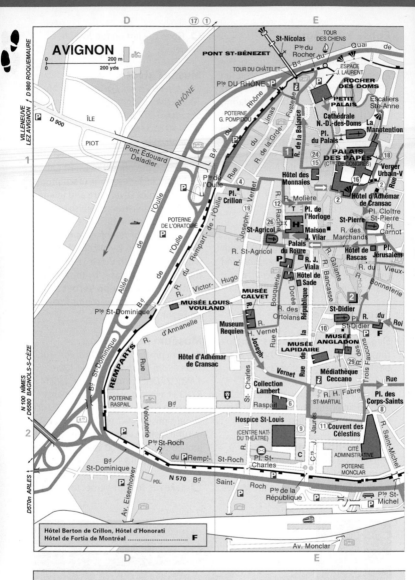

AVIGNON

0   200 m
0   200 yds

WHERE TO STAY

Camping-auberge de jeunesse Bagatelle............①
Chambre d'hôte La Banasterie.........................②
Chambre d'hôtes Lumani..................................③
Hôtel Boquier..⑥
Hôtel Cloître St-Louis......................................⑨

Hôtel Colbert...⑪
Hôtel du Palais des Papes...............................⑮
Hôtel La Ferme...⑰
Hôtel Mignon..⑲

Rue de la République

This lively shopping street, which runs into cours Jean-Jaurès (leading straight to the train station), forms the main axis of the city.

○ Go back towards the tourist office.

From cours Jean-Jaurès turn right (the arcades standing in the neighbouring square are all that remain of the **Abbaye**

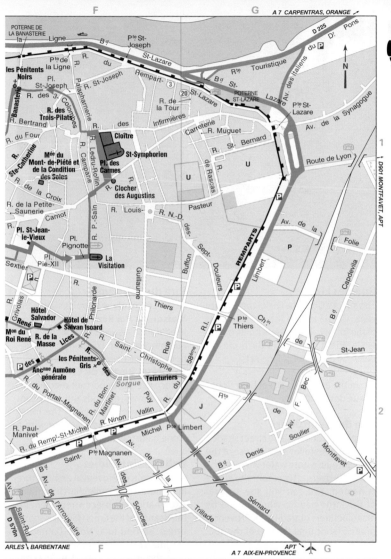

F   G   A 7 CARPENTRAS, ORANGE

St-Martial), then left into rue Agri-col-Perdiguier to reach the 15C **Couvent des Célestins** *(pl. des Corps-Saints)*, built in the northern Gothic style.

▶ Turn back north on to rue des Lices (on the right).

Rue des Teinturiers

© Matthieu Colin/hemis.fr

Rue des Lices

This street follows the line of the 13C city walls. On the left are the 18C buildings of the former almshouse with its galleried façade. It now houses the École des Beaux-Arts (School of Fine Arts).

▷ At the end of the street bear right on rue des Teinturiers.

Rue des Teinturiers

This picturesque cobbled street shaded by plane trees follows the course of the River Sorgue, whose water was used by the cloth-dyers after whom the street is named. You can still see several of the large paddle-wheels used by manufacturers of traditional Provençal printed fabric until the end of the 19C. On the right is the Franciscans' bell tower, all that remains of a convent where Petrarch's unrequited love, Laura, is believed to have been buried.

▷ Turn around and walk back as far as rue de la Masse, on the left.

Rue de la Masse

At no **36** is the **Hôtel de Salvan Isoard**, a 17C mansion with ornately carved window surrounds; and at no 19 **Hôtel Salvador** is an impressive 18C square mansion.

Rue du Roi-René

At the corner of rue Grivolas stands the **Maison du Roi René**, where the king lived during his visits to Avignon.
Further on, four 17C and 18C townhouses form a remarkable **group★**.
The **Hôtel Berton de Crillon (no 7)** is decorated with portrait medallions, masks, flowers, garlands and an elegant wrought-iron balcony. In the inner courtyard is a grand staircase with a stone balustrade.

Église Saint-Didier

An example of Provençal architecture in its purest form, this church contains a dramatic **altarpiece★** representing the Bearing of the Cross (15C). It is sometimes referred to as Notre-Dame-du-Spasme (Our Lady of Spasms), so vividly does the artist Francesco Laurana convey the pain suffered by those depicted in this work. A series of frescoes attributed to artists of the Siennese School decorates the chapel of baptismal fonts.

Livrée Ceccano

To the south of the church you will see the tower (or *livrée*) of the mansion occupied by the cardinal de Ceccano, later incorporated into the collège des Jésuites which is now a multi-media library (*access via rue du Laboureur*).

The Penitent Brotherhoods of Avignon

Appearing as early as the 13C, the penitent brotherhoods were at their peak in the 16C and 17C. The brothers were expected to help each other, do public penance, and perform good deeds. The brotherhood they belonged to was identified by the colour of their sackcloth and by the hood that covered their heads during processions. Avignon was a city where many different brotherhoods – grey, white, blue, black, purple and red – coexisted. The White Penitents were the most aristocratic and included among their members Charles IX and Henri III. Each brotherhood had assets and a chapel: a number of these chapels are still standing (the most interesting are those of the Grey Penitents and Black Penitents). During the Revolution they were disbanded, yet several brotherhoods managed to survive.

From place Saint-Didier, go left into rue des Fourbisseurs.

At the corner of rue des Marchands and rue des Fourbisseurs, note a fine corbelled house dating from the 15C, the **hôtel de Rascas**.

Continue along rue des Fourbisseurs until you reach place Carnot. Then turn right and head for place Jérusalem.

On the small place Jérusalem is the synagogue, which until the 19C was the heart of the Jewish District, also known as the Carrière.

Continue to nearby place St-Jean-Le-Vieux.

Place St-Jean-le-Vieux

Set at one corner of the square is a tall, square tower (14C), all that remains of the Commandery of the Knights of St John of Jerusalem destroyed in the 19C.

From rue St-Jean le Vieux, go to place Pignotte.

Église de la Visitation

This former convent chapel (17C) has a finely carved façade.

Take rue Paul Saïn to the left, then turn right on to rue Carreterie, which leads to place des Carmes.

Place des Carmes

On the south side of the square is the Clocher des Augustins, last vestige of the convent founded here in 1261. The wrought-iron bell tower dates from the 16C.

Église St-Symphorien
pl. des Carmes.

This is worth visiting for the three fine 16C statues in painted wood – Christ, the Virgin and St John – in the first chapel on the left. In the succeeding chapels hang paintings by Pierre Parrocel (*Holy Family*), Nicolas Mignard (*St Eligius*) and Guillaume Grève (*Adoration of the Magi*). Through a wrought-iron gate to the left you can see the 14C cloisters.

On the north side of the square, take rue des Infirmières (on the left), then rue des Trois-Colombes (2nd on the right).

Chapelle des Pénitents noirs
57 r. de la Banasterie. ◷*Open 2–5pm: Apr–Sept Fri–Sat; Oct–Mar Sat only.* ℘*04 90 86 30 62.*

Adding to an exuberantly decorated façade, the head of John the Baptist is a reminder that the Black Penitents' order was founded with his beheading as its symbol. The Baroque interior features some fine decorative woodwork, marble and paintings by Levieux, Nicolas Mignard and Pierre Parrocel.

👣 Passion in Avignon... 👣

Get your **"Avignon PASS'ION" pass,** valid for two weeks, which offers significant price reductions for visitors to Avignon and Villeneuve Lez Avignon.

Rue de la Banasterie

This street is named for the basket-makers' guild (*banastiers* in Provençal). At no 13, the 17C **Hôtel de Madon de Châteaublanc** has a façade adorned with garlands of fruit, eagles and masks.

▶ From place Manguin take the narrow rue de Taulignan to the right.

Hôtel d'Adhémar de Cransac

11 r. de Taulignan. 🗣️*Guided tours (1hr) by prior appointment.* ⊛€6. *𝒸04 90 86 13 28.*
This small private mansion, dating from the 17C, was redecorated in the 18C: its drawing rooms acquired silk hangings and fireplaces with overmantels and painted decorations. Only two rooms retain their original French-style timber ceilings. The mansion used to be a part of the St-Martial cardinal's mansion. It was the residence of one Amélie Palun, Countess René d'Adhémar de Cransac (1873–1955), who, along with her poet and Camargue *guardian* friends, dedicated her life to promoting Provençal folklore. There is a collection of items and documents relating to Frédéric Mistral, as well as two crèches with 18C and 19C santons.

▶ Continue straight to place St-Pierre.

Église Saint-Pierre

pl. St-Pierre.
On the church's west façade are two doors with richly decorated Renaissance **panels★**. Carved in perspective in 1551 by Antoine Valard, the subjects illustrate, on the right, the Virgin and the angel of the Annunciation and on the left St Michael and St Jerome.

▶ Take rue des Marchands, to the left, off place Carnot, to get back to the place de l'Horloge.

ADDITIONAL SIGHTS
Musée Louis-Vouland★

17 r. Victor-Hugo. 🕐*Open Tue–Sun 2–6pm.* 🗣️*Guided tours (45min) available.* 🕐*Closed Feb, 1 Jan, 1 May, 25 Dec.* ⊛€6. *𝒸04 90 86 03 79. www.vouland.com.*
The museum contains a decorative arts collection that concentrates on 18C French **furnishings**: a commode signed by Migeon, an inlaid backgammon table, a money-changer's desk, and an amusing travelling table service stamped with the Countess du Barry's coat of arms A fine collection of **faience★** and porcelain is displayed in two rooms; there are many examples of Moustiers and Marseille wares. Flemish and Gobelins **tapestries** (*Diana the Huntress*, pastoral scenes) hang on the walls. The Far Eastern art collection consists of a number of Chinese vases and plates and ivory polychrome statues. Two galleries are dedicated to the works of Provençal painters.

Musée Angladon★

5 r. du Laboureur. 🕐*Open 1–6pm: mid-Apr–mid-Nov daily except Mon; rest of the year daily except Mon–Tue.* 🗣️*Guided tours (1hr) by appointment.* 🕐*Closed 1 Jan, 25 Dec.* ⊛€6.50. *𝒸04 90 82 29 03. www.angladon.com.*
This lovely 18C mansion was acquired in 1977 by the Avignon painters Jean Angladon-Dubrujeaud (1906–79) and his wife Paulette Martin (1905–88) in order to display their art collections. It contains several paintings by Cézanne, Sisley, Manet, Derain, Picasso, Modigliani and Foujita. Van Gogh's *Train Carriages* (1888), painted during the artist's stay in Arles, is the only work of his to be found in Provence today.
On the first floor you will find a collection of furniture and paintings: a Renaissance dining room, an 18C library with paintings by Joseph Vernet; a Chinese salon,

famous for its collection of porcelain (dating from the reign of Emperor Kangxi, 1661–1722) and the studio where the couple's own work is exhibited.

Collection Lambert★

Hôtel de Caumont, 5 r. Violette.
&Open daily except Mon 11am–6pm (Jul–Aug 11am–7pm). Guided tours available. Closed 1 Jan, 1 May, 25 Dec. €7. 04 90 16 56 20. www.collectionlambert.com.

This fine 18C mansion, previously a college, has been renovated to display the **modern art** collection of prominent Paris art dealer Yvon Lambert. Most of the avant-garde art movements championed by him are represented in a substantial number of works, some of them created specially for this space. Among the names to note are Cy Twombly, Christian Boltanski, Nan Goldin, Sol LeWitt, Anselm Kiefer, Daniel Buren, Robert Combas and Bertrand Lavier.

Musée Lapidaire★

27 r. de la République. &Open Tue–Sun 10am–1pm, 2–6pm. Closed 1 Jan, 25 Dec. €2 (combined ticket: €7 with Musée Calvet). 04 90 85 75 38. www.musee-lapidaire.org.

Located in the former chapel of the 17C Jesuit College (with a superb Baroque façade), this building has a single nave with side galleries where you will find displays of sculpture and stone carvings representing the different civilisations that left their mark on this region.

You will see the "Tarasque" of Noves, a man-eating monster that is a part of the Celtic tradition. There are a number of statues: Greek, Greco-Roman (a remarkable copy of Praxiteles' *Apollo the Python killer*) and local (Gallic warriors from Vachères and Mondragon). Also on view are sculpted portraits of emperors (Marcus Aurelius and Tiberius), bas-reliefs (one of Cabrières d'Aigues represents a tow-path scene), sarcophagi and a remarkable series of masks from Vaison-la-Romaine.

EXCURSION
Montfavet

6km/3.7mi E via the N 100 (route de Morières) at the N 107 turn right.

This imposing **church** was once was a 14C monastery for the cardinal Bertrand de Montfavet.

Epicurium – *Cité de l'alimentation. R. Pierre Bayle.* Open Apr–Nov 10am–12.30pm, 2–6.30pm (Sat–Sun and holidays 2–6.30pm). €7, under 6 free. 04 90 31 58 91. www.epicurium.fr.

This museum offers young gourmands a fun and interactive introduction to fruits and vegetables by way of sensory exhibits, a kitchen, a gardening workshop and some 8 000sq m/86sq ft of gardens.

DRIVING TOUR

Allow 3hr. To visualise this 32km/20mi round trip, consult the map on p253.

▷ Leave Avignon by the D 571.

Châteaurenard

This little town sits below the castle which was built on the hill of Griffon centuries ago. Important as an agricultural centre, it has a worthwhile Sunday morning market. In the restored town centre is a little **Museum of Agricultural Tools** (*open May–Sept daily except Mon and public holidays 2.30–6.30pm (Sun 10am–noon). closed Oct–Apr. no charge. 04 90 90 11 59*). Climb up to the jardin des Tours *(steps to the right of the church)* to reach the **feudal château** of the counts of Provence. Of the old fiefdom of seigneur Reynard (13C–15C) just four towers remain and only one of them is complete. Inside there are five rooms to visit, one of which is devoted to **Pope Benoît XIII**.

▷ Head east along the D 28.

Noves

A small fortified town in medieval times, Noves has retained two gateways from that period (Porte d'Agel and Porte Aurose) and a 12C church.

▶ Leave Noves on the D 7N travelling towards Avignon; then, after you cross the autoroute, turn right towards Cavaillon. You will soon see a sign to the Chartreuse de Bonpas on the left.

Caumont-sur-Durance

This attractive village is worth stopping in for the charming twisting little streets which climb up to the pretty **Romanesque chapel** of Saint-Symphorien, standing against a backdrop of limestone hills. (There is a viewing table.)

Chartreuse de Bonpas

◷*Open Mon–Thu 10am–12.30pm, 2–5pm, Fri 10am–12.30pm, 2–4pm.* ◷*Closed 1 Jan, 25 Dec* ⊛ *€7, tasting included (allow 1hr 30min).* ℘*04 90 23 67 98. www.chartreusedebonpas.com.*
A convent established by the Knights Templar in the 13C, the chartreuse enjoyed a period of prosperity in the 17C; it was during this time that the *salle capitulaire* (capitular hall) was built. The restored buildings are now used for wine production (including popular Côtes-du-Rhône), so you may want to taste and perhaps buy some bottles. First, visit the French-style gardens and have a look at the view. It may provoke some meditation on man's capacity to change the face of the landscape.

Jardin romain

Le Clos de Serre, 6 impasse de la chapelle St-Symphorien. ◷*Temporarily closed for redevelopment.* ℘*04 90 22 00 22. www.jardin-romain.fr.*
Archaeological digs revealed this Roman garden and ornamental pool, the longest (65m) discovered since the pool of the Villa Papyri in Pompeii was unearthed. The bottom of the pool is striking for the many shades of ochre created by over 50,000 clay bricks. Access was gained via five steps which can still be seen in the southwest corner. The pool lies below the remains of an opulent Roman villa (1C); its positioning at right angles to the villa's façade points to Italian influence.
A small museum space displays various other finds (amphorae, Roman coins and

a fresco). Nearby, gardens with themes linked to Greek and Roman divinities have been created to evoke the atmosphere of the Augustan period. The garden is especially delightful in spring when the flowers are out.

▶ Return to Avignon on the N7.

ADDRESSES

⌂ STAY

⊝ **Auberge de jeunesse Bagatelle**– *25 allées Antoine Pinay, Île de la Barthelasse.* ℘*04 90 86 30 39. www. campingbagatelle.com. 150 beds at the hotel, 230 sites at the campground. Prices vary according to accommodation type (camping/half-board/hotel, etc).* Large campsite with a separate hotel. Great setting on an island near Pont St Benezet. ◖*See La Ferme, also on Île de Barthelasse, opposite.*

⊝⊝ **Hôtel Blauvac** – *11 r. de la Bancasse.* ℘ *04 90 86 34 11. www. hotel-blauvac.com. 16 rooms.* Beautifully renovated in a rustic Provençal style, the former residence (17C) of the Marquis de Blauvac bears traces of its historic past, such as original stonework in the guest rooms.

⊝⊝ **Hôtel Boquier** – *6 r. du Portail Boquier.* ℘*04 90 82 34 43. www.hotel-boquier.com. 12 rooms.* Each room is individually and tastefully decorated, housing between one and four people, depending on the size of the bedroom.

⊝⊝ **Hôtel Bristol** – *44 cours Jean-Jaurès.* ℘*04 90 16 48 48. www.bristol-avignon.com. 67 rooms.* The hotel is perfecty situated midway between the train station and Avignon's livelier neighbourhoods. Guest rooms are functional, and most of them are surprisingly large.

⊝⊝ **Hôtel Colbert** – *7 r. Agricol Perdiguier.* ℘*04 90 86 20 20. www. avignon-hotel-colbert.com. Closed 1 Nov –1 Mar. 14 rooms.* A simple hotel with a friendly atmosphere. Bedrooms are decorated with antiques and posters. Don't miss the charming patio and its palm tree.

La Ferme – *110 chemin des Bois, Île de la Barthelasse, 5km/3mi N. ℘04 90 82 57 53. www.hotel-laferme-avignon. com. Closed 1 Nov–14 Mar, Mon lunch, Wed lunch. 20 rooms. Restaurant.* This haven of peace has pleasant rooms with modern Provençal décor, a country-style dining room and a big, shaded terrace.

Hôtel du Palais des Papes – *3 pl. du Palais and 1 r. Gérard Philipe. ℘04 90 86 04 13. www.hotel-avignon.com. 27 rooms.* You'll find beautiful rooms and lovely views at this luxurious, reasonably priced hotel in the heart of the historic centre of Avignon.

Chambre d'hôte La Banasterie – *11 r. de la Banasterie. ℘06 87 72 96 36. www.labanasterie.com. 5 rooms.* A Virgin with Child statue adorns the listed façade of this 16C edifice. A cosy, romantic interior. Rooms are named after chocolate, in tribute to the owner's passion.

Chambre d'hôte Lumani – *37 rempart Saint-Lazare. ℘04 90 82 94 11. www.avignon-lumani.com. Closed 4 Nov–25 Dec and 7 Jan–7 Mar. 5 rooms.* Artists are particularly welcome in this fine 19C manor house, which has an attractive courtyard shaded by a couple of hundred-year-old plane trees. Rooms and suites are individually decorated with taste. Warm welcome.

Chambre d'hôte Le Posterlon – *3 r. du Posterlon. 84510 Caumontsur-Durance. ℘04 90 22 21 20. www. posterlon-Provence.com. 5 rooms.* Standing on a tiny street near the top of the village, this former curial residence (16C) has been tastefully renovated and expertly decorated as an inviting guest house. A pleasant, family atmosphere prevails. Rooms are spacious and quaint. The garden and swimming pool add a grace note of bucolic charm.

Hôtel Mignon – *12 r. Joseph Vernet. ℘04 90 82 17 30. www.hotel-mignon.com. 16 rooms.* A small hotel with sound-proofed rooms in the heart of Avignon's historic centre. Just 5min walk from the palace and 10min walk from the train station.

Cloître St-Louis – *20 r. Portail Boquier. ℘04 90 27 55 55. www. cloitre-saint-louis.com. 80 rooms. Restaurant.* Tucked away in handsome 16C cloisters close to the town centre, this hotel was partly designed by the acclaimed French architect Jean Nouvel. The building uses a variety of materials including glass, steel and stone. Rooms are stylishly minimalist. Pool and solarium top the roof.

⚑ EAT

L'Ami Voyage... en compagnie – *5 r. Prevot. ℘04 90 87 41 51. Closed last 3 weeks Jun, last 3 wks Aug.* Very central but quiet, this café, linked to an antiquarian bookshop, is perfect for a cup of tea or no-fuss, traditional food.

Ginette et Marcel – *27 pl. des Corps-Saints. ℘04 90 85 58 70.* This place is more a bistro/caféteria than a restaurant. You can grab a decent sandwich or salad here to take away.

L'Essentiel – *2 r. Petite-Fusterie. ℘04 90 85 87 12. www.restaurant lessentiel.com. Closed Wed and Sun.* In a contemporary interior with a pretty courtyard, L'Essentiel does indeed focus on what is essential: delicious food that is modern but not irritatingly modish.

Le Grand Café – *4 r. des Escaliers-Ste Anne. ℘04 90 86 86 77. Closed Jan, Sun and Mon (except in Jul).* Backing onto the buttresses of the Palais des Papes, these old barracks have become an key part of local life. Locals and tourists all flock here to savour inventive cooking with a Provençal accent. There is also an attractive terrace.

L'Isle Sonnante – *7 r. Racine. ℘04 90 82 56 01. Closed 22 Feb–1 Mar, 25 Oct–5 Nov, Sun, Mon.* This restaurant near the town hall is proud of its Rabelaisian name. The cosy interior combines rustic style with warm tones. Modern dishes inspired by the region.

Piedoie – *26 r. 3-Faucons. ℘04 90 86 51 53. Closed Aug, 21–30 Nov, Feb school holidays, Tue, Wed.* Beams, parquet flooring and white walls hung with contemporary paintings form the décor, and creative cuisine is based on market produce. A family atmosphere.

Le Jardin de la Tour – *9 r. de la Tour. ℘04 90 85 66 50. www.jardindela tour.fr. Closed Sun–Mon.* Situated near the ramparts, this restaurant has a lovely garden. Very enjoyable Provençal cuisine.

Le Moutardier du Pape – *15 pl. Palais-des-Papes. &04 90 85 34 76. www.lemoutardierdupape.fr.* This 18C building, listed in France's National Heritage, makes an exceptional setting for a simple meal. There is a pleasant atmosphere, both in the bistro room, where frescoes depict the story of "The Pope's mustard maker", and on the terrace facing the Palais des Papes.

Christian Étienne – *10 r. de Mons. &04 90 86 16 50. www.christian-etienne.fr. Closed Sun and Mon except in Jul.* Avignon's best-known chef, avuncular Christian Étienne, has been an inspiration to a whole generation of younger chefs throughout Provence. His stylish restaurant in 13C and 14C buildings adjoining the Palais des Papes is famous for tomato menus in summer and truffle menus in winter.

D'Europe – *12 pl. Crillon. &04 90 14 76 76. www.heurope.com. Closed Sun–Mon. 41 rooms, 3 suites* . Elegant 16C mansion with refined décor in the centre of Avignon. Classic dining rooms serve delicious traditional cuisine and there is a pleasant terrace with a fountain.

La Mirande – *4 pl. Amirande. &04 90 85 93 93. www.la-mirande.fr. Closed 5 Jan–3 Feb, Tue–Wed. 20 rooms* . Lavish 18C Provençal décor, antiques, ornaments and a profusion of refined detail set the stunning scene of La Mirande. Inventive, finely tuned food which you may learn how to cook at one of La Mirande's eagerly sought-out cookery courses.

Flea market, Place des Carmes

© cascoly/Bigstockphoto.com

NIGHTLIFE

Bar de l'Utopia – *Cour Maria-Casarès – La Manutention.* Just beside the Utopia cinema (specialising in avant-garde films), this lively bar feels like a theatre foyer with its plush red seats and dark woodwork. Animated discussions are the order of the day – or evening, rather.

SHOPPING

Markets – Les Halles, *pl. Pie. Open Tue–Sun, 7am–1.30pm.* Covered market in a purpose-built space. Outstanding.

Flower market Sat in *place des Carmes*.
Flea market Sun in *place des Carmes*.

Wine – Le Vin Devant Soi, *4 rue du Collège du Roure. &04 90 82 04 39. www.levindevantsoi.fr.* Great wine shop run by knowledgeable owners. For a small fee, you can taste different styles before deciding what to buy.

Chocolate – Aline Géhant, *15 rue des Trois Faucons. &04 90 02 27 21. www.agchocolatier.e-monsite.com. Open 10am–1pm, 3–7pm.* From a talented young **chocolatier**, an exciting range of chocolates which look almost as good as they taste.

Lavender – Lavande & Co – Pure Lavande – *61 r. Grande Fusterie. &04 90 14 70 05.* A shop full of lavender cosmetics along with demonstrations and information videos.

Home décor – Terre è Provence – *26 r. de la République. &04 90 86 31 59.* In the same family for several generations, this shop is dedicated to all things Provençal: table settings, fabrics, pottery and porcelain.

Les Délices du Luberon – *20 pl. du Change. &04 90 84 03 58. Open 9.30am–1.30pm, 2.30–7pm (all day Sat).* Avignon outlet of a family-run company based in L'Isle sur la Sorgue, famous for its excellent range of tapenades. Also sells attractive Provençal dishes and a fine selection of olive oil-based toiletries.

Les Olivades – *56 r. Joseph-Vernet. &04 90 86 13 42. Open 10am–1pm, 2–7pm. Closed Mon morning and Sun.* The Avignon shop of this highly regarded Provençal fabric company – one of the few still working in the traditional way – is spacious enough to display its wares in attractive room sets.

Place du Palais during the Festival d'Avignon

© Alain Hocquel/L'ADT Vaucluse Tourisme

Distillerie de la liqueur Frigolet – *26 r. Voltaire, 13160 Chateaurenard. Open Mon–Fri 9am–noon, 2–6pm. ☎04 90 94 11 08. www.frigoletliqueur.com.* Established in 1865, this traditional distillery became famous through the stories of Alphonse Daudet; the character Father Gauchet was partial to its main product, Le Frigolet liqueur. Although the recipe has always been a closely guarded secret, it is known to involve macerating some 30 plants in alcohol. An interesting place to visit, with a small museum. Other types of spirits are also on sale.

Miellerie des Butineuses – *189 r. de la Source, 84450 Saint-Saturnin-lès-Avignon. ☎04 90 22 47 52. www.miellerie.fr. Open 10am–noon, 2–6pm. Closed Sun and public holidays.* Everything there is to know about bees and beekeeping will be revealed on a visit to this well-organised honey producer. Free honey tasting in a shop whose shelves are laden with local honey-based products of all kinds.

EVENTS

Festival d'Avignon – *Bureau du Festival d'Avignon, Cloître St-Louis, 20 r. du Portail-Boquier. Information ☎04 90 27 66 50. Reservations ☎04 90 14 14 14. www.festival-avignon.com.* Every July Avignon's world-famous festival promotes France's cultural life through theatre, dance, lectures, exhibitions and concerts in and around the city. Programmes are confirmed in mid-May, and from the first two weeks of June onwards it is also possible to make reservations online, at FNAC booking counters or at the main office.

Festival Théâtr'Enfants – *www.festivaltheatrenfants.com.* In July, while the Festival is on, at the Maison du Théâtre *(20 av. Monclar)*, theatre companies and storytellers put on plays, musical comedies and puppet shows for children – tiny tots included.

Booking "Festival Off" – *☎04 90 85 13 08. www.avignonleoff.com.* The programme for Avignon's Fringe Festival, held at the same time, is available mid-June.

Hivernales d'Avignon – *☎04 90 82 33 12. www.hivernales-avignon.com.* This contemporary dance festival takes place during two weeks in July.

ACTIVITIES

Petit train touristique – *Operates daily Jul–Aug 10am–8pm; Sept–Oct and mid-Mar–Jun 10am–7pm; Nov–mid-Mar Wed and Sat afternoons. €7 (under 9, €4). ☎04 90 06 36 75. www.cars-lieutaud.fr.* A 40-minute commentated tour of Avignon's key highlights. Departure from the Palais des Papes every 20min.

275

Villeneuve-lès-Avignon★

Gard

A tour of Villeneuve-lès-Avignon is the natural complement to a visit to Avignon. This town, the "City of the Cardinals", offers one of the most famous views in the Rhône valley – over the "City of the Popes". The best time to drink it in is at the end of the afternoon, beneath a setting sun, when Avignon appears in all its splendour.

▶ **Population:** 12 471.

🕐 **Michelin Map:** 339: N-5.

ℹ **Info:** 1 place Charles David, Villeneuve-lès-Avignon. ☎04 90 25 61 33. www.ot-villeneuvelezavignon.fr.

🅿 **Parking:** There's a free car park on Place Charles-David, in front of the tourist office.

☺ **Don't Miss:** The excellent view of Avignon from Philippe-le-Bel tower.

🕐 **Timing:** Allow half a day.

A BIT OF HISTORY

In 1271, after the Albigensian Crusade, the King of France, Philip III the Bold, acquired the county of Toulouse, which extended to the banks of the Rhône. On the opposite shore was Provence and the Holy Roman Empire. The river belonged to the Crown, which raised the thorny question of rights: whenever the river flooded parts of Avignon, the French King claimed them as his territory and demanded taxes from the unfortunate citizens.

At the end of the 13C, Philip the Fair founded a new town (in French: *ville neuve*) on the plain, and its population grew rapidly. Grasping the great military importance of the spot, he built a powerful fortification at the entrance to Pont St-Bénézet. The cardinals, arriving at the papal court in the 14C and finding no suitable accommodation in Avignon, began to build magnificent residences

(livrées) across the river in Villeneuve, until eventually there were 15 of these. The prosperity which the cardinals' patronage of churches and monastic houses brought to the town remained long after the papal court had returned to Rome. The kings John the Good and Charles V had built Fort St-André in order to watch over the neighbouring papal kingdom. In the 17C and 18C fine *hôtels* lined the Grande-Rue. In the monasteries, which developed into museums, an active and brilliant lifestyle flourished, until the Revolution swept away the aristocratic and ecclesiastic regimes.

👣 WALKING TOUR

▷ Starting from the tourist office, take rue Fabrigoule, turn left into rue de la Foire then go up to the tower.

Villeneuve Lez Avignon and Fort St-André

©S. Sauvignier/MICHELIN

Tour Philippe-le-Bel

av. Gabriel Péri. ⏱*Open May–Oct Tue–Sun 10am–12.30pm, 2–6pm; Feb–Apr 2–5pm (Wed 10am–noon, 2–5pm.* ⏱*Closed Mon, public holidays, Nov–Jan.* ⬚*€2.50.* ☎*04 32 70 08 57.*

Built on a rock near the Rhône, this tower was the key structure in the defence work at the west end of Pont St-Bénézet, on royal land. The first storey was built between 1293 and 1307. The second floor and watch turret were added in the 14C. The upper terrace *(176 steps)* gives a lovely **view**★★ of Villeneuve and Avignon, Mont Ventoux, the Montagnette hills and the Alpilles.

◗ Walk back up to place de l'Oratoire, then follow rue de l'Hôpital.

Église Collégiale Notre-Dame

pl. Meissonnier. ♿⏱*Open Nov–Apr 2–5pm (Wed 10am–noon, 2–5pm); May–Oct 10am–noon, 2–6pm.* ⏱*Closed Mon, 1 May, 1 and 11 Nov, 25–26 Dec.* ⬚*No charge.*

This collegiate church dedicated to Our Lady was founded in 1333 by Cardinal Arnaud de Via, nephew of Pope John XXII. The tower which ends the building on the east side was built as a separate belfry, the ground floor of which straddled the public footpath. The monks blocked this off, converted it into a chancel and linked it to the existing church by adding an extra bay to the nave.

Inside, a number of works of art can be found: the tomb of Cardinal Arnaud de Via, rebuilt with its original 14C recumbent effigy (second north chapel); a copy of *St Bruno* by Nicolas Mignard (the original is in the Musée Calvet in Avignon); and a copy of the famous 15C Pietà of the Avignon School. Made for this church, the original has been in the Louvre since 1904.

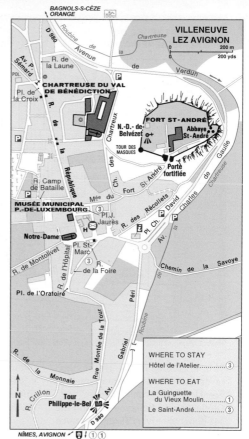

Rue de la République

The street is lined with a number of *livrées* (cardinals' residences) – nos **1**, **2**, **3**, **45** and **53**. One of these palaces houses the local **museum** (◖*see below*), which belonged to Cardinal Pierre de Luxembourg, a cardinal who died having already won saintly repute at the early age of 19 (in 1387). At no 60 a gateway gives access to the Chartreuse du Val de Bénédiction.

Musée Municipal Pierre-de-Luxembourg

2 r. de la République. ♿⏱*Open daily except Mon: May–Oct 10.30am –12.30pm, 2–6pm; rest of year 2–5pm (Wed 10am–noon, 2–5pm).* ⏱*Closed Jan, 1 May, 1 and 11 Nov, 25 Dec.* ⬚*€3.50.* ☎*04 90 27 49 66.*

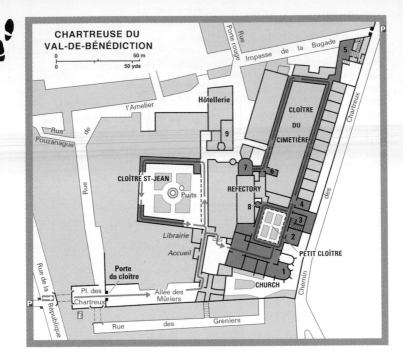

This museum, in the Hôtel Pierre-de-Luxembourg, displays magnificent works of art on four floors.

On the ground floor you will find the 14C polychrome ivory **Virgin★★**, carved from an elephant's tusk; it is one of the finest works of its kind. Also worth admiring are: the marble **Virgin★★** with two faces from the School of Nuremberg (14C); the death mask of Jeanne de Laval, second wife of King René, by Laurana; the chasuble said to have belonged to Innocent VI; and the 17C veil of the Holy Sacrament, adorned with small pearls.

The first floor houses the museum's most beautiful work of art: **Coronation of the Virgin★★**, painted in 1453 by Enguerrand Quarton, from Laon; this artist painted in Aix, then Avignon (from 1447). Fascinated by landscapes and Provençal light, he used bright colours, which emphasised the scene's majesty. The Virgin, with her large cloak, dominates this composition, which encompasses heaven and earth in the subjects painted.

Note interesting paintings by Nicolas Mignard (*Jesus in the Temple*, 1649) and Philippe de Champaigne (*Visitation*, c.1644), Reynaud Levieux (*Crucifixion*), Simon de Châlons and Parrocel (*St Anthony and the Infant Jesus*).

Fort St-André★

Montée du Fort St-Andre. ⏱*Open daily: Oct–May 10am–1pm, 2–5pm; Jun–Sept 10am–6pm.* ⊘*€5.50 (combined ticket with Chartreuse de Villeneuve €9).* ☎*04 90 25 45 35. www.fort-saint-andre.monuments-nationaux.fr.*

This fort encompasses a 10C Benedictine Abbey, the 12C Romanesque Chapelle Notre-Dame-de-Belvézet, and the village of St-André, of which there remain but a few walls. The fort was built in the second half of the 14C by John the Good and Charles V, on an island called Mount Andaon, which became attached to the mainland when the tributary of the Rhône dried up in the Middle Ages. The magnificent **Porte Fortifiée★** (fortified gate), flanked by twin towers, is an exceptionally fine example of medieval fortifications. Access to the west tower of the fortified gate allows visitors to discover the chamber from which the portcullises were controlled, and an 18C bakery.

The terrace *(85 steps)* commands a very beautiful **view★★** of Mont Ventoux, the Rhône, Avignon and the Palais des Papes, the Comtadin plain, the Luberon, the Alpilles and Tour Philippe-le-Bel.

Abbaye St-André

🕐*Access to the gardens: Apr–Sept 10am–12.30pm, 2–6pm; Oct–Mar 10am–noon, 2–5pm.* 🕐*Closed Mon.* ⊛€5. 🕿 *04 90 25 55 95.*

Of the Benedictine abbey founded in the 10C and partly destroyed during the Revolution, there remain the entrance gate, left wing and terraces, held up by massive vaulting. Walk through the **Italian-style gardens★**; the upper terrace offers a lovely **view★** of Avignon, the Rhône valley and Mont Ventoux.

Chartreuse du Val-de-Bénédiction★

60 r. de la République. 🕐*Open daily Apr–Sept 9.30am–6.30pm; Oct–Mar 10am–5pm.* 🕐*Closed public holidays.* ⊛€8. 🕿 *04 90 15 24 24. www.chartreuse.org.*

In 1352 the papal conclave met in Avignon and elected the General of the Carthusian Order as pope, but he refused the throne out of humility. To commemorate this gesture Innocent VI, who became pope instead, founded a charter house on his *livrée* in Val de Bénédiction. The house, enlarged by the Pope's nephews after his death, became the most important in France.

The **Carthusian Order** was founded in 1084 by St Bruno. It consisted of Fathers, who used the title Dom, and Brothers, who lived a communal life like monks in other orders. The Fathers, however, lived individually in cells, spending their time in prayer, study and manual work. Three times a day the monks met to sing the offices; they took their meals alone except on Sundays, when brief periods of conversation were allowed.The charter house now houses *colloquia* and seminars and also the Centre National des Écritures du Spectacle (CNES), established to promote writing for public per-

formance (plays, opera and songs). The Rencontres de la Chartreuse, held annually *(Jul–Sept)*, is linked with the famous annual Avignon theatre festival in July.

Porte du Cloître

The cloister door separates place des Chartreux from allée des Mûriers. The proportions and ornamentation of the 17C door can be admired from inside.

▶ Pass through the reception area at the end of allée des Mûriers.

Church

Go through the nave; the apse opens out with a **view★** on to Fort St-André. The north side apse and nave contain the tomb of Innocent VI **(1)**: the white marble recumbent figure lies on a high plinth of Pernes stone.

Petit Cloître

The east gallery opens into the chapter house **(2)** and the Sacristans' yard **(3)**, with its well and picturesque staircase. The lavabo **(8)**, a circular domed building, has a pretty 18C cupola.

Cloître du Cimetière

The great cloisters, 80m by 20m, with their warm Provençal colouring, are lined with cells for the Fathers, each cell consisting of a small open court and two rooms, one of which communicates with the cloisters by a hatch. The first cell **(4)** can be visited. The others have been restored and are used as lodgings for writers-in-residence. At the northeast end of the cloisters a passage leads to the *bugade* **(5)** or laundry room, which still has its well and chimney for drying clothes. Opening off the west gallery is a small chapel of the dead **(6)**, off which is another chapel **(7)** which was part of Innocent VI's *livrée*; it is decorated with lovely frescoes attributed to Matteo Giovanetti (14C), one of the decorators of the Palais des Papes. They illustrate scenes from the life of John the Baptist and the life of Christ.

Refectory

The Tinel (18C) is used for concerts. On leaving the cloisters, skirt the crenellated east end of the Tinel; note the bakery **(9)** with its hexagonal tower. On the northeast side, the guest house, remodelled in the 18C, features a lovely façade on its north side.

Cloître St-Jean

The cloisters' galleries have disappeared; however, several of the Fathers' cells remain. In the centre stands the monumental Fontaine St-Jean (18C), which has kept its well and lovely old basin.

EXCURSIONS

🧑‍🤝‍🧑 Parc du Cosmos

At Les Angles, 2km/1.2mi from the centre of Villeneuve. Leave Villeneuve heading west towards Nîmes. ⏰*Open Tue–Sun: May–Sept 2.30–6pm (guided tour 3pm, planetarium 4.45pm); Oct–Apr 2–6pm (guided tour 2.30pm, planetarium 4.15pm).* ⏰*Closed 1 Jan, 25 Dec.* ✆*€7.50 (child 6–15, €5), combined ticket with planetarium €13.* ✆*04 90 25 66 82. www.parcducosmos.eu.*

Mapped out amidst pines and green oaks, this activity park dedicated to astronomy invites visitors to make an imaginary journey through space and time. The architecture of the buildings, in stacked terraces, evokes the ziggurats of Ancient Mesopotamia which were believed to symbolise the union of earth and sky. The path through the labyrinth, among planets, stars and asteroids, encapsulates evolution in an entertaining way.

Rochefort-du-Gard

8km/5mi west on D 900 (direction Les Angles), then a very short distance on N 100 (direction Remoulins) and D 111.

You will enjoy strolling in the steep little streets and shady squares of this village whose town hall is in an ancient chapel. Some distance away to the east, the *castellas* around which the village developed is only a memory: all that remains of it is the massive white silhouette of its Romanesque chapel. From the platform, there is a fine **view★** of Notre-Dame-de-Grâce and the dried-up lake of Pujaut against a backdrop of mountains.

🧑‍🤝‍🧑 Musée du Vélo et de la Moto★

14km/9mi west of Villeneuve on D 900, then N 100. After 9km/5mi, turn right on to N 100 at the Château de Bosc. ⏰*Open Feb–May Wed, Sat–Sun, public and school holidays 2–5.30pm; Jun–Sept*

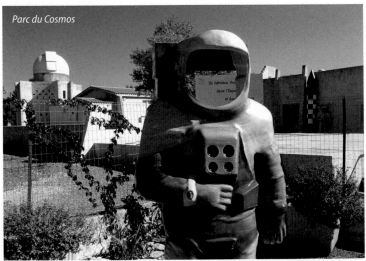

Parc du Cosmos

© Bertrand Rieger/hemis.fr

daily 10am–7pm; Oct–Nov Wed, Sat–Sun, public and school holidays 2–5pm. ⏱*Closed Dec–Jan.* 📷*€8 (child 3–13, €6.50).* 📞*04 66 57 65 11.*

Now in a 19C castle nestling among vines and olive trees in a French-style park, this museum presents an exceptional collection of bicycles and motorbikes including motorised tricycles from 1900, today's racing bikes and everything in between. Among the most astonishing and incongruous items are a velocipede (1869) which belonged to the famous singer and actor Yves Montand; a bicycle with articulated handlebars, forerunner of the scooter; a scooter created specially for clerics (!); a propeller-driven bike (to ride lying down) and a 1980 solar tricycle which has the unusual attribute of working only in theory.

Also on view is a very rare celerifere – a early bicycle prototype. It's a copy. The original existed only in the fertile imagination of a journalist – so, paradoxically, this copy of an imaginary object is original in itself!

Roquemaure

16km/10mi north on D 980.

This large town, centred on wine production (and with an *académie du vin et du goût* – a wine and taste academy), has some interesting old houses, like that of Cardinal Bertrand near the church. This dates from the 13C and has a fine 17C organ. The tower of the Princes of Soubise is the most important remaining part of the château where Clément V, the first Avignon pope, died in 1314. Across the river, the tower of the château de l'Hers looks as if it is keeping watch over precious vineyards.

During the weekend closest to 14 February, Roquemaure celebrates St Valentine by re-enacting the arrival of the saint's relics in 1868. These were bought in Rome by a wine grower and offered to the parish to protect its vines from phylloxera, the deadly vineyard scourge which had made its first European appearance here five years earlier.

ADDRESSES

🛏 STAY

🍽🍽 **Hôtel de L'Atelier** – *5 r. de la Foire.* 📞*04 90 25 01 84. www.hotel delatelier.com. Closed in Jan. 22 rooms.* This charming 16C house features a lovely staircase, antique furniture and exposed beams.

🍷 EAT

🍽🍽 **La Guignette de Vieux Moulin** – *5 r. du Vieux Moulin.* 📞*04 90 94 50 72. www.guinguettevieuxmoulin.com. Closed Mon in Oct–May.* Simple but delicious cuisine. Eat on the patio or in the dining room.

🍽🍽🍽 **Le Saint-André** – *4 bis montée du Fort.* 📞*04 90 25 63 23. Closed weekday lunch in Jul–Aug, Tue and Wed lunch the rest of the year.* ♿. Near the church and the abbey, this restaurant has Provençal décor and tasty food.

ACTIVITIES

Walk – Follow the "abbey paths" (8km/5mi, 12km/7.5mi and 23km/14mi) along the Rhône or the inland "montagne de Villeneuve" path (8km/5mi). Leaflets from the tourist office.

👫 **Parc de loisirs Amazonia**– *Rte d'Orange. Open Jun–Aug daily 10:30am–6pm; Apr–May and Sept Sat–Sun and holidays 11am–6pm. €14 (child under 12, €13).* 📞*04 66 82 53 92.* The forest of Roquemaure has been invaded by Aztecs and Mayas! This family adventure park is organised around various attractions: water toboggans (Machu Picchu), a 4x4 trail (Amazonia trophy), a river trail (Ascent of the Andes), a little train (Cuzco express), boat trips (Crocodile River) and rock-climbing. Snack bar and picnic areas.

EVENT

Rencontres de la Chartreuse – *Villeneuve Lez Avignon.* 📞*04 90 15 24 24. www.chartreuse.org.* In July and August the chartreuse is the setting for a celebration of modern screenplays.

L'Isle-sur-la-Sorgue★

Vaucluse

The pretty town of L'Isle-sur-la-Sorgue is perfect strolling territory. Built on a network of canals linked to the Sorgue river, it was once famous for silk mills, paper mills and tanneries powered by giant water wheels, 14 of which still help to give the town its picture-postcard charm. Today antiques are its main claim to fame, attracting well-heeled visitors in droves. Hundreds of dealers are active here, some headquartered in antiques "villages", others displaying their wares along the quays on Sundays. There is also a worthwhile Sunday morning market for fresh produce.

▶ **Population:** 19 048.
◔ **Michelin Map:** 332: D-10.
▤ **Info:** place de l'Église, L'Isle-sur-la-Sorgue. ℘04 90 38 04 78. www.oti-delasorgue.fr.
ℙ **Parking:** Paying car parks right in centre; free along quays and further out.
⊚ **Don't Miss:** Antique shops, Sunday morning market.

SIGHTS
Hôtel Campredon – Centre d'art★

20 r. du Dr-Tallet. ○*Open Jul–Oct 10am–1pm, 2.30–6.30pm; rest of year: 10am–12.30pm, 2–5.30pm.* ○*Closed Mon, 1 Jan, 1 May, 25 Dec.* ⊕€6.20. ℘04 90 38 17 41.

This magnificent 18C mansion, a fine example of French Classicism, houses temporary exhibitions of contemporary art. The third floor is devoted to the well-known poet **René Char** (1907–88) who was born in L'Isle-sur-la-Sorgue; as well as a permanent exhibition relating to him, and an archive, there is a replica of his study.

Collégiale Notre-Dame-des-Anges

●‿●*Guided tours available Mon–Fri, 10am–noon, 3–6pm.* ⊕*No charge.*

The flamboyant and exceptionally rich **Baroque decoration★** of this 17C church may seem more Italian than French. The single nave is decorated with a huge wooden Gloria attributed to Jean Péru, as are the figures of the Virtues which stand beneath the balustrades. The side-chapels are decorated with exquisite wooden screens and paintings by Mignard, Sauvan, Simon Vouet and Parrocel. In the chantry, a large altarpiece incorporates a painting of the *Assumption* by Reynaud Levieux. There is also a splendid 17C organ.

Water wheels

Of the countless water wheels which once provided power to all the mills and factories of this industrious little town, 14 still remain. Have a look near place Emile-Char; at the corner of the Caisse d'Épargne's garden; on cours Victor Hugo; on rue Théophile Jean and on quai des Lices. More details from the tourist office.

Hôpital

rue Théophile Jean.

Admire the gilded wooden Virgin in the hall, and the grand staircase embellished by an 18C wrought-iron banister. The chapel has impressive 18C woodwork, and there is a lovely 18C fountain in the peaceful garden.

EXCURSIONS
Le Thor

5km/3mi west on N 100 towards Avignon.

Once the capital of the white dessert grape, Chasselas, Le Thor is worth visiting especially for its 12C church, **Notre Dame du Lac**. The exterior is imposing, and, inside, the Gothic vaulting above the nave is among the oldest in Provence. Also remaining from the Middle Ages are some fragments of the town ramparts and belfry.

Grottes de Thouzon

3km/2mi N of Thor on the D 16.
*Guided tours (45min) daily Jul–Aug
10am–6.30pm; Apr–Jun and Sept–Oct
10am–noon, 2–6pm; Mar Sun 2–6pm.
€8.30. 04 90 33 93 65.
www.grottes-thouzon.com.*

The cave opens at the foot of the hill
crowned by the ruins of the Thouzon
priory. It was discovered in 1902 by
chance after a blast on the site of a
former quarry.

The visitor walks 230m along the bed
of the old underground river which
carved this horizontal gallery, ending
in a not very deep chasm. On the cave
roof, which rises to 22m, are delicate
stalactites of rare quality. In addition
there are oddly shaped, beautifully
coloured concretions on the cave's high,
domed roof.

ADDRESSES

STAY

Hôtel Les Névons – *Chemin des
Névons. 04 90 20 72 00. www.hotel-les-
nevons.com. Closed mid-Dec–mid-Jan
44 rooms.* The rooms in this centrally
located hotel are functional (but more
spacious and modern in the new wing).
Some have a balcony. Solarium and
pool on the roof.

EAT

La Marmite Bouillonnante –
*"Passage du Pont-L'Ile aux Brocantes"
antiques village, 7 avenue des Quatre
Otages. 04 90 38 51 05. Open Sat–
Mon and holidays noon–4pm. Closed
Tue–Fri and eves.* With its terrace along
the river and 40 antique dealers as a
backdrop, this is a pleasant place for
an unpretentious lunch. Traditional
Provençal dishes made from market
produce are the backbone of the menu.

L'Oustau de l'Isle –
*147 chemin du Bosquet. 04 90 20 81
36. Closed 12 Nov–4 Dec, 18 Jan–5 Feb,
Tue–Wed.* This old *mas* surrounded
by greenery has a delightful terrace
and two elegant dining rooms. Finely
judged cuisine highlights all the best
flavours of Provence.

Antique Fairs

The biggest antique fairs in
Provence take place in L'Isle-sur-
la-Sorgue during Easter weekend
and the weekend closest to 15
August. Over 1,500 exhibitors
reveal their treasures: old quilts,
Provençal furniture, faïences,
pictures and knick-knacks of all
kinds. Bric-a-brac is also sold
every Sunday along the avenue
des Quatre-Otages.

NIGHTLIFE

Café de France – *14 pl. de la Liberté.
04 90 38 01 45. Closed 1 Jan, 25 Dec.*
This charming old café is a member
of the Association of Historic Cafés
of Europe. Light food is served inside
and out, on a terrace well placed for
people-watching.

SHOPPING

Le Village des Antiquaires de la Gare
– *2 bis av. de l'Égalité. 04 90 38 04 57.
Closed Tue–Fri.* This is one of the biggest
antique centres in town: 80 dealers
grouped together in an old weaving
factory.

Weekly food market – Tuesday and
Sunday morning in the town centre.

Les Délices du Luberon – *1 av. du
Partage-des-Eaux. 04 90 20 77 37.
www.delices-du-luberon.fr. Open daily.*
This family-run business sells mouthwatering local gourmet products
including *tapenades*, aubergine caviar,
sun-dried tomatoes, olive oils, honeys
and jams; also olive-oil-based toiletries.

Fontaine-de-Vaucluse

Vaucluse

Vallis Clausa (the "enclosed valley"), from which the Vaucluse *département* **takes its name, is best known for the famous resurgent spring that is the source of the River Sorgue. In a picturesque spot which was dear to Petrarch, it gushes out, looking its most dramatic in winter or spring, when the rate of flow can rise to 150cu m/39 625 gal per second. By extreme contrast, in summer or autumn the flow may be reduced to a tiny fraction of that.**

▸ **Population:** 668.
◔ **Michelin Map:** 332: D-10.
▯ **Info:** Chemin de la Fontaine, Fontaine-de-Vaucluse. ℘04 90 20 32 22.

A BIT OF HISTORY
Petrarch
On 6 April 1327 in an Avignon church, this great poet and humanist – a familiar member of the pontifical court in Avignon – met the lovely **Laura de Noves**, with whom he fell passionately in love. However, this love remained platonic: Laura was married and virtuous, but she inspired many of the poet's works. Ten years after his first meeting with her, Petrarch, then just 33 years old, retired to the Vaucluse. He remained here for 16 years seeking peace in the tranquil Sorgue valley. During his stay Laura died of the plague in Avignon in 1348. The poet died 26 years later in Arquà Petrarca near Padua. He never forgot her during all that time.

The Fontaine-de-Vaucluse★
⟿*30min return on foot. From place de la Colonne, where a commemorative column of the fifth centenary (1304–1804) of Petrarch's birth stands, take chemin de la Fontaine, which climbs gently, following the River Sorgue.*
The Fontaine-de-Vaucluse is one of the most powerful resurgent springs in the world. It is the outlet of an important underwater river fed by rainwater draining through the Vaucluse plateau pitted with numerous chasms *(avens)*, through which spelaeologists have searched for the underground Sorgue.

The exploration of the fountain's chasm began as early as the 19C and continues to this day. A record depth of 315m was recorded in August 1985 with the help of a small remote-controlled submarine equipped with cameras.
The cave from which the River Sorgue emerges is at the foot of a rocky cirque formed by high cliffs. In front of it stands a pile of rocks through which the waters filter. During heavy flooding the water reaches the level of the fig trees growing in the rock above the cave mouth, before racing away over the rocks in a vivid green fury of tumbling foam.

SIGHTS
Vallis Clausa – Paper mill
Chemin de la Fontaine. ♿◔*Open daily Mar–Jun 9am–12.25pm, 2–6.25pm; Jul–Aug 9am–7.25pm; Sept–Oct 9am–12.25pm, 2–6.55pm; Feb and Nov 9am–12.25pm, 2–5.55pm; Dec–Jan 9.30am–12.25pm, 2–5.25pm.*
◔*Closed 1 Jan, 25 Dec.* ⟿*No charge.* ℘*04 90 20 34 14.*
In the 18C Fontaine-de-Vaucluse had four paper mills. This one uses water directly from the Sorgue, and from a gangway visitors can see paper being made in the traditional way. The **shop** sells beautiful papers for visiting cards, invitations, literary texts and so on.

Le Monde Soutterain
Chemin de la Fontaine. ♿◔*Open Jul–Aug 9.30am–12.30pm, 2–7pm; Sept 9.30am–12.30pm, 2–7pm; Apr–May and Oct 9.30am–12.30pm, 2–6.30pm; Feb–Mar and Christmas holidays 9.20am–12.30pm, 2–6pm.* ◔*Closed Nov–Jan.* ⟿*€6.* ℘*04 90 20 34 13.*
This underground museum presents the **Casteret collection★**: magnficent limestone concretions (calcite, gypsum,

aragonite) assembled during 30 years of exploration by the spelaeologist Norbert Casteret. Visitors can see re-created stalactite and stalagmite caves, rivers, waterfalls and so on. Interesting for young cave explorers in the making.

Musée d'histoire Jean-Garcin (1939–45)

chemin du Gouffre. ♿⏰*Open daily except Tue: Jun–Sept 10am–6pm; Apr–May and 1st 2 weeks of Oct 10am–noon, 2–6pm; Mar and mid-Oct–Dec Sat–Sun 10am–noon, 2–5pm.* ⏰*Closed 1 Jan, 1 May, 25 Dec, Feb.* ⊜€3.50. ☎04 90 20 24 00.

In the same building as the tourist office, this museum offers a historical, literary and artistic view of the years 1939–45. The first section describes daily life in occupied France; the second, the activity of the Resistance in the Vaucluse, with reference to some key literary and artistic figures (including Matisse).

Église Saint-Véran★

This little Romanesque church (11C) has attractive vaulting both above the nave and over the semicircular apse. In the crypt is the sarcophagus of St Véran, famous for having conquered a frightful dragon known as the Coulobre.

Musée-Bibliothèque Pétrarque

Rive Gauche de la Sorgue. ⏰*Open Wed–Mon mid-Mar–May 10am–noon, 2–6pm; Jun–Sept 10am–12.30pm, 1–6pm; 1–15 Oct 10am–noon, 2–6pm; 16–end Oct 10am–noon, 2–5pm.* ⏰*Closed Nov–mid-Mar, Tue.* ⊜€3.50. ☎04 90 20 37 20.

This library–museum is in the heart of the village, in a house said to be built on the very spot where Petrarch once lived. Upstairs, there is an exhibition of drawings and prints (16C–19C) relating to the poet and his life, as well as a collection of old editions of his writings. On the ground floor there are interesting works by Miró, Braque and Giacometti, illustrating the writings of René Char who was involved in opening the museum.

EXCURSIONS
Saumane-de-Vaucluse

4km/2.5mi NW. Leave Fontaine-de-Vaucluse on the D 25, then turn right onto the D 57.

The road follows the hillside across the limestone slopes of the Vaucluse mountains, before arriving at this village perched above the Sorgue valley. Here stands the 15C castle belonging to the family of the **Marquis de Sade**. From the square, which contains a 16C stone cross, there is a **view** across the Sorgue valley, the Luberon and the Alpilles.

Cabrières-d'Avignon

5km/3mi S on the D 100A. 🅿*Leave the car in the car park by the town hall.*

The Château des Adhémar (⚷*closed to the public),* dating from the 11C, was partially rebuilt in the 17C in a Renaissance style. It was the backdrop to the tragic events of 20 and 21 April 1545, when Vaudois Lutheran "heretics", who had taken refuge there, were massacred by Roman Catholic forces.

🚶 Walk around the château *(go along rue du Vieux-Four, then go left up chemin Eustache-Marron skirting open country-side)* to see the ramparts linking the five original towers, vestiges of the original fortifications.

ADDRESSES

🛏 STAY

🍴🍴🍴 **Hôtel du Poete** – *Le Village, Fontaine-de-Vaucluse.* ☎04 90 20 34 05 *www.hoteldupoete.com. 24 rooms. Closed late Nov–Mar.* Named in honour of Petrarch, this comfortable hotel occupies an attractively converted old flour mill right on the river. Expect well-appointed rooms with a mix of old and newer furniture, an excellent breakfast and the soothing sound of waterfalls.

Tucked up in the northwest corner of Provence, Orange and its surroundings are sometimes overlooked by visitors making a headlong dash south; a sad mistake. Gateway to the Midi, the town has two remarkable Roman monuments, both UNESCO World Heritage Sites, while nearby Vaison-la-Romaine harbours an immense area of Gallo-Roman remains. Not far away is the Enclave des Papes, steeped in medieval history, and the pretty old stone villages whose names appear on the labels of so many Côtes du Rhône wines. In between them all is a sea of vines stretching right across the Ouvèze valley to the lower slopes of the craggy Dentelles de Montmirail.

Highlights

Orange, easily accessible as it stands on the main motorway and rail route south, makes a good starting point. Allow plenty of time to admire its magnificent Théâtre Antique, the only Roman theatre whose stage wall has survived practically intact. With its tiered seating and generous stage, it has made a memorable setting for Les Chorégies d'Orange, the town's annual July opera festival, for around 150 years. Almost as impressive is the majestic Arc de Triomphe, built in 20 BCE to commemorate the victories of the veterans of the Second Gallo-Roman legion who made Orange their home.

Wine Country

Orange also marks the northern approach to the Côtes du Rhône, one of the most important wine regions in the south of France. Vineyards planted by the Romans were extended and developed in the 14C by the Avignon popes who created a new summer palace for themselves at Châteauneuf-du-Pape. Their legacy has lasted seven centuries and shows no signs of fading, for Châteauneuf-du-Pape remains the most celebrated of this rich region's many wines. But increasingly these days its supremacy is challenged by impressive bottlings from many other villages – pretty little townships like Gigondas, Rasteau, Cairanne, Vacqueyras, Séguret, Sablet and Beaumes-de-Venise, which are delightful to visit whether you are a wine enthusiast or not.

Dramatic Backdrop of the Dentelles

Many wine villages either nestle up against the picturesque Dentelles de Montmirail or look across the valley at their dramatically irregular limestone peaks. They look mesmerising, especially in the early morning when they seem to float in a veil of mist. The Dentelles are an unspoilt wonderland for casual and serious walkers, as well as for mountain bikers and rock climbers. The higher up you go (it's easy to cheat and drive part of the way), the better you will be rewarded with giddy views out across the vine-filled valley floor and up to the huge pillars of semi-eroded limestone that loom directly overhead.

Vaison, Valréas and the Enclave des Papes

North of the Dentelles, Vaison-la-Romaine is worth visiting not just for its vast stretch of Gallo-Roman remains, or even for its medieval heart, the Haute Ville perched high above the river, but because it is imbued with Provençal charm. Further north still is the fascinating little area known as the Enclave des Papes, another legacy of the Avignon papacy. Its towns and villages – Valréas, Visan, Grignan, Richerenches – combine a fascinating past with a relatively untouristy present. Explore them and you will discover another facet of the real Provence.

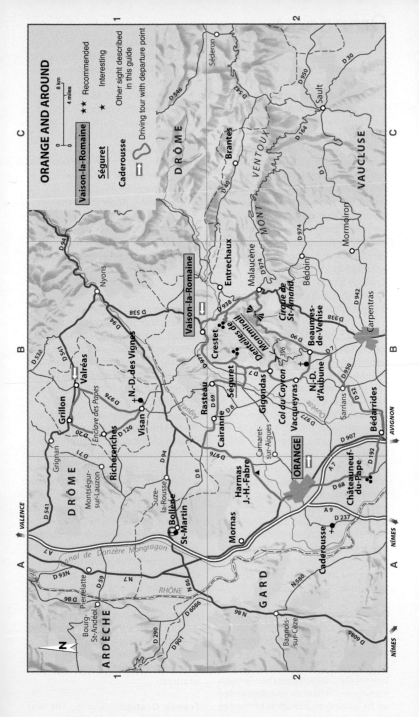

ORANGE AND AROUND

Vaison-la-Romaine
Séguret
Caderousse

★★ Recommended
★ Interesting
○ Other sight described in this guide
⇨ Driving tour with departure point

0 ─── 4 miles
0 ─── 8 km

Orange★★

Vaucluse

Gateway to the Midi, at the crossroads of two motorways, Orange is famous for its prestigious Roman public buildings, including the triumphal arch and the Roman Theatre. These monuments serve as the stage for the international music festival, the Chorégies, which features top international opera singers. An important market centre for fruit, Orange also has industrial (canning, chemicals) and military (air base, Foreign Legion) activities. In 1981 the triumphal arch, Roman theatre and its surroundings were inscribed as a UNESCO World Heritage Site for the remarkable manner in which they have stood the test of time.

▶ **Population:** 29 135.
⚙ **Michelin Map:** 332: B-9.
🛈 **Info:** 5 Cours Aristide-Briand, Orange. ☎04 90 34 70 88. www.otorange.fr.
▶ **Location:** South of Montélimar and north of Avignon, on main motorway and rail routes.
👁 **Don't Miss:** The Roman antiquities, of course!
🕐 **Timing:** Allow at least 2hrs for sightseeing, including 1hr for the Théâtre Antique alone.
👪 **Kids:** 'Les Fantômes du Théâtre.

A BIT OF HISTORY

Roman Orange – Established in 35 BCE, the Roman colony of Orange welcomed veterans of the Second Gallic Legion. The town had a well-ordered urban plan, enhanced by public buildings and surrounded by fortifications which protected some 70ha/173 acres. It was at the head of a vast territory, which the Roman land surveyors laid out with precision. Lots were attributed with priority to the veterans, the next lots were rented out to the highest bidders and the remaining lots belonged to the collective. In this way the Roman state encouraged colonisation and the development of land at the natives' expense. Until 412, when the town was ransacked by the Visigoths, Orange prospered.

Dutch Orange – In the second half of the 12C, the town became the seat of a small principality in Comtat Venaissin; its prince, Raimbaut III d'Orange, was a famous troubadour who sang of his love for the Comtesse de Die. Through marriage and inheritance, Orange ended up belonging to a branch of the Les Baux family, heirs also to the German principality of Nassau. In the 16C the then prince of Orange and Nassau, **William the Silent**, transformed his fiefdom into the United Provinces with himself as first *stadthouder*. At the same time, the town became Protestant and fell victim to the ravages of the Wars of Religion, but it succeeded in preserving its autonomy.

Orange is justly proud of the fact that the preferred title of the glorious royal dynasty of Holland is Prince or Princess of Orange; and its name has been given to a state, cities and rivers in South Africa and the USA. While governing the Low Countries and even England, the House of Orange-Nassau did not forget its tiny enclave in France.

In 1622 Maurice of Nassau surrounded the town with strong ramparts and built a large castle. Unfortunately, for economic reasons as well as through lack of time, he took the stones for his fortifications from the Roman ruins that had not been destroyed by the Barbarian invasions. This time nothing was left standing except the theatre, part of the ramparts and the triumphal arch, which had been transformed into a fortress.

French Orange – During the war against Holland, Louis XIV coveted the Principality of Orange. It was the

Count of Grignan, Lieutenant-General to the King in Provence and Mme de Sévigné's son-in-law, who captured the town. The ramparts were razed and the castle demolished. In 1713 the Treaty of Utrecht ceded Orange to France.

ROMAN MONUMENTS
Allow 2hr.

Arc de Triomphe★★
At the entry to the town on the N 7.
P Free parking at the crossroads.
Restored in 2009, this UNESCO monument creates a dramatic entrance to the town of Orange as it has done for over 2,000 years. The triumphal arch stands on the north side of the city on the old Via Agrippa, which linked Lyon to Arles. It ranks third among the Roman constructions of this type owing to its dimensions – 22m high, 21m wide and 8m deep – and is one of the best preserved, particularly the north face.
Built c.20 BCE and dedicated later to Tiberius, the arch commemorated the campaigns of the Second Legion. It has three openings flanked by columns and displays two unusual architectural features: a pediment above the central opening and two attic storeys. It was surmounted at the time of its construction by a bronze *quadriga* (a

chariot drawn by four horses harnessed abreast) flanked by two trophies.
Its exuberant decoration is linked to Roman Classicism and the plastic beauty of the Hellenistic style. Admire the scenes of battles and arms captured, which recall the conquering of Gaul, and naval symbols evoking Augustus' victory over the fleet of Antony and Cleopatra.

Roman Theatre (Théâtre Antique)★★★
r. Madeleine Roch. ○Open Jan–Feb and Nov–Dec 9.30am–4.30pm; Mar and Oct 9.30am–5.30pm; Apr–May and Sept 9am–6pm; Jun–Aug 9am–7pm. ⊗€9.50 with audioguide. ℘04 90 51 17 60. www.theatre-antique.com.
Built during the reign of Augustus (31 BCE–AD 14), this spectacular building is the pride of Orange. The only Roman theatre which has managed to conserve its stage wall almost intact, it is a UNESCO World Heritage Site. The impressive stage wall (103m long and 36m high), which Louis XIV had qualified as the finest wall of the kingdom, has recently been covered with an immense glass canopy roof that adds to its grandeur. Its upper storey was made up of two rows of corbels pierced with holes to hold up the poles for the *velum*, which shaded the spectators from the sun. Below, 19

Arc de Triomphe, Orange

© Chris Selby/age fotostock

Chorégies at the Théâtre Antique

© Alain Hocquel/L'ADT Vaucluse Tourisme

blind arcades corresponded with rooms inside, corridors and staircases.

The semicircle, the *cavea*, held up to 9,000 spectators seated according to their social station. It was divided into three sections of 37 tiers of seats and separated by walls. Below, the orchestra occupied a semicircle; along it were three low tiers where movable seats were set up for high-ranking citizens.

On either side of the stage, large rooms, one on top of the other, were used as public reception and backstage areas. The stage, fitted with wooden flooring, under which the machinery was kept, measured 61m long and 9m wide; it was raised above the orchestra by about 1.1m, supported by a low wall, the *pulpitum*. Behind was the curtain slot (the curtain was dropped during the performances). The stage wall was as high as the topmost tier, and displayed a richly ornate decoration of marble facing, stucco, mosaics, several tiers of columns and niches for statues, including the imperial one of Augustus (3.5m), which was brought back to its original location in 1951.

The stage wall had three doors, each of which had a particular function. The royal door in the centre was used by the principal actors for their entrances, whereas the two side doors were for secondary actors. So impressive are the acoustics that someone speaking in the semicircle can be heard from the top row. The actors' masks amplified their voices, and the large sloping roof which protected the stage was also useful acoustically.

👥 There is a multimedia presentation, "Les Fantômes du Théâtre" (the Ghosts of the Theatre), in one of the small rooms behind the terraces. With projections and photomontages, it re-creates the spectacles put on in this theatre over a 2,000-year period, from the Roman gladiators of the earliest days up to today's magnificent summer opera festival, the **Chorégies**, held every mid-July through early August (🕐 *see Events under Addresses*).

Musée d'Art et d'Histoire

r. Madeleine Roch. 🕐 *Open Jan–Feb and Nov–Dec 9.45am–12.30pm, 1.30–4.30pm; Mar and Oct 9.45am–12.30pm, 1.30–5.30pm; Apr–May and Sept 9.15am–6pm; Jun–Aug 9.15am–7pm.* 🎫€5.50 *with audioguide,* €9.50 *combined ticket with Roman Theatre.* 📞04 90 51 17 60. *www.theatre-antique.com.*

This museum, which occupies a former palace built in the 17C by a Dutch nobleman, displays in the courtyard and ground floor lapidary vestiges from the Roman monuments (no

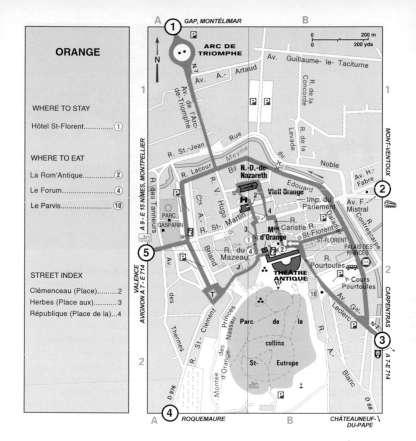

longer standing) and the castle of the Princes of Orange. One gallery contains fragments (meticulously reconstructed) of the renowned Roman **land survey** of Orange (&see A bit of History), unique in France. On these marble tablets, the historians have identified the well-planned grid pattern, the administrative subdivisions and topographical references (roads, mountains, rivers, swamps), and documents describing the judicial and fiscal status of the land. Prime among the museum's other attractions is a collection of fabrics made by the Wetter family, major manufacturers of traditional Provençal printed material which was exported all over Europe in the 18C.

OLD ORANGE

▷ Starting from the theatre, follow rue Caristie until it joins rue de la République, the city's main street.

The streets of the old town centre are very animated and pleasant to stroll along. Turn right into rue Fuseerie and after place du Cloître, left into rue de Renoyer. Note the statue of the troubadour-prince Raimbaut d'Orange while crossing place de la République and heading towards the cathedral, the **ancienne Cathédrale Notre-Dame de Nazareth** (r. de Renoyer. ○open daily 8.30am–5pm).

There are plenty of lively cafés and restaurants with pavement terraces in place Georges-Clemenceau, where you can admire the **Hôtel de Ville** with its 17C belfry. From place de la République,

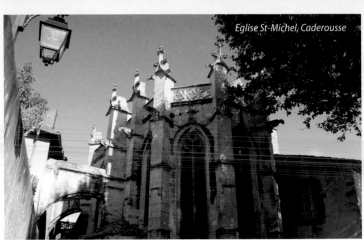
Eglise St-Michel, Caderousse

© Alain Hocquel/L'ADT Vaucluse Tourisme

rue Stassart leads to a little square shaded with plane trees, **place aux Herbes**, which you cross to return to the theatre via rue du Mazeau.

▷ Go down rue Pourtoules to reach the steps on the eastern side.

Colline St-Eutrope (St Eutrope Hill)

The main avenue crosses the moat of the former castle of the Princes of Orange; the excavations (left of square Reine-Juliana) have uncovered important ruins. At the far north end of the park, near a statue to the Virgin, there is a viewing table offering a beautiful **view★** of the Roman Theatre in the foreground, the city of Orange with its tiled roofs, and the Rhône plain enclosed by mountains including majestic Mont Ventoux.

EXCURSIONS
Caderousse

8km/5mi to the W, by the D 17.
Standing at a bend in the Rhône, this village is dubbed "little Avignon" because it is surrounded by a dike and ramparts to protect it from flooding. Don't miss the **Eglise St Michel**, a good example of the Romanesque style in Provence, and the adjoining 16C **Chapelle d'Ancezune**, Flamboyant Gothic.

Harmas Jean-Henri-Fabre

Rte d'Orange, Sérignan du Comtat. 8km/5mi by the N 7 and D 976 to Sérignan. Near the entrance to the village. ◷*Open Jul–Aug 10am–12.30pm, 3.30–7pm; Apr–Jun and Sept–Oct daily except Wed 10am–12.30pm, 2.30–6pm.* ◷*Closed Nov–Mar, 1 May.* ⊛€5. ℘*04 90 30 57 62. www.mnhn.fr.*
This is the house of Jean-Henri Fabre (1823–1915), the renowned entomologist. The visit includes the scientist's office, where display cases contain his collections of flora and fauna, a gallery in which his finely executed watercolours are hung, and a superb botanical garden.

Bollène

23km/14.3mi north of Orange.
This hill town has been an agricultural marketing centre since the days of the Avignon popes, when it was one of their richest possessions.
A few houses and fine doorways remain as mementoes of the past in what is now a typical Provençal town, with wide shaded boulevards marking the line of the ancient ramparts and a web of narrow streets at the centre.

Collégiale St-Martin

Montée de la Paroisse. ℘*04 90 30 11 38.*
The former parish church (12C–16C) is now used for exhibitions. Its robust bell

The Homer of Insects

This was Victor Hugo's description of **Jean-Henri Fabre**, a remarkable person who devoted his entire life to insects and dedicated to them his fascinating *Souvenirs entomologiques* (*Entomological Recollections* – 2,360 pages which fans of *Microcosmos* have a duty to devour!). This self-taught scientist, who funded his studies by selling lemons from door to door, was forced to give up teaching because, horror of horrors, he had delivered a lecture on the sex life of plants in the presence of young ladies! Although he proudly proclaimed his love of all living insects (apart from cicadas which were too noisy for his taste), he had no hesitation in suggesting that they be cooked for him exactly as he wished at meals, which his guests particularly dreaded.

tower stands atop the hill overlooking the town's rooftops from the east.
Go through the lovely Renaissance doorway to admire the size of the nave covered with a vast timberwork saddleback roof.

Belvédère Pasteur
From this small public garden, set around the former Romanesque **Chapelle des Trois-Croix** (which houses the Musée Pasteur, with art exhibtions), there is a pleasant view of the town and its surrounding countryside.

Mornas
11km/7mi S via the D 26, which cuts through Mondragon and is dominated by the castle ruins. Then take the N 7.
The village of Mornas clings to the foot of a sheer cliff (137m) on which lie the ruins of a **fortress**.

♣♣ Fortress
Guided tours (1hr) Apr–Sept 11am–12.30pm, 2–5pm. €8 (child under 11, €6). ℘04 90 37 01 26. www.forteresse-de-mornas.com.
The fortress features a vast curtain wall, 2km/1.2mi long, flanked by both semicircular and square towers. The castle was also the scene of a terrible episode during the Wars of Religion: it fell into the hands of the sinister Baron des Adrets, who forced all the Catholic inhabitants to jump off the top of the cliff! Themed visits by guides in medieval costume.

🚗 DRIVING TOUR

THE CÔTES DU RHÔNE
In order to visualise this 85km/53mi round-trip starting from Orange, see the map on p287. Allow half a day if possible.

▷ Leave Orange on the south side, following the D 68.

Châteauneuf-du-Pape
It is thanks to the popes who made Avignon their base from 1309 to 1377 (⌖see Avignon, panel) that Châteauneuf-du-Pape came to be associated with the most prestigious wine in the Southern Rhône: a reputation that it still holds internationally today.
Keen to escape the city heat, Pope John XXII chose this elevated spot in the 14C to build a fortified summer residence (the "new château of the pope"). Around it, vineyards were planted to supply papal appetites for quality wines. Much later, in the 1920s, Baron Le Roy, a local wine producer, founded a growers' association whose strict rules relating to such things as vineyard management, harvest dates and grape varieties (13 are permitted here) led to the establishment of the **French Appellation Contrôlée** system. Today, Châteauneuf-du-Pape's precious 3,300ha/8,154 acres of vines are shared by 320 growers.
The town, spilling down the hill from the château, is compact and pleasant for a stroll through narrow streets lined with wine shops and cellars. Around it are the

Famous Côtes du Rhône

The wine producers of **Gigondas** (rivals to Châteauneuf-du-Pape), **Vacqueyras** (structured reds, poised whites), **Rasteau** (rich reds), **Cairanne** (elegant reds and whites) and **Beaumes-de-Venise** (admired for red wine as well as sweet muscat) have brought this region international renown – and deserve a visit! Plan ahead if possible, or consult the tourist office.

vineyards, some of them remarkable for their carpet of large, round stones known as *galets*. These stones soak up the sun during the day and reflect it back at night to the heat-loving Grenache vines whose grapes are the main ingredient of red Châteauneuf-du-Pape wine.

Château des Papes

The ruined papal fortress commands a splendid **view★★** of the valley of the Rhône; Roquemaure and ruins of Château de l'Hers; Avignon with Notre-Dame-des-Doms and the Palais des Papes against the Alpilles; the Luberon and the Vaucluse plateau; the Dentelles de Montmirail and, further off, Mont Ventoux.

Musée du Vin

av. Pierre-de-Luxembourg. ⏱*Open daily mid-Apr–mid-Oct 9am–1pm, 2–7pm; mid-Oct–mid-Apr 9am–noon, 2–6pm.* 👥*Guided tours available.* ⏱*Closed 1 Jan, 25 Dec.* 🎫*No charge.* 📞*04 90 83 59 44. www.brotte.com.* This museum, owned by the wine-producing Brotte family, has a comprehensive collection of interesting old tools and other equipment used traditionally in wine production.

▷ Leave Châteauneuf-du-Pape on the D 192.

Bédarrides

This quiet little town on the banks of the Ouvèze is within the Châteauneuf-du-Pape appellation. Pleasant picnic areas on the river and a farmers' market at the quays in July and August (*Fri 5pm–8pm*).

▷ Take the Sarrians road (D 52), crossing the "Roman bridge" (17C) over the Ouvèze. It takes its name from the old structure which it replaced. At Sarrians, follow the signs to Beaumes-de-Venise.

Beaumes-de-Venise

👉*See Dentelles de Montmirail, Vaison-la-Romaine Tour.*

▷ Take the D 81 to Vacqueyras (5km/3mi to the northwest).

Châteauneuf-du-Pape

© Alain Hocquel/LADT Vaucluse Tourisme

Vineyards of Gigondas

©Sunset/Tips Images

Vacqueyras

Like Châteauneuf-du-Pape and Gigondas (*see below*), this hillside village has also given its name to one of the *crus* (the most highly ranked wine villages) within the Côtes du Rhône. Note its strange clock tower, created out of a 12C watch tower, and the remains of its ramparts.

▷ Continue on the D 7.

Gigondas

Second to Châteauneuf-du-Pape in terms of its reputation as a Côtes-du-Rhône *cru*, Gigondas is worth visiting for more than its meaty red wine. *See Dentelles de Montmirail, Vaison-la-Romaine Tour.*

▷ Continue on the D 7 towards Sablet, on a road that winds through vineyards. On the way you will have great views of the Dentelles de Montmirail (*see Dentelles de Montmirail*), and the attractive wine villages of Sablet and Séguret. Turn left on to the D 977. After 3km/2mi, bear right on to the D 69, in the direction of Rasteau.

Rasteau

Elevated to *cru* status for its red wines since 2010, the village of Rasteau seems to bask in a hillside sun bowl all day long. There are still traces of its medieval past

in cobbled streets, a ruined château and a Romanesque church at the top of the hill. From here there are sweeping views across vines to Mont Ventoux and the Dentelles de Montmirail.

Wine enthusiasts will enjoy the **Musée du Vigneron** (*Route de Roaix;* ♿ 🕐 *open Jul–Aug 10am–6pm, Apr–Jun and Sept 2–6pm;* 🕐 *closed Sun and Tue.* ♿ €2, *guided visit* €5. ☎ *04 90 46 11 75. www. beaurenard.fr*) with its collection of old vineyard tools. Wines are also available to taste and buy, as the museum is run by Domaine de Beaurenard, an excellent biodynamic estate with vineyards in both Rasteau and Châteauneuf-du-Pape.

▷ Continue on the D 69.

Cairanne

Noted for its finely tuned, elegant wines, the Cairanne appellation is crowned by an attractive old village, also with a medieval past.

Parcours Sensoriel des Vin

Quartier de la Laune. 🕐 *Open mid-Jun–mid-Sept 9am–6pm; Jan–mid-Jun 9am–12.30pm, 2–5pm (Sun and public holidays 9am–5pm).* 🕐 *Closed 1 Jan, 25 Dec.* ♿ €5. ☎ *04 90 30 82 05. www.maisoncamillecayran.com.*

In the basement of the Cairanne wine co-op, this interactive "wine route" focusing on the senses is well worth following but available only to groups of 10 or more if booked ahead.

▶ Return to Orange via the D 8, then the D 976.

ADDRESSES

🛏 STAY

🍽🛏 **Camping "La Simioune"** – *Quartier Guffiage - 84500 Bollène* ☎*06 70 73 50 54. www.la-simioune.fr.* Ideally located in a triangle formed by Mont Ventoux, the gorges of Ardeche and Drome Provençal, Camping "The Simioune" offers year round cottages and mobile homes, and from February through November 80 shaded or sunny stands for caravans, motorhomes and tents.

🍽🛏 **Hôtel St-Florent** – *4 r. du Mazeau.* ☎*04 90 34 18 53. www.hotel-orange-saint florent.com. 16 rooms. Closed Dec–Feb.* A st one's throw from the Roman Theatre, this is an attractive little hotel with individually decorated rooms and paintings by the owner.

🍽🛏🛏 **Chambre d'hôte Le Clos des Grenadiers** – *400 rte des Plaines, 84350 Courthézon.* ☎*04 90 70 29 76. www.closdes grenadiers.fr. 2 rooms.* Representing the seventh generation at Châteauneuf-du-Pape estate Mourre du Tendre, Florence Paumel has two very well-appointed rooms for guests in her lovely home. Each has a private terrace and a luxurious bathroom, and breakfasts are delicious. A fine garden with pool and views to Mont Ventoux, plus Châteauneuf wine estates on the doorstep add to the appeal.

🍽🛏🛏 **La Bastide des Princes** – *chemin de Bigonnet, 84860 Caderousse.* ☎*04 90 51 04 59. www.bastide-princes.com. Restaurant (table d'hote)* 🍽🛏🛏. In quiet countryside near Orange, well-known local chef Pierre Paumel and his wife have created attractively traditional rooms in this old bastide. Its greatest feature, however, is M Paumel's cooking – to be enjoyed in the evening or at cookery classes.

🍴 EAT

🍽 **Le Pistou** – *15 r. Joseph-Ducos, 84230 Châteauneuf-du-Pape.* ☎*04 90 83 71 75. Closed Sun eve and Mon.* A cosy, unpretentious little bistro whose menu focuses on traditional Provençal dishes.

🍽🍽 **Auberge Le Tourne au Verre** – *Rte de Ste-Cécile, 84290 Cairanne.* ☎*04 90 30 72 18. www.letourneauverre.com. Closed Sun and Wed.* In the heart of a wine village, what better thing than a terrific wine bar! An impressive selection of Côtes du Rhone wines, simple but tasty food and a relaxed atmosphere attract almost as many wine producers as visitors.

🍽🍽 **La Rom'Antique** – *5 pl. Silvain.* ☎*04 90 51 67 06. www.la-romantique.com.* ♿. *Closed 3 weeks in Jan, 2 weeks in Oct, Sat lunch, Sun eve, Mon.* Sit on the terrace if possible so that you can take in views of the Roman Theatre. Good-quality food with particularly tempting desserts.

🍽🍽 **La Garbure** – *3 r. Joseph-Ducos - 84230 Châteauneuf-du-Pape.* ☎*04 90 83 75 08. www.la-garbure.com. Closed Sun–Mon except in Jul–Aug.* 🅿 Regional dishes, and some Provençal-themed rooms for a longer stay.

🍽🍽🍽 **Le Forum** – *3 r. de Mazeau.* ☎*04 90 34 01 09. Closed 20 Aug–3 Sept, 23 Feb–5 Mar, Sun and Tue.* Small restaurant hidden in a tiny, narrow street near the Roman theatre. Elegant Provençal-style décor. Traditional cuisine prepared with fresh produce.

🍽🍽🍽 **Le Parvis** – *55 cours Pourtoules.* ☎*04 90 34 82 00. Closed 8 Nov–1 Dec, 10 Jan–1 Feb, Sun–Mon.* Polished parquet flooring and contemporary paintings create an elegant atmosphere in this restaurant. Contemporary cuisine with a Provençal note.

SHOPPING

🛈 **Good to know** – Many wine estates in the Côtes-du-Rhône are open to visitors for tastings, cellar visits and other activities. Check with tourist offices in wine villages for details.

Vinadéa – Maison des vins – *8 r. du Mar.-Foch, 84230 Châteauneuf-du-Pape.* ☎*04 90 83 70 69. www.vinadea.com. Open daily Jul–Aug 10am–7pm; rest of the year 10.30am–12.30pm, 2–6.30pm.* Linked to the Maison des Vins, this excellent shop right in the centre of town sells about 200 wines from 90 producers (including many of Châteauneuf 's ritziest names), all at cellar-door prices. Tasting mini-tutorials (*€5*) are also on offer.

Cave de Rasteau – *Rte des Princes d'Orange, 84110 Rasteau.* ☎*04 90 10 90 10. www. cavederasteau.com. Open Apr–Jun and Oct 9am–12.30pm, 2pm–7pm; Jul–Sept*

9am–7pm; rest of the year 9am–12.30pm, 2pm–6pm. Closed 25 Dec, 1 Jan. In operation since 1925, the Rasteau co-op is also quite well geared to visitors.

Vignerons de Caractère – *Rte de Vaison-la-Romaine, 84190 Vacqueyras.* ℘04 90 65 84 54. www.vigneronsdecaractere.com. *Open Apr–Sept 10am–7pm; Oct–Mar 10am–12.30pm, 2pm–6pm.* One of the most go-ahead co-ops in the region, the strikingly modern Vignerons de Caractère set-up includes a first-rate shop with gourmet products as well as wines and an imaginative programme of tastings and other activities. There's a play area for children, too.

Vin Chocolat et Compagnie – *Rte de Sorgues, 84230 Châteauneuf-du-Pape.* ℘04 90 83 54 71. www.vin-chocolat-castelain. com. *Open daily 9am–noon, 2pm–7pm. Closed Sun (Sept–Jun).* This sizeable chocolate company has a spacious shop, chocolate and ice-cream bar and tasting area where you can explore wine and chocolate matching *(reservation required).*

ACTIVITIES

Wine tasting – École de dégustation Mouriesse– *2 r. des Papes, 84230 Châteauneuf-du-Pape.* ℘04 90 83 56 15. www.oenologie-mouriesse.com. *€40/60 pp (for 2hr tasting). Reservation required.* Situated in a wine producer's cellar, this wine school runs courses at all levels.

Vineyard bike rides – The Châteauneuf-du-Pape tourist office suggests four easy routes across the vineyards (from 12 to 28.5km/7.5 to 19mi). Free leaflet.

Vineyard walks – The tourist offices of Châteauneuf-du-Pape, Vacqueyras and Cairanne all have free leaflets mapping out suggested routes through their vineyards.

EVENTS

Chorégies – *pl. Silvain.* ℘04 90 34 24 24. www.choregies.fr. World-famous opera festival in the magnificent setting of the Roman Theatre, mid-Jul–early Aug.

Orange se Met au Jazz – *every year in late June.* Annual jazz festival.

Valréas

Vaucluse

Right in the north of Provence, Valréas is a delightful town whose historic centre (encircled by a road built on the former ramparts) is worth exploring on foot. Famous today for truffles and vineyards, in the 19C it was an important centre for printing and the production of cardboard – as its museum reveals.

A BIT OF HISTORY

The story goes that in 1317 Pope Jean XXII visited Valréas and, feeling rather unwell, drank some local wine which restored him to good health. Impressed (and perhaps keen to secure a steady supply of it), he decided to buy the town for the Avignon papacy. Over the succeeding 150 years, the so-called "Enclave des Papes" (the Popes' Enclave) acquired neighbouring villages such as Visan, Richerenches and Grillon. After the Revolution, when the *département* boundaries were drawn up, the people of the Enclave asked to remain within

▶ **Population:** 9 800.

⚑ **Michelin Map:** 332: C-7.

🛈 **Info:** Av. Maréchal Leclerc, Valréas. ℘04 90 35 04 71. www.ot-valreas.fr.

▶ **Location:** Although in the heart of the Drôme, Valréas (10km/6mi E of Grignan on the D 941) is attached to the Vaucluse.

🕐 **Timing:** From November to March, the truffle market takes place here on Wednesdays and in Richerenches on Saturdays.

the Vaucluse, even though their small area was entirely surrounded by the *département* of the Drôme.

SIGHTS

The town lies within plane tree-shaded boulevards planted on the site of former ramparts of which only the **Tour du Tivoli** *(cours Tivoli)* remains. In the old town are several fine houses: at no 36

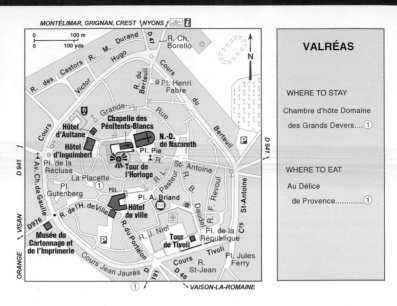

MONTÉLIMAR, GRIGNAN, CREST \ NYONS /

VALRÉAS

WHERE TO STAY

Chambre d'hôte Domaine
des Grands Devers....①

WHERE TO EAT

Au Délice
de Provence.............①

VAISON-LA-ROMAINE

Grande-Rue is the **Hôtel d'Aultane**, its door topped by a coat of arms; on the corner of rue de l'Échelle is **Hôtel d'Inguimbert**, adorned with modillions and mullioned windows; and on place Gutenberg stands **Château Delphinal**, with its fine machicolations.

Château de Simiane (Hôtel de Ville)

8 pl. Aristide Briand. ⏰Open mid-Jul–mid-Aug daily except Tue 11am–8pm. No charge. ℘04 90 35 04 71.
This former 18C mansion belonged to the Marquis de Simiane, who married the granddaughter of Mme de Sévigné.

The oldest part of the mansion dates back to the 15C; a majestic Renaissance façade overlooks place Aristide Briand. The library, on the first floor, with its 17C wood panelling from the former hospital, contains papal bulls and manuscripts.

Musée du Cartonnage et de l'Imprimerie

3 av. Maréchal Foch. ⏰Open daily except Tue: Apr–Oct 10am–noon, 3–6pm (Sun 3–6pm); Nov–Mar 10am–noon, 2–5pm (Sun 2–5pm). ⏰Closed public holidays. €3.50. ℘04 90 35 58 75.

Château de Simiane

© Hemis/Photoshot

This museum is dedicated to the two industries on which the wealth of Valréas depended in the 19C – the production of cardboard and printing.

Chapelle des Pénitents Blancs

pl. Pie. ◐Open: phone tourist office for details.
A lovely wrought-iron gate announces the way to the 17C chapel. The chancel is adorned with carved stalls and a lovely coffered ceiling.

Église Notre-Dame de Nazareth

The most interesting part of this church is its south door, a fine example of Provençal Romanesque architecture.

🚗 DRIVING TOUR

L'ENCLAVE DES PAPES

To visualise this 22km/14mi round trip starting from Valréas, have a look at the map on p287. Allow about 2hr to meander along roads edged with vines and truffle oaks.

▷ Leave Valréas on the D 941, heading west towards Grillon (5km/3mi).

Grillon

Surrounded by vines, this peaceful village has two different aspects. In the lower part, there is the place de la Bourgade with its neo-Gothic bell tower, plane trees and café. Higher up is the medieval heart of Grillon (known as the "Vialle"). Note the belfry with its fine wrought-iron campanile and the restored village walls.

▷ Leave Grillon on the south side, following the D 20 for 4km/2.5mi.

Richerenches

This pretty little village developed around the massive 12C château which was the commanderie of the Knights Templar. Built to a rectangular plan, it has retained its outer wall with four round towers. The entrance is via the

Le Petit Saint-Jean

This is a charming tradition which has survived 500 years. Every year, on the night of 23 June, a small boy (3–5 years old) is crowned Le Petit St-Jean (Little St John). Symbolising St Martin, the city's patron saint, Le Petit St-Jean parades through torch-lit streets on a litter, blessing people along the way. A procession of 300 costumed figures follows him in a colourful and animated atmosphere. For one year Valréas is placed under his protection.

belfry *(starting point for a signposted walk which explains the history of the town)*. Today Richerenches is famous for its winter truffle market (♿see p300).

▷ Leave Richerenches heading south-east and follow the D 120.

Visan

The streets of this substantial village, lined with grand mansions, fan out around the ruins of a medieval castle (the Marot'). It is perched on a hill with caves which make convenient, natural cellars for the storage of Visan wine.

▷ Follow signposts in the direction Vaison-la-Romaine.

In a little valley near the village, separated from a modern housing development by a thick hedge, stands the **chapelle Notre-Dame-des-Vignes** with 13C chancel and statue of the Virgin in woods of various colours. The woodwork in the nave is 15C.

▷ Return to Valréas via the D 976.

"Caveurs" and "Rabassiers"

These are the names given locally to mad-keen truffle hunters. You may see them on winter days, in amongst truffle oaks, armed with a sharp tool for digging and accompanied by a dog (pigs are no longer used to sniff out truffles in Provence). They are out looking for the famous "mélano", or *Tuber melanosporum*, otherwise known as the black truffle. At truffle markets in the Vaucluse, you may see them conducting negotiations with chefs and dealers, following a precise and, to the uninitiated, quite mysterious ritual. Voices are kept low; the truffles, hidden in hessian sacks, are weighed on old-fashioned scales and payment is in cash. Outsiders may feel they have landed in the midst of a secret society.

ADDRESSES

STAY

Chambre d'hôte Domaine des Grands Devers – *Rte de St-Maurice par la Montagne, 84600 Valréas.* 04 90 35 15 98. *www.grandsdevers.com.* 4 rooms. An old Provençal *mas*, surrounded by vines and charming in its authenticity. The four brothers who own it are wine growers. Excellent quality–price ratio.

Le Mas du Sillot – *Les Plans, 84600 Grillon, 8km/5mi W.* 04 90 28 44 00. *www.lemasdusillot.com.* 18 rooms. Restaurant. Set in the heart of orchards on the edge of the Enclave des Papes, this old farm offering hostel-type accommodation is lovely. Rooms are a bit small, but quite well fitted out. Prices very reasonable for the area.

Chambre d'hôte Le Mas des Sources – *chemin Notre-Dame-des-Vignes, rte de Vaison-la-Romaine, 84820 Visan.* 06 98 10 13 00. *www.mas-des-sources.com.* 5 rooms. Restaurant. Situated among the vines, this restored farm offers cosy, antique-filled rooms (including one family room). Special theme weekends around wine, olive oil and, of course, truffles.

Chambre d'hôte Domaine de Château Vert – *84820 Visan.* 04 90 41 91 21. *www.hebergement-chateau-vert.com.* 5 rooms. Restaurant. An imposing 18C residence on a wine and truffle estate. Themed truffle weekends are run from late December to mid-March; reservation essential.

EAT

Au Délice de Provence – *6 La Placette.* 04 90 28 16 91. *Closed Wed.* A pleasant little place to stop and cheer yourself up with classic cooking, in the town centre. A good choice of menus at very reasonable prices.

L'Escapade – *Av. de la Rabasse, 84600 Richerenches.* 04 90 28 01 46. *Closed Mon (from mid-Jun–end Sept) Mon–Tue, Wed eve, Thurs eve, Sun eve (from Oct–mid-Jun).* The HQ of truffle hunters who take refuge here when the mistral is blowing. A good restaurant it is, too, run by Jeannot, the queen of the southern speciality pieds paquets, featuring lamb trotters and tripe. Not for the fainthearted!

SHOPPING

Market – Traditional market on Wednesday morning in historic downtown Valreas, Friday morning in Visan, Saturday morning in Grillon and Richerenches (Nov–Mar).

Truffle market – *Cours du Mistral, 84600 Richerenches.* 04 90 28 05 34. *www.richerenches.fr.* Small though it may be, the village of Richerenches is widely regarded as the truffle capital; there is even a truffle Mass in its church on the third Sunday in January. While the Valréas and Carpentras truffle markets are essentially for dealers, anybody can buy fresh truffles at Richerenches (Saturday morning, November–March).

More information about local truffles can be found in the Comtat Venaissin and Ventoux Discovering section, p314.

Chocolates – Jef Challier – *16 pl. A.-Briand, 84600 Valréas.* 04 90 35 05 22. *www.enclave-passion.com.* One of the most talented chocolatiers in Provence is based in Valréas. Jef Challier has developed a range of chocolates with unusual and exquisite flavours as well as superb (sometimes surprising) ice creams and irresistible patisseries.

Goat's cheese – *C. And V. Charansol, chemin des Étangs, 84600 Valréas. ℘04 90 35 58 25. Open Apr–Dec 5–8pm.* Christian and Véronique Charransol make goat's cheeses of outstanding quality on their farm. They also grow vegetables and keep other animals, making this a fun place for children to visit – especially around 5pm when the cows are milked.

ACTIVITIES

Walking and cycling itineraries – The tourist office in Valréas provides a free booklet suggesting 18 circuits which you can follow by bike or on foot. Among them are walking routes for Valréas, Grillon, Richerenches and Visan; and the **circuit des Bornes papales** (11.8km/7.3mi), taking in the engraved stones which marked the boundaries of the Enclave des Papes in the 14C.

EVENTS

Festival des Nuits et Salon de l'Enclave – From mid-July to mid-August, concerts, stage plays, and painting and sculpture exhibitions.

Fête médiévale – In mid-August, artists and artisans return Richerenches to its medieval past.

Cuvée du Marot – On the second Sunday in July, 10,000 magnums of red Visan wine are released from the caves underneath the château (the "Marot") where they have been held for the past year.

Corso de la Lavande – *first week of Aug, Valréas.* A celebration of lavender including a float parade, concerts and a wine festival.

Vaison-la-Romaine★★

Vaucluse

Built along the banks of the River Ouvèze, in the middle of a corrie of wooded hills, charming and prosperous Vaison-la-Romaine will enchant those who love historical places. Rarely does a town offer such a complete and picturesque ensemble: vast fields of ancient ruins, a Romanesque cathedral and cloisters, and, high up on a hill above the river, the old town dominated by its castle.
As well as becoming a busy tourist hub during the music festivals, Vaison thrives as an agricultural centre producing wine, fruit, honey, lavender and truffles.

A BIT OF HISTORY

The City of the Vocontii – Southern capital of the Vocontii, a Celtic tribe, Vaison (Vasio Vocontiorum) became part of Roman Provence, which was conquered at the end of the 2C BCE and covered all southeastern Gaul. Very early on it received the status of federated city (and not colony), which allowed it a great deal of autonomy. Allied with Caesar during

- ▶ **Population:** 6 169.
- ⊙ **Michelin Map:** 332: D-8. Local map *see Dentelles de Montmirail.*
- ℹ **Info:** Place du Chanoine Sautel, Vaison-la-Romaine. ℘04 90 36 02 11. www.vaison-ventoux-tourisme.com.
- 🅿 **Parking:** Arriving from Orange (28km/17.4mi SW) or Carpentras (27km/16.8mi S), use the car park in place Burrus.
- ⊛ **Don't Miss:** The Roman ruins, the old town, the cloisters.
- ⊙ **Timing:** Allow 2hrs to visit the Roman ruins and more if you want to explore the old town; there's a market here on Sundays in summer.

the Gallic Wars (58–51 BCE), the Vocontii lived side by side with the Romans; and among them illustrious men appeared: the historian Trogus-Pompeius and Nero's tutor Burrhus.
Cited as one of the Narbonensis' most prosperous cities under Roman rule,

Vaison covered some 70ha/173 acres and had a population of approximately 10,000. Unlike the colonial examples of Arles, Nîmes and Orange, the city did not expand with a Romanised urban plan, as was customary, because a pre-existing rural plan prevented the surveyors from tracing a regular grid plan and placing living quarters and public buildings in their rightful place. The result was a very loose urban layout. Immense dwellings were built right in the centre of the city, replacing the earlier buildings.

It was not until the last third of the 1C AD, under the Flavians, that it was decided to create straight streets: properties had to be remodelled accordingly, the façades of houses were realigned and their axes modified, while porticoes and colonnades were erected. Archaeologists have established that the luxurious domi were much larger than those in Pompeii. They were built over a period of 250 years, and yet Vaison was not restricted to just this kind of dwelling; excavations have unearthed small palaces, modest dwellings, huts and tiny shops. The large public buildings, except for the theatre and baths, have not been traced.

Over the Centuries – Partially destroyed in the late 3C, Vaison rose again during the 4C with a reduced urban plan. The seat of a bishopric, it ranked highly in the 5C and 6C in spite of Barbarian occupation, and two synods took place here in 442 and 529.

The following centuries were marked by a sharp decline and by the desertion of the lower town, to the profit of the old town on the river's south bank where the Count of Toulouse built a castle. The medieval upper town was abandoned in the 18C and 19C and the modern town fortified the Gallo-Roman city. In September 1992 disaster struck Vaison when the Ouvèze River burst its banks, destroying 150 houses and causing about 30 deaths. Miraculously, or perhaps because it was so stoutly constructed, the Roman bridge survived, losing only its parapet.

WALKING TOURS

THE TOWN

The exceptional archaeological site for which Vaison is justly famous should not allow visitors to neglect the delightful medieval town, starting with the cathedral, which is reached from Quartier de la Villasse by following avenue Jules-Ferry.

Ancienne Cathédrale Notre-Dame-de-Nazareth

This beautiful Provençal Romanesque-style building still has its 11C chevet, made from a solid rectangular block of masonry, its apsidal chapels and its walls, reinforced in the 12C at the same time that the nave was covered in by a barrel vault. The discovery of Gallo-Roman architectural fragments leads experts to believe that the cathedral was built on the ruins of a civic building with a basilical ground plan.

Outside, the chevet is decorated with cornices and foliated friezes imitating Antique decoration. Inside, the nave includes two bays with pointed barrel vaulting and one bay topped by an octagonal dome on squinches decorated with the symbols of the Evangelists. It is lit through windows cut at the base of the vaulting.

Cloître★

Open Mar–Sept daily 9.30am–6pm; Oct 10am–noon, 2–5.30pm. Closed Nov–Feb. No charge.
04 90 36 50 05.

The cloisters are adjacent to the cathedral and were originally built in the 12C and 13C; the southeast gallery is a 19C reconstruction. The capitals in the east arcade are the most elaborately decorated: acanthus leaves, interlaced designs or figures.

▷ Return to the avenue and turn right along quai Pasteur, which runs along the right bank of the Ouvèze.

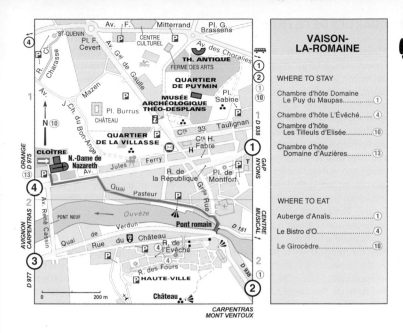

CARPENTRAS
MONT VENTOUX

Pont Romain

The Roman bridge has only one arch, 17.20m wide. Apart from the parapet, rebuilt after the dramatic flood on 22 September 1992, the bridge is as it was 2,000 years ago.

HAUTE VILLE★ (UPPER TOWN)

▷ Start from place du Poids and go through the 14C fortified gateway, dominated by the belfry tower and its 18C wrought-iron bell cage.

The 14C fortifications which surround the city's steeply sloping streets were built in part using stones from the ruins of the Roman town. Take the time to amble through the picturesque maze of alleyways (rue de l'Église, rue de l'Évêché, rue des Fours) and squares (place du Vieux Marché) decorated with lovely fountains. The successful restoration of the creamy stone houses roofed with old Roman-style tiles evokes a typical Provençal village of yesteryear.The church dates from the 15C and there is a fine view of Mont Ventoux from the parvis. A steep path leads to the castle, built by

the Counts of Toulouse at the end of the 12C on a rock above the upper town.

ROMAN RUINS★★

◐ open daily: Jun–Sept 9.30am–6.30pm; Mar and Oct 10am–12.30pm, 2–5.30pm; Apr–May 9.30am–6pm; Nov–Dec and Feb 10am–noon, 2–5pm. ◐Closed Jan and early Feb. ✆€8 (combined ticket with Roman Theatre in Orange €12.50). ☎04 90 36 50 05.

The ancient ruins are spread over 15ha/37 acres. The centre of the Gallo-Roman city (forum and precincts) is covered by the modern town, so only the peripheral quarters, rich with information on life at Vaison and its inhabitants in the 1C AD, have been uncovered. At present the excavations are progressing towards the cathedral in the La Villasse quarter and around Puymin hill, where a shopping district and a sumptuous *domus*, the **Peacock villa** with its mosaics, were unearthed. On the northern boundary of the ancient town, the excavated baths (some 20 rooms) have revealed that they were used until the late 3C and then destroyed.

QUARTIER DE PUYMIN

Maison à l'Apollon Lauré

This *domus*, a large urban dwelling belonging to a wealthy Vaison family (partly buried under the modern road network), features a very elaborate interior which favoured a sumptuous and comfortable lifestyle. As one enters, via the Roman street, a vestibule and then a corridor lead to the *atrium* (1) around which the various rooms have been laid out, including the *tablinum* (study and library reserved for the head of the family). The atrium had in its centre, under the open section, a square basin *(impluvium)* which caught rainwater. Note the room (2) where Apollo's head (in the museum) was found, the main reception hall or *oecus* (3), the peristyle and its basin. The annexes include the kitchen (4) with its twin hearths, and the private bath (5) with its three rooms: *caldarium, tepidarium, frigidarium*.

Portique de Pompée

This elegant public promenade, a sort of public garden, 64m x 52m, consisted of four galleries with niches *(exedra)*, covered originally with a lean-to roof, surrounding a garden and pool, in the centre of which stood a square aedicule. The well-excavated north gallery presents three *exedra* into which were placed the casts of the statues of Sabina, Diadumenos (Roman copy of the statue by Polyclitus which is exhibited at the British Museum) and Hadrian. The west gallery is also almost entirely excavated, while the other two galleries are buried under the modern buildings.

Rented Houses (Maisons de rapport)

This residential complex consists of a block of dwellings (to rent) several storeys high, for citizens of modest means. Note the large urn *(dolium)* for provisions.

Nymphaeum

This features various buildings of a cistern set around a spring, which was collected into an elongated basin, called a *nymphaeum*. Further on to the east the shopping district and Peacock villa were excavated (o⚊ *closed to the public*).

Musée Archéologique Théo-Desplans★

&⏲*Open daily Nov–Feb 10am–noon, 2–5pm; Mar and Oct 10am–12.30pm, 2–5.30pm; Apr–May 9.30am–6pm; Jun–Sept 9.30am–6.30pm.* ⊛€8 *(including Roman Ruins).* ☎04 90 36 50 05. www.vaison-la-romaine.com.
This fascinating archaeological museum displays the finds excavated at Vaison.

Mosaics in Peacock villa, Quartier de Puymin

© World Pictures/Photoshot

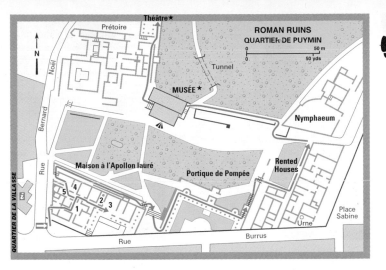

ROMAN RUINS
QUARTIER DE PUYMIN

Different aspects of Gallo-Roman civilisation are presented thematically: religion, living quarters, pottery, glassware, arms, tools, ornaments, toiletries and imperial coins. The statues are remarkable. They are all in white marble; in chronological order: Claudius (dating from 43) wearing a heavy oak crown; Domitian in armour; naked Hadrian (dating from 121) in a majestic pose in the Hellenistic manner; Sabina, his wife, represented more conventionally as a great lady in state dress. Two other pieces are worthy of interest: the 2C marble head of Apollo crowned with laurel leaves, and a 3C silver bust of a patrician and mosaics from the Peacock Villa.

▷ Go to the theatre by following the west slope of the Puymin.

Théâtre Romain★

The theatre was built in the 1C, repaired in the 3C and dismantled in the 5C. Its dimensions (95m diameter, 29m high) reveal that it was slightly smaller than the one in Orange; it had a seating capacity of 6,000 people (Orange held 9,000 to 10,000 spectators).

Also like the theatre in Orange, it was built against the hillside; its tiers were rebuilt by Jules Formigé (1879–1960; Inspector-General of Historical Monuments). The entire stage was hewn out of the rock and the pits containing the

machinery and curtain have been well preserved. Discovered amid the ruins were the fine statues exhibited in the museum. Another feature, unique among the Roman theatres in Provence, is the existence of part of a top gallery portico.

QUARTIER DE LA VILLASSE

Main Street and Baths

On entering the site of the excavations, walk on the paved main street, under which runs a drain going down towards the Ouvèze and the modern buildings. On the west side of the street is a parallel passageway lined with colonnades reserved for pedestrians only; shops, located in the main houses' outbuildings, lined it. On the east side of the street lie the baths, which are surrounded by deep drains. The great room has a pilastered arcade.

Maison au Buste d'Argent (House of the Patrician of the Silver Bust)

Across from the baths in the shopping street is the entrance (1) to the vast *domus*, in which was discovered the silver bust (&see Musée Archéologique Théo-Desplans, p304) of its opulent owner. Sprawled over about 5,000sq m/53,820sq ft, the *domus* is complete: paved vestibule, *atrium* (2),

Maison au Buste d'Argent

© S. Sauvignier/MICHELIN

tablinum **(3)**, a first peristyle with garden and pool and then a second larger peristyle also enhanced with garden and pool.

On the south side of the house stands another where mosaics **(4)** were found as well as frescoes around an *atrium*. North of the second (larger) peristyle is the private bath **(5)**, which is preceded by a courtyard. Nearby, to the east, lies a large hanging garden which enhanced the wealthy property.

Maison au Dauphin (Dolphin House)

In its early stages, c.40 BCE, this house occupied the northeastern section of a large enclosure in a non-urban setting. The central part of this vast house, which covers 2,700sq m/29,066sq ft, is laid out around a peristyle **(7)** decorated by a pool in dressed stone. To the north, covering 50sq m/538sq ft, there are the private baths **(8)** with the *triclinium*, a large dining room used for banquets, along the west edge. The *atrium* **(6)** led into the colonnaded street; this was one of the entrances to the house.

To the south stands another peristyle, a pleasant garden complemented by a large pool, with three *exedra* and faced with white marble, as well as fountains and formal gardens.

Colonnaded Street

Not completely excavated, this street borders the Maison au Dauphin. It was not a paved street; its surface, like many other streets, was made of gravel.

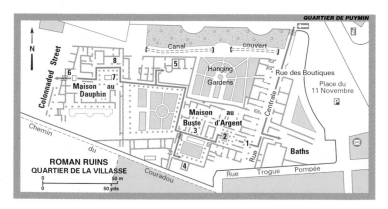

ROMAN RUINS
QUARTIER DE LA VILLASSE

EXCURSIONS

There are two signposted footpaths which loop around the surrounding countryside, one of 18km/11.2mi and one of 37km/23mi. Maps are available at the tourist office.

Entrechaux

6km/3.7mi southwest on the D 938, then the D 54.

A former possession of the bishops of Vaison, this village is noteworthy for its ruined château with a dungeon 20m deep.

Brantes

28km/17.4mi E by the D 938, then left onto the D 54 until Entrechaux. There take the D 13 towards Mollans and finally turn right onto the D 40.

This isolated village, popular with artists, occupies an impressive **site★** in the Toulourenc valley, up against the north face of Mont Ventoux. It has a chapel of the Pénitents Blancs, the remains of a Renaissance manor house (lovely sculpted doorway) and a richly decorated church.

ADDRESSES

🛌 STAY

⊜⊜ **Chambre d'hôte Domaine le Puy de Maupas** – *7km/4.3mi NE, rte de Nyons, 84110 Puyméras.* ☏*04 90 46 47 43. www. puy-du-maupas.com. Closed Nov–Mar.* 🅿️. *5 rooms.* A house set among vines, next to the cellar of this wine-producing property. Breakfast is served facing Mont Ventoux. Evening meals offer the opportunity to taste the house wines. Swimming pool.

⊜⊜⊜ **Chambre d'hôte Domaine des Auzières** – *84110 Roaix, 9km/5.6mi W.* ☏*04 90 46 15 54. www.auzieres.fr.* 🅿️🏊. *5 rooms. Table d'hôte* ⊜⊜⊜. It's hard to find somewhere more isolated than this B&B on a wine estate high up above the village of Roaix. A sizeable house with spacious rooms. Table d'hôte dinners feature the estate's wines. Swimming pool.

⊜⊜⊜ **Chambre d'hôte L'Évêché** – *14 r. de l'Évêché.* ☏*04 90 36 13 46. http:// eveche.free.fr.* 📧. *5 rooms.* This pleasant 16C house in the upper part of town was

once part of the bishop's palace. Carefully decorated rooms, prettily furnished, arranged on several levels. Lovely views.

⊜⊜⊜ **Chambre d'hôte Les Tilleuls d'Elisée** – *1 av. Jules-Mazen (behind the cathedral).* ☏*04 90 35 63 04. www.vaison chambres.info.* 🅿️. *5 rooms.* Close to the centre of Vaison yet in a peaceful location surrounded by olive trees, this B&B in an old farmhouse has very pretty, well-appointed rooms. Breakfast is served in the attractively restored dining room or in the garden.

🍽️ EAT

⊜⊜ **Auberge d'Anaïs** – *Le Péreyrus, 84340 Entrechaux, 5km/3mi SE.* ☏*04 90 36 20 06. www.aubergeanais.com. Closed Dec–Feb, Mon Apr–Sept, Sat Mar, Oct–Nov.* ♿🅿️🏊. Surrounded by vines and olive trees, this inn is a popular meeting place for locals. Relaxed dining room, tasty cooking and lively, down-to-earth atmosphere.

⊜⊜ **Le Girocèdre** – *Montée du Portalet, 84110 Puyméras, 6km/3.7mi NE.* ☏*04 90 46 50 67. www.legirocedre.fr. Closed Nov–Dec, Mon, Tue Oct–Easter.* ♿🅿️. At the top of the village is this building perched on an outcrop of rock, whose caves, originally hollowed out to raise silkworms, now serve as wine cellars. Lovely terrace where grilled or barbecued meat and fish are served in summer.

⊜⊜⊜ **Le Bistrot du'O** – *1 r. du Château.* ☏*04 90 41 72 90. Closed Jan, Mon lunch, Sun.* An elegant, modern bistro with contemporary cooking. Décor mixes old and new under a vaulted ceiling. Carefully chosen wine list.

⊜⊜⊜⊜ **Le Grand Pré** – *rte Vaison-la-Romaine.* ☏*04 90 46 18 12. www.legrandpre. com. Closed Apr–mid-Nov Wed and Sat lunch and Tue; mid-Nov–Mar Thu–Sun lunch and Mon–Wed.* The most sophisticated, subtle cooking around Vaison comes from chef Raoul Reichrath who runs a charming restaurant on the edge of Roaix with his wife Flora, an accomplished sommelier.

SHOPPING

Markets – *Tue mornings in the town centre.*

Moulin à huile Chauvet – *Porte Major, 26170 Mollans-sur-Ouvèze.* ☏*04 75 28 90 12. Open Jul–Sept daily 10am–12.30pm and 2.30pm–7pm; Apr–Jun Sat–Sun and public holidays 10am–12.30pm, 2.30pm–7pm.* Selling and tasting of olive oil.

ACTIVITIES

Walks – *Check with the Vaison tourist office.* Several itineraries enable walkers to discover the countryside around Vaison-la-Romaine.

Bike rides – There are three itineraries, starting from the Vaison tourist office. You can download them from www.escapado.fr.

EVENTS

Choralies – *Information from the À Cœur Joie association.* ℘*04 72 19 83 40. www. choralies.fr.* Every three years, Vaison holds Les Choralies, a choral music festival that attracts singers and choirs from far and wide. They perform in studios by day and on the stage of the Théâtre Antique by night. The festival is typically held the first week of August.

Dentelles de Montmirail★
Vaucluse

The jagged peaks of the Dentelles de Montmirail are a Vaucluse landmark, visible for many kilometres. Although they look like huge molars, their name has nothing to do with *dents* (the word for teeth) but, much more poetically, compares them to pieces of lace. Formed when upper layers of Jurassic limestone were forced upright by the folding of the Earth's crust, then eroded by wind and weather into thin spikes and ridges, the Dentelles provide dramatic scenery, particularly as vines, green oaks and, in late spring, yellow broom cover the slopes below their grey-white summits. They attract painters and naturalists as well as walkers and rock climbers of all abilities.

- **Michelin Map:** 332: D-8 to D-9.
- **Info:** 122 place du Marché, Beaumes-de-Venise. ℘04 90 62 94 39. www.ot-beaumesdevenise.com.
- **Don't Miss:** Séguret, Gigondas' wine-tastings, Beaumes-de-Venise.

Séguret★

This picturesque old village, built on a ledge against the side of a steep hill, is well worth a visit. At the village entrance, walk through the covered passage into the main street and continue past the 15C Mascarons fountain and the 14C belfry to the 12C St-Denis church.
From the square *(viewing table)* the view embraces the Dentelles, the Comtat Venaissin and, to the far north, the line of the Massif Central. A ruined castle and a network of steep, narrow streets lined with old houses all add character.

◗ On leaving Séguret turn left onto the D 23 for Sablet and then take the D 7 and the D 79 for Gigondas.

Gigondas

About 90 percent of the Dentelles lie within the commune of Gigondas, so this lovely wine village occupies a prime position on your route. Perched on a hill with the craggy peaks of the Dentelles de Montmirail rising up behind, it is one

🚗 DRIVING TOUR

VAISON-LA-ROMAINE TOUR
60km/37mi round trip.
About half a day.

◗ Leave Vaison-la-Romaine on the D 977, the road towards Avignon. Turn left after 5.5km/3.4mi onto the D 88.

The road climbs into the mountains, disclosing views of the Ouvèze valley to the west.

15C Mascarons fountain, Séguret

© Nicolas Thibaut/Photononstop

of the prettiest villages in this area of breathtaking vineyard and mountain scenery. Consider making it the starting point for a walk in the Dentelles, or climb up to the church and ramparts right at the top of the village, where there is a sculpture trail. There are plenty of wine estates to visit too, of course.

Afterwards you can recover at one of the cafés or restaurants in the flower-filled square.

▶ Drive via Les Florets (where there is a mountaineering hut and a hotel/restaurant, *see* Addresses), to the Col de Cayron.

Col de Cayron
Alt 396m.

This pass is at the centre of the Dentelles' principal peaks which, with faces rearing nearly 100m high, offer all the complexity of features relished by rock climbers. Park the car and bear right *(1hr return journey on foot)* on the unsurfaced road which winds through the Dentelles. There are splendid **views★** of the Rhône plain backed by the Cévennes, Vaucluse plateau and Mont Ventoux. The road passes below a ruined Saracen tower (Tour Sarrazine).

▶ Return to the car and take the D 7, then turn left towards Vacqueyras.

ChapelleNotre-Damed'Aubune

This Romanesque chapel sits on a small terrace at the foot of the Dentelles de Montmirail, near Fontenouilles farm. It has an elegant **bell tower★** ornamented on each side by long pilasters inspired by Antiquity.

The four bays are framed by pillars or small columns elaborately decorated with fluting, grapes, vine branches, acanthus leaves and grimacing faces.

▶ On the left, follow the D 81 which meanders among vines and olive trees.

Beaumes-de-Venise

This terraced village on the other side of the Dentelles from Gigondas is famous for delicious sweet white wine made from the Muscat grape, and for red wine too. You can taste the different styles of Muscat in its excellent wine co-op, Balma Venitia.

▶ Leave Beaumes-de-Venise eastwards on the D 21, bear left on the D 938 and left again on the D 78. Leave Le Barroux N towards Suzette and meet up with the D 90.

After Suzette the road enters the vertically walled Cirque de St-Amand. The road rises to a small pass which

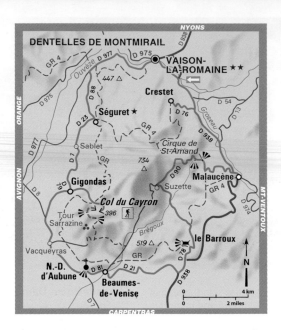

in the main car park and have a look at the village's 14C church, arcaded square and fountain. Narrow streets between Renaissance houses climb the hill up to a 12C **castle**, from where there is a fantastic **view** of the village, the Ouvèze, Mont Ventoux and the Baronnies.

affords a good **view★** on one side of the Dentelles and on the other of Mont Ventoux, the Ouvèze valley and the Baronnies.

▷ The D 938 NW climbs the fertile Groseau valley. Turn left onto the D 76.

Crestet
The climb up to this little village is steep and twisting but worth the effort. Park

▷ Return to the D 938 and turn left for Vaison-la-Romaine.

Dentelles de Montmirail

© minicel73/Fotolia.com

ADDRESSES

STAY

Chambre d'hôte La Farigoule –
*Le Plan-de-Dieu, 84150 Violès, 10km/6mi
W of Gigondas.* ☎*04 90 70 91 78. Closed
Nov–Easter.* 🅿 ⬜. *5 rooms.* This 18C *maison
vigneronne* has kept its authenticity. Each
room is named after a Provençal poet.
Breakfast is served in a fine vaulted room
or on the terrace.

**Chambre d'hôte Le Mas de la
Fontaine** – *Rte de Vacqueyras, 84260
Sarrians.* ☎*04 90 12 36 63. www.lemasdela
fontaine.fr. Closed mid-Nov–end Jan.* 🅿 ⬜.
5 rooms. Restaurant ⬤⬤. Among vines,
this huge, attractively renovated mas is
an agreeable place to stay, its 300-year-
old plane tree and old fountain creating
a pleasantly cool terrace in summer. The
bedrooms, all on the first floor, are calm
and simply decorated. Provençal-style
table d'hôte.

**Chambre d'hôte Mas de la
Lause** – *40 Chemin de Geysset, rte de
Suzette, 84330 Le Barroux.* ☎*04 90 62 33
33. www.Provence-gites.com. Closed Nov–
mid Mar.* 🅿. *5 rooms. Restaurant* ⬤⬤.
Surrounded by vines and olive trees,
this old mas dating from 1883 has been
renovated in a modern way. Family-style
cuisine, based on local products.

Hôtel-restaurant Les Florets –
rte des Dentelles, 84190 Gigondas. ☎*04
90 65 85 01. www.hotel-lesflorets.com.* 🏊.
Closed Jan–mid-Mar. Restaurant ⬤⬤⬤.
Well run by the Bernard family, this hotel
above the village with the vine-clad slopes
of the Dentelles almost within touching
distance has been a Gigondas landmark
for decades. A delightful terrace facing the
hills, comfortable rooms and very good
food help to maintain its popularity. And
there's a swimming pool on the premises.

EAT

Le Dolium – *pl. Balma-Vénitia,
Cave des Vignerons, Beaumes-de-Venise.*
☎*04 90 12 80 00. www.dolium-restaurant.
com. Closed Sun, Wed, Thu dinner (mid-Jun–
mid-Sept).* Attached to Balma Venitia, the
Beaumes wine growers' co-operative, is
this excellent restaurant serving confident,
modern food in a stylish contemporary
interior. Very pleasing price.

Restaurant le Gajulea – *201 cours
Louise Raymond, Le Barroux.* ☎*04 90 62 36
94. www.gajulea.fr. Closed 2 weeks in Mar,
Sun evening (except Jul–Aug) and Mon.* If
you long for excellent cooking without
any fiddly flourishes, this restaurant run
by Michel Philibert, one of the most
experienced chefs for many kilometres
around, deserves a visit. Extensive cellar
and close-up views of Mont Ventoux. Next
door, the Philiberts' bistro Entre' Potes
suits those with more modest budgets.

L'Oustalet – *Pl. du village,
84190 Gigondas.* ☎*04 90 65 85 30. www.
restaurant-oustalet.fr. Closed 22 Dec–20 Jan,
Sun eve, Mon eve, Tue apart from mid-Jun–
Aug, Tue eve in Nov–Mar, Wed eve.* Now
owned by the Perrin family of acclaimed
Châteauneuf-du-Pape estate Château de
Beaucastel, this restaurant situated on the
square in Gigondas is better than ever.
Delightful terrace, competent cooking
and a good list of local wines.

ACTIVITIES

Climbing – Two experienced guides
offer rock-climbing courses and training
programs: **Régis Leroy** (☎*07 77 31 69
60. www.rocdentelles.com*) and **André
Charmetant** (☎*04 90 82 20 72.
www.charmetant.org*).

Walking – Some 40km/24mi of marked
trails lace the slopes of les Dentelles de
Montmirail. The tourist information offices
at Beaumes-de-Venise and Gigondas offer
trail maps (*€5 and €2.50 respectively*)
and recommended walking routes for the
mountain and the surrounding areas.

Good to Know – Access to the mountain
may be restricted during the summer
season. *For information:* ☎*04 88 17 80 00.*

*Walking on the Dentelles
de Montmirail*

© Alain Hocquel/L'ADT Vaucluse Tourisme

COMTAT VENAISSIN *and Ventoux*

Lying between the Rhône and Durance rivers and the mightiest mountain in Provence, the Comtat Venaissin and Ventoux are delightful areas to visit. At their heart is Carpentras, as interesting for its Jewish past as for the bountiful weekly market that contributes so handsomely to its appeal today. Around it to the north, east and south lies countryside enriched both by the fields and orchards that have made this area famous for vegetables and fruit, and by a whole series of fascinating villages. Above it all, sometimes dramatically close, looms magnificent Mont Ventoux.

Highlights

1 The fantastic Friday market and the old town: **Carpentras** (p315)

2 A tour of 40 fountains: **Pernes-les-Fontaines** (p321)

3 The Baptristy, one of the oldest in France: **Venasque** (p324)

4 A drive or walk to the summit: **Mont Ventoux** (p326)

5 The dramatic Gorges de la Nesque: **Sault** (p330)

First, explore Carpentras with its intriguing mix of buildings, including the moving and beautiful 14C synagogue (a reminder that under the popes, this area welcomed Jews); the Gothic cathedral, begun in 1404 and completed a century later; the majestic 18C Hôtel-Dieu and from the same period, the Classical façades of some fine houses. The reward for the exertion of a walking tour should be a stop for coffee and a cake in a superb patisserie, or for picnic supplies in a great cheese shop or deli, because Carpentras is a *ville gourmande*: food heaven.

Small Townships to Stroll In

Within easy reach of Carpentras, to the south and east especially, small towns and villages steeped in history are laid out in a lush and fertile landscape like jewels scattered on a cape of mottled green. Particularly charming are Pernes-les-Fontaines with, as its name suggests, an extraordinary abundance of fountains; and Venasque, perched on an outcrop of rock and powerful enough, in the era of the popes, to have given

its name to the Comtat Venaissin. Today its reputation rests on its sheer beauty.

Fruits, Truffles, Vines

Few parts of Provence can claim to be so blessed with outstanding produce. If strawberries top the list (the *fraises de Carpentras* which brighten markets from early spring are eagerly sought all over France), they have plenty of other locally grown fruits for company. No wonder Carpentras became a key centre for *fruits confits*, heartstoppingly sweet candied fruits. It is also an important truffle town, gateway to some of the most productive truffle territory in all of France. The illustrious winter truffle draws food enthusiasts to restaurants celebrated for their all-truffle menus besides attracting buyers to the Carpentras truffle market. As if all that were not enough, the large *appellation* of the Ventoux has become one of the most exciting wine regions in the Southern Rhône, thanks to ambitious young talent and realistic pricing.

The Giant and Gushing Gorges

Unmissable from almost every perspective is the Giant of Provence, Mont Ventoux. This mountain, enjoyed as much by climbers as it is dreaded by cyclists in the Tour de France, provides the centre of Provence with some of its most spectacular scenery. Fields of lavender and wheat on its lower slopes create an alluring patchwork around the little town of Sault, where the smell of fresh lavender permeates the summer air. Not far away to the west, the Gorges de la Nesque deliver scenic drama of a quite different kind as the fast-flowing Nesque River carves its way through deep limestone chasms.

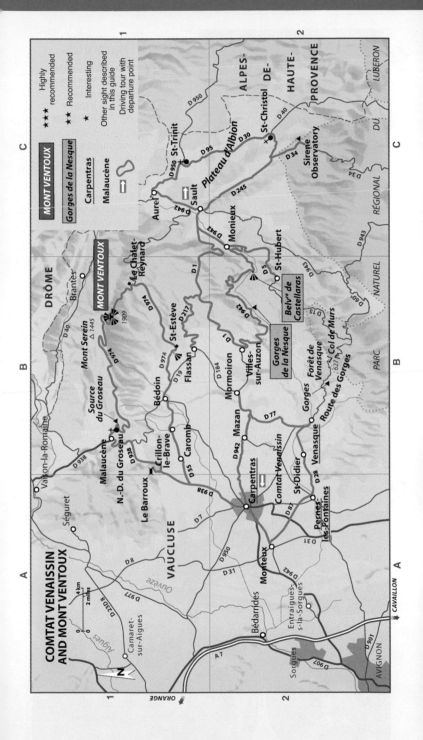

COMTAT VENAISSIN AND MONT VENTOUX

VAUCLUSE

DRÔME

ALPES-HAUTE-PROVENCE

Highly recommended ★★★
Recommended ★★
Interesting ★
Other sight described in this guide
Driving tour with departure point

MONT VENTOUX
Gorges de la Nesque
Carpentras
Malaucène

N

ORANGE

Camaret-sur-Aigues

Séguret

Vaison-la-Romaine

Brantes

Mont Serein △ 1445

Source du Groseau

Malaucène

N.-D. du Groseau

Le Barroux

Crillon-le-Brave

Bédoin

Caromb

St-Estève

Flassan

MONT VENTOUX 1909

Le Châlet-Reynard

Aurel

St-Trinit

Plateau d'Albion

St-Christol

HAUTE-PROVENCE

Sault

Monieux

Sirène Observatory

Mormoiron

Villes-sur-Auzon

St-Hubert

Belv.r de Castellaras

Mazan

Gorges de la Nesque

Forêt de Venasque

Col de Murs

Carpentras

Comtat Venaissin

Venasque

St-Didier

Pernes-les-Fontaines

Monteux

Bédarrides

Entraigues-s-la-Sorgues

Sorgues

AVIGNON

CAVAILLON

Route des Gorges

Gorges

PARC

NATUREL

RÉGIONAL

DU LUBERON

Ouvèze

Aigues

313

Black Truffles

© Marco Mayer/Fotolia.com

Black Diamonds

Although most visitors explore Provence between April and October, the winter months hold a special appeal for gourmets. November to March is the season of the black truffle, *tuberum melanosporum*, a highly prized and highly priced delicacy best eaten fresh. And the Vaucluse is prime territory for these knobbly tubers, accounting for almost 80 percent of France's total truffle output. All winter long, restaurants stud their menus with dishes designed to show off the so-called *diamant noir* (black diamond), a commodity so precious that prices currently run from €800 to €1,000 per kilo.

Well worth visiting for their sheer fascination are the two most important truffle markets in the Vaucluse: one in Carpentras, essentially for dealers (🐌 *see p320*), and the other in Richerenches (🐌 *for customers of all kinds, see p300*). While individual shoppers focus on buying just one or two truffles, key customers negotiate with major dealers for booty by the hessian bagful, discussing terms in hushed tones and flashing wads of banknotes. All around, the heady, earthy smell that drives gastronomes wild with desire hangs in the crisp winter air.

If you are tempted to buy, be aware that the *brumale* variety, less intense or refined in aroma and flavour, also makes its appearance in winter; so if you want the real thing, be sure to check that what you are about to buy is indeed a *melanosporum*. A single truffle costing around €50 can make a thrilling dish for four to six people.

The paler, larger summer truffle, *tuberum aestivum*, while pleasant enough, is much less flavoursome than its ritzy winter cousin, which no doubt explains why it commands only a fraction of its price.

In both winter and summer, it is possible to arrange an outing with a truffle hunter and his dog: an intriguing way to spend a couple of hours. Check with truffle town tourist offices for details.

Truffle market, Carpentras

© Camille Moirenc/hemis.fr

Carpentras★
Vaucluse

The superb market that spills through the centre of Carpentras every Friday morning is testament to this town's role as a thriving agricultural centre. But the capital of the Comtat Venaissin has a fine old centre whose interesting buildings are also well worth visiting.

A BIT OF HISTORY

Market centre for a Celtic-Ligurian tribe, then a Gallo-Roman city and a bishopric, which was temporarily moved to Venasque, Carpentras blossomed when the popes came to Provence.

Pope Clement V stayed here frequently from 1309 to 1314, as did the cardinals. Capital of the Comtat Venaissin in 1320, the town profited from papal munificence. It expanded and protected itself, under Innocent VI, with powerful ramparts consisting of 32 towers and 4 gates, demolished in the 19C. With Avignon, Cavaillon and Isle-sur-la-Sorgue, it had a Jewish ghetto up until the Revolution.

The most famous local figure was the 18C Bishop Malachie d'Inguimbert, benefactor and founder of the hospital (Hôtel-Dieu), who also founded, in 1745, the famous library named after him, the Bibliothèque Inguimbertine.

Carpentras grew prosperous from the production of madder, a dye-plant introduced in 1768, and the surrounding plain became a fertile garden when a canal, a branch of the Durance, was built in the 19C, enabling the area to be irrigated.

◂● WALKING TOUR

THE OLD TOWN
Allow 3hr. Start south of town in place Aristide Briand.

Hôtel-Dieu
pl. Aristide Briand. ◂● *Guided tours of the hospital and pharmacy Apr–Oct.* ◉€4. ℘04 90 63 00 78 (tourist office).

▸ **Population:** 29 278.
◔ **Michelin Map:** 332: D-9.
▯ **Info:** 97 place du 25-Août. ℘04 90 63 00 78. www.carpentras-ventoux.com. Ask about 90min tours conducted Apr–Sept.
◔ **Location:** Best town view is from D 950 from Orange (*24km/15mi to the NW*).
▣ **Parking:** Free parking on allée des Platanes.

This majestic building housing the former hospital dates from the 18C. To the left of the chancel, the Baroque chapel houses the tomb of Monseigneur d'Inguimbert, the hospital's founder. The Hôtel-Dieu was built outside the city wall, to the south, so that the sick inmates were not subject to the foul air of the city. The tour includes a visit to the **pharmacy★**, largely in its original state, containing cabinets painted with landscapes and amusing figures, in which there is a large collection of Moustiers faïence (glazed earthenware) jars.

▸ Cross place du 25-Août-1944 and enter the city along rue de la République, a pedestrian street.

Medicine cabinets, Hôtel-Dieu

© S. Sauvignier/MICHELIN

In place Ste-Marthe note the fine 17C and 18C **Classical façade** to the right along rue Moricelly, to the left the **Chapelle du Collège** (r. du Collège; ℘04 90 60 22 36), built in the Jesuit style. It houses contemporary art exhibits.

▷ Continue along rue de la République, into place du Général-de-Gaulle.

Cathédrale St-Siffrein★
r. St-Siffrein.
The cathedral was started in 1404, on the orders of Pope Benedict XIII of Avignon, and is a good example of the southern Gothic style. It was finished in the early 16C, and its façade was completed in the 17C with the Classical doorway. Inside, the balcony on the nave's end wall connects with the bishop's apartments, and from the small room above the first bay he could follow services.

Palais de Justice
pl. du Général-de-Gaulle. ➳Guided *tours (1hr30min) from Apr–Oct: book ahead at the tourist office.* ᴄᴄ€4.
Adjoining the cathedral is the old bishop's palace from the 17C, which now houses the law courts. The halls are decorated with French-style painted ceilings and a frieze of canvases painted in the 17C.

▷ Take a right and go along the south side of the cathedral.

Note the cathedral's Gothic south door (late 15C), known as the **Porte Juive★** or Jewish door, after the Jewish converts who passed through it to be baptised.

▷ Continue around the cathedral's east end via rue de la Poste to reach place d'Inguimbert.

Near the east end of the present church are the remains of the original Romanesque cathedral surmounted by an ornate dome (from the railing, look up to see the twisted column topped by a historiated capital).

Arc de Triomphe
pl. d'Inguimbert.
The Roman municipal arch behind the law courts was probably built in the 1C. Its damaged decorations are particularly interesting on the east face, where two prisoners are chained to a tree hung with military trophies.

▷ Take rue d'Inguimbert to the left, past place du Colonel Mouret, then turn right into rue Raspail.

This road traces the line of the old city walls.

▷ After 50m turn left onto rue des Frères-Laurens.

After running alongside the chapelle des Visitandines (16C), the street comes to some steps, from the top of which there is a good view of the **Auzon valley** with the Dentelles de Montmirail in the distance (ᴸsee Dentelles de Montmirail).

▷ At the bottom of the steps, take bd. Leclerc to the right.

Porte d'Orange
pl. Porte d'Orange.
North of the old town centre, this gateway was one of four fortified gateways leading into Carpentras. It is 26m high, and is all that remains of the fortified wall punctuated by 32 towers built at the end of the 14C.

▷ Take rue de la Porte d'Orange again and turn left into rue des Halles.

Rue des Halles
This street is lined with shopping arcades, making it an ideal place for refuge from the heat of summer. Note the **Tour de l'Horloge** (Clock Tower) at the entrance to the street, a remnant of the first town hall (15C).
For a better view of the clock tower, go into the courtyard terrace of the Atelier de Pierre restaurant (access via rue du Château). Further on, **passage Boyer** opens off to the right. This glass-covered passage was built in 1848 by a group of

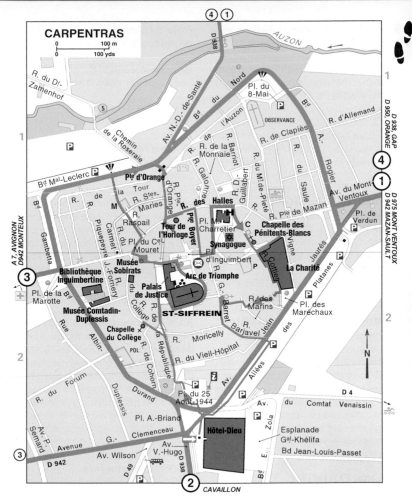

unemployed members of the national workshops, *Ateliers Nationaux*.

▶ At the far end of passage Boyer turn left onto rue d'Inguimbert. This leads into place Maurice Charretier, standing in the place of the old Jewish ghetto. Note the **façade** of the synagogue on the right.

Synagogue★

pl. Maurice-Charretier. ◷*Open: ask for details.* ⊛€4. ◷*Closed Sat–Sun and Jewish holidays.* ℘*04 90 63 39 97.*
The synagogue, dating from 1367, was rebuilt in the 18C. On the first floor is the panelled sanctuary, simple yet richly decorated. On the ground floor is the

oven for baking unleavened bread. In the basement is the pool, dating from the 14C, for women's purification rites.

▶ Rejoin rue des Halles and walk around the town hall into rue Bidauld.

Rue Bidauld leads down to the **Chapelle des Pénitents Blancs**, a 17C chapel with a triangular front door.

▶ Take rue Cottier.

La Charité
77 r. Cottier.
Built in 1669 to shelter the poor, the building today houses temporary exhibits in its cellars *(access via r. Vigne)*.

▷ Head to place des Maréchaux, turn right, and rejoin rue des Marins.

This street is lined with fine mansions, such as the Hôtel de Bassompierre with its caryatids.

▷ Take rue Gaudibert-Barret to the left, an extension of rue Barjavel. Cross avenue Jean Jaurès to rejoin allée des Platanes and return to the Hôtel-Dieu.

ADDITIONAL SIGHTS
Musée Sobirats
112 r. du Collège. ⊙*Open Wed–Mon Apr–Sept 10am–noon, 2–6pm; Oct–Mar by appointment.* ⊛€2. ℘*04 90 63 04 92. www.carpentras.fr.*
Lovely reconstruction of an 18C mansion: furniture, faïences and tapestries.

Musée Comtadin-Duplessis
234 bd Albin-Durand. ⊙*Same hours and prices as Musée Sobirats.*
One level displays regional mementoes, such as coins and seals, local headdresses and bells for cattle and sheep. Another level exhibits a collection of 16C–20C paintings including those by Parrocel, Rigaud and the Carpentras artists Duplessis and Laurens.

🚗 DRIVING TOUR

EASTERN COMTAT
To visualise this 50km/31mi round trip starting from Carpentras, have a look at the map on p313. Allow about half a day.

▷ Leave Carpentras on the southwest side, heading for Monteux.

Monteux
4.5km/3mi W via the D 942.
This market-garden centre was visited by Pope Clement V in the early 14C. A tower remains from the castle where he stayed. Also standing are two gates from the 14C ramparts. The town is also the birthplace of St Gentius, patron saint of

Provençal farmers, who reputedly had the ability to bring on rain.

▷ Leave Monteux to the north and take a right turn down D 87.

Pernes-les-Fontaines★
ⓘ*See Pernes-les-Fontaines.*

▷ Leave Pernes East, via the D 28.

Saint-Didier
Previously used only by hunters, *appeaux* (little whistles used as decoys) have taken on a new lease of life thanks to a new generation of nature lovers. It was in the hills of the Ventoux, in the middle of the 19C, that Théodore Raymond developed his prototypes; today, 80 different types are manufactured in the workshop of his great-grandson Bernard.
👥In his **écomusée des Appeaux (Appeaux Ecomuseum)**, he does **demonstrations**, replicating the sounds of all sorts of animals and birds (from the thrush to the wild boar) by making about 40 *appeaux* vibrate expertly in his mouth (⊙*Open daily 9am–noon, 2–5pm.* ⊛€5 (under 10 free). ℘*04 66 46 28 10. www.appeaux-raymond.com*).

▷ Continue on the D 28.

Venasque★
ⓘ*See Venasque.*

▷ Go north on the D 4 , then bear right on the D 77 until you reach the D 942, which you take on the right.

Mormoiron
Don't miss the 👥**Musée de la musique méchanique** (Mechanical Music Museum) (*Rte de Carpentras (on the right, before the Centre Ville signs).* ♿ ◐*Guided tours (1hr) Wed 3pm.* ⊛€5 (under 12, €4). ℘*04 90 61 75 91*) with its collection of mechanical musical instruments. The mill provides historical background, technical explanations (it may be worth having a look into the

workshop where old instruments are restored), and you can hear a serenade from 1740, an orchestration with 9 instruments from 1900, a fairground organ and a barrel-organ whose handle you may turn yourself.

▶ Continue on the D 942 towards Carpentras.

Mazan

Only a short distance from Carpentras, Mazan is an attractive and interesting little town with a number of good wine estates on its fringes. Sixty-six Gallo-Roman sarcophagi surround the **churchyard** (*pl. du 8-Mai, just before the exit of the village in the direction of Villes-sur-Auzon, following the slope*) of the 12C Notre-Dame-de-Pareloup, which has an underground chapel. From here there is a fine **view★** of the Dentelles de Montmirail, Mont Ventoux and the Montagne de Lure. The **Château de Mazan** once witnessed the extravagant debaucheries of the notorious Marquis de Sade (*now a luxury hotel, see Addresses*). Near the church, the 17C Chapelle des Pénitents Blancs houses a **museum** (*r. Saint-Nazaire Mazan;* ○ *open mid-Jun–mid-Sept 3–6pm;* ○ *closed Tue and public holidays;* ○ *no charge.* ☎ *04 90 69 75 01*) exhibiting Stone Age articles found during the excavations on the south face of Mont Ventoux and a 14C bread oven in the courtyard.

▶ Continue on the D 942 back to Carpentras.

ADDRESSES

◎ STAY

○○ **Chambre d'hôte Bastide Ste-Agnès** – *1043 chemin de la Fourtrouse. 3km/2mi NE via D 974 for Bédoin and D 13 for Caromb.* ☎ *04 90 60 03 01. www.sainte-agnes.com.* ☒☐. *5 rooms.* This old country house of mellow stone is imbued with Provençal tradition, from antique floor tiles to a scented garden. Rooms are

simple but pleasant. Pretty swimming pool in what used to be the water cistern.

○○ **Hôtel du Fiacre** – *153 r. Vigne. -* ☎ *04 90 63 03 15. www.hotel-du-fiacre.com.* ☐. *18 rooms.* Housed in an 18C mansion in the Old Town, this hotel preserves its original bourgeois atmosphere. The décor is in a mixture of styles, but the guest rooms, spacious and comfortable, are all individually appointed. Some rooms have a pleasant patio or a private balcony.

○○○ **Safari Hôtel** – *1060 av. J.H.-Fabre.* ☎ *04 90 63 35 35. www.safarihotel.fr.* ☒ ☐. *29 rooms.* Situated at the entrance of town, near the hospital, this new property features a sleek, contemporary style throughout the interior. Spacious bedrooms are decorated in soothing pastels, while the restaurant/bar features crisp white furnishings and boldly colored wall art. There's an on-site spa and outdoor pool.

○○○○ **Château de Mazan** – *pl. Napoléon, 84380 Mazan, 21km/13mi N.* ☎ *04 90 69 62 61. www.chateaudemazan.com.* ☒☐. *30 rooms. Restaurant* ○○○○ *closed Jan–early Mar, Tue, Mon in spring and fall.* Built in 1720 by the family of the Marquis de Sade (who visited in 1772), this imposing place marries 18C grandeur with 21C comfort. Confident, modern cuisine is served in a splendid dining room or on an elegant terrace. Swimming pool.

♀/EAT

○○○ **La Petite Fontaine** – *13 pl. du Col.-Mouret.* ☎ *04 90 60 77 83. Closed 2 weeks in Feb, 3 weeks in Nov, Wed, Sun.* Small dining room decorated with several paintings on the theme of Provence. Food is traditional Provençal cuisine. You can eat lunch on the terrace.

○○○ **Chez Serge** – *90 r. Cottier.* ☎ *04 90 63 21 24. www.chez-serge.com.* A bistro with simple but trendy décor, and the same is true of the food which ranges from pizzas to more elaborate dishes. Serge is a big fan of summer truffles, and, as an ex-sommelier, runs an interesting wine list.

○○○ **Le Saule Pleureur** – *145 chemin de Beauregard, 84180 Monteux, 23km/ 14.3mi NW.* ☎ *04 90 62 01 35. www.le-saule-pleureur.fr. Closed 2–8 Jan, Sat lunch, Sun eve, and Mon apart from public holidays and 3 Jun–27 Sept.* Set back a little from a busy road, this restaurant is housed within a villa surrounded by a large garden. The kitchen is noted for creative, fashionable cuisine.

TAKING A BREAK

Pâtisserie Jouvaud – *40 r. de l'Éveché. ℘04 90 63 15 38. Open Tue–Sun 9am–7.30pm, Mon 10.30am–7.30pm.* This is the perfect place to pause for tea, coffee or superb ice cream. Exceptionally delicious cakes, chocolates and candied fruits are all made on the spot. Presents you buy will be exquisitely wrapped.

SHOPPING

Market – *Throughout town centre, Fri 8am–12.30pm.* Running since 1155, the Carpentras market is so outstanding that it was elected *marché exceptionnel* in 1996. There is also a producers' evening market in summer *(square de Champeville, Apr–Sept, Tue 5–7pm).*

Truffle Market – *pl. Artistide Briand. Mid-Nov–Mar Fri 9am, for about 1hr. ℘04 90 60 33 33. www.carpentras.fr.* Although essentially for dealers, this important truffle market is fascinating to observe.

👥 **Confiserie du Mont-Ventoux** – *1184 av. Dwight-Eisenhower. ℘04 90 63 05 25. www.berlingots.net. Open Tue–Sat 9am–noon, 2–6.45pm. Closed 1 week in Feb, 1 week in Jun and public holidays.* Thierry Vial is one of the very few confectioners still using artisan methods to make top-quality *berlingots,* the hard, striped sweets which have been a Carpentras speciality since the 14C. Stop by in the morning to watch them being made.

Chocolaterie Clavel – *allées Jean-Jaurès. ℘04 90 29 70 39. Open Tue–Sat 8.30am–12.30pm, 2.30–7pm.* In the premises previously occupied by the famous Confiserie Bono, Serge Clavel continues to make *fruits confits* (candied fruits) in the traditional, artisan way (which can involve 10–12 boilings in sugar syrup). He also makes *berlingots de Carpentras.*

Nougats Silvain – *rte de Venasque, 84210 Saint-Didier. ℘04 90 66 09 57. Open Jul–Aug daily 10am–noon, 3–7pm.* The Silvain brothers make some of the very best nougat in Provence, using almonds, honey and fruits from their own farm. Visitors can watch the process and buy nougat in the shop. There is also an ice cream parlour.

EVENTS

Trans'Art – The umbrella name for a whole range of festivals that run through the summer, including music, theatre, dance and street performances. *Details from the tourist office.*

Festival of Jewish Music – *Details from tourist office.* Early August, in the synagogue and the Espace culturel.

Truffle and Wine Festival – Truffle tastings, cooking demonstrations and more on the first weekend in Feb.

TOURS

Guides conduct 90min tours Apr–Sept. *Enquire at the tourist office.*

Berlingots

© Philippe Michel/age fotostock

Pernes-les-Fontaines★

Vaucluse

A town with 40 fountains, Pernes-les-Fontaines is a pretty place where water features decorate many small streets and squares. Most of them were built in the middle of the 18C, following the discovery of a large spring near Chapelle St-Roch. The older fountains have since been restored. Pernes-les-Fontaines was the capital of Comtat Venaissin (968–1320) before Carpentras. Its economy depends mainly on fruit-growing. Cherries, strawberries (including the famous *fraises de Carpentras*), melons, grapes and almonds are especially abundant.

🐾 WALKING TOUR

Allow 1hr. Take the route for the old town below or get the free "Circuit des Fontaines" map from the tourist office.

▷ Start at the church of Notre-Dame de Nazareth.

Notre-Dame de Nazareth
pl. Église Notre-Dame.
The oldest parts of the church date from the late 11C. Opposite, the willow-shaded River Nesque is spanned by an old bridge, which leads to the Porte Notre-Dame.

Porte Notre-Dame★
On one of the bridge's piles is the small 16C chapel of Notre-Dame-des-Grâces with its elegant cast-iron bell tower. On the left is the 17C covered market.

Fontaine du Cormoran
Quai de Verdun.
This, the most interesting of the fountains in Pernes (**E** *on map*), owes its name to the cormorant with outspread wings which is perched on top of it. The base is decorated with low reliefs and masks.

▶ **Population:** 10 405.
⚭ **Michelin Map:** 332: D-10.
🚺 **Info:** place Gabriel Moutte, Pernes-les-Fontaines. ℘04 90 61 31 04. www.tourisme-pernes.fr.
🅿 **Parking:** Best to park in the car park near the tourist office.
👓 **Don't Miss:** The fountains – there are 40 of them!

▷ Turn right onto rue Victor-Hugo, which runs parallel to the Nesque River. Take rue de Brancas and immediately turn right.

Tour de l'Horloge
Montée du Donjon. 🕐*Open daily late Apr–Oct 9am–5pm (except in bad weather).* ✍*No charge.* ℘*04 90 61 31 04. www.tourisme-pernes.fr.*
This keep was part of the fortified wall which protected the castle of the Counts of Toulouse. From the top of the clock tower there is a panorama to the west over the Comtat plain and the countryside around Avignon; in the background, to the north and east,

One of many fountains in town

© S. Sauvignier/MICHELIN

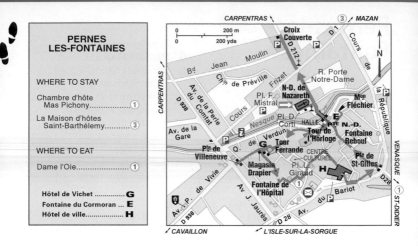

PERNES LES-FONTAINES

WHERE TO STAY

Chambre d'hôte
Mas Pichony.................(1)

La Maison d'hôtes
Saint-Barthélemy..........(3)

WHERE TO EAT

Dame l'Oie.....................(1)

Hôtel de Vichet ....**G**
Fontaine du Cormoran ... **E**
Hôtel de ville..................**H**

the Dentelles de Montmirail and Mont Ventoux.

◗ Continue down rue Victor-Hugo where you will pass in front of the Clos de Verdun, a minuscule park which stands on the site of an old olive press.

Tour Ferrande
r. Victor-Hugo. ◗◗*Guided tours (1hr) mid-Jun–mid-Sept by appointment with the tourist office.* €2. ℘04 90 61 31 04. This 13C tower overlooks a small square which contains the Gigot fountain. Go up a staircase to the third floor, which is decorated with 13C frescoes depicting the Virgin and Child, St Christopher and Charles of Anjou.

◗ Go to the end of rue Gambetta.

Porte de Villeneuve
This 16C gate is flanked by two round, machicolated towers.

◗ Turn back and take rue de la République on the right.

On the corner of rue Gambetta and rue de la République, the magasin Drapier houses the Musée du Costume Comtadin. Opposite, notice the 16C Hôtel de Vichet with its wrought-iron balcony.

◗ Take rue de la République and turn right.

13C frescoes, Tour Ferrande

© S. Sauvignier/MICHELIN

Maison du Costume Comtadin

🕐*Open end Jun–mid-Sept 10am–12.30pm, 3–6.30pm; May–end Jun 3–6.30pm.* 🕐*Closed Tue and Oct–Apr.* ✎*No charge.* ✆*04 90 61 45 14.*
On the ground floor, the shop still looks much as a drapery might have looked in the 19C. The shelves are filled with costumes, headwear, traditional Comtadin shawls and other garments. On the first floor, 11 typical costumes from past times (peasant, bourgeois, noble and so on) were all donated by Pernes families. On the top floor, a workshop making traditional costumes is open to the public a few afternoons each week.

Opposite, a doorway topped with an elegant wrought-iron balcony leads to the 16C **Hôtel de Vichet** (G). Pass in front of the 17C Hôtel de Villefranche. Turn left on to rue Barrau, where the **fontaine de l'Hôpital**, dating from 1760, faces the hôtel of the ducs de Berton, lords of Crillon. Soon you reach place Louis-Giraud where the centre culturel des Augustins has been set up in an old church.

▶ Follow rue des Istres until you reach place des Comtes-de-Toulouse, then turn right on to narrow rue Brancas.

Hôtel de Ville

pl. Aristide Briand. 🕐*Open Mon–Fri 8.30am–noon, 1.15–5.15pm (Fri until 4pm).* 🕐*Closed public holidays.* ✎*No charge.* ✆*04 90 61 31 04.*
This 17C mansion (H) once belonged to the Dukes of Brancas. The courtyard is further enhanced by a striking fountain and its vast portico (1750). In fine 17C vaulted cellars is the little **Musée Comtadin du Cycle** (🕐*open daily except Tue Jul–Aug 10am–12.30pm, 3–6.30pm; May–Jun and Sept 3–6.30pm*). About 50 old bicycles are exhibited, the oldest of which is a Grand Bi dating from 1870.

▶ Turn left into rue du Bariot, which leads to Porte de St-Gilles.

Porte de St-Gilles

This square tower was part of the 14C fortifications.

▶ Cross the tower and continue towards rue Raspail.

At no 214, set back on the right, lies the Hôtel de Jocas with its beautiful Louis XV doorway. Note the 17C **Fontaine Reboul**, also known as the "Grand' Font" (Big Fount), with its fish-scale ornamentation.

▶ Before returning to porte Notre-Dame, turn right on to place Fléchier.

Maison Fléchier

🕐*Open daily except Tue: Jul–Aug 10am–12.30pm, 3–6.30pm; May–Jun and Sept 3–6.30pm; rest of year call for hours.* 🕐*Closed 1 May and 25 Dec.* ✎*No charge.* ✆*04 90 61 45 14.*
Birthplace of orator Esprit Fléchier, this 17C mansion celebrates Provençal traditions on two floors. There is a 19C dining room where the table is laid for the Christmas *gros souper*; a bedroom evoking the good wishes bestowed on a new baby; the re-created workshop of a *santonnier,* and also of a *magnanerie* (where silk worms were raised).

▶ Return to porte Notre-Dame, cross the bridge and continue for about 200m after cours Frizet.

Croix Couverte

This elegant four-sided monument was erected in the 15C by Pierre de Boët, a native of Pernes.

ADDRESSES

🛏 STAY

🛏 **Maison d'hôtes Saint-Barthélemy** – *1623 chemin de la Roque.* ✆*04 90 66 47 79.* ⌲🅿. *5 rooms.* This fine Provençal mas stands in parkland with a waterfall. Attractive rooms and good breakfasts.

⊜⊜⊜ **Chambre d'hôte Mas Pichony** – *1454 rte de St-Didier. ℘04 90 61 56 11. www.maspichony.com. Closed Nov–Mar.* 🅿🍽🗲. *5 rooms. Table d'hôte* ⊜⊜⊜. From this 17C Provençal farmhouse, guests get a great view of Mont Ventoux: the house, which is surrounded by vineyards, is picture-postcard Provence. Rooms are comfortable and alluring.

ᵠ/ EAT

⊜⊜ **Dame l'Oie** – *56 r. Troubadour, Durand. Open daily except Mon lunch and Sun evening. Set-price lunch.* This typically Provençal-style restaurant has a cheerful ambiance and a whimsical collection of decorative geese. Diners can savour classic flavours in lamb, rabbit, chicken, fish and other dishes along with local wines.

⊜⊜⊜ **Au Fils du Temps** – *pl. Louis Giraud. ℘04 90 30 09 48. Closed Tue, Wed lunch all year, Mon–Thu lunch in Jul–Aug.* The ideal time to visit this charming little *bistro-gastro* is summer, when you can eat outside soothed by the sound of the square's fountain. Flavoursome cooking with original touches.

TAKING A BREAK

Le Haricot magique – *95 pl. Louis-Giraud. ℘04 88 50 85 05. www.leharicot magique.com. Open Tue–Fri 3pm–6.30pm, Sat 10.30am–1pm, 3pm–6.30pm. Closed 15–31 Aug.* This tearoom and gallery offers numerous film screenings and exhibitions. Organic produce.

Venasque★

Vaucluse

Built on the edge of a cliff which towers above the valley of the Nesque, Venasque is a *village perché* which held an important defensive position for thousands of years. Ranked among the most beautiful villages in France, it has strikingly unified architecture which includes fine houses and attractive fountains as well as the famous Baptistry which is one of France's oldest religious buildings. Many houses have been tastefully restored, in some instances by the painters and potters who have been capitvated by Venasque's charm.

▶ **Population:** 1 156.
🖢 **Michelin Map:** 332: D-10.
🖪 **Info:** Grand'Rue, Venasque. ℘04 90 66 11 66. www.tourisme-venasque.com.
🆎 **Don't Miss:** The Baptistry.
🕓 **Timing:** Allow 2hr.

A BIT OF HISTORY

The village was, before Carpentras, the Comtat's bishopric and gave its name to the Comtat Venaissin. Located between the Rhône and Durance rivers and Mont Ventoux, the territory was under the Counts of Toulouse's rule; and like all the county's other possessions it was affected by the Albigensian heresy and united under the Crown in 1271. It was ceded three years later to Pope Gregory X by Philip III, the Bold, and remained under papal authority until 1791 when it once again became part of France.

 WALKING TOUR

Stroll through the peaceful streets of the village, among artists' workshops and well-maintained houses, many of them decorated with pergolas and window boxes. During the walk, admire **place des Fontaines** and the small streets branching off it. From **esplanade de la Planette** and **Tours Sarrasines**, remains of medieval fortifications, there are fine views to be had of Mont Ventoux and the Dentelles de Montmirail.

Baptistry★

Entrance right of the presbytery.
🕓*Open Apr–Oct 9am–1pm, 2–6.30pm; Nov–Mar 9.15am–1pm, 2–5pm.*

Baptistry

© Gerth Roland/age fotostock

🕒*Closed mid-Dec–early Jan.* 🎫€3.
📞*04 90 66 62 01. www.venasque.fr.*
Built during the 6C and remodelled in
the 11C, this Baptistry ranks alongside
those of Aix-en-Provence, Fréjus, Poitiers and Riez as one of the most ancient
religious edifices in France. The Greek
cross plan, with groined vaulting over
the centre square, has unequal arms
ending in apsidal chapels, each oven-
vaulted with blind arcading on slender
marble columns with Antique or, in the
case of the east apsidal chapel, Merovingian capitals. The hollow in the floor
was for the font.

Église Notre-Dame
The church, which is connected to the
Baptistry by a long corridor, contains
a 17C carved altarpiece and a 15C
Avignon School **Crucifixion★**.

EXCURSION
Route des Gorges
10km/6mi E on the D 4 towards Apt.
This route goes up the gorges through
the **Forêt de Venasque**. After climbing
400m the road reaches **Col de Murs** pass
(alt 627m). Beyond the pass there are
views of the Apt basin and Roussillon.

ADDRESSES

🛏 STAY
😊😊 **Hôtel Restaurant Les Remparts –**
r. Haute, 84210 Venasque. 📞*04 90 66 02 79.*
www.hotellesremparts.com. Closed mid-Nov
–mid-Mar. 🅿. *8 rooms. Restaurant*😊😊.
This quaint hotel is ensconced within old
fortifications built on the hilltop village.
Eat in the restaurant or out on the terrace:
both permit remarkable views. Guest
rooms are simply furnished but charming,
with private bathrooms.

🍴 EAT
😊😊😊 **Auberge du Beaucet –** *r. Coste*
Chaude, 84210 Le Beaucet. 📞*04 90 66 10 82.*
www.aubergedubeaucet.fr. Closed Sun
dinner, Mon, and Tue lunch, mid–end
Nov, 6 Jan–6 Feb. This well-established
restaurant up in the centre of the nearby
village of Le Beaucet attracts customers
from the Comtat Venaissin and further
afield. Carefully prepared, elegantly
presented food is matched by a well-
chosen wine list. Bread comes from the
wonderful Boulangerie du Beaucet at the
foot of the hill.

Mont Ventoux★★★

Vaucluse

With its bold, sloping silhouette and its crown of white limestone (or, in winter, snow), Mont Ventoux dominates the landscape. The climb to its summit is one of the loveliest excursions in Provence, providing magnificent views over the entire countryside. In summer, fields of lavender and wheat look like a vast chequerboard of purple and gold spread out at the mountain's foot. With a height of only 1 909m, Mont Ventoux cannot rival the Alps for altitude; yet its isolated situation, far from any rival peak, and its broad, solid outline give it an astonishing majesty. Every year it provides riders in the *Tour de France* with one of the most gruelling stages in the race.

🚗 DRIVING TOUR

THE GIANT OF PROVENCE

To visualise this 78km/49mi circuit starting from Carpentras, have a look at the map on p313. Allow about 1hr30min, excluding time for stops.

▶ Leave Carpentras on the D938 leading north.

- ⚲ **Michelin Map:** 332: E-8.
- 🗉 **Info:** Espace Marie-Louis-Gravier, Bédoin. ℘04 90 65 63 95. www.bedoin.org.
- ▶ **Location:** Three ways to drive to the summit: Malaucène to the west, Bedoin to the south (D 974) and Sault to the east.
- 🕐 **Timing:** Allow half a day to do the circuit described.

Le Barroux

🅿 *Car park at entrance to the village.*
This picturesque village, with sloping streets, is dominated by the lofty silhouette of its **castle** (🕐*open Apr–May Sat–Sun 10am–7pm; Jun 2.30–7pm; Jul–Sept 10am–7pm; Oct 2–6pm.* 🕐*closed Oct–Mar.* ⊚€5. ℘04 90 62 35 21. *www.chateau-du-barroux.com*). This huge quadrilateral construction, flanked by round towers, originally (12C) guarded the Comtat Venaisson plain. Remodelled in the Renaissance, burnt down during World War II, then restored once more, the castle was, until the 18C, the seat of several lordships, including that of Rovigliasc (note the coats of arms above the square tower doorway). After visiting the chapel, the lower rooms and the guard room, walk through the different floors, where contemporary exhibitions are on display in several of the rooms. There is a fine view from the gardens.

Aerial view of Mont Ventoux

© Camille Moirenc/hemis.fr

Malaucène

This typical Provençal town is surrounded by an avenue shaded by plane trees. The 14C **fortified church** was once a part of the ramparts. Go through **Porte Soubeyran**, the gate beside the church, into the old village of fountains and oratories, with a belfry crowned by a wrought-iron bell cage. The path to the left of the church to the Calvary for a view of Mont Ventoux.

◐ Take a right on to D 974.

Source Vauclusienne du Groseau

This spring forms a pool of clear water as it emerges from several fissures at the foot of a steep slope (over 100m), beneath trees to the left of the road. The Romans built an aqueduct to carry the water to Vaison-la-Romaine.

The road continues up the northern slope revealing a good view of the Vaucluse plateau, climbing up the steepest and most ravined face of the mountain; it crosses pastures and pinewoods near the Mont Serein refuge. The viewpoint beyond the Ramayettes hut offers a fine **view★** of the Ouvèze and Groseau valleys, the Massif des Baronnies and Plate summit.

Mont Serein

This is a popular place among sports enthusiasts, both in summer, for walks, and in winter, for skiing (◐ *see Activities, p329*). The vast panorama that opens up as you climb includes the Dentelles de Montmirail and the Alps. Two long hairpin bends lead to the top.

Mont Ventoux Summit★★★

In summer the summit may be shrouded in cloud or midday mist; it is advisable to set out early or remain at the top until sunset. In winter the atmosphere tends to be clearer, but the last stage of the ascent may well have to be made on skis.

The summit, which rises to an altitude of 1 909m, is spiked with scientific equipment: an air force radar station and a television mast.

The view from the car park extends over the Alps, particularly the Vercors range *(viewing table)*. The platform on the south side offers a **panorama★★★** *(viewing table)*, which swings from the Pelvoux massif to the Cévennes by way of the Luberon, Ste-Victoire, the Chaîne de l'Estaque, Marseille, the Étang de Berre, the Alpilles and the Rhône valley. On very clear days, the Canigou is visible to the southwest in the Pyrenees. At night the Provençal plain is transformed into a dark carpet studded with clusters of glittering lights. The sight extends to the Étang de Berre and coast where lighthouses punctuate the darkness.

The corniche road, which winds down the south face through a vast tract of shining white shingle to woods, is the oldest road built (c.1885) to serve the observatory. In 22km/13.7mi of hairpin bends to Bédoin (alt 310m), it descends 1 600m.

Three **ascent routes** are suggested: From **Bédoin** *(from the hamlet of Ste-Colombe, 4km/2.5mi from Bédoin)*, the climb of 1 450m in elevation is difficult, so allow 4hr30min (yellow and white and red markers). Plan to leave a vehicle at the arrival point and allow 3hr30min for the descent.

The Weather

There is nearly always a wind on Mont Ventoux, as its name suggests (*vent* means wind), particularly when the *mistral* is blowing. The temperature at the top is on average 11°C/20°F lower than at the foot; rainfall is twice as heavy and filters through the fissured limestone of the Vaucluse plateau. In winter the temperature may drop at the observatory to -27°C/-17°F, the mountain is usually snow-capped above 1 300m from December to April, and the slopes at Mont Serein on the north side and Chalet-Reynard on the south provide good skiing. ☎08 92 68 24 84 *for weather info.*

Flora

The lower slopes of Mont Ventoux are covered with trees and plants typical of Provence, while at the summit polar species such as Spitzbergen saxifrage and Icelandic poppy flourish. The flowers are at their best in early July. The forests which once covered the mountainside were felled from the 16C on, to supply the naval shipyards in Toulon; replanting has continued since 1860. Aleppo pine, holm and downy oaks, cedar, beech, pitch pine, fir and larch form a forest cover which at about 1 600m is replaced by a vast field of white shingle. During the autumn a climb to the top through a multicoloured landscape is enchanting.

From **Mont-Serein** (campsite east end of the station), an intermediate-level ascent of 500m elevation requires 2hr (yellow, then white/red markers).

From **Brantes** (from the village of Frache, opposite Brantes): allow 5-6hr for a difficult-level ascent; take the trail that skirts the Serres-Gros, then the GR9, which joins the Mont-Serein GR4, from which point it climbs to the summit.

Le Chalet-Reynard

Excellent local slopes have made Le Chalet-Reynard a popular resort for skiers from Avignon, Carpentras and other nearby towns.

The road goes through the forest; pine trees, beeches, oaks and cedars give way to vines, peach and cherry orchards and a few small olive groves. The view extends across the Comtadin plain; beyond the Vaucluse plateau you can see the Luberon.

▶ Leave the D 164 on the left to return to Sault (&see Sault) by the Nesque Valley.

St-Estève

From the famous sharp bend, now straightened, which featured in the Ventoux car racing competition to the summit, there is a good **view★** on the right of the Dentelles de Montmirail, the Comtat plain, and left onto the Vaucluse plateau.

Bédoin

This village, which is perched on a hill, has picturesque small streets, leading to the classical Jesuit-style church, which contains several elegant altars.

▶ Take the D 138.

Flowers at the summit of Mont Ventoux

© Christian Mueringer/Dreamstime.com

Crillon-le-Brave

On an overhang facing Mont Ventoux, Crillon-le-Brave is a quaint perched village with remains of former fortifications.

▶ Continue on the D 138.

Caromb

Surrounded by orchards and olive groves, this likeable village is slightly off the main tourist trail. There are great views from the **du Paty dam**, the oldest dam in France, built for irrigation in 1766.

▶ Return to Carpentras on the D 938.

ADDRESSES

🏨 STAY

Le Chalet Liotard – *Station du Mt-Serein, 84340 Beaumont-du-Ventoux. ℘04 90 60 68 38. www.chaletliotard.fr.* 🅿. *8 rooms. Restaurant*🍽. The ambience comes straight from the mountains: family rooms with pine bunks, rustic chalet look and restaurant specialising in robust, sustaining dishes.

Hôtel La Garance – *Sainte-Colombe, 84410 Bédoin. ℘04 9012 81 00. www.lagarance.fr.* ♿🅿. *Open 1 Apr–31 Oct. WiFi. 13 rooms.* A restored old farm in a hamlet surrounded by vines and orchards, overlooked by Mont Ventoux. The rooms have contemporary furniture, Provençal colours and old floors. Those at the back are preferable, with a view of the "Giant of Provence". Swimming pool.

Domaine des Tilleuls – *Rte du Mont-Ventoux (D 974), 84340 Malaucène. ℘04 90 65 22 31. www.hotel-domaine destilleuls.com.* 🅿👶. *19 rooms.* In the heart of the village, this impressive, tastefully renovated building offers modern and personalized rooms. In the large grounds, a few sunloungers and hammocks are scattered among the trees. Enjoy other amenities such as pétanque, swing and a home accessories shop.

Hotel Crillon-le-Brave – *pl. de l'Église, 84410 Crillon-le-Brave. ℘04 90 65 61 61. www.crillonlebrave.com. Closed Dec–early Mar. 34 rooms. Restaurant*🍽. This alluring hotel has been created out of a cluster of half a dozen old houses at the top of the village. The rooms are extremely comfortable and beautifully decorated in a low-key, modern style with Provençal touches. Excellent cuisine served in a lovely vaulted dining room; elegant Italian garden and fantastic terrace with immense views.

🍽 EAT

Le Vieux Four – *Le Village, 84410 Crillon-le-Brave. ℘04 90 12 81 39. Closed 11 Nov–13 Feb, Jun and lunch except Sun.* 🏃🍽. A dynamic young chef has set up this restaurant in the old village bakery. She will welcome you into the bakehouse, where she has retained the ovens, or onto the terrace on the remparts, from which there is a fine view of Mont Ventoux.

Le Mas des Vignes – *Au virage de St-Estéve, 84410 Bédoin. 6km/3.7mi E of Bédoin. ℘04 90 65 63 91.* 🅿🍽. *Closed Dec–Mar, Jul–Aug lunch except Sun and public holidays, Mon except in Jul–Aug; Tue.* From this pretty *mas* overlooking the valley, the view extends as far as the Dentelles de Montmirail and the Comtat plain. Enjoy the simple cooking in the dining room or on the terrace.

ACTIVITIES

Cycling – Two guides detailing circuits for all levels are available from tourist offices.

Horse-riding centre Le Ménèque – *583 rte du Ménèque. 9km/5.6mi E of Bédoin. ℘04 90 65 66 39. Closed Thu afternoon.* Horse-riding excursions and lessons.

Night climbs – The tourist offices of Bédoin and Malaucène organise night climbs (3hr) on Fridays in Jul and Aug to see the sunrise from the summit.

Winter sports – *Details from tourist office of Beaumont-du-Ventoux: ℘04 90 65 21 13, or visitor centre: ℘04 90 63 42 02. www.stationdumontserein.com.* Between December and April Mont Ventoux is capped with snow, providing excellent terrain for winter sports. On the north slope, at Mont Serein, there is snow skiing with mechanical lifts.

Safran des Papes – *Domaine de la Madelène, Rte de Malaucène, 84410 Bédoin. ℘06 81 30 84 13.* Besides buying saffron here, you can learn how to cultivate it by taking a course in this beautiful domaine at the foot of Mont Ventoux. The saffron is grown on terraces around a Romanesque chapel.

Sault

Vaucluse

The small town of Sault stands high up on a rock promontory towering over the Val de Sault between Ventoux, Lure and Luberon. Its position makes it an ideal base for excursions to Mont Ventoux. Sault is at the centre of an important lavender- and wheat-growing region associated especially with *petit épeautre*, an ancient, nutty grain rather like spelt which is currently undergoing a revival. The area is also famous for its lamb (which carries a red label), as well as for nougat and honey.

▶ **Population:** 1 362.
Michelin Map: 332: F-9.
Info: Avenue de la Promenade, Sault. 04 90 64 01 21. www.saultenprovence.com.

SIGHTS
Old Town
There is a signposted one-hour walk through the old town, under the title *1hr sur les pas du loup*. A free leaflet is available from the tourist office.

Museum
r. du Musée. Open Jul–Aug Mon–Sat 3–6pm. No charge. 04 90 64 02 30. Located on the first floor of the library, the museum contains prehistoric and Gallo-Roman remains, coins, arms, geological finds and a collection of old documents, as well as a mummy and other Egyptian artefacts.

Centre de découverte de la nature et du patrimoine cynégétique (Nature and Hunting heritage discovery centre)
Av. de l'Oratoire. Open daily Jul–Aug 10am–noon, 3–7pm; Sept–Jun 10am–noon, 2–6pm. Closed Sat–Sun, mid-Dec–mid-Feb and public holidays. €3. 04 90 64 13 96.
With interactive screens, slides and posters, this centre provides insights into the flora, fauna and geology of the region as well as traditional activities (farming, hunting etc) and local produce (honey, lavender). Permanent and temporary exhibits.

DRIVING TOURS

MONT VENTOUX★★★
Allow 2hr – ascent via the eastern face. Leave Sault on the D 164 and join route at Le Chalet-Reynard. See Mont Ventoux.

PLATEAU D'ALBION
Round trip of 30km/18.6mi – 1hr30min.

▷ Leave Sault on the D 30 towards St-Christol.

The Albion plateau, with its fissured calcareous landscape, has all the physical characteristics of a limestone *causse*. Over 200 underground caves or *avens* have been discovered here, many with narrow openings which are difficult to spot. The most beautiful viewed from above is the "Crirvi" cave near St-Christol; the deepest in the region include the Aven Jean-Nouveau with its 168m vertical shaft at its entrance, and the 600m-deep Aven Autran, also near St-Christol, with abundant water flowing at its base. The distinctive feature of these caves is their ability to absorb rainwater down into the branches of an underground system buried deep in the calcareous rock: the main branch of this vast system emerges in the famous Fontaine-de-Vaucluse.

Aurel
From the D 950 the village, overlooking the Sault plain and its fields of lavender, appears suddenly below, along with its old fortifications and robust church of light-coloured stone. The source of the Nesque River is close to Aurel at Les Fontaines.

▶ Leave Aurel going west on the D 95, then take the D 1, and finally, on the left, the D 950.

Saint-Trinit

This 12C church is all that remains of an old medieval priory which was accountable to the Abbaye St-André at Villeneuve-lez-Avignon. It is a fine example of Romansque architecture in Haute Provence.

Saint-Christol

This village has several lavender distilleries (not open for visits, however, whereas two in Sault do accept visitors), and a beautiful Romanesque **church** built in the 12C (a second nave was added in the 17C). Interesting decoration on the apse, featuring creatures of fantasy, and altar carvings dating from the Carolingian period.

▶ Leaving Saint-Christol, take the D 34 towards Lagarde-d'Apt.

The road climbs steeply up to the plateau, at 1 100m of altitude, through a landscape dominated by Mont Ventoux and, in the distance, the Alps, towards **Lagarde-d'Apt**.

Sirene Observatory

Before the sign marking the entrance to Lagarde-d'Apt, after the small road leading to Notre-Dame-de-Lamaron. ✎ *Group visits with advance booking; check the website for details.* ✆ *04 90 75 04 17. www.obs-sirene.com.*
"A silo rehabilitated for starry nights": such is the poetic description of this observatory, housed in a former military post and benefiting from 360° views as well as extraordinarily pure air. It's the ideal place to discover the beauty of the sky at night, thanks especially to a fully automated telescope.

▶ Follow the D 34 in the opposite direction, then go left on to the D 245 to return to Sault.

GORGES DE LA NESQUE★★
75km/46.6mi. Allow about 3hr.

▶ Leave Sault to the SE along the D 942, a scenic road that runs along the Nesque River.

The River Nesque has cut a spectacular gorge through the calcareous rock of the Vaucluse plateau, especially in its picturesque upper reaches. It rises on the east face of Mont Ventoux and after some 70km/43mi flows into a tributary of the Sorgue, west of Pernes-les-Fontaines.

Monieux

This picturesque old village perched above the Nesque is overlooked by a high 12C tower connected to the village by what remains of a defensive wall. Some of the village's medieval houses have retained their old doors. A little truffle museum, the **Musée de la Truffe du Ventoux**, at nearby Le Moustier is well worth a visit. (⊙*open Mon–Fri 9am–noon, 2–6pm.* ✆ *no charge.* ✆*04 90 64 16 67).*

The Aiguiers of the Pays de Sault

Evidence of a harsh way of life without much help from nature, **aiguiers** were hollowed out of the ground by farmers to collect run-off water, sometimes preceded by an impluvium and fed by channels cut into the rock. Often covered by dry-stone vaulting (in much the same way as the *bories* of the Luberon), they no doubt existed primarily to water animals, but also in certain cases to provide drinking water to people living in isolated places. You can see them in the Gorges de la Nesque (the aiguiers of Puits-Verrier, Fayol and Les Annelles; then, continuing on from those at Castellaras, a path leads to the superb aiguiers of the Champ-de-Sicaude).

Gorges de la Nesque

© Catherine Hansen/Photononstop

Gorges de la Nesque ★★

🚶 *3hr circuit marked in yellow, red and white (GR 9), 9km/5.5mi. Only for serious walkers as there are some steep sections. Starting point is the Monieux reservoir ("plan d'eau").*

The beauty of this delightful walk is that it reveals a landscape dominated by olive trees and green oaks, very different from what is to be seen on the D 942. Go along the left bank, following the direction "chapelle Saint-Michel", then cross the fast-flowing river. Opposite you on the right bank is the **troglodyte chapelle Saint-Michel**, a Romanesque building tucked under a rock. You will be moved by the beauty of its simple architecture and by the little altar with a statue of the archangel flooring the dragon. The path continues on the right bank. A steep climb leads back to the D 942. If you go left, you can reach the Castellaras viewpoint in 15min; going straight ahead, it's a 30min walk back to Monieux.

◖ Leaving Monieux on the south side, take the first turn on the right towards the reservoir (signposted "plan d'eau"). Go around it. At the stop sign, turn right towards "Méthamis" and continue on this road for 10km/6mi until you reach the Saint-Hubert hostel. Park there.

Saint-Hubert botanical trail

🚶 *Allow 2h30min for 4.5km/2.8mi circuit; easy.* This well-signposted walk has panels at intervals to explain the local flora, with details of the many different types of plants to be found in the biosphere of Mont Ventoux. Halfway along, you will see the ruins of a 15C farmhouse constructed with dry-stone walls.

◖ Return to the Gorges de la Nesque the way that you came.

Castellaras Viewpoint (Belvédère)★★

Alt 734m.

The viewpoint *(left of the road)*, signalled by a stela bearing verses from Mistral's *Calendau*, overlooks the gorges and the jagged **Cire rock** (872m high). The descent begins with a passage through three tunnels, between which the road affords beautiful views of the site. At this point the Nesque runs in a cleft buried so deep in lush vegetation that only the murmuring of the fast-flowing crystal-clear waters over its pebble-strewn bed can be heard.

The D 942 moves slightly away from the gorge to cross the Coste Chaude coomb. At the exit to the fourth tunnel there is a good **view** back along the gorge to the Rocher du Cire. The road runs below the ruined hamlet of Fayol, buried beneath luxuriant Provençal vegetation. The landscape then changes suddenly as the river emerges into the Comtat Venaissin plain, and the horizon expands to include Mont Ventoux to the east and Carpentras and its countryside straight ahead.

The beautiful Hermitage coomb leads to the village of **Villes-sur-Auzon**, an important agricultural centre which lies on the wooded slopes of Mont Ventoux. It is centred on a large square overlooked by old houses and is ringed by a street of plane trees and splashing fountains.

▶ Take the D 1 towards La Gabelle.

As the road crosses the plateau, Mont Ventoux, the Dentelles de Montmirail and the Carpentras basin fill the horizon. At the entrance to La Gabelle the view extends to the opposite slope, with the Nesque gorges in the foreground and the Luberon mountains in the background.

▶ From La Gabelle continue north, cross the D 1 and head towards Flassan.

The road descends into a cool valley studded with pines and spruce.

Flassan
The minute village has ochre-walled houses and a typically picturesque Provençal square.

▶ The D 217 and D 1 on the left lead back to Sault.

ADDRESSES

🛏 STAY

😊😊 **Ferme Les Bayles** – *84390 Saint-Trinit, 9km/5.6mi E of Sault via D 950 and a secondary road. ℰ04 90 75 00 91. http://lesbayles.com. ⛷ℙ🚲. 5 rooms.* An old sheepfold set in nature. Chicken, guinea-fowl, duck and rabbit are usually on the menu at this farm-inn. Simple rooms and a cottage are available for hikers, cyclists and riders. Riding centre and pool.

😊😊 **Hôtel-Restaurant Signoret** – *Av. de la Résistance. ℰ04 90 64 11 44. www.le signoret.fr. ⛨. 26 rooms. Restaurant 😊😊 (closed Sun eve and Fri off season).* Nothing fancy, certainly, but a chat and a clean room at a reasonable price.

😊😊😊😊 **Hostellerie du Val de Sault** – *Ancien chemin d'Aurel. Head towards St-Trinit then turn left after the fire station. May–Sept half-board only. Open Easter–Nov. ℰ04 90 64 01 41. www.valdesault.com. ⛷ℙ 20 rooms. Restaurant 😊😊😊.* A member of the Relais du Silence group, this comfortable hotel sits just outside Sault. The best suites have private terraces with views across the valley (even from the bathroom). Chef proprietor Yves Gattechaut loves cooking with Sault lavender, lamb and *petit épeautre.* Full spa and fitness room, swimming pool and tennis court.

♈EAT

😊😊 **Le Provençal** – *r. Porte-des-Aires. ℰ04 90 64 09 09. ⛨🚲🏠. Closed mid-Nov–Dec, 1 week of Feb school holidays, Mon evening, and Tue except mid-Jul–mid-Aug.* Don't be fooled by the simple façade: this restaurant is well liked locally for its unpretentious, friendly atmosphere.

SHOPPING

Andre Boyer – *Pl. de l'Europe, Sault. ℰ04 90 64 00 23. www.nougat-boyer.fr. Open daily 7am–7pm. Closed Feb. Production visits Jul–Aug Tue and Fri 3pm.* This old company remains a top address for nougat made with locally produced honey and almonds. Macaroons, biscuits, *galettes* made with *petit épeautre* flour and artisan ice creams are also tempting.

TerraVentoux – *Rte de Sault, 84570 Villes sur Auzon. ℰ04 90 61 79 47. www. terraventoux.fr. Apr–Jun 9am–noon, 2pm–6.30pm, (Sun and public holidays 3pm–6pm); rest of the year 9am–noon, 2pm–7pm. Closed Sun (Oct–Mar).* One of Ventoux's dynamic wine co-operatives. Good wines. Activities include wine walks, picnics and cycling.

EVENT

Fête de la lavande (Lavender festival) – On 15 August, a procession with traditional costumes and demonstrations of lavender customs including how it is hand-cut and dried. At the race track.

South of Mont Ventoux but north of Aix-en-Provence and Marseille, the wide sweep of the Luberon is in some ways a microcosm of Provence. The precariously perched hilltop villages which have helped to make it famous are set in glorious countryside where lush orchards, melon fields and vineyards contrast with the stark, grey, rocky spine of the Montagne du Luberon.

Highlights

These ravishing landscapes, wild in some parts and tamed by agriculture in others are cherished and protected as the vast Parc Naturel Régional du Luberon which stretches right across the heart of the region is, like Mont Ventoux (*see p326*), a UNESCO Biosphere Reserve. Unlike other parts of Provence, the Luberon has become well known only in relatively recent times.

First popular with Marseille city dwellers fleeing summer crowds, it began, in the late 1960s, to attract Parisians who migrated south to restore some of its quaint old villages. But it was Peter Mayle's book *A Year in Provence*, published in 1989, which rapidly earned the

Silvacane Abbey

© Riccardo Sala/age fotostock

© S. Sauvignier/MICHELIN

Sentier des Ocres, Roussillon

Luberon the international renown that it enjoys today. Celebrities of all kinds are drawn towards the area's natural beauty, its wonderful food and wine, its slow pace of life – and, not least, because the low-key Luberon grants them the privacy they need in order to relax.

From the Rock: Ochre and Bories

Clinging to outcrops of rock and built out of it centuries ago, *villages perchés* like Gordes, Ménerbes, Lacoste and Oppède-le-Vieux have become the Luberon's most compelling images – and they could hardly be more charming, their narrow, stepped, medieval streets stacked up in hazardous tiers. But rock is important in other ways, too. Around Roussillon, rich seams of ochre led to the development of a local mining industry which has left dramatic, cathedral-like spaces chipped out of orange rock as well as an ochre-clad village that blazes at sunset on a crimson and gold cliff.

Equally symbolic of the Luberon are its *bories*, ancient dwellings with dry-stone walls built out of shallow slabs of limestone. Arranged in clusters, they provide fascinating insights into a pastoral way of life so far back in time that it still remains shrouded in mystery.

Sublime Cistercian Abbeys

In striking contrast to these primitive huts are the Luberon's architectural glories from the early Middle Ages, especially the Abbaye de Sénanque and the Abbaye de Silvacane. These two Cistercian abbeys, as remarkable for their unadorned simplicity as for their awe-inspiring proportions and perfect acoustics, are ranked with the Abbaye de Thoronet in the Var as the three finest buildings of their kind in the south of France – the "three sisters of Provence". It is impossible to visit them without being moved by their austere beauty.

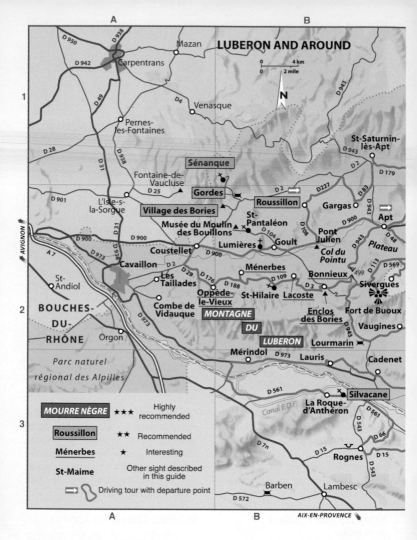

LUBERON AND AROUND

0 — 4 km
0 — 2 mile

N

D 950, D 938, Mazan, D 942, Carpentrans, D 49, Venasque, D 4, Pernes-les-Fontaines, D 28, D 31, D 938, Fontaine-de-Vaucluse, **Sénanque**, St-Saturnin-lès-Apt, D 943, D 2, D 179, D 901, L'Isle-s-la-Sorgue, D 25, **Gordes**, **Roussillon**, D 227, D 83, **Gargas**, D 943, **Apt**, **Village des Bories**, **Musée du Moulin des Bouillons**, St-Pantaléon, D 104, Goult, D 108, **Pont Julien**, D 900, D 48, AVIGNON, D 900, Coustellet, Lumières, Col du Pointu, D 943, **Plateau**, D 37, D 973, D 900, Cavaillon, D 2, Ménerbes, D 109, Bonnieux, D 499, D 113, D 569, St-Andiol, A 7, Les Taillades, D 29, D 176, D 188, Oppède-le-Vieux, St-Hilaire, Lacoste, D 3, **Sivergues**, **MONTAGNE**, Enclos des Bories, Fort de Buoux, **BOUCHES-DU-RHÔNE**, Combe de Vidauque, D 973, **DU**, **LUBERON**, Lourmarin, Vaugines, Orgon, Mérindol, D 973, Lauris, Cadenet, *Parc naturel régional des Alpilles*, D 561, Canal E.D.F., D 561, Silvacane, La Roque-d'Anthéron, D 543, D 66, Rognes, D 15, D 543, Barben, Lambesc, D 572, AIX-EN-PROVENCE

MOURRE NÈGRE	★★★	Highly recommended
Roussillon	★★	Recommended
Ménerbes	★	Interesting
St-Maime		Other sight described in this guide
		Driving tour with departure point

Melons and Goat's Cheese

Food for the soul is matched, of course, by nourishment for the body of the most delicious kind. With its market gardens and orchards watered by the Durance River, the Luberon is noted for outstanding produce: not just celebrated Cavaillon melons but peaches, apricots, cherries and other fruits as well as spring vegetables of all kinds. Goat's cheeses are exceptional here too, led by Banon, which is easily recognisable with its chestnut-leaf packaging, tied together with raffia. With first-rate ingredients like these on hand, it is hardly surprising

that supremely talented chefs like Reine Sammut, Edouard Loubet and Eric Sapet have chosen the Luberon as their base.

Wine

To accompany all this good food, there are excellent wines. The Luberon may be the southernmost *appellation* in the Rhône valley but, thanks to the cool mass of the Luberon mountain, it is certainly not the warmest. Grapes ripen slowly and perfectly here, delivering crisp whites, delicate rosés and poised reds whose overall hallmark is elegance.

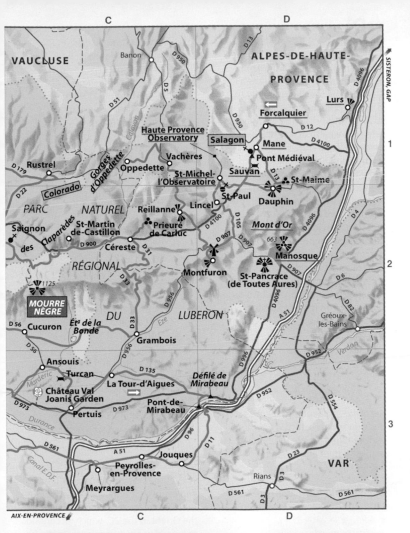

C · D

VAUCLUSE

Banon

D 950

ALPES-DE-HAUTE-

PROVENCE

SISTERON, GAP

D 13

D 4096

Lurs

← Forcalquier

D 51

D 5

D 950

D 12

Haute Provence
Observatory

Salagon

Mane

D 4100

D 179

Rustrel

Gorges d'Oppedette

Vachères

St-Michel-
l'Observatoire

Sauvan

Pont Médiéval

Oppedette

D 13

St-Maime

Colorado

Dauphin

D 22

Claparèdes

PARC

NATUREL

Reillanne

Lincel

St-Paul

Saignon

St-Martin
de-Castillon

Prieuré
de Carluc

D 4100

D 105

Mont d'Or

D 4096

D 4

des

D 900

Céreste

D 31

D 907

663

Manosque

RÉGIONAL

Montfuron

St-Pancrace
(de Toutes Aures)

D 907

D 6

1125

D 33

Eze

LUBERON

A 51

D 82

MOURRE
NÈGRE

DU

Gréoux-
les-Bains

D 56

Cucuron

Étg de la
Bonde

D 956

Grambois

D 996

Verdon

D 56

Marderic

Ansouis

Turcan

D 135

Défilé de
Mirabeau

D 952

Château Val
Joanis Garden

La Tour-d'Aigues

→

D 973

Pertuis

D 973

Pont-de-
Mirabeau

D 952

D 554

Durance

D 561

A 51

D 96

D 11

VAR

Canal E.D.F.

Peyrolles-
en-Provence

Jouques

D 23

Meyrargues

Rians

D 3

D 561

D 561

AIX-EN-PROVENCE

C · D

1

2

3

Market in Apt

© S. Sauvignier/MICHELIN

337

Apt

Vaucluse

The Roman colony of Julia Apta was a prosperous town on the Via Domitia, the road linking Italy to Hispania, and important enough to be a bishopric in the 3C. Much later, the wealth of Apt was based on crystallised fruit, manufacturing, pottery and ochre mining – industries recently in decline – as well as lavender essence and truffles. Today this attractive town straddling several rivers at the heart of the Luberon is an important tourist centre. Visitors are drawn to its narrow streets, exceptional Saturday market and its location as a base for trips through the Luberon in all directions. A traditional pilgrimage takes place on the last Sunday in July.

- ▶ **Population:** 11 755.
- **Michelin Map:** 332: F-10 or 114 fold 2 or 528 fold 31.
- **Info:** 20 avenue Philippe de Girard, Apt. ℘04 90 74 03 18. www.luberon-apt.fr.
- ▶ **Location:** Arriving from the west (Gordes is 25km/15.5mi E via D 2 and D 4, Cavaillon at 34km/ 21mi E via N 100), you must go through suburbs before arriving in the centre of town: place de la Bouquerie.
- **Parking:** Paid parking on the quays, free on the banks. Free shuttle bus on Saturday mornings (market day) every 30min from 9am, leaving from Viton car park and train station.
- **Don't Miss:** Saturday's market, Luberon National Park Centre, the Ochre Tour.
- **Timing:** Allow 1–2hr to walk around town or half a day for the ochre tour.
- **Kids:** Unique landscapes of Colorado de Rustrel.

🐾 WALKING TOUR

Allow at least 2hr on market days.

▶ From place de la Bouquerie take rue de la République until you reach place du Septier, which is adorned with beautiful private residences. Go to place Carnot and turn right onto rue Ste-Anne.

Cathédrale Sainte-Anne

104 r. Cassin. ◷*Open 10am–noon, 3–6pm.* ℘*04 90 04 85 44. www.apt-cathedrale.com.*

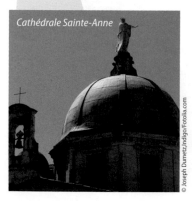
Cathédrale Sainte-Anne

© Joseph Dumetz,Indigo/Fotolia.com

This cathedral is the first sanctuary dedicated to St Anne in France. It holds the saint's reliquaries brought back from the Orient in the 3C, which, according to legend, were miraculously found by Charlemagne during a trip in 776.

Chapelle Sainte-Anne – The first chapel off the north aisle was built in 1660, when Anne of Austria came on pilgrimage. The furnishings include a large reliquary bust of St Anne; a marble group of St Anne and the Virgin by the Italian Benzoni; and the family tomb of the Dukes of Sabran.

Treasury (Trésor) – In the sacristy of St Anne's chapel are displayed 11C and 12C liturgical manuscripts, shrines decorated with 12C and 13C Limoges enamels, 14C Florentine gilded-wood

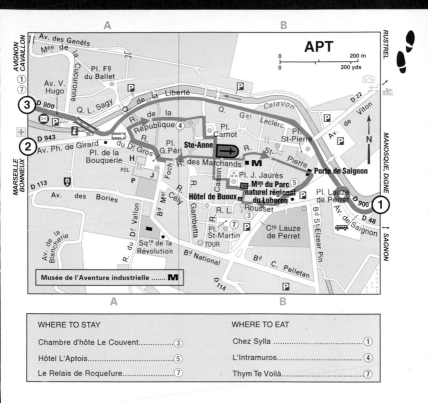

caskets, St Anne's shroud, and an 11C caliph's coat brought back from the First Crusade (1096–99).

Crypt – Composed of two floors: the upper crypt is in the Romanesque style and contains an altar supported by a Romanesque capital and 13C sarcophagi; the lower crypt is Pre-Romanesque. At the back of the two crypts stand two tombstones.

◗ Continue along rue des Marchands, which passes through the bell gate, to place du Postel.

Porte de Saignon

Rue St-Pierre leads to this medieval gate, part of the town's remaining fortifications.

◗ Go right onto cours Lauze-de-Perret which goes along a wonderful Provençal area for playing boules until you reach r. Louis-Rousset, which leads back into the old town.

On the corner of rue P.-Achard, note on the left the Classical façade of the 17C **chapelle des Récollets**, before going on to rue P.-Achard. La Maison du Parc naturel régional du Luberon is in a fine old mansion on place Jean-Jaurès.

Maison du Parc naturel régional du Luberon

60 pl. Jean-Jaurès. ⏱*Open Apr–Sept Mon–Fri 8.30am–noon, 1.30–6pm, Sat 8.30am–noon; Oct–Mar daily except Sat 8.30am–noon, 1.30–6pm.* ⏱*Closed Sun and public holidays.* ✆*No charge.* ☎*04 90 04 42 00. www.parcduluberon.fr.* A good place to arm yourself with information about the activities and aims of the Luberon Natural Park as well as gaining insights into nature, geography and geology.

◗ Go as far as place du Postel, on your right.

Musée de l'Aventure industrielle

14 pl. du Postel. &Open Jun–Sept 10am–noon, 2–6.30pm; rest of the year daily except Sun–Mon 10am–noon, 2–5.30pm. Guided tours (1hr) with advance booking. Closed Tue and holidays. €4. 04 90 74 95 30. www.apt.fr.

In a former fruit processing factory, this museum (M) focuses on Apt's three most important industrial activities and traces their evolution from the 19C to the present day: the production of **crystallised or candied fruits** (with utensils, old labels etc); the mining of **ochre** (showing how dyes were extracted and refined); and **faïencerie** (with an exhibition of Apt's famous marbled earthenware from the 17C to the 20C.

▶ On the left, go back up rue des Marchands.

On **place Gabriel-Péri**, the sous-préfecture has a fine Classical façade flanked by two fountains with dolphins.

▶ Via rue du Dr-Gros, return to place de la Bouquerie.

ADDRESSES

⌂ STAY

Hôtel L'Aptois – *289 cours Lauze-de-Perret. 04 90 74 02 02. www.aptois.fr. Closed 25 Dec–1 Jan. 29 rooms.* Facing a large square right in the centre of town, this is a simply decorated, functional hotel. The best rooms are the ones which have been renovated. These include good value family rooms.

Le Relais de Roquefure – *Quartier de Roquefure, 3km/1.8mi west of Apt via the D 900. 04 90 04 88 88. Closed Dec–mid-Feb. 16 rooms.* This fine big pink house stands in parkland, surrounded by hundred-year-old cedars. Individually decorated rooms and pool.

Chambre d'hôte Le Couvent – *36 r. Louis-Rousset. 04 90 04 55 36. www.loucouvent.com. 5 rooms.* In this 17C convent building enclosed by high walls, you will forget that you are in the middle

of town. Attractive, minimalist rooms, vaulted refectory for breakfast and a small garden with a pool.

⟨⟩ EAT

Chez Sylla – *D 900, leaving Apt. 04 90 04 60 37. www.sylla.fr. Open noon–2pm. Closed Sun.* Besides selling its wines, this co-operative serves simple lunches – salads, cheese plates and so on. Plus wine, of course.

Thym te Voilà – *59 pl. St-Martin. 04 90 74 28 25. http://thymtevoila.free.fr. Open Tue–Sat lunch and Thu–Sat eve (lunch and eve mid-Jun–mid-Sept). Closed Sun and Mon, Jan–Mar.* This small restaurant has built up a strong local following. Charming, slightly funky décor and tasty food which marries local flavours with exotic touches from further afield.

L'Intramuros – *120–124 r. de la République. 04 90 06 18 87. Closed 10 Jan–28 Feb, Sun and Mon (open Sun in season).* In a delightful interior which looks rather like an antiquarian bookshop, you will sample Provençal fare based on fresh market produce. Interesting set lunch menu. Food also available to take away.

SHOPPING

Market – *Place Lauze-de-Perret.* The traditional Saturday morning market is one of the best in the region; there is also a small farmers' market on Tuesday morning.

Confiserie Le Coulon – *24 quai de la Liberté. Open Apr–Sept 9.15am–12.15pm, 3–7pm; rest of the year 9.15am–12.15pm, 2.30–6.30pm. Closed Sun and Mon, 2 weeks in Jan and 2 weeks in Jun. 04 90 74 21 90.* This smart shop attached to one of the few confiseries still working in a traditional, small-scale way is one of the best places to buy crystallised fruits. Apricots and mandarins are the star attractions.

ACTIVITIES

Leisure centre, Apt's artificial lake – *Rte de St-Saturnin-lès-Apt. 04 90 04 85 41. Mid-Mar–Oct daily 8.30am–noon, 1.30–7pm.* Numerous activities are on offer here: sailing, windsurfing, kayaking, mountain biking, rock climbing etc.

Good to know: Swimming is not permitted on this lake.

La Montagne du Luberon★★★

Vaucluse, Alpes-de-Haute Provence

Midway between the Alps and the Mediterranean lies the long spine of the Luberon range. This region is full of charm, with its rocky mountains, picturesque hilltop villages, quiet woods, expansive vineyards and dry-stone huts.

ACTIVITIES IN THE PARK
Walking

The Maison du Parc (*see p339*) provides a range of guides with details of many **walking routes** starting from Roussillon, Bonnieux, Buoux, Apt, Cavaillon, Robion, Les Taillades, Cheval Blanc, Merindol, Murs and Rustrel. Information about guided walks is also available (*charges vary*).

Cycling

Also on offer from the Maison du Parc and from the association **Vélo Loisir en Luberon** (*see p383*): a wide range of itineraries to suit cyclists. Covering 450km/280mi of marked trails in total, with signposts at every crossroads, these range in distance from just 18km/11mi to an ambitious 236km/147mi. Maps and other practical information for cyclists are now on view in about 40 villages.

DRIVING TOURS

1 GRAND LUBERON★★

Round trip from Apt – 119km/74mi. Allow half a day (not including climb to Mourre Nègre). Route marked in green on maps on p337 and p345.

Leave Apt on the D 48 going southeast on avenue de Saignon.

As the road climbs, the hilltop site of Saignon, the Apt basin, the Vaucluse plateau and Mont Ventoux all come into view.

Michelin Map: 332: E-11 to G-11.

Info: La Maison du Parc, 60 place Jean-Jaurès, Apt. 04 90 04 42 00. www.parcduluberon.fr.

Don't Miss: The Petit Luberon with its pretty perched villages such as Bonnieux and Ménerbes.

Timing: Allow half a day for the Petit Luberon circuit and a day for the Grand Luberon.

Saignon

The village, close to a tall rock, contains a Romanesque church.

Continue along the D 48.

The road skirts Claparèdes plateau with its scattered *bories* (dry-stone huts).

Leave the car at Auribeau; exit from town northwards and bear left on the unsurfaced road towards Mourre Nègre. The **GR 92** leads to the summit.

Mourre Nègre★★★

Half a day return journey on foot.

You need to be fit to climb to the Luberon's highest point, the summit of Mourre Nègre (1 125m), but what a reward!

The **panorama★★★** embraces four points of the compass: the Montagne de Lure and Digne pre-Alps (northeast), the Durance valley with Montagne Ste-Victoire in the background (southeast), Étang de Berre and the Alpilles (southwest), Apt basin, Vaucluse plateau and Mont Ventoux (northwest).

Return to the D 48 and continue through Auribeau. Bear right on to the D 900, then, after 2km/1.2mi, bear left on to the D 48, heading for Saint-Martin-de-Castillon.

Enclos des Bories, Bonnieux

© Alain Hocquel/L'ADT Vaucluse Tourisme

Nature Protected

Created in 1977 and a UNESCO World Biosphere Reserve since 1997 (as is Mont Ventoux), the Parc Naturel Régional du Luberon is a vast protected area encompassing 77 communes and covering 175,000 ha/432,500 acres, taking in the towns of Pertuis, Apt, Cavaillon, Manosque and Forcalquier. Its objective is to preserve the balance of nature in this magnificent, unspoilt sweep of countryside while at the same time raising living standards for local people. Agriculture is extremely important: the area encompasses 12 *appellations d'origine contrôlée* or *indications geographiques protégées* for its produce, including Ventoux and Luberon wines, Banon cheese, Sisteron lamb, the Muscat grape and Haute-Provence olive oil. Also of interest to visitors may be the fact that the park is charged with developing information centres and marked trails for walking and cycling, restoring buildings, putting together publications on the area and encouraging farmers' markets.

Geology and climate – The Montagne du Luberon is a gigantic anticlinal fold of calcareous rock of the Tertiary Era, running from east to west. The range is divided from north to south by the Lourmarin coomb into two unequal parts: to the west the Petit Luberon forms a plateau carved by gorges and ravines where the altitude rarely exceeds 700m; whereas to the east, the massive summits of the Grand Luberon rise up to 1 125m at Mourre Nègre.

The contrast between the north and south slopes is equally striking. The northern face, steep and ravined, is cooler and more humid, cloaked with a forest of downy oaks. The southern side, turned toward Aix-en-Provence, is more Mediterranean in its vegetation (oak groves and rosemary-filled *garrigue*), and with its sunny slopes, crops and cypresses, announces the delightful countryside along the River Durance.

Natural Habitat – The diversity of the vegetation is a delight to nature lovers: oak forests, Atlas cedar (planted in 1862) on the heights of the Petit Luberon, beech, Scots pine, moors of broom and boxwood, *garrigue*, an extraordinary variety of aromatic plants (herbs of Provence) clinging here and there to the rocky slopes. The *mistral* contributes, provoking unusual local changes: holm oaks are blown onto the northern exposed slopes and downy oaks onto the southern exposed slopes. In winter the contrast between the evergreens and deciduous trees is striking. The fauna is equally rich: snakes (seven different varieties), lizards, warblers, blue rock thrushes, owls and eagles.

Hilltop Villages – The Luberon has been inhabited by humans since prehistoric times. Villages appeared during the Middle Ages, clinging to the rock face near a waterhole. The tall houses with their imposing walls huddled close together at the foot of a castle or church; most of them had rooms cut out of the rock. Men left their homes to work in the surrounding countryside and when necessary they lived in dry-stone huts called *bories*. Their livelihood was obtained mostly from sheep, olives, grain and vineyards as well as lavender and silkworms. Each parcel of cultivated land was carefully cleared of stones – the stones were grouped into piles called *clapiers* – and bordered by low walls which served to protect the land from soil erosion. The flocks were also contained within a close of dry stone. Traces of these arrangements are still visible in the rural landscape. This traditional economy was swept away by the agricultural improvements of the 19C and 20C: villages lost their inhabitants and fell into ruins. Nowadays, the trend is reversing itself: village populations are increasing at an almost constant rate, and the villages themselves have been well restored.

Bories – On the slopes of the Luberon and the Vaucluse plateau stand curious dry-stone huts, one or two floors high, called *bories*. They are either alone or in groups forming a very picturesque unit; there are about 3 000 of them. They were sometimes just tool sheds or sheep pens but many were inhabited over the different periods from the Iron Age until the 18CE.

The *bories* were built with thin slabs of limestone. These stones, called *lauzes*, are on average 10cm thick. Specialised stonemasons knew how to select the *lauzes* and assemble them without either mortar or water. As the walls were raised, each stone course was carefully made to underhang the preceding one, so that at a height of 3 to 4m, the diameter diminished to the point of being reduced to a small opening which could be closed by placing one slab on it. To avoid the infiltration of water, the different layers of stone were slightly inclined towards the exterior.

The *bories* came in several forms. The simplest are round, ovoid or square, consisting of one room and one opening to the east or southeast. The interior was limited to hollow niches used for storage. The temperature of the *borie* remained constant whatever the season. Larger dwellings exist, especially at Gordes. They are rectangular, with a few narrow openings, and their organisation was similar to that of a traditional farm: disposed around a courtyard encircled by a high wall were the living quarters, bread oven and outbuildings.

Luberon countryside

© C. Chillio/Comité Régional de Tourisme Provence-Alpes-Côte d'Azur

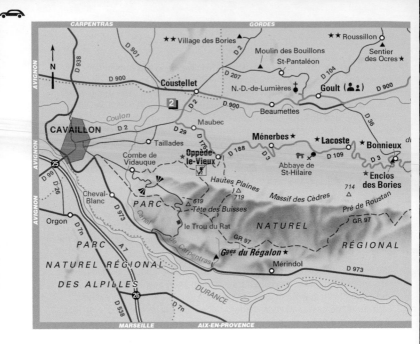

Saint-Martin-de-Castillon

Alt. 551m. As well as a pleasant café and delicatessen where you can restore your energy, this village perched on a hillside ledge provides a pretty **view★** over the Calavon plain and the Grand Luberon.

◗ Turn around to come back on the D 900, heading towards Céreste. Immediately after crossing the Calavon, take the first little road on the right (direction camping de Sibourg) and follow it for 2km/1.2mi.

After you have passed the campsite you will arrive in front of the imposing, almost windowless façade of the **tour d'Embarbe** (12C).

◗ Turn around to go to Céreste on the D 900.

Céreste

This old village was on Via Domitia, the first road built by the Romans through Gaul. It still has some of its fortifications and constitutes a lovely architectural unit. The surrounding earth is rich in remarkable fossils (fish, plants) which

have formed in the calcareous strata. On the road out of Céreste leading to Forcalquier is the old square of the **église primitive**; note the beautiful Romanesque porch with arcatures all the way round. After the church, take the first little road on the left which will bring you, after 300m, to the **pont romain** which crosses the Encrème River at an angle.

◗ Continue on the route du pont romain. Poorly indicated, the priory is half hidden 5km/3mi from here, just before you reach a stream running along the side of a clearing, on a rise hidden by trees (follow the signs for cyclists pointing towards Forcalquier).

Prieuré de Carluc

⊶ *Interior closed.* ☜ *Guided tour may be booked at the tourist office in Céreste.*
Set above what looks like a natural harbour, the Cure ravine, the strange remains of the Carluc priory have not yet revealed all their secrets. Built in the 12C, this priory was under the control

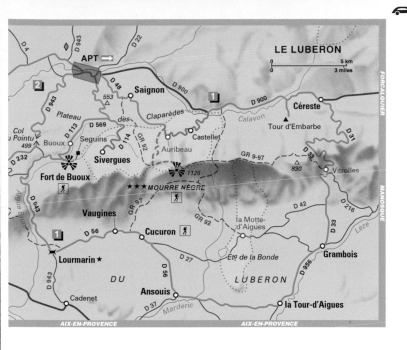

of the abbey of Montmajour. Of the three churches included in it, only one is still standing, its nave carved out of the cliff face. On its left side, hollowed out of the rock, is a mysterious gallery. **Anthropomorphid tombs** can be seen on the floor. This gallery led to a second church, of which only the rock face remains. The pretty clearing nearby looks as if it might have been created specially for picnics.

▷ Return on the D 900 and cross the village of Céreste again. Take the D 31 heading for Vitrolles-en-Luberon (13km/8mi).

The road winds around the north slope of the Grand Luberon, affording lovely **views★** over the Calavon plain and the Vaucluse plateau. It reaches the col de l'Aire deï Masco (alt. 696m), before veering off down the south slope of the Luberon, covered in rosemary-rich *garrigue*.

▷ Go down the south slope towards Vitrolles and take the D 33 towards Grambois (18km/11.2mi).

There is a nice view of the hilltop village as you arrive.

Grambois

More rustic (some people would say more authentic) than Ménerbes or Bonnieux, this old village perched on the top of a hill is every bit as seductive, huddled around a charming square which is dominated by the silhouette of the fortified **église Notre-Dame-de-Beauvoir**. Inside *(1st chapel on left)*, there is a *Life of John the Baptist,* a triptych of the Gothic Aix school attributed by some to André Tavel, a painter from Pont-Saint-Esprit. If you are visiting around Christmas time, you will see in the church the very expressive **santons** of **Pierre Graille**. Not much wonder they are life-like: he used the villagers as his models!

▷ Leave Grambois heading west on the D 27, towards Saint-Martin-de-Brasque. Pass la Motte d'Aigues and the étang de la Bonde, going towards Cucuron (15km/9.2mi).

Cucuron

This delightful village with its large pond in the centre and its olive oil mill is well worth strolling through. Opposite the church, on the first floor of the 17C Hôtel de Bouliers, is a small museum: the **Musée Archéologique Marc Deydier** (*r. de l'Église;* ⊙*open May–Oct 10.30am–noon, 2–5.30pm (Tue 2–5.30pm); Nov–Apr call for details of times.* ℘*04 90 77 25 02*), which is dedicated to prehistory, the Gallo-Roman period and later local traditions. From the terrace below the keep, there is a fine view over the Cucuron basin to Montagne Ste-Victoire on the horizon.

▷ Leave Cucuron on the D 56 going southeast.

Vaugines

At the entrance to the village (where there are a few old dwellings), romantically positioned in a hollow, the Romanesque church **Saint-Pierre-et-Saint-Barthélemy★** and the ancient cemetery beside it create an extraordinarily serene picture. Cinema buffs will easily recognise it as the church in *Jean de Florette* and *Manon des Sources*.

Lourmarin★

This pretty village at the foot of the Montagne du Luberon is dominated by its château built high on a rock bluff. Various writers and artists have been so won over by its charm that they ended up living here, from **Albert Camus** (1913–60), author of *L'Étranger* (The Stranger) and *La Peste* (The Plague), who is buried in the cemetery, to **Peter Mayle** whose bestselling book *A Year in Provence* played a major part in publicising the appeal of the Luberon.

Château de Lourmarin★

⊙*Open daily: Jun–Aug 10am–6.30pm; May–Sept 10.30am–12.30pm, 2.30–6pm; Mar–Apr and Oct 10.30am–12.30pm, 2.30–5pm; Feb and Nov–Dec 10.30am–12.30pm, 2.30–4.30pm; Jan Sat–Sun only 2.30–4.30pm.* ⌂*Guided tours (1hr) available with advance booking.* ⊙*Closed 25 Dec.* ⊷€7 (children under 10 free). ℘04 90 68 15 23. www.chateau-de-lourmarin.com.*

The château is partly 15C and partly Renaissance. The Renaissance wing has remarkable stylistic unity and contains large chimney-pieces ornamented with caryatids or Corinthian columns.

The grand staircase ends dramatically with a slender pillar supporting a stone cupola. The château offers a lovely view of the Durance valley and the olive grove lying within the grounds.

▷ The D 943 travels northwest up the Lourmarin coomb.

The River Aigue Brun has cut narrow gorges through the rock. The road goes through a children's holiday camp (16C–18C château) before crossing a bridge and reaching a group of houses.

▷ Just before these houses, turn right onto the narrow path (car park).

Fort de Buoux

⚡ *20min there and back on foot plus 1hr visit. From the gate follow the path beneath a vertical rock wall to the porter's lodge.* ⊙*Open daily dawn–dusk (weather permitting).* ⊷€4 (under 12 free). ℘04 90 74 25 75. www.buoux-village.com.* ⊙*Try to be here for sunset.*

The rock spur on which the fort stands is a natural defence which has, in succession, been occupied by Ligurians, Romans, Catholics and Protestants. Louis XIV ordered its demolition in 1660; there nevertheless remain three defensive walls, a Romanesque chapel, houses, silos hewn out of the rock, a keep, a Ligurian sacrificial altar and a concealed staircase.

From the rock spur, where a medieval keep once stood, there is a fine view of the Upper Aigue Brun valley.

▷ Return to the holiday camp and turn right onto the D 113. Turn right on to the D 569, then right again on to the D 114.

Sivergues

Set back from the road, this hilltop village on the slopes of the Grand Luberon was inhabited by **Vaudois** who benefited from its isolation to escape from religious repression, before joining forces with mainstream Protestantism (🕯️ *see Introduction*). Perhaps it is here, in this village described by the writer Henri Bosco as perched "damnably" on a hilltop, that you will come closest to communing with the soul of the Luberon.

▷ Turn around and head for Apt on the D 114.

2 PETIT LUBERON★★

Round trip from Apt – 101km/63mi. About 6hr. Route on map, p345.

To experience the charm of the Luberon's hilltop villages fully, take this trip at a slow pace. Have a coffee on the terrace of a little bar, stroll the narrow streets, look at the flowers, walk in the vineyards stopping at the cellars of some Luberon wine producers, and take in the panoramas afforded by these hilltop villages.

Bonnieux★

This popular perched village, situated on a Luberon promontory, is an ideal base to explore the area.

Upper Bonnieux – *Start from pl. de la Liberté by the steep vaulted passage-way, rue des Pénitents Blancs, to reach the terrace situated below the old church. By car take the road to Cadenet and a steep surfaced path on the left.*

Terrasse – *From the terrace there is a lovely* **view★** *of the Calavon valley; to the left, you can see the hilltop village of Lacoste; and further to the right, the edge of the Vaucluse plateau to which cling the hilltop villages of Gordes and Roussillon. In the background, Mont Ventoux stands out.*

Musée de la Boulangerie

12 r. de la République. 🕐*Open end Mar– Oct 10am–12.30pm, 2.30–6pm.* 🚫*Closed Tue and public holidays.* ✆€1.50. 📞*04 90 75 88 34.*

The museum illustrates the work of a baker, with utensils and literature on the bakery trade.

Enclos des Bories★

15min from the Bonnieux campsite, following the signs. By car, take the Lourmarin road as far as the cedar forest (forêt de cèdres), then follow a path on the right for 1km/0.6mi.
🕐*Open Apr–Nov daily 10am–7pm.*
✆€5 (children under 12, free).
🚶*Guided tours on request.* 📞*06 08 46 61 44. www.enclos-des-bories.fr.*
It took the owners 10 years to uncover this extraordinary collection of **drystone dwellings**, buried under vegetation. The 4ha/10-acre site, planted with oaks and partly covered by *garrigue*, is separated into two parts by an impressive 250m **wall**. Looking at some 20 bories encircled by a wall, it is not difficult to imagine the pastoral life that must have been lived in this place with its superb **beehive**, cattle enclosure and circular area for grinding wheat. An **aiguier** collected rain water and wells were hollowed into the rocks to a depth of 7m. Strange **twin bories** (sharing the same entrance) are next to bories that witnessed murder scenes when the Vaudois took refuge here in the 16C. At the end of your visit, don't miss the fine **view★** over the village of Bonnieux, the Petit Luberon and Mont Ventoux.

Cedar Forest

5km/3mi along the Loumarin road. Allow 2hr.
Imported from the Moroccan Atlas, these cedars were planted in upper Bonnieux in 1862. A botanical **footpath** features eight stopping points with information about the plants of the Luberon area.

▷ Return towards Bonnieux, then continue on the D 109 towards Lacoste. Leave your car at the bottom of the village.

Lacoste★

This tiny hilltop village has an elegant 17C belfry and is dominated by the remnants of a 42-room château, which belonged to the de Sade family. The **Marquis de Sade** (1740–1814), author of erotic works, was the Lord of Lacoste for 30 years. Extremely fond of the stage, he gave orders to build an extravagant theatre here. Condemned several times, he escaped and hid in Lacoste; but in 1778 he was caught and imprisoned.

The château is now owned by fashion designer Pierre Cardin and used as the setting for cultural events. The village is also known internationally for the **Lacoste School of Arts**, founded in 1970 by American art professor Bernard Pfriem.

Abbaye de St-Hilaire

Located on a pretty site facing the Luberon, this former monastery (o━ now private property) was occupied by the Carmelites in the 13C–18C.

◐ Continue to Ménerbes via the D 109; note, near Lacoste, the quarries which extract high-quality stone suitable for carving.

Ménerbes★

This old village occupies a picturesque site on a promontory high up on the Luberon's north face. In 1573 the Calvinists captured the stronghold by a ruse, and it took five years and a large ransom to dislodge them.

Place de l'Horloge – The square is overlooked by the town hall's bell tower with its simple wrought-iron bell cage. In one corner of the square stands a Renaissance mansion with a round-arched doorway. This is the **Maison de la Truffe et du Vin** (⌂ see Addresses).

Église Saint-Luc – The church stands at the end of the village and dates back to the 14C when it was a priory dependent on St-Agricol of Avignon. Behind the east end there is a fine **view★** of Coulon valley, the villages of Gordes and Roussillon (with its ochre cliffs), Mont Ventoux, the Vaucluse plateau and the Luberon.

Citadelle – This 13C fortress (rebuilt in the 16C and 19C) has preserved part of its defence system with its corner towers and machicolations. Owing to its strategic position it played an important part during the Wars of Religion.

Musée du Tire-Bouchon – *On the D 3 towards Cavaillon.* ◐ *Open Apr–Oct daily 10am–noon, 2–7pm; Nov–Mar daily except Sun and public holidays 9am–noon, 2–5pm.* ◈€4. ✆ 04 90 72 41 58. www.domaine-citadelle.com. On the highly regarded wine-producing estate of La Citadelle, owned by former film producer Yves Rousset-Rouard (of *Emmanuelle* fame), this museum holds a remarkable collection of over 1 000 corkscrews from the 17C to today, created out of different materials and ranging in style from elegant to bawdy. (One features an effigy of Senator Volstead, who promoted the laws on Prohibition in the United States in the 1920–1930s.) The various methods used to uncork wine are well illustrated. Visitors may also arrange a tour of the wine cellars, complete with a tasting of Luberon wine, and there is an excellent shop.

Oppède-le-Vieux★

Leave the car in the car park just after the village, to explore it on foot.

Once largely abandoned, this old, terraced village on a picturesque rocky spur has come to life again, having been carefully restored by numerous artists and writers. An old gateway in the walls leads from the original village square to the upper village, crowned by its 13C collegiate church and ruined castle (founded by the Counts of Toulouse and rebuilt in the 15C and 16C).

The fine **view★** from the church terrace is of the Coulon valley and Vaucluse plateau, Ménerbes and, from the rear of the castle, the north face of the Luberon with its deep ravines.

◐ Cross the Maubec wine region (D 176, D 29). Turn left instead of right onto the D 2 and, on leaving Robion, bear left on the D 31 to the intersection with the Vidauque road, which you take to the left.

This very steep, winding road (one-way; speed limit 30kph/18mph) skirts the wild Vidauque coomb and offers magnificent plunging **views**★★ of the surrounding countryside: the tip of the Vaucluse plateau and Coulon valley (north), Alpilles and Durance valley (south and west), and below, Cavaillon plain with its market gardens.

▷ The road branches off to the right on the so-called Trou-du-Rat road leading to the D 973, which you take to the right in the direction of Cavaillon. Here, turn right to rejoin the D 2.

Coustellet

This village has become well known for its excellent farmers' market (the first in France), held on Sunday mornings. Nearby is the lavender museum.
Musée de la Lavande (276 rte de Gordes, on the D2, on right after crossing D900.&⊙open Feb–Apr and Oct–Dec daily 9am–12.15pm, 2–6pm; May–Sept daily 9am–7pm. ⊛€7. ℘04 90 76 91 23. www.museedelalavande.com). This attractive little museum demonstrates the lavender distillation process in an interesting way, besides selling a wide range of lavender-related products.

Goult

Leave the car in the church car park.
Less elevated than other villages and on not as steep a site, Goult is dominated by its château (o–▪private). You might enjoy a drink at one of the café terraces on the church square before going to the upper part of the village where the mill has had its sails restored. This is the departure point for a walk which explains Goult's heritage, but you will see the same explanatory panels if you walk at random through the narrow streets.
▬◣1hr. Departure point beside the mill. On the walk, look out for examples of the dry-stone walls which were built so widely around here to create terraces for agriculture, and which are preserved

and explained by the **Conservatoire des terrasses de cultures**.

▷ Return to Apt on the D 900, which goes back over the Cavalon plain.

On the left you will see the **pays de l'ocre** (ochre territory, ⟲see Roussillon).

▷ 3.5km/2.2mi from Goult, turn right on the D 149 towards Bonnieux.

Pont Julien

This bridge, situated close to the ancient Roman road, the Via Domitia, was built across the Coulon (or Cavalon) in the 3C BCE. Note the openings which were made in the piers so that water could escape more rapidly when floods threatened.

▷ Return to the D 900 towards Apt.

ADDRESSES

◈STAY

◉ **Hostellerie L'Aiguebelle** – pl. de la République, 04280 Céreste. ℘04 92 79 00 91. www.hotel-luberon-aiguebelle.com. Closed 14 Nov–13 Feb. 12 rooms. Restaurant◉◉. Before or after visiting the medieval ruins, take a break in this unpretentious hotel in the heart of the village. Rooms are simple and bright. Simple local cooking which is both tasty and very reasonably priced.

◉ **Auberge des Seguins** – 84480 Buoux. ℘04 90 74 16 37. www.aubergedesseguins. com. 27 rooms. Restaurant◉◉. This huge country inn at the foot of the orange Buoux cliffs is popular with hikers, climbers and more casual walkers. Simple, even rather spartan rooms and a small pool.

◉◉ **Chambre d'hôte La Ferme de l'Avellan** – Chemin St-Jean, 84480 Lacoste. ℘04 90 75 85 10. http://lavellan.free.fr. 5 rooms. Restaurant◉◉. With a rustic ambience, this B&B on a farm pursuing an organic approach has five simple rooms and a small pool.

◉◉ **Chambre d'hôte La Lombarde** – Puyvert, 84160 Lourmarin, D 973. ℘04 90 08 40 60. www.lalombarde.com. Closed Nov–Feb. ⬜☂. 4 rooms. In a very quiet setting on a 10ha/25-acre estate, this old house has 4 rooms and 2 gîtes for guests. Private terraces and swimming pool. Breakfasts are served at a big, communal table. Flights over the surrounding countryside can be arranged.

⊜⊜ **Chambre d'hôte Domaine de Layaude Basse** – *Chemin de St-Jean, 84480 Lacoste, 1.5km/0.9mi north of Lacoste in direction of Roussillon.* ℘*04 90 75 90 06. www.domainedelayaude.fr. Closed Dec–Feb.* 🍴. *5 rooms.* Your hosts will accommodate you in the pretty rooms of their 17C family *mas,* at the centre of an extensive farm facing Mont Ventoux.

⊜⊜ **Chambre d'hôte Les Grandes Garrigues** – *84160 Vaugines, 3km/1.9mi west of Cucuron via D 56 and D 45 (rte de Cadenet).* ℘*04 90 77 10 71. Closed Oct–Apr.* 🛏🍴. *5 rooms.* On an 11ha/27-acre estate at the foot of the Luberon mountain, this fine ochre-walled property has comfortable rooms. Guests may use the summer kitchen as well as the pool. Lovely views of the Alpilles and Montagne Sainte-Victoire.

⊜⊜ **Chambre d'hôte Chambre de Séjour avec Vue** – *1 r. de la Burgade, 84400 Saignon.* ℘*04 90 04 85 01. www. chambreavecvue.com. Closed Dec–Feb. 5 rooms.* This unusual guesthouse doubles as an art gallery and residence for artists, some of whom have left their works *in situ.* Minimalist rooms decorated with the precision of an art collector.

⊜⊜⊜ **Le Clos du Buis** – *r. Victor-Hugo, 84480 Bonnieux.* ℘*04 90 75 88 48. www. leclosdubuis.com.* ♿🛏🅿. *Closed mid-Nov– Feb. 8 rooms. Restaurant*⊜⊜⊜. Situated near the church, this old house used to be a grocery and bakery and there is still a bread oven in the sitting room. The attractive bedrooms are bright and airy and have terra-cotta flooring. Behind the house there is a pleasant garden and swimming pool.

⊜⊜⊜ **L'Hostellerie du Luberon** – *Cours St-Louis, 84160 Vaugines.* ℘*04 90 77 27 19. www.hostellerieduluberon.com. Closed 11 Nov–9 Mar.* ♿🛏🅿. *16 rooms. Restaurant*⊜⊜⊜ *(Closed Tue and Wed lunch).* Facing the Durance valley, this family-run hotel has pretty rooms with Provençal décor. Library and games for all ages. Meals are served in the large dining room or on the terrace beside the pool.

🍽 EAT

⊜ **Bar de la Fontaine** – *84750 St-Martin-de-Castillon.* ℘*04 90 75 24 67. Lunch year round, dinner summer only.* A member of the excellent "Bistrot de Pays" group (dedicated to promoting local produce), this village bar has tasty *plats du jour.*

⊜⊜ **L'Escanson** – *450 av. A.-Briand, 84440 Robion.* ℘*04 90 76 59 61. Closed 2 Jan–2 Feb, Wed lunch and Tue.* Pastel tones and wrought iron give the dining room of the little restaurant a Provençal feel. Good traditional cuisine, lifted by a dash of creativity. Shaded terrace.

⊜⊜ **Maison de la Truffe et du Vin du Luberon** – *Pl. de l'Horloge, 84560 Ménerbes.* ℘*04 90 72 38 37. www.vin-truffe-luberon.com. Closes 6pm. Closed Nov–Mar.* In a wonderful setting (a beautiful 18C mansion on the village square with superb views from its garden terrace), the wine bar here serves salads and other light dishes. Excellent wine tastings are also on offer, and the bottlings of all the region's key producers can be bought at cellar-door prices.

⊜⊜ **Le Garage à Lumières**– *Hameau de Lumières, 84220 Goult.* ℘*04 32 50 29 32.* An old garage has been converted to provide the setting for this hip, stylish restaurant whose walls are decorated with little cars, modern art and film projections. Creative modern cooking.

⊜⊜⊜ **Bistrot la Cour de Ferme** – *Auberge la Fenière, 84160 Lourmarin. 2km/ 1.2mi via rte de Cadenet.* ℘*04 90 68 11 79. www.reinesammut.com. Closed 17 Nov– 4 Dec and Jan.* Reine Sammut, one of the Luberon's most respected chefs, offers a relaxed and affordable alternative to her famous Auberge de la Fenière nearby. Although the dishes here are simpler, her ability to conjure exquisite flavours from the best local produce still shines through.

⊜⊜⊜ **Le Fournil** – *5 pl. Carnot. Pl. Carnot, 84480 Bonnieux.* ℘*04 90 75 83 62. Closed Dec–Jan, Sat lunch and Mon (Apr–Sept), Mon and Tue (Oct–Mar). Booking advised.* The cave-like dining room of this house, which is built on the rock, ensures coolness which may be welcome during a summer meal. For sun worshippers, there is a terrace in the square. Regional dishes.

⊜⊜⊜ **Auberge de la Bartavelle** – *R. du Cheval-Blanc, 84220 Goult, 6km/3.7mi northeast of Ménerbes via D 218 and D 145.* ℘*04 90 72 33 72. Closed mid-Nov–early Mar, Tue, Wed.* This small restaurant in a vaulted dining room with a floor of traditional terra-cotta tiles serves carefully prepared food, based on local produce and marrying tradition with modernity.

L'Auberge des Tilleuls – *Moulin du Pas, 84240 Grambois. ℰ04 90 77 93 11. www.tilleuls.com. Closed Mon and Tue.* **P**. *5 rooms* ⬭⬭⬭⬭. This country inn has been taken over by a chef who has breathed new life into the cuisine, adding some modern touches without sacrificing Provençal tradition.

La Petite Maison – *Pl. de l'Étang, 84160 Cucuron. ℰ04 90 68 21 99. www. lapetitemaisondecucuron.com. Closed Mon and Tue.* Talented chef Eric Sapet has made his restaurant in an old house in the centre of Cucuron a top address for gourmets. Exquisite food, carefully selected wines and friendly, well-trained staff in a relaxed ambience. Prices are reasonable given the high standards.

La Bastide de Capelongue – *84480Bonnieux. ℰ04 90 75 89 78. www. capelongue.com. Open mid-Mar–mid-Nov. Closed Tue lunch and Wed.* ⬭⬭**P**. This splendid big Provençal *mas* above Bonnieux is the flagship property among several run by flamboyant chef Edouard Loubet. Ambitious, inventine cooking of the highest order in an elegant country-house setting, simple and refined rather than chi-chi.

TAKING A BREAK

Le Thé dans l'Encrier - *R. de la Juiverie, 84160 Lourmarin. ℰ04 90 68 88 41. Open Tue–Sat 10.30am–6.30pm.* This bookshop and café offers delicious food, all home-cooked. Soups, well-filled quiches, savoury crumbles and salads form the backbone of the lunch menu, with desserts such as raspberry and almond tart, a red fruit crumble or a devilish chocolate mousse.

SHOPPING

La Ferme de Gerbaud – *Campagne Gerbaud, 84160 Lourmarin. ℰ04 90 68 11 83. Open daily 2–7pm. Guided tours Apr–Oct.* A bumpy track leads to this estate, dedicated to growing plants and herbs for perfume and medicinal purposes. Guided visit available; the shop sells herbs, honey, essential oils and so on.

MARKETS

Coustellet – Apr–Nov Sun mornings.
Saint-Martin-de-la-Brasque – Apr–Nov Sun mornings.

EVENTS

International Festival of String Quartets – *ℰ04 90 75 89 60. www.festival-quatuors-luberon.com. Mid-Jul–mid-Sept.* In Goult, Roussillon and the abbaye de Silvacane.

LacosteFestival – *ℰ04 90 75 93 12.* This festival of music and theatre takes place in the château from early July to early August.

Market in Lourmarin
© Steven Morris/age fotostock

Roussillon★★
Vaucluse

Standing high up on cliffs of ochre rock whose rich tones of crimson, orange and gold are replicated in its ochre-washed houses, Roussillon is a sight to behold. Try to visit it late in the day when both village and cliffs are set ablaze by the glowing light of the setting sun. There will be fewer tourists at this time, too. Spring and autumn are also less crowded.

SIGHTS
The Village★
With its narrow little streets, splendidly colourful ochre-coated houses, galleries where potters and artists exhibit their work, and unexpected views at every turn, Roussillon is a continual enchantment from dawn to dusk.
Start at the pharmacy and go right into rue des Bourgades, then follow rue de l'Arcade, a partially covered stepped street. Pass under the belfry to get to the castrum.

Castrum
Viewing-table. From this platform a magnificent view extends northwards to the white crest of Mont Ventoux, southwards to the Grand Luberon with Mourre Nègre and, perched on its rock to the northwest, the village of Gordes.

▷ Go via place Pignotte to reach the far end of the watchpath, from where

▶ **Population:** 1 305.
Michelin Map: 332: E-10.
Info: Place de la Poste.
℘04 90 05 60 25.
Location: Coming from Apt (12km/7.4mi SE) or Gordes (10km/6mi W), you will reach the village. There are paying car parks in several locations.
Timing: The village looks its best at sunset.
Kids: The Sentier des Ocres, the Conservatoire des Ocres.

there is a lovely view of the **Aiguilles du Val des Fées**, vertical clefts in an ochre cliff-face.

OCHRE LAND
Besides providing an opportunity to explore one of the Luberon's most beautiful villages, a visit to Roussillon also gives a good overview of ochre production, covering every stage including extraction from the quarries and processing to giving the walls of the village their brilliant colours. Ochre had many industrial uses apart from pigment and plaster: rubber and sausage skins were just two.

Sentier des Ocres★★
Departure in front of the cemetery opposite place du Pasquier. Open beginning Feb school holidays–Dec. Closed if raining. €2.50 (under 10 free). *Taking samples of the ochre, smoking and picnicking are prohibited. Wear clothes and shoes that you don't mind dirtying.*
Signposted footpaths *(circuits of either 30min or 50min available)*, dotted with information panels, provide an introduction to the flora and landscape of the ochre hills whose dramatic shapes have been created partly by man and partly by erosion. Note the **aiguilles des fées**, which dominate the famous **chaussée des géants★★**, imposing jagged cliffs.

Roussillon
© M.Raynaud/Comité Régional de Tourisme Provence-Alpes-Côte d'Azur

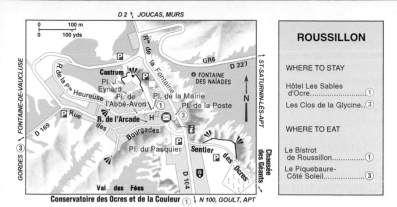

D 2 \ JOUCAS, MURS

ROUSSILLON

WHERE TO STAY

Hôtel Les Sables
d'Ocre..........................①
Les Clos de la Glycine..③

WHERE TO EAT

Le Bistrot
de Roussillon..............①
Le Piquebaure-
Côté Soleil..................③

Conservatoire des Ocres et de la Couleur ① \ N 100, GOULT, APT

👥 Conservatoire des Ocres et de la Couleur★

Ancienne usine Mathieu - rte d'Apt D 104. 🚹🕐*Open Apr–Jun and Sept 9am–6pm; Jul–Aug daily 9am–7pm; rest of the year daily except Sat–Sun 9am–1pm, 2–6pm.* 🕐*Closed first 2 weeks Jan and 25 Dec.* 🎫€6 (under 10 free). 📞04 90 05 66 69. www.okhra.com.
This workshop, established in 1921, was used to process ochre extracted from the quarries. Ochre in its natural state is a mixture of argillaceous sand and iron oxide. To obtain a pure ochre product, the mineral is washed and the heavier sandy impurities settle to the bottom. The lighter-weight mixture of iron oxide and clay is passed through a filter and into settling tanks where the clay gradually accumulates in layers. The water is evacuated and the ochre is left to dry all summer; it is then cut into blocks. To finish the drying process and to darken the pigmentation, the ochre is baked in ovens (to obtain a red colour, yellow ochre is baked at 450°C/842°F). Finally it is crushed, sifted and put in sacks or barrels.
The adjoining **Jardin des Teinturiers (garden of the dyers)** provides an introduction to the vegetable-based pigments which were also produced over a long period in this region.
Ôkhra Société coopérative d'intérêt collectif – This cultural co-operative, founded by the Conservatoire in 1994, organises visits and other activities related to Roussillon's ochre heritage throughout the year. Exhibitions, colour workshops

and activities for children are included. There is a bookshop specialising in colour-related themes, and pigments are for sale.

🚗 DRIVING TOUR

OCHRE TOUR★★
49km/30.5mi. Allow about 4hrs. Route shown in green on regional map p336–37.

▷ Leave Roussillon by the D 227 (good views to the right of the ochre cliffs and the Luberon, and to the left of the Vaucluse plateau), then bear right onto the D 2, then immediately right again on to the D 101.

Mines de Bruoux à Gargas
Rte de Croagne. 💬*Guided tours available, contact for times.* 🕐*Open May–Oct 10am–6pm (7pm in Jul–Aug).* 🎫€8. 📞04 90 06 22 59. www.minesdebruoux.fr. ⏱*Note that the temperature is just 11°C/52°F inside: bring a sweater.*
Ochre is still extracted in Gargas today (it is the last quarry of its kind in Europe), but on an infinitely smaller scale than when it was at the height of its production in the 19C. Do not be misled by the name: these "mines" are nothing of the kind. Although you will walk along underground galleries (there are 40km/24.8mi in total), these were chipped out with picks, eventually creating huge, vaulted, cathedral-like spaces. The monumental scale of these

and the extent of the galleries created in pursuit of the richest seams of ochre are truly impressive. After they had been abandoned, these quarries were used for mushroom-growing for a time.

▶ Go back the way you came to return to the D 2.

St-Saturnin-lès-Apt

This tiny village is overlooked by old castle ruins and a Romanesque chapel. Take the alley left of the village church and climb to the chapel for a view of the Apt countryside and Luberon range.

▶ Follow D 179 and then D 30.

👥 Colorado de Rustrel★★

Guides and maps available at the Maison du Colorado ✆04 90 04 96 07 or 06 81 06 82 20. Leave your car in one of the paying car parks, either by the banks of the Dôa, or on D 22. Footpaths are well marked; walking time for each loop is indicated by a signpost at the start of the trail.

This gigantic canyon, with its ochre-coloured landscape of cliff faces, clay-capped earth pillars with jagged crowns (Cheminées de Fées – fairies' chimneys), the spot known locally as "the Sahara", the Cirque de Barries, waterfalls, and the "river of sand", can be explored on different walks.

The 2hr loop *(recommended for experienced walkers)* begins at the Colorado campsite, on D22. Follow the yellow blaze marks. Leave the Rustrel iron foundry to the right. The slope down into the valley of the Lèbre contains vermilion rocks. Climb back up the valley to the foot of the old phosphate quarries known as "Terres Vertes" (green earth). Later, be sure to stop in the village of Rustrel for a well-deserved refreshment.

▶ Return to Roussillon via Apt on D 22.

ADDRESSES

🛏 STAY

Hôtel Les Sables d'Ocre – *Rte d'Apt. ✆04 90 05 55 55. www.sablesdocre.com.* 🅿. *22 rooms. Restaurant* 😊😊. *Closed Nov–Mar.* Situated in the heart of a 1ha/2.5-acre park area, this hotel offers comfortable, air-conditioned guest rooms with terraces overlooking the garden or the swimming pool.

Hôtel Les Clos de la Glycine – *Pl. de la Poste. ✆04 90 05 60 13. www. luberon-hotel.com.* 🅿. *9 rooms. Restaurant* 😊😊😊. High up in the village, this is a charming hotel with fresh, comfortable rooms which have superb views over the Chaussée des Géants and Mont Ventoux. The restaurant serves Provençal dishes under a canopy of wisteria on a terrace with a magnificent panorama.

Chambre d'hôte La Forge – *Notre-Dame-des-Anges, 84400 Rustrel, 2km/1.2mi on route d'Apt and route secondaire. ✆04 90 04 92 22. Open 1 Apr–5 Nov. 🏊. 5 rooms.* Within the Colorado, this old foundry, partly restored, has been converted into a welcoming B&B. Spacious rooms decorated in an original, colourful style. Flower-filled garden and fine pool.

🍴 EAT

Auberge de Rustréou – *3 pl. de la Fête, 84400 Rustrel. ✆04 90 04 90 90. Closed 24 Dec–1 Jan. 7 rooms😊. Restaurant 😊😊.* This restaurant close to the Colorado has had a reputation for good food for a long time. Enjoyed carefully prepared food in the air-conditioned dining room.

Le Bistrot de Roussillon – *pl. de la Mairie. ✆04 90 05 74 45. Closed winter evenings.* The terrace looks out over the roofs of the village and the Val des Fées. This creates an ideal setting in which to savour Provençal cuisine prepared by the owner, not forgetting the local wines. The dining room is ochre coloured and there are also tables outside in the lively square.

Le Piquebaure-Côté Soleil – *Quartier les Estrayas, rte de Gordes. ✆04 90 05 79 65. Closed Jan, mid-Nov– mid-Dec, Tue, Wed (out of season).* This restaurant takes its name from one of the rocks along the circuit de l'Ocre. Smart, rustic interior, nice covered terrace facing the valley, and *cuisine du marché*.

ACTIVITIES

Cycling– Two signposted itineraries: **Autour du Luberon** (236km/146mi circuit from Cavaillon, via Apt, Forcalquier, Manosque, Lourmarin) and **Les Ocres à vélo** (51km/31.6mi, via Apt, Rustrel and Roussillon). Information from Parc naturel régional du Luberon.

👪 **Colorado Aventures**– Forêt N.-D.-des-Anges, 84400 Rustrel. ✆06 78 26 68 91. www.colorado-aventures.fr. Open Jul–Aug daily 9.30am–7.30pm; rest of the year with advanced booking 10am–4.30pm. €19: access to Canyon, Forest and Indiana (children €14: access to Mempapeur and Pasifacile). Forest adventure park for children from age 6 with snack bar and picnic areas.

Gordes★★

Vaucluse

Rising in picturesque tiers above the Imergue valley, facing the Luberon mountain, Gordes has been classified as one of the most beautiful villages in France. On a site already occupied by humans as far back as the Neolithic era, it looks alluring with its old stone houses weathered to golden tones, its wonderful views, its narrow streets and château. Although Gordes can be crowded with tourists, many of them do not stray beyond its most commercial streets.

SIGHTS
The Village★

It is pleasant to walk through this charming town along the *calades* – small paved, sometimes stepped alleyways lined with gutters defined by two rows of stone – with vaulted passageways, arcades of old, tall houses and rampart ruins. The shops, craftshops and lively market add to the atmosphere.

Château

pl. du Château. 🕐*Open daily 10am–noon, 2–6pm.* 🕐*Closed 1 Jan and 25 Dec.* ⊛€4. ✆04 32 50 11 41.
The Renaissance château stands on the village's highest point. It was rebuilt by Bertrand de Simiane on the site of a 12C fortress. The north face, flanked by round machicolated towers, is austere, the south monumental, relieved by mullioned windows and small turrets. In the courtyard note the fine Renaissance

▶ **Population:** 2 113.
◉ **Michelin Map:** 332: E-10.
🄸 **Info:** Place du Château, Gordes. ✆04 90 72 02 75. www.gordes-village.com.
🅿 **Parking:** From April–November you'll have to park in one of the paying car parks.
🕐 **Timing:** Spring and autumn are the best times to visit.
👪 **Kids:** Village des Bories.

door (the soft limestone has been worn away by erosion). Inside, in the great hall (first floor) two flanking doorways show off a splendid **chimney-piece★** (1541) with ornate pediments and pilasters, shells and flowers.
In July and August, plays and concerts are held in the courtyard of the castle.

Caves du palais Saint-Firmin

Access from place Genty-Pantaly via the little rue de l'Église, the rue du Belvédère, in the direction of "point de vue". 🕐*Open May–Sept Wed–Mon 10am–6pm.* ⊛€6 (children €4.50). ✆04 90 72 02 75. www.caves-saintfirmin.com.
A son et lumière presentation is laid on in the underground passages of this "palace" (actually a large village house). It highlights a little-known aspect of Gordes history: the artisan work carried out by troglodytes. Water tanks, stairs, and the remains of a very old olive oil mill, probably dating from the 15C, are testament to their stone-hewing skills.

Gordes

© Franck Guiziou/hemis.fr

EXCURSIONS
♣♦ Village des Bories★★

3km/1.8mi south via the D 15 in the direction of Cavaillon. A little after the junction of the D 2, take a right down a tarmacked country road before a dry-stone wall. Continue for approximately 2km/1.25mi. ○Open daily 9am–8pm (5.30pm in winter). ○Closed 1 Jan and 25 Dec. ☞€6 (child under 17, €4). ℘04 90 72 03 48. www.gordes-villages.com. This village is now a Museum of Rural Life with about 20 restored *bories* (☞see *Le Montagne du Luberon*) between 200

and 500 years old, grouped around a communal bread oven. The larger *bories* served as dwellings; others were either sheep-folds or outbuildings. They were inhabited until the early 19C but their origin and use remain a mystery. They were certainly used as refuges during troubled times.

Musée du Moulin des Bouillons

5km/3.1mi south via the D 15 (direction Cavaillon), D 2 then the D 103, right, towards Beaumettes. Turn right again

Village des Bories

© Alain Hocquel/L'ADT Vaucluse Tourisme

on the D 148 towards Saint-Pantaléon; continue straight 100m following "Moulin des Bouillons" signs. ♿🕐Open Apr–Oct Wed–Mon 10am–noon, 2–6pm. ⚭€5. 𝒫04 90 72 22 11. www.musee-verre-vitrail.com.
This *bastide* (16C–18C) has been transformed into a museum dedicated to the history of olive oil. An **olive press★** made from an oak tree trunk weighs seven tonnes; Gallo-Roman in appearance, it is the oldest preserved press of its kind. The history of lighting and olive oil through the ages is explained.

St-Pantaléon

7km/4.3mi southeast via the D 104, then right on the D 148.
The tiny Romanesque church is built out of the rock with a central nave dating back to the 5C. Surrounding the church is a rock necropolis, or cemetery, where most of the tombs are child-size. It may have been a "sanctuary of grace" where children who died before they were baptised were brought by their parents; according to legend, they revived for the duration of a Mass during which they were baptised, then they died again and were buried here.

ADDRESSES

🏠 STAY

⊖⊖ **Chambre d'hôte Les Hauts de Véroncle** – 84220 Murs, 8.5km/5.3mi north to Gordes via D 15. 𝒫04 90 72 60 91. Closed 4 Nov–1 Mar. 🍴. 3 rooms. Restaurant⊖⊖. Nothing disturbs the calm of this isolated *mas* with *garrigue*. Pleasant, elegant rooms and a *gîte* for 4. Dinner is served under the pergola in summer or by the fire in winter.

⊖⊖⊖ **Chambre d'hôte la Badelle** – 7km/4.3mi S of Gordes via D 104 for Goult. 𝒫04 90 72 33 19. www.la-badelle.com. Reservations obligatory in winter. 5 rooms. The outbuildings of this ancestral farm have been converted into bedrooms. They are pleasantly simple with antique furniture and terra-cotta floor tiles. A kitchen is available for guests' use in the summer.

⊖⊖⊖ **Chambre d'hôte Le Mas de la Beaume** – 84220 Gordes. 𝒫04 90 72 02 96. www.labeaume.com. 5 rooms. Table d'hôte ⊖⊖⊖. Peace, a view of the village and the song of cicadas will seduce most city dwellers. This Provençal *mas* has a garden with olive and almond trees, lavender, and nice, spacious rooms. Swimming pool and Jacuzzi.

⊖⊖⊖ **Hôtel Le Mas des Romarins** – Rte de Sénanque. 𝒫04 90 72 12 13. www. masromarins.com. Closed mid-Nov–mid-Dec, Jan–Feb. 13 rooms. The terrace of this 100-year-old farm overlooking Gordes is sunny enough for breakfast early on. Attractive rooms, each with its own character.

🍴 EAT

⊖⊖ **La Farigoule** – Les Imberts (D 2, between Gordes and Cabrières-d'Avignon), 84220 Gordes. 4km/2.5mi from Gordes. 𝒫04 90 76 92 76. Closed Wed eve, Thu. On a beautiful covered terrace, this restaurant offers Provençal dishes that are bursting with flavour at fair prices.

⊖⊖ **L'Artegal** – Pl. du Château. 𝒫04 90 72 02 54. Delicious *plats du jour*, generous salads and home-made pâtisseries can be enjoyed on the terrace in fine weather, just below the château. Pleasant bistro-style interior with some modern touches.

⊖⊖⊖ **Le Mas Tourteron** – Chemin de St-Blaise. 𝒫04 90 72 00 16. Open 4 Mar– 11 Nov, Sat–Sun in Nov–Dec. Closed Sun eve Oct and Mar, Mon–Tue. "A cook in her own home" is how the owner of this *mas* with a bucolic garden sums up her approach, which marries culinary skill with conviviality. Attractive rustic setting.

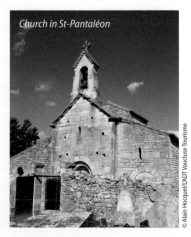
Church in St-Pantaléon

© Alain Hocquel/ADT Vaucluse Tourisme

Abbaye de
Sénanque★★

Vaucluse

One of the most iconic postcard photographs of Provence shows the beautiful, isolated Cistercian Abbaye de Sénanque surrounded by a sea of lavender. Nestling right down in the hollow of a small canyon of the Senancole River, the harmonious ensemble of buildings is a moving sight, the simplicity of the architecture and the tranquillity of the setting together evoking an atmosphere perfectly in tune with Cistercian monasticism. If you come via the D 177, you will have a splendid view of Gordes en route.

A BIT OF HISTORY

Foundation and Development – The foundation, in 1148, of Sénanque by a group of monks who had come from Abbaye de Mazan (Haut-Vivarais) fits into the great Cistercian expansion of the 12C. This monastic movement, directed and inspired by St Bernard of Clairvaux, preached an ascetic ideal and prescribed the strict application of Benedictine rule involving isolation and poverty in its monasteries.

The way of life of the Cistercians was thus demanding: divine service, prayer and pious reading alternated with man-

ⓑ **Michelin Map:** 332: E-10.
🅱 **Info:** Abbaye Notre-Dame de Sénanque, Gordes.
𝄞 04 90 72 05 72.
www.senanque.fr.
ⓣ **Timing:** Allow 1hr. To respect the silence of the monks who live here, only guided visits are allowed (in French).

ual labour to fill long days where rest did not exceed seven hours; meals were taken in silence and the monks slept in a dormitory without any comfort.

Cistercian austerity influenced the architectural and artistic conceptions of the Order. St Bernard decreed that buildings be plain and stripped of all ornamentation that could divert the attention of those who prayed: no coloured stained-glass windows, statues, paintings or carved tympana. This characteristic can be found in the other two Cistercian abbeys of Provence: Abbaye du Thoronet *(ⓒsee The Green Guide French Riviera)* and Abbaye de Silvacane *(ⓒsee Abbaye de Silvacane)*. They are collectively known as "les Trois Soeurs Provençales" (the Three Sisters of Provence).

Sénanque prospered rapidly to the point that, as early as 1152, the community had enough members to found another abbey in the Vivarais. It profited from

Abbaye de Sénanque

© Alain Hocquel/LADT Vaucluse Tourisme

numerous gifts, starting with the land of the Simiane family and later the land of the Lords of Venasque. The monastery set up outlying farms (granges) worked by lay brothers recruited from the peasant population.

Sénanque's peak occurred in the early 13C, but prosperity led to corruption: the order accumulated wealth incompatible with its vow of poverty.

Decadence and Renaissance – In the 14C Sénanque entered a decadent period. Recruitment and fervour diminished while lack of discipline increased. Yet, thanks to the energetic rule of an abbot during the end of the 15C, the situation improved and until the mid-16C the monastery once more strove to respect the ideals of its founders.

Unfortunately, in 1544, Sénanque fell victim to the Vaudois Revolt: monks were hanged by the heretics and several buildings were razed. These actions were the final blow; the abbey was never able to recover. At the end of the 17C, in spite of the efforts of the abbots, the community numbered only two monks. Nevertheless, the south wing of the monastery was rebuilt at the beginning of the 18C.

Sold as state property in 1791, Sénanque miraculously fell into the hands of an intelligent owner who not only preserved it from destruction but also consolidated it. Bought by an ecclesiastic in 1854, it was returned, soon after, to its monastic vocation; new buildings were added flanking the older ones and 72 monks were installed. The anticlerical beliefs of the Third Republic brought about their eviction twice. In 1927 a dozen monks returned, and since then there has been a small community in Sénanque.

🐾 WALKING TOUR

🕐Guided tours by reservation; check website for times. 𝄞04 90 72 05 72. www.senanque.fr. 🕐Closed on religious holidays. ✆€7.50.

The abbey is a very fine example of Cistercian architecture. The early monastery is complete with the exception of the lay brothers' wing, which was rebuilt in the 18C. The medieval parts are built in local ashlar stone. The abbey church has kept its original roof of limestone slabs (lauzes) surmounted by a square bell tower; contrary to custom, it was built facing north rather than east, as the builders had to compensate for the rigours of the local terrain.

▶ The tour starts on the first floor of the dormitory, northwest of the cloisters (Cloître).

Dormitory (Dortoir)

This vast pointed barrel-vaulted room with transverse arches, lit by a 12-lobed oculus and narrow windows, is paved in brick. This is where the monks slept fully dressed on a simple straw pallet. They were roused in the middle of the night for the first service (nocturns), which took place at 2am, soon followed by matins at dawn. The dormitory now houses an exhibition on the abbey's construction.

Abbey Church (Église)★

Begun in 1160 with the sanctuary and transept, the church was completed in the early 13C with the nave. The purity of line and remarkable, austere beauty, emphasised by the absence of all decoration, create a place of worship and meditation.

Stand at the back of the nave to admire the harmony of the proportions and masses. The transept crossing is crowned by a large dome on elaborate squinches (small arches, curved stone slab, fluted pilasters which recall the style of churches from Velay and the Vivarais). The sanctuary ends with a semicircular apse pierced by three windows, symbolising the Trinity, and flanked by four apsidal chapels. Nave, transept and aisles are covered with flat stones resting on the vault itself.

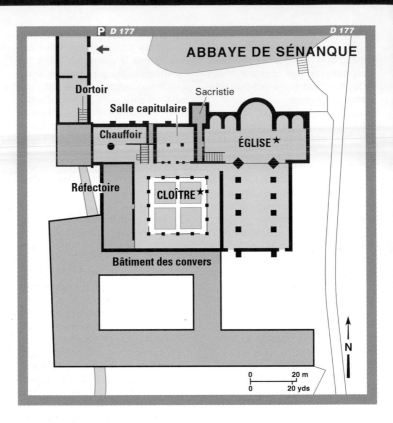

ABBAYE DE SÉNANQUE

Dortoir

Sacristie

Salle capitulaire

Chauffoir

ÉGLISE★

Réfectoire

CLOÎTRE★

Bâtiment des convers

N

0   20 m
0   20 yds

Cloisters (Cloître)★

Late 12C. The cloisters' galleries are covered with rounded barrel vaulting with transverse arches held up by carved brackets. Decoration appears on the capitals (leaf-work, flowers, rope and palm-leaf moulding and interlacing) and yet it remains discreet.

The cloisters open onto the different rooms of the conventual buildings, each of which has its specific function.

Conventual Buildings★
Chapter house (Salle capitulaire)

The room is roofed with six-pointed vaults held up at the centre on two pillars. Under the abbot's leadership the monastic community met here to read and comment on the Scriptures, receive the novices' vows, to keep vigil over the dead and to make important decisions.

Warming room (Chauffoir)

Access via a narrow passage. One of the two original chimneys remains in a corner. The heat was essential to the transcribers, who were bent over their manuscripts all day.

Refectory (Réfectoire)

Parallel to the west gallery of the cloisters. It was extensively damaged in the 16C and has recently been restored to its original appearance.

Lay brothers' wing (Bâtiment des convers)

South of the cloisters, this building, which was remodelled in the 18C, housed the lay brothers, who lived separately from the monks, meeting them only during certain services or when working in the fields.

Cavaillon

Vaucluse

Even though Cavaillon produces far fewer melons now than it did at the height of its golden era a century ago, its name is still associated with the perfumed, succulent fruits that made it famous. Throughout Provence and further afield, juicy, orange-fleshed Cavaillon melons are still regarded as a perfect antidote to the summer heat. They are grown, along with other produce, in the extensive market gardens that surround the town. The fields are irrigated with water from the Durance River, through an elaborate system of channels created by the Romans. Cavaillon also has an interesting Jewish aspect to its history, like Carpentras.

▶ **Population:** 24 951.
Michelin Map: 332: D-10.
Info: Place François-Tourel, Cavaillon. ℘04 90 71 32 01. www.cavaillon-luberon.com.

WALKING TOUR

LOWER CAVAILLON

▷ From place Tourel walk towards the adjacent place du Clos, which used to be the site of a melon market.

Arc Romain

pl. du Clos.
On the square lie the ruins of a small, delicately carved Roman arch dating from the 1C BC. It stood near the cathedral at the intersection of the main streets of the Roman town and was re-erected here in 1880.

▷ Take cours Sadi Carnot and turn right into rue Diderot.

Cathédrale Saint-Véran

pl. Joseph d'Arbaud. Open Apr–Sept Mon–Fri 8.30am–noon, 2–6pm, Sat 2–5pm, Oct–Mar Mon–Fri 9am–noon, 2–5pm, Sat 2–5pm. Closed Sun, public holidays. ℘04 90 78 03 44.
The cathedral is dedicated to the patron saint of shepherds, who was Bishop of Cavaillon in the 6C. The original Romanesque structure was enlarged by side chapels, from the 14C to the 18C. The façade was almost entirely rebuilt in the 18C, and the east end has a fine pentagonal apse.

▷ Take Grand-Rue, which crosses the old part of Cavaillon.

Pass the façade of the Grand Couvent before going through the Porte d'Avignon, part of the town's remaining fortifications.

Musée de l'Hôtel-Dieu

Open May–Sept 2–6pm. Closed Tue. €3 (free for under 18s); ticket includes admission to the Synagogue et Musée Juif Comtadin. ℘04 90 76 00 34. www.cavaillon.com.
There is an area in the chapel given over to engravings; information about the history of the old hospital (including pots for unguents, made of faïence and glass), and, on the first floor, an **archeological collection★** of objects found on the hill of Saint-Jacques: ceramics, coins and so on.

▷ Turn right along cours Gambetta to reach the square of the same name, then turn right again into the pedestrian-only shopping street, rue de la République.

This area was known as the *carrière*, formerly the Jewish ghetto. On the right is rue Hébraïque, which leads to the **synagogue**.

Synagogue et Musée Juif Comtadin

r. Hébraïque. Open daily except Tue: May–Sept 9.30am–12.30pm, 2–6pm; Oct 10am–noon, 2–5pm. Closed Tue,

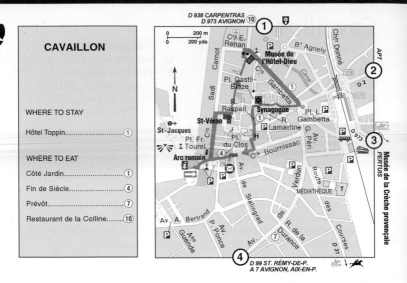

CAVAILLON

WHERE TO STAY

Hôtel Toppin.............................①

WHERE TO EAT

Côté Jardin..............................①

Fin de Siècle...........................④

Prévôt......................................⑦

Restaurant de la Colline........⑩

1 Jan, 1 May and 25 Dec. ⊛€3 *(ticket includes admission to Hôtel-Dieu). ℘04 90 72 26 86. www.cavaillon.org.*
The original synagogue was built on this site in the 14C, making it the oldest in France. Rebuilt in 1772–74, this synagogue, together with that of Carpentras, is one of the last examples of Baroque Provençal synagogue architecture. The interior is ornamented with beautiful wood panelling painted grey and decorated with blue and yellow touches. A superb wrought-iron balustrade encircles the gallery. The museum contains a miscellaneous collection of objects and documents: manuscripts, prayer books and sacred articles. In the basement are the baths reserved for the women's purification rites.

▷ Return to place Tourel by rue Raspail and, on the right, cours Bournissac.

ADDITIONAL SIGHT
Colline St-Jacques

The hill can be reached on foot taking a signposted footpath which starts at the Roman arch (allow 30min).

▷ It is also accessible by car (5.5km/3.4mi) by way of the D 938 towards Carpentras; then via a road to the left uphill, just beyond a crossroads.

From the viewing table the **view★** embraces the Cavaillon plain, Mont Ventoux, the Coulon valley, the Vaucluse plateau, the Luberon (quite near), the Durance valley and the Alpilles. Continue to the **Chapelle St-Jacques** *(colline St-Jacques;* ◷*open daily 10am–6pm)*, a 12C chapel, which stands in an attractive garden among cypresses, pines and almond trees.

Napoleon's Woes

Fleeing Avignon in April 1814, **Napoleon Bonaparte**, on his way to exile on the island of Elba, stopped at an inn in Orgon, south of Cavaillon. A hostile crowd, alerted by the Royalist drummers, gathered. The excited mob wanted to lynch him but he was saved by the mayor of Orgon and fled. He was able to reach the Auberge de La Calade near Aix.

Arc Romain

© Di Rosa G./ARCO/age fotostock

EXCURSIONS
Les Taillades

5km/3mi E via the D 143. At the roundabout, follow signposts to "Vieux Village". **P** *Park the car on the square in the front of the town hall.*

At the far end of the Petit Luberon range, this little village comes as a surprise with its houses perched on what look like enormous stone stalagmites, creating a striking yet serene **site★**. Quarrymen literally hacked away at the foundations of their homes to obtain molasse, a highly prized sandstone.

Follow the road that climbs in a spiral to the church and go past the tower. To your left you will see a strange statue, the "Morvellous", supposedly of St Veranus. A former graveyard opposite the church of St-Luce overlooks the village: ancient dwellings, troglodyte constructions and, wherever you look, vertical partitions carved into the rock.

▶ Retrace your steps and turn right after Auberge des Carrières into rue des Carrières.

A vaulted archway leads into this quarry hollowed out of the village itself. Its sheer rock walls form a roughly circular space, the **théâtre des carrières** *(place de la mairie. www.lestaillades.fr).* This forms a striking setting for open-air concerts every summer.

▶ Continue on the D 143 to the Cavaillon crossroads.

The road comes to **moulin St-Pierre**, a watermill on the canal de Carpentras that still features its great paddle-wheel. It was used for grinding madder before becoming a flour mill, a role it played until 1870.

Combe de Vidauque

5km/3mi southeast. Leave Cavaillon on the D 973 and fork left towards Vidauque.

The road is very steep and takes a hairpin course *(one-way traffic, speed limit of 30kph/18mph)*, skirting the wild Vidauque combe and offering magnificent plunging **views★★** of the surrounding countryside: the tip of the Vaucluse plateau and Cavalon valley (north), the Alpilles and Durance valley (south and west), and below, the Cavaillon plain.

▶ Take the Trou-du-Rat road down to D 973 into which you turn right towards Cheval-Blanc to return to Cavaillon.

ADDRESSES

🏠 STAY

◌◌ **Hôtel Toppin** – *70 cours Léon, Gambetta.* ℘*04 90 71 30 42. www.hotel-toppin.com.* **P***. WiFi. 32 rooms.* Right in the city centre, this straightforward hotel is a

The Melon Festival

This festival takes place the weekend before 14 July. There are exhibitions, tastings, processions of flowered carts, reconstructions of an old market and fireworks all centred on the theme of the melon, the symbol of Cavaillon. This town is a welcoming one, so contingents from other cities are invited to join the festivities, including candied fruit makers from Apt and vintners from Beaumes-de-Venise. *Délice de Melon* is the name of an aperitif made from the pulp of melon steeped in alcohol with the addition of sugar, served with crushed ice. *www.melondecavaillon.com.*

© S. Sauvignier/MICHELIN

convenient place to collapse. Simple, clean rooms, a big terrace and welcoming staff. The bedrooms to the back are best.

⊉/EAT

☺☺ **Le Fin de Siècle** – *46 pl. du Clos (1st floor). ℘04 90 71 12 27.* The décor inside this restaurant is inspired by the Empire, with images of Napoleon III. Somewhat kitsch. Traditional cuisine and friendly service. Patio-terrace.

☺☺ **Côté Jardin** – *49 rue Lamartine. ℘04 90 71 33 58. Closed Sun, Tue eve, Feb.* Slightly out of the town centre, the discovery of this restaurant with its wall friezes will come as a pleasant surprise. In the summer tables are laid out around a fountain in a pretty courtyard. Mediterranean cuisine.

☺☺☺ **Restaurant Prévôt** – *353 av. Verdun. ℘04 90 71 32 43. Closed Sun and Mon Sept–Jun, public holidays.* Passionate about melons, chef Jean-Jacques Prévôt has made his elegant restaurant a Cavaillon institution. Formal décor. Themed menus include an all-melon one in summer.

☺☺☺ **Restaurant de la Colline** – *chemin des Chênes Verts, Ermitage St-Jacques, 4km/2.5mi dir. Avignon-Carpentras. ℘04 90 71 44 99. www.la-colline-luberon.com. ⅁ꔥ. Closed Jan, Mar and Mon eve Oct–May.* Peaceful, bright environment combined with local wines and a varied menu of good-quality dishes.

TAKING A BREAK

Sole Pan – *61 cours Bournissac. ℘04 90 78 06 54. Open daily 7am–7.30pm. Closed Mar.* Cavaillon people have been buying their bread in this boulangerie for over a century. The current baker has introduced a vast range of flavours, but the traditional approach and quality of the results remain the same. The café/salon de thé is open all day.

SHOPPING

🛒 **Choosing the right melon** – The scientific approach is to check that the melon feels heavy (the riper it is, the more sugar there will be in the flesh, and the heavier it will feel), and the stem *(le pécou)* should be ready to snap off easily. If there are cracks in the melon's skin, it will probably taste great.

Pâtissier-chocolatier Étoile du Délice – *57 pl. Castil-Blaze. ℘04 90 78 07 51. www. etoile-delice.fr. Open Thu–Tue 7am–1pm, 3–7.30pm.* Melons of course, this time enrobed in chocolate and baptized *melonettes*. The melon sorbet (seasonal) smells wonderful *(call ahead to order).*

Markets – Traditional market every Monday morning. Farmers' market Apr–Sept Thu 5pm–7pm, on place du Clos.

La Tour d'Aigues

Vaucluse

At the foot of the Luberon mountains, the region around Aigues is delightful countryside made up of fertile, sun-drenched vineyards, cherry orchards and market gardens, in stark contrast to the wild barrenness of the neighbouring hills. Founded in the 10C or 11C, the town owes its name to a tower which was a precursor of the keep of the present castle. In high season the Festival du Sud Luberon is held here.

▶ **Population:** 3 947.
⚙ **Michelin Map:** 332: G-11.
🛈 **Info:** Le Château, La Tour-d'Aigues. ℰ04 90 07 50 29. www.souriredu luberon.com.

SIGHTS
Château

🕐*Open mid–Jun–mid-Sept Tue–Sat 10am–1pm, 3–6pm, Sun–Mon 3–6pm; Apr–mid-Jun 10am–12.30pm, 2–6pm (Sun–Mon 3–6pm).* 🕐*Closed 1 Jan, 24, 25, 31 Dec.* ﷼€5. ℰ04 90 07 50 33. www.chateaulatourdaigues.com.

Replacing a medieval château on the same site, this proud Renaissance-style edifice was built in 1555–75 by an Italian architect (Ercole Nigra) on a vast terrace overlooking the Lèze; Catherine de' Medici stayed here in 1579. Burned in 1782 and again in 1792 when it was ruined, it is now being progressively restored by the Vaucluse *département*. The monumental entrance gate takes the form of a richly decorated triumphal arch: Corinthian columns and pilasters, a frieze of the attributes of war and an entablature surmounted by a triangular pediment. In the centre of the bailey is the keep restored to its 16C Italian plan. Inside, the network of underground cellars now houses exhibition, projection and conference rooms as well as collections from the two museums below.

Musée des Faïences

During the course of the restoration work carried out on the château's cellars a large quantity of glazed earthenware was discovered. The finest pieces have been brought together in this museum which offers the visitor a comprehensive illustration of the work produced in Jérôme Bruny's Tour d'Aigues factory between 1750 and 1785.

Musée de l'Habitat Rural du Pays d'Aigues

This museum contains a modern display drawing heavily on audiovisual methods: a history of Provençal man's evolution from his origins to the present. Slides, illuminated maps, miscellaneous objects (early casts, tools, reconstruction of a silkworm farm) and models depict the development of local rural life.

🚗 DRIVING TOUR

LEISURELY DRIVE ALONG THE DURANCE

112km/69.5mi. Allow 1 day.
⚙*See local map on p367.*

At the foot of the **Luberon** mountains flows the Durance, the great fluctuating river which follows a course parallel to the Mediterranean before joining the Rhône at Avignon. This was not always the case, however: at the end of the last Ice Age, the swollen waters burst through the Lamanon gap on a more direct route to the sea, depositing a huge mass of rock and stone over the wide expanse of what is now the Plaine de la Crau. The Durance's flow is irregular, with violent rainstorms provoking devastating flood-waters, though the river is gradually being harnessed to serve the local economy. The Serre-Ponçon reservoir helps to control its course as well as maintaining irrigation of the plains of the Basse-Durance during dry periods.

Château de la Tour d'Aigues

© Camille Moirenc/hemis.fr

It is rare for any one region to be as well served by canals as Provence is between the Durance and the sea. Each was constructed for one of three purposes: irrigation (such as the 16C Canal de Craponne, one of the oldest in Provence), the provision of town and factory water, and the production of electricity.

The river's waters have regained their purity, as shown by the numerous fish, cormorants, herons and beavers which make it their home.

▷ Leave Tour d'Aigues by the D 135 eastwards and proceed towards Mirabeau.

On the left after the village, the N 96 goes through the **Défilé de Mirabeau** where the river bends sharply to the west and emerges from Haute-Provence into the Vaucluse through this dramatic narrow channel cut out by the action of the water.

▷ After crossing the Durance by the **Pont Mirabeau**, turn left at the roundabout in the direction of Saint-Paul-lès-Durance, then a right on to D 11, in the direction of Jouques.

Jouques

Rising in terraces from the banks of the Réal, this village with its grand avenue of majestic plane trees, houses with façades in warm colours, steep, flower-bedecked streets, sometimes straddled by arches, and roofs of Roman tiles evokes the archetypal Provençal village in an irresistible way. A pleasant walk will take you to the top of the village where, from the 11C church of **Notre-Dame-de-la-Roque**, you will be rewarded with a pretty view of this village's harmonious architecture with green countryside all around.

▷ Take D 561 in the direction of Peyrolles.

Peyrolles-en-Provence

Little remains of the town's medieval fortifications except for a belfry crowned by a wrought-iron bell cage and a round tower (in ruins) near the church.

Château de Peyrolles-en-Provence

◐ *Open: check at tourist office for information.* ℘ *04 42 57 89 82.* *www.peyrolles-en-provence.fr.*
Once a residence of King René and today the local town hall, this castle was converted into a mansion in the late 17C.

The interior features a grand sweeping staircase and 18C gypsum furnishings. From the east terrace, decorated with a fountain portraying a gladiator, there is a pretty view of the Durance valley.

At the foot of the château a grotto has been discovered, with astonishing traces of **fossilised palms** dating from the tertiary era, unique in Europe (*Visits on request, book ahead at the tourist office, ℘04 42 57 89 82*).

The **église Saint-Pierre**, rebuilt many times, has retained a Romanesque nave. On a rocky spur, the **chapelle du Saint-Sépulcre**, erected in the 12C, is in the form of a Greek cross. On the walls, note the frescoes of the creation of Adam and Eve (above the door) and a procession of haloed saints.

▶ Take the D 96 in the direction of Meyrargues.

Meyrargues

The town is dominated by its château (now a hotel), rebuilt in the 17C. A pleasant walk leads to the remains of a Roman aqueduct (below the castle) which brought water to Aix-en-Provence and continues to the wild Étroit gorges.

▶ On leaving the town, turn right onto the D 561 in direction of Roque-d'Anthéron, then left onto the D 15 towards Puy-Ste-Réparade.

Rognes

Rognes is located on the north face of the Chaîne de la Trévaresse. It is famous on two accounts: for the well-known Rognes stone much used for construction locally, and, more recently, for its truffles (market in December). The **church** (23 place de l'Eglise. ℘04 42 57 01 01 ⏰open: check at the tourist office for details) built in the early 17C is decorated with a remarkable group of **ten altarpieces★** (17C–18C).

▶ Take the picturesque D 66 to return to the D 561, and turn left.

Centrale de St-Estève-Janson (power station)

This is where the Canal de Marseille begins. Dug in the 19C, it supplied the city with drinking water for many years.

Bassin de St-Christophe

A vast reservoir in a setting of rocks and pine trees, at the foot of the chaîne des Côtes.

▶ The road crosses and then follows the EDF canal.

Abbaye de Silvacane★★

👜see Abbaye de Silvacane.

La Roque-d'Anthéron

At the centre of this small town stands the 17C **Château de Florans** (place Louis Auguste Forbin. ⛓now a private clinic) flanked by round towers. The château acts as a backdrop to the prestigious International Piano Festival (last week Jul and first 3 weeks Aug. www.festival-piano.com).

On Place Paul-Cézanne, the **Centre d'évocation vaudois et huguenot** acts as a reminder that the Vaudois (*see Introduction, p71*) settled in La Roque between 1514 and 1545. (To have a fuller picture, you can visit the protestant church in old Vaudois quarter, dating from 1825.)

On Cours Foch, a recently renovated space, is the **musée de Géologie et d'Ethnographie**, retracing 300 million years of Provençal geological history. Fossils, impressions and reconstructions will fascinate both adults and children. *Cours Foch.* ○*Open Jul–Aug 3–7pm; Sept–Jun Sat, 2.30–5.30pm, Sun 10am –noon 2.30–5.30pm.* ○*Closed public holidays.* ☞€4 (children under 18, €2). ℘04 42 53 41 32. www.musee-geologie-ethnographie-laroque.com.

▶ Continue along the D 561 to the D 23C on the right. Beyond the town of Mallemort turn onto the D 32 to cross the river; turn left onto the D 973. Continue for 2km/1.2mi and just before a bridge, bear right onto a small road which skirts a quarry.

Mérindol

On an embankment along the Durance, a wooden viewing hut provides a unique view of hundreds of birds, frolicking happily quite unaware of your presence. This **bird observatory** (☞*no charge, information panels about the various species*) was created by the Parc naturel régional du Luberon. Morning is the best time to come here. Don't forget your binoculars!

▶ Continue on the D 973.

Lauris

A picturesque village with streets lined with 16C–18C houses. From the promenade de la Roque, visitors can explore the terraced gardens of the castle, overlooking the Durance Valley. The **church** has one of the prettiest wrought-iron campaniles in the region.

The **château** (18C), at the highest point of the cliff, controlled the Durance valley. After you have visited

the courtyard where there are eight artists' studios, take the time to stroll in the terraced gardens. On the second level is the **Conservatoire des plantes tinctoriales (Conservatory of dye-producing plants)**, with 300 species from all over the world. These are the source of vegetal dyes used in the manufacture of food, cosmetics, paints, fabric dyes and so on. ○*Open mid-May–Oct Tue–Sun 9am–noon, 3–7pm (6.30pm in Sept–Oct).* ○*Closed Mon.* ☞€5 (under 12 free). ✱*Guided tours (1hr30mins) on request* ☞€8. ℘04 90 08 40 48. www.couleur-garance.com.

Cadenet

This town was an important centre for basket making, thanks to the proximity of the Durance; from the beginning of the 19C until the mid-20C, its willow beds were harvested for the production of wicker. The industry reached its zenith between the 1920s and 1930s after which, as a result of competition from rattan imported from the Far East, production diversified into household items and various decorative objects. You can find out all about it at the **Musée de la Vannerie** (*av. Philippe de Girard;* ♿○*open mid-Mar–mid-Nov daily except Tue 10am–noon, 2.30–6.30pm (Wed and Sun 2.30–6.30pm)* ☞€3.50. ℘04 90 68 06 85), which is situated on the site of the former La Glaneuse workshop. On the main square, a statue perpetuates the memory of a local hero, André Estienne, known as the **Arcole drummer boy** (*see box, right*).

A fine square tower supports the bell tower of the **church** (14C but rebuilt several times). Inside, don't miss the beautiful **baptismal font★** fashioned out of a 3C Roman sarcophagus decorated with bas-reliefs.

▶ After Villelaure, on the D 973, turn left in the direction of Pertuis and follow signs to Château Val Joanis (3km/1.8mi). Note: take care crossing the road when you reach the château entrance.

Château Val Joanis Garden

Open Apr–Oct 10am–1pm, 2–7pm (6pm in Oct) (Jul–Aug 10am–7pm); rest of year Mon–Fri 9am–noon, 2–4.30pm. Guided visits possible with advanced booking. €4.50 (free under 16). 04 90 09 69 52. www.val-joanis.com. Follow a visit to the garden with a local Côtes-du-Luberon wine tasting.

Behind the cellars of this huge wine estate lies a magnificent 18C-style garden. It is laid out on three terraces: the first has a potager with fruit and vegetables; the second is given over to flowers and the third is for ornamental trees and shrubs. A long arbour covered with roses runs down one side while an olive grove has been planted at the other. A serene, refreshing and colourful place to visit, with vines all around. You can also taste and buy wine here in a shop well stocked with local products.

▷ Turn back towards Villelaure and bear right on the D 37 to Ansouis (4km/2.5mi).

Ansouis

Located between the River Durance and the Grand Luberon foothills, the town was built on the southern slope of a rocky spur crowned by an imposing castle.

Château★

pl. du Château. Guided tours only (1hr) Apr–Oct daily except Tue–Wed 3pm, 4.30pm. €10. 04 90 77 23 36. www.chateau-ansouis.com.

Towering over the village, the château of Ansouis is well worth visiting because, apart altogether from its beauty, it encapsulates several periods of history, each marked by a different architectural style. Built by the Counts of Provence in the 13C on the site of an older fortification, its medieval core (which includes a lovely chapel and intriguing 15C kitchen) was added to in 1630 with the creation of a magnificent Classical façade in the Aixoise style. In the 18C (during which period Louis XV gave the Sabran family who lived here for centuries an elegant altar), it was further extended and embellished with exquisite plasterwork.

Le Tambour d'Arcole

In the main square there is a statue of André Estienne, the famous drummer boy, born in Cadenet in 1777. He served in Napoleon's northern Italy campaign of 1796 and, in the midst of the battle against the Austrians and Italians for the Arcole Bridge, he swam the river and beat such a tattoo that the Austrians mistook it for artillery fire; as they retreated, the French advanced to capture the bridge and win the battle.

Now in the hands of new owners who are carrying out extensive restoration work, the château feels more like a family home, albeit on a grand scale, than many castles that are open to the public. The delightful garden was designed by Lenôtre and the terrace has superb views over the valley.

Musée Extraordinaire

r. du Vieux Moulin. Open daily 2–6.30pm. Guided tours available. €3.50. 04 90 09 82 64.

The 15C vaulted cellars of this ancient building house a small museum devoted to underwater life. Works displayed are by painter, ceramicist and stained-glass artist **G Mazoyer**.

Ansouis and the château

© Alain Hocquel/L'ADT Vaucluse Tourisme

▶ Leave Ansouis heading towards La Tour d'Aigues, then turn immediately right onto D 56 towards Pertuis. After 2km/1.2mi, turn left (signposted) onto a gravelled track lined with cypress trees.

Château Turcan: Musée de la Vigne et du Vin

&⊙*Open Jul–Aug daily 9.30am–noon, 2.30–6pm.* ⊙*Rest of year closed Mon am, Wed and Sun.* ⊛€5. *℘04 90 09 83 33. www.chateau-turcan.com.* Established in the 1860s by Louis Turcan, a self-professed "pharmacist winegrower", this wine estate has become famous for its wine museum. It has a very extensive collection of tools and equipment including some of the oldest wine presses in France.

▶ Return to the D 56 towards Pertuis.

Pertuis

Capital of the pays d'Aigues, the town has a rich history, as evidenced by a 14C battlemented tower (St-Jacques), a 13C clock tower, a castle ruin and the **Église St-Nicolas**. This church, rebuilt in the 16C, contains a 16C triptych and two 17C marble statues given to the monks of the town by Cardinal Barberini.

▶ Return to La Tour d'Aigues by the D 956.

ADDRESSES

🏠 STAY

⊖⊜ **Hôtel-restaurant Le Petit Mas de Marie** – *Quartier Revol, 84240 La Tour-d'Aigues. ℘04 90 07 48 22. www.lepetitmas demarie.com. Closed mid-Nov and mid-Feb.* 🅿. *15 rooms. Restaurant for guests* ⊖⊜. This welcoming country house is surrounded by a peaceful garden. Impeccably maintained Provençal rooms and cuisine to match.

⊖⊜ **Chambre d'hôte Un Patio en Luberon** – *R. du Grand-Four, 84240 Ansouis. ℘04 90 09 94 25. www.unpatioenluberon. com. Closed 1 Jan–15 Mar.* ⊡. *5 rooms. Restaurant* ⊖⊜. At the centre of medieval

Ansouis, this renovated 16C inn has retained character and charm. Pretty rooms, vaulted dining room and sweet patio with fountain.

⊖⊜⊜ **Chambre d'hôte La Maison des Sources** – *Chemin des Fraisses, 84360 Lauris. ℘04 90 08 22 19 or 06 08 33 06 40. www. maison-des-sources.com. Closed end Nov–early Jan.* ⊡. *4 rooms.* In a *bastide* on a hill, a B&B whose brightly decorated, spacious rooms all have green views. Sustaining breakfasts and a kitchen area for guests.

♀/ EAT

⊖⊜ **La Table des Mamées** – *1 r. du Mûrier, 84360 Lauris. ℘04 90 08 34 66. www.latabledesmamees.com. Closed 17 Nov–8 Dec, Sun eve and Mon. Booking recommended.* Recipes handed down from grandmothers are the basis for the tasty dishes served in this 14C–15C coaching inn with rough stone walls and vaulted ceilings.

⊖⊜⊜ **La Closerie** – *Bd des Platanes, 84240 Ansouis. ℘04 90 09 90 54. Closed Nov–Jan.* This small Ansouis restaurant is sought out for its flavoursome food; best to book in advance. Pretty terrace facing the Luberon.

⊖⊜⊜ **Restaurant du Lac** – *Lieu-dit Pied-Bernard, 84240 La Motte d'Aigues. ℘04 90 09 14 10. www.restaurantdulac.eu. Closed 1 week Christmas, 2 weeks Feb, Wed lunch Oct–May, Tue lunch Jun–Sept, Mon. 2 rooms, 1 suite* ⊖⊜⊜. Chef Philippe Sublet worked with the Roux brothers in England before setting up his smart restaurant with rooms. Deft cuisine with subtle Asian touches in a delightful lakeside setting. Low-key luxury in the bedrooms.

SHOPPING

Markets – Traditional market in Pertuis *(Fri am)*, Rognes *(Wed am)*, La Roque-d'Anthéron *(Thu am, on cours Foch)*. Producers' market in Cadenet *(Apr–Nov, Sat am)*, Pertuis *(Wed and Sat am)*, La Tour-d'Aigues *(Jul–Aug Tue am, Thu eve)*.

Abbaye de Silvacane★★

Bouches-du-Rhône

Set in a pastoral landscape on the Durance's south bank, the Abbaye de Silvacane, with its pink-tiled roofs and small square bell tower, offers a spellbinding example of plain Cistercian beauty, in much the same way as does the Abbaye de Sénanque (see p358). It is a perfect setting for musical events (see panel, p372).

- **Michelin Map:** 340: G-3.
- **Info:** Abbaye de Silvacane, La Roque-d'Anthéron. 04 42 50 41 69. www.abbaye-silvacane.com.
- **Timing:** Allow 1hr.

A BIT OF HISTORY

From its Founding to the Present – In the 11C the monks from St-Victor of Marseille established themselves on land surrounded by "a forest of reeds" *(Sylva cana)*, from which the monastery derives its name.

The monastery became affiliated with Cîteaux and in 1144 received a donation from two benefactors: Guillaume de la Roque and Raymond de Baux, allowing a group of Cistercians from the Abbaye de Morimond to settle here.

Protected by Provence's great lords, the abbey prospered; it accomplished large land improvement projects in the region and in turn founded Abbaye de Valsainte near Apt. In 1289 a violent confrontation occurred between it and the powerful Abbaye de Montmajour of the Benedictine Order; monks pursued each other and some were even taken as hostages. The conflict ended in a trial and Silvacane was returned to its rightful owners, the Cistercians.

But even more serious were the pillaging of the abbey in 1358 by the Lord of Aubignan and the severe frosts of 1364, which destroyed the olive and wine crops. This set off a period of decline, which ended in 1443 with the annexation of the abbey to the chapter of St-Sauveur Cathedral in Aix.

It became the village of Roque-d'Anthéron's parish church in the early 16C, and suffered during the Wars of Religion. When the Revolution broke out the buildings were already abandoned; the abbey was sold as state property and converted into a farm.

In 1949 the buildings were bought by the state, and since then extensive restoration work has been carried out on the foundations discovered in 1989, the monastic buildings, the fortified wall in coated quarry-stone, and the monks' guest house.

Abbaye de Silvacane

S. Sauvignier/MICHELIN

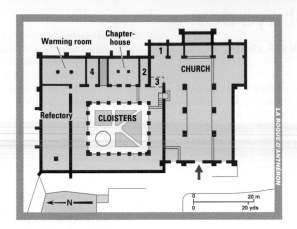

LA ROQUE-D'ANTHÉRON

Music in the Monastery

Buildings which once echoed the chanting of monks now echo classical music as the abbey hosts the **Festival International de Quatuors à Cordes du Luberon** (www.quatuors-luberon.org) and the **Silvacane Festival of Vocal Music**, among other events.

VISIT

🕐 *Open Jun–Sept daily 10am–6pm; Oct–May Wed–Mon 10am–1pm, 2–5pm.* 🕐 *Closed 1 Jan, 1 May, 25 Dec.* ⊛ €7.50.

Church (Église)

The church, built on a slope between 1175 and 1230, features different levels, which are noticeable when one views the west façade with its several openings: a central door, two side doors topped with small off-centred windows, three windows and an oculus adorned with mouldings on the upper floor.

The three-bayed nave ends in a flat east end. Each arm of the transept has two chapels. Note how the architect had to take into account the very steep slope of the land by placing the south aisle, nave, the north aisle and the cloisters at different levels.

In the north chapel of the north arm of the transept **(1)** are the fragments of the tomb of Bertrand de Baux (c.1137–81), grandson of the founder, who began the church's construction.

Cloisters

Located at a lower level (1.6m) than the church, the cloisters date from the second half of the 13C, although the gallery vaulting is still Romanesque. Powerful rounded arches open on to the yard; they were originally adorned with paired bays.

Conventional Buildings

Except for the refectory these were all built from 1210 to 1230. The **sacristy (2)** is a long narrow room next to the **library (3)**, under the north arm of the transept. The **chapter house** recalls the one at Sénanque: six-pointed vaults falling on two central pillars. After the **parlour (4)**, which was used as a passage to the exterior, comes the **warming house**; also with pointed vaulting, it has kept its chimney. Above is the **dormitory**. The magnificent **refectory**, rebuilt in the 15C, and still with its pulpit, has large windows and more elaborately decorated capitals than the other rooms. The lay brothers' wing has completely disappeared. Excavations have uncovered the ruins of the gatehouse and the abbey's precinct wall.

Manosque★

Nestling among foothills at the edge of the Luberon massif, a stone's throw from the River Durance, this peaceful town has expanded owing to its position in the rich agricultural valley and the proximity of new, high-tech industries; in only twenty years its population has grown from 5 000 to 20 000. This modernisation has altered the rural setting of Manosque, celebrated by the town's most famous son, novelist Jean Giono (1895–1970), and visitors will need sharp eyes to spot the charming little Provençal streets that the writer would have known.

WALKING TOUR

OLD TOWN★

Wide boulevards have replaced the ramparts which once enclosed the old town; the typically Provençal streets are narrow and lined with tall houses concealing secluded gardens, patios, beautiful cellars and galleries. The streets are linked by covered passages and extremely narrow alleyways known as *androns*. A colourful **market** enlivens the square three times a week.

▶ **Population:** 22 105.

◔ **Michelin Map:** 334: C-10.

▤ **Info:** Place du Dr Joubert, 04100 Manosque. ℘04 92 72 16 00. www.manosque-tourisme.com.

◗ **Location:** At 80km/50mi from Marseille, Manosque is set among five hills. A circular boulevard on the site of the former ramparts encloses the old town.

☺ **Don't Miss:** The Saturday morning market at Place Terreau; frescoes in the Fondation Carzou and a view of the town from the top of the Mont d'Or.

◷ **Timing:** Spend at least a half-day here.

👥 **Kids:** The lake at Les Vannades has activities all year long.

Porte Saunerie★

This 12C gate, which formed part of the original town walls, owes its name to the salt warehouses which once stood nearby. Note the twinned openings supported on slender columns and the machicolated side turrets.

Street of Manosque

© M. Raynaud/Comité Régional de Tourisme Provence-Alpes-Côte d'Azur

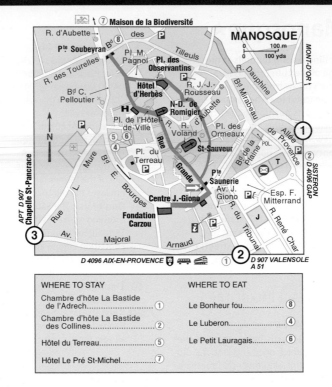

WHERE TO STAY		WHERE TO EAT	
Chambre d'hôte La Bastide de l'Adrech............	(1)	Le Bonheur fou...............	(8)
Chambre d'hôte La Bastide des Collines............	(2)	Le Luberon.....................	(4)
Hôtel du Terreau....................	(5)	Le Petit Lauragais.............	(6)
Hôtel Le Pré St-Michel............	(7)		

Rue Grande

This lively, picturesque high street offers a wealth of old doorways, fine stairwells, courtyards and balconies. **No 14** was the workshop where Giono's father used to mend shoes and where his mother ironed clothes. Note the wrought-iron balconies of the 16C–17C house at **no 23**.

Église St-Sauveur

The plain façade overlooks a square decorated with a fountain. Look for two blocks of stone set into the north wall of the church; one shows a pilgrim with his staff, the other a cockerel fighting with a snake. The square belltower is surmounted by a famous wrought-iron **campanile**, which was made in 1725 by a blacksmith from Rians.

Église Notre-Dame-de-Romigier★

The church has a Renaissance doorway, but the nave was remodelled in the 17C and the aisles were added. The altar is a splendid 4C or 5C **sarcophagus★** in

Carrara marble. According to legend, the **Black Madonna statue★** from which the church takes its name was discovered at the end of the 10C under a bramble bush, where it had been hidden when the Saracens invaded Provence in the 9C; it was later placed inside the church.

Hôtel de Ville

The town hall, with its elegant 17C **façade★** and beautiful staircase, is one of the finest buildings in Manosque.

Porte Soubeyran

The 12C gate, remodelled in the 14C, was later decorated with a lovely stone balustrade and a tower surmounted by an onion-shaped top in wrought iron.

Place des Observantins

A former monastery has been turned into the music and dance conservatory. The square holds a lovely old fountain. The library and municipal archives are housed in the **Hôtel d'Herbès**, which has a fine 17C staircase inside.

Centre Jean-Giono

© Sylvain Grandadam/age fotostock

ADDITIONAL SIGHTS
Centre Jean-Giono

3 bd Élémir-Bourges. ⬥◷Open Oct–Mar 2–6pm; Apr–Sept Tue–Fri 9.30am–12.30pm, 2–6pm, Sat 9.30am–noon, 2–6pm. ◷Closed Sun and public holidays. ☞€4. ✆04 92 70 54 54. www.centrejeangiono.com.

This fine Provençal house, dating from the 18C, houses a museum devoted to the life and works of Jean Giono.

Those who wish to walk in the footprints of the great novelist can participate in **literary excursions** to sites in the area connected with his work.

Fondation Carzou

7–9 bd Élémir-Bourges. ◷Open Nov–Mar Wed–Sat 2–6pm; Apr–Oct Tue–Sat 10am–12.30pm, 2–6pm. ◷Closed public holidays and 23 Dec– 2 Jan. ☞€3. ✆40 92 87 40 49. www.fondationcarzou.fr.

Jean Carzou (1907–2000), a French painter of Armenian descent, departed from Abstract painting and evolved his own intricate style, full of fantasy, against a monochrome background.

Start your visit to the right of the entrance. It took Carzou seven years to complete **The Apocalypse★**. Each panel of this striking fresco illustrates a particular theme. The unity of the whole is reinforced by the strong blue-green backgrounds which natural light from the windows emphasises. The left side of the chancel focuses on massacres and acts of destruction carried out by man; the apse represents lust; the cupola over the choir is supported by four historiated pillars showing the four Evangelists. The right side evokes the work of women. Carzou also created the **stained-glass windows★** (except for the one above the main door). Some depict the wars of Vendée and Napoléon. The four horsemen of the Apocalypse symbolise great genocides in history: the massacre of the Indians in America; that of the Armenians, killed by the Turks in 1915; the St Bartholemew's Day massacre of Huguenots in Paris in 1572 (small panel); and the concentration camps of World War II.

The right-hand side shows the reconstruction of the world, thanks to love and hard work. Notice the discreet tribute to Millet and his **Angélus** in the corner of the wall on the left.

Maison de la Biodiversité

Chemin de la Thomassine. From the centre, follow signs for "Dauphin" (or for the Hôtel Pré Saint-Michel), pass the cemetery and the station, take a right onto the chemin de la Thomassine for 2km/1.25mi. ☛Guided tours 10.30am and 4.30pm. ✆04 92 87 74 40. www.parcduluberon.fr. ☞€4 (free under 18).

Romance and Literature

Jean Giono was wasting his time when he maintained that François I never set foot in Manosque. According to ingrained tradition, the king was received at porte Saunerie by Péronne de Voland, daughter of the consul. This young lady, who presented him with the keys of the town on the customary velvet cushion, was so beautiful that the king was smitten. But rather than yield to his advances, she preferred to disfigure herself by exposing her face to sulphurous fumes. Since then, Manosque has been referred to as "la Pudique" ("the modest one").

One thing is certain: a large part of the work of **Jean Giono** (1895–1970) is set in and around Manosque. "At the bottom of the hill lay the town, like the back of a tortoise in the grass", he wrote. In *Jean le Bleu* especially, he evokes the face of his shoemaker father, the streets of Manosque, his childhood on the banks of the Durance and the times he spent with shepherds in the hills.

👥 Standing alone in a beautiful amphitheatre of wooded hills high above Manosque, this former wine estate has been converted into a conservation orchard by the Parc régional naturel du Luberon. In three exhibition rooms, information panels paint a picture of biodiversity. But it is when you step outside that you understand the concept better. In eight terraced gardens, 500 heirloom varieties of fruit are grown and harvested: figs, apples, pears, cherries, olives... All are on sale here in season. When you have strolled around the little potager garden of forgotten vegetables and seen the pretty rose garden, head for the renovated farmhouse, which has a permanent exhibition on biodiversity.

EXCURSIONS
Chapelle Saint-Pancrace (de Toutes Aures)

2km/1.25mi to the southwest. Leave Manosque where ③ is indicated on the map.

From the Chapel at the summit, the **panorama★** gradually extends to embrace the old town and its roofs, the Durance Valley, the Luberon and, in the distance, the Valensole plateau and the Préalpes de Digne.

🚶 Mont d'Or★

1.5km/0.9mi northeast. Starting from rue Dauphine, climb up Montée des Vraies-Richesses then follow a no-through-road on the right to the last house on the right, known as Le Paraïs.

It would be a pity to leave Manosque without going up this hill planted with olive trees. Close to the town and yet delightfully rural, it provides splendid views.

Maison de Giono Le Paraïs

Montée des Vraies-Richesses.
♿🚶 *Guided visits (1hr) Fri afternoons with 1 week advance booking.* 🕐 *Closed public holidays.* 📞 *04 92 87 73 03.*
🙂 *As the Giono family still lives here, it is essential to be quiet and discreet.*
Having lived in the area since 1930, Giono acquired the property in 1968. In his library, the wall of which is covered by a fresco painted by Lucien Jacques, note the importance of a collection of Chinese literature which shows how open Giono was to other cultures. On the mantelpiece, a pre-Columbian head smiles enigmatically. In the writer's study are touching mementoes: the cobbler's hammer that belonged to his father, as well as his pipes and a mould of his right hand. From the mansard window you will see the layered rooftops of the old town.

▶ Return to the road and park in the car park before the summit.

The Summit★
🚶 *10min round trip.*

The summit, crowned by a ruined tower and the remains of a château of the Counts of Forcalquier, provides a splendid **view★** of Manosque, the orchards of the Durance valley, the Luberon mountain and, in the distance, Montagne Sainte-Victoire and the Sainte-Baume.

ADDRESSES

🛏 STAY

🍽 **Hôtel du Terreau** – *Pl. du Terreau.* ℘*04 92 72 15 50. www.hotelmanosque.fr. Closed 27 Dec–17 Jan.* 🅿. *19 rooms.* This hotel on a pretty square at the centre of old Manosque continues to improve on the comfort it offers. Rooms are soundproofed. Many are decorated using traditional whitewash and wood.

🍽🍽 **Chambre d'hôte la Bastide de l'Adrech** – *Av. des Serrets.* ℘*04 92 71 14 18.* 🅿 ⇥. *5 rooms.* In the middle of the countryside not far from Manosque, this imposing bastide dating from the early 18C has recovered its past lustre. Fireplaces, big windows, doors, beams, floor tiles and steps of a magnificent and monumental staircase, all original, give it great character. Rooms are decorated in Provençal style with whitewashed walls, old furniture and pretty fabrics. An olive oil estate, cookery classes and themed excursions add to the appeal.

🍽🍽 **Chambre d'Hôte La Bastide des Collines** – *82 chemin de Valvéranne.* ℘*04 92 87 87 67.* ♿🅿⇥. *3 rooms. Restaurant* 🍽🍽. Enjoy home cooking using organic produce. Rooms are decorated in coloured themes. Lovely green lawn for a moment of repose.

🍽🍽 **Hôtel Le Pré St-Michel** – *1.5km/1mi N of Manosque.* ℘*04 92 72 14 27. www.presaintmichel.com.* ♿🅿. *24 rooms.* This modern hotel with a Provençal appearance offers a panorama overlooking Manosque. The rooms are large, with painted furniture, Provençal fabrics, wrought-iron details. Swimming pool.

🍽 EAT

🍽🍽 **Le Luberon** – *21 bis pl. du Terreau.* ℘*04 92 72 03 09. Closed 12–26 Oct, Sun eve, Mon and Thu eve.* This restaurant in the old town offers tasty local food alongside an extensive wine list. Rustic furniture, and paintings by local artists are on show.

🍽🍽 **Le Petit Laurageais** – *6 pl. du Terreau.* ℘*04 92 72 13 00. Closed Sat and Wed lunch and Sun.* This understated restaurant offers excellently prepared specialities from southwest France, as well as Provençal dishes.

🍽🍽 **Le Bonheur fou** – *11 bis bd des Tilleuls.* ℘*04 92 87 77 52. Closed Wed eve and Thu. Booking recommended.* The work of Jean Carluc may have given this intimate, convivial place its name, and it suits because it is the setting for exhibitions, talks and other cultural events besides being a restaurant. In the kitchen, David Arcos draws on his travel experience to create fusion food based on fresh produce.

SHOPPING

Market – *Plasce du Terreau, de l'hôtel de ville and Marcel-Pagnol. Sat 5am–1pm.* This colourful market, rich with the scent of lavender and olive oil, embodies the essence of Provence. You will find almost everything here that features in Provençal cuisine and everyday life.

Le Moulin de l'Olivette – *Pl. de l'Olivette.* ℘*04 92 72 00 99. www.moulinolivette.fr. Open Apr–Sept 8am–12.30pm, 1.30–7pm; Oct–Mar 8am–noon, 2–6.30pm. Closed Sun and public holidays.* This mill is one of the most important in the Alpes-de-Haute-Provence. Since 2000, its extra-virgin oil has regularly been awarded a gold medal at the Concours général agricole. The shop also sells regional gourmet specialities, pottery, and items carved from olive wood.

ACTIVITIES

Les Vannades – *Quartier St-Jean-Mairie, 5km/3mi N of Manosque via the D4096.* ℘*04 92 70 34 25.* At the end of a long and difficult road lies this 11ha/27-acre leisure centre. Swimming (supervised), sailing and rowing courses, rambling, volleyball, boules and miniature golf.

Forcalquier★

Surrounded by the hills of Haute Provence, Forcalquier is an off-the-beaten-track small town with a fascinating past. Although little remains of the ancient citadel at the top of the hill to which Forcalqiuer clings, it acts as a reminder that it was once a place of immense influence, becoming in the 12C the capital of an important territory run by counts whose power rivalled that of the Counts of Provence. It has an interesting cathedral, museum and cemetery. Nearby is the observatory of Haute Provence. Among the villages in the quiet countryside around Forcalquier, the best known is Banon: its distinctive *appellation contrôlée* goat's cheese, wrapped in a chestnut leaf, then carefully bound with raffia, is to be found at every market in the Luberon and beyond.

▶ **Population:** 4 680.
◔ **Michelin Map:** 334: C-9.
▯ **Info:** 13 pl. du Bourget, 04300 Forcalquier.
℘ 04 92 75 10 02. www.haute-provence-tourisme.com.
▷ **Location:** 47km/29.2mi S of Sisteron, it is an ideal base for exploring the surrounding area.
👁 **Don't Miss:** The panorama from the Notre-Dame-de-Provence, the Simiane rotunda, Banon goat's cheese and the Oppedette rooftops.
◕ **Timing:** The best time to visit is Monday morning for the market, one of the best for many kilometres around. To fill in the rest of the morning take a stroll through town. The afternoon can be spent discovering the Pays de Banon.

Forcalquier lies at the heart of a low area of rolling hills, a pretty **site★** bordered by the Montagne de Lure, the River Durance and the Luberon. The town, built in the shape of an amphitheatre, surrounds a hill once crowned by a citadel.

Today, Forcalquier is a thriving agricultural centre whose Monday market is one of the biggest in the area. If you plan to overnight in Forcalquier, opt for the "pays du Contadour" excursion in the afternoon, with "pays de Forqualquier" the following morning.

Forcalquier with the Chapelle Notre-Dame-de-Provence on the right

© Günter Lenz/imageBROKER/age fotostock

Forcalquier the Capital

At the end of the 11C, the fortified town of Forcalquier became the capital of a *comté* (county) created by a branch of the Comtes de Provence dynasty and extending along the Durance from Manosque north to Sisteron, Gap and Embrun. The bishopric of Sisteron was split into two and the church of Forcalquier became a co-cathedral, a unique precedent in the history of the Church. The Comté de Forcalquier and the Comté de Provence were united at the end of the 12C, under the leadership of **Raymond Bérenger V**. The two territories were eventually bequeathed to the French Crown in 1481.

OLD TOWN
Notre-Dame Cathedral

This former co-cathedral offers an interesting contrast between the Romanesque character of its massive rectangular tower and the slender appearance of its steeple crowned by a lantern. A lofty nave in typical Provençal Romanesque style dates from the same period as the transept and the chancel, which, built some time before 1217, are the oldest examples of Gothic architecture in the area. The massive organ, dating from the 17C, is considered one of the finest in Provence.

The Visitandines convent sits opposite the cathedral.

◗ Walk round the cathedral by the bd des Martyrs; turn to face the Couvent des Cordeliers opposite.

Couvent des Cordeliers

Franciscan friars settled in Forcalquier in 1236. Their monastery, one of the first of its kind in Provence, was occupied until the 18C. It now houses a training centre for the **European University for Scents and Flavours**, which organises courses and workshops for the public. *04 92 72 50 68. www.uess.fr.*
The **cloisters** have a lovely garden with clipped boxwood. The Lords of Forcalquier were buried in these Gothic crypts. The chapter house has twin bays which frame a Romanesque doorway.

Cité Comtale

The **Porte des Cordeliers** gate is all that remains of the town's fortifications and marks the beginning of the medieval town. The narrow streets were laid out to offer the best protection from the *mistral*. Some houses have kept their paired windows and Gothic, Classical or Renaissance doorways. A 16C **Renaissance fountain**, in the shape of a pyramid crowned by St Michael slaying the dragon, decorates place St-Michel.

Cimetière★

The yews have been clipped into amazing arched shapes in the cemetery.

EXCURSIONS
St-Michel-l'Observatoire★

On the D 305 north of the village of Saint-Michel l'Observatoire. ♿Visitors will be required to walk up 60 steps. ☞Guided tours (1hr) Jul–Aug Tue–Thu 2–5pm; Apr–Jun and Sep–Nov Wed 2.15–4pm. ◷Closed public holidays. ▨€4.50 (children €2.50) from tourist office, access via free shuttle bus (departs every 30min). ℘04 92 70 64 00. www.obs-hp.fr.
On a plateau near the village of St-Michel l'Observatoire, the **Haute Provence Observatory★** was established in 1937 as a national facility for French astronomers. Its cupolas are

The City of Four Queens

The daughters of **Raymond Bérenger V** all became queens. Marguerite married St Louis, King of France, Éléonore married Henry III, King of England, Sanche married Richard of Cornwall, King of the Romans, and Beatrix married Charles, King of Deux-Siciles.

said to shine beneath the clearest skies in France. In the village itself, narrow streets lead to the elegant, white **Église haute** crowning the hill. From the terrace of this 12C "upper church" there is a **view** of the area around Forcalquier. ♣♦The **astronomy centre** at Saint-Michel, part of the observatory of Haute-Provence, offers activities and evening star-gazing. ℘04 92 76 69 09. www.centre-astro.fr. Open Jul–Sept "l'été astro" is a star-gazing festival with conferences (booking recommended). Observations of the sun Oct–May once or twice a month 2pm ⊜€7 (children, 6–16 €5); evening events where you will receive an introduction to the equipment occur once a month 9pm or 9.30pm. ⊜€11 (6–16 years €9).

Chapelle Saint-Jean-des-Fuzils

A path to the right of the observatory entrance leads to this modest 11C building with strange spiral decoration and a roof tiled with *lauzes* (thin flat stones).

Lurs★

11km/6.8mi E of Forcalquier.
This village occupies a remarkable **position**★ on top of a rocky spur overlooking the Durance and the area around Forcalquier. Once a medieval stronghold belonging to the bishops of Forcalquier, it was gradually deserted and became derelict until it was "revived" by a group of graphic designers and is today the summer rendezvous of the printing profession through the **Rencontres internationales de Lurs** and a centre of graphic arts.
Go through the clock gate surmounted by a campanile, past the church with its interesting belltower and along the winding streets lined with bay-windowed houses; there are traces of the old fortifications. Note the **chancellerie des compagnons de Lure**, the rustic open-air theatre, the restored **priory**, now a cultural centre, and the partly rebuilt bishops' castle.
After you have walked around the castle go along the **Promenade des Évêques**, lined with 15 oratories dating from 1864, to the Chapelle Notre-Dame-de-Vie offering fine **views** of the Durance and

Préalpes de Digne on one side, of the Montagne de Lure and Forcalquier Basin on the other.

🚗 DRIVING TOURS

1 FORCALQUIER TO BANON

Drive of 100km/62mi shown on the regional map (♦ see p336–37). Allow 3hrs.

This rich rural area, in striking contrast with the austere surrounding plateaux and Montagne de Lure, is dotted with charming hilltop villages, most facing east or south to shelter from the north-westerly wind.

▷ From Forcalquier, follow D 13 in the direction of Manosque and bear right on to the D 13.

Mane★

Clustered around its medieval citadel, the village stands on a peak overlooking the plain to which it has given its name.
The **église Saint-André** dates from the 16C. Its Florentine doorway is decorated with palms. Inside there is a beautiful, polychrome altar. To the left of the church, take the **Grande Rue** lined with Renaissance houses whose doorways have carved lintels. When you reach the fountain, continue on the rue Haute and take the stepped chemin de Palissat on the left.
The **citadel** (not open to visitors) dates from the 12C. It is striking because of the two sets of ramparts which rise in a helix, one superimposed on the other. You can walk all the way round. Enjoy the lovely **view** over the plateaux of the Vaucluse and Luberon, the Saint-Michel observatory and on towards the Durance valley.

▷ Continue on the D 13.

St-Maime

A few ruins and the castle chapel overlooking the village are the only remains of the Comtes de Provence's castle, in which the four daughters of Raymond Bérenger V *(see panel p379)* were brought up in the traditional way.

▶ Return to D 13 and cross it to reach Dauphin.

Dauphin
Built on another hilltop facing St-Maime, Dauphin has retained part of its 14C fortifications, its medieval streets and its keep, crowned by a balustrade and a statue of the Virgin Mary; from the top there is a wide-open **panorama** of the surrounding area.

▶ Follow D 5 and cross N 100.

St-Michel-l'Observatoire★
see p379.

▶ Follow D 105 south.

Chapelle St-Paul
This simple oratory has thick columns with Corinthian captials, the remains of a 12C priory.

▶ Turn right onto D 205.

Lincel
This village, which nestles in a fold, has retained a small Romanesque church and a castle with a few 16C features.

▶ Cross N 100, continue along D 105, then turn right onto D 907 and left towards Montfuron.

Montfuron
Fine restored **windmill**. From the village, **view** of the heights of Haute-Provence to the northeast and of Montagne Ste-Victoire to the southwest.

▶ Return to D 907 and turn left; drive across N 100 and follow D 14.

Reillanne
This village is built on the side of a hill crowned by the 18C Chapelle St-Denis, which replaced the castle; avenue Long-Barri leads past the Portail des Forges (all that remains of the castle) to the

viewing table: panoramic **view** of the old village, of the Ste-Victoire Mountain to the south and Luberon to the west.

▶ Continue along D 14 and make a detour to Vachères.

Vachères
This old hilltop village acquired fame when the statue of a Gallo-Roman warrior, now in the Calvet Museum in Avignon, was discovered nearby. The **Musée paléontologique et archéologique** (& *open Jul–Aug daily 3–6pm; Sept–Jun Wed, Sun and public holidays 2.30–5.30pm.* *closed mid-Dec–mid-Feb.* €2.50. 04 92 75 67 21) contains archaeological finds going back to prehistoric times, including flint, axes and a copy of the famous **Vachères warrior**, as well as fossils discovered locally.

▶ From Notre-Dame-de-Bellevue on D 14, take a small road to Oppedette.

Oppedette
This tastefully restored hamlet overlooks the **Gorges d'Oppedette★**, 2.5km/1.5mi long and 120m/394ft deep in places, through which flows the Calavon. There is a fine **view★** from the viewpoint near the cemetery; a marked path, starting beneath the viewpoint, leads to the bottom of the gorge.

▶ Take the D 201, then D 155, leading back along the Calavon River to the D 4100. Head towards Forcalquier again.

Château de Sauvan★
Guided tours at 3.30pm: Jul–Aug daily; Apr–Jun and Sept–mid-Nov Thu–Sun; Feb–Mar Sun 3.30pm. *Closed mid-Nov–Jan.* €7.50 (under 14 €3). 04 92 75 05 64. www.chateaudesauvan.com.
This 18C château has been magnificently restored, down to every last detail. The furniture, dating from the 17C, 18C and 19C, highlights the beauty of the rooms (in some of which the original wallpaper has been discovered).

Prieuré de Salagon

© Franck Guiziou/hemis.fr

From the windows on the north side or from the terrace which faces Mane and Forcalquier, the vegetation and luminosity may make you imagine that you are in Tuscany.

▷ Continue on the D 4100.

Prieuré de Salagon★★

⊙*Open Jun–Aug daily 10am–8pm; May and Sept daily 10am–7pm; Feb–Apr and Oct–mid-Dec daily 10am–6pm.* ⊙*Closed mid-Dec–Jan.* ⊛€7. ℘04 92 75 70 50. www.musee-de-salagon.com. This Benedictine **priory**, founded in 1105, rebuilt in the 15C and used as a farmhouse during the Revolution, was finally restored and turned into an ethnological museum in 1981. A medieval garden, and two gardens for medicinal and aromatic herbs, were planted when the museum was opened.

The west front of the 12C **church★** is decorated with an inset rose-window and a doorway, similar to that of the Ganagobie Monastery (&*See French Alps Green Guide*). There are contemporary stained-glass windows by Aurélie Nemours.

In the **priory lodge** that replaced the monastery at the end of the 15C, you will see a strange angled window and the tower of the spiral staircase. This tower adjoins the **Musée départemental ethnologique,** which features two permanent exhibitions: one describes the artisans of the village while the other is about the aromatic plants of Haute-Provence.

The buildings where these are based are built around a fine **pebbled courtyard**, the lower part of which has been listed as a heritage structure. There are various temporary exhibitions, events and other activities presented here all year.

👥 During school holidays the museum runs workshops for children aged 6–12. Finally, there are numerous **themed gardens** around the priory, including a medieval potager filled with herbs and medicinal plants; an old-fashioned cottage garden; and a scented garden. There are more than 2,000 kinds of plants on the premises.

▷ Return to Forcalquier via the D 13.

ADDRESSES

🛏 STAY

🍽🍽 **Auberge Charembeau** – *Rte de Niozelles. 📞04 92 70 91 70. www. charembeau.com. Open Mar–mid-Nov. 25 rooms. ♿🅿.* An 18C farm in delightful, undulating parkland. A relaxing place with generous rooms decorated in typical Provençal style.

🍽🍽 **Chambre d'hôte le Relais d'Elle**– *Rte de La Brillanne, 04300 Niozelles. 📞04 92 75 06 87. www.relaisdelle.com. Closed 7 Jan– 7 Feb. 🅿🍴. 5 rooms. Table d'hôte 🍽🍽.* Sitting at the foot of the montagne de Lure, between La Brillanne and Forcalquier, this early 19C farm-turned-inn has been attractively restored. A convivial ambience and attention to detail: cosy salons with open fires; spacious, comfortable bedrooms with views of the hills or the park. Breakfasts make good use of local products. Nice pool.

🍽🍽🍽 **Hôtel du Mas du Pont Roman** – *Chemin Châteauneuf (rte Apt), 04300 Mane. 📞04 92 75 49 46. www.pontroman.com. 🏊🅿. 9 rooms.* Set back from the N 100 near an old Romanesque bridge, this restored *mas* has a charming salon, pretty bedrooms, modern bathrooms and a fine pool with a counter-current.

🍴 EAT

🍽🍽 **L'Aïgo Blanco**– *5 pl. Vieille. 📞04 92 75 27 23. Closed Mon eve (except school holidays) and Jan.* This unassuming restaurant is in the centre of Forcalquier, behind the église Notre-Dame. Provençal-style dining room and a terrace is set out on a little square in fine weather. Robust regional dishes including, in winter, a menu of Savoyard specialities.

🍽🍽 **La Tourette**– *20 bd Latourette. 📞04 92 75 14 00. Closed Sun.* Traditional Provençal dishes, usually served with a smile in a brightly coloured interior, make this a popular address in the town centre. The mulberry-shaded terrace is pleasant on hot days.

SHOPPING

🕐 **Good to know:** The area around Forcalquier has been labelled "Site remarquable du goût" taking into account its top-quality food specialities and markets.

Market – *Mon 8.30am–1pm.* Among its regional produce is famous Banon goat's cheese.

Farmers' markets – At Forcalquier *(Thu pm)* and Pierrerue *(Sat am).*

La Fontaine sucrée – *Pl. St-Michel. 📞04 92 75 02 50. Open Mon and Thu– Sat 8am–12.30pm, 3.30–7.30pm, Tue 8am–12.30pm, Sun 8am–12.30pm, 4–7.30pm, . Closed Wed (except Jul–Aug), Feb and Oct.* Among the many treats at this excellent pâtisserie, look out for its speciality, the Pierre du Luberon.

Distilleries et Domaines de Provence – *9 av. St-Promasse. 📞04 92 75 15 41. www. distilleries-provence.com. Open Jul–Aug Mon–Sat 9am–7pm; Sept–Dec and Apr–Jun Mon, Wed–Sat 10am–12.30pm, 2–7pm. Closed Jan–Mar.* A century-old still enhances the rustic appearance of this distillery established in 1898. Today, its artisan approach is better appreciated than ever.

ACTIVITIES

Hiking – There are many hiking trails around Forcalquier and the montagne de Lure including four GR paths: GR4, GR6, GR97 and the GR of Saint-Jacques de Compostelle.

Cycling – There is a 78km/48mi itinerary called *Le pays de Forcalquier et la montagne de Lure à vélo*, signposted in both directions. Leaflet from the tourist office. From Forcalquier, you can also follow the circuit right around the Luberon (*see Manosque*).

Vélo Loisir en Luberon – *203 r. Oscar-Roulet, 84440 Robien. 📞04 90 76 48 05. www.veloloisirluberon.com.* This professional group offers a range of services for cyclists holidaying in the Luberon.

Hot-air ballooning – *France Montgolfières. 📞08 10 600 153. www.france-montgolfiere. com. Mar–Nov, ascents from Forcalquier daily in early morning, weather permitting. €360/couple, €158 children aged 6–12 years.* Gain a thrilling new perspective on the landscape from high above.

EVENTS

🕐 **Good to know** – Festivities are listed in the monthly magazine "Le Petit Colporteur" available at the tourist office.

INDEX

INDEX

INDEX

INDEX

INDEX

INDEX

🛏 STAY

INDEX

⚘ EAT

INDEX

MAPS AND PLANS

COMPANION PUBLICATIONS

REGIONAL AND LOCAL MAPS

To make the most of your journey, travel with Michelin maps at a scale of 1:200 000: **Regional maps nos 512 and 518** and the new local maps, which are illustrated on the map of France below. And remember to travel with the latest edition of the **map of France no 721** (1:1 000 000), also available in atlas format: spiral bound, hard back, and the new mini-atlas – perfect for your glove compartment.

INTERNET

Michelin is pleased to offer a route-planning service on the Internet: **www.viamichelin.com** **www.travel.viamichelin.com**. Choose the shortest route, a route without tolls, or the Michelin recommended route to your destination; you can also access information about hotels and restaurants from *The Michelin Guide*, and tourist sites from *The Green Guide*.

MAP LEGEND

	Sight	Seaside resort	Winter sports resort	Spa
Highly recommended	★★★	⚏⚏⚏	✸✸✸	♯♯♯
Recommended	★★	⚏⚏	✸✸	♯♯
Interesting	★	⚏	✸	♯

Additional symbols

🛈		Tourist information
═══ ═══		Motorway or other primary route
❶	❶	Junction: complete, limited
⊏══⊐ ═══		Pedestrian street
⊥══⊥		Unsuitable for traffic, street subject to restrictions
▭▭▭▭	- - - -	Steps – Footpath
🚂	🚉	Train station – Auto-train station
🚌	S.N.C.F.	Coach (bus) station
──────		Tram
Ⓜ		Metro, underground
🅿		Park-and-Ride
♿		Access for the disabled
✉		Post office
☎		Telephone
✉		Covered market
⋅⋅✕⋅⋅		Barracks
△		Drawbridge
◡		Quarry
⚒		Mine
B	F	Car ferry (river or lake)
⛴		Ferry service: cars and passengers
⛴		Foot passengers only
③		Access route number common to Michelin maps and town plans
Bert (R.)...		Main shopping street
AZ B		Map co-ordinates

Sports and recreation

🐎		Racecourse
⛸		Skating rink
🏊	🏊	Outdoor, indoor swimming pool
🎥		Multiplex Cinema
⛵		Marina, sailing centre
⛺		Trail refuge hut
▭■▬■▭		Cable cars, gondolas
▭┼┼┼┼▭		Funicular, rack railway
🚂		Tourist train
◆		Recreation area, park
🎢		Theme, amusement park
🦌		Wildlife park, zoo
❀		Gardens, park, arboretum
🐦		Bird sanctuary, aviary
🚶		Walking tour, footpath
😊		Of special interest to children

Selected monuments and sights

◉ ⟹	Tour - Departure point
🛉 ⚑	Catholic church
🛉 ⚑	Protestant church, other temple
⬛ ⬛ 🛕	Synagogue - Mosque
⬛⬛	Building
■	Statue, small building
⚑	Calvary, wayside cross
◎	Fountain
━●━■►	Rampart - Tower - Gate
⋈	Château, castle, historic house
∴	Ruins
⌣	Dam
✿	Factory, power plant
☆	Fort
∩	Cave
▣	Troglodyte dwelling
⌁	Prehistoric site
▼	Viewing table
ᙎ	Viewpoint
▲	Other place of interest

Abbreviations

A	Agricultural office (Chambre d'agriculture)
C	Chamber of Commerce (Chambre de commerce)
H	Town hall (Hôtel de ville)
J	Law courts (Palais de justice)
M	Museum (Musée)
P	Local authority offices (Préfecture, sous-préfecture)
POL.	Police station (Police)
🛡	Police station (Gendarmerie)
T	Theatre (Théâtre)
U	University (Université)

YOU ALREADY KNOW THE GREEN GUIDE, NOW FIND OUT ABOUT THE MICHELIN GROUP

The Michelin Adventure

It all started with rubber balls! This was the product made by a small company based in Clermont-Ferrand that André and Edouard Michelin inherited, back in 1880. The brothers quickly saw the potential for a new means of transport and their first success was the invention of detachable pneumatic tires for bicycles. However, the automobile was to provide the greatest scope for their creative talents. Throughout the 20th century, Michelin never ceased developing and creating ever more reliable and high-performance tires, not only for vehicles ranging from trucks to F1 but also for underground transit systems and airplanes.

From early on, Michelin provided its customers with tools and services to facilitate mobility and make traveling a more pleasurable and more frequent experience. As early as 1900, the Michelin Guide supplied motorists with a host of useful information related to vehicle maintenance, accommodation and restaurants, and was to become a benchmark for good food. At the same time, the Travel Information Bureau offered travelers personalised tips and itineraries.

The publication of the first collection of roadmaps, in 1910, was an instant hit! In 1926, the first regional guide to France was published, devoted to the principal sites of Brittany, and before long each region of France had its own Green Guide. The collection was later extended to more far-flung destinations, including New York in 1968 and Taiwan in 2011.

In the 21st century, with the growth of digital technology, the challenge for Michelin maps and guides is to continue to develop alongside the company's tire activities. Now, as before, Michelin is committed to improving the mobility of travelers.

MICHELIN TODAY

WORLD NUMBER ONE TIRE MANUFACTURER
- 70 production sites in 18 countries
- 111,000 employees from all cultures and on every continent
- 6,000 people employed in research and development

Moving
for a world

Moving forward means developing tires with better road grip and shorter braking distances, whatever the state of the road.

CORRECT TIRE PRESSURE

RIGHT PRESSURE

- Safety
- Longevity
- Optimum fuel consumption

-0,5 bar

- Durability reduced by 20% (- 8,000 km)

-1 bar

- Risk of blowouts
- Increased fuel consumption
- Longer braking distances on wet surfaces

forward together
where mobility is safer

It also involves helping motorists take care of their safety and their tires. To do so, Michelin organises "Fill Up With Air" campaigns all over the world to remind us that correct tire pressure is vital.

WEAR

DETECTING TIRE WEAR

The legal minimum depth of tire tread is 1.6mm.
Tire manufacturers equip their tires with tread wear indicators, which are small blocks of rubber moulded into the base of the main grooves at a depth of 1.6mm.

Tires are the only point of contact between the vehicle and road.

The photo below shows the actual contact zone.

If the tread depth is less than 1.6mm, tires are considered to be worn and dangerous on wet surfaces.

NEW TIRE

WORN TIRE
(1,6 mm tread)

Moving forward
means sustainable mobility

INNOVATION AND THE ENVIRONMENT

By 2050, Michelin aims to cut the quantity of raw materials used in its tire manufacturing process by half and to have developed renewable energy in its facilities. The design of MICHELIN tires has already saved billions of litres of fuel and, by extension, billions of tons of CO_2.

Similarly, Michelin prints its maps and guides on paper produced from sustainably managed forests and is diversifying its publishing media by offering digital solutions to make traveling easier, more fuel efficient and more enjoyable!

The group's whole-hearted commitment to eco-design on a daily basis is demonstrated by ISO 14001 certification.

Like you, Michelin is committed to preserving our planet.

Chat with Bibendum

Go to
www.michelin.com/corporate/en
Find out more about
Michelin's history and the
latest news.

QUIZ

Michelin develops tires for all types of vehicles.
See if you can match the right tire with the right vehicle...

Solution : A-6 / B-4 / C-2 / D-1 / E-3 / F-7 / G-5

DISCARD

Michelin Travel Partner

Société par actions simplifiées au capital de 11 288 880 EUR
27 cours de l'Ile Seguin - 92100 Boulogne Billancourt (France)
R.C.S. Nanterre 433 677 721

No part of this publication may be reproduced in any form
without the prior permission of the publisher.

© Michelin Travel Partner
ISBN 978-2-067203-55-6
Printed: March 2015
Printed and bound in France : Imprimerie CHIRAT, 42540 Saint-Just-la-Pendue - N° 201503.0285

Although the information in this guide was believed by the authors and publisher to be accurate
and current at the time of publication, they cannot accept responsibility for any inconvenience,
loss, or injury sustained by any person relying on information or advice contained in this guide.
Things change over time and travellers should take steps to verify and confirm information,
especially time-sensitive information related to prices, hours of operation, and availability.